Israel Smith Clare

The World's History Illuminated - Vol. 01

Israel Smith Clare

The World's History Illuminated - Vol. 01

ISBN/EAN: 9783744651509

Printed in Europe, USA, Canada, Australia, Japan

Cover: Foto ©ninafisch / pixelio.de

More available books at **www.hansebooks.com**

HERODOTUS

THE WORLD'S HISTORY
ILLUMINATED

CONTAINING A RECORD OF THE HUMAN RACE FROM THE EARLIEST HISTORICAL PERIOD TO THE PRESENT TIME. EMBRACING A GENERAL SURVEY OF THE PROGRESS OF MANKIND IN NATIONAL AND SOCIAL LIFE, CIVIL GOVERNMENT, RELIGION, LITERATURE, SCIENCE AND ART

COMPLETE IN EIGHT VOLUMES

Compiled, Arranged and Written by....... **ISRAEL SMITH CLARE** Author of "THE WORLD'S HISTORY ILLUMINATED," and "COMPLETE HISTORICAL COMPENDIUM."

REVIEWED, VERIFIED AND ENDORSED BY THE PROFESSORS OF HISTORY IN FIVE AMERICAN UNIVERSITIES, WITH AN INTRODUCTION ON THE EDUCATIONAL VALUE OF HISTORICAL STUDY

By MOSES COIT TYLER, A.M., L.H.D.
PROFESSOR OF AMERICAN HISTORY IN CORNELL UNIVERSITY.

"NOT TO KNOW WHAT HAPPENED BEFORE WE WERE BORN IS TO REMAIN ALWAYS A CHILD; FOR WHAT WERE THE LIFE OF MAN DID WE NOT COMBINE PRESENT EVENTS WITH THE RECOLLECTIONS OF PAST AGES?"—*CICERO.*

Volume I.—Ancient Oriental Nations
ILLUMINATED WITH MAPS, PORTRAITS AND VIEWS.

ST. LOUIS
WESTERN NEWSPAPER SYNDICATE

COPYRIGHT, 1897,

BY

R. S. PEALE AND J. A. HILL.

THE EDUCATIONAL VALUE
OF THE
STUDY OF HISTORY.

BY MOSES COIT TYLER,

Professor of American History in Cornell University.

N order to do justice to the claims of historical study, it can never be necessary for us to depreciate those of any other branch of learning. Properly considered, there is no such thing as rivalry between different spheres of knowledge; only emulation, a noble and helpful emulation.

All real knowledge is good, being in one way or another a source of power and happiness. The various realms of things known or knowable are but co-equal and fraternal states in that vast confederation which we may call the republic of science. No single member of this confederation is strong, none is sufficient, standing alone. Each is necessary to all, all are necessary to each.

While, therefore, no one study may assert for itself the whole of what is valuable, every study doubtless has its own special value; and this value, as in the case of a study like history, it may sometimes be worth our while to place clearly before our minds, modestly, tolerantly, and for the rightful purpose of forming a just idea of the particular good we ought to expect and to work for, in our pursuit of it.

I.

Probably that use of the study of history which will first occur to most persons, is the one suggested by the common conception of history as an enormous body of facts about the past,—the effort to know and retain a considerable number of these facts being regarded as a fine gymnastic exercise for the faculty of memory. It is, indeed, quite astonishing how great a multitude of historical details—dates, names, and other precise items about persons, cities, nations, armies, political parties, institutions, and so forth—almost any person is capable of carrying in his memory, if only he patiently sto.es and trains it in that way. Moreover, no one will deny that there is much convenience and delight in the possession of a memory like that,—a memory enriched with precise and various historical facts, all labeled, and pigeon-holed, and ready for service at a moment's call. Certainly, a brilliant accomplishment this for conversation; a weapon of victory for public speech; in hours of loneliness and suffering, a great solace,—all of which may be seen in the cases of certain famous men in our country who had such a memory, as John Quincy Adams, Theodore Parker, Charles Sumner, Garfield.

On the other hand, this particular use of historical study is somewhat discredited among persons of mature sense, whenever it is associated with either of two practical mistakes, to which, indeed, young students of history are liable. One of these mistakes arises from a lack of discrimination as to the relative value of different historical facts; the other from the notion that the work of memorizing historical facts is the principal part of historical study. It can hardly be wise to make the memory serve the purpose of an old fashioned garret in a country house, — a receptacle for all sorts of odds and ends of property, precious and worthless. Surely, such indiscriminate memorizing must be a waste of energy, and the perversion of a noble faculty. What is the use of making an effort to remember what is useless? Besides, however valuable it may be to store the memory with well selected dates and names and other historical items, this at best belongs among the lower and more mechanic uses of history.

With these qualifications upon the primary claim put forward on behalf of historical study, we may now pass on to consider some claims which point to mental and even spiritual discipline of a far higher and more complex kind.

II.

One of these higher benefits may be described as that of training the critical faculty, through the effort to test the evidence for and against particular historical facts, or what are alleged to be such. Perhaps the very hardest thing to get at in this world is the truth, the very truth, especially the very truth concerning the past transactions of the human race. From this point of view, it is plain that the study of history is something more than the passive reading of certain finished and fascinating books, like Livy, for instance, or Gibbon, or Thiers, or Macaulay, or Prescott, or Parkman; it is indeed, the resolute and attentive application of the whole mind to an immense and complicated subject, — a process which cannot be carried on very long without our running up against questions of disputed fact. To deal with these questions in a manner to satisfy a truth-loving mind, it will be necessary for us to look keenly into problems of conflicting testimony, of personal character, of the validity of documents, of the meaning of words, of the right method of construction. I am not now speaking of the labors of professional historians, the intricacy and arduousness of which are admitted to be great, just in proportion to the quality of their results. Even pupils at school, however, and college students, and the members of historical clubs, and solitary readers of history, if they would pursue this study in the wisest and most fruitful way, must all be, to some extent, historical critics; must be alert, inquisitive, cautious, never credulous, always intolerant of slovenly ways; and as far as possible, they must try the text they are reading by earlier texts, and especially by those nearest to the times that happen to be under consideration.

Who is likely to overstate the educational value of such a method of study? On the moral side, how great it must be! It is produced and is nourished by a conviction of the incomparable worth and sacredness of mere truth in itself, as against all baser stuff in the form of half-truth, guess work, fables, or lies, and this conviction is sure to grow and to strengthen under such honest toil in its service. On the purely mental side, how great must be the effect of such study, — since it calls forth and taxes powers so important as those of analysis and comparison, nicety of verbal sense, literary insight, logical acuteness and precision, soundness of judgment, and saving common sense.

III.

In the next place, it should not be overlooked that the mental and moral discipline involved in the study of history, is of a kind even broader and more complex than that required for the ascertainment and verification of particular historical facts.

That alone, as we have just seen, is a great task, calling for fine and strong powers of mind; it is a task that can perhaps never be perfectly done by any finite being; and yet, even that, when it is done as well as we can do it, is not the end of historical study, but rather the beginning of it. For, after you have verified and defined your facts, comes the still more subtle process of discovering their causal relations,—the great play of influence among human events, the interdependence of events, the action and reaction and counteraction of events. Of course, to do this sort of work hastily, recklessly, with that tone of easy infallibility which some historical students have when passing judgment upon groups of facts in relation to the past, is probably not very hard,—at least for persons who can do it all; but to one who realizes the worthlessness, the misleading character, of all mere assumption in statements professing to be historical, and how hard it must be even approximately to discover the actual relations of events, it will be obvious that, aside from the intrinsic value of such generalizations, is the disciplinary value of the mental and spiritual process of arriving at them. Certainly, to generalize wisely from sound historical data, is a great exercise of the philosophic powers; it is a test and a development of broad-mindedness, lucidity, and vigor in reasoning.

IV.

Another benefit from historical study will occur to us, when we reflect that such study compels one to investigate and to reason within the realm, not of the exact and of the absolute, but of the approximate and the probable.

No doubt there is a peculiar educational value in the study of those sciences in which the data are precise or absolute; in which the conclusions are so, likewise. History, however, deals with data of a different kind, — with mixed deeds, and mixed motives, and traits of character, and experiences of human beings; looking back into the past, it draws some general conclusions from these data and applies them to the present and the future; it aims to formulate some general principles relating to the collective human life of this world, to government, to the working of the social organism. But whatever history requires of its student or does for him, it keeps him mostly within the sphere of the approximate and the probable. You cannot weigh a human motive or impulse as precisely as you can a chemical substance. In much of your work as an historian, you have to balance one probability against another; to estimate the operation of spiritual forces, to deal with the inscrutable mysteries of personal character. In so many parts of your work, you are obliged to reason with caution, slowly, circumspectly, not dogmatically; and to realize the limitations upon the definiteness and certainty of many of your conclusions.

Well, is there any special value in such training as this? It seems to me that, in a rather peculiar sense, this gives the very training required for real life; since in real life we are in the sphere not of the absolute, but of the relative, and we have to deal with the very problems which the historian has to deal with, — human character, human feelings and motives, probabilities, and other data more or less indefinite. I would say no word to imply any disparagement of the educational value of mathematics, for example. It has its value, unrivaled in its kind; but he who should apply the methods of mathematical reasoning to the questions which come up between man and man in real life, would often make most absurd mistakes and go far astray. Historical study, on the other hand, is a study of human nature on a broad field, and for all ages; it is exactly the sort of training which helps us to know persons and affairs in real life, the great types of human character, the limited worth of testimony, the play of passion in interfering with reasonable and prudent conduct, the probable consequences of any particular set of outward conditions. History is the great teacher of human nature by means of object lessons drawn from the whole recorded life of human nature.

V.

This brings us naturally to the fifth benefit to be got from historical study,— the cultivation of fair-mindedness as a habit, and the suppression of intellectual partisanship with respect to all subjects whatsoever.

No one can pursue this study in the right way, or with any real success, who does not learn to acquire the mental attitude, not of an attorney standing for one side of the question, but of a judge standing for what is true on both sides. The historical spirit is the judicial spirit. However vast may be his learning, however splendid his style, whoever writes history in a partisan fashion, spoils to that extent the genuineness and value of his work, as any one may observe by the brilliant examples of Macaulay and Froude.

We must not, we cannot, tolerate in history, what we are obliged to tolerate in contemporary comment. Such comment is almost inevitably colored by contemporary passion, is biased this way and that through contemporary prejudice, through the stormy likes and dislikes that are irrepressible among men actually engaged in the conflicts of their own time, and having great personal interests at stake. But when it comes to history, we demand something different. History is the comment made afterward, when the fight is over and ended and the combatants are cold in their graves; and the duty of history is to hear all sides and all persons, to weigh all pleas, to sift all testimonies, to be fair to all. If, with regard to living controversies, this attitude of fairness between opposite persons and opinions is almost impossible to attain, it is by no means easy of attainment even with regard to dead controversies; it is, for every topic in history, one of the last and choicest results of spiritual discipline.

I do not know any other study more likely than the study of history, to help us to acquire intellectual poise, justice in thought and word, freedom from the warp of undue sympathy or antipathy, the judicial habit. And this, after all, is a quality of great influence and esteem in this world, overridden, as it is, with partisanship of all sorts, and yet conscious that there is a mental attitude nobler and wiser.

VI.

For the sixth benefit to be got from historical study, I would call attention to its incomparable use in enlarging one's mental horizon.

He who does not know history must have a very limited mental horizon—a horizon as wide only as the time during which he has lived. The whole vast realm of the past is to him as if it never had been: he knows only what has been done and enjoyed and suffered by the human family since he arrived here. Even in the case of the oldest man, what is that by comparison with all the years, decades, centuries, epochs, which have rolled over this planet before the sound of his footstep was heard upon it, and which have been crowded with stupendous transactions that he is totally ignorant of except by some sort of hearsay, by broken fragments of knowledge picked up from casual tradition?

The man who knows only the time immediately around him, is in a mental condition somewhat like that of the man who knows only the place immediately around him — the man who has never traveled, who knows nothing of other neighborhoods and other peoples. Such a man must have a very false notion of himself and others;

his mind can hardly fail to be full of local prejudice and conceit; he lacks the necessary standards by which to estimate his own size and quality and that of the men and things around him. Such a man is necessarily provincial, parochial; his intellect is the intellect of a villager. So, the man who knows but little of human time, except what has elapsed since his own birth, is provincial-minded with respect to vast tracts of human experience; his mental horizon is necessarily limited to the petty circle of time which surrounds his own life in the world. To such a man history comes with its power to enlarge his own horizon by annexing to it the horizons of all the generations before him. History is for time, what travel is for space; it is an intellectual journey across oceans and continents of duration, and of ages both remote from our own and vitalized and enriched by stupendous events. There is an old aphorism to the effect that, "ignorance of what has been done in the world before he came into it, leaves a man always a child." This, perhaps, is but a far-away echo of the saying of the Chinese moralist, Lao-Tse: "Man is an infant born at midnight, who, when he sees the sun rise, thinks that yesterday has never existed." To him who has not studiously opened those books which tell of the world's yesterday, it is as though the world had never had a yesterday — as though the world had begun only when he began.

There have been many attempts to define the essential difference between man and the other animals known to us here. What is to be thought of this definition? Man is the history-knowing animal — the only animal that can know the past. Therefore, our conscious and cultivated relation to the past, through historical study, develops in us as human beings that very attribute which distinguishes us from those animals that are called the brutes.

VII.

Perhaps the most impressive consideration touching the benefit to be derived from historical study, is the one which still remains to be mentioned: history enables each generation of men to profit, if they will, by the experience of their predecessors, — especially to avoid their costliest and most painful mistakes. Without history, nearly all the practical wisdom of mankind, gained through innumerable blunders and mishaps, would be lost, and the same blunders and the same mishaps would have to be repeated and to be suffered over and over again on the part of successive generations ignorant of what had happened before.

Let us suppose that the human family should now agree that history is an undesirable branch of knowledge; that it should no longer be cultivated or taught; that all the books of history which have been written, from Herodotus down to Ranke and Stubbs and George Bancroft, should be burned up, and that no more should be written; that even the documentary sources of history should be destroyed. What would be the effect of this gigantic piece of Vandalism? Of course, before many years, the men who now know something of the past would be dead, and would have left no successors to their knowledge; and, gradually, nearly all remembrance of former times and of the men and the deeds and the sufferings of former times, of their mistakes and triumphs and failures, would be blotted out. Nearly all the lessons taught by the experience of the human family would be forgotten. Consequently, to a large extent, progress would cease; each generation, knowing but little of what men had learned before themselves, would have to begin nearly all experiments over again; and each generation would be liable to keep on repeating the errors of its predecessors, treading over again the same round of blundering attempts and

knowledge of the history of Europe during the Middle Ages and in the ancient times. But how shall we know the history of mediæval and of ancient Europe, unless we become acquainted with the remoter races from whom these earliest Europeans were derived, and the countries from which they came, and the ideas they brought with them thence, and their subsequent relations therewith?

Thus, we reach the broad principle that, as there is a certain unity in the life of the human family, so there is a certain unity in its history also; that no nation has ever lived without an original kinship with other nations, without more or less contact with other nations, without having its destinies interfered with and influenced by other nations. Consequently, no part of history can be truly known without knowing something of all parts. The ideal of the historical student should be to know the life of his own country as a constituent part of the general life of mankind. Thus, the study of American history must be preceded or at least accompanied by the study of Universal History.

Moses Coit Tyler

TABLE OF CONTENTS.

INTRODUCTION.

History, Its Departments, Aids and Divisions.—Its Sources.—Races of Mankind.—Origin of Civilisation.—Historical Nations.—Oriental and European Civilization.—Forms of Government.—Varieties of Religion.—Ethnological Table of the Caucasian Race. 25–34

PART I.—ANCIENT HISTORY—VOL. I.

CHAPTER I.—ANCIENT EGYPT.

SECTION I.

THE COUNTRY AND PEOPLE, ... 41–42

Egyptian Civilization and History the Oldest.—Fertility of the Nile Valley and Cause.—Origin and Character of the Ancient Egyptians.—Geographical Divisions of Ancient Egypt.—Chief Cities.

SECTION II.

SOURCES OF EGYPTIAN HISTORY, ... 43–44

Ancient Egyptian Myths.—Historical Writings of Herodotus, Diodorus, Eratosthenes, Apollodorus, and Manetho.—Modern Discovery of the Rosetta Stone and Deciphering of Hieroglyphic Inscriptions.—Difference Among Modern Egyptologists as to the Antiquity of Egypt.

SECTION III.

POLITICAL HISTORY, ... 44–62

Periods of Egyptian History.—Founding of the First Dynasty at Memphis by Menes.—Contemporary Dynasties.—Fourth Dynasty at Memphis and the Great Pyramids.—High Civilization under the Fourth Dynasty.—Contemporary Dynasties.—Five Kingdoms in Egypt.—Great Power of Thebes.—Conquest of Lower Egypt by the Shepherd Kings.—Greatness of Thebes under the Twelfth Dynasty.—The Labyrinth and Lake Mœris.—Conquest of Upper Egypt by the Shepherd Kings.—End of the Old Empire.—The Middle Empire under the Shepherd Kings.—Their Barbarous Rule.—Absence of Records.—Expulsion of the Shepherd Kings.—All Egypt United under the New Empire Over a Thousand Years.—Prosperity, Power and High Civilization of Egypt under the Eighteenth, Nineteenth and Twentieth Dynasties.—Amasis, Amenset, Thothmes IV.—Great Sphinx.—Amunoph III. and the two Colossi.—Vocal Memnon.—Horus.—Rameses I.—Seti and the Great Hall of Karnak.—Rameses the Great.—Rameseum at Thebes.—Height of Egyptian Art.—Menepta and the Exodus.—Rameses III. and the Temple-Palace at Thebes.—His Successors.—Decline of Egypt.—The Priest-Kings.—Temporary Revival under the Twenty-second Dynasty Founded by Sheshonk I.—Disturbed Condition of Egypt under the next two Dynasties.—Conquest of Egypt by Sabaco the Ethiopian.—His Defeat by Sargon of Assyria at Raphia.—Assyrian Conquest of the Delta.—Tirhakah.—Assyrian Conquest of Egypt.—Psammetichus Recovers the Independence of Egypt.—Migration of the Warrior Caste to Ethiopia.—Reign of Neko.—Commerce.—Circumnavigation of Africa.—Neko Defeated by Nebuchadnezzar of Babylon at Carchemish.—Reign of Uahabra.—Egypt Tributary to Babylon.—Amasis Throws off the Babylonian Supremacy.—Defeat of Psammenitus at Pelusium and Persian Conquest of Egypt.—Table of Kings.

SECTION IV.

EGYPTIAN CIVILIZATION, ... 63–89

Origin of the Egyptians.—Their Physical Characteristics.—Egyptian Tribes.—Intellectual and Moral Qualities of the Egyptians.—Government.—The King.—His Sacred Character.—His Rights and Duties Strictly Prescribed by the Sacred Books.—Castes.—Priests.—Their Mode of Life.—Their Ascendency over the People.—Priestly Professions.—Physicians.—Military Caste.—Common People.—Egyptian Castes Not Absolutely Fixed.—Intermarriages and Transitions.—Evils of the Caste System.—Its Tendency to National Decay.—Egyptian Land System.—Agricultural Laborers.—Egyptian Laws.—Egyptian Army.—War Chariots.—Archery.—Weapons of Warfare.—Treatment of Prisoners.—Mutilation of the Enemy's Slain.—Climate of the Nile Valley.—Vegetables.—Animals.—M'nerals.—Causes of Egypt's Productiveness.—Cause of its Dense Population.—Agriculture.—Song to Oxen.—Care of Animals.—Field Sports.—Beasts of Burden.—Egypt an Object of Interest in All Ages.—Density of the Ancient Population.—Memphis and Thebes.—Architecture.—Pyramids and Obelisks.—Egypt the Ancient World's School.—Progress in Science.—Skill in the Finer Mechanical Arts.—Egyptian Language.—Art of Writing.—Three Kinds of Writing.—Hieroglyphics and Papyrus.—Discovery of the Rosetta Stone and the Key to the Hieroglyphics.—Dr. Young and Champollion.—Egyptian Custom of Recording Everything in Pictures and Writing.—Sources of our Knowledge of the Ancient Egyptians.—Revelation of Domestic Scenes from the Egyptian Tombs.—Progress in the Arts thus Demonstrated.—High State of Civilization thus Shown.—Curious Scenes.—Egyptian Dress.—Trades and Occupations.—Stone Cutting.—Commerce.—Sculpture and Painting.—Religious Character of Egyptian Art.—The Great Temple-Palace at Medinet-Abu.—Egyptian Tombs—Custom of Embalming the Dead.—Paintings and Sculpture in the Tombs.—Chambers in the Tombs.—Scenes Represented in the Tombs.—Process of Embalming.—Mummies of Animals.—Methods of Embalming.

(xi)

SECTION V.

EGYPTIAN MYTHOLOGY AND RELIGION, . 89–100

Religious character of the Ancient Egyptians.—Character of their Religion.—Two Kinds of Religion.—Three Orders of Gods.—The Eight Gods of the First Order.—Amun.—Kneph.—Phthah. —Khem.—Phrah.—Reason for Two Systems.—Second Order of Gods.—Third Order.—Change in the Third Order.—Typhon.—Myth of Osiris and Isis.—Plutarch's Explanations.—Allegorical Meaning.—Phthah the Chief God in Lower Egypt.—Amun in Upper Egypt.—Comparison of Amun with Phthah.—Phrah the Life-Giving God.—God's of Upper Egypt.—Comparison of Egypt's Gods with those of Greece.—Local Deities.—Animal Worship.—Sacred Animals.—Sacred Bull, Apis, of Memphis.—Place of Burial.—Animals Sacred in One Place not so in Another Place.—Mummies of Sacred Animals.—Reasons for Animal Worship.—Religious Festivals.—Religious Daily Life of the People.—Priests.—Orders of the Priesthood.—Gloomy Character of the Egyptian Religion.—Egyptian Temples.—Temple of Amun.—Doctrine of the Soul's Immortality.—Transmigration of the Soul.—Comparison with the Hindoo Doctrine.—Reasons for Ornamenting the Egyptian Tombs and Embalming the Dead.—Ritual for the Dead.—Belief in Future Rewards and Punishments.—Embalming the Dead.—Funeral Ceremonies.—Trial of the Dead.—Burial of the Wicked.—Of the Good.—Sacred Lakes.—Influence of these Ceremonies on the People.—The Soul's Trial before the Tribunal of the Gods.—Hall of the Two Truths

SECTION VI.

THE ANCIENT ETHIOPIANS, ... 100–103

The Ancient Ethiopians and their Country.—Their Antiquity.—Savage and Civilized Ethiopians. —Fertility of Ethiopia.—Monuments.—Meroe and Its Caravan Trade.—Its Red Sea Ports.—Animals. —Kingdom of Meroe.—Its History.—Ethiopian Kings of Egypt.—Egyptian Migration to Ethiopia. —Destruction of the Persian Army of Invasion by Famine.—Ethiopian Religion.—The Priesthood and Their Influence.—Temples.—Power of the Priests Over the Kings.—Ethiopian Queens.—Candace and her War with the Romans.—Judaism and Christianity Successfully Established in Ethiopia. —Christianity Still the Religion of Abyssinia.—Pyramids of Meroe.—Kingdom of Axume and Its Capital, Axum.—Ruins of Axum.—Inscription on a Stone Slab.—King Aeizemus.—Nubian Pyramids.—Temples near Merawe.—Great Rock Temple of Ipsambul.—Ruins of Barkal.—Rock-hewn Temples.—Meroe as an Ancient Commercial Emporium.—Causes of its Extinction.

CHAPTER II.—CHALDÆAN EMPIRE.

SECTION I.

GEOGRAPHY OF CHALDÆA, ... 105–107

Cradle of Asiatic History and Civilization.—Ancient Date in Chaldæan History.—Testimony of the Hebrew Scriptures.—Land of Shinar.—The Tigris and Euphrates Rivers.—Geographical and Political Divisions in the Tigris-Euphrates Valley. —Mesopotamia.—Chaldæa, or Babylonia.—Susiana.—Assyria.—The Three Great Empires in the Tigris-Euphrates Valley.—Antiquity of Chaldæa.—Its Fertility and Productions.—Testimony of Herodotus and Other Writers.—Brick and Bitumen.—Climate of Chaldæa, or Babylonia.—Animals.—Cities.—Testimony of the Book of Genesis.—Ur of the Chaldees and Its Ruins.—Other Cities.

SECTION II.

SOURCES OF CHALDÆAN HISTORY, . . . 107–108

Berosus.—The Old Testament.—Herodotus, Ctesias and Diodorus Siculus.—Modern Investigation. —Explorations of Layard and Others at Nineveh, Babylon and Other Ancient Cities.—Cuneiform Inscriptions.—The Canon of Ptolemy.—Assyrian Canon.—Modern Writers.

SECTION III.

POLITICAL HISTORY, ... 108–113

Origin of Chaldæa.—Dynasties According to Berosus.—Mosaic Account of Nimrod.—His Character and Deification.—Universal Tradition of Nimrod.—Migrations from Chaldæa.—Urukh and His Great Temples.—Ilgi.—His Signet-cylinder in the British Museum.—Conquest of Chaldæa by a Susianian or Elamite Dynasty.—Kudur-Nakhunta. —Kadur-Lagamer and His Conquest of Canaan.—His Successors.—Third and Fourth Dynasties.—New Style of Architecture.—Conquest of Chaldæa by an Arabian Dynasty.—Khammurabi and His Great Canal.—His Successors.—Wars and Marriage-Alliances with Assyria.—Assyrian Conquest of Chaldæa.—Table of Kings.

SECTION IV.

CHALDÆAN CIVILIZATION, ... 113–120

Nimrod, Urukh, and Chedorlaomer.—Rawlinson on Chaldæan Civilization.—Chaldæan Architecture.—Brick and Bitumen.—Temples.—Dwellings. —Tombs.—Brick Vaults.—Dish-cover Coffins.—Double-jar Coffins.—Sepulchral Mounds.—Drainage of the Mounds.—Cuneiform Writing.—Clay Tablets.—Legends on Bricks.—Pottery.—Figures on Clay Tablets.—Arms, Implements and Ornaments.—Implements of Stone and Bronze.—Cloths and Textile Fabrics.—Gem Engraving.—Signet-cylinders and Their Seals and Legends.—Commerce.—Caravan Trade.—" Ships of Ur."—Articles of Food.—Astronomy and Arithmetic.—Weights and Measures.—Chaldæa's Legacy to Posterity.

SECTION V.

CHALDÆAN COSMOGONY AND RELIGION , 120–132

Chaldæan Account of the Creation as Given by Berosus.—Likeness Between Chaldæan and Jewish Legends.—Assyrian Account of the Creation as Deciphered from the Tablet Inscriptions.—Mythical Antediluvian Dynasty of Berosus.—Chaldæan Account of the Deluge as Related by Berosus.—Assyrian Account from the Tablets.—Traditions of a Great Flood in Countries Subject to Overflows.—Link Between Chaldæan and Jewish Legends.—Account of the Tower of Babel by Berosus.—Rawlinson's View of Chaldæan Mythology.—Polytheistic Religion of Chaldæa.—Grouping of the Chaldæan Deities.—Chief Deity.—First Triad and Their Wives.—Second Triad and Their Wives.—Five Planetary Deities.—Inferior Deities.—Relationship of the Deities.—Il or Ra.—Ana and Anata.—Bel-Nimrod.—Beltis or Mulita.—Hea or Hoa and Davkina.—Sin or Hurki, and the Great Lady.—San or

Sansi, and Gula or Anunit.—Vul or Iva, and Shala or Tala.—Nin or Ninip.—Merodach.—Nergal.—Ishtar or Nana.—Symbolical Myth of Ishtar.—Nebo.—Astronomical Character of the Chaldæan Worship.—Origin of Astrological Signs and Superstitions.

CHAPTER III.—THE ASSYRIAN EMPIRE.

SECTION I.

GEOGRAPHY OF ASSYRIA, ... 137-138

Location of Assyria.—Productions of Assyria.—Mineral Products.—Climate.—Wild and Domestic Animals.—Extent of Assyrian Ruins.—Scriptural Account of Early Assyrian Cities.—The Four Great Cities.—Ruins of Nineveh, Calah, Asshur and Dur-Sargina.—Other Ruins.—Arbil or Arbela.—Other Assyrian Cities.

SECTION II.

SOURCES OF ASSYRIAN HISTORY, ... 139-140

Herodotus and Ctesias.—The Canon of Ptolemy and the Assyrian Canon.—Their Harmony and Authenticity.—Inscriptions on Assyrian Tablets, Bricks, Sculptures.—Chronologies of Berosus and Herodotus. — Disagreement between Herodotus and Ctesias.—Their Respective Ancient and Modern Supporters.—The Fidelity and Accuracy of Herodotus.—The Temper and Disposition of Ctesias Toward Herodotus.—Herodotus Sustained by the Other Historical Sources.—Origin and Duration of the Assyrian Empire According to Herodotus.—According to Berosus.

SECTION III.

POLITICAL HISTORY, ... 140-195

Periods of Assyrian History.—Chaldæan Origin of the Assyrians.—First Evidence of Assyrian Independence.—Shalmaneser I.—Tiglathi-Nin I.—His Successors.—Mutaggil-Nebo and Asshur-risilim.—Tiglath-Pileser I.—His Wars.—His Restorations and Temples.—His Invocation.—Religious Tone of His Inscription.—General Condition of Assyria.—Tiglath-Pileser's War with Babylon.—Rock Tablet of Tiglath-Pileser I.—Asshur-bil-kala and Shamas Vul I.—Obscure Interval.—Asshurdayan II., Vul-lush II. and Tiglathi-Nin II.—Asshur-izir-pal.—His Wars.—His Edifices.—His Great Palace.—His Sculptures.—His Stelæ and Obelisks—Shalmaneser II.—His Wars. — Tribute Taken from Jehu, King of Israel.—His Palace.—The Black Obelisk.—Rebellion of Asshur-danin-pal.—Extent of Assyrian Dominion.—Shamas Vul II.—Vul-lush III.—His Sculptures.—His Wife, Semiramis.—Pul.—Nabonassar at Babylon.—The Prophet Jonah at Nineveh.—End of the Old Assyrian Empire and Beginning of the New or Lower Assyrian Empire under Tiglath-Pileser II.—His Wars.—Shalmaneser IV.—His Wars.—Siege of Tyre and Samaria.—Sargon's Revolt and Usurpation.—His Wars.—Capture of Samaria.—His War with Sabaco, King of Egypt.—Assyrian Victory at Raphia.—Capture of Ashdod.—Sargon's Other Conquests.—His War with Susiana.—Sargon's Town and Palace.—Sennacherib.—His Wars.—His Victory over the Egyptians and Ethiopians at Altaku.—His War with Hezekiah, King of Judah.—Siege of Jerusalem.—Submission of Hezekiah.—Sennacherib's Second Syrian Expedition.—Destruction of His Army at Pelusium.—Its Effects.—Sennacherib's War with Susiana.—Babylonian Revolt under Susub.—Susub's Defeat.—Renewed Defection of Babylon.—Sennacherib's Palace at Nineveh.—His Employment of Forced Labor.—Assassination of Sennacherib.—Esar-haddon.—His Wars.—His Invasion of Arabia.—His Conquest of Egypt.—Colonization of Palestine.—Esar-haddon's Palace at Calah.—Asshur-bani-pal.—His Wars.—His Conquest of Egypt, Tyre, Cilicia and Susiana.—His Relations with Lydia.—His Love of Hunting.—His Literary Tastes.—His Edifices.—His Great Palace at Nineveh.—His Sculptures.—Asshur-bani-pal Known to the Greeks.—His Cruelties.—Decline of Assyria.—Scythian Inroad.—Asshur-emidilin, the Last Assyrian King.—Effects of the Scythian Invasion on Assyria.—Cyaxares, King of Media, Attacks Nineveh.—Treachery of Nabopolassar.—Capture and Destruction of Nineveh and Fall of the Assyrian Empire.—Table of Kings.

SECTION IV.

ASSYRIAN CIVILIZATION, ... 196-219

Rawlinson on the Character of the Assyrian Empire.—The Assyrians a Semitic Race.—Their Kinship with the Jews.—Resemblances Between the Two Races in Physiognomy, Character, Customs, etc.—Valor of the Assyrians.—Ferocity Tempered by Clemency.—Their Treachery.—Their Pride.—Greek Accounts of their Voluptuousness and Sensuality Exaggerated.—Their Mental Power.—Their Superiority Over the Egyptians.—Their Mental and Physical Vigor.—Assyrian Writing.—Stone Slabs and Clay Cylinders.—Inscribed Bulls and Lions.—Obelisks.—Durability of the Tablets.—Assyrian Bas-reliefs.—Their Varieties.—Mimetic Art.—Painting.—Taste for Display.—Modern Excavations in Assyria.—Description of an Assyrian Palace.—Architecture.—The Present Condition of the Ruins of Nineveh.—Its Walls.—Palaces and Temples on its Mounds.—Ancient Accounts of Nineveh.—Assyrian Warfare.—War Chariots.—Cavalry.—Infantry.— Weapons.—Sieges. — Battering Rams and Movable Towers.—Catapult or Balista.—Treatment of Captives.—Spoils of War.—Despotism.—The Sovereign.—Musical Instruments—Dress.—Food.—Entertainments.—Commerce.—Practical Character of their Arts and Civilization.—Their Architecture Practical.—Their Palaces Superior to Their Temples.—Manufactures and the Useful Arts.—Metallurgy. — Mechanical Knowledge.—Rawlinson on Their Progress.—Their Military and Material Greatness.

SECTION V.

ASSYRIAN RELIGION, ... 220-230

Identity of the Assyrian and Chaldæan Religions.—Few Differences.—Asshur the Supreme God of Assyria.—Asshur's Deification.—Asshur's Emblems.—The Sacred Tree.—The Next Deities.—Anu.—His Temples.—Bel.—His Emblem.—His Temples.—Hea or Hoa.—His Emblem.—His Temples.—Beltis.—Her Temples.—Sin, the Moon-god.—His Emblem. — His Temples. — His Wars. — His Emblem. — His Temples.—Vul or Iva.—His Emblem.—His Temples.—Gula.—Her Emblem.—Her Temples. — Niu or Ninip. — His Emblem. — His Temples. — Merodach.—His Emblem. — Nergel.—His Emblem.—His Temples.—Ishtar.—Her Temples.—Nebo.—His Statues.—His Temple.—Inferior Deities.—The Female Divinities.—Character of the Goddesses.—Minor Male Deities.—Genii.—Good Genii. — Evil Genii. — Their Figures. — Assyrian

TABLE OF CONTENTS.

Idols.—Mode of Worship.—Sacrifices of Animals.—Altars.—Thank-Offerings.—Religious Perform- ances of the King.—Priests.—Festivals.—Fasts.—Religious Character.—Religious Ostentation.

CHAPTER IV.—THE MEDIAN EMPIRE.

SECTION I.

GEOGRAPHY OF MEDIA, ... 231-234
Situation of Media.—Geographical Description.—Climate.—Minerals.—Animals.—Media Magna and Media Atropatênê.—The Two Ecbatanas.—The Southern Ecbatana.—Its Royal Palace.—The Northern Ecbatana.—Other Median Cities.

SECTION II.

POLITICAL HISTORY, ... 234-244
Origin of the Medes.—Greek Legends Respecting the Medes.—Early Assyrian Accounts of Media.—Median Kings According to Ctesias.—According to Herodotus.—Founding of the Median Empire by Cyaxares.—His Unsuccessful Attack on Assyria.—Scythian Invasion of Media.—Expulsion of the Scyths.—Legend of Zarina.—Duration of the Scythian Supremacy According to Herodotus.—According to Eusebius.—Capture of Nineveh and Overthrow of the Assyrian Empire.—Division of the Assyrian Empire between Media and Babylonia.—Conquests of Cyaxares.—War between Media and Lydia.—Peace Caused by a Solar Eclipse on the Eve of a Battle.—Alliance and Friendship between Media, Lydia and Babylonia.—Alyattes, the Successor of Cyaxares.—His Character.—His Court.—The Magi.—Peaceful Reign of Astyages.—Contradictory Accounts of Astyages.—His Domestic Relations.—Early Connection of Media and Persia.—Cyrus the Great at the Median Court.—His Escape into Persia.—Revolt of the Persians under Cyrus.—Defeats of the Medes and Death of Astyages.—End of the Median Empire and Beginning of the Medo-Persian Empire.—Extent of the Median Empire.

SECTION III.

MEDIAN CIVILIZATION, ... 245-248
The Medes and Persians a Kindred Aryan Race.—Testimony of the Persian Sculptures.—The Median Women.—Rawlinson on the Modern Persians.—Bravery of the Medes.—Simple Life of the Early Medes.—Later Luxury and Degeneracy.—Military Costume and Arms.—Dress of the Medes in Peace.—Later Luxury in Dress and Banquets.—Court Ceremonial.—Royal Amusement.—Hunting.—The Royal Harem or Seraglio.—Corruption and Degeneracy of the Medes.—Median Architecture and Sculpture.

SECTION IV.

ZOROASTRIANISM AND MAGISM, ... 248-263
Zoroaster and Zend-Avesta.—Testimony of Greek Writers.—Plutarch's Account.—Translation of the Zend-Avesta into French by Anquetil du Perron.—Modern Orientalists on the Zend-Avesta.—Uncertainty Concerning Zoroaster's Country and Time.—His Wonderful Influence.—His Personality Impressed on his Religion.—His Belief Concerning the Dualism of Good and Evil.—Change in the Climate of Northern Asia.—Character of the Zend-Avesta.—Its Books.—Ahura-Mazda and Angra-Mainyus.—The Great War between Them.—Zoroastrianism Free from Idolatry.—Teachings of the Zend-Avesta.—Worship.—Sacrifice.—Purity.—Truth.—Later Corruption of Zoroastrianism by its Contact with Magism.—Worship of the Elements.—The Magi.—Fusion of Zoroastrianism and Magism.—Disposition of the Dead.—Rawlinson on this Mixed Religion.—Extracts from the Zend-Avesta.

CHAPTER V.—THE BABYLONIAN EMPIRE.

SECTION I.

EXTENT OF THE BABYLONIAN EMPIRE, . 264-266
Babylonia or Chaldæa.—The Countries Included in the Babylonian Empire.—Agricultural Products of Babylonia.—Of Susiana, Northern Mesopotamia, and Northern Syria.—Of Southern Syria and Palestine.—Mineral Products of the Empire.—Building Stone.—Wild Animals.—Climate.—Countries Bordering on the Empire.—Great Cities.

SECTION II.

POLITICAL HISTORY, ... 266-278
Beginning of the Babylonian Empire.—Babylonia under Assyrian Rule.—The Assyrian Dynasty in Babylonia.—Early Wars between Babylonia and Assyria.—Nabonassar.—His Successors.—Merodach-Baladan.—Revolt of Nabopolassar and his Alliance with Cyaxares of Media.—Overthrow of Assyria and Founding of the Babylonian Empire by Nabopolassar.—His Peaceful Reign and His Alliance with Media.—Neko, King of Egypt, Invades the Babylonian Empire.—His Defeat at Carchemish by Nabopolassar's Son, Nebuchadnezzar.—Nebuchadnezzar's Great Reign.—Nebuchadnezzar Attacks Jehoiakim, King of Judah.—Nebuchadnezzar's Campaign against Apries, King of Egypt, and Zedekiah, King of Judah.—Siege and Capture of Jerusalem.—Siege and Capture of Tyre.—Conquest of Phœnicia and Palestine.—Nebuchadnezzar's Invasions of Egypt.—Results of His Victories.—His Great Works.—The Walls of Babylon.—The "Hanging Gardens."—Other Works.—Nebuchadnezzar's Private Life.— His Personal Character. — His Wealth. — His Occasional Piety.—His Cruelties.—His Devotion to His Median Wife.—His Lycanthropy.—His Recovery.—Brilliancy of the End of his Reign.—Evil-Merodach. — Neriglissar. — Laborosoarchod. — Nabonadius the Last Babylonian King.—Lydian Embassy.—Nabonadius Strengthens Babylon.—His Ally, Crœsus, King of Lydia, Defeated by Cyrus the Great of Persia.—Nabonadius Attacked and Defeated by Cyrus.—Belshazzar's Feast.—Capture of Babylon by Cyrus, and End of the Babylonian Empire.—Table of Kings.

SECTION III.

BABYLONIAN CIVILIZATION, ... 279-298

Professor Rawlinson on the Babylonian Empire.—The Later Babylonians a Mixed Race.—Semitizing of the Old Chaldæan Population.—Physical Characteristics of the Later Babylonians.—Their Hair and Beards.—Babylonian Women.—Physical Similarity of the Assyrians and Babylonians.—Intellectual Ability of the Babylonians.—Enterprise.—Luxurious Habits.—Warlike Bravery and Skill.—Violence and Cruelty.—Pride.—Religious Feeling.—Honesty and Calmness.—Extent of the Ruins of Babylon.—Walls of Babylon.—Gates.—Houses.—Quays, River Walls, and Bridge.—Palaces of Babylon.—Temple of Bel.—Great Palace.—Hanging Gardens.—Smaller Palace.—Walls of Babylon.—Its Ruins at Present.—Babil, Kasr and Amran Mounds.—Lines of Rampart and Low Mounds.—El Homeira Mound.—Extent of Ruins.—Recent Explorations.—Identification of Sites.—Birs-i-Nimrud.—Ingenuity of the Babylonians.—Babylonian Architecture.—Temples.—Palaces.—Hanging Gardens.—Domestic Architecture.—Bricks.—Cement.—Mimetic Art.—Mechanical Arts.—Stone Cutting.—Pottery.—Textile Fabrics.—Carpets and Muslins.—Astronomy. — Observations. — Constellations.—Uranography.—Zodiacal Constellations.—Eclipses.—Catalogue of Fixed Stars.—Sun Dials.—Other Astronomical Instruments.—Astrology.—Influence of Stars on Individuals and Nations.—Changes of Weather.—Mathematics.—Manners and Customs.—The King's Tiara.—Priests' Attire.—Weapons of Warfare.—Babylonian Armies.—Cavalry.—Character of the Babylonian Armies.—The Priests.—"Wise Men."—The Chaldæans as Priests and Philosophers.—The Priests a Learned Body.—Their Learning.—Their Social Standing.—Babylonian Manufactures and Commerce.—Their Imports.—Agriculture.—Cultivation of the Date-Palm.—Food.—Babylonian Music.—Babylonian Women.—Implements.

SECTION IV.

BABYLONIAN RELIGION, ... 299-302

Identity of the Early Chaldæan and the Later Babylonian Religion.—Difference in the Ranks of Deities.—Nebuchadnezzar's Preference for Merodach.—Bel Restored to his Former Place by Nabonadius.—Confounding of Beltis and Ishtar.—Bel, Nebo and Merodach the Chief Deities of the Later Babylonians. — Nergal.—Local Character of the Gods.—Babylonian Images.—Material of the Idols.—Magnificence of the Worship.—Festivals.—Religious Prostitution.—Cleanliness and Uncleanliness.—Symbolism in Religion.—Mystic Numbers.—Pictorial Symbols.—Sacred Names of Temples.

CHAPTER VI.—KINGDOMS OF ASIA MINOR.

SECTION I.

GEOGRAPHY OF ASIA MINOR, ... 305-307

Situation. — Boundaries. — Extent. — Climate.—Productions.--Rivers.—Mountains.—Lakes.—Minerals.—Islands along the Coast.—Asia Minor in History.—Geographical and Political Divisions.

SECTION II.

PHRYGIA AND CILICIA, ... 307-308

Early Races of Asia Minor.—Phrygians.—Cilicia.

SECTION III.

KINGDOM OF LYDIA, ... 308-314

Rank and Situation of Lydia.—Its Cities.—The Lydians and their Wealth.—Their Origin.—The Three Dynasties of Lydia.—Lydian Traditions.—Beginning of the Real History of Lydia.—Gyges.—Invasion of the Cimmerians.—Defeat and Death of Gyges.—Ardys.—Sadyattes.—Alyattes.—Expulsion of the Cimmerians.—Founding of the Great Lydian Empire.—War with Media.—Peace in Consequence of a Solar Eclipse on the Eve of a Battle.—Alliance and Friendship of Lydia, Media and Babylonia.—War with the Greek Colonists.—Crœsus.—His Wars and Conquests.—Greatness of Lydia.—Wealth of Crœsus.—Story of Crœsus and Solon.—War With Cyrus the Great of Persia.—Defeat and Captivity of Crœsus.—End of the Lydian Kingdom.—Table of Kings.

CHAPTER VII.—PHŒNICIA AND SYRIA.

SECTION I.

PHŒNICIA AND ITS PEOPLE, ... 315-316

Situation and Extent of Phœnicia.—The Phœnicians a Semitic People.—The Phœnician Cities.—Sidon.—Tyre.

SECTION II.

HISTORY OF TYRE, ... 316-320

Short Duration of Phœnician Independence.—Supremacy of Tyre.—King Abibaal.—Hiram.—Baaleazar. — Abdastartus. — Eth-baal. — Matgen.—Pygmalion and Dido. — Flight of Dido, Who Founded Carthage.—Assyrian Conquest of Phœnicia.—Hiram II.—Elulæus.—Five Years' Siege of Tyre by the Assyrians, Who Finally Retire.—Recovery of Phœnician Independence.—Second Assyrian Conquest of Phœnicia.—Capture of Tyre by Sennacherib.—Revolt of Sidon.—Its Reconquest by Esar-haddon of Assyria.—Revolt of the Phœnician Cities Subdued by Asshur-bani-pal.—Egyptian Supremacy over Phœnicia.—Babylonian Supremacy.—Thirteen Years' Siege of Tyre by Nebuchadnezzar.—Defeat of the Egyptians.—Phœnicia under Medo-Persian Rule.—Siege and Capture of Tyre by Alexander the Great.—Phœnicia under the Macedonian Dominion.—Subsequent History.

SECTION III.

PHŒNICIAN COMMERCE AND COLONIES, . 321-323

The Phœnicians the Leading Manufacturing, Commercial, Colonizing and Maritime People of Antiquity. — Rapid Growth of Phœnician Commerce.—Carrying-Trade.— Extent of Phœnician Colonies. — Phœnician Land Trade. — Precious Metals from Spain.—Tin from Cornwall.—Phœnician Voyage Around Southern Africa.—Commercial Enterprise of the Phœnicians.

SECTION IV.

PHŒNICIAN ARTS AND CIVILIZATION, . . 323-325

Phœnician Manufactures.—Tyrian Purple.—Veg-

xvi   TABLE OF CONTENTS.

etable Dyes.—Glass-blowing.—Pottery.—Bronze-work.—Jewelry.—Ivory-carvings.—Agriculture.—Letters.—Phœnician Alphabet.—Phœnician Language.—Literature.—Architecture.—Statuary.—Paintings.—Dress.—Testimony of the Egyptian Paintings.—Of Isaiah.

SECTION V.

PHŒNICIAN RELIGION, ... 326-327
Limited Sources of Information Concerning the Phœnician Religion.—The Works of Philo Byblus.—Origin and Character of the Phœnician Religion.—A Narrow Polytheism.—Gods.—Baal.—Astarte.—Sun and Star Worship.—Cruel and Licentious Rites.—No Idolatry.—Praise, Prayer and Sacrifice.—Festivals.—General Tendency of the Worship to Lower and Debase Man.—Rawlinson's View.

SECTION VI.

GEOGRAPHY OF SYRIA, ... 328-330
Situation of Syria.—Mountains.—Productions.—Climate.—Animals.—Damascus.—Antioch.—Hierapolis.—Emessa.—Tadmor, or Palmyra.—Baalbec, or Heliopolis.—Earliest Inhabitants.—Petty States of Ancient Syria.—Syria under Foreign Dominion.—Syria the Theatre of Important Events.

SECTION VII.

HISTORY OF DAMASCUS, ... 331-333
Five Great States of Ancient Syria.—Syria of Damascus.—Remote Antiquity of Damascus.—Origin of the Kingdom of Damascus.—Reigns of Hadad, Rezon, Tab-rimmon, Ben-hadad I., Ben-hadad II., Hazael, Ben-hadad III. and Rezin.—Assyrian Conquest of Damascus.—Table of Kings.

CHAPTER VIII.—THE HEBREW NATION.

SECTION I.

THE HEBREW PATRIARCHS, ... 337-345
Semitic Origin of the Hebrews.—Abraham's Migration from Ur of the Chaldees to the Promised Land of Canaan.—Abraham in Egypt.—Invasion of Canaan by Chedorlaomer, King of Chaldæa.—Abraham's Victory near Damascus.—Hagar Driven into the Wilderness.—Birth of Ishmael.—Lot's Flight from Sodom.—Destruction of Sodom and Gomorrah.—Birth of Isaac.—Abraham's Residence at Beer-sheba.—Attempted Sacrifice of Isaac.—Death and Burial of Sarah.—Isaac's Marriage with Rebekah.—Birth of Esau and Jacob.—Abraham's Second Marriage.—His Death and Burial.—Character of Esau and Jacob.—Esau Sells his Birthright for a Mess of Pottage.—Jacob Defrauds Esau of the Blessing which his Father Intended for him.—Esau's attempts on Jacob's Life.—Jacob's Flight to Mesopotamia.—His Sojourn with his Uncle Laban.—His Wives and Children.—His Return to Canaan.—Esau's Welcome to his Brother.—Jacob's Trouble with His Children.—Joseph Sold as a Bond Slave into Egypt.—He Becomes Prime Minister to the Reigning Pharaoh.—Famine in Egypt.—Jacob and His Family Settle in Egypt.—Jacob's Death.

SECTION II.

THE EXODUS AND WANDERINGS, . . . 346-355
Growth of the Hebrew Nation in Egypt.—Their Condition in the Land of Goshen.—Expulsion of the Shepherd Kings.—Severe Oppression of the Hebrews by Rameses the Great.—Birth of Moses.—His Education as an Egyptian Prince.—He Kills an Egyptian.—His Flight to the Land of Midian.—His Sojourn at Mount Sinai.—The Burning Bush.—Moses Undertakes the Deliverance of His Countrymen.—He Seeks Pharaoh Menepta's Court.—His Demand Rejected.—The Ten Plagues.—Institution of the Passover.—The Exodus.—The Passage of the Red Sea.—The March to Sinai.—The Laws of Moses.—Founding of the Hebrew State.—The March Resumed.—Return of the Spies.—Rebellion of the Israelites.—Their Defeat by the Canaanites.—The Wanderings in the Wilderness.—Death of Aaron.—The Advance to the Promised Land.—Conquest of the Country East of the Jordan.—Defeat of the Moabites.—Death of Moses.

SECTION III.

CONQUEST OF CANAAN—THE JUDGES, . . 355-366
Joshua, the Successor of Moses.—Passage of the Jordan.—Canaanitish Nations.—Description of Canaan, or Palestine.—Capture of Jericho, Ai and Shechem.—Joshua Conquers Canaan by the Two Decisive Battles of Beth-horon and the Waters of Merom.—Division of the Promised Land among the Twelve Tribes of Israel.—Joshua's Death.—Evils which Followed.—Period of Anarchy.—The Judges.—Character of the Office of Judge.—Exploits of Ehud.—Barak's Victory over Sisera.—Gideon's Triumph over the Midianites.—Eli, High-Priest.—Wickedness of his Sons.—Samson the Strong.—The Prophet and High-Priest, Samuel.—Defeat of the Israelites by the Philistines.—Capture of the Ark of the Covenant.—Eli's Death.—Samuel, Judge.—The Israelites Demand a King.—Samuel's Warning.—Saul Anointed King of Israel.

SECTION IV.

THE UNITED KINGDOM OF ISRAEL, . . . 366-373
Character of Saul.—Discontent of the Tribes.—Rescue of Gilead.—Saul Acknowledged by the Hebrew Nation.—Saul's Usurpation of the High-Priest's Power.—His Quarrel with Samuel.—Wars with the Philistines and Other Nations.—Extermination of the Amalekites.—Samuel Kills Agag.—He Curses Saul.—Saul's Madness.—David Anointed King.—Saul's Fondness for David.—David Kills Goliath.—Saul Seeks the Life of David.—David's Flight.—His Adventures.—Saul Massacres the Priests.—Battle of Mount Gilboa and Death of Saul and Jonathan.—David Becomes King of Judah.—The Other Eleven Tribes Adhere to Ishbosheth, Saul's Surviving Son.—Civil War.—David King of All Israel.—David Takes Jerusalem from the Jebusites and Makes it the Capital of his Kingdom.—David's Conquests.—Extent of His Empire.—His Civil Administration.—His Psalms.—His Sins.—Rebellion and Death of Absalom.—Tragic Deaths of Two Other Sons of David.—David's Death.—Solomon's Brilliant Reign.—Splendor of His Court.—Commerce of the Hebrews.—Solomon's Temple.—His Wisdom and Early Virtues.—His Proverbs.—Visit of the Queen of Sheba.—Solomon's Harem, or Seraglio.—His Luxury and Sensuality.—Its Corrupting Influence.—Decline of Solomon's Power.—His Sins.—His Death.—Accession of Rehoboam and Revolt of the Ten Tribes.

SECTION V.

THE KINGDOM OF ISRAEL, ... 373-375
Character of the Kingdom of Israel.—Idolatrous

Reign of Jeroboam.—Complete Separation of the Two Hebrew Kingdoms.—Baasha's Reign.—War with Damascus.—Omri's Reign.—The City of Samaria Founded by Omri.—Ahab and Jezebel.—Jehu's Reign.—Israel Subject to Syria.—Reign of Jeroboam II.—Shallum's Reign.—His Invasion of Assyria.—He is Conquered and Made Tributary to Assyria.—Assyrian Conquest of the Trans-Jordanic Country.—Israel Invaded by Shalmaneser IV. of Assyria.—Capture of Samaria and Assyrian Captivity Ends the Kingdom of Israel.—The Depopulated Country Colonized by Other Subjects of Sargon, King of Assyria.

SECTION VI.

THE KINGDOM OF JUDAH, ... 375-381
Advantages of Judah over Israel.—Reign of Rehoboam.—Capture of Jerusalem by Shishak, King of Egypt.—Reign of Abijah.—Asa's Good Reign.—His Victory over the Egyptians. — The Levites Join Judah.—Alliance with Damascus.—Wars with Israel.—Jehoshaphat's Reign.—Alliance with Israel.—Athaliah.—Reign of Joash.—Reign of Amaziah.—Conquest of Edom.—Uzziah's Sin.—Reign of Ahaz.—Judah Becomes Tributary to Assyria.—Hezekiah's Good Reign.—Invasion of Judah by Sennacherib, King of Assyria. — Destruction of Sennacherib's Army.—Manasseh's Wicked Reign. —His Captivity in Assyria and His Release by Esar-haddon, the Assyrian King. — Ammon's Reign. — Judah Tributary to Babylon. — Josiah's Reign and Death.—Judah Subject to Egypt.—Judah Comes under the Dominion of Babylon.—Revolts of Judah.—Zedekiah the Last King of Judah.—Capture of Jerusalem by Nebuchadnezzar of Babylon.—The Babylonian Captivity Ends the Kingdom of Judah.—Table of Kings.

SECTION VII.

BABYLONIAN CAPTIVITY AND RETURN, . 381-384
The Jews in Babylon.—Capture of Babylon and Overthrow of the Babylonian Empire by Cyrus the Great of Persia.—His Friendship for the Jews. —His Edict Permitting Them to Return to Palestine.—The Return of the Jews under Zerubbabel, Ezra and Nehemiah.—The Temple of Jerusalem Rebuilt.—Darius Hystaspes, King of Persia, Permits the Jews to Rebuild Jerusalem.—Ezra, High-Priest.—Judæa under Persian Rule.—Loyalty of the Jews to Jehovah.—End of the Old Testament History.—Jewish Civilization.—Manners and Customs.

MAPS IN VOLUME I.

World according to Strabo 21	Earliest Historic Regions..... 104
World according to Pomponius Mela 22	Ancient Egypt.. 135
World according to Dionysius Periegetes......... 23	First Great Empires............................. 134, 135
World according to Ptolemy 22, 23	Ancient Asia Minor................................... 303
World according to Eratosthenes.................... 24	Primitive Settlements.................................. 334
World according to Herodotus...................... 35	Canaan, Egypt and Route of the Israelites.... 335
Ancient Historical World............................. 36, 37	Ancient Palestine... 336
World according to Hecatæus....................... 38	Solomon's Kingdom and Phœnicia............. 385

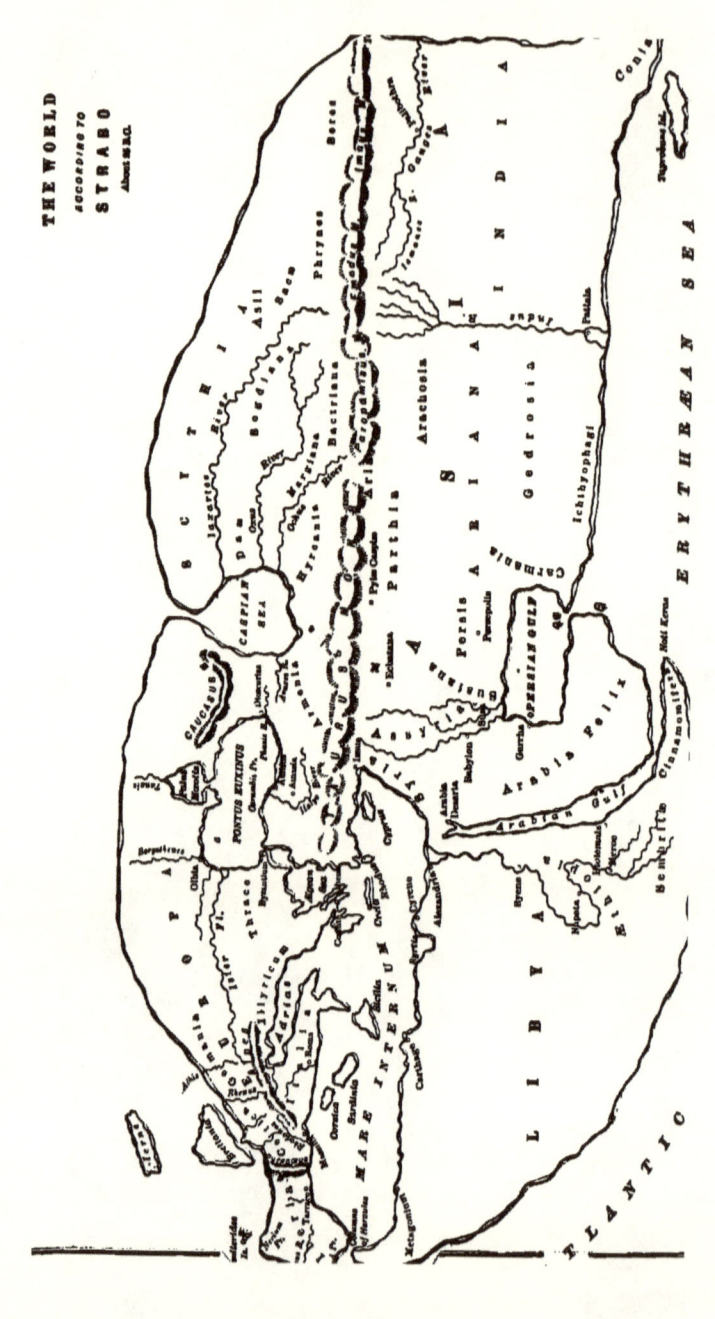

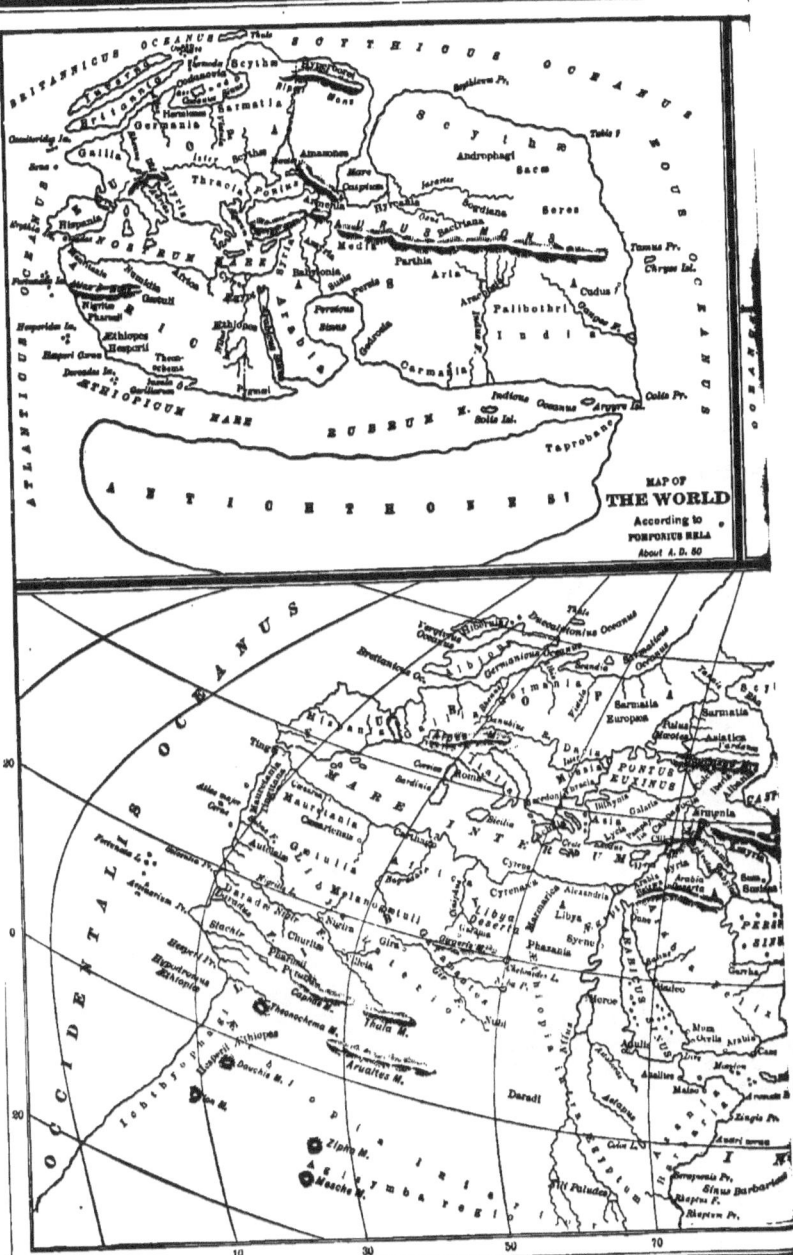

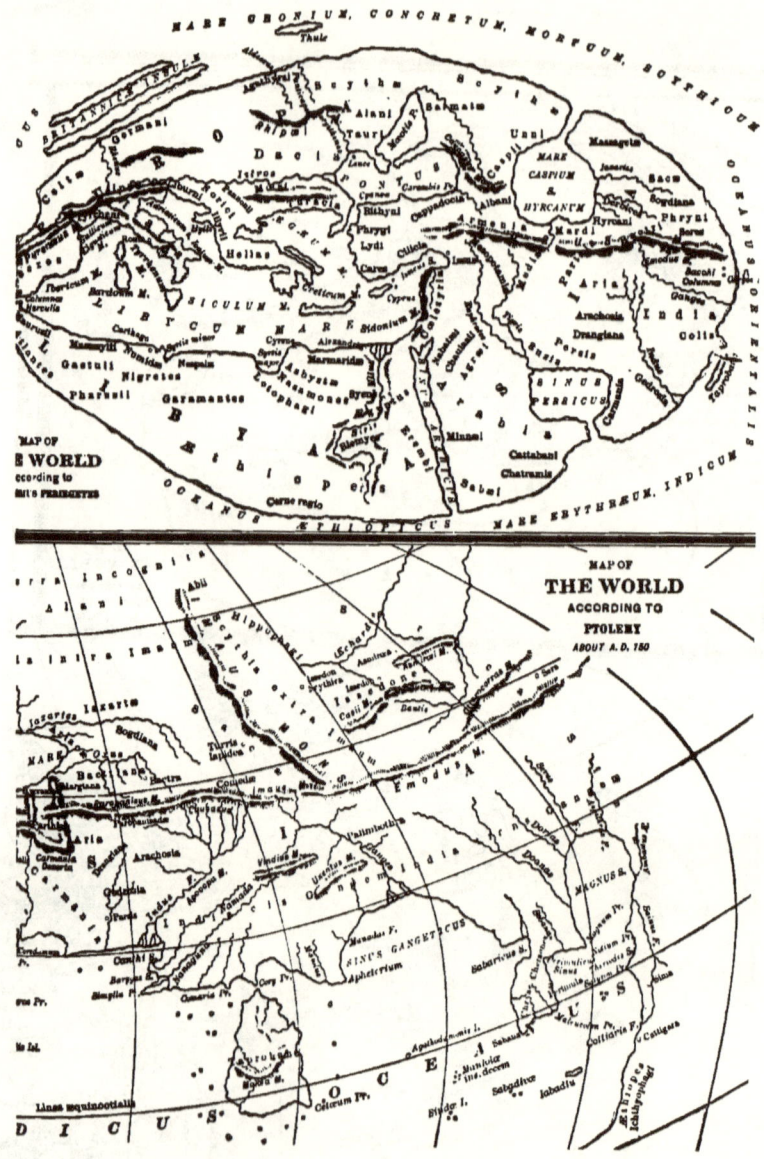

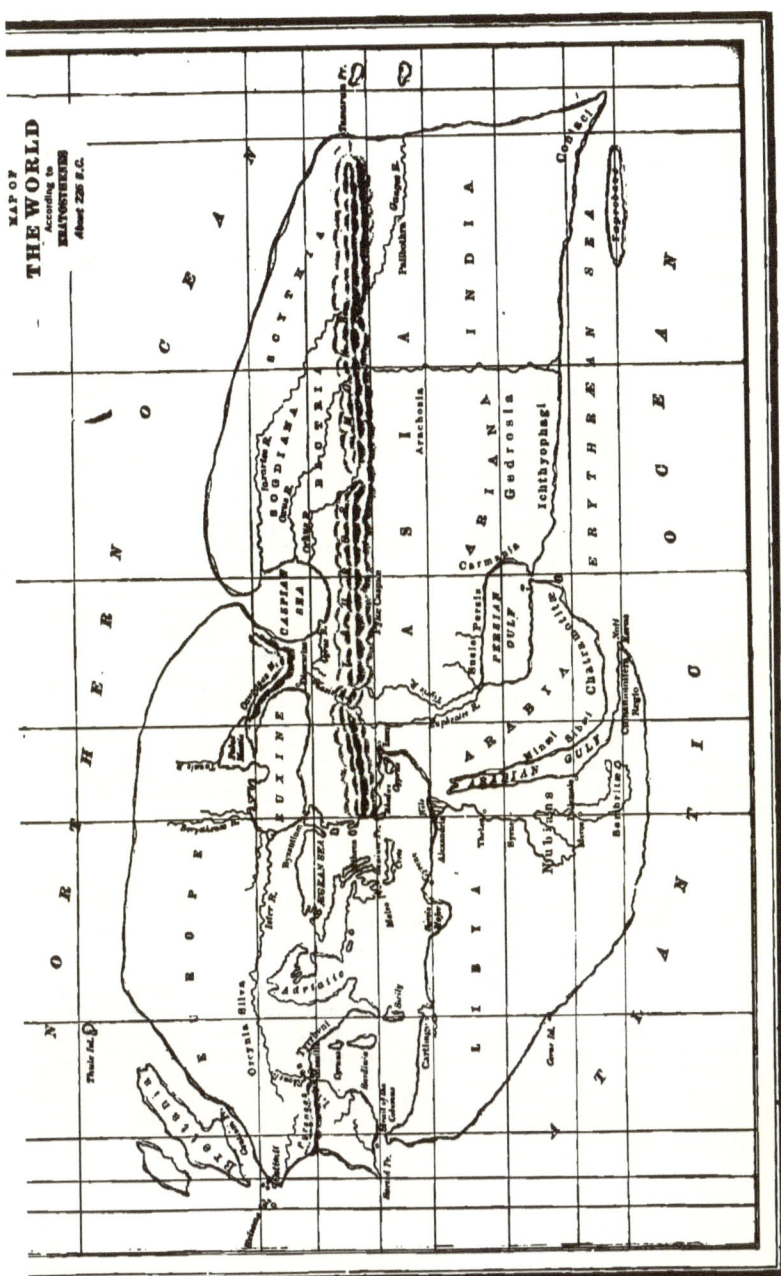

INTRODUCTION.

ISTORY is a record of events which have occurred among mankind; embracing an account of the rise and fall of nations, and other great mutations which have affected the political and social condition of the human race. In a more limited sense, History is a record of the progress of mankind in civilization; and, therefore, deals especially with those nations which have performed great achievements and exerted a commanding influence upon the fortunes of the human race. The *History of Civilization* is that department of History which treats of the progress of different nations in the arts, sciences, literature and social culture. The *Philosophy of History* treats of the events of the past in connection with their causes and consequences, and deduces from them certain principles, which may serve as a guide to statesmen in conducting the affairs of nations. Thus, History has been called "philosophy teaching by example;" and, as a celebrated writer has observed: "Social advancement is as completely under the control of natural law as is bodily growth. The life of an individual is a miniature of the life of a nation." *Sacred History* is that which is contained in the sacred scriptures; as distinguished from *Profane History*, as recorded in other books. *Ecclesiastical History* is the History of the Christian Church; while *Civil* or *Political History* deals with the rise, progress and fall of nations.

Chronology is that department of History which treats of the precise time or date of each event with respect to some fixed time called an *era* or *epoch*. Chronology and Geography have been called the two eyes of History. The one tells when, the other where, events have occurred. Christian nations compute time from the birth of Christ; while Mohammedan nations reckon from the Hegira, or Mohammed's flight from Mecca, which event occurred in the year 622 of the Christian era. The Ancient Greeks dated from the first Olympiad, 776 years before the Christian era; the Ancient Romans from the founding of Rome, 753 years before the Christian era; and the Ancient Babylonians from the *Era of Nabonassar*, 747 years before the Christian era. No dates can be established with certainty for events in Ancient History of any period more than five centuries before Christ.

Concerning the human race outside of nations, there is much important and interesting knowledge furnished by different sciences. Among these sciences, as aids to History proper, are *Ethnology*, or the science of the various races or types of mankind; *Archæology*, or the science of the ancient works of man; *Philology*, or the science of language; and *Anthropology*, or the science which deals with man in natural history.

History is generally divided into three great epochs—*Ancient History*, *Mediæval History*, and *Modern History*. Ancient History begins with the first appearance of historic records, and ends with the fall of the Western Roman Empire, A. D. 476. Mediæval History, or the History of the Middle Ages, extends from the fall of Rome, A. D. 476, to the Discovery of America, A. D. 1492. Modern History embraces the period from the Discovery of America to the present time. Sometimes, however, the world's history is divided into only two great periods—*Ancient* and *Modern;* Ancient History embracing the whole period before the fall of Rome, A. D. 476, and Modern History comprising the entire period since that event. This double division is perhaps the more logical of the two, as ancient civilization passed away with the extinction of the Western Roman Empire, while modern nations and modern institutions took their rise

INTRODUCTION.

from that point. The triple division, however, is the more convenient, and for that reason we shall follow it in this work.

The three sources of History are written records, architectural monuments and fragmentary remains. Several races of men have disappeared from the globe, leaving no records inscribed upon stone or parchment. The existence and character of these people can only be inferred from fragments of their weapons, ornaments and household utensils, found in their tombs or among the ruins of their habitations. Among these races were the Lake-dwellers of Switzerland; the prehistoric inhabitants of the Age of Stone and the Age of Bronze of the British Isles; the builders of the shell-mounds of Denmark and India; and the Mound-builders of the Mississippi Valley.

The discovery of monuments of great antiquity has aided vastly in ascertaining the date of ancient events. The *Parian Marble*, brought to England from Smyrna by the Earl of Arundel, contains a chronological arrangement of important events in Grecian history from the earliest period to 355 B. C. The *Assyrian Canon*, discovered by Sir Henry Rawlinson, the great English antiquarian, consists of a number of clay tablets, constructed during the reign of Sardanapálus, and containing a complete plan of Assyrian chronology, verified by the record of a solar eclipse which must have occurred June 15, 763 B. C. The *Fasti Capitolini*, discovered at Rome, partly in 1547 and partly in 1817 and 1818, contains in fragmentary records a list of Roman magistrates and triumphs from the beginning of the Roman Republic to the close of the reign of Augustus. The *Rosetta Stone*, discovered by a French military engineer during Bonaparte's expedition to Egypt in 1798, contains inscriptions in the Greek and Egyptian languages, the deciphering of which has led to the discovery of a key to the meaning of the hieroglyphic inscriptions on the Egyptian monuments. The fragmentary writings of Sanchoniathon give us some light on Phœnician history; those of Berosus on Babylonia and Assyria; Manetho's lists of the thirty dynasties of Egyptian kings afford us valuable information; and the works of Herodotus, the "Father of History," have given us a graphic account of the ancient nations —their annals, manners and customs, as well as a geographical description of the countries which they inhabited.

The imposing temples and palaces of Egypt, Assyria, and India have only afforded historic materials since the diligent research of European scholars and antiquarians has succeeded in deciphering the inscriptions which they bore. Within the present generation the discoveries of these European orientalists have added wonderfully to our knowledge of primeval ages, and explained in a remarkable manner the brief allusions of the Hebrew Scriptures. Thus within the last century the discovery of the Rosetta Stone, the deciphering of the Egyptian hieroglyphics, and the labors of those learned French Egyptologists Champollion and Mariette, have given us a flood of new light upon ancient Egyptian times; while the exhumations and discoveries of those celebrated English archæologists and antiquarians, Layard and Rawlinson, in the Tigris-Euphrates valleys, have almost recast the history of Assyria, Chaldæa, and Babylonia; and the patient explorations and exhumations of that German savant, Dr. Schliemann, upon the site of ancient Troy, between the years 1869 and 1873, have been rewarded with the discovery of many interesting architectural remains and furnished new illustrations of the "tale of Troy divine."

The oldest remaining books are the Hebrew Scriptures, which, in the Mosaic cosmogony, describe the origin of the universe and the creation of the first pair, Adam and Eve, and their fall from a state of innocence and purity; the murder of their son Abel by his brother Cain; the genealogy of the patriarchs of the antediluvian period; the destruction, by a great Deluge, of the whole human race, except Noah and his wife and his three sons and their wives, and their salvation in the Ark, which rested on Mount Ararat, in Armenia; the vain attempt of Noah's descendants to avert a similar pun-

MEN DURING THE STONE AGE.

MEN DURING THE BRONZE AGE.

PREHISTORIC MAN.

MEDEAN NOBLE.

ASSYRIAN HIGH PRIEST—ASSYRIAN KING.

THE EARLIEST HISTORICAL TIMES.

ishment by building the great Tower of Babel, and the consequent Confusion of Tongues and the Dispersion of the human race, which led to the peopling of every quarter of the globe by the descendants of Noah's sons, Shem, Ham, and Japheth. The writings of Berosus, the Babylonian historian, also describe the Creation, the Deluge and the Confusion of Tongues. Every civilized nation and savage tribe has some vague idea of a great flood that once covered the earth, but they all differ in their details.

We have already alluded to the writings of Sanchoniathon, the Phœnician historian; Berosus, the Babylonian; Manetho, the Egyptian; Herodotus, the "Father of History," and the great Hebrew lawgiver, Moses, the earliest sacred historian. Herodotus was the first of Grecian historians. Other Greek writers of history were Thucydides, the great philosophic historian; Xenophon, the writer of charming historical romances; Ctesias; Diodorus Siculus; Polybius; and Plutarch, the charming biographer of antiquity. Ancient Rome produced Livy, Tacitus, Sallust, and Cornelius Nepos, who have given us the facts of Roman history. For the history of the ancient Hebrews we are indebted to the books of the Old Testament and the works of Josephus, the celebrated Jewish historian, who wrote a complete history of his countrymen in Greek. Among early Christian church historians were the Roman Eusebius and the Anglo Saxon, the "Venerable Bede." The Frenchmen Comines and Froissart were celebrated chroniclers of the Middle Ages. The Italian Macchiavelli achieved fame by his historical writings. Among modern historians have been many who have acquired celebrity by their works. Such were the great trio of British historians who flourished a century ago—Hume, Gibbon and Robertson, whose works have ever since been regarded as standards. In the present century England has produced many famous writers of history; such as Macaulay, Carlyle, Grote, Thirlwall, Froude, Lingard, Arnold, Alison, Freeman, Rawlinson, Green,

Knight, Merivale, Milman, Hallam and others. France, in the last century, produced Rollin and Voltaire; and in the present century have flourished Thiers, Guizot, Sismondi, Mignet, Michelet and the brothers Thierry. In the last century Germany gave the world a great ecclesiastical historian in the person of Mosheim; and in the present century a number of German historians have given the world the benefit of their scholarly researches, among whom we may mention Niebühr, Neander, Rotteck, Heeren, Schlosser, Mommsen, Curtius and Leopold von Ranke. Among American historians the most renowned have been Hildreth, Prescott, Bancroft, Motley, Lossing and Parkman.

All traditions and written accounts point to Asia as the cradle of the human race. According to the prevalent belief of modern scholars, mankind spent its infancy in the region between the Indus and the Euphrates, the Arabian Sea and the Jaxartes. The exact location of the Garden of Eden, or Paradise, is not known. The Oriental nations reckon four Paradises in Asia—one near Damascus, in Syria; another in Chaldæa; a third in Persia; and a fourth in the island of Ceylon, where there is a lofty mountain called Adam's Peak.

Mankind has been classed by different ethnologists into a variety of races or types of humanity; the most generally accepted classification for the last century being Blumenbach's division into five races—the Caucasian, or white race; the Mongolian, or yellow race; the Ethiopian, or black race; the American, or red race; and the Malay, or brown race. The only race which has figured in history is the Caucasian. The history of the civilized world is the history of the Caucasian race. The great historical nations have belonged to this race. The only nations outside of the Caucasian race which have attained to any degree of civilization or played the least part in history have been several Mongolian nations, as the Chinese, the Japanese, the ancient Parthians, and the modern Tartars, Turks, and Magyars or Hungarians, and two American

Indian nations, the ancient Peruvians, and the Aztecs or ancient Mexicans. The Ethiopian and Malay races have never had any history nor any civilization.

The origin of nations has been involved in obscurity, which has only quite recently been removed by the diligent study and the patient research of modern European scholars. Investigation into the affinities of the various languages has given us some new knowledge upon this interesting and important subject. Comparing the languages of most of the modern European nations with those spoken by the ancient Romans, Greeks, Medes and Persians, and Hindoos, we observe that all these languages had a common origin, entirely different from those spoken by the ancient Chaldees, Assyrians, Phœnicians, Hebrews, Arabs and Egyptians; these latter being related to each other, but not to those of the nations previously named. The former of these languages are called *Aryan*, the latter *Semitic* and *Hamitic;* while the Central Asian Tartar nomads have a language called *Turanian.* Modern philologists have divided the Caucasian race into three great branches—the Aryan, Indo-European, or Japhetic; the Semitic, or Shemitic; and the Hamitic. The Aryan, or Indo-European, branch embraces the Brahmanic Hindoos, the ancient Medes and Persians, and all the European nations, except the Laps and Fins of Northern Europe, the Magyars or Hungarians, the Ottoman Turks, and the Basques of Northern Spain, all five of whom belong to the Turanian or nomadic branch of the Mongolian race. The descendants of Europeans and European colonists in America and other quarters of the globe of course also belong to the Aryan race. The Semitic branch comprises the Hebrews or Israelites, the Arabs, and the ancient Syrians, Assyrians, Babylonians, Phœnicians and Carthaginians. The Hamitic branch included the ancient Chaldees, Egyptians and Ethiopians.

The Aryan branch is called Japhetic, because it has been supposed to be descended from Japheth; while the Semitic branch is regarded as the posterity of Shem, and the Hamitic branch as the children of Ham. The name Aryan means *tiller of the soil;* wherein this race has differed from the Turanian, or nomadic races of Central Asia. The ancestors of the Indo-European nations, the primitive Aryans in prehistoric ages, occupied that region of Central Asia in which was located the ancient city of Bactra, the modern Balk, in Turkestan. Here this primeval race lived and attained to a considerable degree of civilization; practicing agriculture and cattle-raising, and some of the mechanical arts, such as weaving and sewing, metallurgy, pottery-manufacture, etc. They were also somewhat skilled in architecture, navigation, mathematics and astronomy. They considered marriage a sacred contract; and, unlike other Asiatic peoples, they shunned polygamy. Children were regarded as the light of the family circle, as shown by the meaning of the names —boy, *bestower of happiness;* girl, *she that comes rejoicing;* brother, *supporter;* sister, *friendly.* With regard to the Aryan or Indo-European race, it is found that the names of many common objects are very much alike in all the languages and dialects spoken by these people. Thus the word *house* in Greek is *domos;* in Latin *domus;* in Sanskrit, or ancient Hindoo, *dama;* in Zend, or ancient Persian, *demana;* and from the same root is derived our word *domestic.* The words for ploughing, grinding corn, building houses, etc., are also found almost similar. This demonstrates that these nations must have had a common origin, and that they engaged in farming, making bread and building houses. They also counted up to one hundred, and domesticated the most important animals—the cow, the horse, the sheep, the dog, etc.; and were acquainted with the most useful metals, and armed with iron hatchets. The primitive Aryans were monotheists in religion and worshiped a personal God. The Aryan or agricultural races had the patriarchal form of government, like the Turanian or nomadic races of Central Asia; but the father, or head of the family, was subject to a council of seven elders, whose

FUNERAL IN THE BRONZE AGE.

LAKE DWELLERS DURING THE BRONZE PERIOD.

chief was king, and from whose decision there was an appeal to heaven in the ordeal of fire and water. The Aryans followed their leaders and kings, and fixed the distinction between right and wrong by laws and customs. All these facts can be proven by the evidence of language, on the authority of Max Müller and other eminent philologists.

The rapid increase of the Aryan population in its primeval home led to a division of this primitive people into three branches—one crossing the Hindoo-Koosh and overspreading the plateau of Iran and laying the foundations of the great Median and Medo-Persian Empires; another moving southeastward across the Indus and becoming the ancestors of the Brahmanic Hindoos; and a third migrating into Europe in successive hordes, as represented by the Pelasgic, Celtic, Teutonic and Slavonic nations, whose descendants now occupy the greater part of Europe. These Aryan immigrants into Europe seized the lands of the original Turanian inhabitants, whose descendants are represented by the modern Basques of Northern Spain and the Laps and Fins of Northern Russia and Scandinavia.

The Aryan immigrants into Europe occupied different portions of the continent. The Pelasgians settled in the Grecian and Italian peninsulas of Southern Europe, and founded the Greek and Roman nations. The Celts spread over Western Europe, embracing the Spanish peninsula, Gaul and the British Isles; and became the ancestors of the ancient Spaniards and Gauls, and the Welsh, Irish and Highland Scotch. The Teutons occupied Central Europe and the Scandinavian peninsula; and became the progenitors of the Goths and Vandals, and the modern Germans, Danes, Swedes, Norwegians, Dutch or Hollanders, and the Anglo-Saxons or English. The Slavonians overspread the vast steppes of Eastern Europe; and their descendants are represented by the ancient Sarmatians and the modern Russians, Poles, Bohemians, Servians, Bulgarians, Bosnians and Croatians.

The Aryan or Indo-European branch of the Caucasian race has always played the leading part in civilization; and has been the most active, enterprising and intellectual in the world's history. The Aryans have always been peculiarly the race of progress; and have surpassed all others in the development of civil liberty, the perfection of law, social advancement, and their progress in art, science, literature, invention, and mode of living. The Aryans alone have originated, developed and perfected constitutional, representative and republican government. The present and the future belong wholly to this highest type of human development.

The Semitic branch has been noted for religious development, having given rise to three great monotheistic religions—Judaism, Christianity, and Islam or Mohammedanism. The Hamitic branch were famous builders, and their architectural structures in Chaldæa and Egypt were noted for their massive grandeur. The Semitic and Hamitic nations, after attaining a certain degree of civilization, remained stationary; and their civilization has utterly perished.

After the dispersion of mankind into various quarters, men chose different occupations and modes of living, according to the diversities of their places of residence. The inhabitants of steppes and deserts, interspersed only here and there with fertile pasture grounds, became shepherds and roved with their tents and herds from place to place, thus becoming nomads or wanderers; and their occupation was the breeding of cattle and sheep. Those who occupied favorable districts on the sea-coast soon discovered, as population increased and their resources developed, the advantages of their situation. They accordingly practiced navigation and commerce, and sought for wealth and comfort, in furtherance of which objects they erected elegant dwelling houses and founded cities; whilst the inhabitants of less hospitable shores subsisted by means of fisheries. The dwellers upon plains adopted agriculture and the peaceful arts; whilst the rude mountaineer gave himself up to the chase, and, moved by a violent im-

INTRODUCTION.

pulse for freedom, found his delight in wars and battles. By taming wild cattle, man very early procured for himself domesticated animals.

Commerce was a mighty factor in the development and civilization of the human race, and the intercourse among nations. Those who occupied fruitful plains, or the banks of navigable rivers, carried on an inland trade. The inhabitants of the sea-shores conducted a coasting trade. At first men exchanged, or bartered, one article for another. At a later period they adopted the plan of fixing a certain specified value upon the precious metals, and employed coined money as an artificial and more convenient medium of exchange. The dwellers in towns occupied themselves with mechanical employments and inventions; and cultivated the arts and sciences for the comfort, happiness and refinement of life and for mental culture and development.

In the course of time nations became divided into civilized and uncivilized, as their intellectual development was furthered by talents and commerce, or retarded and cramped by dullness and by isolation from the rest of mankind. Uncivilized nations are either wild hordes under an absolute and despotic chief who wields unlimited power over his followers, or wandering nomadic tribes, guided by a leader, who, as father of the family, exercises the functions of lawgiver, governor, judge and high-priest. Neither the wild hordes under their despotic chiefs, occupying the unknown regions of Africa (Negroes), the steppes and lofty mountain ranges of Asia, the primeval forests of America (Indians), and the numerous islands of Oceanica (Malays), nor the nomadic races with their patriarchal government, find any place in history. This subject only deals with those nations who have attained to some degree of civilization and have from similarity of customs and for mutual advantage engaged in peaceful intercourse with each other, and who have made considerable progress in the science of civil government and the development of political institutions.

The oldest civilizations were those found in the Tigris-Euphrates and Nile valleys, in the Hindoo peninsula, and in the remote empire of China. The exact origin of the ancient nations and civilizations is lost in the dimness of their remote antiquity. These regions were richly endowed by nature with the resources necessary for sustaining a dense population; and the oldest historic empires accordingly took their rise in the rich alluvial lands watered by the Tigris and the Euphrates in South-western Asia and by the Nile in North-eastern Africa.

Historical Asia is South-western Asia; where the great Hamitic and Semitic empires of Chaldæa, Assyria and Babylonia successively flourished, in the Tigris-Euphrates valleys; where the Hebrews and the Phœnicians played their respective parts in the world's historic drama; and where the Aryan race finally came upon the scene in the appearance of the great Median and Medo-Persian Empires and the Græco-Macedonian Empire of Alexander the Great and his successors, followed by the Parthian, Eastern Roman and New Persian Empires; after which the Semitic race again prevailed in the sudden rise of Mohammed's religion and the great empire founded by his successors; followed by the conquests of the Seljuk Turks from Tartary, the two centuries of warfare between Christendom and Islam for the possession of the Holy Land as represented in the Crusades, the terrible scourges of the conquering Mongol and Tartar hordes of Zingis Khan and Tamerlane; and, lastly, the rise of the now-decaying Mohammedan empires of the Ottoman Turks and the modern Persians.

All that part of Asia north of the Altai mountains, now known as Siberia, is a comparatively barren region and was unknown in antiquity. Central Asia, now called Tartary and Turkestan, was anciently known as Scythia, and was then as now occupied by nomadic hordes who have roamed over those extensive pastoral lands for countless ages with their flocks and herds, having no fixed abodes or cities and no other polit-

INTRODUCTION.

ical arrangements than the patriarchal form of government. Accordingly, the Turanian races inhabiting that region have played no part in history, except that the Tartar and Mongol races inhabiting those vast steppes have at times overrun and conquered the civilized countries of Southwestern and Southern Asia.

Thus, with the single exception of Egypt, all the ancient Oriental nations had their seat in Asia. The populous empires of India, China and Japan—though they contributed their jewels, spices, perfumes and silks to the luxury of the people of Southwestern Asia—were almost unknown to the ancient Greeks and Romans; and though their art and literature are vast, these had no influence upon the general course of the world's progress. China and Japan are two ancient empires which have continued to exist with but little change to the present time. The nations of Farther India are almost unknown to history; while Hindoostan, the seat of a dense Aryan population from the earliest antiquity, and one of the oldest civilizations, as attested by vast architectural remains and a copious religious literature, was unknown to history until Alexander's invasion, and became successively the prey of Arabian, Afghan, Tartar, Mongol, Portuguese and British conquest.

The only historical part of Africa is Northern Africa, or that part of the continent bordering on the Mediterranean sea and watered by the Nile; and the only great nations of ancient Africa were Egypt, Ethiopia and Carthage. All the rest of the vast continent was a dark region wholly unknown to the ancient civilized nations of South-western Asia and Europe; and only within the last four centuries have its Western, Southern and Eastern coasts been discovered, explored, taken possession of and colonized by Europeans; while the interior has been but partially visited by European explorers, within the last hundred years.

Southern Europe was the seat of the greatest two nations of antiquity—the Greeks and the Romans—the former by their literature and philosophy and their political freedom, and the latter by their laws and political institutions, influencing all future European nations. The other nations of ancient Europe were barbarians, many of whom were conquered and civilized by the Romans. The overthrow of the Roman dominion in the fifth century after Christ entirely changed the current of European history by a redistribution of its population through the migrations and conquests of its vast hordes of Northern barbarians, who fourteen centuries ago laid the foundations of the great nations of modern Europe. America and Oceanica were wholly unknown to the ancient inhabitants of the Old World, and have only occupied the field of history since their discovery and settlement by Europeans within the last four centuries.

History deals only with civilized man, and history proper only begins with the origin of civilized nations and with the commencement of historical records. Accordingly, the cradle of civilization—if not the cradle of the human race—was the fertile alluvial Tigris-Euphrates and Nile valleys, where, with the dawn of civilization, flourished the old Chaldæan and Egyptian empires—the most remote of historical states of antiquity. History begins with Egypt, the oldest of historical nations.

Civilization and human progress have in the main followed the course of the sun. In the East arose those great nations and cities from which other lands have derived a part of their civil institutions, their religion and their culture. In the East, the land of the camel, the "ship of the desert," originated that caravan trade which contributed so vastly to human progress. To protect themselves against the rude Bedouins, the Oriental merchants traveled in large companies, often armed, conveying their wares upon the backs of camels from place to place. These commercial journeys gave rise to many commercial cities and centers of trade, occasioned the erection of store-houses and caravansaries, and led to intercourse between distant nations and to an interchange of productions, religious institutions and social policy. Temples and oracles of celebrity often served for markets and warehouses. In the East all the great religions took their rise and gained their full development, as the Orientals have always been the most contemplative on all that concerns man's relations to the Deity. In the East the patriarchal and despotic governments alone prevailed. Where the system of castes prevailed, the priests and soldiers constituted the privileged classes, from both of which ultimately arose the unlimited kingly power; and the officers of state were regarded as slaves and menials, without personal rights or property. The king, who was regarded with almost as much reverence as the Deity, disposed of the lives and possessions of his subjects at will. He gave and took away at his pleasure, and no one dared to appear before him without prostrating his body on the ground. He lived like a god, in the midst of pleasure and enjoyment, surrounded by hosts of slaves, who obeyed his wishes, executed his orders, and submitted themselves to his pleasures; and he was surrounded by all the wealth and possessions, by all the pomp and splendor, of the world. In these Oriental governments laws and human rights were nowhere; despotism and slavery prevailed; and consequently there was no incentive to vital energy and no capability of permanent civilization. For this reason all Oriental states have become the easy prey of foreign conquerors, and their early civilization has perished or remained stationary.

By original disposition, the Orientals are more inclined to contemplative ease and enjoyment than to active exertion; and for this reason they have never attained to freedom and spontaneous activity, but have quietly submitted to their native rulers, or groaned under the yoke of foreign oppressors. After reaching a certain degree of civilization, they submitted themselves to an unenterprising pursuit of pleasure, and thus by degrees became slothful and effeminate. Their practice of polygamy further promoted their effeminacy. Oriental architecture was noted for its gigantic designs and its imposing grandeur; but it did not display the symmetry, harmony and utility characteristic of the architecture of a free people. Slavery paralyzed every outward manifestation of Oriental life.

Besides being the cradle of the human race, Asia is the birth-place of the great religions and the home of absolute despotism. The two great pantheistic religions—Brahmanism and Buddhism; also the great monotheistic religions—Zoroastrianism, Judaism, Christianity and Mohammedanism—arose in Asia; while Asiatic governments to-day are what they have been from time immemorial—absolute monarchies, or despotisms; no republic or constitutional monarchy ever having flourished on Asiatic soil.

Europe, on the contrary, inhabited by the progressive Aryan race, has carried political institutions to the highest state of development; civil, political, and religious liberty having had a steady growth. Asiatic civilization has been stationary, while European civilization has been progressive. The Asiatics are passive, submissive, given to contemplative ease and disinclined to active exertion. The Europeans are active, energetic, vigilant and aggressive. Europe has also colonized other portions of the globe; the greater part of the present populations of North and South America being the descendants of Europeans who settled in the New World, and drove away, or assimilated with, the aborigines; while Europeans have also settled in portions of Africa, Asia and Oceanica. The Asiatics, on the other hand, do not colonize.

In the Prehistoric Ages—that is, the ages before recorded history—the *patriarchal* form of government prevailed; each father, or head of a family, governing the whole family. Since the formation of nations there have been various forms of governments—*Autocracy, despotism,* or *absolute monarchy,* where the supreme power is vested in the monarch himself, without any restraint or limitation; *Limited, or constitutional monarchy,* where the power of the monarch is limited by law or by constitutions giving the nobility, or aristocracy, and the masses some share in

INTRODUCTION.

the government; *Aristocracy*, or government by nobles or aristocrats; *Theocracy*, or government by the Church in the name of the Deity; *Hierarchy*, or government by priests; *Pure democracy*, or government by the people directly; and *Representative democracy*, or *republicanism*, or government by the people through their chosen representatives. There have been several kinds of republics—*aristocratic*, where the few have governed, and *democratic*, where the masses through their chosen representatives are the rulers. The best examples of pure democracy were the governments of ancient Athens and ancient Rome, where the people themselves assembled in a body for purposes of legislation. This form of democratic government can only exist where a state consists of but a single city with its surrounding territory, as in the cases of the two ancient republics just cited; and is utterly impossible among a population distributed over a vast extent of country.

Monarchs are called by different titles, as Emperor, King, Prince, Duke, Sultan, or Czar. The savage and barbarous tribes of Asia, Africa, America and Oceanica are governed by their chiefs; and their governments are simple, as were those of all the original nations. Even the civilized Asiatic nations have always been despotisms. It was only on the soil of Europe, occupied by the progressive Aryan race, that civil liberty was born, and where the masses first obtained any share of political power. A great hindrance to civil freedom among ancient Asiatic and African nations was the system of castes, by which men were separated according to their occupations and conditions, which were transmitted without the slightest change from generation to generation. The priests, who alone possessed a knowledge of religious customs and institutions, and who bequeathed their knowledge to their descendants, comprised the first caste. The soldiers constituted the second caste, and shared with the priests the government of the people. The third caste were the tillers of the soil, the fourth caste the artisans, and the fifth caste the shepherds, who were universally despised. Any one who violated the rules of caste became an outcast. The system of castes prevailed for the longest time in its purest state in India and Egypt.

Man is naturally a religious being. A world-wide religious sentiment seems to prevail, but there have been many varieties or manifestations of this sentiment. Thus we have *Monotheism*, or the belief in one God; *Polytheism*, or the belief in many gods; *Pantheism*, or the system which regards the whole universe, with all its laws and the different manifestations of nature, as the Supreme Being. Many polytheistic and pantheistic nations have made idols, or images, as figures or representations of their deities; and for this reason have been called *idolators*, *pagans* or *heathen*. The four great monotheistic religions of the world have been the *ancient Persian religion* of Zoroaster; *Judaism*, or the religion of the Jews; *Christianity;* and *Islam*, or Mohammedanism. The leading polytheistic religions were those of the ancient Egyptians, Chaldæans, Assyrians, Babylonians, Phœnicians, Greeks, Romans and Scandinavians. The chief pantheistic religions have been the two great religions of Hindoo origin—*Brahmanism* and *Buddhism*.

It is believed that originally monotheism was universal; but that sometime during the prehistoric ages, after the dispersion of mankind into various quarters, most nations fell into polytheism and idolatry. Even among polytheistic religions there is one Supreme Being, who is superior to and above all the other deities; and for this reason all religions have been to some extent regarded as monotheistic. There are also some polytheistic features about all monotheistic religions, as the belief in the existence of angels, who, as dwelling in the celestial world, are beings superior to mortals. Among ancient nations the only truly monotheistic religions were those of the Hebrews and the Medo-Persians—the one a Semitic and the other an Aryan people.

From time immemorial the custom has prevailed among pagan and polytheistic

INTRODUCTION.

nations of making idols or images of wood, stone, metal or clay, to represent their deities; and these have been fashioned into a great variety of forms. Temples and altars have been erected for the worship of these deities; and sacrifices have been offered to them, partly to appease their wrath, and partly to obtain their favor. These sacrifices have varied in character with the civilization of the people who have offered them. The ancient Greeks and Romans, in their joyous festivals to their gods, socially consumed the fruits of the earth and animals from the firstling of a flock to the solemn sacrifice of a hecatomb (a hundred oxen). Savage tribes have slaughtered human beings upon their altars, to appease by blood the wrath of their offended deities. The Phœnicians and Syrians placed their own children in the arms of a red-hot idol, Moloch. At first the image or idol was only a visible symbol of a spiritual conception or of an invisible power; but this higher signification often gave way in the progress of time to the worship of the inanimate image itself; the priests only being sensible of any deeper meaning, which they kept from the people for purposes of their own.

To further delude the masses, the priests invented legends, fables and myths about their gods, clothed them in poetic fancy, and thus originated mythology, or the science of their gods. In these legends, fables and myths, the deeds of the different gods and their dealings with men were described in enigmatical allusions, allegories and figurative expressions. The nations with the greatest amount of creative imagination and religious impulse possessed the richer mythology. These stories of the gods incited the people to superstition; and the solemn worship in the temples and sacred groves, with their mysterious ceremonies and symbolical usages, maintained a feeling of veneration and religious awe. To inspire in the people a feeling of the divine presence, sacred places and temples were provided with oracles, from which the superstitious multitude might get light into the mysteries of the future, in obscure and ambiguous language. In this way and by such means the priesthood swayed the masses in most countries; and thus secured power, honor and wealth for themselves. The people were enslaved by ignorance, credulity, superstition and fear.

BRANCHES OF THE CAUCASIAN, THE ONLY HISTORICAL RACE.

I. ARYAN, OR INDO-EUROPEAN BRANCH.
  1. HINDOOS.
  2. MEDES AND PERSIANS.
  3. HELLENES, OR GREEKS.
  4. LATIN, OR ROMANIC NATIONS.
    1. ANCIENT ROMANS.
    2. ITALIANS.
    3. FRENCH.
    4. SPANIARDS AND SPANISH AMERICANS.
    5. PORTUGUESE AND BRAZILIANS.
    6. FLEMINGS, OR BELGIANS.
    7. ROUMANIANS.
  5. GERMANIC OR TEUTONIC NATIONS.
    1. GERMANS.
    2. DANES.
    3. SWEDES. } SCANDINAVIANS.
    4. NORWEGIANS.
    5. DUTCH, OR HOLLANDERS.
    6. ENGLISH AND ANGLO-AMERICAN (Anglo-Saxon).
    7. SCOTCH LOWLANDERS.
    8. NORMAN-FRENCH.

  6. CELTIC NATIONS.
    1. ANCIENT BRITONS, GAULS AND SPANIARDS.
    2. IRISH, WELSH, AND SCOTCH HIGHLANDERS.
    3. BRETONS (West of France).
  7. SLAVONIC NATIONS.
    1. RUSSIANS.
    2. POLES.
    3. BOHEMIANS.
    4. SERVIANS.
    5. BULGARIANS.
    6. BOSNIANS.
    7. CROATIANS.

II. SEMITIC BRANCH.
  1. HEBREWS, OR ISRAELITES.
  2. ARABS.
  3. SYRIANS.
  4. ASSYRIANS AND LATER BABYLONIANS.
  5. PHŒNICIANS AND CARTHAGINIANS.

III. HAMITIC BRANCH.
  1. CHALDEES, OR EARLY BABYLONIANS.
  2. EGYPTIANS AND ETHIOPIANS.

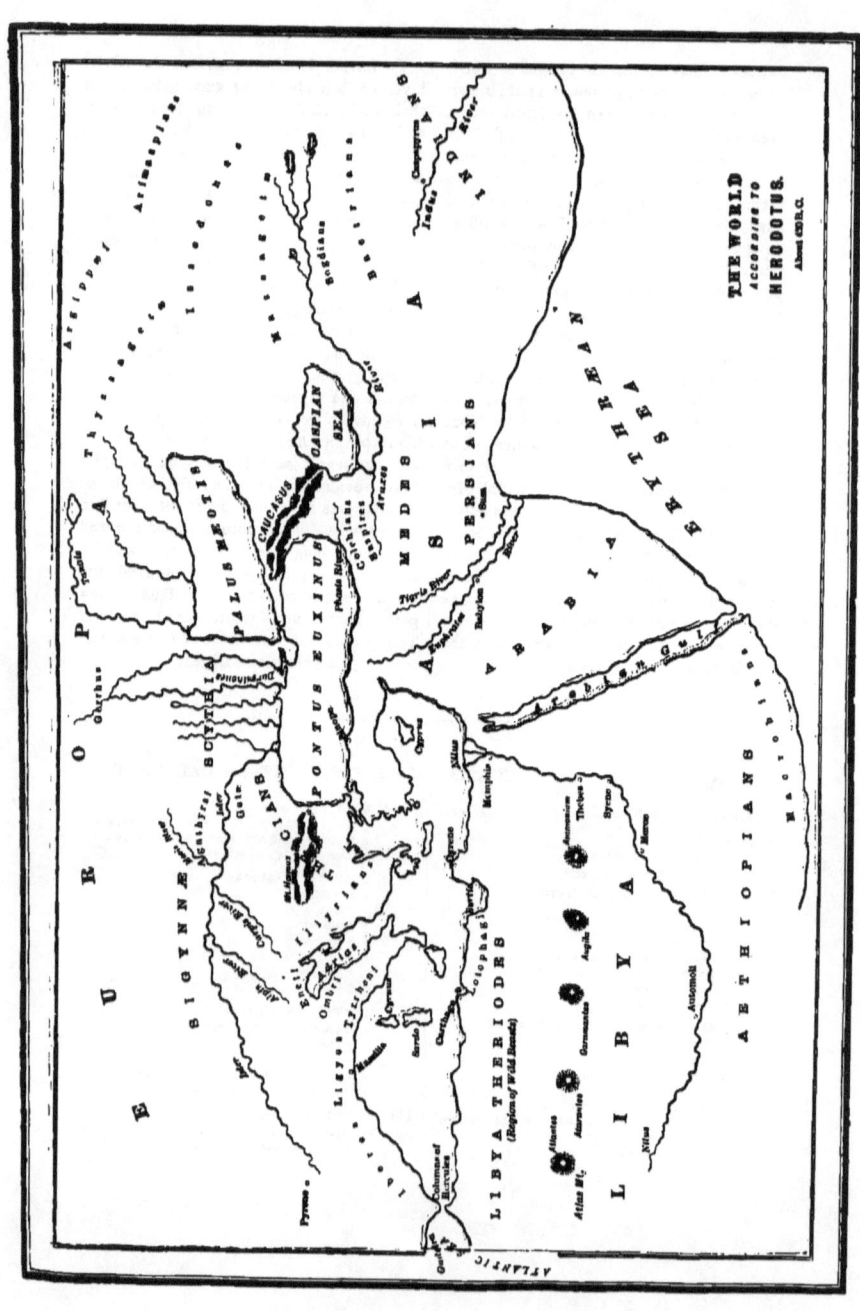

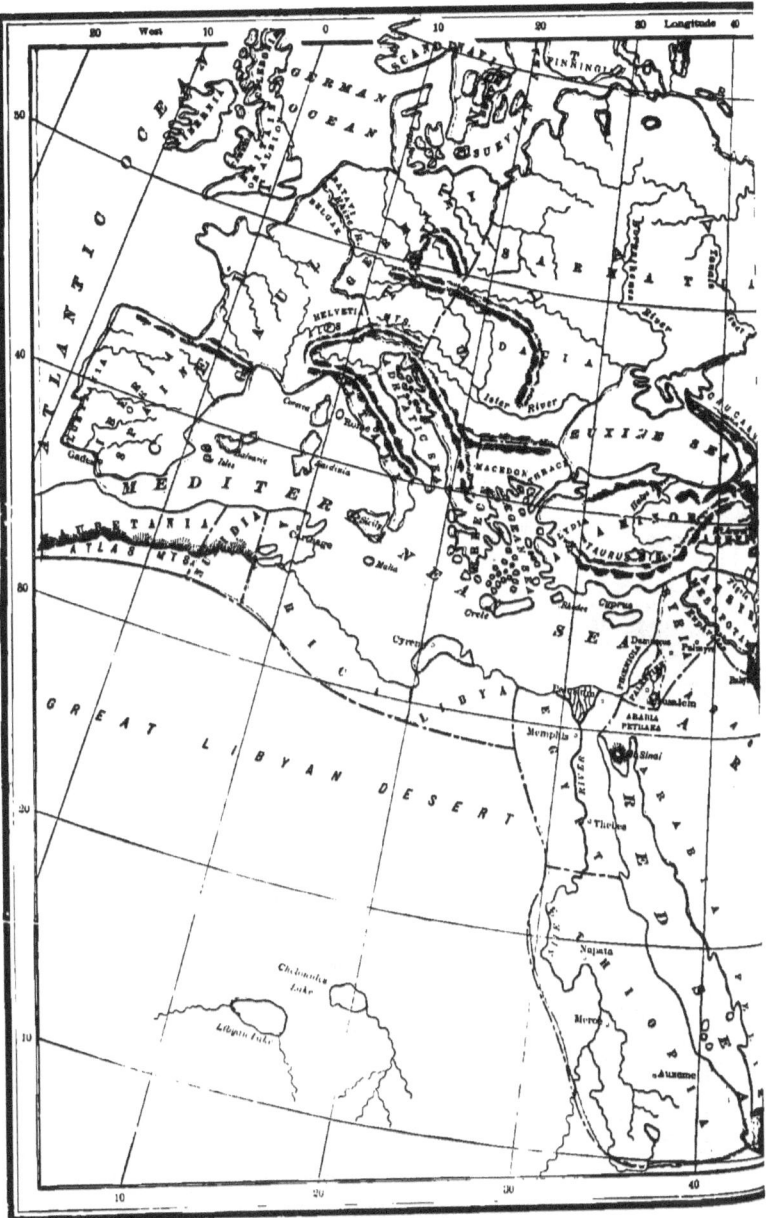

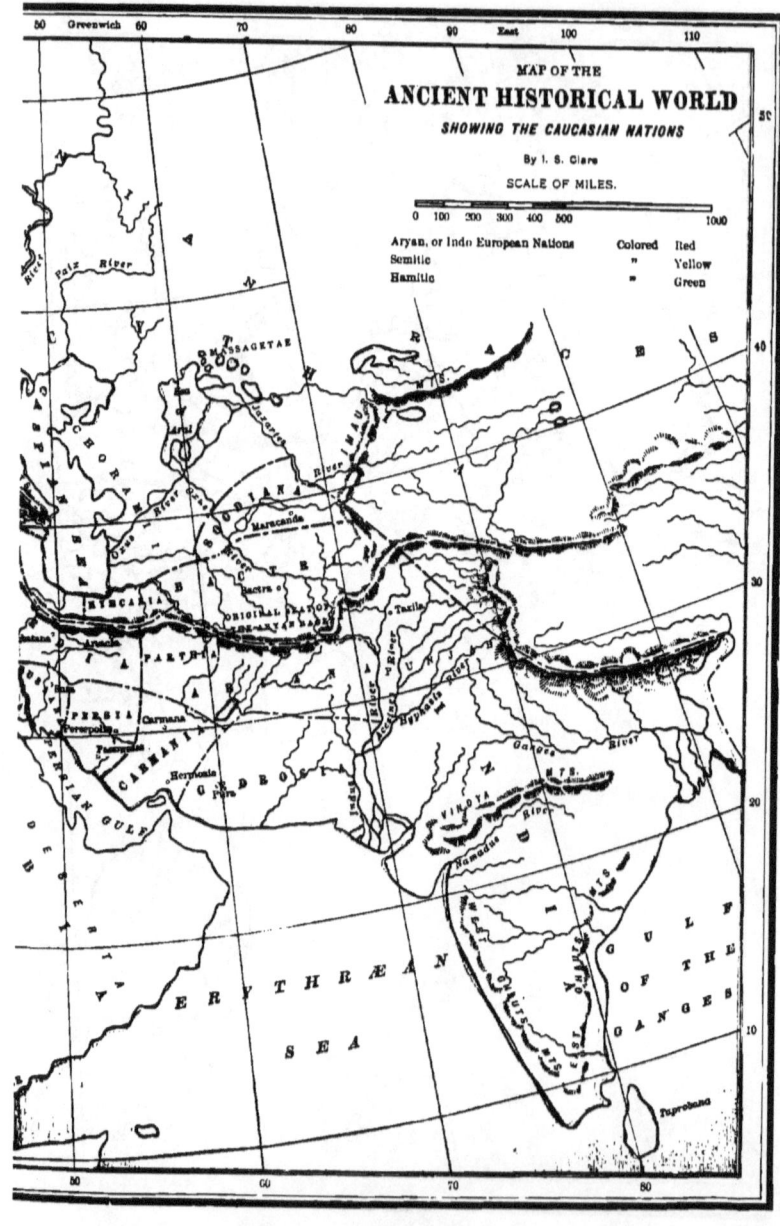

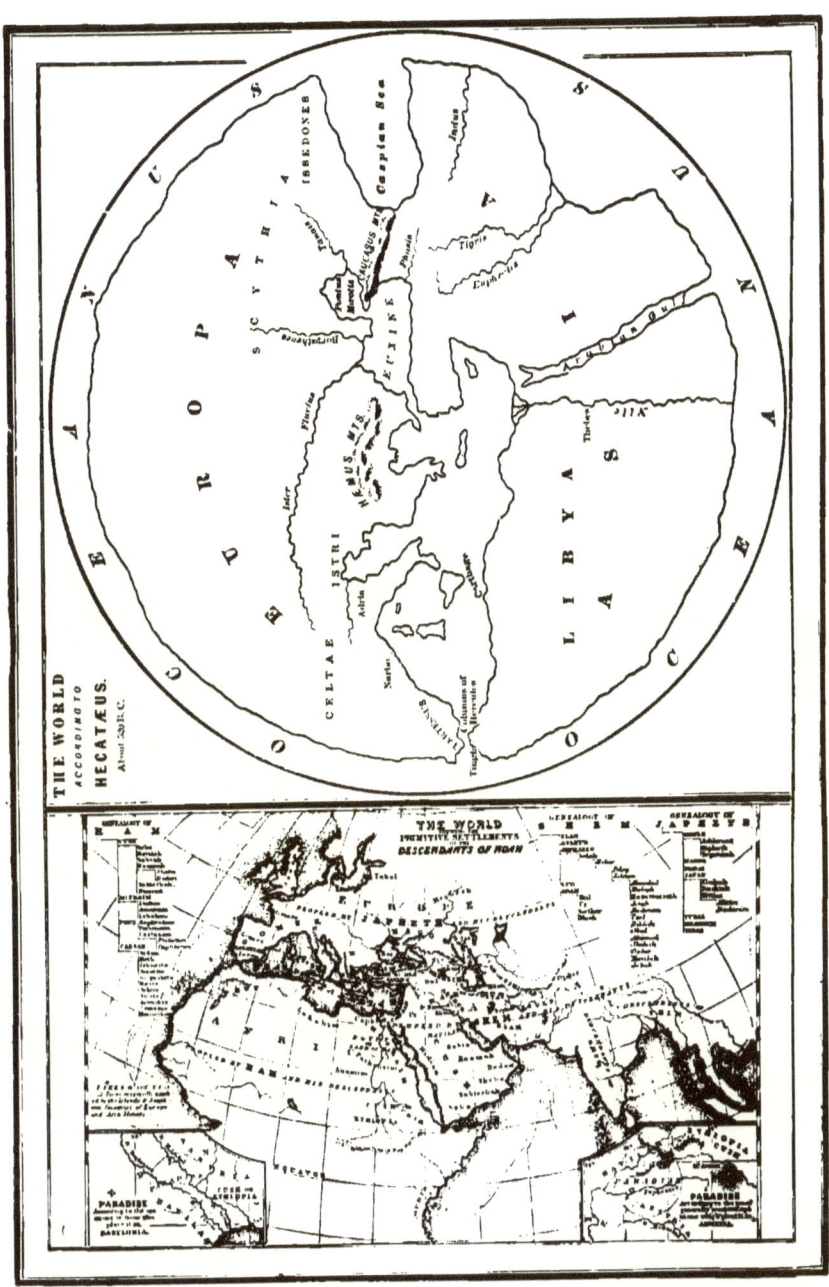

PART FIRST.

ANCIENT HISTORY.

MEDEAN NOBLE—PERSIAN NOBLE—PERSIAN.

ASSYRIAN WARRIOR WITH WICKER SHIELD—WARRIOR WITH ROUND SHIELD—ARCHER.

ASSYRIAN—ASSYRIAN NOBLE—ASSYRIAN COURTIER

PERSIAN WARRIOR—PERSIAN NOBLE—PERSIAN WARRIOR.

MEDIA, ASSYRIA, PERSIA.

CHAPTER I.

ANCIENT EGYPT.

SECTION I.—THE COUNTRY AND PEOPLE.

LTHOUGH Asia was the cradle of the human race, the cradle of civilization was in the Nile valley, which, from the island of Elephantine, in the Nile, northward to the Mediterranean sea, a distance of five hundred and twenty-six miles, was the seat of ancient Egypt, "the mother of the arts and sciences." In Egypt we first find a civil government and political institutions established; and although Egypt may not be the oldest nation, Egyptian history is the oldest history. The monuments, records and literature of Egypt are far more ancient than those of Chaldæa and India, the next two oldest nations. The ruins and monuments of ancient civilization found in the Nile valley render that country one of the most interesting on the globe. While the progress of other nations from ignorance and rudeness to art and civilization may be easily traced, Egypt appears in the earliest twilight of history a great, powerful and highly civilized nation; and her gigantic architectural works are the most wonderful, as well as the most ancient in the world, showing a skill in the quarrying, transporting, carving and joining of stone which modern architects may admire but are unable to surpass.

From the earliest antiquity Egypt has been called "the Gift of the Nile." From time immemorial this renowned land, in the midst of surrounding deserts, has been one of the most fertile regions of the globe, and was in consequence the great granary of antiquity. This unsurpassed fertility is attributable to the annual overflow of the Nile, occasioned by the heavy rainfalls in the uplands of Abyssinia; so that this mighty stream, the only river of Egypt, in its whole course through the country from south to north, by its mud deposits renews yearly the soil of this narrow valley, which really constituted ancient Egypt, and whose average width, from the modern city of Cairo south to the First Cataract, does not exceed fifteen miles. The Nile discharges its waters into the Mediterranean through three distinct channels, which branch off from each other about ninety miles from the sea, and which enclose the region called the Delta, from its resemblance in form to the Greek letter of that name. The Delta has always been a region of unsurpassed fertility. The spontaneous growth of the date-palm furnished the people with a cheap and abundant article of food; and the immense yield, with comparatively slight labor, of large crops of cereals, because of the natural fertility of the soil, rendered this region, from primitive times, capable of sustaining a dense population, and made it the primeval seat of organized human society.

Ancient Egypt was divided into three geographical sections—the Thebaïs, or Upper Egypt, in the south; the Heptanomis, or Middle Egypt, in the centre; and the Delta, or Lower Egypt, in the north. The chief city of the Thebaïs was the "hundred-gated Thebes," whose ruins, extending for seven miles on both banks of the Nile, astonish the modern traveler, as he gazes upon the remains of magnificent temples, splendid palaces, colossal statues, obelisks, sphinxes, tombs hewn in the solid rock, subterranean catacombs, and the gigantic statue of Memnon. Karnak and Luxor are the portions of Thebes which present the most stately ruins, the most imposing being the great temple at the former place. The most ancient city of Upper Egypt was This, afterward called Abydos. Other cities of this section were Lycopolis, Latopolis, Antæopolis and Ombos. The southernmost points of Egypt were Syene and the island of Elephantine, in the Nile. The leading city of the Heptanomis was Memphis, on the west side of the Nile, founded by Menes, the first Egyptian king, and whose wonderful ancient splendor is now attested by its ruins. In the vicinity of Memphis was the famous Labyrinth, and here also are the great Pyramids of Ghizeh—the most imposing monuments ever erected by human hands. Other famous cities of Middle Egypt were Heracleopolis, Hermopolis and Letopolis. The Delta was, in ancient times, thickly studded with cities, chief of which were Avaris, or Tanis, Sais, Bubastis, Mendes, Rameses, Heliopolis, Magdolon, Pelusium, Canopus and Hermopolis. The famous Greek city of Alexandria, on the western side of the Delta, was, in the later days of antiquity, the metropolis of Egypt, and from its location it became the great commercial center of the civilized world, while being also the seat of learning and civilization.

To the south of ancient Egypt, in the region now embracing Nubia and Abyssinia, was the ancient Ethiopia, whose people had also attained a high state of civilization, as is fully proven by the existence of ruins along that portion of the Nile valley similar to those of Egypt. On the west of Egypt was the great Libyan Desert, now called the Sahara.

The population of ancient Egypt is known to have been at least five millions, and may have been seven millions. They belonged to the Hamitic branch of the Caucasian race, and originally came from Asia, being, according to the Hebrew account, the descendants of Misraim, the grandson of Ham. They were a brown race, mild in their general character, polished in their manners, and were by nature obedient and religious. They were cleanly in their habits and food, and in consequence were a healthy, hardy people.

SECTION II.—SOURCES OF EGYPTIAN HISTORY.

THE history of Egypt dates back to the most remote antiquity. The early Egyptians believed that there had been a time when their ancestors were savages and cannibals, dwelling in caves in those ridges of sandstone which border the valley of the Nile on the east; and that their greatest benefactors were Osiris and Isis, who raised them into a devout and civilized people, eating bread, drinking wine and beer, and planting the olive. For this reason the worship of Osiris and Isis became general throughout Egypt, while the different cities and nomes had their own respective local deities. According to Manetho, a native Egyptian historian of the later days of antiquity, the first rulers of Egypt were gods, spirits, demigods, and *manes*, or human souls; which amounts to saying that the earliest history of Egypt, like that of most other countries, is unknown or involved in the obscurity and uncertainty of legend and fable.

The history of this great ancient people has been derived from several sources—the historical writings of the ancient Greek historians, Herodotus and Diodorus, and the native Egyptian priest Manetho, and in modern times from the deciphering of the inscriptions on the Egyptian monuments and from the discovery of the records on rolls of papyrus found in the tombs.

The ancient sources of Egyptian chronology are obscure and conflicting. The Greek historians represented the Egyptians as the

SOURCES OF EGYPTIAN HISTORY.

first race of men. When Herodotus visited Egypt, about the middle of the fifth century before Christ, the native priests read to him, from rolls of papyrus, the names of three hundred and forty-one kings, from Menes, the founder of the monarchy, to Seti. In the great temple of Thebes the priests showed Herodotus the wooden images of three hundred and forty-five priests, who, from father to son, had held the sacerdotal office during the reigns of these kings. From these data Herodotus estimated the antiquity of Egypt to have been nearly twelve thousand years, counting three hundred and forty generations from Menes to Seti, with three generations to each century, and reckoning a century and a half from the beginning of Seti's reign to the Persian conquest of Egypt, B. C. 525, which latter event had occurred about seventy-five years before the visit of the "Father of History" to this celebrated land. According to this computation, based upon the recorded traditions of the Egyptian priests, the founding of the Egyptian monarchy by Menes occurred more than twelve thousand five hundred years before Christ.

In the first century before Christ, Diodorus Siculus, another Greek historian, also visited this renowned land, and to him the priests read from their sacred books the names of four hundred and seventy kings, beginning with Menes, with accounts of their appearance, stature and actions. From the information he thus received, giving three generations to a century, Diodorus computed the founding of the kingdom by Menes at nearly seventeen thousand years before his time. But careful research revealed to him many errors in the traditionary records, and his corrected accounts assign the founding of the Old Empire by Menes at 4800 B. C.

About three centuries before Christ, the learned Greek antiquarian, Eratosthenes, librarian of Alexandria, copied the names of thirty-eight Theban kings from the holy books of Thebes, which list was finished by Apollodorus by adding the names of fifty-three more, thus giving a full list of ninety-one kings.

In the third century before Christ, an Egyptian priest, named Manetho, compiled a history of his country in three volumes, giving the reigns of all the kings from the founding of the monarchy by Menes to the first Persian conquest of Egypt, 525 B. C., through twenty-six dynasties, and through four more dynasties until the final Persian conquest in 346 B. C., making thirty dynasties in all. This work was afterward lost, but fragments of it were transcribed by Josephus, Julius Africanus, Eusebius, Syncellus, and other historians, and thus handed down to future generations. According to Manetho's calculation, the founding of the kingdom by Menes occurred in the year 5706 B. C. in the Egyptian reckoning, and in the year 5702 B. C. of the Julian calendar. Manetho's record of the first seventeen dynasties, embracing the periods of the Old Empire and the Middle Empire, is very obscure, on account of facts and dates found recorded in the monumental inscriptions of that long period of over twelve centuries; and it is hard to decide whether the thirty dynasties were consecutive, or whether several of them were contemporaneous. This fact has made it difficult to fix the exact or approximate date of the establishment of the Old Empire by Menes.

A list of the names of kings was also preserved in the Turin Papyrus, recorded more than a thousand years before the Christian era. Other sources of ancient Egyptian history are the allusions made to that country in the Hebrew Scriptures.

In the past century our knowledge of this famous land has been immensely extended by the discovery of the art of deciphering the inscriptions which this ancient people lavishly carved on their buildings and monuments, particularly their obelisks, painted on the frescoed insides of their tombs, and actually cut on nearly all objects of art or use. These writings and carvings were in the character of what are known as *hieroglyphics*, a Greek word signifying sacred carvings or priestly writing The knowledge of the reading of these inscriptions perished with the decay of ancient Egypt, and for many centuries the term "hieroglyphics" was synonymous with everything mysterious.

The unraveling of this mystery was brought about by an interesting incident. During Bonaparte's invasion of Egypt in 1798, a French engineer, while engaged in digging the foundation of a fort near the Rosetta mouth of the Nile, discovered a stone tablet about three feet long, on which was carved an inscription in three different characters. This tablet has become celebrated as the *Rosetta Stone*. The lower of the three texts was Greek, and easily translated; the upper text was in the hieroglyphic style, while the middle text was in a character since styled *demotic*, meaning the writing of the common people (from *demos*, the people). Copies of this inscription were circulated among the learned men of Europe, and after long and patient efforts the alphabet of the hieroglyphics was discovered; so that these carved inscriptions on old Egyptian works of art and architecture can now be easily and correctly read, thus giving an abundance of new light on the history of this wonderful land of antiquity. The Rosetta Stone was carved about 196 B. C., and was an ordinance of the Egyptian priests decreeing honors to Ptolemy Epiphanes, one of the famous Greek dynasty who governed Egypt during the first three centuries before Christ, and that accounts for the existence of the three texts on the tablet. The great task of deciphering these inscriptions was chiefly the work of the noted French savant, Champollion.

On account of the obscurity and uncertainty of early Egyptian chronology, modern historians and Egyptologists have differed widely as to the antiquity of this most ancient monarchy. The French Egyptologists, headed by M. Mariette, place the founding of the First Dynasty by Menes at 5004 B. C. The German Orientalists and Egyptologists differ, Böckh fixing the date at 5702 B. C., Dr. Brugsch at 4455 B. C., Lauth at 4157 B. C., Professor Lepsius at 3892 B. C., Baron Bunsen at 3059 B. C., and Dr. Duncker at 3233 B. C. The English Egyptologists, at the head of whom stands Sir Gardner Wilkinson, regard the year 2700 B. C. as about the approximate date; and, as it is necessary to have some fixed chronological basis, we will follow the English view in the present work.

SECTION III.—POLITICAL HISTORY.

THE history of ancient Egypt has been divided into three distinctive periods. The Old Empire extended from the establishment of the First Dynasty at Memphis by Menes, in the very earliest times, to the conquest of all Egypt by the Hyksos, or Shepherd Kings, about 1900 B. C. The Middle Empire—the epoch of the rule of the Hyksos over the whole country—embraced the period from 1900 B. C., to the expulsion of the Shepherd Kings in 1600 B. C. The New Empire lasted over a thousand years, from 1600 B. C. to the Persian conquest of Egypt in 525 B. C.; since which time this famous land has not been governed by a native prince. The New Empire was the most brilliant period of Egyptian history, and may be subdivided into two sharply-distinguished epochs—the grand age, from 1600 B.C. to 1200 B. C.; and the age of decay, from 1200 B. C. to 525 B. C.

Egypt was originally divided into a number of *nomes* or petty states, independent of each other, and each having for its nucleus a temple and an established priesthood. One historian mentions fifty-three nomes, another thirty-six. The gradual absorption of the weaker nomes by the more powerful finally resulted in the establishment of this first consolidated monarchy of Africa.

The first mortal king of Misraim, the "double land," was MENES, who, according

POLITICAL HISTORY.

to Manetho, founded the First Egyptian Dynasty at This (afterwards Abydos), in Upper Egypt. This was the beginning of the OLD EMPIRE, which lasted from the earliest times to the conquest of all Egypt by the Hyksos, about 1900 B. C. Menes, the first Egyptian king, conquered and improved Lower Egypt, and on a marshy tract which he had drained and protected by dykes against the annual overflow of the Nile, he founded the great city of Memphis, which, for many centuries, remained the capital of the flourishing kingdom which he had established. At Memphis Menes built the temple of Phthah, and there were won the

—who was skilled in medicine and wrote works on anatomy, of which portions still exist, and who built the citadel and palace of Memphis. KENKENES, the third king, was succeeded by UENEPHES, who built the Pyramid of Kokome, believed to be the oldest of all those wonderful structures, and who bore the name of the Sacred Calf of Heliopolis. Altogether the First Dynasty comprised eight kings.

The Third Dynasty reigned at Memphis and embraced nine kings. The first of these was NECHEROPHES, who is said to have conquered Libya; the superstitious Libyans having been frightened into submission by

THE GREAT PYRAMID.

first recorded triumphs of this very oldest of ancient civilized nations. On the north and west sides of his capital, Menes caused artificial lakes to be constructed for the defense of the city, and on the south side a large dyke protected it against the annual overflow of the Nile. The public treasures were established in the city, the laws were revised and the civil administration improved. After a reign of sixty-two years, Menes is said to have perished in a struggle with a hippopotamus, and was deified by his admiring countrymen.

Menes was succeeded by his son ATETA —called Athothis, or Thoth, by the Greeks

an eclipse of the moon as they were preparing for battle. TOSORTHRUS, the second king of this dynasty, encouraged writing, medicine and architecture, and introduced or improved the art of building with hewn stone, previous structures having been made of rough stone or brick. He was known to the Greeks as the "Peaceful Sesostris," the later two monarchs bearing that name being great warriors and conquerors.

His son and successor, SASYCHIS, or Mares-sesorcheres, was a renowned lawgiver, who is said to have organized the worship of the gods, and to have invented the sciences of geometry and astronomy.

He is likewise said to have made the remarkable law that a debtor might give his father's mummy as security for a debt. If the debt was not discharged, neither the debtor nor his father could ever rest in the family sepulcher, and this was regarded as the most disgraceful fate that could befall a mortal.

The monumental and more certain history of Egypt commences with the Second, Fourth and Fifth Dynasties, which reigned contemporaneously; the Second at This, in Upper Egypt; the Fourth at Memphis, in Middle Egypt; and the Fifth in the Isle of Elephantine, in Upper Egypt. Of these the Fourth Dynasty, established at Memphis about 2450 B. C., was the most powerful and exercised a certain degree of supremacy over the other two. This Memphite dynasty consisted of eight kings, and its greatness is fully attested by the gigantic structures of stone which it left in Middle Egypt between the Libyan Mountains and the Nile; so that it was the Fourth Dynasty that immortalized itself as that of the Pyramid-builders, and this period is one of the most brilliant in the history of ancient Egypt.

The great increase in the population had placed at the king's disposal a large amount of unemployed labor, and the natural productiveness of the soil had given all ranks far more leisure than was enjoyed by any other people of antiquity. The long duration of the yearly overflow of the Nile caused a perceptible suspension in the various industrial channels, and allowed the sovereigns larger opportunities to employ the labor of the people in works which might carry their fame to countless future ages. Such were the circumstances that led to the building of the great Pyramids—the most gigantic structures ever erected by human hands, and which the kings designed for their tombs.

These Pyramids are in the vicinity of the site of the ancient Memphis, about ten miles west of the Nile, on a barren elevation, in the sides of which were chambers hewn out of the solid rock, in which the bodies of the ordinary dead were interred. The kingly sarcophagus was assigned a more pretentious sepulcher under more imposing monuments of stone. Gradually the heap of royal tombs assumed the form of the Pyramids, the structure becoming, by degrees, more regular internally and externally, so that the finished pile has been the wonder of succeeding ages. Along the elevation west of Memphis about seventy of these stupendous structures were erected. Of these, three were specially celebrated because of their size and grandeur. These are the Pyramids of Ghizeh, near which city they are located. They were built in the twenty-fifth century before Christ. These three are more conspicuous than the remaining seven of the same group in that vicinity. The oldest and largest of the three great Pyramids of Ghizeh is that of KHUFU—the Cheops of Herodotus—who was the successor of SENEFERU or Soris, the first king of the Fourth Dynasty, and the builder of the northern Pyramid of Abousir.

The Pyramid of Cheops was originally four hundred and eighty feet high, but as the apex has been broken off it is now but four hundred and fifty feet high. The base covers about thirteen acres, and each side of the base is seven hundred and sixteen feet long, and the inclination is five hundred and seventy-four feet. The vast structure is located exactly on the thirtieth parallel of north latitude, and its four sides face the cardinal points of the compass. On the north side, exactly in the middle, a rectangular opening is cut, being the entrance of a descending passage three feet wide and four feet high. The passage leads downward to a chamber cut in the solid rock of the foundation, over a hundred feet under the ground-level of the base. The chamber is precisely under the apex of the pyramid, at a distance of six hundred feet. At points in the main passage to this chamber diverging passages lead to two other chambers, which also lie directly under the apex of the Pyramid and above the first chamber. In these chambers were placed the stone coffins containing the mummies of these ancient monarchs. Upon the walls were sculptures recounting the departed king's deeds. The door of the passage was sealed with a stone, and the name of the dead sovereign was added to

BUILDING OF THE PYRAMIDS.

THE PYRAMIDS AND SPHINX.

POLITICAL HISTORY.

the list of deities in the temple. Herodotus says that the building of the "Great Pyramid" occupied thirty years, that one hundred thousand men were forced to work upon it at a time, and that a new army of laborers was employed every three months.

The second of the three great Pyramids was built by Khufu's celebrated successor, SHAFRA, and was originally four hundred and fifty-seven feet high, and resembles the Pyramid of Cheops in general proportion and internal structure. The third Pyramid of Ghizeh was erected by MENKAURA, the successor of Shafra, and is only two hundred feet high and thirty-three feet at the base, and the inclination is two hundred and sixty-two feet. Some of the outside portions of this Pyramid consist of polished slabs of granite. It has a double chamber within, one behind the other. In the farther chamber was recently found the sarcophagus containing the mummy of Menkaura himself, by General Howard Vyse; and the hieroglyphic inscription on the case containing, with the monarch's name, the myth of the god Osiris, has been deciphered and translated into English. It is only in recent times that other royal mummies have been found.

The Pyramids are built of successive layers of stone from two to six feet thick, in proportion to the size of the structure. The layers decrease in size from the ground upwards, so that the monument appears on each side in the form of a series of stone steps receding to the top. Diodorus says he was informed by the Egyptian priests that the gigantic masses of stone which were used in building the Pyramids were brought from Arabia, and were put into place by building under them vast mounds of earth, from which the blocks of stone could be moved into their respective places. This statement seems to be substantiated by the fact that no stone of the kind used in the construction of these vast monuments can be found within many miles from the place where the Pyramids were erected.

Khufu and his successor, Shafra, oppressed the people and despised the gods, crushing the former by the severe toils required by these great works, and closing the temples of the latter and putting an end to their worship; but Menkaura, who was the son of Khufu, and who, as well as his father, reigned sixty-three years, differed from him in being a good and humane sovereign. Menkaura reopened the temples which his father had closed, restored the religious rites of sacrifice and praise, and put an end to oppressive labors. He was, in consequence, highly reverenced by the people, and his name was celebrated in many hymns and ballads. After the reigns of four more kings, known to us only by names and dates, the Fourth Dynasty, whose eight reigns aggregated about two hundred and twenty years, ended about 2220 B. C.

The Second Dynasty, ruling Middle Egypt from This, or Abydos, and the Fifth, ruling Upper Egypt from the Isle of Elephantine, were probably related by blood to the powerful sovereigns ruling Lower Egypt from Memphis, as the tombs of all three of these royal races are found in the vicinity of Memphis. The Arabian copper mines of the Peninsula of Sinai were worked by Egyptian colonies established there by the Pyramid-kings, and at this period Egyptian arts and architecture had attained their highest degree of perfection. Painting, sculpture and writing, as well as modes of living and general civilization, were about the same as fifteen centuries later. The reed pen and the inkstand are among the hieroglyphics employed, and the scribe appears, pen in hand, in the paintings on the tombs, making notes on linen or papyrus. In the tombs of Beni-Hassan, belonging to this period, five different kinds of plows are shown, and agricultural life is fully illustrated. Thus we have figures of sheep and goats treading seed into the ground; of wheat bound into sheaves, threshed, measured, and carried in sacks to the granary; of bundles of flax on the backs of asses; of figs gathered; of grapes thrown into the press; of wine carried into the cellar; of the overseer and laborers in field and garden; and of the bastinado applied to the backs of laggards. We also have scenes of flocks and herds, of bullocks, calves, asses, sheep, goats; and also domestic fowl, such as geese and ducks. The making of butter and cheese is likewise shown. Other works of sculpture show us the spinners and weavers at their looms, the potter working the clay or burning his ware in the furnace, the smith making javelins and lances, the painter at work with his colors, the mason with his trowel, the shoemaker at his bench, the glass-blower plying his art. The various grades of domestic life are illustrated, and we see servants at work,

The Fourth Dynasty at Memphis was succeeded by the Sixth Dynasty about 2220 B. C. The Second Dynasty continued to reign at This or Abydos, and the Fifth in the Isle of Elephantine, while the Ninth arose at Heracleopolis and the Eleventh at Thebes; so that Egypt was now divided into five separate kingdoms, the Theban gradually becoming the most powerful, as the Memphite was losing its preëminence. Thus weakened by division and exhausted by the great architectural works which had

OBELISK OF USURTASEN I. AT HELIOPOLIS.

the kitchen implements used, also domestic apes, dogs, cats, etc. In military life we have exhibited soldiers practicing in arms, fighting battles, battering walls and storming towns. Various sports and amusements are likewise depicted, and we have here exhibited wrestlers, jugglers, musicians, male and female dancers, fishing parties with hooks and spears and nets. Dwarfs and deformities can also be seen, and every condition of human life is found represented upon imperishable tablets of stone.

withdrawn the people from the practice of arms, the country easily fell a prey to the barbarous nomad hordes from the neighboring regions of Syria and Arabia. These entered Lower Egypt from the north-east by way of the Isthmus of Suez about 2080 B. C., and soon became masters of the country from Memphis to the sea. They were called the Hyksos, or Shepherd Kings. They carried on their conquests in the most cruel manner, burning the cities, razing the temples to the ground, slaying the inhabitants and

POLITICAL HISTORY.

reducing the women and children to slavery.

The Hyksos founded the Fifteenth Dynasty at Memphis and the Sixteenth at Avaris, in the Delta, near the site of the later city of Pelusium. Native dynasties continued to reign in Middle and Upper Egypt, the Ninth at Heracleopolis, the Fifth in the Isle of Elephantine, while the Twelfth had succeeded the Eleventh at Thebes, and the Fourteenth arose at Xois, in the Delta, in the very heart of the conquests of the Shepherd Kings, and maintained its independence during the whole period of the dominion of the Hyksos.

Under the vigorous rule of the Twelfth Dynasty, Thebes rapidly grew into a powerful and prosperous kingdom and extended its supremacy over the kingdoms of Elephantine and Heracleopolis, conquered the peninsula of Sinai and carried its arms triumphantly into Arabia and Ethiopia. USURTASEN I. reigned over all Upper Egypt, and under USURTASEN II. and USURTASEN III. Thebes attained its highest prosperity. Usurtasen III. enriched the country by numerous canals; and monuments of his power at Senneh, near the southern border of the kingdom, still excite the wonder of the traveler. His successor, AMMENEMES III.—the Maris or Lœmaris of Manetho, and the Mœris of Herodotus—built the Labyrinth in the Faioom, the most superb and gigantic edifice in Egypt, which contained three thousand rooms, one half of which number were underground, and were the receptacle of the mummies of kings and of the sacred crocodiles, and are known as the Catacombs. The walls of the fifteen hundred apartments above ground were of solid stone and entirely covered with sculpture. Herodotus, who visited this magnificent structure, declared that it surpassed all other human works. He says: "The roof throughout was of stone like the wall, and the walls were carved all over with figures. Every court was surrounded with a colonnade, which was built of white stones exquisitely fitted together."

The same king constructed the Lake Mœris, a natural reservoir near a bend of the Nile, which he so improved by means of a canal and dykes as to retain, for purposes of irrigation, a large part of the waters from the annual inundation, and thus increased the fertility of the surrounding country.

Architecture and the arts flourished in Upper Egypt, and numerous canals were constructed to increase the fruitfulness of the soil by irrigation, while Lower Egypt continued to groan under the oppressive rule of the Hyksos, or Shepherd Kings. The Thirteenth Dynasty, which succeeded the Twelfth at Thebes, was compelled to give way before the Shepherd Kings and to seek refuge in Ethiopia, thus leaving Upper Egypt also to the mercy of the barbarous Hyksos, who now ruled all Egypt, except Xois, in the Delta (B. C. 1900). The barbarous conquerors burned cities, destroyed temples, and massacred or enslaved the inhabitants. During the MIDDLE EMPIRE—from 1900 B. C. to 1600 B. C.—this barbarous race held the native Egyptians in subjection; the Thirteenth Dynasty at Thebes, the Seventh and Eighth at Memphis, and the Tenth at Heracleopolis, holding their crowns as tributaries of the Shepherd Kings of the Seventeenth Dynasty.

This was the darkest period of Egyptian history. The Hyksos destroyed the monuments of their predecessors and left none of their own, so that there is a gap of three centuries between the Old and the New Empire, during which the Holy City of Thebes was in the hands of the barbarians; the annals ceased, and the names of kings, either native Egyptian or Hyksos, are for the most part unknown to us. Late writers suppose the Hyksos to have been the same as the Hittites of Syria. After their expulsion from Egypt some of them found refuge in Crete, and reappeared in Palestine about the same time that the Israelites entered that country from the west. It is believed by some that Joseph and the family of Jacob settled in Lower Egypt during the reign of one of the Shepherd Kings; others, however, place that event a little later.

After their long humiliation under the oppressive rule of the Shepherd Kings, the

Egyptian people rallied for a great national uprising under the Theban king AMOSIS, Ames, or Aahmes; and the Hyksos were driven from Egypt, after a desperate contest, B. C. 1600. Then began the NEW EMPIRE —the most brilliant period of Egyptian history—which lasted a little more than a thousand years (B. C. 1600–525). Amosis united all Egypt into one kingdom, with Thebes for its capital, and founded the Eighteenth Dynasty. He married Nefruari, the daughter of the King of Ethiopia—"the good and glorious woman"—who held the highest honor ever accorded a queen.

tial spirit wrought up by the struggle against the Hyksos displayed itself in warlike enterprises against neighboring nations, which were again obliged to acknowledge the supremacy of Egypt, whose arms were carried in triumph into Ethiopia, Arabia and Syria, and even beyond the Euphrates.

Amosis, the first king of the Eighteenth Dynasty, reigned twenty-six years. The next king, AMUNOPH I., married the widow of Amosis, and reigned twenty-one years. THOTHMES I., the third king of the Eighteenth Dynasty, won great victories over the Ethiopians and conquered the Canaanites of

AN EGYPTIAN KING DESTROYING HIS ENEMIES.

For the next eight centuries Egypt remained a single united kingdom; and during the Eighteenth, Nineteenth and Twentieth Dynasties Egyptian sculpture and architecture reached their highest degree of perfection. During this period the hundred-gated Thebes attained the height of its splendor. Its great temple-palaces were then built; and numerous obelisks, "fingers of the sun," pointed heavenward. The horse and the war-chariot were now introduced into Egypt, and the military caste for a time held a higher rank than the priestly. The mar-

Palestine, and even carried his arms eastward against the Assyrians in Mesopotamia. He reigned twenty-one years.

Royal women were held in higher esteem in Egypt than in any other ancient monarchy. Thothmes I. was succeeded by his daughter, AMENSET, Mesphra, or Hatasu, who acted as regent for her younger brother, THOTHMES II., who died a minor. Amenset held the regency for her next brother, THOTHMES III. Her reign of twenty-two years was brilliant and successful. She completed the temple of Amun, and her

POLITICAL HISTORY.

fame is commemorated by the two gigantic obelisks at Karnak.

After the death of Amenset, her brother, THOTHMES III., reigned alone. Envious of his sister's fame, he caused her name and image to be effaced from all the sculptures in which they had appeared together. Thothmes III. reigned alone forty-seven years (B. C. 1510-1463). He carried on wars in Ethiopia, Arabia, Syria and Mesopotamia, and defeated the Syrians in a great battle at Megiddo, in Canaan, twice took Kadish, the chief city of the Kheta tribes, and led his armies as far as Nineveh, from which city, according to inscriptions on his monuments, he took tribute. Thothmes III. is no more distinguished for his military exploits than for the magnificent temples and palaces which he erected at Karnak, Thebes, Memphis, Heliopolis, Coptos, and in every other city of Egypt and Ethiopia.

CLEOPATRA'S NEEDLE.
As it stood in Alexandria (now in New York).

The records of his twelve successive campaigns are inscribed in sculpture upon the walls of his palaces at Thebes. The two obelisks near Alexandria, which some Roman wit called Cleopatra's Needles, one of which is now in London and the other in New York, bear the name of this king.

Thothmes III. was succeeded by his son, AMUNOPH II., in the beginning of whose reign the Egyptians took Nineveh. He is said to have brought to Egypt the bodies of seven kings whom he had slain in battle, and whose heads were placed as trophies upon the walls of Thebes. After a short reign he was succeeded by his son, THOTHMES IV., who is believed by some writers to have caused the carving of the great Sphinx near the Pyramids. AMUNOPH III., the son and successor of Thothmes IV., who ascended the Egyptian throne B. C. 1448, reigned thirty-six years, and was one of the greatest monarchs of the Eighteenth Dynasty. He conducted successful wars against the Libyans and Ethiopians, and adorned his kingdom with many magnificent architectural works, and improved its agriculture by the construction of tanks or reservoirs to regulate irrigation. New temples were built at Thebes, where also two great Colossi, one of which is known as the *Vocal Memnon*, also belong to this reign; but the Amenopheum, of which they were ornaments, is now in ruins. The two Colossi were huge granite statues of Amunoph III., with his mother and queen in relief on the die, in front of the sanctuary of Osiris, and may still be seen among the surrounding ruins. The Vocal Memnon, according to a Greek tradition founded on the story of travelers who visited the spot, was said to utter a musical sound at sunrise like the twanging of harp-strings. The pedestal is fifty-nine feet high from base to crown. The palaces of Luxor and Karnak, now among the most conspicuous of the ruins of those famous places, were connected by an avenue of a thousand sphinxes, while at Thebes a colonnade in the same style was lined with colossal sitting statues of the cat-headed goddess Pasht, or Bubastis. In the monumental inscriptions of his times, Amunoph III. is styled "Pacificator of Egypt and Tauner of the Libyan Shepherds."

The reign of Amunoph III. was marked by great internal troubles, in consequence of his unsuccessful efforts to change the national religion. His son, HORUS, was his legitimate successor, but his claims were disputed by many pretenders, most of whom were princes or princesses of the blood royal, and for thirty years the kingdom was in an unsettled and distracted condition. Horus ultimately triumphed over and outlived all his rivals, and died after reigning seven years in peace. He conducted successful wars in Africa and enlarged the palaces at Karnak and Luxor. With the next king, RESITOT, or Rathotis, the Eighteenth Dynasty came to an end, B. C. 1400.

The Nineteenth Dynasty was founded B. C. 1400 by RAMESES I., who was descended from the first two kings of the Eighteenth Dynasty. He reigned less than two years, and was succeeded by his son SETI, or Sethos I., who inherited all the national hatred toward the Syrian invaders of his country, reconquered Syria, which had revolted forty years before, and extended his conquests as far as the borders of Cilicia and the Euphrates. Seti built the great Hall of Columns at Karnak, in which the whole Cathedral of Notre Dame, in Paris, could stand without touching walls or ceiling; and his tomb is the most magnificent of all the royal sepulchers of ancient Egypt.

The most renowned king of Egypt was RAMESES II., (1388-1322 B. C.), surnamed the Great, whom the Greek writers named Sesostris, and who, during his father's lifetime, subdued both Libya and Arabia. Upon ascending the throne he entered upon a career of conquest with the ultimate design of universal dominion. Herodotus, Diodorus, and Manetho relate, with some variation in their narrative, his subjugation of the neighboring nations. After dividing his kingdom into thirty-six nomes and assigning his brother Armais to the regency in his absence, Rameses set out with an army

THE TWIN COLOSSI OF AMUNOPH III. NEAR THEBES.

of six hundred thousand foot-soldiers, twenty-four thousand horse, and twenty-seven thousand war-chariots, to conquer the world.

He first reduced Ethiopia under subjection and imposed upon that country a heavy tribute of ebony, ivory and gold. He founded the Egyptian navy by building a fleet of four hundred war vessels on the Red Sea, and reduced under his dominion the islands and shores as far as India. After carrying his victorious arms eastward beyond the Ganges, he rapidly subdued Asiatic and European Scythia, and was only checked in his conquering career in Thrace by the severity of the climate and the scarcity of food. Wherever he conquered he

THE RAMESSEUM AT THEBES.

erected monuments with the inscription: "Sesostris, king of kings and lord of lords, has conquered this territory by the power of his arms." After nine years of conquest, this triumphant warrior-king returned to his kingdom with a vast booty and captives from the subjugated nations.

HALL OF COLUMNS IN THE GREAT TEMPLE AT KARNAK.

Modern investigation has shown the military exploits of Rameses the Great, as narrated by Herodotus and Diodorus, to have been highly exaggerated. By deciphering the inscriptions in the Rameseum at Karnak, in the temple erected by Rameses in Ethiopia, in the ruins of Tanis, and on the Rocks of Beyreut, it has been shown that the principal scenes in his triumphant career were enacted in the neighboring countries of Ethiopia, Arabia and Syria.

The noted works of Rameses the Great were the building of a great wall from Pelusium to Heliopolis, to protect Egypt on the east against the inroads of the Syrians and Arabs; the cutting of a system of canals from Memphis to the sea; the completion of the famous Hall of Columns at Karnak, begun by his father; and the magnificent temple of Amunoph III. at Luxor. Before this temple were placed two sitting colossi of Rameses and two red granite obelisks, both of which still remain with their hieroglyphic inscriptions as perfect as when they were cut, one still standing on the original spot, and the other greeting the eye of the beholder in the Place de la Concorde, in Paris.

In every part of Egypt may be found monuments commemorating the achievements and greatness of this celebrated monarch. At Ipsambul, in Nubia, in a valley with walls of yellow sandstone, two temples are cut in the solid rock, one dedicated to Ra by Rameses the Great, and the other to Hathor by his queen. Before the temple of Rameses are four stupendous colossi of himself, over seventy feet high, and seated on thrones. The shoulders of these colossal statues are twenty-five feet wide, and they measure fifteen feet from elbow to finger-tip. The image of Rameses stands conspicuous among those of the long line of deified sovereigns of Ancient Egypt, on the walls of the great temple of Abydos, while before the altar another image represents Rameses as a mortal offering sacrifice to himself and his ancestors.

Under the Nineteenth Dynasty, the magnificence and greatness of Thebes, then the capital, surpassed the former splendor of Memphis. In Thebes the wonderful works of Thothmes IV., Amunoph III., Seti, Rameses II., and Rameses III., rose in majestic grandeur, on both sides of the Nile, around a circle of fifteen miles.

MENEPTA, who succeeded Rameses the Great in 1322 B. C., and reigned twenty years, is now generally regarded as the Pharaoh of the Exodus of the Israelites. In 1550 B. C., the family of Jacob, the grandson of Abraham, the founder of the Hebrew race, had settled in that part of Lower Egypt on the east side of the Delta, known as the Land of Goshen, while Jacob's favorite son, Joseph, was prime minister to the Egyptian king, a post to which he is said to have been elevated on account of his services in saving the land from famine. Here the posterity of Jacob or Israel multiplied during a period of two and a half centuries. For a while the new race of strangers were highly esteemed by the Egyptian kings and nation, but during the reigns of Seti I. and Rameses the Great, the Egyptian authorities grew jealous of the rapidly increasing Hebrew race and began to exercise a systematic oppression toward them. The strangers were set to work at building and digging. Their labor enlarged the treasure cities of Pithom and Rameses. They aided in the construction of the great canal from the Nile, at Bubastis, to the Red Sea. They toiled in the brickyards and were beaten by the Egyptian task-masters until they rose in open rebellion. The revolt was heightened by the withdrawal of religious privileges. Their great leader, Moses, who had been compelled to save his life by flight to the Land of Midian because he had slain an Egyptian whom he had seen ill-treating a Hebrew, had now returned to his people and sought to obtain King Menepta's permission to lead them in a three days' march into the desert to sacrifice to Jehovah. It was only after Moses had performed signs and wonders in the king's house that Menepta allowed the Israelites to depart.

They followed the bank of the canal, gathering their people along the route of the Hebrew towns, but upon reaching the Gulf of Suez were hemmed in by the hosts of the Egyptian king.

COLOSSUS OF AMUNOPH III., NEAR THEBES—THE VOCAL MEMNON.

By the receding of the waters at that shallow point of the sea, by means of a "strong east wind," as told in Exodus, the fleeing Israelites, numbering two millions, were enabled to cross the bare, sandy bottom and reach the opposite shore in safety. But the hosts of Menepta, while crossing the shallow bottom in pursuit of the fugitives, were suddenly drowned by the returning waters.

The account of the Exodus of the Ismelites, as related by Manetho and quoted by Josephus, differs from the Mosaic account in detail. Manetho states that Menepta desired to see the gods, and was informed by a priest of the same name that his wish could only be gratified when he cleansed the land of lepers. The Pharaoh Menepta, therefore, priest Osarsiph, of Heliopolis, for their leader. He gave them laws, one of which gave them permission to kill and eat the gods, the sacred animals of the Egyptians. He then directed them to fortify Avaris, and also sent an embassy to Jerusalem to inform the banished Hyksos of the course of events in Egypt, to invite them to return, and to promise them the keys of Avaris. The Shepherd Kings gladly availed themselves of the offer and returned with an army of two hundred thousand men to recover the kingdom of their ancestors. When informed of this invasion of the Hyksos, King Menepta, influenced by superstition and fear,

RAMESES III. HUNTING THE LION.

cast eighty thousand of the lepers into the stone-quarries east of the Nile. When the son of Papius heard that some priests and men of learning had thus perished, he feared the displeasure of the gods for having plotted to ruin or enslave holy men. But a vision informed him that others would come to aid the lepers and govern Egypt thirteen years. After writing this on a roll of papyrus, he committed suicide.

Menepta, becoming alarmed, liberated the lepers from the quarries. He assigned them Avaris, which had remained in ruins since the expulsion of the Shepherd Kings. After rebuilding the city, the lepers chose the fled in terror into Ethiopia, there to remain until the thirteen years of leper rule should have passed. Thus Egypt was sacrificed to the unclean, who rioted in the sacred places until King Menepta returned with an army of Egyptians and Ethiopians and expelled the lepers and their allies, the Hyksos, from the kingdom. The name of the priest-leader of the lepers had, in the meantime, been changed to *Moyses*, or Moses. The Egyptian historians always spoke of the Hebrews as lepers.

After the reigns of SETI II. and SIPHTHAH, the Twentieth Dynasty ascended the throne of Egypt in 1269 B. C., in the person of SET-

NEKHT. The next king was RAMESES III., who, during a reign of thirty-two years and in ten victorious campaigns, restored to Egypt the glory which she had possessed under the elder kings of the preceding dynasty, subduing the Hittites and Amorites of Canaan and the Ethiopians, Libyans and Negroes of Africa. Naval battles were fought during this reign, as attested by hieroglyphic inscriptions. Rameses III. built the palace of Medinet-Abu at Thebes, of which every pylon, every gate, and every chamber gives some account of his brilliant exploits. Rameses III. had four sons, each named RAMESES, who reigned in succession. RAMESES VIII., who succeeded them, conducted some successful wars. He was followed by seven other kings bearing the same name, but their reigns were short and uneventful. Egypt, which had reached the pinnacle of its greatness under the Nineteenth Dynasty, rapidly declined during the Twentieth. The hieroglyphic inscriptions no longer recount the grand military exploits of kings, and art and architecture decayed. Egypt's conquests in Asia and Ethiopia were gradually lost. From its long contact with Asiatic nations, Egypt had lost its national feeling, and foreign influence was marked in the civil administration of the kingdom. The Pharaohs at this time became allied by marriage with foreign courts, and foreign colonies—Assyrian, Babylonian and Phœnician—settled in the country; and the constant intercommunication between the Egyptians and the Semitic nations of Asia is shown by the presence of Semitic names and the admission of Semitic words to the Egyptian language, as well as by the admission of foreign gods into the Egyptian sanctuaries, hitherto inaccessible to any deity outside of the Egyptian pantheon. The overwhelming predominance of the priesthood, whose influence pervaded all ranks, from the highest to the lowest, was a barrier to thought and progress of every kind. The people were slavishly held to the old forms of religion, architecture languished, no new buildings were erected, nor additions made to the magnificent structures of former ages. Sculpture and painting derived no new life from the study of nature, but confined themselves to slavish copies of old models or dull and meaningless imitations. The priestly caste aimed to hold all things at a certain level, fixed and unchangeable. Thus, when progress ceased, decay at once commenced. The later monarchs of the Twentieth Dynasty were but instruments in the hands of the priestly class.

During this period of general military and intellectual decline the priestly order augmented its power and influence to such an extent that it seized the throne, and the Twenty-first Dynasty reigning at Tanis, in the Delta, was a race of priest-kings. They wore the sacerdotal robes and called themselves High Priests of Amun. PISHAM I., one of this priestly race, gave his daughter in marriage to Solomon. The seven kings of this dynasty generally had short and uneventful reigns (B. C. 1091-990).

SHESHONK I.—the Shishak of the Old Testament and the founder of the Twenty-second Dynasty—married the daughter of PISHAM II., the last king of the previous dynasty, and also called himself High Priest of Amun. He made Bubastis, in the Delta, his capital, and restored the military strength of the kingdom. It was to Sheshonk that Jeroboam fled after his unsuccessful rebellion against King Solomon; and Sheshonk espoused the cause of Jeroboam in his revolt against Solomon's son and successor, Rehoboam, and invading Judah, took Jerusalem, plundered the treasures of the Temple and the palace, and compelled Rehoboam to pay tribute. One of the inscriptions at Karnak gives a list of one hundred and thirty towns and districts reduced by Sheshonk in Syria. He made the office of High Priest of Amun hereditary in his family.

Sheshonk died in 972 B. C., and was succeeded by his son OSORKON I., who reigned fifteen years and was succeeded by his son PEHOR. OSORKON II., the fourth king of this dynasty, is believed by some writers to have been the Zerah of Scripture, who invaded Syria and was defeated by Asa, King of

EGYPTIAN COURTIER — EGYPTIAN KING — FAN BEARER.

JEWISH WARRIORS—JEWISH KINGS.

JEWISH HIGH-PRIEST—LEVITES.

ALEXANDER THE GREAT.

EGYPT, JEWISH KINGDOM, GREECE.

Judah, in the battle of Mareshah (2 Chron. xiv. 9-14). The remaining kings of the Twenty-second Dynasty, which ended with TAKELOT II. in 847 B. C., were insignificant personages; and the process of decay and disintegration rapidly went on and was aggravated by the employment of Libyan mercenaries in preference to native soldiers. Semi-independent principalities sprang up in different parts of the kingdom, successfully defying every effort of the Pharaohs to preserve the unity of the nation. The utter decay of the national spirit paralyzed both sovereign and people.

The Twenty-third Dynasty, (B. C. 847-758), which ruled at Tanis, comprised four kings, none of them famous, and whose reigns were characterized by revolutions and civil wars. The Northern Ethiopian kingdom, which had Napata for its capital, was founded by Piankhi, a descendant of the priest-kings of the Twenty-first Egyptian Dynasty. Piankhi became virtual master of Egypt, which, according to his stélé found at Gebel-Berkal, was at this time divided into seven kingdoms, each ruled by a native Egyptian prince, who reigned under the suzerainty of Piankhi. Tafnekht, who ruled in the Western Delta and held Sais and Memphis, endeavored to cast off the yoke of Piankhi, and headed a revolt which was joined by the other native Egyptian princes. Piankhi's army took Thebes, defeated the rebel fleet, besieged and took Hermopolis, defeated the rebel fleet a second time at Sutenseneu and gained another great victory on land. Namrut, the Hermopolitan king, besieged the Ethiopian garrison in Hermopolis and recovered the city. Thereupon Piankhi, in person, led an army against Hermopolis, and laid siege to the city, which he finally compelled Namrut to surrender. Piankhi also forced Pefaabast, king of Heracleopolis Magna, to surrender, and then attacked Memphis, which was defended by a strong garrison devoted to Tafnekht. After a desperate resistance and frightful slaughter Memphis was taken, and its fall hastened the restoration of Piankhi's authority over all Egypt. The revolt ended with the submission of Osorkon, king of Bubastis, and Tafnekht, the rebel leader, both of whom were generously pardoned by Piankhi, after taking a new oath of allegiance to the Ethiopian sovereign, who allowed all the native rebel kings to retain their respective thrones. But in a few years, Egypt revolted under the leadership of BEK-EN-RANF, called Bocchoris by the Greeks, a native of Sais, who was the only king of the Twenty-fourth Dynasty. Bocchoris, however, was soon conquered by Sabaco, or Shabak, the Ethiopian king reigning at Napata, and was burned alive in punishment for his rebellion.

SABACO, the Ethiopian, thus founded the Twenty-fifth Dynasty, and is known in the Hebrew Scriptures as So, or Sevah. He entered into an alliance with Hoshea, King of Israel, and the Syrian princes against Sargon, King of Assyria, but was defeated by the Assyrian monarch in the great battle of Raphia, near the eastern borders of Egypt, B. C. 711. Sabaco fled to Ethiopia, retaining possession of Upper Egypt; while the sway of the Assyrians was established over the Delta and Middle Egypt, over which they placed tributary native princes, their policy being to weaken Egypt by dividing it as much as possible. Sabaco's son and successor, SHABATOK, for a short time ruled all Egypt, but was deprived of the Ethiopian crown by TIRHAKAH, or Tehrak; while the petty native Egyptian princes formed an alliance with Hezekiah, king of Judah, against Sennacherib, King of Assyria, but the allies were defeated in the South of Palestine and submitted to the sway of the victorious Assyrians. Instigated by Tirhakah, the Egyptian princes and the King of Judah again rose in arms against the Assyrian king. Again Sennacherib took the field against the allies and advanced to Pelusium, in the eastern part of Lower Egypt, but his army of one hundred and eighty-five thousand men was destroyed by a strange panic which seized them in the night, and which the Jews and Egyptians considered a miraculous interposition, B. C. 698. Senuacherib fled in dismay to Nineveh and abandoned his conquests. The Assyrian defeat enabled

Tirhakah to invade Egypt, kill Shabatok and reduce the whole land under Ethiopian dominion. Tirhakah was at once involved in a struggle with Esarhaddon, King of Assyria, Sennacherib's son and successor, who, in 672 B. C., invaded Egypt, captured Memphis and Thebes, drove Tirhakah back into Ethiopia, and established the Assyrian sway once more over all Egypt, whose twenty native princes were reduced to a state of vassalage under the Assyrian monarch. A few years afterward, however, Tirhakah returned and expelled the Assyrian garrisons from Egypt, which again acknowledged the Ethiopian dominion; but his triumph was of short duration, as he was again deprived of his Egyptian conquest by Esarhaddon's successor, Asshur-bani-pal, who won the native Egyptian princes over to the Assyrian interest. Being allowed more local freedom by the Assyrian king, they preferred his rule to that of the more oppressive Ethiopian monarch. Tirhakah's stepson and successor, RUT-AMMON—the Urdamané of the Assyrian inscriptions—endeavored to maintain the Ethiopian power in Egypt; and descending the Nile, he re-occupied Thebes and Memphis, drove the Assyrians out of Egypt and made himself master of the country; but was soon driven back into Ethiopia by Asshur-bani-pal. Rut-ammon's successor, MI-AMMON-NUT, tells us that in the first year of his reign (about B. C. 660), he dreamed that a serpent appeared on his right hand and another on his left, and when he woke they had disappeared. The interpreters informed him that this signified that he would rule all Egypt. Thereupon Mi-ammon-Nut led a hundred thousand men into Egypt, being hailed as a deliverer in Upper Egypt, against the Assyrians, who had allowed the temples to go to decay, overturned the statues of the gods, confiscated the temple revenues, and restrained the priests from exercising their offices. Mi-ammon-Nut proclaimed himself the champion of religion, visited the temples, led the images in procession, offered rich sacrifices and paid every respect to the priestly colleges. For this reason he was everywhere received with acclamations in Upper Egypt. In Lower Egypt he was opposed, but after a great victory at Memphis, he occupied that city and enlarged and beautified the temple of Phthah. The chapel to Phthah-Sokari-Osiris, recently uncovered by M. Mariette, is full of Mi-ammon-Nut's sculptures and inscriptions, its stones being inlaid with gold, its paneling made of acacia-wood scented with frankincense, its doors of polished copper and their frames of iron. The princes of the Delta submitted and were generously pardoned, governing their towns as Ethiopian and no longer as Assyrian vassals. Mi-ammon-Nut returned to Ethiopia, and the Ethiopian yoke was soon shaken off by the Egyptians. The petty native Egyptian states for many years remained tributary to Assyria, as the employment of foreign mercenaries, which had so long prevailed in Egypt, had deadened the national spirit and patriotism of the Egyptian people, and thus made it easy for the Assyrians to hold the country in subjection.

PSAMMETICHUS, one of the native viceroys under the Assyrian monarch, encouraged by the growing weakness of the Assyrian Empire, which was obliged to recall its garrisons from Egypt to defend itself against the destructive inroads of Scythian hordes from Central Asia, seized the opportunity to throw off his allegiance to Assyria, and crushing the opposition of the native viceroys, founded the Twenty-sixth Dynasty, thus placing Egypt once more under the sway of its native kings, after a century of foreign dominion, Ethiopian and Assyrian, B. C. 632. Psammetichus conciliated the Ethiopian party by marrying the daughter and heiress of the King of Thebes, whom he had deposed, and thus secured the adhesion of Upper Egypt, where the Ethiopians were still popular. He was a wise and liberal sovereign, and under his rule the arts and sciences began to revive. He constructed many great works throughout the kingdom. The new culture was not purely native Egyptian. Foreign wars, colonization and commercial intercourse had brought immense numbers of foreign settlers—Ethiopians, Phœnicians, Jews and Greeks—into the Egyptian cities. The new art was widely different from the classic art of Old Egypt. The Egypt of the Pharaohs was beyond resurrection, the old civilization had perished, and the native tongue had been corrupted.

Psammetichus was also a great warrior. He reduced part of Ethiopia and subdued the Philistines, but his continuance of the use of foreign troops and his employment of Greek mercenaries offended the warrior class of Egypt, of whom two hundred and forty thousand emigrated to Ethiopia, rejecting every entreaty of Psammetichus to return to their native land, and thus striking a fatal blow at the reviving prosperity of Egypt. Psammetichus attempted the conquest of Palestine and Syria, but was thwarted in his designs by the stubborn resistance of the Philistine city of Ashdod, which endured a siege of twenty-nine years before it was taken. He encouraged commerce and friendly intercourse with other nations.

Psammetichus died in 610 B. C., and was succeeded by his son NEKO, under whom the navy and commerce of Egypt were largely augmented. The great increase in the number of foreign colonists in Egypt gave rise to a new class of interpreters, through whose medium foreign intercourse was immensely facilitated. Neko endeavored to reopen the great canal from the Nile to the Red Sea, which had been constructed during the reign of Rameses the Great, but abandoned because the oracle had instructed him that he was laboring for the barbarian. Under Neko's auspices, an Egyptian fleet, manned by Phœnician seamen, sailed down the Red Sea, and after an absence of three years, during which they twice landed, sowed grain and gathered a harvest, they returned to Egypt by way of the Pillars of Hercules (Straits of Gibraltar) and the Mediterranean; thus making the circumnavigation of Africa two thousand years before the famous voyage of Vasco da Gama around the same continent.

Neko's military enterprises were blessed with but varied fortune. The great empire of Assyria had already fallen before the conquering arms of Media and Babylon. Neko prepared to dispute the dominion of the world with the Babylonian monarch. After invading Palestine and defeating and killing Josiah, King of Judah, at Megiddo, Neko conquered all the country eastward to the Euphrates; but Nabopolassar, King of Babylon, sent his son Nebuchadnezzar, with a large army, to drive the Egyptians out of Asia. In the great and decisive battle of Carchemish, Neko was totally defeated by Nebuchadnezzar, and Egypt's power in the East was ended forever, all of Neko's Asiatic conquests falling into the hands of Babylon, B. C. 605.

Neko died in 594 B. C., and was succeeded by his son, PSAMMIS, whose short reign of six years was only distinguished for an expedition into Ethiopia. His son and successor, UAHABRA—the Pharaoh Hophra of Scripture and the Apries of Herodotus—who reigned nineteen years, renewed the warlike schemes of his grandfather, besieged Sidon and fought a naval battle with Tyre, but failed in his attempt to conquer Phœnicia. He formed an alliance with Zedekiah, King of Judah, who endeavored to free himself from the Babylonian yoke; but the great Babylonian king, Nebuchadnezzar, quickly invaded Palestine, besieged and took Jerusalem, pillaged the city and the Temple, and thus broke the power of the allies and put an end to the struggle by driving the Egyptian monarch back into his own kingdom. Uahabra was afterward defeated in an expedition against the Greek colony of Cyrene, west of Egypt, in consequence of which his native soldiers revolted and dethroned him; and the revolutionary leader, AMASIS, with the aid of Nebuchadnezzar, who had twice invaded Egypt, (B. C. 581 and 570), was placed upon the Egyptian throne as king, tributary to the Babylonian monarch.

Amasis reigned forty-one years, at first as a tributary to Babylon, but he afterward cast off this yoke and increased his influence by marrying Nitocris, the sister of his predecessor. He adorned Sais, his capital, with magnificent buildings; and numerous monuments of his reign, found in all parts of the country, attest his liberal patronage of the arts; while his friendly foreign policy toward Cyrene and the other Greek states, and his encouragement to Greek merchants to settle in Egypt, added immensely to the wealth of the country. He conquered the island of Cyprus and reduced it to tribute.

Alarmed by the growing power of Persia under its renowned monarch, Cyrus the Great, who had conquered Media and Babylon, Amasis allied himself with Crœsus, King of Lydia, and Polycrates of Samos; but before his policy was productive of any results, he died, B. C. 525, and was succeeded on the throne of Egypt by PSAMMENITUS. Cambyses, King of Persia, the son and successor of Cyrus the Great, was already on the march toward Egypt. The Egyptian army advanced to Pelusium to meet the invader, but was there defeated in a pitched battle and driven back to Memphis, the capital, which was besieged and taken by the Persian king. Psammenitus was taken prisoner after a reign of only six months, and soon afterward put to death by the hardhearted Cambyses, who suspected him of a design to recover his power. With the tragic end of Psammenitus perished the ancient kingdom of Egypt, which had existed for over two thousand years, from the time of the founding of the Old Empire by Menes; and the celebrated land of the Pharaohs became a mere province of the vast Medo-Persian Empire (B. C. 525).

The tyranny and cruelty of Cambyses produced in the hearts of the Egyptians the most implacable hatred of Persia; and during a period of two centuries they constantly plotted against the Twenty-seventh, or Persian Dynasty, and under three native dynasties—the Twenty-eighth, Twenty-ninth and Thirtieth—regained their independence, which they as often lost. The accounts of these revolts and short spasms of independence will be narrated in the history of the Medo-Persian Empire. Since its conquest by the Persians, the land of the Pharaohs has been successively under the sway of the Persians, the Macedonians, the Romans, the Saracens, the Mamelukes, and the Ottoman Turks; the last of whom have held the country tributary for the last three and a half centuries.

MANETHO'S THIRTY EGYPTIAN DYNASTIES.

OLD EMPIRE.

CONTEMPORARY DYNASTIES FROM ABOUT B. C. 2700 TO ABOUT B. C. 2450.

FIRST DYNASTY (THINITE).			THIRD DYNASTY (MEMPHITE).		
KINGS.	YEARS ACCORDING TO		KINGS.	YEARS ACCORDING TO	
	EUSEBIUS.	AFRICANUS.		EUSEBIUS.	AFRICANUS.
MENES,	60	62	NECHEROPHES,	...	28
ATHOTHIS, or THOTH,	27	57	TOSORTHRUS,	...	29
UNEPHES,	39	31	TYREIS,	...	7
KENKENES,	42	23	MESOCHRIS,	...	17
USAPHÆDUS,	20	20	SUPHIS,	...	16
MIEBIDUS,	26	26	TOSERTASIS,	...	19
SEMEMPSES,	18	18	ACHES,	...	42
BIENECHES,	26	26	SEPHURIS,	...	30
			KERPHERES,	...	26
	258	263		298	214

POLITICAL HISTORY.

Contemporary Dynasties from about B. C. 2450 to about B. C. 2220.

SECOND OR BRANCH DYNASTY (THINITE).		FOURTH OR CHIEF DYNASTY (MEMPHITE).		FIFTH OR BRANCH DYNASTY (ELEPHANTINE).	
	YEARS.		YEARS.		YEARS.
Boethus, or Bochus,	38	Seneferu, or Sorus,	29	Userscheres, or Osirkef,	28
Kœechus, or Kekeou,	39	Khufu, }		Sephres,	13
Binothris,	47	Shafra, }	66	Nephercheres, or Nofr-	
Tlas,	17	Menkaura, or Mencheres	63	ir-ke-re,	20
Sethenes,	41	Ratoises,	25	Sisires, or Osir-n-rê,	7
Chæres,	17	Bicheris,	22	Cheres,	20
Nephercheres,	25	Sebercheres,	7	Rathures,	44
Sesochris,	48	Thamphthis,	9	Mencheres,	9
Cheneres,	30			Tancheres,	44
	—		—	Onnus, or U-nus,	33
	302		221		—
					218

Contemporary Dynasties from about B. C. 2220 to about B. C. 2080.

SECOND DYNASTY (THINITE).	SIXTH DYNASTY (MEMPHITE).	FIFTH DYNASTY (ELEPHANTINE).	NINTH DYNASTY (HERACLEOPOLITE).	ELEVENTH DYNASTY (THEBAN).
	YEARS.			
Continuing under the last three kings.	Othoes, . . . 30 Phios, . . . 53 Methosuphis, 7 Phiops, or Pepi, ... 100 Menthesuphis, 1 Nitocris, or Neit-akret, 12 —— 143	Continuing.	Achthoes, the Anteps, and the Mentu-hoteps.	Sixteen Kings. Ammenemes or Amun-m-hê.

Contemporary Dynasties from about B. C. 2080 to B. C. 1900.

FIFTH DYNASTY (ELEPHANTINE).	NINTH DYNASTY (HERACLEOPOLITE).	TWELFTH DYNASTY (THEBAN).	FOURTEENTH DYNASTY (XOITE).	FIFTEENTH DYNASTY (HYKSOS).	SIXTEENTH DYNASTY (HYKSOS).
Continuing till about B. C. 1850.	Continuing.	YEARS. Sesonchosis, . . . Usurtasen I., . . 46 Ammenemes II., or Amun-m-hê II., . 38 Usurtasen II., . . 48 Mœris, or Amun-m-hê III., . . 8 Ameres, ... 8 Ammenemes III., or Amun-m-hê IV., 8 Skemiophris, . . 4 —— 160 THIRTEENTH DYNASTY (THEBAN).	Seventy-six Kings in 484 years.	YEARS. Salatis, . 19 Bnon, . . 44 Apachnas, 36 Apophis, . 61 Jannas, . 50 Asses, . . 49 —— 259	Thirty Kings in 518 years.

ANCIENT HISTORY.—EGYPT.

MIDDLE EMPIRE.—(HYKSOS, OR SHEPHERD KINGS.)

CONTEMPORARY DYNASTIES FROM ABOUT B. C. 1900 TO ABOUT B. C. 1600.

SEVENTH AND EIGHTH DYNASTIES (MEMPHITE).	TENTH DYNASTY (HERACLEOPOLITE).	SEVENTEENTH DYNASTY (HYKSOS).

NEW EMPIRE.

EIGHTEENTH DYNASTY—THEBAN.
(B. C. 1600-1400.)
AMOSIS, AAHMES, or AMES, (B. C. 1600-1575).
AMEN-HOTEP I., AMENOPHIS I., or AMUNOPH I., (B. C. 1575-1562).
THOTHMES, I.
THOTHMES II., and HATUSA or AMENSET, (B. C. 1562-1547).
THOTHMES III., (B. C. 1547-1493).
AMEN-HOTEP II., AMENOPHIS II., or AMUNOPH II., (B. C. 1493-1485).
THOTHMES IV., (B. C. 1485-1477).
AMEN-HOTEP III., AMENOPHIS III., or AMUNOPH III., (B. C. 1477-1441).
AMEN-HOTEP IV., AMENOPHIS IV., or AMUNOPH IV.
SAANEKHT.
AI.
TUTANKHAMEN.
HOREMHEB-MERIENAMMON, or HORUS.
RESITOT, or RATHOTIS.

NINETEENTH DYNASTY—THEBAN.
(B. C. 1400-1280).
RAMESES I.
SETI I.
RAMESES MERIAMON, or the GREAT (SESOSTRIS).
MENEPTA, or MENEPHTHAH.
SETI II.
SIPHTHAH.

TWENTIETH DYNASTY—THEBAN.
(B. C. 1280-1100).
SETNEKHT.
RAMESES III., (B. C. 1269-1237).
RAMESES IV.
RAMESES V.
RAMESES VI., and MERI-TUM.
RAMESES VII.
RAMESES VIII.
RAMESES IX.
RAMESES X.
RAMESES XI.
RAMESES XII.
RAMESES XIII.

TWENTY-FIRST DYNASTY—TANITE.
(B. C. 1100-993).
PEHOR, HERHOR, or SMENDES.
PIANKH, or PISHAM I.
PINETEM I.
MEN-KHEPR-RA.
PA-SEB-EN-SHA.
PINETEM II., or PISHAM II.
HOR-PASEBENSHA.

TWENTY-SECOND DYNASTY—BUBASTITE.
(B. C. 993-847).

SHESHONK I., or SHISHAK I., (B. C. 993-972).
OSORKON I., (B. C. 972-957).
TAKELOT I., (B. C. 957-956).
OSORKON II., (B. C. 956-934).
SHESHONK II.
TAKELOT II.
SHESHONK III.
PIMAI.
SHESHONK IV.

TWENTY-THIRD DYNASTY—TANITE.
(B. C. 847-756).
PETUBASTES, or PETSUPASHT, (B. C. 847-807).
OSORKON IV., (B. C. 807-799).
PSAMMUS, or PSEMUT, (B. C. 799-789).
ZET, or SETI III., (B. C. 789-756).

TWENTY-FOURTH DYNASTY—SAITE.
(B. C. 758-730).
BEKENHAUF, or BOCCHORIS.

TWENTY-FIFTH DYNASTY—ETHIOPIAN.
(B. C. 724-650).
SABACO, or SHABAK, (B. C. 724-712).
SHABATOK, (B. C. 712-698).
TIRHAKAH, or TEHRAK, (B. C. 698-667).
RUT-AMMON. (B. C. 667-660).
MI-AMMON-NUT, (B. C. 660-650).

TWENTY-SIXTH DYNASTY—SAITE.
(B. C. 650-525).
PSAMMETICHUS, or PSAMATIK I., (B. C. 665-610).
NEKO, (B. C. 610-594).
PSAMMIS, or PSAMATIK II., (B. C. 594-588).
UAHABRA, APRIES, or PHARAOH HOPHRA, (B. C. 588-569).
AMASIS, AAHMES, or AMES, (B. C. 569-525).
PSAMMENITUS, or PSAMATIK III., (B. C. 525).

TWENTY-SEVENTH DYNASTY—PERSIAN.
(B. C. 525-332).

TWENTY-EIGHTH DYNASTY—NATIVE.
(B. C. 460-455).
AMYRTÆUS.

TWENTY-NINTH DYNASTY—MENDESIAN.
(B. C. 405-384).
NEFERITES, or NEFAOROT, (B. C. 405-399).
ACHORIS, or HAKAR, (B. C. 399-386).
PSAMMUTHIS, (B. C. 386-385).
NEPHERITES II., (B. C. 384).

THIRTIETH DYNASTY—SEBENNYTIC.
(B. C. 384-346).
NECTANEBO I., or NEKHT-NEBEF, (B. C. 384-366).
TEOS, or TACHOS, (B. C. 366-364).
NECTANEBO II., (B. C. 364-346).

SECTION IV.—EGYPTIAN CIVILIZATION.

ODERN ethnologists, in general, regard the ancient Egyptians as of Asiatic origin, since they differed so much from other African races, such as the Berbers and the Negroes, in language, the shape of their skulls, and their physiognomy. The skulls of the ancient Egyptians, and of their legitimate descendants, the modern Copts, are eminently Caucasian; while the Egyptian language has analogies connecting it with the Aryan and Semitic tongues. The conclusion that the Egyptians, at least the upper and middle classes of them, were Asiatic immigrants into the Nile valley, is therefore a safe one. They are believed to have been kindred with other races of South-western Asia, such as the Canaanites, the primitive Chaldæans, and the Southern Arabs. We must accordingly conclude that Syria or Arabia was the cradle of the Egyptian nation.

Some have maintained that the immigration was from the south of the Nile valley, and that the Egyptians were of Ethiopian origin; but recent research has shown conclusively that the movement of the Egyptians was from north to south. Says Mr. Birch, the latest English historian of Egypt: "The study of the monuments furnishes incontrovertible evidence that the historical series of Egyptian temples, tombs and cities, constructed on either bank of the Nile, follow one upon another in chronological order, in such sort that the monuments of the greatest antiquity, the Pyramids for instance, are situated furthest to the north; while the nearer one approaches the Ethiopian cataracts, the more do the monuments lose the stamp of antiquity, and the more plainly do they show the decline of art, of beauty, and of good taste. Moreover, in Ethiopia itself the existing remains present us with a style of art that is absolutely devoid of originality.

At the first glance one can easily see that it represents Egyptian art in its degeneracy, and that art ill understood and ill executed. The utmost height to which Ethiopian civilization ever reached was a mere rude imitation, alike in science and in art, of Egyptian models."

The color of the ancient Egyptians was brown, like that of the modern Copts. For this we have the authority of the monuments. The women were lighter than the men, being depicted on the monuments as yellow. The hair was usually black and straight, though sometimes it grew in short, crisp curls. Men generally shaved both hair and beard, and went about with their heads perfectly bare, or else wore wigs or a close-fitting cap. Women always wore their own hair, and plaited it in long tresses, sometimes extending down to the waist. The

DRESSES OF EGYPTIAN WOMEN.

hair of the wigs, and that found sometimes on the heads of mummies, is coarse.

The features of the Egyptians resembled those of their Syrian neighbors. The forehead was straight, but low; the nose generally long, though sometimes slightly aquiline. The lips were over full, but the upper lip was short, and the mouth was seldom too wide. The chin was good, being well rounded, and neither receding nor extending too far. The eye was a long, narrow slit, like that of the Chinese, but placed horizontally, instead of obliquely. The eyebrow, likewise long and thin, shaded the eye. The coloring was always dark; the hair, eyebrows, eyelashes, and beard (where there was one), being black, or nearly so, and the eyes black or dark brown.

The Egyptians resembled the modern Arabs in form. They were tall, with long and supple limbs, and with the head well placed upon the shoulders. Their movements were graceful, their carriage dignified. Generally, however, their frames were spare, and their hands and feet unduly large. The women were as thin as the men, and their forms were almost similar. Children, however, were sufficiently plump.

The Egyptians were divided into distinct tribes. We read in the Mosaic account of Ludim, Anamim, Lebahim, Naphtuhim, Pathrusim, Casluhim and Caphtorim as distinct "sons of Misraim"—as separate tribes of the people who occupied the "two Egypts."

The Egyptians ranked high intellectually among the ancient nations. In art they exhibited wonderful power. Mr. Birch says that their architecture "was on the grandest scale, and dwarfs the Greek in comparison." The Egyptians had a high moral standard theoretically, but practically their morals were very lax. Says Brugsch, the eminent German Egyptologist: "The forty-two laws of the Egyptian religion, contained in the 125th chapter of the Book of the Dead, fall short in nothing of the teachings of Christianity." The same authority further says that Moses, in compiling his code of laws, did only "translate into Hebrew the religious precepts which he found in the sacred books" of the Egyptians, among whom he had been brought up. The Egyptian women were notoriously loose in their character, exceedingly immodest and licentious. The men openly practiced impurity, and boasted of it in their writings. An inclination to luxurious living was also a defect in the Egyptian character; and drunkenness was a common vice among both sexes, all the appeals and exhortations of the priests in favor of temperance being unavailing to stem the tide of general debauchery. Sensual pleasure and amusement seemed the ends of existence among the upper classes in general. False hair was worn, dyes and cosmetics were used to produce artificial beauty, magnificent dress was worn, equipages were splendid, great banquets were frequently held, games and sports were constant, and life was passed in feasting, sport and a continual succession of enjoyments. The effect of self-indulgence is seen in the national decay of these people, and their successive subjections to hardier races, such as the Ethiopians, Assyrians, Babylonians, Persians, and Macedonian Greeks.

Their family affection is shown by the paintings, where husbands and wives are everywhere represented with their arms around each other's necks. The Egyptians were industrious, cheerful and gay even under hardships; but they were cruel, vindictive, treacherous, avaricious, superstitious and servile. The use of the bastinado was universal, being employed to inflict punishment for minor offenses, while superiors freely beat inferiors. The poor peasantry were forced by blows to yield to the extortions of the tax-gatherers, and slaves were impelled to labor under fear of the rod, which the taskmaster freely applied to the backs of laggards. The passions of the Egyptians often broke out in riot, insurrection and murder. They were extremely fanatical in religious belief, and ready to wipe out in blood any insult to their religion.

They were at times timid, submissive and sycophantic. The lower classes prostrated themselves before their superiors, tamely submitting to blows. The great nobles were equally servile to their sovereign, addressing him as a god, and ascribing to him their continued existence in this life.

Though successful in their early wars, when their disciplined troops attacked un-

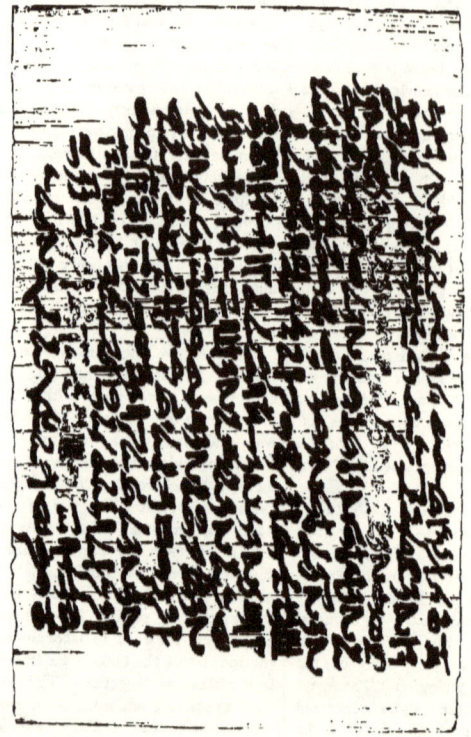

THE PRISSE PAPYRUS.

CHAPTER ON THE VIRTUE OF OBEDIENCE.

FROM THE WRITINGS OF PRINCE PTAHHOTEP, CITY GOVERNOR AND STRATEGIST UNDER ASA, KING OF EGYPT.

(FIFTH DYNASTY, 4,000 B.C.)

(THE LIGHT LETTERS ARE WRITTEN IN RED IN THE ORIGINAL.)

disciplined hordes, they were defeated whenever they encountered a brave and skillful enemy. Their readiness to break engagements when their fulfillment was inconvenient, made them unreliable allies; and for this reason the Hebrew prophet Isaiah spoke of Egypt as a "bruised reed, whereon if a man lean, it will go into his hand and pierce it."

The government of Egypt was a theocratic monarchy, the king being the earthly representative of the Deity. His body was considered sacred, and he was worshiped as a god. His title of Phrah, or Pharaoh, signifying the Sun, ranked him as the emblem

DRESS OF THE EGYPTIAN KING.

of Helios, or Phrah, or Ra, the Sun-god. His right and duty was to preside over the sacrifices and to pour out libations to the gods. He was thus the head of the national religion, as well as the civil and political head of the state. The kingly office was hereditary, but the monarch was not an absolute ruler; and the political system was a combination of theocracy, monarchy and hierarchy, the king's power being more or less curtailed by the power of the priesthood, or hierarchical class. In this respect Egypt differed from an Asiatic despotism, where the sovereign was unlimited lord and master over his subjects. An Egyptian Pharaoh did not possess unlimited power over the lives and property of his people but his authority was strictly defined and limited by law, and nothing was left to passion or caprice. The monarch, however, possessed the right to make new laws. The king's public duties and personal habits were minutely defined by religious regulations, the sacred books prescribing his food, drink, dress and the employment of his time, thus allowing him less individual freedom than was enjoyed by the humblest and most degraded of his subjects. He was not permitted to give way to excessive indulgence of any kind. No slave or hireling was permitted to hold office about his person, for fear that he might be contaminated by such unworthy presence, but those of the highest rank only were accorded the privilege of attending him and ministering to his wants. The ritual of every morning's worship constantly refreshed his memory with a knowledge of the virtues of former kings, and reminded him of his own kingly and personal duties. After his death his body was placed in an open court, where any and every one of his subjects might bring accusations against him; and if his conduct in life was proven to have been unworthy his exalted station, he was forever excluded from the tombs of his ancestors.

The ancient Egyptians were divided into classes or *castes*, distinguished by their ranks and occupations; the priests forming the highest caste, the warriors the second caste, and husbandmen, gardeners, boatmen and herdsmen the lowest caste.

The priesthood possessed great authority in the state and were the "power behind the throne." So far as the sovereign was concerned they used their power wisely and well. Their habits of life were simple and moderate. Their diet was plain in quality and limited in quantity, and they abstained from fish, mutton, swine's flesh, beans, peas, garlic, leeks and onions, which were articles of food among the common people. They bathed twice a day and twice during the night, some of the more strict in water tasted by their sacred birds, the ibis, to make sure of being purged of all uncleanness. Their abstinence, purity and humility, and their reputation for learning, enabled the priests to hold the people in religious, political and mental subjection. By their knowledge of physical science they could frighten and terrorize the superstitious and ignorant lower classes by optical illusions and other tricks. By their power to try the dead they could decide the fate of any man, from the king to the swineherd, by refusing him a passport to the outer world. The priests prescribed the religious ritual of every Egyptian, from the king to the meanest of his subjects.

The Egyptian priesthood embraced an order including many professions and occupations. They alone were acquainted with the arts of reading and writing, and with medicine and the other sciences. They cultivated the science of medicine from the earliest ages. The universal practice of embalming was exercised by the physicians, thus enabling them to study the effects of various diseases by examining the body after death. Asiatic monarchs sent to Egypt for their physicians, and the fertile soil of the Nile valley furnished drugs for the whole ancient civilized world. Even in our own time the characters used by druggists to denote drams and ounces are the Egyptian ciphers adopted by the Arabs.

The soldiers, or military caste, which ranked next to the sacerdotal, or priestly order, numbered about four hundred thousand persons. When not engaged in military service, either in foreign wars, in garrisons or at the royal court, these were settled on their lands, which were located principally on the east side of the Nile or in the Delta, which portions of the country were the most exposed to hostile invasion by a foreign foe. Each soldier was allotted about six and a half acres of land, exempt from all taxation or tribute; and from the proceeds of this land he defrayed the expenses of his arms and equipments. The soldier, however, could not engage in any art or trade. The lands of the priests and soldiers were considered privileged property, while all other lands were regarded as the king's property, and were rented by him to farmers, who paid a yearly rent of one-fifth of the produce.

Below the priests and warriors were the various unprivileged castes, embracing husbandmen, gardeners, boatmen, artisans of various kinds, and herdsmen, comprising shepherds, goatherds and swineherds. These latter were intensely despised as the most degraded of human creatures, and were not allowed to enter the temples. All castes below the priesthood and the warrior class were deprived of all political rights and disqualified from ownership in land.

The two privileged castes, the priests and warriors, are believed to have been the descendants of the Asiatic conquerors and immigrants into Egypt, while the lower classes were the descendants of the Ethiopian abo-

EGYPTIAN SOLDIERS OF DIFFERENT CORPS.

Cyrus the Great.

Egyptian King in War Chariot — Egyptian Warriors.

Egyptian Lady — Egyptian Queen — Egyptian Lady.

Egyptian Priest — Men and Woman of Low Caste.

MEDIA AND EGYPT.

rigines of the Nile valley. The Egyptian castes were not as fixed as those of the Hindoos, as the educational system enabled any one of superior talent to rise above his native rank. Says Rawlinson: "Castes, in the strictest sense of the word, did not exist in Egypt, since a son was not absolutely compelled to follow his father's profession." Intermarriages sometimes occurred between members of the priestly and warrior castes, and transitions between them were common. The same was the case between members of the various unprivileged orders. Still, in the main, the same rank, professions and occupations remained in the same families for hundreds and hundreds of years, and the evils of class distinction were almost equal to those of the fixed castes of India. The upper classes despised all handicrafts, and "every shepherd was an abomination in the sight of an Egyptian." There were many slaves who had been captives taken in war. The class system tended to discourage personal ambition, and thus to check all progress and improvement after the earliest high state of civilization had been attained, and was the principal cause of the final national decay of this renowned ancient people.

The land in Egypt belonged exclusively to the king, the priests and the soldiers, during the period of the New Empire; all other land-owners having surrendered their proprietorship to the king, while the Hebrew Joseph was prime minister, occupying them only afterward as tenants of the crown by paying an annual rental of one-fifth of the produce.

The lot of the agricultural laborer in Egypt was a hard one. There were few Egyptian peasants rich enough to rent their farms and till them for themselves. Most of them were hired laborers working on the estates of others, under the supervision of brutal overseers or taskmasters, who applied the bastinado to the backs of the idle or refractory on the slightest pretext. The peasant farmer was not much better off. Writes Amenemun to Pentaour: "Have you ever represented to yourself the estate of the rustic who tills the ground? Before he has put the sickle to the crop, the locusts have blasted a part of it; then come the rats and the birds. If he is slack in housing his grain, the thieves are upon him. His horse dies of weariness as it drags the wain. Anon, the tax-gatherer arrives; his agents are armed with clubs; he has Negroes with him, who carry whips of palm branches. They all cry, 'Give us your grain!' and he has no easy way of avoiding their extortionate demands. Next, the wretch is caught, bound and sent off to work without wage at the canals; his wife is taken and chained; his children are stripped and plundered." Tuaufsakhrat, in the "Praise of Learning," gives a similar account in these words: "The little laborer having a field, he passes his life among rustics; he is worn down for vines and pigs, to make his kitchen of what his fields have; his clothes are heavy with their weight; he is bound as a forced laborer; if he goes forth into the air, he suffers, having to quit his warm fire-place; he is bastinadoed with a stick on his legs, and seeks to save himself; shut against him is the hall of every house, locked are all the chambers."

Thus it will be seen that the small cultivator was oppressed with extortionate taxation, collected by the brutal tax-gatherers; that forced labors were exacted of him, and that he was bastinadoed with a stick on the back or legs if he resisted. He was torn from his family and homestead, and forced to labor under the hot Egyptian sun at cleaning out or banking up the canals. No wages being paid him, and insufficient food being furnished him, he often perished under the hardships imposed upon him by a merciless government. If an iron constitution saved him and he returned home, he frequently found his family dispersed, his wife carried off, and his mud cabin in ruins. He was regarded with contempt, not alone by the privileged classes, but also by their servants, and even by their slaves.

The laws of Egypt were remarkable, and are another evidence of the high civilization of the people. Bossuet has said that "Egypt was the source of all good government."

ANCIENT HISTORY.—EGYPT.

Perjury was considered the most heinous of all crimes—an offense alike against gods and men—and was punishable with death. Any one seeing a person defending his life against a murderer, and failing to render him assistance, was also capitally punished, as being equally guilty with the assassin. If the witness were unable to assist the defendant, he was bound to report the assailant to the lawful authorities. A person falsely accusing another was punished as a calumniator. Every Egyptian was bound to furnish the authorities with a written statement of his means of livelihood; and any one giving a false account, or following an unlawful pursuit, was punished with death. A wilful murderer was likewise put to death. A judge who condemned an innocent person to death was punished as a deliberate murderer. A soldier who deserted his ranks was punished with infamy, but could recover his lost honor by future gallant behavior. Making counterfeit money, false weights, scales or measures, falsifying public records, or forging documents, were crimes punished with the loss of both hands. A man's property could be seized for debt, but not his person; and if a debtor swore that he owed nothing to a creditor who was without a bond, the debt was void. The interest was never permitted to exceed the principal.

The Egyptians were the first people to organize a regular army, and thus to lay the foundation for the whole system of ancient warfare, including the military systems of the ancient Asiatic monarchies. The war-chariots formed the most important part of an Egyptian army, and were used instead of

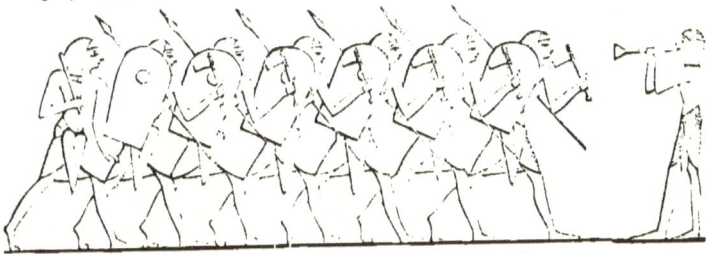

DISCIPLINED TROOPS OF THE EIGHTEENTH DYNASTY.

cavalry. These chariots were mounted on two wheels, and were very carefully made. They were hung low, were open behind to enable the warrior to step in and out with ease, and had no seat. They were drawn by two horses, and usually contained two war-

EGYPTIAN WAR-CHARIOT.

riors, one to manage the horses, and the other to fight. The war-chariots of different nations differed from each other. The harness and housings of the horses were elegantly decorated. A quiver and bow-case, tastefully and skillfully decorated, were fixed to the chariot on the outside. The

CIVILIZATION.

Egyptian national weapon was the bow, used by infantry and charioteers.

The Egyptians were the most skillful archers of antiquity. Their bows were the most powerful, and their arrows, drawn to the ear, were the best aimed, of those of all ancient nations. The children of the military caste were trained to the practice of archery from the earliest infancy. The heavy arms of the Egyptian infantry were a spear, a dagger, a short sword, a pole-ax, a battle-ax, a helmet and a shield. Some of the principal officers used coats of mail for protection. The light troops were armed with swords, battle-axes, maces and clubs. Every battalion had its standard, with some symbol or sacred object represented thereon, generally the emblem of the nome or tribe. The soldiers were called out by conscription, drilled to the sound of the trumpet, and taught to march in measured time. In the most ancient period cavalry were used as skirmishers, videttes and expresses. In attacking walled cities battering-rams, besieging-towers and scaling-ladders were used. The Egyptians, like other ancient nations, treated their captives very cruelly, putting them to death or reducing them to slavery.

The Egyptians readily gave quarter when an enemy submitted, and thousands of prisoners were often taken in their military expeditions. If they ran down an enemy's ship they exerted themselves to rescue the men on board from the waves, and took them to their own vessels at the risk of their own lives. Enemies who laid down their weapons on land and sued for mercy were usually spared. Their arms were bound together by a cord passed round them a little above the elbows, and they were led from the field to the camp, usually in long strings, each conducted by one Egyptian. Laggards were urged forward by fear of the bastinado,

1—5.-U. H.

which was freely applied by those in charge of the captives. All captives were considered as belonging to the king, and consequently became his slaves, being employed by him in forced labors during the rest of their lives; but sometimes the monarch rewarded individual captors by allowing them to hold their own prisoners, who thus passed into private servitude.

ASSAULT ON A FORT—TESTUDO AND SCALING-LADDER.

The Egyptians, in order to ascertain the number of slain among an enemy's army on the battle-field, mutilated them, cutting off and carrying to the camp the right hand, the tongue or some other portion of the body. Heaps of each of these are shown in the sculptures, which the royal scribes are represented as counting in the king's presence, before registering them. Each soldier received a reward upon showing these proofs of his prowess.

The climate of the Nile valley is warm

and dry. In Southern Egypt the heat is excessive. In Northern Egypt several causes combine to give a lower summer temperature. In the desert tracts the air is much drier than in the Nile valley itself, with greater alternations of heat and cold. In summer the air is suffocating, while in winter the days are cool and the nights actually cold. Heavy rains and violent thunder-storms are frequent at this season. At certain seasons green herbage and flowers cover the torrent-beds after the water has flowed into the Nile; but the solar heat and the *Khamseen*, or hot desert wind, wither the herbage and flowers at other seasons.

The vegetable productions of Egypt are trees, shrubs, esculent plants, grain, artificial grasses and medicinal plants. The trees are the date-palm, the sycamore, the tamarisk, the myxa, the acanthus and several kinds of acacias. Among shrubs and fruit-trees are the fig, the pomegranate, the mulberry, the vine, the olive, the apricot, the peach, the pear, the plum, the apple, the orange, the lemon, the banana, the locust-tree, the persea, the castor-oil plant and the prickly pear. These, excepting the orange, lemon, apricot and banana, are believed to have all been productions of ancient, as well as of modern, Egypt. The esculent plants which grew wild were the byblus, or papyrus, the *Nymphæa lotus* and the *Lotus cærulea*. The papyrus plant, which was used for writing, is not now found in Egypt. The cultivated vegetables are mainly the same as those of other countries. Artificial grasses of ancient Egypt were clover, vetches, lupins and the *gilbán* of the Arabs, or the *Lathyrus sativus* of Pliny.

The wild animals indigenous in Egypt were the hippopotamus, the crocodile, the lion, the hyena, the wolf, the jackal, the fox, the ichneumon, the hare, the jerboa, the rat, the mouse, the shrew-mouse, the porcupine, the hedgehog, and perhaps the bear, the wild boar, the ibex, the gazelle, three kinds of antelopes, the stag, the wild sheep, the *Monitor Niloticus*, and the wild cat. The domestic animals were the horse, the ass, the camel, the Indian or humped ox, the cow, the sheep, the goat, the pig, the cat and the dog.

The birds of Egypt are the eagle, the falcon, the Ætolian kite, the black vulture, the bearded vulture, the *Vultur percnopterus*, the osprey, the horned owl, the screech-owl, the raven, the ostrich, the ibis, the pelican, the vulpanser or fox-goose, the Nile duck, the hoopoe, the sea-swallow, the Egyptian kingfisher, the quail, the oriental dotterell, the benno, the sicsac, the swallow, the sparrow, the wagtail, the crested plover, the heron and other wading birds, the common kite, the hawk, the common vulture, the common owl, the white owl, the turtle-dove, the missel thrush, the common kingfisher, the lark, and the finch.

There were different kinds of fish in the Nile; and various reptiles were found in the country, such as turtles, iguanas, geckos or small lizards, the horned snake, the asp, the chameleon, and others. The most remarkable insects are the scorpion, the locust and the *solpuga* spider.

Among minerals in Egypt are many excellent kinds of stone, such as magnesian limestone, sandstone, porphyry, alabaster, granite and syenite. The inexhaustible supply of stone made that gift of nature the great building material of Egypt. The different kinds of stone were conveyed from one end of Egypt to the other by being floated on rafts along the Nile. It was easy to float down the river the granite and syenite of the far South of Egypt to Thebes, Memphis, and the cities of the Delta. There were few metals in Egypt. Among these were gold, silver, copper, iron and lead. Other mineral productions were natron, salt, sulphur, petroleum, chalcedonies, carnelians, jaspers, green breccia, emeralds, agate, rock-crystal, serpentine, compact felspar, steatite, hornblende, basanite, actinolite and the sulphate of barytes.

The fertilizing of the soil by the annual inundation of the Nile, and the irrigation of the country by means of numerous canals, contributed to make Egypt the great gran-

CIVILIZATION.

ary of antiquity, from which other nations drew their supplies in times of famine. The naturally fertile soil and the spontaneous growth of the date-palm furnished the people with cheap and abundant food, and agriculture received much attention.

The rapid increase and density of the Egyptian population, which, as we have already said, was about seven millions, crowded in the narrow valley of the Nile, only seven miles in width, was due to the abundance and cheapness of food and the readiness with which it could be obtained.

trodden in by sheep, goats or pigs, and then simply awaited the harvest. Plows, of a simple construction, and hoes were used in preparing the ground in other portions of the country. The plows were drawn by two oxen or two cows, yoked to it by the shoulders or by the horns. Sometimes a single plowman guided the plow by holding one handle in his left hand, and carrying a whip in his right; but generally there were two plowmen, one holding the two handles, and the other driving the animals with the whip. In light and loose soils the hoe was used

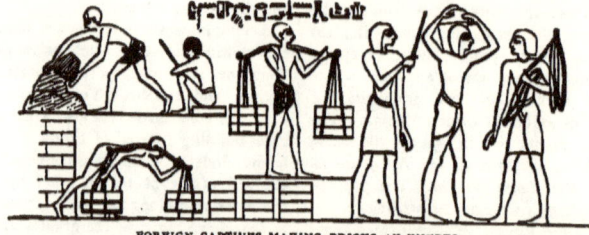

FOREIGN CAPTIVES MAKING BRICKS AT THEBES.

This fact accounts for the ease with which great public works like the Pyramids, that were useless, could be built; as the monarchs were thus enabled to employ the labor of hundreds of thousands of men, who were not required by necessity to labor in any other way.

The non-interference of the government with agriculture was an advantage. The grain was sowed when the inundation had disappeared. In some parts of Egypt the husbandman only scattered the seed upon the rich Nile deposit and caused it to be

instead of the plow. The hoes and plows were of wood. The grain cultivated was wheat, barley, and what Herodotus called *zea* or *olyra*, probably the modern *doora*. The wheat and barley were used by the rich, and the *doora* by the poor. The wheat was cut with a toothed sickle, a little below the ear, and put in baskets or bound in sheaves. The filled baskets were carried in by men or donkeys to the threshing-floor, and there emptied on a heap. Sometimes the corn was conveyed from the harvest-field to the granary or storehouse, and kept there a month.

ANCIENT HISTORY.—EGYPT.

Threshing was done by means of cattle, which were driven round and round the threshing-floor, while a laborer, with a pitchfork, threw the unthreshed ears into their path. The threshed corn was at once winnowed, by being tossed into the air with shovels, in a place where the draught of air would blow off the chaff as the corn fell. After this operation the cleansed grain was carried in sacks to the granary, and there stored until used.

In a harvest song, discovered by Champollion at Eilethyias, the oxen are represented as mainly threshing *for themselves*. The following is the song in hieroglyphics, with its translation into English:

SONG OF THRESHERS TO OXEN.
Translated as Follows:
Thresh for yourselves,
Thresh for yourselves,
O Oxen!
Thresh for yourselves,
Thresh for yourselves,
Measures for yourselves,
Measures for your masters.

The cultivation of barley was similar to that of wheat, and barley bread was in great demand. Beer was also brewed from the grain. The *doora* was pulled up by the roots, and the earth was then shaken off by the hand. It was bound in sheaves and carried to a storehouse; and after it was dry it was unbound and drawn by the hand through an instrument, armed at one end with a set of metal spikes, which separated the heads from the straw. These were, perhaps, then also threshed and winnowed.

Beans, peas and lentils were also raised. Artificial grasses, such as clover, lupins and vetches, were grown to furnish provender for the cattle during the inundation. Flax was raised in great abundance for the linen out of which garments were made. Cotton, indigo, safflower, sesame, the castor-oil plant, and various medicinal herbs were also cultivated. Esculent vegetables, such as garlic, onions, leeks, endive, radishes, melons, cucumbers, lettuces, etc., were likewise raised in considerable quantities, and formed a large element in the food of the people. The raising and harvesting of these different crops employed the agricultural class for the greater part of the year. In addition to the yearly overflow of the Nile, the country was fertilized by irrigation in the form of a system of canals, with embankments, sluices and flood-gates, by which the overflow was retained in vast reservoirs, and thus utilized. This system of irrigation was established at an early date, and was maintained with the greatest care by the government. In the district of the Faioom, a natural depression in the Libyan desert, eight or ten miles from the Nile valley, a canal was cut from the Nile, thus filling this depression with water, and forming an artificial lake, known as the "Lake Mœris." From this immense reservoir, canals were cut in all directions to irrigate the surrounding desert. In this region, by this system of irrigation, the cultivation of the olive was rendered possible. In the edge of the Nile valley, toward the desert of *Hâger*, where the soil was light and composed of sand mixed with gravel, the vine was cultivated all the way from Thebes to Memphis. It was also grown in the Faioom, and in the western part of the Delta. The fruit, after being gathered, was carried in baskets to the storehouse, where the juice was extracted by treading or squeezing in a bag. After fermentation, the wine was stored away in vases or amphoræ of an elegant shape, closed with a stopper and then hermetically sealed with moist clay, pitch, gypsum or other substance.

In the large estates of the rich land-owners the herdsmen were under the supervision of overseers. The peasant who cultivated the land on which the flocks and herds fed was responsible for their proper support and for the exact account of the amount of food which they consumed. Some persons were wholly employed in taking care of the sick animals, which were kept at home in the farm-yard. The overseer of the shepherds attended, at stated periods, to give a report to the scribes connected with the estate, by whom it was submitted to the steward, who was accountable to his employer for this and all his other possessions. The paintings represent the head shepherd rendering his account, and behind him we see the flocks assigned to his charge, consisting of the sheep, goats and wild animals belonging to the person in the tomb. In one painting the expressive attitude of this man, with his hand at his mouth, is imagined to convey the idea of his effort to remember the numbers which he is giving, from memory, to the scribes. In another painting the numbers are written over the animals. The oxen are numbered eight hundred and thirty-four, the cows two hundred and twenty, the goats three thousand two hundred and thirty-four, the asses seven hundred and sixty, and the sheep nine hundred and seventy-four. These are followed by a man carrying the young lambs in baskets slung upon a pole. The steward, in a leaning posture upon his staff, and accompanied by his dog, stands on one side; while the scribes, writing over their statement, occupy the other side. Another painting shows us men bringing baskets of eggs, flocks of geese, and baskets full of goslings. An Egyptian "Goose Gibbie" is represented as making obeisance to his master. In still another painting we see persons feeding sick oxen, goats and geese. The ancient Egyptians carried the art of curing diseases in all kinds of animals to great perfection; and the testimony of ancient writers and paintings is sustained by a discovery of Cuvier, who found the left shoulder of a mummied ibis fractured and reunited, thus showing that human art intervened in this case.

The ancient Egyptians of every class delighted in field-sports, and the peasants considered it a duty, no less than amusement, to hunt and kill the hyena and other wild animals which annoyed them. The paintings show us numerous hunting scenes and various devices for catching birds and beasts. The hyena is usually represented as caught in a trap. Wild oxen were caught by a noose or lasso, in very much the same manner as the South Americans catch horses and cattle, though the Egyptians are not represented as riding on horseback when they used it. The introduction of a bush in one painting, just behind the man throwing the lasso, would seem to imply that the huntsman was concealed. Other wild animals hunted were the hippopotamus, the jackal, the fox, the crocodile, the porcupine, the gazelle, the ibex, the hare, the antelope, and even the ostrich. Wild cattle were also hunted. Lions, upon the borders of Egypt, were hunted by a few of the kings, but there is only one representation of a royal lion hunt. Sometimes lions were tamed, and were used in the chase of other animals, according to a single painting. One king is represented as having "hunted a hundred and twenty elephants on account of their tusks." Fishing and fowling were also favorite sports among the Egyptians. Hounds were likewise used in pursuing game.

All the departments of agriculture, farming, breeding cattle, etc., are illustrated in the paintings with wonderful accuracy and detail. We observe oxen lying on the ground, with legs pinioned, while herdsmen are branding marks upon them with hot irons, and other men are heating irons in the fire. The paintings give us full accounts of the king's kine, which are generally copied after the fattest specimens. One of these represents the Pharaoh as himself a tolerably extensive grazier, the king's ox being marked eighty-six. Another illustrates a regular cattle-show; another the actual operation of the veterinary art, cattle doctors being exhibited as performing operations upon sick oxen, bulls, deer, goats and geese. The hieroglyphic denoting a physician is

ERECTION OF PUBLIC BUILDINGS IN EGYPT.

RUINS IN THE TEMPLE-DISTRICT OF KARNAK.

CIVILIZATION.

the fowl whose cry is "Quack! quack!"

Egyptian beasts of burden were asses, cows and oxen. Horses were used for riding, for drawing curricles and chariots, mainly by men of the upper classes, and for drawing the plow. Multitudes were required for the war-chariots and for the cavalry service. A brisk trade in horses was carried on with Syria and Palestine, where they were in great demand and commanded high prices. The horses of ancient Egypt were kept constantly in stables, fed on straw and barley, and were not allowed to graze in the fields. The larger land-owners also possessed wild animals, such as wild goats, gazelles and oryxes; and also wild fowl, such as the stork, the vulpanser and others. Egyptian farmers also bred large numbers of sheep, goats and pigs.

Egypt has been an object of interest to mankind in every age, as the birth-place of civilization, art and science. In this narrow strip of country, "the Gift of the Nile," only seven miles wide and five hundred and twenty-six miles long, were seven million inhabitants. The Nile valley is studded with the ruins of ancient cities. Memphis, the chief city of Middle Egypt, or the Heptanomis, so called from its seven nomes, was situated about twelve miles south of the apex of the Delta, and as we have said, was founded by Menes, the first Egyptian king. In the vicinity of Memphis are the most splendid of the pyramids, which extend for seventy miles on the west bank of the Nile, and among which are the famous Pyramids of Ghizeh, already described. In this vicinity is also the Great Sphinx, or woman-headed lion, one hundred and forty-six feet long and thirty-six feet wide across the shoulders. Here are also the ruins of the famous Labyrinth, and miles on miles of rock-hewn temples. The magnificent and stately Thebes, the hundred-gated city of Upper Egypt, or the Thebaïs, is said to have extended over twenty-three miles. On its site are the villages of Karnak and Luxor, where the ruins of magnificent and spacious temples, splendid palaces, colossal statues, avenues of obelisks and lines of sphinxes, tombs of kings hewn in the solid rock, subterranean catacombs and the gigantic statue of Memnon, still bear witness to the immense size and splendor of this great and celebrated city, whose ruins extend for seven miles along both banks of the Nile.

The ancient Egyptians had a wonderful building instinct, and architecture was the greatest of all their arts. The distinguishing features were massiveness and grandeur, in which they have never been surpassed. This great people delighted in pyramids, sphinxes, obelisks and stupendous palaces and temples, with massive columns and spacious halls of solemn and gloomy grandeur, in which our largest cathedrals could stand, adorned with elaborately-sculptured colossal statues, and connected with which were avenues of sphinxes and lines of obelisks. Their pyramids are the oldest, as well as the largest and most wonderful of human works yet remaining, and the beauty of their masonry, Wilkinson declares, has never been surpassed. An obelisk of a single stone now standing in Egypt weighs three hundred tons, and a colossus of Rameses the Great nearly nine hundred tons; and Herodotus describes a monolithic temple weighing five thousand tons, which was carried hundreds of miles on sledges, as were also the huge blocks of stone, sometimes weighing sixteen thousand tons each, with which the pyramids were built. In one instance two thousand men were employed three years in conveying a single stone from the quarry to the structure in which it was to be placed. There is a roof of a doorway at Karnak covered with sandstone blocks forty feet long. Sculpture and bas-reliefs thirty-five or forty centuries old, in which the granite is cut with exquisite delicacy, are yet to be seen throughout this famous land. The pyramids were all built on strictly scientific and mathematical principles.

The obelisks, so called on account of their peculiar shape, were tall and slender monoliths erected at the gateways of temples, one standing on each side. From the quarries of Syene they were floated down the Nile on rafts during an annual overflow.

ANCIENT HISTORY.—EGYPT.

They were formed in accordance with a certain rule of proportion, and were from twenty to one hundred and twenty-three feet high. was taken to Paris in 1833 and erected in the Place de la Concorde. Several others had previously been removed to Rome.

RUINS OF OMBOS.

The names and titles of the kings who erected them were recorded in hieroglyphic carvings on the sides. An obelisk at Luxor Two famous obelisks, after standing for eighteen centuries at the gate of the temple of the sun at Heliopolis, where they had

CIVILIZATION. 77

been erected by King Thothmes III., were removed to Alexandria by the Romans just after their conquest of Egypt, in the time of Augustus Cæsar. These were known at Alexandria as Cleopatra's Needles, and one was transported to London a few years ago. The other was shortly after transported to New York, and is now one of the objects of interest greeting the eye of the beholder in Central Park.

RUINS OF TEMPLE AT KARNAK.

Egypt, renowned for its discoveries in art and science, was the ancient world's university, where Moses, Lycurgus and Solon, Pythagoras and Plato, Herodotus and Diodorus—lawgivers, philosophers and historians—were students. The ancient Egyptians had made considerable progress in the sciences, particularly astronomy, geometry, arithmetic, chemistry, medicine and anatomy. Their knowledge of astronomy is proven by the accuracy with which they calculated solar and lunar eclipses; by their mode of reckoning time and their knowledge of the length of the year as being three hundred and sixty-five days; by their knowledge of the spherical shape of the earth; and by their ability to compute latitude and longitude, as demonstrated by the fact that the tomb of Cheops, Suphis, or Khufu, the king who built the largest of the three great Pyramids of Ghizeh, is located exactly on the 30th parallel of north latitude.

The ancient Egyptians had attained great skill in many of the finer mechanical arts, such as pottery, the manufacture of glass and porcelain, dyeing and the making of linen and cotton goods. They likewise excelled in the polishing and engraving of precious stones, and in metallurgy. Mining was one of their industries. Their walls and ceilings were painted in beautiful patterns, which moderns yet imitate; and in the production of useful and ornamental articles they have never been surpassed, either in ancient or modern times.

The language of the ancient Egyptians was related to the languages of the Semitic nations, but differed from them in many particulars. There were different dialects in Upper and Lower Egypt.

The Egyptians practiced the art of writing far more extensively than any other ancient people. The pyramids and monuments, even to the most remote antiquity, bear inscriptions, and it was the custom to mark every article of use or ornament. There were three kinds of writing in use. For monumental inscriptions hieroglyphics were used. For documents the writing was executed on leaves of the papyrus plant, from which our word *paper* is derived. The third kind of writing was the demotic, that of the common people, so called from *demos*, the people. The writing was executed with a reed pen. The hieroglyphics were traced in black, but commenced in red, and the sculptured hieroglyphs were also embellished with colors. The hieroglyphic signs are pictorial, and are of four kinds—representative, figurative, determinative and phonetic. Much of this ancient literature has come down to us in a fragmentary and disconnected form. Remnants of papyrus manuscripts of the most ancient Theban dynasties—about four thousand years old—are still in existence. The professional scribes were from the priestly class.

The discovery of the famous *Rosetta Stone*, during Bonaparte's Egyptian campaign, in 1798, led to the deciphering of the hieroglyphic inscriptions on the monuments, which has been the means of throwing a flood of new light upon the history of ancient Egypt. All three forms of hieroglyphic writing were unknown to the Greeks, to whom the monumental inscriptions were interpreted by the Egyptian priests. The key to these writings was lost, thus concealing the treasures of Egyptian learning from the civilized world for centuries. The copies of the three kinds of inscriptions on the Rosetta Stone—the hieroglyphic, the demotic and the Greek—given to European scholars, were the means of opening this long-sealed library on stones and papyri. In 1815 Dr. Young, the English Egyptologist, discovered the key to the texts, and the distinguished French Egyptologist, Champollion, made a successful application of the newly-discovered key. The Rosetta Stone is now in the British Museum.

The ancient Egyptians surpassed all other nations in their love for recording all human actions. They preserved in writing, on papyrus, a record of all the details of private life with surprising zeal, method and regularity. Every year, month, week and day had its record of transactions. This inclination fully accounts for Egypt being the monumental land. No other human records

CIVILIZATION.

—whether of Chaldæa, India or China—go as far back into remote antiquity as do those of Egypt. Bunsen says: "The genuine Egyptian writing is fully as old as Menes, the founder of the Old Empire, perhaps three thousand years before Christ." Lepsius saw the hieroglyph of the reed and inkstand on the monuments of the Fourth Dynasty. Herodotus remarked: "No Egyptian omits taking accurate note of extraordinary and striking events." Everything was recorded. Scribes are everywhere seen on the monuments, taking accounts of the products of the farms, going into the most minute details, even so far as to giving account of every single egg and chicken. Bunsen further says: "In spite of the ravages of time, and though systematic excavation has scarcely yet commenced, we possess chronological records of a date prior to any period of which manuscripts are preserved, or the art of writing existed in any other quarter."

It is owing to their fondness for recording everything, both in pictures and in three kinds of writing; also to their fondness for building and excavating temples and tombs in imperishable granite; and lastly, to the dryness of the air which has preserved for us these paintings, and to the sand which has buried the monuments, thus preventing their destruction—it is owing to all these circumstances that we have so wonderfully preserved, for forty-five centuries, the account of the everyday life, thoughts and religious belief of this renowned ancient people.

The most ancient mural paintings reveal a state of the arts of civilization so perfect as to excite the wonder of archæologists, who therefore know how few new things there are under the sun. We find houses with doors, windows and verandas, likewise barns for grain, vineyards, gardens, fruit trees, etc. We also see pictures of marching troops, armed with spears and shields, bows, slings, daggers, axes, maces and the boomerang. We also notice coats of mail, standards, war-chariots, and the assault on forts by means of scaling-ladders.

The ancient Egyptian tombs likewise exhibit scenes of domestic life and customs similar to those of our own times. We observe monkeys trained to gather fruit from the trees in an orchard, houses furnished with a great variety of chairs, tables, ottomans, carpets, couches, as elegant and elaborate as any used at the present day. There are likewise seen comic pictures of parties, where ladies and gentlemen are sometimes represented as being the worse for wine; of dances, where ballet-girls in short dresses perform pirouettes of the modern kind; of exercises in wrestling, games of ball, games of chance like chess or check-

EGYPTIAN MEN CARRIED HOME FROM A DRINKING PARTY.

ers; of throwing knives at a mark; of the modern thimble-rig, wooden dolls for children, curiously-carved wooden boxes, dice and toy-balls. We have likewise presented to our view men and women playing on harps, flutes, pipes, cymbals, trumpets, drums, guitars and tambourines. We find glass to have been in general use by this great people nearly four thousand years ago, as early as the reign of Usurtasen I., and we can see pictures of glass-blowing and glass bottles as far back as the Fourth Dynasty. The most skillful Venetian glass-workers can not rival some of the old Egyptian glass-work; as the Egyptians could combine all colors in one cup, place gold between two surfaces of glass, and finish in glass details of feathers, etc., which can not be distinguished without the use of the microscope. This last fact demonstrates that they must have understood the use of the magnifying-glass. The Egyptians likewise imitated with success the colors of precious stones, and were even able to make statues thirteen feet high, closely resembling an emerald. They made mosaics in glass of colors of wonderful brilliancy. They were able to cut glass in the most ancient periods. Chinese bottles have also been found in previously-unopened tombs of the Eighteenth Dynasty, showing that there must have been commercial intercourse as far back as that period. The Egyptians could spin and weave and color cloth, and understood the use of mordants, as in modern calico printing. Pliny described this art as practiced in Egypt.

The art of making writing-paper from the papyrus, or paper-plant, is as ancient as the Pyramids. The Egyptians tanned leather and made shoes; and the shoemakers are represented as working on their benches precisely as do our own. Their carpenters used axes, saws, chisels, drills, planes, rulers, plummets, squares, hammers, nails, and hones for sharpening. They likewise knew the use of glue in cabinet-making, and there are paintings in veneering, in which a piece of thin, dark wood is fastened by glue to a coarser piece of light wood. Their boats were propelled by sails on yards and masts, as well as by oars. They used the blow-pipe in making gold chains and other ornaments. They had rings of gold and silver for money, and weighed it in carefully-constructed scales. Their hieroglyphics are carved on the hardest granite so delicately and accurately as to indicate the use of metallic cutting instruments harder than our best steel. The siphon was known to these people as early as the fifteenth century before Christ. The wig was worn by all the higher classes, who constantly shaved their heads, as well as their chins, and frequently wore false beards. In the tombs are found sandals, shoes and low boots, some of them very elegant. Loose robes, ear-rings, finger-rings, bracelets, armlets, anklets and gold necklaces were worn by women. Vases for ointment, mirrors, combs, needles, etc., are found in the tombs. These people also had their doctors and drugs. The prevalence of the passport system is also shown by the careful descriptions of the person contained in their deeds, in precisely the same style as those required by travelers in Europe. The description of Egyptian customs and manners here given is but a small part of that revealed to us in painting or sculpture in the tombs, or upon the walls of Thebes or Beni-Hassan.

At their feasts, which were numerous among the rich, the host and hostess presided. The seats were single or double chairs, but numbers sat on the ground. The servants decked the guests with lotus flowers, and placed meat, cakes, fruits and other articles of food on the small tables in front of them. Hired musicians and dancers entertained the company. Their games were something like our chess or checkers. The rich rode in chariots, or in heavy carriages drawn by oxen. Women received more respectful treatment and enjoyed more freedom in Egypt than in any of the Asiatic nations.

Games of ball were played by females, as well as by males, and one picture shows us that the loser was obliged to allow the winner to ride on her back.

Egyptian shops furnished many curious scenes. Poulterers suspended geese and other fowls from a pole in front of the shop, which also supported an awning to shade them from the sun. Many of the shops resembled our stalls, being open in front, with the goods set on the shelves or hanging from the inner wall; a custom still prevailing in the East. In the Egyptian kitchens were likewise exhibited singular scenes, among which we find representations of a cook roasting a goose. He holds the spit with one hand, and blows the fire with a fan in the other. Another person is seen cutting up joints of meat and putting them into the pot, which is boiling close at hand; while other joints of meat are lying on the table.

Egyptian artists and scribes put their reed pens behind their ears, when examining the effect of the painting or listening to a person on business, as in a modern counting room. The paintings in some instances represent the scribe at work with a spare pen behind his ear, his tablet upon his knee, and his writing-case and inkstand on the table in front of him.

CIVILIZATION.

The dress of the highest class consisted of the *shenti*, a short linen or woolen garment, folded or fluted, and worn around the loins, being fastened with a girdle. A fine linen robe, reaching to the feet, was worn over this, being provided with long sleeves reaching to the elbows. A second girdle fastened the outer robe to the waist. The arms and lower parts

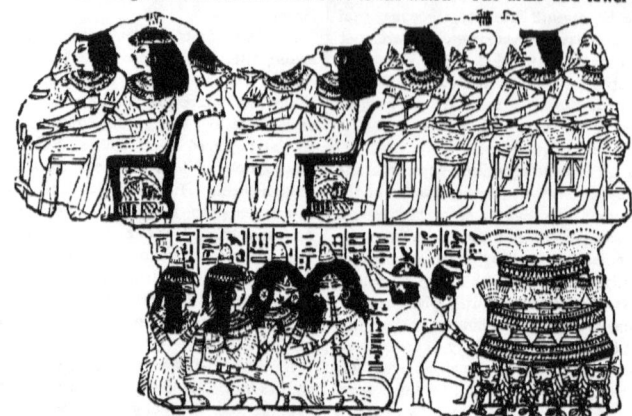

EGYPTIAN GUESTS ENTERTAINED WITH MUSIC AND DANCING.

EGYPTIAN GUESTS TO WHOM WINE, OIL AND GARLANDS ARE BROUGHT.

of the legs were left bare. Sandals or shoes of leather, or of palm-leaves or papyrus stalks, were worn by the rich of both sexes. The Egyptian lords wore ornaments, such as collars of beads or gold chains round their necks, armlets and bracelets of gold round the arms, rings upon the fingers, and anklets round the ankles. The Egyptian women wore a single garment, tied at the neck or fastened by straps over the shoulders, and reaching

ANCIENT HISTORY.—EGYPT.

from the neck or breast to the feet; but those of the upper class wore over this a colored sash, passed twice around the waist and tied in front, and over this second garment a large, loose, fine linen robe with full open sleeves, reaching to the elbow. They wore sandals like the men, and the same ornaments, with the addition of ear-rings in the form of serpents or ending in the heads of animals or of goddesses. Elegant head-dresses were worn.

The most important trades among the Egyptians were those of building, stone-cutting, weaving, furniture-making, chariot-making, glass-blowing, pottery, metallurgy, boat-building and embalming. The builders worked in wood, stone and brick. The mechanical excellence of their works is fully attested by their continuance to the present day.

The paintings frequently allude to the occupations of the mason, the stone-cutter and the sculptor. Workmen are represented polishing and painting statues of men, sphinxes and small figures. In two cases are illustrated large granite colossi, surrounded with scaffolding, on which are represented men employed in polishing and chiseling the stone; the painter coloring the hieroglyphics which the sculptor had engraved on the back of the statue.

Stone-cutting embraced the occupations of quarrying and shaping blocks for the builder, and of cutting, polishing and engraving gems. The Egyptians are still without rivals in the former branch. Blocks of stone were usually cut with a single-handed saw in the hands of a single sawyer. Sometimes the pick and chisel were used to a considerable extent, after which wedges of dry wood were inserted; and these expanded on being wetted, and split off the required block from the mass of stone in the quarry. The tools used were mostly of bronze. Blocks of stone, obtained from the quarries, were finally smoothed and prepared for use by means of the chisel and mallet.

The Egyptians carried on an extensive commerce with other countries; importing gold, ivory, ebony, skins and slaves from Ethiopia and Central Africa, incense from Arabia, and spices and gems from India; and exporting, in exchange for these articles, grain and cloth. As the Egyptians had not attained much skill in the art of ship-building, their trade was carried on principally by Greek and Phœnician merchants.

Egyptian sculpture was designed to illustrate the religious faith of the people, and for this reason was characterized by grandeur and sublimity rather than beauty. Their peculiar taste was the outgrowth of their religious ideas, for the aim was to inspire awe rather than please the eye with graceful and elegant forms. This checked all progress in art, for all inventive genius was fettered by conventional rules founded on religious beliefs. Colossal statues, uncouth allegorical

EGYPTIAN HEAD-DRESSES.

figures and strange ideal forms of animals supplied the place of nature and beauty in Egyptian art. Painting, as illustrated by the specimens in the interiors of temples and sepulchers, was likewise intended to serve the cause of religion, and was trammeled by the same conventional rules, certain colors being strictly prescribed in representing the bodies and draperies of the gods, thus sacrificing variety of form to an ideal monotony. The painting was often executed in brilliant coloring, but the drawing lacked accuracy, exhibiting no compliance with the rules of perspective or the plainest laws of vision. The pigments used were characterized by durability and often by brilliancy.

Ancient Egyptian scu.pture embraces *statuary; reliefs*, or representations of forms on a flat surface by means of a certain projection; and *intaglios*, or representations by cutting the forms into stone or marble, thus sinking them below the surface. Completely detached statues are rare in Egypt. The statues were cut out of stone. There are grotesque figures of Phthah and Bes, which produce disgust and aversion. Egyptian statuary was distinguished for massiveness and strength. The statuettes, in bronze, basalt or terra-cotta, are less dignified than the statues, but possess more elegance and grace. The Great Sphinx, near the Pyramids of Ghizeh, is a striking monument, and impresses the beholder with its air of impassive dignity. Other sphinxes have a certain calmness and grandeur. There are also statuettes of bulls, monkeys and dogs, which are fairly good.

Animal forms are excellent, but the chief defects of Egyptian drawings are improper proportion and incorrect perspective. The bas-reliefs have the same defects in this respect as their statues and statuettes; and there is a frequent intrusion of hideous forms, as seen in the three huge and misshapen figures, so frequently seen upon the ceilings of temples, and which are supposed to represent "the heavens." Bes in all his forms is fearful to behold; as are also Taouris, Savak, Cerberus, Khem, and sometimes even Osiris. The forms of the gods are all more or less repulsive; the stiff outlines, the close-fitting robes, the large hands and feet, the frequent animal heads and immense head-dresses, the ugly or inexpressive faces, recall the monstrosities of the religious representations of Brahminism and Buddhism.

The drawings, mostly of a serious nature, are of four kinds—1, *religious*, where worship, especially sacrifice, is offered to the gods, or where the gods sustain the king, or where the soul passes through scenes it will endure after death; 2, *processional*, where the monarch goes in state, or where tribute is brought to him, or where the pomp of a funeral, or the installation of an official, or some other civil ceremony, forms the subject; 3, *war scenes*, such as land and naval battles, sieges of forts, marches of armies, the return home with booty and captives, etc.; 4, *scenes of ordinary life*, as exclusively represented in the tombs, where the houses and goods, the occupations, the hunting scenes, the entertainments, and the amusements of the deceased are depicted. These tomb scenes are the most numerous and the most interesting; and here the Egyptians are sportive and amusing, exhibiting playfulness and humor, and even approaching caricature.

In painting the Egyptians drew figures of men and animals, and also of other objects, in outline on a white background, and then filled in the outline, wholly or partially, with masses of uniform hue, practicing no shading or softening of the tints. All the exposed parts of a man's body were colored with a uniform red-brown; all the exposed portions of a woman's body, with a lighter red or a yellow. Except in the case of foreigners, the hair and beard were pitch-black. Dresses were mostly white, with their folds marked by lines of red or brown, and were sometimes striped or otherwise patterned, generally red or blue. Most large surfaces were more or less patterned, generally with small patterns of various colors, including much of white. The stone on which the Egyptians painted—whether sandstone, fossiliferous limestone, or granite —was covered with a coating of stucco, which was white or whitish and prevented the colors from being lost by sinking into the background. Besides black, white, red, blue and yellow, they used green, brown and gray, as colors in their paintings. The black is a bone-black. The white is prepared from pure chalk with a light trace of iron. The red and the yellow are ochres, the coloring matter being iron mixed with the earthy substance. The blue is derived from the oxide of copper combined with pulverized glass. The green is the same preparation combined with yellow ochre. The brown is a mixture of blue-black with the red. The colors were mixed with water and with a moderate amount of gum, to make the mixture adhesive and tenacious. They were applied to a stuccoed flat surface, or to figures in relief or intaglio.

The great temple-palace of Rameses III. at Medinet-Abu fully illustrates the combined effects of painting and sculpture in Egypt. On the north-east wall of this ruined structure is represented, in painting, the king on a throne, inscribed with a hawk-headed figure leading a lion and sphinx. Behind the king are the winged effigies of Truth and Justice. Twelve royal princes bear the shrine, and high officers of state wave their *labella* before their august sovereign, while priests carry his arms and insignia. The monarch's sons bear the footstool of his throne, and are accompanied by scribes and great warriors. There is likewise seen a procession of scholars, fan-bearers and soldiers. A great scribe delivers a proclamation from a roll of papyrus, and the high-priest burns incense before the shrine. Birds fly in every direction, as if to spread Pharaoh's fame to every quarter of the world. This is but a part of the elaborate sculpture, the effect of which is heightened by the painter's art, on the inside walls of the great temple-palace. The temples and palaces of Thebes exhibit a similar degree of form and color, which appear almost as perfect as if they had just come from the artist's hand.

As we shall observe, the belief of the future reunion of the soul and body was the reason

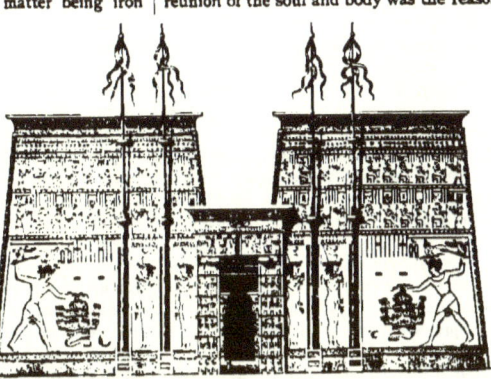

SCULPTURED FAÇADE OF THE TEMPLE OF EDFU.

taken to preserve the latter from decay, as exemplified in the singular custom of embalming the dead, which was the universal practice among this celebrated people, and also in the great pains taken to ornament the insides of the rock-hewn sepulchers, the belief prevailing that the dead body in the tomb was not entirely unconscious.

While other nations embellished the temples and palaces of the living, the ancient Egyptians decorated their tombs, the receptacles of the dead, with lavish splendor. Many of these highly-ornamented sepulchral chambers seem only accessible through long, narrow and intricate passages. The entrances to others seem to be closed with the strictest care, and hidden with reverential sanctity. A necropolis, or "city of the dead," belonged to each city or nome. In the rock-hewn sepulchers of Memphis and Thebes were treasured up all the scenes in which the living monarch and his subjects had figured. Egypt abounds with immense tombs, whose walls, like those of the temples, are adorned with the most wonderful paintings, executed three and four thousand years ago. In these paintings, the entire country, with all its natural productions, its vegetables, animals, birds, fishes, and the people in all their private and domestic occupations, are delineated with a remarkable fidelity of outline and an extraordinary richness of coloring.

Religion was at the foundation of the extraordinary care which the Egyptians bestowed upon their dead. The whole art of embalming the body—the preparing, the bandaging, the anointing, in fact the entire process of forming the mummy—was a duty of the priests. This remarkable custom was a universal national usage among the ancient Egyptians, and had an inseparable connection with their religious dogmas and sentiment. The origin of this singular practice has been traced to the local circumstances of the country. In Egypt the customs of burning and burying the dead, which have prevailed among other nations, were impracticable,—the first, because the country produces little timber, and its fruit-trees, such as the date-palm and others, are too valuable for ordinary consumption; and the second, because in the narrow Nile valley all the land available for agricultural purposes was required for the sustenance of the dense population, and also because the annual inundation of the Nile would have washed up the bodies and generated pestilence. The rocky mountain ranges on each side of the river seemed designed by nature for sepulchers; but the multitudes of the dead could not with safety be heaped together in a state of decomposition, even in the inmost chambers of their rocks, without breeding pestilence. Ancient Egypt was remarkably free from the epidemic plagues which now desolate the Nile land, on account of the universal practice of embalming the dead, which cut off one chief source of noxious vapors. This peculiar custom was, therefore, a wise sanitary regulation, adopted by the priestly lawgivers, and incorporated with the civil and religious institutions of the nation.

1—6.-U. H.

The Egyptian lawgivers, having recognized this provision as essential to the public health, secured its universal and permanent practice by associating it with the doctrines of the soul's immortality and the metempsychosis, or transmigration of the soul. It was believed that every spirit, upon leaving the body, must pass through a predestined cycle of three thousand years, entering successively into the bodies of various animals, until it returned to the human body from which it had departed. Whenever the body which it had last left became subject to corruption the course of its migrations was suspended; the end of its long journey and its ardently-wished-for return to more exalted states of existence was delayed. For this reason the utmost care was taken to preserve the bodies of human beings and animals, and secure them forever from decomposition and putrefaction. Thus this usage was enforced by stringent and sacred laws, and certain orders of the priesthood were expressly empowered with the duty of carrying it into execution. Embalming was performed with solemn religious rites. Herodotus tells us that when a body was found seized by a crocodile, or drowned in the Nile, the city upon whose territory the body was cast was obliged to take it in charge and to cause it to be embalmed and interred in a sepulcher.

The tombs of the wealthy consisted of one or more chambers, ornamented with paintings and sculpture, the place and size o which depended on the expense which the family of the deceased incurred, or on the wishes of the persons who purchased them during their lifetime. These sepulchers were owned by the priests; and as a sufficient number were always held in readiness, the purchase was made at the shortest possible notice, even the sculptures and inscriptions being so far complete as to require only the insertion of the name of the deceased, and a few statements concerning his family and profession. The numerous subjects illustrating agricultural life, the trades and occupations of the people, their diversions, etc., were already introduced. These were the same in all the tombs, differing only in their details and the manner of their execution, and were probably designed as a brief epitome of human life, being adapted equally to every future occupant. In some cases all the paintings of the tomb were completed, and even the small figures representing the tenant were introduced, only those of larger size being left unsculptured, because they required more accuracy in the features to give a correct portrait. In some instances even the large figures were finished before the tomb was sold, only the hieroglyphic legends containing the names of the tenant and his wife remaining to be inserted. The priests often sold old mummy-cases and tombs belonging to other persons, altering the hieroglyphics and giving the name of the new tenant. This was especially the case when the purchaser was satisfied, from motives of economy, with a second-hand tenement for the remains of his departed friend.

The tomb was invariably prepared as a resting-place for the bodies of a husband and his wife. Whichever died first was interred in the sepulcher, or was kept embalmed in the house until the death of the other. The manner in which husband and wife are always represented, with their arms around each other's waist or neck, illustrates the affectionate disposition of the ancient Egyptians. The presence of the different relatives, who are introduced in the performance of some tender office to the deceased friend, shows the attachment of a family to its departed relatives.

Besides the upper rooms of the Egyptian tombs, which were ornamented with the paintings already described, there were pits, from twenty to seventy feet deep, at the bottom and sides of which were recesses, like small chambers, for the reception of the coffins. The pit was closed with masonry after the interment of the body, and was, in some cases, reopened to receive the other members of the family. The upper apartments were profusely ornamented with painted sculptures, thus bearing the character of a monument in honor of the deceased, rather than his sepulcher. These apartments served for the reception of the friends of the deceased, who often met there, and accompanied the priests when performing the services for the dead. Tombs were built of brick or stone, or cut in the solid rock, according to the position of the necropolis. The rock-hewn tombs were preferred wherever the mountains were near enough to the Nile, and these were usually the most elegant in design and variety of sculpture. The sepulchers of the poorer classes had no upper chamber. The coffins of these were laid in pits in the plain, or in recesses at the side of a rock. Mummies of the lower orders were interred together in a common repository, and the remains of those whose relatives were too poor to defray the expenses of a funeral, after being cleansed and kept in an alkaline solution for seventy days, were wrapped up in coarse cloth, in mats or in a bundle of palm sticks, and laid in the earth.

We have the following account of the funeral of Nophri-Othph, a priest of Amun. at Thebes, from the walls of his tomb. The scene of the funeral was on the lake, and on the way from the lake to the sepulcher. At the head of the procession was a large boat conveying the bearers of flowers, cakes and many things relating to the offerings, tables. chairs and other articles of furniture, as well as the friends of the deceased, these being conspicuous by their dresses and their long walking-sticks, the distinguishing mark of Egyptian gentlemen. Next came a small skiff, carrying baskets of cakes and fruit, with a supply of green palm-branches, which it was the custom to strew in the way as the body was being conveyed to the tomb; the smoothness of the palm-leaves and stalks making it easy for the sled to glide over them. The love of caricature, so general among the Egyptians, even in so serious a matter as a funeral, is exemplified in this portion of the scene. A large boat having run aground and being pushed off the bank, struck a smaller one with its rudder, and overturned a large table, loaded with cakes and other things, upon the heads of the rowers seated below, notwithstanding all the exertions of a man in the prow, and the vehement cries of the frightened helmsman.

In another boat were men carrying bunches of flowers and boxes supported by yokes on their shoulders. Then followed two other boats, one conveying the male mourners, and the other the female mourners, standing on the roof of the cabin, beating themselves, uttering cries and making other demonstrations of grief. At last came the consecrated boat, carrying the hearse, around which were the chief mourners and the female relatives of the deceased. Upon arriving at the opposite shore of the lake, the procession marched to the catacombs. On their way, several women of the vicinity, carrying their children in shawls, suspended from the side or back, joined in the lamentations of the funeral train. The mummy was set in a standing position in the chamber of the tomb; and the sister, wife or nearest relative, embracing it, began a funeral dirge, calling upon the deceased with every expression of affection, extolling his virtues and bewailing her own great loss. The high-priest presented a sacrifice of incense and libation, with offerings of cakes and other usual gifts for the dead; and the male and female mourners continued the wailing, throwing dust upon their heads, and making other demonstrations of grief.

Another painting represents the judgment of a wicked soul, which is condemned to return to earth in the form of a pig, having been weighed in the scales before Osiris and found wanting. It is put in a boat, and, attended by two monkeys, is expelled from heaven, all intercourse with which is symbolically cut off by a man hewing away the ground behind it with an axe.

During the whole period of seventy-two days of mourning for the dead, the process of embalming the body was performed. This embalming was performed by the physicians, who, as we have observed, were of the priestly order. Vast numbers of sacred animals—bulls, apes, dogs, cats, sheep, etc.

—were likewise embalmed. It is said that more than four hundred million mummies of human beings were made in Egypt. In recent years many of these mummies have been brought from the land of the Pharaohs to our museums. Tombs have been opened revealing thousands of them in rows one upon another, without coffins. Shiploads of them have been transported to England, and ground up for fertilizers for the soil.

EGYPTIAN MUMMIES.

The embalmers of dead bodies constituted a numerous class among the ancient Egyptians, and must have carried on a prosperous trade, if the prices mentioned by Diodorus were actually those usually exacted. According to the Sicilian historian, the most improved method of preparing a corpse for interment cost a sum which, in our money, would amount to about a thousand dollars. A secondary and much inferior method required an expenditure amounting to about four hundred dollars. The lowest and poorest classes had a third method, the price of which was comparatively moderate; but the vast numbers of this class must have made the profits to the embalmers considerable. It has been estimated that between B. C. 2000 and A. D. 700, when embalming ceased, there may have been interred in Egypt four hundred and twenty million mummied corpses, averaging one hundred and fifty-five thousand yearly. If five-sixths of these, or one hundred and thirty thousand, belonged to the lower classes, while two-fifteenths, or twenty thousand, may have been furnished by the middle classes, and one-thirtieth, or five thousand, by the wealthy classes, and if the poor man paid one-twentieth of the price paid by those of the upper middle class, the annual amount received by the embalmers would have exceeded fifteen million dollars of our money.

The process of embalming was very ancient in Egypt, and by the time of the Eighteenth Dynasty the art had reached a remarkable degree of perfection. In the most expensive system, the brain was extracted with great skill by a curved, bronze implement through the nostrils, after which the skull was washed out with certain medicaments. The nostrils were plugged up, the eyes were removed and their places supplied with artificial ones of ivory or obsidian, and the hair was likewise sometimes removed and placed in a separate packet, covered with linen and bitumen. An opening was cut in the right side with a flint knife, through which the entire intestines were removed by the hand and deposited in sepulchral urns. The cavity was then cleansed by an injection of palm-wine, and sometimes by a subsequent infusion of pounded aromatics; after which it was filled with bruised myrrh, cassia, cinnamon and other spices. The whole body was then immersed in natron for seventy days. The finger-nails were kept in place with thread, or by means of silver gloves or stalls placed over the fingers. A tin plate, inscribed with the symbolic eye, was laid over the incision in the right side. The arms were arranged symmetrically along the sides, or on the breast or groins. The body was then bandaged. Linen bandages were always used, and were generally three or four inches wide and several yards long. The coarser linen was nearest the body, the finer towards the outside. In some instances the bandages in which a single corpse was swathed were over seven hundred, or, according to Pettigrew, over a thousand yards long. The bandages were joined together and kept in place with gum. After the bandaging, an outer linen shroud, dyed red with the *carthamus tinctorius*, and ornamented with a network of porcelain beads, was put over the entire body; or the bandaged body was covered by a "cartonnage," composed of twenty-four layers of linen tightly pressed and glued together, thus forming a kind of pasteboard envelope, which was then thinly coated with stucco, and painted in bright colors with hieroglyphics and figures of deities The body was then placed within a wooden coffin shaped similarly, and in most instances similarly ornamented; and this coffin was often enclosed within another, or within several, each just capable of holding the preceding one. In the funerals of the wealthy the coffined body was placed within a stone chest, or sarcophagus, which might be of granite, alabaster, basalt, breccia or other good material, and was either rectangular or in the form of the mummied body. Some sarcophagi were plain, but many were adorned with sculptures in relief or intaglio, embracing mainly scenes and passages from the most sacred of Egyptian writings, the "Ritual of the Dead."

When the family or relatives were unable or indisposed to incur the large expense required by this costly mode of embalming, a cheaper method was adopted. The viscera, instead of being deposited with spices in separate urns, could be returned into the body, accompanied by wax images of the four genii. The abdominal cavity could be only cleansed with cedar oil, and not filled with spices. The silver finger-stalls and artificial eyes could be dispensed with. The bandages could be reduced in number and made of coarser linen. The ornamentation could be simpler. A single wooden coffin would be sufficient, and the sarcophagus might be done without. Thus the expense of funerals could be reduced within moderate limits.

A still cheaper mode was necessary for the poorer classes. Sometimes the bodies of the poor were submerged in mineral pitch. Often they were only dried and salted. Bodies prepared in this manner are in some cases swathed in bandages, but are frequently only wrapped in coarse cloths or rags. These bodies are not enclosed in coffins, and have been only buried in the ground, some singly, others in layers, one above the other. The expense of these modes of embalming was so trifling as to be within the reach of the poorest.

SECTION V.—EGYPTIAN RELIGION AND MYTHOLOGY.

ONCERNING the Egyptians, Herodotus says: "They are of all men the most excessively attentive to the worship of the gods." Much of the theology, mythology and ceremonies of the Hebrews and Greeks had their origin in Egypt. Herodotus further says: "The names of almost all the gods came from Egypt to Greece." He also states that the Greek oracles, especially that of Dodona, were brought from Egypt, and that the Egyptians first introduced public festivals, processions and solemn supplications, which the Greeks learned from them. He goes on to say: "The Egyptians are beyond measure scrupulous in matters of religion." They invented the calendar and connected astrology with it. Says Herodotus: "Each month and day is assigned to some particular god, and each person's birthday determines his fate." He likewise says: "The Egyptians were also the first to say that the soul of man is immortal and that it transmigrates through every variety of animal." The Greek Mysteries of Eleusis were taken from those of Isis, and the story of the wanderings of Ceres in pursuit of Proserpine was borrowed from that of Isis in search of Osiris. Modern writers agree with Herodotus. Wilkinson says: "The Egyptians were unquestionably the most pious nation of all antiquity. The oldest monuments show their belief in a future life. And Osiris, the Judge, is mentioned in tombs two thousand years before Christ." Bunsen says: "It has at last been ascertained that all the great gods of Egypt are on the oldest monuments." He goes on to say: "It is a great and astonishing fact, established beyond possibility of doubt, that the empire of Menes, on its first appearance in history, possessed an established mythology, that is, a series of gods. Before the empire of Menes the separate Egyptian states had their temple worship regularly organized."

M. Maury, the French Egyptologist, says that everything among the Egyptians took the stamp of religion. Their writing was so full of sacred symbols as to render it almost useless for any other purpose. Literature, science and art were branches of theology and worship. The most common labors of daily life were constantly inter-

EGYPTIAN TRINITY.

rupted by some reference to priestly regulation. The future fate of every Egyptian was perpetually before him, so that he only lived to worship the gods. When the sun set, it seemed to die; when it arose, it seemed a symbol of the resurrection. Religion penetrated so deeply into the people's habits that it became an instinct. It was of all polytheisms the last to give way to Christianity, retaining its votaries as late as the sixth century of the Christian era.

The ancient Egyptian religion was a perplexing mixture of monotheism and polytheism, of lofty and noble conceptions and of degrading superstitions.

The sacred books of the ancient Egyptians contained the religion of the priests, who were monotheists and considered it impious to represent the Supreme Being by images and idols; but they made him known to the masses by personifying his various attributes and manifestations, as Phthah the Creator, Amun the Revealer, and Osiris the Benefactor and Judge, and so on through an innumerable list of primary, secondary and tertiary characters, which, to the untutored masses, became so many separate deities, thus accounting for the polytheistic faith of the lower classes. Some portion of the divine life was believed to pervade plants and animals, which were consequently cherished and worshiped by the ignorant; for what to the wise and learned were merely symbols became to the people distinct objects of adoration; and the Egyptian priests, like other ancient philosophers, disdained to enlighten the people, whom they despised and deemed incapable of comprehending their grand conceptions, and whom they desired to hold in subservience to their own and the kingly authority.

Thus there were two kinds of Egyptian theology—esoteric, or an interior theology, for the initiated, and exoteric, or an exterior theology, for the uninitiated. The interior hidden theology for the priests and the wise related to the unity and spirituality of the Deity. The exterior theology for the masses consisted of mythological accounts of Osiris and Isis, the judgment of the dead, the metempsychosis, or transmigration of the soul, and everything pertaining to the ceremonial worship of the gods.

Herodotus tells us that the Egyptian masses believed in three orders of gods, and Bunsen and Wilkinson thought that they had succeeded in tracing them from the monuments. Thus there were eight gods of the first order, twelve gods of the second order, and seven gods of the third order. The gods of the first order were of a higher and more spiritual class; those of the second order were a transition from the first order to the third—children of the first and parents of the third. The first order of gods was for the priesthood, and taught them the unity, spirituality and creative power of the One True and Indivisible Supreme Being.

The gods of the third order were for the masses of the people, and were the personal agents which represented the forms and forces of external nature, which was believed by the ignorant masses to work through this third series of gods, the most popular of which were Osiris and Isis. The gods of the second or intermediate order were neither so abstract as those of the first order, nor so concrete as those of the third order—not representing either the spiritual characteristics of the gods of the first class, or the natural qualities and forces of those of the third class, but rather the powers and faculties of human beings. For this reason most of the deities of this second class were adopted by the Greeks, whose religious system was essentially founded on human nature, and whose gods and goddesses were mainly the imaginary representations of human characteristics.

The eight gods of the first order were believed to constitute a process of divine development, and were supposed to exercise the power of revealing themselves. These eight divinities, according to Bunsen, were arranged in the following order: 1. Amn, or Ammon; 2. Khem, or Chemmis; 3. Mut, the Mother Goddess; 4. Num, or Kneph; 5. Seti, or Sate; 6. Phthah, the Artist God; 7. Net, or Neith, the Goddess of Sais; 8. Ra, the Sun, the God of Heliopolis. According to Wilkinson, they are classed in a different order: 1. Neph, or Kneph; 2. Amun, or Ammon; 3. Phthah; 4. Khem; 5. Sate; 6. Maut, or Mut; 7. Pasht, or Diana;

RELIGION AND MYTHOLOGY.

8. Neith, or Minerva. In Wilkinson's list, Pasht, or Diana, is classed in the first order instead of the second, while Ra is not classed in this series.

Ammon, or Amun, was "the Revealer," "the Concealed God," "the Absolute Spirit," "the Father of all the other gods;" corresponding to the Zeus of the Greeks. He is styled "the King of the Gods," "the Lord of Heaven," "the Ruler," "the Lord of the Two Thrones," "the Horus or God of the Two Egypts." His city was Thebes. Manetho says his name signifies concealment. The root "*Amn*" signifies to veil or conceal. His original name, as standing in the rings of the Twelfth Dynasty, was Amn. After the Eighteenth Dynasty he was called Amn-Ra, signifying the Sun. Says Bunsen: "Incontestably, he stands in Egypt as the head of the great cosmogonic development."

Kneph, the God of Spirit, was also called Knubis, or Num. His name, according to Plutarch and Diodorus, means Spirit. At Esna he was called "the Breath of those in the Firmament." At Elephantine he was styled "Lord of the Inundations." He is represented as wearing the ram's head with double horns, and was universally worshiped in Ethiopia. The sheep were sacred to him, and large flocks of them were kept in the Thebais for their wool. The serpent or asp were also sacred to Kneph. He was called Creator, and was represented in the figure of a potter with a wheel. In Philæ he is represented as forming on his wheel a figure of Osiris, bearing the inscription: "Num, who forms on his wheel the Divine Limbs of Osiris." He is likewise called "the Sculptor of all men," "the god who made the sun and the moon to revolve." According to Porphyry, Phthah sprang from an egg which came from the mouth of Kneph, and in this declaration he is sustained by the authority of the monuments. Phthah thus represents the Absolute Divine Being as Spirit, the Spirit of God moving on the face of the waters, a moving spirit intertwined and interwoven with the chaotic and shapeless mass of matter.

Phthah—called Hephæstus by the Greeks, Vulcan by the Romans—represents creation by the truth, formation, stability; and is called in the inscriptions "Lord of Truth," "Lord of the Beautiful Face," "Father of Beginnings, moving the Egg of the Sun and Moon." Horapollo and Plutarch considered the scarabæus, or beetle, the sign of this god, as an emblem of the world and its creation. In an inscription he is called "Creator of all things in the world." Says Iamblicus: "The God who creates with truth is Phthah." He was also related with the sun, having thirty fingers, representing the thirty days of the month. He is also represented as a deformed dwarf.

Khem, whom the Greeks called Pan, the principle of generation, is sometimes represented as holding a plowshare. Amun has no female companion. Mut, the mother, is the partner of Khem, the father. Seti, the Ray or Arrow, a feminine figure with the horns of a cow, is the consort of Kneph. Neith, or Net, the Goddess of Sais, is the companion of Phthah. The Greek Athênê, Pallas, or Minerva, is believed to be derived from Neith, and her name signifies: "I came by myself." Clemens Alexandrinus says that her great shrine at Sais has an open roof bearing this inscription: "I am all that was and is and is to be, and no mortal has lifted my garment, and the fruit I bore is Helios." This signifies her identity with Nature.

Helios, or Ra, or Phrah, the Sun-god, the God of Heliopolis (City of the Sun), is the eighth and last of the first order of gods, according to Bunsen. It is from Ra, or Phrah, that the name Pharaoh is derived. As we have already seen, Wilkinson excludes Ra from the first order, substituting Pasht, or Bubastis, the Diana of the Greeks, instead. If we accept Bunsen's classification, taking the Sun-god as the eighth and last of the first series, we shall then see in Ammon, the Concealed God, the pure Spirit, from which emanates Kneph, the creative power; followed by Khem, the generative power; followed by Phthah, the artistic principle; after which come the three feminine creative principles of Nature in Neith, the nourishing principle in Mut the mother, the developing principle in the goddess Pasht, and the completion of the whole cycle in Helios, or Ra, or Phrah, the Sun-god.

The reason for the difference between the priestly and popular religions of Egypt is to be attributed to the difference of race origin between the priesthood and the masses. The priests are believed to have been the descendants of the Asiatic immigrants into the Nile valley, while the great body of the people are supposed to have been of Ethiopian extraction. The Asiatic immigrants and conquerors brought with them the spiritual ideas represented by the first order of gods, while the Ethiopian occupiers of the Nile valley held fast to the African instinct of nature-worship. The combination of these two principles formed the Egyptian religious system. The first order of gods was therefore for the priests, the initiated; the third order was for the people, the uninitiated; while the second order was a transition between the first and third—children of the first and parents of the third.

As we have said, the second order of Egyptian gods was incorporated into the Greek pantheon. Thus Khonso, the child of Ammon, was the same as the Greek Hercules, God of Strength; Thoth, child of Kneph, was the equivalent of the Greek Hermes, God of Knowledge; Pecht, child of Phthah, was represented by the Greek Artemis, or Diana, the Goddess of Birth, who protected women; Athor, or Hathor, was the same as the Grecian Aphroditê, or Venus, the Goddess of Love; Seb was the Greek Kronos, or Saturn, the God of Time; and Nutpe was the Grecian Rhea, the wife of Kronos.

The third order of gods were the children of the second order, and were manifestations of the Divine Spirit in the external universe. These, as we have said, were the popular gods, though worshiped by the untutored masses. The gods of the third class, though lowest in the scale, had more of individuality and personality about them, and their worship throughout Egypt was universal from the most remote antiquity. Says Herodotus: "The Osiris deities are the only gods worshiped throughout Egypt." Says Bunsen: "They stand on the oldest monuments, are the center of all Egyptian worship, and are perhaps the oldest original objects of reverence." Wilkinson says the only change in the Egyptian religious system was during the fourteenth century before Christ, when Amun, or Ammon, was made chief of the third class of gods, in place of Typhon, or Seth, the God of Destruction, who had previously held the first place and had been the most highly reverenced of the popular deities. Seth's name was then chiseled off the monuments, and Amun's substituted instead. This religious revolution was the final result of the amalgamation of the two races and religions in Egypt—the Asiatic Semitic and Aryan immigrants, with their higher spiritual ideas, and the Ethiopian Hamitic aborigines, with their gross African nature-worship. It was very natural that the priests, the descendants of the Asiatic immigrants, should place their religion above that of the descendants of the aboriginal inhabitants, and that they should have permitted for a time the external worship until the public was prepared for the reception of a higher religious faith in the substitution of Amun, the Revealer, for the God of Terror and Destruction.

The most popular of ancient Egyptian myths was that of Osiris and Isis, as given us by Plutarch. Seb and Nutpe, or Nut—the Kronos and Rhea of the Greeks, the Saturn and Cybele of the Romans—were the parents of the third group of deities. Seb is Time, and Nut is Space. The Sun pronounced a curse upon them, in not permitting them to be delivered on any day of the year. This symbolizes the difficulty of the thought of Creation. But Hermes, or Wisdom, who loved Rhea, won at dice, of the Moon, five days, the seventieth part of all her illuminations, which he added to the three hundred and sixty days, or twelve months. This implies the correction of the calendar. The five days added were the birthdays of the gods. Osiris was born on the first of these five days,

THE HATHOR TEMPLE OF DENDERAH.

TEMPLE OF ISIS, ISLAND OF ELEPHANTINE.

RELIGION AND MYTHOLOGY.

when a voice proclaimed: "The Lord of all things is now born." Arueris-Apollo, the elder Horus, was born on the second of these days; Typhon on the third; Isis on the fourth; Nepthys-Venus, or Victory, on the fifth. Osiris and Arueris were children of the Sun; Isis was the daughter of Hermes; and Typhon and Nepthys were children of Kronos, or Saturn, the God of Time.

Osiris took Isis for his wife, and went through the world civilizing and refining mankind by means of music, poetry and oratory. On his return Typhon took seventy-two men and likewise an Ethiopian queen and constructed an ark as large as the body of Osiris, and at a feast he offered it to the one whom it should fit. Osiris got into the ark, and they closed the lid and soldered it fast, after which they cast the ark into the Nile. Then Isis, putting on mourning, went to look for the ark. As her inquiries were made to little children, these were thought by the Egyptians to possess the power of divination. She then found Anubis, child of Osiris by Nepthys, wife of Typhon, who informed her that the ark was entangled in a tree which grew up around it and concealed it from view. The king constructed from this tree a pillar to support his house. Isis sat down and wept, whereupon the queen's women came to her, and she stroked their hair, thus causing fragrance to pass into it. She became nurse to the queen's child, feeding him with her finger, and burning his impurities by means of a lambent flame during the night-time. After this she converted herself into a swallow, and flying around the house, bewailed her fate. The queen watched her proceedings and cried out in alarm, thus depriving her child of immortality. Isis then begged the pillar, and taking it down, took out the chest and cried so loud as to frighten the king's younger son to death. Then taking the ark and the king's elder son she sailed away. Being chilled by the cold air of the river she became angry and cursed it, so that it became dry. Then opening the chest, she put her cheek to the cheek of Osiris, weeping bitterly. The little boy coming and peeping into the chest, she gave him such a terrible look as to frighten him to death. Then Isis went to her son Horus, who was at nurse at Buto. Typhon, while hunting by moonlight, saw the ark, with the body of Osiris, which he tore into fourteen pieces and cast them around. Isis went in a boat made of papyrus to look for the parts of her husband's body, and finding them, buried them all in different places. The soul of Osiris then returned from Hades to train up his son, Horus. Then Horus conquered Typhon in battle, but Isis allowed Typhon to make his escape. It is also said that Isis had another son by the soul of Osiris after his death, the god Harpocrates, who is represented as lame and with his finger on his mouth, signifying childhood.

Plutarch says that Osiris afterward became Serapis, the Pluto of the under-world. Plutarch, in explanation of the myth of Osiris and Isis, says that Osiris is the personification of Water, especially the Nile, and that Isis is the Earth, especially the Nile valley of Egypt overflowed by the river. Horus, the son, is the Air, especially the moist, mild air of Egypt. Typhon is Fire, especially the summer heat which dries up the Nile and parches the land. His seventy-two companions are the seventy-two days of most intense heat, as viewed by the Egyptians. Nepthys, Typhon's wife, sister of Isis, is the Desert out of Egypt, but which, when overflowed by a higher inundation of the Nile, becomes productive and has a child by Osiris, named Anubis. The confinement of Osiris in the ark signifies the summer heat drying up the Nile and confining it to its channel. The entanglement of the ark in a tree means the division of the Nile into many mouths at the Delta and the overhanging of the river by the wood. Isis nursing the king's child, the fragrance, etc., signifies the nourishment of plants and animals by the earth. The tearing of the body of Osiris into fourteen parts by Typhon means either the division of the Nile at its mouths or the pools of water left after the inundation has dried up.

Besides this geographical explanation of this allegory, Plutarch gives a scientific and astronomical view. Thus Osiris is the productive and creative principle in nature. Isis is the feminine quality in nature, and for this reason is called by Plato the nurse. Typhon is the destructive principle in nature. Horus is the mediator between creation and destruction. This gives us the triad of Osiris, Typhon and Horus, corresponding to the Hindoo triad of Brahma, Siva and Vishnu, and likewise to the Persian triad of Ormazd, Ahriman and Mithra. In this way the Egyptian myth symbolizes the struggle between the principles of good and evil in the world of nature.

The priests sought to turn the worship of Osiris and Isis into an allegory of the struggles, trials, sorrows and self-recovery of the human soul. After death every human soul adopted the name and symbols of Osiris, after which he retired to the under-world, there to be judged by that god. Closely related with this was the doctrine of the soul's transmigration through various bodies—which doctrine Pythagoras brought from Egypt. These doctrines were taught in the Mysteries. Herodotus says: "I know them, but must not tell them." Iamblicus, in his work on the Mysteries, says that they taught that One God existed before all things, and that this One God was to be venerated in silence. Then Emeph or Neph was god in his self-consciousness. After this in Amun his mind became truth, diffusing light. Phthah represents truth working by art, and Osiris symbolizes art producing good.

Bunsen says that according to the monuments Osiris and Isis, besides emanating from the second order of gods, are themselves the first and second order. Osiris, Isis and Horus embrace all Egyptian mythology, excepting Amun and Neph. In Lower Egypt Phthah was the highest god, corresponding to the Greek Hephæstus, the Roman Vulcan, the god of fire or heat, the father of the sun. In Upper Egypt Amun was the chief god. According to Manetho, Phthah reigned nine thousand years before the other gods, signifying that this was the oldest worship in Egypt. Amun is the head of a cosmogony proceeding by emanation from spirit to matter, while Phthah is at the origin of a cosmogony ascending by evolution from matter to spirit. From Phthah, or heat, comes light; from light comes life; from life proceed gods, men, plants, animals and all organic existence. In the inscriptions Phthah is called, "Father of the Father of the Gods," "King of both Worlds," "God of all Beginnings," "Former of Things." The egg, as containing the germ of life, is one of his symbols. The scarabæus, or beetle, which rolls its ball of earth, supposed to contain its egg, is sacred to Phthah. Memphis was his sacred city. His son, Ra, the Sun-god, had his temples at On, which the Greeks called Heliopolis, meaning "City of the Sun," so named from Ra's Greek name Helios. The cat was sacred to Ra. As Phthah is the god of all beginnings in Lower Egypt, so Ra is the life-giving god, the active ruler of the world, holding in one hand a sceptre and in the other the symbol of life.

The goddesses of Lower Egypt were Neith at Sais, Leto, the goddess whose temple was at Buto, and Pasht at Bubastis. As we have already said, the chief god in Upper Egypt was Amun, or Ammon, the Concealed God; and next to him is Kneph, or Knubis, the Spirit of God. Their companions were Mut, the mother, and Khonso. The two oldest gods were Mentu, the rising sun, and Atmu, the setting sun.

In Egypt, as in Greece, the earliest worship was of local divinities, who were afterwards united in a Pantheon. As in Greece Zeus was at first worshiped in Dodona and Arcadia, Apollo in Crete and Delos, Aphroditê in Cyprus, Athênê at Athens, and afterwards these local deities were united in one company as the twelve great gods of Olympus, so in Egypt the different early theologies were combined in the three orders of gods, with Ammon at their head. But in Egypt, as in Greece, each city and district retained the special worship of its own local deity. As in Greece Athênê continued to be the protecting goddess of Athens, and Aphroditê of Cyprus, so, in Egypt, Set continued to be the god of Ombos, Leto of

Buto, Horus of Edfu, Khem of Coptos, etc.

The one great singular feature about the Egyptian religion was animal-worship. Herodotus says: "All animals in Egypt are accounted sacred, and if any one kills these animals willfully he is put to death." This account of Herodotus is not strictly correct, as many animals were not considered sacred, though most of them were. Wilkinson mentions more than one hundred Egyptian animals, over one-half of which number were sacred. Hunting and fishing being favorite amusements of the Egyptians, the killing of some animals must have been tolerated. If, however, any one killed any of the sacred animals, either accidentally or willfully, he was immediately put to death. In different parts of Egypt different animals were accounted sacred. Besides the sacred bull at Memphis, the most striking sacred animals were the Mnevis, or sacred calf at Heliopolis, the sacred sheep at Sais and Thebes, and the sacred crocodiles at Ombos and Arsinoe. Thus the animal sacred in one place was not so regarded in another. The cat, the ibis and the beetle were particular objects of worship. The death of a cat in a private house caused the whole family to shave their eyebrows in token of their grief. The Persian king Cambyses was enabled to conquer the Egyptians by placing in the van of his army multitudes of cats, which the Egyptians were fearful of killing, so that they abandoned all resistance.

Cows were sacred to Isis, and this goddess was represented in the form of a cow. The gods often wore animals' heads. Amun is represented with the ram's head. The worship of Apis, the sacred bull of Memphis, the representative of Osiris, was one of the most striking and imposing among Egyptian religious ceremonies. Plutarch describes him as a fair and beautiful image of the soul of Osiris. He was a bull with black hair, a white spot on his forehead, and some other distinguishing marks. He was kept in a magnificent temple at Memphis. The festival in his honor continued seven days, during which time a great multitude of people assembled. When he died his body was embalmed and buried with great pomp, and the priests went in quest of another Apis, which, when discovered by the distinguishing marks, was taken to Memphis, fed with care and exercised, and consulted as an oracle. The burial-place of the sacred bulls was in recent years discovered near Memphis. It consists of an arched gallery cut in the solid rock, two thousand feet long, twenty-five feet high and twenty-five feet wide. On each side is a series of recesses, each of which contains a large sarcophagus of granite, fifteen by eight feet, in which the body of a sacred bull was deposited. In 1852 thirty of these had been discovered. Before this tomb is a paved road, with lions in rows on each side, and before this is a temple with a vestibule. As we have previously remarked, the animals sacred in one place were not so regarded in another, and this difference of worship often led to bitter enmities between the several nomes. Thus at Ombos the crocodile was worshiped, while at Tentyra it was hunted and abhorred. The ram-headed Amun was adored at Thebes, and the sheep was there a sacred animal, while the goat was killed for food. In Mendes the goat was worshiped and the sheep killed and eaten. Mutton was likewise eaten at Lycopolis, in compliment to the wolf, which was there an object of veneration.

The sacred animals at death were embalmed by the priests and buried, and thousands upon thousands of mummies of dogs, cats, wolves, sheep, crocodiles, birds and other animals are found in the tombs. The sacred animals were reverenced as containing a divine element. Says Wilkinson: "The Egyptians may have deified some animals to insure their preservation, some to prevent their unwholesome meat being used as food." The cow, the ox, the dog, the cat, the ibis, appeared to the Egyptians as gifted with supernatural powers. This people reverenced the mysterious manifestation of the Divine presence in all external nature. Animals were considered expressions of Divine thoughts. This belief reached its extreme point in the Egyptian reverence for animal life. This people saw something divine and found Deity in nature.

The Egyptians had more religious festivals than any other ancient people, every month and day being governed by a god. There were two feasts of the New Year; twelve of the first days of the months; one of the rising of the dog-star; and others to the great gods, to seed time and harvest, to the rise and fall of the Nile, as the nine days' feast in honor of Osiris, the Benefactor of men. The feast of the lamps at Sais was in honor of Neith, and was observed throughout Egypt. Other noted festivals were the feast of the death of Osiris, and the feast of his resurrection, when the people exclaimed: "We have found him! Good luck!" One of the feasts of Isis lasted four days. The great feast at Bubastis was the most noted of all the Egyptian festivals. On one of these occasions seven hundred thousand persons sailed on the Nile with music. At another bloody conflicts occurred between the armed priests and the armed men who conveyed the image of the god to the temple.

The daily life of the people was an embodiment of the history of the deities. The French Egyptologist, De Rouge, describes an old papyrus which says: "On the twelfth of Choràk no one is to go out of doors, for on that day the transformation of Osiris into the bird Wennu took place; on the fourteenth of Toby no voluptuous songs must be listened to, for Isis and Nepthys bewail Osiris on that day. On the third of Mechir no one can go on a journey, because Set then began a war." None must go out on another specified day. The day on which the other gods conquered Set was regarded

EGYPTIAN PRIESTS.

as lucky, and the child born on that day was believed to be sure to live to a good old age.

The priests, of which every temple had its own separate body, did not form an ex-

SACRED WOMEN.

clusive caste, though the priestly office was generally continued by inheritance in certain families. Priests could be military commanders, provincial governors, judges or architects. The sons of soldiers were often priests, while soldiers frequently married daughters of priests. Joseph, who was a foreigner naturalized in Egypt, married the daughter of the High Priest of On, or Heliopolis. The Egyptian priests were of different grades—the chief priests, or pontiffs, the prophets, the judges, the scribes, those who examined victims, the keepers of the robes, the keepers of the sacred animals, and others. Women also performed official duties in the temples.

The priests were exempt from taxation and were supported out of the public stores. Their duties were to superintend sacrifices, processions, funerals, etc. They were initiated into all the religious mysteries, and were taught surveying. They were particular as to their food, refraining from eating peas, beans, onions and garlic, while fish and swine-flesh were strictly forbidden. They bathed twice a day and twice during the night, and shaved the head and body every third day. Their fasts, which lasted from one to six weeks, took place after their purification. They offered prayers for the dead.

The priestly dress was simple, made chiefly of linen, and consisted of an undergarment and a loose upper robe, with full sleeves, and the leopard-skin above; while sometimes there were one or two feathers in the head.

Chaplets and flowers were placed upon the altars, such as the lotus and papyrus; likewise baskets of figs and grapes, and alabaster vases of ointment. Necklaces, bracelets and jewelry were also offered as invocations and thanksgivings.

Oxen and other animals were offered as sacrifices, and the blood was permitted to flow over the altar. Incense was offered to all the gods and goddesses in censers.

Religious processions were another characteristic feature of the Egyptian system. In one of these shrines were carried on the shoulders by means of long staves passed through rings. In others the statues of the gods were carried, and arks overshadowed by the wings of the Goddess of Truth were spread over the sacred beetle.

The most highly esteemed of the priestly order were the prophets, who studied the ten hieratical books. The stolists dressed and undressed the images, attended to the vestments of the priests, and marked the beasts chosen for sacrifice. The scribes served for the Apis, or sacred bull, and their chief requirement was great learning.

The priests, whose life was full of duties and restrictions, had only one wife, and were circumcised like other Egyptians. They devoted all their time to study or religious service. The gloomy character of the Egyptian religion was in strong contrast with the cheerful worship of the Greeks. One Greek writer says: "The gods of Egypt rejoice in lamentations, those of Greece in dances." Another says: "The Egyptians offer their gods tears."

The Egyptian temples surpassed in grandeur all other architectural monuments in the world. The temple of Amun, in the fertile oasis of Siwah, in the Libyan desert, was one of the most celebrated oracles of antiquity. Near this temple, in a grove of palm-trees, rose a hot spring, the Fountain of the Sun, whose bubbling and smoking were believed to betoken the Divine presence. The oasis was a stopping-place for caravans passing between Egypt and Central Africa, and many rich offerings were left in the temple by traveling merchants, who thus showed their gratitude for escaping the perils of the desert, or thus sought the favor of Amun for their journey when just begun.

The immortality of the soul and the belief in a future state, based on rewards and punishments for good or evil in this life, formed a cardinal point of Egyptian religious faith from the earliest period; and the belief in the transmigration of the soul was closely connected with the reverence for animals. Bunsen says the Egyptians viewed the human soul and the animal soul as the same, and for this reason the animal was considered sacred to man. The Egyptian doctrine of transmigration differed from that of the Hindoos in one essential point; there being no idea of retribution in the Egyptian doctrine, as in the Hindoo. The Egyptian doctrine, according to Herodotus, was that every human soul must pass through all animals, fishes, insects and birds, thus completing the whole circuit of animated existence, after which it would again enter the human body from which it came. The Hindoo doctrine regards transmigration as a punishment for sin and wickedness, and that only those who lead an unholy life are subjected to this punishment, from which the only release is the leading of a pure and holy life. Herodotus further says that the complete circuit of transmigration is performed by the soul in three thousand years, and that it does not begin until the body decays. This explains the extraordinary care taken in ornamenting the tombs, as the permanent resting-places for the dead during a long period. Diodorus says that the Egyptians ornamented their tombs as the enduring residences of mankind. The doctrine of transmigration also accounts for the custom of embalming the dead, in order to preserve the body from decay, and to render it fit to receive the soul on its return.

Mr. Birch says that the doctrine of the soul's immortality is as old as the inscriptions of the Twelfth Dynasty, of which many contain extracts from the Ritual for the Dead. Mr. Birch has translated one hundred and forty-six chapters of this Ritual from the text of the Turin Papyrus, which is the most complete in Europe. Chapters of it are seen on mummy-cases, on mummy-wraps, on the walls of tombs, and on papyri within the sarcophagi. This Ritual is the only remnant of the Hermetic Books constituting the library of the priests. This liturgy represents Osiris and his triad as struggling with Set and his devils for the soul of the departed, in the presence of the Sun-god, the source of life.

The Egyptians believed that happiness in the future state depended upon well-doing in this life. As we have seen, the belief that the soul, after making the circuit of transmigration through the animal creation, would return to the body from which it had departed, caused the universal national custom of embalming the dead to preserve their bodies from decay. The period of mourning for the dead lasted seventy-two days, during which the body of the deceased was in the charge of the embalmers. After the process of embalming had been finished, the mummy thus formed was returned to the house of its earthly abode, where its friends kept it for a month or a year, and where feasts were given in its honor, it being always present in the company of guests. The mummy, in its stone chest, or sarcophagus, was then carried in an imposing funeral procession to the borders of the sacred lake, where occured the trial of the deceased by a priestly tribunal of forty-two judges, symbolizing the soul's trial before the judgment-seat of the gods presided over by Osiris. Masked priests represented the gods of the underworld. Typhon is represented as accusing the deceased and demanding his punishment. The intercessors plead for him. Any one was at liberty to bring accusations against the deceased. A large pair of scales was brought forward, on one side of which was placed the conduct of the deceased in a bottle, and on the other side was set the image of truth. If it was clearly shown that the deceased had led an evil life, the priestly judges pronounced an unfavorable verdict upon it as to its future fate, in which case the body was denied the privilege of burial with the just opposite the sacred lake and was returned to its friends, who usually buried it on the side of the sacred lake opposite the resting-place of the just. If, however, the verdict of the judges was favorable, the lamentations of the funeral train gave way to songs of triumph, and the deceased was congratulated upon being admitted into the happy companionship of the friends of Osiris; and the body in its sarcophagus was ferried across the sacred lake and interred with those of its ancestors in a tomb richly ornamented. These ceremonies are represented on the funeral papyri. The forty-two judges who tried the dead represented the forty-two nomes, or provinces of Egypt; and every nome had its sacred lake, across which all funeral processions must pass on their way to the city of the dead. On the sides of these sacred lakes nearest the abodes of the living have been found the remains of great numbers who were rejected by the judges at their trial, and whose bodies were in consequence returned in disgrace to their friends, to be disposed of in the most speedy manner possible. At death all became equal, and every one, from the king and highest pontiff to the lowest swineherd, was subject to the same solemn judgment passed at death, and the fear which it inspired exercised a wholesome influence over all classes.

The soul's trial before the judgment-seat of the gods, as represented in the papyrus Book of the Dead, and before which the soul had to pass an acquittal before it could enter the abode of the blessed, is described as follows: Forty-two gods occupy the judgment-seat, over which Osiris presides, and before whom are the scales, in one of which is placed the statue of perfect Justice, while in the other is the heart of the deceased. The soul of the departed stands watching the balance, while Horus examines the plummet showing on which side the beam inclines; and Thoth, the Justifier, records the sentence. If the decision of this divine tribunal is favorable, the soul is sealed as "justified."

The Hall of the Two Truths, described in the Book of the Dead, recounts the scene when the soul appears before the gods, forty-two of whom are ready to feed on the blood of the wicked. The soul, addressing the Lord of Truth, denies having done evil, saying: "I have not afflicted any. I have not told falsehoods. I have not made the laboring man do more than his task. I have not been idle. I have not murdered. I have not committed fraud. I have not injured the images of the gods. I have not taken scraps of the bandages of the dead. I have not committed adultery. I have not cheated by false weights. I have not kept milk from sucklings. I have not caught the sacred birds." He then says to each god: "I have not been idle. I have not boasted. I have not stolen. I have not counterfeited, nor killed the sacred beasts, nor blasphemed, nor refused to hear the truth, nor despised God in my heart." In other texts the soul is represented as saying: "I have loved God. I have given bread to the hungry, water to the thirsty, garments to the naked, and an asylum to the abandoned."

Many of the virtues taught by Christianity appear to have been the ideal of the ancient Egyptians. Brugsch tells us that a thousand voices from the tombs declare this. One inscription in Upper Egypt says: "He loved his father, he honored his mother, he loved his brethren, and never went from his home in bad temper. He never preferred the great man to the low one." Another says: "I was a wise man, my soul loved God. I was a brother to the great men and a father to the humble ones, and never was a mischief-maker." An inscription at Sais, on a priest who lived in the days of Cambyses, says: "I honored my father, I esteemed my mother, I loved my brothers. I found graves for the unburied dead. I instructed little children. I took care of orphans as though they were my own children. For great misfortunes were on Egypt in my time, and on this city of Sais." The following is an inscription on a tomb of a nomad prince at Beni-Hassan: "What I have done I will say. My goodness and my kindness were ample. I never oppressed the fatherless nor the widow. I did not treat cruelly the fishermen, the shepherds or the poor laborers. There was nowhere in my time hunger or want. For I cultivated all my fields, far and near, in order that their inhabitants might have food. I never preferred the great and powerful to the humble and poor, but did equal justice to all." A king's tomb at Thebes describes the religious creed of a Pharaoh thus: "I lived in truth, and fed my soul with justice. What I did to men was done in peace, and how I loved God, God and my heart well know. I have given bread to the hungry, water to the thirsty, clothes to the naked, and a shelter to the stranger. I honored the gods with sacrifices, and the dead with offerings."

A rock at Lycopolis pleads for an ancient ruler in these words: "I never took the child from its mother's bosom, nor the poor man from the side of his wife." Hundreds of stones in Egypt declare the best gifts which the gods bestow on their favorites to be "the respect of men, and the love of women."

On a monumental stele discovered at Karnak by M. Mariette, and translated by De Rouge, is an inscription recording the triumphs of Thothmes III. in strains sounding like the song of Miriam or the Hymn of Deborah, the king recognizing his power and triumph as the work of the great god Amun. A like strain of religious poetry is found in the Papyrus of Sallier, now in the British Museum. This is an epic poem by the Egyptian poet Pentaour, celebrating the campaigns of Rameses the Great, and was carved in full on the walls of Karnak. It especially describes an incident in a war with the Kheta, or Hittites, of Syria, who had revolted against Rameses. Rameses being separated from his main force by a stratagem, was in extreme peril; and Pentaour describes him as calling upon Amun, God of Thebes, for aid, recounting the sacrifices he had offered to the god, and imploring the god not to leave him to the mercy of the cruel Syrian tribes. Rameses is represented as pleading thus: "Have I not erected to thee great temples? Have I not sacrificed to thee thirty thousand oxen? I have brought from Elephantine obelisks to set up to thy name. I invoke thee, O my father, Amun. I am in the midst of a throng of unknown tribes, and alone. But Amun is better to me than thousands of archers and millions of horsemen. Amun will prevail over the enemy." After defeating his enemies, Rameses, in his song of triumph, says: "Amun-Ra has been at my right and my left in the battles; his mind has inspired my own, and has prepared the downfall of my enemies. Amun-Ra, my father, has brought the whole world to my feet."

SECTION VI.—THE ANCIENT ETHIOPIANS.

SOUTH of Egypt—in the region now called Nubia and Abyssinia—lived the ancient Ethiopians, some tribes of whom were as highly civilized as the ancient Egyptians, but we know very little of their history, and their origin is involved in the impenetrable obscurity of a remote antiquity. The ruins of splendid monuments, obelisks, sphinxes, colossal statues, rock-cut temples, etc., along that portion of the Nile valley, fully attest the progress of this ancient Hamitic people in the art of architecture.

Besides the civilized Ethiopians, this region was occupied in ancient times, as now, by various Arab tribes in different stages of advancement from the complete savage to the hunting and fishing tribes, and from these to the nomadic herdsmen and shepherds. The civilized Ethiopians dwelt in cities, possessed a civil government and laws, were acquainted with the use of hieroglyphics, and the fame of their progress in knowledge and the social arts had in the earliest ages spread over a considerable portion of the earth.

The soil of the portion of the Nile valley occupied by the ancient Ethiopians was in their day as fertile as the richest part of Egypt, and where protected it yet continues to be so, but the hills on both sides are bordered by sandy deserts, against which they afford but a scanty protection. The navigation of the Nile is impeded by the windings of the river, and by the obstruction of cataracts and rapids, so that intercourse is more generally maintained by caravans than by boats. In the southern part of the valley the river incloses a number of fertile islands. The productions of the Nile valley in Nubia are essentially the same as those of Egypt. All along this portion of the valley is a succession of stupendous monuments, rivaling in beauty those of Thebes, and surpassing them in grandeur.

The island of Meroe—so called because it was almost surrounded with rivers—possessed large numbers of camels, which were used in its immense caravan trade; and the ivory, ebony and spices which the Ethiopians sent down the river into Egypt were obtained by traffic with the inhabitants of Central Africa. Meroe had better harbors for commerce with India than had Egypt, as the Ethiopian ports on the Red Sea were superior to the Egyptian, and the caravan-routes to them were shorter and the perilous portion of the navigation of that sea was entirely avoided. In the wild tracts of country in the vicinity of Meroe are animals which were hunted by the ancient savage tribes, as they are by the modern, such as the giraffe, or camelopard. The elephant is found in Abyssinia, not far south of the neighborhood of Meroe.

About one thousand years before Christ, Meroe was the seat of a flourishing Ethiopian kingdom, which for a time held Upper Egypt under sway, but its early history is shrouded in the obscurity of a dim past. The monuments of Meroe are believed to have been modeled from the wonderful architectural structures of Egypt; but cut off from the rest of the civilized world by Egypt, the Ethiopians can only be traced in history when their country is invaded, or when they themselves invade other lands. We have seen that several Egyptian kings conquered Ethiopia and ruled the country for short intervals. The fabled Assyrian queen, Semiramis, is said to have invaded Ethiopia in the eleventh century before Christ. This is doubtful, but we have certain knowledge that the Ethiopians at this time were a powerful nation, and that they aided Shishak, King of Egypt, in his war against Rehoboam, King of Judah, in 957 B. C. Sixteen years later Zerah, King of Ethiopia, is said to have invaded Judah with an immense army, but was totally defeated. According to the Scripture narrative, the Ethiopians had made considerable progress in the art of war, controlled the Red Sea navigation, and held sway over a large portion of Arabia. The expense of so vast and distant an expedition bears evidence to the fact that the Ethiopian kingdom must then have been in a flourishing condition.

The gradual increase of the Ethiopian power finally enabled the King Sabaco, or Shebak, to conquer Egypt, over which he and his two successors, Sevechus and Tarakus, reigned successively. Sevechus, called So in Scripture, was so powerful a monarch that Hoshea, King of Israel, rose in revolt against the Assyrians, relying upon the aid of So; but, not being supported by his Ethiopian ally, Hoshea and his subjects were carried into the Assyrian Captivity. Tarakus, the Tirhakah of Scripture, was a more warlike sovereign, for he led an army against Sennacherib, King of Assyria, who was then besieging Jerusalem; and the Egyptian traditions, preserved in the time of Herodotus, give the account of the destruction of Sennacherib's army of one hundred and eighty-five thousand men in a night panic, as mentioned in the Hebrew Scriptures.

In the reign of Psammetichus in Egypt, in the seventh century before Christ, two hundred and forty thousand Egyptians of the warrior-caste, offended at their king's favor to Greek merchants whom he had invited to settle in Egypt, migrated to Ethiopia, and were settled in the extreme southern part of that country, where they added immensely to the prosperity of the state. These useful colonists instructed the Ethiopians in the improvements then recently made in the art of war, and thus prepared them for resisting the formidable invasion by the Persians.

No sooner had the Persian king, Cambyses, conquered Egypt, in 525 B. C., than he invaded Ethiopia without preparing any store of provisions, ignorant of the deserts through which he had to pass, so that when the invasion took place the Persian army was destroyed by famine.

The religion of the ancient Ethiopians was in early times similar to that of Egypt. Ammon was the chief of the Ethiopian gods, and several temples were erected to his worship. The political power was vested in a priesthood, who comprised a sacred caste. They chose the king from one of their own number, and could take his life at pleasure in the name of their gods. The Ethiopian priests possessed such influence over the superstitious African tribes that a solitary priest at the head of a caravan was able to secure a safe passage of untold wealth through the countries occupied by the most ferocious savages. The temples, also, were a safe place for the deposit of merchandise; and here, under the shadow of an inviolable sanctuary, people of hostile nations met to transact their business in absolute peace and security. At any place where it was considered necessary to have a commercial emporium a temple was built for its protection.

Whenever the Ethiopian priests became tired of their king they sent a courier with orders for him to die. Ergamenes, who reigned early in the third century before Christ and had been instructed in the Greek philosophy, resisted this foolish custom, stormed the fortresses of the priests, massacred many of them, and founded a new religion.

The sovereigns of Ethiopia were frequently queens. An Ethiopian queen named Candace made war on Augustus Cæsar about twenty years before the birth of Christ, and, although the superior discipline of the Romans brought them an easy triumph, Queen Candace obtained an honorable peace. During the reign of another Queen Candace the Jewish religion prevailed in Meroe, as a result of the change made by Ergamenes; and the queen's confidential adviser went to worship at Jerusalem, and when he returned, A. D. 53, he was converted to Christianity by St. Philip, and thus became the means of introducing that religion into Ethiopia. Ever since that time the Christian religion has prevailed among the Ethiopians and their descendants, the modern Abyssinians.

The pyramids of Meroe, though not as large as those of Middle Egypt, exceed them in architectural beauty, and the Ethiopian sepulchers exhibit the greatest purity of taste. The use of the arch by the Ethiopians fully attests their progress in the art of building. Mr. Hoskins has asserted that the Ethiopian pyramids are more ancient than the Egyptian, but this is disputed by the best authorities. The Ethiopian vases depicted on the monuments, though not richly ornamented, exhibit a taste and elegance of form that has never been surpassed. In sculpture and coloring, the edifices of Meroe, though less profusely adorned, rival the best specimens of Egyptian art.

Another famous Ethiopian kingdom was that of Axume, an offshoot of Meroe. Its capital, Axum, is still in existence, and contains remarkable antiquities, among which is an obelisk eighty feet high, in the great square, beside forty others of smaller size. Some of the ruins of Axum are believed by the inhabitants to be as old as the time of Abraham. A stone slab, eight feet by three and a half, found here, has an antique Greek inscription, which, translated, begins as follows:

"We Aeizamus, king of the Axomites, and of the Homerites, and of Raeidan, and of the Ethiopians, and of the Sabeans, and of Zeyla, and of Tiamo, and the Boja, and of the Taguie, King of Kings, Son of God, etc."

Aeizamus was King of Ethiopia in the time of the Roman Emperor Constantine the Great, who wrote him a letter. Adulis, the port of Axume, was celebrated for its ivory trade.

All along the banks of the Nile in Nubia are strewn pyramids of unknown antiquity, ruins of temples and monuments similar to those of Egypt. Near the present Merawe are seven or eight temples, adorned with sculpture and hieroglyphics. One of these temples is four hundred and fifty by one hundred and fifty-nine feet in extent. Near Shendy are forty pyramids.

The most remarkable of all the monuments of Nubia is the rock-temple of Ipsambul, near Derr. This temple is cut from a mountain of solid rock, adorned inside with colossal statues and painted sculptures, representing castles, battles, triumphal processions and religious pageants. On the outside are four colossi, larger than any sculptured figures in Egypt, except the Sphinx. One of these colossi is sixty-five feet high. This temple is one hundred and seventy feet in depth, and contains fourteen apartments, one of which is fifty-seven feet by fifty-two, and is supported by images with folded arms, thirty feet high. The rock in which this temple is built is six hundred feet high.

The great rock-temple of Ipsambul is said to resemble the famous excavated structures on the island of Elephanta, near Bombay, on the west coast of Hindoostan. The general plan is the same in both—massive pillars, stupendous figures, symbolic devices and mystic ornaments. It is also asserted that a frequent resemblance is discovered between the religious vestiges of Egypt and Ethiopia and those of India.

Among the numerous other remarkable antiquities of this region we must mention those of Barkal, about a mile from the Nile, and near the village of Merawe, the ancient Napata, the capital of Queen Candace. Here is a rock rising four hundred feet perpendicularly toward the river, at the foot of which are huge rock-hewn temples, the walls of which are covered with hieroglyphics in high relief, representing figures of kings and gods, among which we are able to distinguish Isis, Ammon, Apis, Horus and Mendes. There are other gigantic ruins in this region.

Meroe, on account of its favorable situation for commercial intercourse with India and Central Africa, by its location on the intersection of the leading caravan-routes of ancient commerce, was the emporium of trade between the north and the south, between the east and the west, while the fertility of its soil enabled the Ethiopians to purchase luxuries with native productions. Fabrics were woven in Meroe, and the manufactures of metal were here as flourishing as in Egypt.

The great changes in the lines of trade, the ravages of successive conquerors and revolutions, the fanaticism of the Saracens, and the ruin of the fertile soil by the moving sands of the desert, together with the pressure of nomadic hordes, all contributed to the extinction of this powerful ancient empire.

ROCK TEMPLE OF IPSAMBUL.

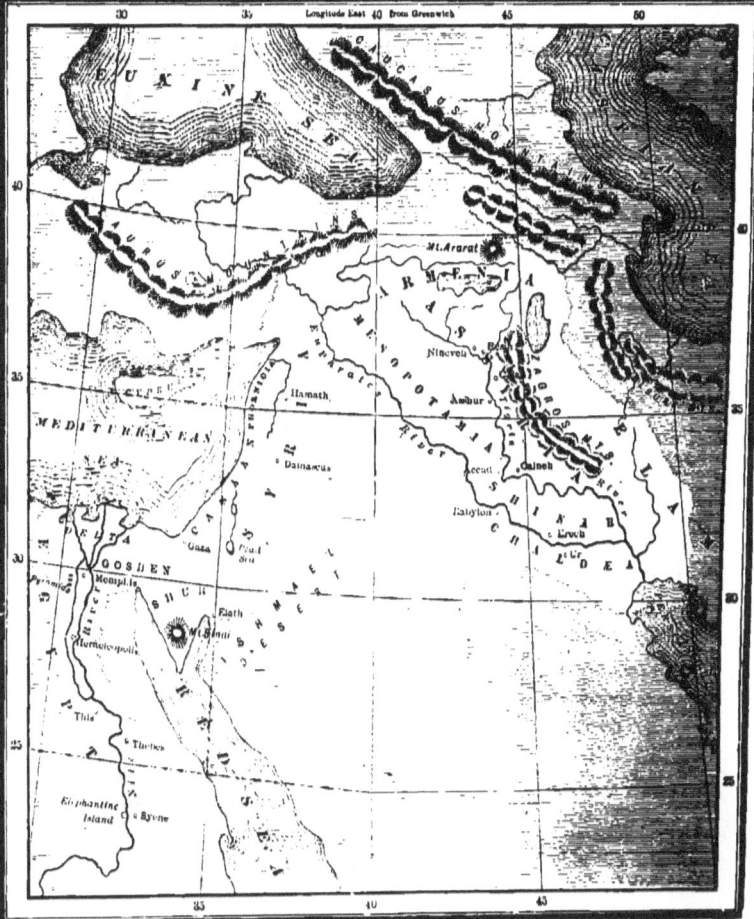

CHAPTER II.

THE CHALDÆAN EMPIRE.

SECTION I.—GEOGRAPHY OF CHALDÆA.

SIA, as we have noticed, was the cradle of the human race. The cradle of Asiatic history and civilization was the valley of the Tigris and Euphrates rivers. This region was early occupied by Semitic and Hamitic tribes. The civilization which grew up in the Tigris-Euphrates valley was almost as ancient as that which arose in the Nile valley. There is an actual date in Chaldæan history as far back as 2234 B. C.; while authentic Egyptian history—the period of the Pyramid-builders, the Fourth Dynasty—antedates this date by only two centuries, B. C. 2450.

The Hebrew Scriptures assign the beginning of the history of the human race in the Tigris-Euphrates valley. Speaking of the immediate posterity of Noah and his sons, Shem, Ham and Japheth, after the Deluge, the Book of Genesis says: "And it came to pass, as they journeyed from the east, that they found a plain in the Land of Shinar, and dwelt there." Shinar was the southern portion of the Tigris-Euphrates valley. In this region the Scriptures place the building of the Tower of Babel, and the "Confusion of Tongues" and dispersion of the human race. The record of this event is preserved in the Babylonian tradition, as well as in the Mosaic narrative; and an account of this has been recently discovered among the cuneiform inscriptions on the Babylonian tablets now in the British Museum.

The Tigris and Euphrates rivers rise in the highlands of Armenia and unite near the head of the Persian Gulf, into which their waters empty after the Euphrates has flowed about 1780 miles and the Tigris about 1146 miles. Both these rivers, like the Nile, overflow their banks in the lower part of their courses; and though these inundations do not deposit a fresh soil, as in the case of the Nile, they are the cause of the fertility of the plain of Mesopotamia, and in ancient times they were conducted throughout its entire extent by a system of canals, by which these overflows were utilized and the country thus irrigated. The Tigris-Euphrates valley comprises a fertile region in the midst of the great belt of desert extending from the western shores of Africa almost to the northeastern coast of Asia.

This fertile valley anciently embraced a number of territorial and political divisions, whose boundaries were often very indefinite. The region between the two rivers was called Mesopotamia by the Greeks (from *mesos*, midst, and *potamoi*, rivers). This was merely a geographical or territorial district, and not a political division. Chaldæa, or Babylonia, was a political as well as a territorial division, situated between the lower course of the Tigris on the east and Arabia on the west, and corresponding to the geographical region which the Hebrews designated as the Land of Shinar. As the Persian Gulf in ancient times extended about 120 or 130 miles farther north than at present, ancient Chaldæa was quite a small section of country compared with that region in our day. The district east of the lower course of these rivers, immediately east of Babylonia, was a territorial and political division called Susiana, or Elam, the chief city of which was Susa. Assyria proper, as a territorial division, lay to the east of the Euphrates, west of the Zagros mountains, north of Susiana and Chaldæa, and south of Armenia; while Assyria as a political power, or the Assyrian Empire, varied in territorial extent at different times, and often comprised the entire region from the Mediterranean to the plateau of Iran.

Three great empires successively flourished in the Tigris-Euphrates valley—the Chaldæan, or Early Babylonian Empire, from 2400 B. C. to 1300 B. C.; the Assyrian Empire, from 1300 B. C. to 625 B. C.; and the Later Babylonian Empire, from 625 B. C. to 538 B. C.

The Chaldæan, or Early Babylonian Empire, was the first great monarchy of Southwestern Asia. As we have seen, its seat was the great alluvial plain lying to the north-west of the Persian Gulf. The population of this region increased very rapidly in the most ancient times, because of the extreme natural fertility of the soil, which produced everything requisite for man's support. Groves of date-palm lined the banks of the rivers, and such cereal grains as wheat, barley, millet, sesame and vetches grew in luxuriant abundance, as did also various other grains. Says a certain writer: "According to a native tradition, wheat was indigenous in Chaldæa. Its tendencies to grow leaves was so great that the Babylonians used to mow it twice, and then pasture their cattle on it for a while, to keep down the blade and induce the plant to turn to ear." Speaking of this country, Herodotus says: "Of all the countries that we know of, there is none so fruitful in grain. It makes no pretension indeed of growing the fig, the olive, the vine or any other tree of the kind; but in grain it is so fruitful as to yield two hundred fold. The blade of the wheat plant and barley plant is often three or four fingers in breadth. As for the millet and the sesame, I shall not say to what height they grow, though within my own knowledge; for I am not ignorant that what I have already written concerning the fruitfulness of Babylonia must seem incredible to those who have never visited the country."

Says another writer: "Babylonia, in the neighborhood of the Euphrates, rivaled the fertility of the valley of the Nile; the soil was so peculiarly suited for corn that the husbandman's returns were sometimes three hundred fold, and rarely less than two hundred fold. The rich oily grains of the pancium and sesamum were produced in luxuriant abundance; the fig-tree, the olive and the vine were wholly wanting; but there were large groves of palm-trees on the banks of the river. From the palms they obtained not only fruit, but wine, sugar and molasses, as the Arabs do at the present time. Dwarf cypress-trees were scattered over the plains; but these were a poor substitute for other species of wood. To this deficiency of timber must be attributed the neglect of the river navigation, and the abandonment of the commerce of the Indian seas, by the Babylonians."

Chaldæa produced no stone or minerals of any kind. The stone used in building was brought there from other lands. But the country yielded an abundant supply of clay, from which were manufactured excellent bricks for building purposes, while the wells of bitumen afforded an inexhaustible amount of admirable cement. These materials supplied the place of wood, stone and mortar. Considering its luxuriant yield of cheap and abundant food and its never-failing supply of building material, it is not surprising that Chaldæa in primeval times became densely populated and abounded in great cities. Assyria was better supplied with minerals than Chaldæa; good qualities of stone, iron, copper, lead, silver, antimony and other metals existed in abundance; while bitumen naphtha, petroleum, sulphur, alum and salt, were also yielded.

As regards climate, the winters of Chaldæa are mild, frosts being light and snow unknown; while the summers are hot and dry; and heavy rains fall in November and December. The wild animals indigenous in Chaldæa were the lion, the leopard, the hyena, the lynx, the wild cat, the wolf, the

SOURCES OF CHALDÆAN HISTORY.

jackal, the wild boar, the buffalo, the stag, the gazelle, the jerboa, the fox, the hare, the badger and the porcupine. The domestic animals of the country were the camel, the horse, the buffalo, the cow, the ox, the goat, the sheep and the dog.

The Book of Genesis, in speaking of Nimrod, "the mighty hunter before the Lord," says: "And the beginning of his kingdom was Babel, and Erech, and Accad, and Calneh, in the Land of Shinar." The southern tetrarchy of four cities consisted of Ur or Hur, Huruk, Nipur, and Larsa or Larancha, which are believed to be identical with the Scriptural "Ur of the Chaldees," Erech, Calneh, and Ellasar. The northern tetrarchy consisted of the cities of Babel or Babylon, Borsippa, Cutha and Sippara.

Ur, or Hur, in the southern part of Chaldæa, between the Euphrates and the Arabian border, was the early capital and metropolis of Chaldæa, and is celebrated as the birth-place of Abraham. Its stately ruins, now called Mugheir by the Arabs, and chief among which are the remains of a great temple, consist principally of a series of low mounds of an oval shape with the largest diameter running from north to south. Thirty miles north-west of Ur, on the east bank of the Euphrates, are the ruins of Larsa or Larrak, the Biblical Ellasar, the Laranchæ of Berosus, and the Larissa of Apollodorus; now called Senkereh or Sinkara. On the same side of the river, fifteen miles north-west of Larsa, are the ruins of Huruk, the Scriptural Erech and the Greek Orchoë; called by the present natives Urka or Warka, and celebrated for the ruins of its massive temple. Sixty-five miles north-west of Warka, thirty miles east of the Euphrates, are the ruins of Nipur, called Calneh by Moses, and Niffer by the present inhabitants. About sixty miles from Niffer, on the west bank of the Euphrates, are the remains of the ancient Borsippa, chiefly its temple, whose modern name is Birs-i-Nimrud. Fifteen miles north-west, on both banks of the Euphrates, are the ruins of "Babylon the Great," which cover a space three miles long by between one and two miles wide, and which consist of three mounds now called Babil, Kasr and Amram by the Arabs. The ancient Sippara, the Scriptural Sepharvaim, was twenty miles north-west of Babylon, on the east bank of the Euphrates, and is now called Sura. Dur-Kurri-galzu, now called Akkerkuf, on the Saklawiyeh canal, was six miles from the site of the present Bagdad. About twenty miles north-east of Babylon was Cutha, now Ibrahim. Ihi, or Ahava, was the modern Hit, about one hundred and twenty miles north-west of Babylon, on the Euphrates. Chilmad was the present Kalwadha, near Bagdad. Rubesi was probably Zerghul. There were a large number of smaller cities in every part of Chaldæa, of which nothing is known.

SECTION II.—SOURCES OF CHALDÆAN HISTORY.

EGARDING the great antiquity of Chaldæa we have the authority of Berosus, the native Babylonian historian, who was a priest of Bel at Babylon, and flourished during the first half of the third century B. C. Soon after Alexander the Great took Babylon, Berosus wrote a *History of Chaldæa* in Greek, in three books, and dedicated the work to Antiochus, King of Syria. Unfortunately this work has been lost, excepting a few fragments which were copied by Apollodorus and Polyhistor, two Greek writers of the first century before Christ, and these fragments were afterwards quoted by Eusebius and Syncellus, and from them we learn the Babylonian historian's account of his country's annals. Other ancient sources of Chaldæan, Assyrian and Babylonian history are the Old Testament and the writings of the Greek historians, Herodotus, Ctesias and Diodorus Siculus.

As in the case of Egypt, our knowledge of the history of the three great successive empires in the Tigris-Euphrates valley has been vastly enlarged through the diligent research of modern historians, antiquarians and Orientalists. By the diligence of the great explorers, beginning with Layard nearly half a century ago, Nineveh, Babylon and the buried cities of the plain have been excavated; their temples and palaces have been exposed to view; the mysterious inscriptions in the *cuneiform*, or wedge-shaped and arrow-headed characters, which were discovered on the slabs that lined the insides of the palaces and temples, have, by a grand triumph of modern scholarship, been deciphered, so that a new flood of light has been shed upon the darkness of these famous ancient monarchies. Specimens of the cuneiform inscriptions have been published in the *British Museum Series*, edited by Sir Henry Rawlinson and Mr. E. Norris. Many of these inscriptions have been deciphered by M. Oppert, the French Orientalist. The evidence of both classical writers and the monumental inscriptions shows that the Chaldæans, Assyrians and Later Babylonians paid great attention to chronology. The *Canon of Ptolemy*, which contained an exact Babylonian computation of time from 747 B. C. to 331 B. C., is generally credited as a most authentic document. The *Assyrian Canon*, discovered by Sir Henry Rawlinson, and consisting of a number of clay tablets, contains a complete system of Assyrian chronology from 911 B. C. to 660 B. C., verified by the record of a solar eclipse which must have occurred June 15, 763 B. C.; and is regarded as equally reliable. Among the eminent modern writers on these ancient Oriental monarchies are the English historians, George Rawlinson and P. Smith, and the renowned German historians and Orientalists, Niebuhr, Bunsen and Duncker.

SECTION III.—POLITICAL HISTORY.

III. Chaldæans were a Semitic and Hamitic race, and their origin is involved in the obscurity of an unknown antiquity. The Chaldæan monarchy probably began about 2400 B. C., as we have an account of astronomical observations dating back to 2234 B. C. Berosus assigns nine dynasties to Chaldæa and Babylonia from the Deluge to the Persian conquest of Babylonia in 538 B. C. The first of these dynasties is largely traditional, and ended, according to Rawlinson, in the year 2286 B. C., and according to Duncker in the year 2458 B. C.

The Hebrew Scriptures mention NIMROD, the son of Cush and the grandson of Ham, as the founder of this most ancient Asiatic empire. Says the Mosaic narrative: "And Cush begat Nimrod; he began to be a mighty one in the earth; he was a mighty hunter before the Lord; wherefore it is said, Even as Nimrod, the mighty hunter before the Lord; and the beginning of his kingdom was Babel, and Erech, and Accad, and Calneh, in the land of Shinar." Nimrod's capital was the celebrated "Ur of the Chaldees," which at this early period was a greater city than the four which Nimrod is said to have founded. By means of his personal prowess and strength, as "a mighty hunter before the Lord," Nimrod had earned the gratitude of his countrymen by reducing the number of wild animals which roamed over that region in primitive times. Evidently one of the greatest characters of antiquity, Nimrod was deified by the Chaldæans after his death, and was worshiped by them and by the Assyrians and Later Babylonians for two thousand years, under the title of *Bilu-Nipru*, or Bel-Nimrod, "the god of the chase," or "the great hunter."

POLITICAL HISTORY.

Rawlinson thinks that the title assigned by the Arab astronomers to the constellation of Orion—*El Jabbar*, "the giant"—was in memory of Nimrod. The ignorant people who occupy that region at the present day still remember Nimrod, Solomon and Alex-

NIMROD.

ander the Great as the three great heroes of antiquity, while all others have been forgotten. Calah, one of the Assyrian capitals, was regarded as Nimrod's sacred city, and the town which now occupies its site bears his name slightly corrupted—*Nimrud*. Although the tradition concerning Nimrod is almost universal, his name has not yet been found among any of the monuments or cuneiform inscriptions.

We have no account of the immediate successors of Nimrod. Some time after his death there followed a migration of Semitic and Hamitic tribes from Chaldæa to the northward and westward. Thus the Assyrians, a Semitic people, migrated to the middle portion of the Tigris valley, where they laid the foundations of their kingdom; the Phœnicians, a Hamitic race, descended from Canaan, a son of Ham, settled on the western shores of the country afterwards called Canaan, or Palestine, where they became the most famous commercial and colonizing people of antiquity; while the Semitic tribe which produced Abraham, the shepherd and native of "Ur of the Chaldees," and from whom are descended the Hebrews and Arabs, passed into Northern Mesopotamia, whence Abraham journeyed westward with his flocks and herds into the "promised land" of Canaan.

One of the successors of Nimrod was URUKH, or Urkham. He is the first Chaldæan king of whom any traces have been discovered in the country. The exact time of his reign is uncertain. He erected many stupendous edifices, which appear to have been designed as temples. These structures are gigantic in dimensions, but rude in workmanship. The bricks of which they are built are rough, and put together awkwardly, moist mud or bitumen being used for mortar. In speaking of the works erected by this monarch, Professor Rawlinson says: "In his architecture, though there is much that is rude and simple, there is also a good deal which indicates knowledge and experience." Astronomy was cultivated during the reign of Urukh. Ur was still the capital of the Chaldæan monarchy, Babylon having not yet risen into importance. At Warka, on the site of the ancient city of Huruk—the Erech of the Book of Genesis—is the famous mound called *Bowariyeh* by the present inhabitants. The general form of the ruin is pyramidal, but the ravages of ages have destroyed its symmetry. Recent discoveries have brought to light the fact that this massive structure was a tower two hundred feet square at its base and two stories high. The lower story was built of bricks baked in the sun and cemented together with bitumen, in which were placed layers of reeds every four or five feet. In the upper story, which is now in ruins, the middle portion was likewise of sun-baked brick, but on the outside were burnt bricks. As it now stands, this ancient temple is about one hundred feet above the level of the plain, and not much is known of the original dimensions of the massive edifice, but the ruins indicate that it must have been of immense altitude and grandeur. All the bricks of the buttresses are stamped with cuneiform inscriptions, and the layers are strongly cemented with bitumen. The solid dimensions of the whole structure have been estimated at three million cubic feet, and the number of bricks used in its erection have been computed at thirty millions. The name of its royal builder frequently occurs on the burnt bricks of this ruined temple. In some places his name is stamped in the baked clay, and in other places the inscription records that "Urukh, King of Ur, King of Sumir and Accad, has built a temple to his lady, the goddess Nana," or that "Urukh has built the temple and fortress of Ur in honor of his Lord, the god Sin," or that "The mighty Lord, King of Ur, may his name continue!"

The temple of Ur was also built by Urukh, and is like the one just described. Recent excavations have unearthed the ruins of this old Chaldæan structure after it lay buried for centuries beneath the mounds of rubbish. In the portion of the structure which has escaped the ravages of time may be seen the traces of the temple of Hurki, the Moon-god. The four corners of the vast edifice, and not its four sides, face the four cardinal points of the compass, and the ground-plan of the structure is in the form of a parallelogram, with its longest sides facing to the north-east and south-west. The foundation of this temple is raised twenty feet above the level of the plain. The longer sides of the base measure one hundred and ninety-eight feet, and the shorter sides one hundred and thirty-three feet. The first story above the basement is about forty feet high, and is secured outside by a wall ten feet thick, made of burnt brick cemented together with bitumen. The second story, now mostly in ruins, had the same form and character originally. According to a local tradition this immense structure had a third story, said to be the shrine of the god to whose worship the temple had been erected. Tiles glazed with a blue enamel and copper nails have been found in such a position as to indicate that they were used in the construction of this third story.

Similar ruins have been discovered in other parts of Chaldæa, of which the most important are those of Calneh and Larsa. Heaps of rubbish, the ruins of wrecked temples, are seen in every part of this famous land of remote antiquity. In Calneh the fragments of temples erected during the reign of Urukh are buried beneath two mounds. The first of these temples was dedicated to the goddess Beltis and the other to Bel-Nimrod. In Larsa the ruins indicate that San, the Sun-god, was adored as the tutelary divinity of that city. In the cuneiform inscriptions of Ur, his capital, Urukh is sometimes called "King of Ur," and also "King of Accad." It was chiefly at Ur that his great architectural works were erected. The ruins of this once-famous city—his great capital—display his inscriptions in greater profusion than those of any other Chaldæan monarch.

Urukh, at his death, was succeeded on the Chaldæan throne by his son, ILGI, or Elgi, who also styled himself "King of Ur." The royal seal or signet of the Chaldæan and Assyrian monarchs was formed in the shape of a small cylinder, with figures and characters engraven in the surface. When rolled upon wax or any other plastic material this cylinder left the king's name and emblems in relief upon the substance employed in sealing. In one of the mounds near Erech, or Orchoë, the signet-cylinder of Ilgi has been found, and is now in the British Museum. The legend inscribed upon it has been deciphered as follows: "For saving the life of Ilgi, from the mighty Lord, the King of Ur, son of Urukh." Ilgi finished the great architectural structures commenced by his father, and is reputed to have repaired two of the great temples of Erech. The inscriptions testify to the fame of both Urukh and Ilgi as architects and warriors.

After Ilgi's reign there is a blank in Chaldæan history, broken by the conquest of the kingdom by a Susianian, or Elamite dynasty, the second in the lists of Berosus, about 2286 B. C. The first monarch of this dynasty was KUDUR-NAKHUNTA, who governed Chaldæa through viceroys, while he held his court at Susa, his capital. One of his successors was KUDUR-LAGAMER—the Chedorlaomer of Scripture—who likewise reigned at Susa, and divided Chaldæa into several provinces, which he governed by means of viceroys. Kudur-Lagamer, or Chedorlaomer, was the first great Oriental conqueror. After conquering Assyria he invaded Canaan, or Palestine, where he was opposed by the Canaanitish princes, Bera, King of Sodom; Birsha, King of Gomorrah; Shinab, King of Admeh; Shemeber, King of Zeboüm; and the King of Bela or Zoar. A great battle in the valley of Siddim, near the Dead Sea—the first great battle recorded in history—resulted in a victory for Chedorlaomer, who for twelve years held the Canaanitish kings in vassalage. At the end of this period these kings attempted to free themselves from this yoke, whereupon Chedorlaomer again led an expedition into Palestine, and defeated the Canaanites in a second battle in the valley of Siddim, on which occasion Lot, Abraham's nephew, was taken prisoner. After plundering the cities of Palestine, the victorious Chaldees set out upon their march home; but encumbered by their captives and plunder, they were routed near Damascus by Abraham, who with a small band had made a night attack upon the retreating Chaldæan host, and driven them in a panic across the Syrian desert, recovering the booty they had taken.

This repulse secured Canaan against any further attack from the King of Chaldæa.

Only three of the succeeding Chaldæan kings of this Susianian, or Elamite dynasty are known. The first of these, Sinti-shil-khak, is known only by name. The second, Kudur-Mabuk, whom the inscriptions call "Conqueror of the West," is credited with having enlarged and beautified the city of Ur, which he made his capital, thus ingratiating himself with his Chaldæan subjects. Tradition also gives him the honor of restoring the old Chaldæan religion, which his predecessors of the Elamite dynasty had discouraged. The temples were repaired and the worship of the old deities once more prevailed. Kudur-Mabuk was succeeded by his son, ARID-SIN, the last of the known monarchs of the Susianian, or Elamite dynasty, which ended in the year 2052 B. C.

Then came the third dynasty mentioned by Berosus, a dynasty consisting of eleven monarchs, whose aggregate reigns embrace a period of only forty-eight years; but neither monumental inscriptions nor tradition afford us any knowledge concerning the events of their reigns. The fourth dynasty recorded by Berosus, one embracing forty-nine native Chaldæan kings, reigned for four hundred and fifty-seven years, from 2004 B. C. to 1546 B. C.

One of the first kings of the fourth dynasty was ISMI-DAGON, who probably reigned during the first half of the nineteenth century before Christ, and who subjected Assyria to the Chaldæan supremacy. His son, Shamas-Vul, was the Chaldæan viceroy over Assyria, and built a temple at Asshur. The monumental inscriptions prove the Chaldæan ascendency over Assyria at this early period, the last-named country being governed by Chaldæan viceroys. Ismi-Dagon was succeeded on the Chaldæan throne by his son, GURGUNA, who is chiefly distinguished as the builder of the great cemeteries at Ur, among the most wonderful of the ruins of Chaldæa. The next king was NARAM-SIN, who erected the great temple at Agana and fixed his capital at Babylon, which had at this time become the largest city of Chaldæa. Ur had for some time ceased to be the Chaldæan capital; Erech, or Huruk, having taken its place; but the latter city now gave way to Babylon, which thenceforth remained the capital of the empire.

After Naram-Sin, who reigned about the middle of the eighteenth century before Christ, followed the reign of SIN-SHADA, who built the upper terrace in the temple of Erech, now the ruins of Bowariyeh, already described. The next king was ZUR-SIN, the most celebrated sovereign of his time. He founded the city of Abu-Shahrein, the ruins of which testify to the adoption of a new style of architecture, much in advance of the previous style, both in the character of its structure and in its ornamental richness. Here also we get a better idea of the simple arts of life prevalent among this celebrated people in the early times. Stone knives, chisels and hatchets are everywhere found among the ruins, and some samples of gold and bronze have also been discovered. Ornaments for the person were also made out of iron. Of NUR-VUL, the next to the last of the kings of this dynasty, as mentioned by Berosus, no trace has been found on the monuments. RIM-SIN, the last of this dynasty, is mentioned on a single tablet discovered in the ruins of Ur.

In the year 1546 B. C., Chaldæa was conquered by an Arab chief named KHAMMURABI, who founded the Arabian dynasty of Chaldæan monarchs—the fifth dynasty in the lists of Berosus, and in which he includes nine kings; but the names of fifteen monarchs of this race have been deciphered from the cuneiform inscriptions and from the tablets. Khammurabi reigned twenty-six years, and was a wise and able sovereign. He fully appreciated the benefits accruing to the country from a proper system of artificial irrigation. He constructed a canal from one of the rivers for this purpose; and a white stone tablet, now in the Louvre at Paris, bears an inscription which says that the canal cut by Khammurabi proved a blessing to the Babylonians, that "it changed desert plains into well-watered fields; it spread around fertility and abundance." Khammurabi also erected several important edifices, one of which was a new palace at Kalwadha, in the vicinity of the present city of Bagdad. He likewise repaired the great temple of the Sun at Larsa, or Larrak (now Senkereh). He was succeeded by his son, SAMSU-ILUNA, whose name has only been found on one series of inscriptions, and of whose immediate successors no traces can be found for three quarters of a century.

The next known Chaldæan king is KARA-IN-DAS, the first of five monarchs during whose reigns intimate relations were maintained with Assyria, which was now gradually rising into importance, and which eventually shook off the Chaldæan supremacy. Chaldæa and Assyria were during this period sometimes united by treaties of alliance or by royal marriages, and were sometimes at war with each other. When the Chaldæan king, KARA-KHAR-DAS, was overthrown and killed in an insurrection headed by Nazi-bugas, an Assyrian army destroyed the insurrectionary chief and placed the brother of the murdered sovereign upon the Chaldæan throne. Some time afterward PURNA-PURIYAS, King of Chaldæa, married the daughter of Asshur-upallit, King of Assyria. The last of the five kings just mentioned was KURRI-GALZU, of whose reign relics have been discovered at Mugheir, the ancient Ur, and at Akkerkuf, the latter of which cities is said to have been founded by this monarch. The remaining kings of the fifth, or Arabian dynasty are SAGA-RAKTIGAS, the builder of the temple of the Sun at Sippara, AMMIDI-KAGA, and six others whose reigns were unimportant.

In the year 1300 B. C., Tiglathi-Nin, King of Assyria, invaded Chaldæa, took Babylon, and extended his supremacy over this ancient Asiatic kingdom. Thus ended the Arabian dynasty in Chaldæa; and the sixth dynasty, according to Berosus, probably Assyrian, ascended the throne of Chaldæa, which, with occasional intermissions,

CIVILIZATION.

remained in dependence upon Assyria thenceforth until 625 B. C., the forty-five kings of the sixth dynasty being merely Assyrian viceroys. The Assyrian conquest of Chaldæa in the year 1300 B. C. is generally regarded as the end of this most ancient of Asiatic empires—this great mother of Asiatic civilization.

KINGS OF CHALDÆA.

DYNASTY.	B. C. to B. C.		KINGS.	EVENTS, ETC.
I. (Chaldæan).		2286	NIMROD, * * * *	Founded the Empire.
			URUKH, * * * * ILGI (son).	Built numerous temples.
II. (Elamite).	2286	2052	KUDUR-NAKHUNTA, (Zoroaster). * * *	Conquered Chaldæa B. C. 2286.
			KUDUR-LAGAMER, * * *	{ Contemporary with Abraham. Led two expeditions into Syria.
			SINTI-SHIL-KHAK. KUDUR-MABUK (son), ARID-SIN (son).	Wars in Syria.
III.	2052	2004	* * * * *	
IV. (Chaldæan).	2004	1546	* * * * * ISMI-DAGON, * * * GURGUNA (son), * * * NARAM-SIN. * * * BILAT * * AT (a queen). SIN-SHADA (son). ZUR-SIN. * * *	{ Reigned from about B. C. 1850 to about B. C. 1830. His brother, Shamas-Vul, ruled in Assyria.
V. (Arab).	1546	1300	NUR-VUL, * * * * RIM-SIN, * * * * KHAMMU-RABI, * * * SAMSU-ILUNA (son), * *	Reigned from about B. C. 1586 to B. C. 1566. Reigned from about B. C. 1566 to B. C. 1546. Reigned from about B. C. 1546 to B. C. 1520. Reigned from about B. C. 1520 to B. C. 1500.
			KARA-IN-DAS, * * * *	{ Contemporary with Asshur-bel-nisi-su, B. C. 1440.
			PURNA-PURIVAS, * * *	{ Contemporary with Buzur-Asshur, B. C. 1420–1400.
			KARA-KHAR-DAS (son) NAZI-BUGAS, * * * * KURRI-GALZU (brother of Kara-khar-das). * * * *	Contemporary with Asshur-upallit, B. C. 1400-1380.
		1300	* * * *	Chaldæa conquered by Tiglathi-Nin.

SECTION IV.—CHALDÆAN CIVILIZATION.

HUS we have seen that the Chaldæan monarchy was the first civil government in Asia, and that its three most illustrious characters were Nimrod, the founder of the kingdom, "the mighty hunter before the Lord;" Urukh, the great architect, the mighty temple-builder; and Chedorlaomer, the warrior, the mighty conqueror, who nearly four thousand years ago marched an army a distance of twelve hundred miles, and held Syria and Palestine in subjection for twelve years, and who was the first of all those great Oriental conquerors who within the last forty centuries have built up vast empires in Asia, which have in larger or shorter spaces of time successively crumbled to decay.

In speaking of this ancient empire, Professor Rawlinson says: "The Chaldæan monarchy is rather curious from its antiquity than illustrious from its great names, or admirable for the extent of its dominions. Less ancient than the Egyptian, it claims the advantage of priority over every empire or kingdom which has grown up upon the soil of Asia. The Aryan, Turanian, and even Semitic tribes, appear to have been in the nomadic condition when the Cushite settlers of lower Babylonia betook themselves to agriculture, erected temples, built cities and established a strong and settled government. The leaven which was to spread by degrees through the Asiatic peoples was first deposited on the shores of the Persian Gulf at the mouth of the 'Great River;' and hence civilization, science, letters, art, extended themselves northward and eastward and westward. Assyria, Media, Semitic Babylonia, Persia, as they derived from Chaldæa the character of their writing, so were they indebted to the same country for their general notions of government and administration, for their architecture, for their decorative art, and still more for their science and literature. Each people no doubt modified in some measure the boon received, adding more or less of its own to the common inheritance. But Chaldæa stands forth as the great parent and original inventress of Asiatic civilization, without any rival that can reasonably dispute her claim."

It was believed by such eminent German scholars and antiquarians as Heeren, Niebuhr, Bunsen, and Max Müller, that the ancient Chaldæans belonged to the Aramaic, or Semitic race, and that they were thus kindred with the Assyrians, Syrians, Hebrews and Arabs. Herodotus regarded the Assyrians and Babylonians, from the earliest times, as belonging to the same race; but Berosus, Diodorus and Pliny considered them as ethnologically different peoples. Classical and other traditions—sustained by such Greek poets as Homer, Hesiod and Pindar—represent the early inhabitants of the shores of the Persian Gulf and the occupants of the Nile valley as the same race, calling them all Ethiopians.

The Hebrew Scriptures also regard the people of these two regions as belonging to a kindred race, namely, Hamites, or Cushites; Cush, the father of Nimrod, being a son of Ham; and the ancient Ethiopians being called the people of Cush; while the Egyptians were regarded as the posterity of Misraim, also a son of Ham. Recent philological investigations demonstrate the truth of the Scripture view of the national affinities of these primitive nations, and show the language of the primeval Chaldees to have been Ethiopic or Cushite, thus ranking them as belonging to the same Hamitic race as the Egyptians and Ethiopians. Although the predominant portion of the early Chaldæan population was Cushite, or Hamitic, there was an infusion of Semitic, Aryan and Turanian elements. The Semites—such as the Syrians, Assyrians, Hebrews and others—migrated from Chaldæa at a very early period to the northward and westward. Accad was a Turanian settlement, and the Aryans occupied the portions of the country bordering on Cissia, likewise called Susiana, or Elam, whose people were also Aryans. The name Chaldæans was unknown to these early people, but was given them by Berosus and has been used by writers ever since. The Hebrew prophets—such as Isaiah, Habakkuk and others—spoke of the Babylonians, even to the latest times, as Chaldæans. Isaiah called Babylon the "daughter of the Chaldæans," and "the beauty of the Chaldees' excellency." In a restricted sense, the term *Chaldæans* was applied to the learned men of Babylon to the latest ancient times. After the Assyrian conquest of Chaldæa, in B. C. 1300, there was an admixture of new Semitic elements from the north, so that in the process of time the Chaldæans became Semitized; and the preponderating portion of the later Babylonian population was Semitic, while the Hamitic, Aryan and Turanian elements occupied a subordinate place. The language of the learned in Babylon in later times was the classic Chaldee, while the national language of the Semitized Babylonians was akin to that of the Hebrews.

At an early period—earlier than 2,000 B. C.—the Chaldees had made considerable progress in the arts, especially in architecture, and from the first they showed the building tendency which seemed to be instinctive in other famous Hamitic nations, such as the Egyptians and Ethiopians. The attempt to build a tower "which should reach to heaven," made here, as mentioned in the Mosaic narrative, was in accordance with the general spirit of the Chaldees. Out of such simple and rude building material as brick and bitumen they constructed edifices of vast size, the ruins of which have recently been discovered by the explorations of Layard and Botta. These vast structures were pyramidal in design, and were built in successive steps or stages to a considerable altitude, and so placed as to face the four cardinal points of the compass.

Speaking of the building material of the Chaldees, a certain writer says: "Stone and marble were even more rare in this country than wood, but the clay was well adapted for the manufacture of bricks. These, whether dried in the sun or burnt in kilns, became so hard and durable that now, after the lapse of so many centuries, the remains of ancient walls preserve the bricks uninjured by their long exposure to the atmosphere, and retaining the impression of the inscriptions in the arrow-headed character as perfectly as if they had only just been manufactured. Naphtha and bitumen, or earthy oil and pitch, were produced in great abundance above Babylon, near the modern town of Hit. These served as substitutes for mortar and cement; and so lasting were they, that the layers of rushes and palm-leaves laid between the courses of bricks as a building material, are found at this day in the ruins of Babylon as perfect as if a year had not elapsed since they were put together."

The most imposing ruins of ancient Chaldæa are their temples, two of which have been described. The temple of Abu-Shahrein was similar in character to those of Erech and Ur, and was one of the few Chaldæan edifices built of stone, which may be accounted for by the proximity of a stone-quarry in the neighboring Arabian hills. In this massive structure are also marble, alabaster and agate, skillfully cut and polished, while gold plates and gilt-headed nails have also been discovered in the ruins. In the sacred shrine of the deity to whose worship the temple was consecrated, the wood-work and images of the god were ornamented. Like the Egyptian Pyramids, the Chaldæan edifices were chiefly remarkable for their grandeur and massive proportions, while architectural beauty was wanting.

In the cities the dwellings were built of brick, but in the rural districts they consisted of reed huts plastered with slime. The houses of even the rich seem to have been rude and coarse. The remains of a dwelling-house have been found among the excavations at Ur, in which the foundation was a brick platform raised above the surface, the floors were of burnt bricks well cemented with bitumen, and the walls were plastered with gypsum. In the apartments of a house discovered at Abu-Shahrein the walls were frescoed with designs in red, black and white; and figures of birds, beasts and men were skillfully drawn on the plaster of the walls. The Chaldæan dwellings usually had flat wooden roofs, though sometimes there were arched roofs built of bricks cemented with bitumen.

Next to their architectural structures, the most remarkable remains of the ancient Chaldæans are their burial-places. The immense number of ancient tombs discovered in what was Chaldæa proper is truly wonderful. Large sepulchers are filled with the bones and relics of the dead. At Warka, the ancient Erech, except the triangular space between the three principal ruins, the whole remainder of the platform, the space within the walls, and a wide extent of the neighboring desert, are filled with human bones and sepulchers. Coffins are heaped upon coffins from thirty to sixty feet, and there are miles on miles of tombs in portions of this once-famous land. The most striking of these burial-places are those at Warka, the ancient Erech; at Mugheir, the ancient Ur; at Abu-Shahrein and Tel-el-Lahm.

The tombs are of three kinds—brick vaults, clay coffins shaped like a dish cover, and clay coffins formed of two large jars placed mouth to mouth and cemented together with bitumen. The brick vaults, principally found at Mugheir, are seven feet long, three and a half feet wide, and five feet high. The floors and walls of these vaults were made of sun-dried bricks cemented together with mud or bitumen, and the side walls were closed in above with an arch. The body was laid to rest on its left side on a matting of reeds spread upon the floor. The fingers of the right hand were placed upon a copper bowl set in the palm of the left. The head rested upon a brick for a pillow. Articles of use and ornament were placed in the vault, and vessels with food and drink were set near the head of the departed. The remains of several bodies are in many cases found in the same vault, and one vault contained eleven skeletons. It is believed from this that the brick vaults were family sepulchers.

Where the dish-cover clay coffins were used, the body was laid on a mat spread over a sun-dried brick platform, disposed of in the same manner as in the brick vaults, and surrounded with articles of food and ornaments. The large clay coffins shaped like a dish-cover, seven feet long, two and a half wide at the bottom, and two or three feet high, then covered the body, matting, utensils, ornaments and all. Never were more than two skeletons, one male and the other female, discovered under one cover. Children were interred under covers half the size of those for adults. These tombs were found seven or eight feet under ground at Mugheir. The clay coffins consisting of two large jars, from two and a half to three feet deep and two feet in diameter, and cemented together with bitumen, as found at Mugheir and Tel-el-Lahm, readily contained a full-sized corpse and had an air-hole at each end to allow the gases generated by decomposition to escape.

The coffins containing the bodies of the dead were placed in rows, and then covered with earth so as to form a mound. These mounds were repeatedly covered with fresh earth, so that they were often elevated to a height of sixty feet above the original level of the plain. The mounds were carefully drained by means of tube-like shafts of pottery, consisting of a succession of rings or joints, two feet in diameter and a foot and a half wide, skillfully put together and cemented with bitumen, and filled with masses of broken pottery to resist external pressure. These drains reached from the surface to the original ground-level; and by their means the sepulchral mounds have been protected from dampness, and their utensils, ornaments and skeletons have been preserved to the present day, and appear perfect on opening the tombs, but usually crumble to dust when touched.

Monuments have also been exhumed bearing inscriptions in the *cuneiform*, or wedge-shaped characters, the deciphering of which, as we have said, has given us new light on early Chaldæan history. This kind of writing was used for monumental records, and was either hewn or carved in rocks and sculptures, or impressed on tiles and bricks. The legends stamped upon the baked bricks of this ancient period prove the extent to which this kind of writing was in use. The earliest date that can be assigned to its use was about 2000 B. C., and it was little, if at all, used as late as 300 B. C. A vast deal of labor and erudition have been spent in deciphering these cuneiform inscriptions. The great inscription of Behistun, in Persia, is of special interest. It is engraved in three forms of cuneiform writing, upon the perpendicular face of a mountain, at a height of three hundred feet; and gives an account of the genealogy of Darius, his exploits,

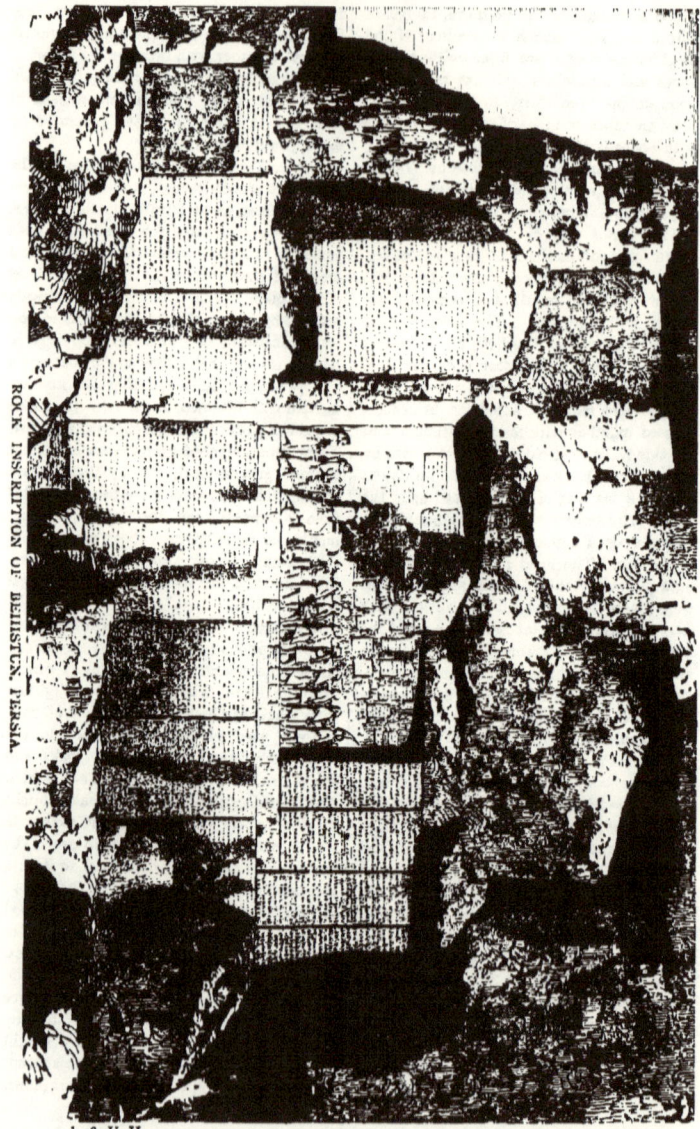

ROCK INSCRIPTION OF BEHISTUN, PERSIA.

and the provinces of his empire. This inscription was deciphered by Sir Henry Rawlinson.

The writing of the Chaldees is well-nigh as abundant as that of their Hamitic kinsmen, the Egyptians. The writing was impressed on the clay while it was moist and plastic. The inscriptions on the bricks record the history of the building in which they are found, the name of the monarch who built it, his titles and his fame. The inscriptions on the clay tablets are usually of a private character, relating to such matters as deeds, contracts and personal records. The writing is from left to right, except on signet-cylinders, on which it is reversed, because of the manner in which it was stamped, as described in a previous section. The legend on the bricks was always stamped in the form of a square in the center; and was in some cases impressed upon the clay, and in others was cut or engraved in the surface with some implement. On many of the tablets the signet-cylinder of the maker or contractor was rolled across the surface, showing the wearer's motto and seal in relief. These tablets were preserved as family records, just as moderns file important documents for preservation. These inscriptions abound in all the ruins of ancient Chaldæa.

The earthenware coffins and drainage-shafting, besides the many jars, vases and drinking-vessels, attest the skill of this ancient people in pottery from the earliest ages of their history. On many burnt-clay tablets are figures representing lions, bulls and men; in most of which are illustrated deadly combats between men and lions.

The Chaldees fashioned arms, implements and ornaments from various metals. In the oldest ruins are discovered flint knives, hatchets, stone hammers and occasional articles of bronze, such as arrow-heads, knives, hatchets and sickles. Articles of iron, gold and copper have been discovered in great abundance in the mounds. Ornaments were usually made of iron or gold, while arms and weapons were generally fashioned from copper or bronze. The primitive Chaldees were also celebrated for the fine cloths and delicate textile fabrics manufactured by their looms, showing that the spinner's and weaver's art had attained a high degree of skill and perfection among this renowed primeval race.

The Chaldees were also skillful in the art of cutting, polishing and engraving gems, some of their work in this art rivaling the best modern specimens. The signets and seals were of this class, and several of them have been deciphered and rendered in English. The inscription on the seal of Urukh has been translated as follows: "The signet of Urukh, the pious chief, King of Ur, High Priest of Niffer." On Ilgi's seal was the following legend: "To the manifestation of Nergal, King of Bit-Zida, of Zurgulla, for the saving of the life of Ilgi, the powerful hero, the King of Ur, son of Urukh * * * May his name be preserved." A signet-cylinder of one of the Sin kings bears this inscription: "Sin, the powerful chief, the King of Ur, the King of the four races * * * his seal." Some of the cylinders bear neither figures nor inscriptions; while others have no legend, but bear figures and symbols. They were usually of jasper or chalcedony, and were used to impress the seals of their owners on clay tablets. They were half an inch in diameter and three inches long. The cylinder was rolled upon the tablet by means of a copper or bronze parallelogram, one side of which was passed through a hole bored through its axis. It was suspended from the owner's neck or waist by means of a string or chain attached to a metal frame. The design of the wearer's seal was cut in reverse on the surface of the signet, leaving the impression in relief.

The Chaldees likewise engaged in commerce with other countries. Their trading caravans journeyed to the Aryan and Turanian countries of Central Asia, and the "ships of Ur" navigated the Persian Gulf and traded with the people on its shores.

The Chaldæans found cheap and abundant articles of food in the luxuriant growth of the date-palm and the abundant yield of such cereals as wheat, barley, millet and sesame; in addition to which the wealthier classes indulged in animal food, such as fish, chickens and the wild boar.

The worship of the heavenly bodies led the primitive Chaldees at an early day to the study of astronomy and chronology. Diodorus declares that the Chaldæans were far in advance of all other ancient nations in their knowledge of the starry heavens. This celebrated people discovered and recorded the relation of the sun's circuit to the other cycles of the solar system. They observed that the sun's apparent course through the firmament equals about twelve rounds of the moon, and for this reason they divided the year into twelve months of thirty days each, and when they discovered the inaccuracy of this system they introduced new calculations, rectifying the calendar so as to agree with the sidereal year of three hundred and sixty-five days and six hours. By their observation of the sun's course through the heavens they were able to establish the twelve signs of the Zodiac; and by observing the variation of the orbits of the planets from that of the sun they were enabled to fix the limits of the zodiacal signs, and to divide each sign into thirty degrees by the progress of the sun. By watching the moon's phases they adopted seven days as the length of the week. They further divided each day into twelve hours; each hour into sixty, or five times twelve, minutes; and thus established the basis of the duodecimal method of calculation. Two times twelve, or twenty-four, finger-widths was fixed upon as the measure of a *cubit*. A cycle of sixty years was called a *soss*; ten times sixty was a *ner;* and the square of sixty, or thirty-six centuries, was a *sar*.

They measured distances in the heavens by taking the width of the sun's disc as a unit. By comparing the quantity of water discharged through an orifice in a jar in the time occupied by the sun in crossing the horizon on the morning of the equinox with the amount discharged through the same orifice at the next sunrise, they discovered that the amount discharged between the two risings of the sun was seven hundred and twenty times the amount discharged during sunrise on the equinoctial morning. They thus inferred that the sun's orbit measured seven hundred and twenty times his disc, and from this they derived a unit to measure space and time. In regard to space this unit constituted half a degree, and in the calculation of time the same unit equaled two minutes, or one-thirtieth of an hour. A *stadium* was the distance an active foot-courier could walk in one unit of time, or two minutes; and the distance he could walk in thirty units, sixty minutes, or one hour, at the same ratio of speed, was called a *parasang*. The stadium was divided into three hundred and sixty *cubits*, and sixty cubits was called a *plethron*.

The Chaldæans discovered and recorded the fact that each cycle of the moon's eclipses is completed in a period of two hundred and twenty-three months, and from this discovery they computed the length of the synodic and periodic months so accurately that modern astronomers have found the calculation to fall short of less than five seconds of our time. They carefully recorded all the results of their observations. The Greek Callisthenes, who had accompanied the expedition of Alexander the Great, sent to Aristotle from Babylon a series of tablets on which were inscriptions recording astronomical observations dating as far back as 1903 years before the year 331 B. C., the year that Alexander entered that city. These observations would therefore reach back 2234 years before Christ.

The Chaldæans had also made considerable progress in arithmetic, and they employed two systems of notation—decimal and duodecimal. They used cuneiform, or wedge-shaped and arrow-headed characters, to represent numbers. Their system of weights was based upon their system of measures. A cubit of water, which weighed sixty-six pounds, was divided into sixty *logs*, each *log* measuring about five-sixths of a pint. The *log* was the unit of measure; and its weight, called a *mina*, was the unit of weight. A duck-shaped stone belonging to King Ilgi has been discovered bearing the inscription, "Ten minæ of Ilgi." Like most other nations, the Chaldæans had one system of weights for the ordinary articles of the market-place, and another system for the precious metals and gems. Circular pieces or rings, called *talents*, *shekels*, etc.—names afterwards used by the Hebrews and the Greeks—were taken as units in weighing gold and silver.

Although the brilliant intellectual activity of Chaldæa ceased more than three thousand years ago, and its massive architectural structures have slumbered in eternal repose beneath the sands and dust of more than thirty centuries, the grand mental triumphs of its venerable civilization yet remain, as a permanent legacy to posterity—the groundwork of the science and learning in which they have ever since been recognized as the pioneers—the wonder and admiration of the ages.

SECTION V.—CHALDÆAN COSMOGONY AND RELIGION.

BEROSUS begins his history by recounting the Chaldæan traditions regarding the creation of the world and the origin of the human race. The following is an account of the Chaldæan cosmogony: "In the beginning all was darkness and water, and therein were generated monstrous animals of strange and peculiar forms. There were men with two wings, and some even with four, and with two faces; and others with two heads, a man's and a woman's, on one body; and there were men with the heads and horns of goats, and men with hoofs like horses, and some with the upper parts of a man joined to the lower parts of a horse, like centaurs; and there were bulls with human heads, dogs with four bodies and with fishes' tails, men and horses with dogs' heads, creatures with the heads and bodies of horses, but with the tails of fish, and other animals mixing the forms of various beasts. Moreover, there were monstrous fish and reptiles and serpents, and divers other creatures, which had borrowed something from each other's shapes; of all which the likenesses are still preserved in the temple of Bel. A woman ruleth them all, by name Omorka, which is in Chaldee Thalatth, and in Greek Thalassa (or 'the sea'). Then Bel appeared, and split the woman in twain; and of the one half of her he made the heaven and of the other half the earth; and the beasts that were in her he caused to perish. And he split the darkness, and divided the heaven and the earth asunder, and put the world in order; and the animals that could not bear the light perished. Bel, upon this, seeing that the earth was desolate, yet teeming with productive power, commanded one of the gods to cut off his head, and to mix the blood which flowed forth with earth, and form men therewith, and beasts that could bear the light. So man was made, and was intelligent, being a partaker of the divine wisdom. Likewise Bel made the stars, and the sun and moon, and the five planets."

There is a remarkable likeness between certain Chaldæan and Jewish legends, such as the traditions of the destruction of mankind by a great Flood, because of its wickedness, and the Tower of Babel and dispersion of the human race. Among some clay tablets brought from Assyria to London by Mr. George Smith are a series of fragments which, joined to some smaller pieces in the British Museum collection, give the history of the world from the Creation down to some period after the fall of man. Mr. Smith succeeded in translating these legends in 1875, and the following is his brief account of the contents of the tablets: "Whatever the primitive account may have been from which the earlier part of the Book of Genesis was copied, it is evident that the brief narrative given in the Pentateuch omits a number of incidents and explanations—for

COSMOGONY AND RELIGION.

instance, as to the origin of evil, the fall of the angels, the wickedness of the serpent, etc. Such points as these are included in the cuneiform narrative."

Mr. Smith then proceeds to give a sketch of the Assyrian cosmogony, as follows: "The narrative on the Assyrian tablets commences with a description of the period before the world was created, when there existed a chaos or confusion. The desolate and empty state of the universe and the generation by chaos of monsters are vividly given. The chaos is presided over by a female power named Tisalat and Tiamat, corresponding to the Thalatth of Berosus; but as it proceeds the Assyrian account agrees rather with the Bible than with the short account from Berosus. We are told, in the inscriptions, of the fall of the celestial being who appears to correspond to Satan. In his ambition he raises his hand against the sanctuary of the God of heaven, and the description of him is really magnificent. He is represented riding in a chariot through celestial space, surrounded by the storms, with the lightning playing before him, and wielding a thunderbolt as a weapon. This rebellion leads to a war in heaven and the conquest of the powers of evil, the gods in due course creating the universe in stages, as in the Mosaic narrative, surveying each step of the work and pronouncing it good. The divine work culminates in the creation of man, who is made upright and free from evil, and endowed by the gods with the noble faculty of speech. The Deity then delivers a long address to the newly-created being, instructing him in all his duties and privileges, and pointing out the glory of his state. But this condition of blessing does not last long before man, yielding to temptation, falls; and the Deity then pronounces upon him a terrible curse, invoking on his head all the evils which have since afflicted humanity."

After his mythical account of the Creation, Berosus mentions a sea-monster, half man and half fish, named Oan, who came out of the deep to teach men language and letters, astronomy, the arts, agriculture and all that pertains to civilization. During the fabulous reigns of the ten antediluvian kings of Chaldæa, there appeared at different times six other fish-monsters who, like Oan, instructed mankind. The ten kings whom Berosus mentions as reigning in Chaldæa during the antediluvian period, and who correspond in number with the ten patriarchs of the same period mentioned in the Mosaic record, will now be named with the lengths of their reigns. Alorus, a Chaldæan, reigned 36,000 years; Aloparus, son of Alorus, 10,800 years; Almelon, a native of Sippara, 46,800 years; Ammenon, a Chaldæan, 43,200 years; Amegalarus, of Sippara, 64,800 years; Daönus, of Sippara, 36,000 years; Edorankhus, of Sippara, 64,800 years; Amempsinus, a Chaldæan, 36,000 years; Otiartes, a Chaldæan, 28,000 years; and Xisuthrus, the Chaldæan Noah, 64,800 years—the ten reigns covering a period of 432,000 years.

The Chaldæan or Babylonian account of the Deluge, as narrated by Berosus, is as follows: "The god Bel appeared to Xisuthrus (Noah) in a dream, and warned him that on the fifteenth day of the month Dæsius, mankind would be destroyed by a deluge. He bade him bury in Sippara, the City of the Sun, the extant writings, first and last; and build a ship, and enter therein with his family and his close friends; and furnish it with meat and drink; and place on board winged fowl, and four-footed beasts of the earth; and when all was ready, set sail. Xisuthrus asked 'Whither he was to sail?' and was told, 'To the gods, with a prayer that it might fare well with mankind.' Then Xisuthrus was not disobedient to the vision, but built a ship fifteen stadia (3125 feet) in length, and six stadia (1250 feet) in breadth; and collected all that had been commanded him, and put his wife and children and close friends on board. The flood came; and as soon as it ceased, Xisuthrus let loose some birds, which, finding neither food nor a place where they could rest, came back to the ark. After some days he again sent out the birds, which again returned to the ark, but with feet covered with mud. Sent out a third time, the birds returned no more, and Xisuthrus knew that land had reappeared; so he removed some of the covering of the ark, and looked, and behold! the vessel had grounded on a mountain. Then Xisuthrus went forth with his wife and his daughter, and his pilot, and fell down and worshiped the earth, and built an altar, and offered sacrifice to the gods; after which he disappeared from sight, together with those who had accompanied him. They who had remained in the ark and not gone forth with Xisuthrus, now left it and searched for him, and shouted out his name; but Xisuthrus was not seen any more. Only his voice answered them out of the air, saying, 'Worship the gods; for because I worshiped them, am I gone to dwell with the gods; and they who were with me have shared the same honor.' And he bade them return to Babylon, and recover the writings buried at Sippara, and make them known among men; and he told them that the land in which they then were was Armenia. So they, when they had heard all, sacrificed to the gods and went their way on foot to Babylon, and, having reached it, recovered the buried writings from Sippara, and built many cities and temples, and restored Babylon. Some portion of the ark still continues in Armenia, in the Gordiæan (Kurdish) mountains; and persons scrape off the bitumen from it to bring away, and this they use as a remedy to avert misfortunes."

The Assyrian inscriptions discovered by George Smith give an account of the Deluge much resembling the narrative of the same event by Berosus. Among the ruins of the palace of the Assyrian king Asshurbani-pal, tablets have been discovered from which the account of the Deluge has been deciphered, agreeing in some particulars with the Chaldæan tradition. The legend found recorded on the tablets states that the god Hea commanded Sisit to build a ship of specified size and to launch it on the deep, as he intended to detroy the wicked. Then Hea said: "When the flood comes which I will send thou shalt enter the ship, and into the midst of it thou shalt bring thy corn, thy goods, thy gods, thy gold and silver, thy slaves male and female, the sons of the army, the wild and tame animals; and all that thou hearest thou shalt do. And Sisit gathered together all his possessions of silver and gold, all that he had of the seeds of life, and caused all of his slaves, male and female, to go into the ship. The wild and tame beasts of the field also he caused to enter, and all the sons of the army. And Shamas, the Sun-god, made a flood, and said: 'I will cause rain to fall heavily from heaven; go into the ship and shut the door.' Overcome with fear Sisit entered into the ship, and on the morning of the day fixed by Shamas the storm began to blow from the ends of heaven, and Vul thundered in the midst of heaven, and Nebo came forth, and over the mountains and plains came the gods, and Nergal the Destroyer overthrew, and Nin came forth and dashed down; the gods made ruin; in their brightness they swept over the earth. The storm went over the nations; the flood of Vul reached up to heaven; brother did not see brother; the lightsome earth became a desert, and the flood destroyed all living things from the face of the earth. Even the gods were afraid of the storm, and sought refuge in the heaven of Ana; like hounds drawing in their tails, the gods seated themselves on their thrones, and Ishtar, the great goddess, spake: 'The world has turned to sin, and therefore I have proclaimed destruction. I have begotten men, and now they fill the sea like the children of fishes.' And the gods upon their seats wept with her. On the seventh day the storm abated, which had destroyed like an earthquake, and the sea began to dry. Sisit perceived the movement of the sea. Like reeds floated the corpses of the evil-doers and all who had turned to sin. Then Sisit opened the window, and the light fell upon his face, and the ship was stayed upon Mount Nizir, and could not pass over it. Then on the seventh day Sisit sent forth a dove, but she found no place of rest, and returned. Then he sent a swallow, which also returned; and again a raven, which saw the corpses in the water and ate them, and returned no more. Then Sisit released the beasts to the four winds of heaven, and poured a libation, and built an altar upon the top of the mountain, and cut seven herbs, and the sweet savor of the sacrifice caused the gods to assemble, and Sisit prayed that Bel might not come to the altar. For Bel had made the storm and sunk the people in the deep, and wished in his anger to destroy the ship, and allow no man to escape. Nin opened his mouth, and spoke to the warrior Bel: 'Who would then be left?' And Hea spoke to him: 'Captain of the gods, instead of the storm let lions and leopards increase, and diminish mankind; let famine and pestilence desolate the land and destroy mankind.' When the sentence of the gods was passed, Bel came into the midst of the ship and took Sisit by the hand and conducted him forth, and caused his wife to be brought to his side, and purified the earth, and made a covenant; and Sisit and his wife and his people were carried away like gods, and Sisit dwelt in a distant land at the mouth of the rivers."

Traditions of a great Flood have been prevalent in all countries subject to overflows of rivers, with the exception of Egypt, where the annual inundation was so regular. Legends like those of Chaldæa and Assyria have been discovered among the inhabitants of Armenia, Greece, India and all countries exposed to dangerous floods. The account of the Deluge as narrated by Moses is a record of the same story as given by Berosus and as found inscribed upon the Assyrian tablets. It is not known when the great Flood occurred in Chaldæa, and the dates assigned by Berosus are fabulous, as are his accounts of the antediluvian dynasty and the first postdiluvian dynasty in Chaldæa.

"In a valuable contribution to the London *Academy*, in the year 1875, Mr. Sayce showed that the Phœnician legends form, as it were, the link between the Chaldæan and the Hebrew so far as the so-called Elohistic portion of Genesis is concerned; this being especially noticeable in the legend of the Creation and the sacrifice of Isaac. Mr. Sayce also explained the very close resemblance between the Babylonian and Jewish legends of the Garden of Eden, the Deluge and the Tower of Babel, the Phœnician analogies failing us here altogether."

The following is the Chaldæan account of the Tower of Babel, as related by Berosus: "The earth was still of one language, when the primitive men, who were proud of their strength and stature, and despised the gods as their inferiors, erected a tower of vast height, in order that they might mount to heaven. And the tower was now near to heaven, when the gods caused the winds to blow and overturned the structure upon the men, and made them speak with divers tongues; whereupon the city was called Babylon."

Says Rawlinson, concerning Chaldæan mythology:"The striking resemblance of the Chaldæan system to that of classical mythology seems worthy of particular attention. This resemblance is too general, and too close in some respects, to allow of the supposition that mere accident has produced the coincidence. In the Pantheons of Greece and Rome, and in that of Chaldæa, the same general grouping is to be recognized; the same genealogical succession is not unfrequently to be traced; and in some cases even the familiar names and titles of classical divinities admit of the most curious illustrations and explanations from Chaldæan sources. We can scarcely doubt but that, in some way or other, there was a communication of beliefs—a passage in very early times, from the shores of the Persian Gulf to the lands washed by the Mediterranean, of mythological notions and ideas. It is a probable conjecture that 'among the primitive tribes who dwelt on the Tigris and Euphrates, when the cuneiform alphabet was invented, and when such writing was first applied to the purposes of religion, a Scythic or Scytho-Arian race existed, who subsequently migrated to Europe and brought with them those mythical traditions which, as objects of 'popular belief, had been mixed up in the nascent literature of their native country,' and that these traditions were passed on to the classical nations, who were in part descended from this Scythic or Scytho-Arian people."

ANCIENT HISTORY.—CHALDÆA.

The religion of Chaldæa, or Babylonia, was from the most ancient times a gross polytheism, and was a kind of Sabæan worship, the heavenly bodies being objects of adoration and represented by their special deities. Local divinities abounded, every town being under the protection of some particular deity. The Chaldæan gods and goddesses therefore dwelt in the sky. The deities of the first order were grouped as follows: At the head of the Chaldæan Pantheon stood *El*, or *Il*, or *Ra;* after whom was named the great city, Babylon, or Bab-El, meaning *Gate of El*. Next to the chief deity was a triad of gods—*Ana*, or *Anu; Bil*, or *Bel*, or *Belus;* and *Hea*, or *Hoa*—who corresponded to the classical Pluto, Jupiter and Neptune. Each of these three gods was accompanied by a female principle, or wife; *Anat*, or *Anata*, being the wife of Ana; *Mulita*, or *Beltis*, the wife of Bel; and *Davkina* the wife of Hoa. These were followed by a second triad of gods, consisting of *Sin*, or *Hurki*, the Moon-god; *San*, or *Sansi*, the Sun-god; and *Vul*, or *Iva*, or *Bin*, the Air-god. Each of this second triad was also accompanied by a feminine power, or wife; a goddess called "the Great Lady," whose name is uncertain, being the consort of Sin, or Hurki; *Gula*, or *Annnit*, the companion of San; and *Shala*, or *Tala*, the wife of Vul. Next to these great gods and goddesses at the head of the Pantheon were a group of five minor deities representing the five planets then known—Nin or Ninip (Saturn), Merodach (Jupiter), Nergal (Mars), Ishtar (Venus), and Nebo (Mercury). All the deities thus far named constituted the principal gods and goddesses, and after them were numerous divinities of the second and third order.

The chief Chaldæan gods and goddesses were not all descended from the same parentage, like the Egyptian, or the Greek or Roman deities, yet some relationship existed among them. Ana and Bel were brothers, the sons of Il. Vul was the son of Ana; and Sin, or Hurki, the Moon-god, was the son of Bel. Nebo and Merodach were sons of Hoa. Among the many deities without parentage were Il, the chief god; Hoa; San, the Sun-god; Ishtar, the planetary Venus; and Nergal, the representative of the planet Mars. Sometimes the relationship is confused and contradictory; Nin, the planetary Saturn, being represented as the son and father of Bel, and as the son and husband of Beltis.

El, or Il, is the root of the well-known Biblical *Elohim*, and also of the Arabic or Mohammedan *Allah*. It is the name which Diodorus represents as *Elus;* and Sanchroniathon, or rather Philo-Byblius, under the name of *Elus*, or *Ilus*. The meaning of the word *El*, or *Il*, is simply "God," or "the God." *Ra* had the same meaning in Chaldæa, but in Egypt it was the special designation of the Sun-god. The Semitic name of Babylon was *Bab-Il*, signifying "The gate of Il, " or "the gate of God." Ra was a sort of fount or origin of deity and had few attributes. He was not much worshiped, and does not appear to have had any temple in early times. He was the common father of Bel and Ana. Though Babylon, from its name *Babil*, was originally under Il's protection, Bel was the god chiefly worshiped in that city in early times, and Merodach in later times. El, or Il, was the lord of heaven. He was styled "the Warrior," "the Prince of the gods," "the Lord of the universe." In an Assyrian tablet he is styled "the Lamp of the divinities." In his anger at the wickedness of mankind Il sent the great Flood to destroy the human race, and Sisit with the rest.

The residence of Ana, the first god of the first triad, was in the concave dome of the sky, to which the other gods fled to escape the ravages of the Flood, which the wrath of Il had sent against the wicked world. On some tablets Ana was called "the Old Ana," "the Original Chief," "the Father of gods," "the Lord of spirits and demons," "the King of the lower world," "the Lord of darkness," "the Ruler of the far-off city," etc. The old city of Erech, or Huruk (now Warka), was the chief seat of Ana's worship, and here was a favorite burial-ground of the Chaldees, over which Ana was believed to preside as a tutelary divinity. He was worshiped in the most remote antiquity, and Urukh alluded to him as one of the gods of Ur. King Shamas-Vul built a temple to Ana at Asshur, (now Kileh-Sherghat), about 1830 B. C. The temple of Erech bore the name of Bit-Ana, or House of Ana; and the goddess Beltis, whose worship superseded that of Ana, in this temple, was the companion of Ana and was called "the Lady of Bit-Ana."

Anat, or Anata, the wife of Ana, was but a reflection of her husband, and had no distinguishing characteristics, being nothing but the feminine form of the masculine Ana. All his epithets were applied to her with only a distinction of gender, and she had no personality different from his, and is rarely, if ever, mentioned in the historical or geographical inscriptions. One tablet represents Ana and Anata as having nine children. Two of Ana's sons were Vul, the Air-god, and *Martu*, the representative of "Darkness," "the West," etc., corresponding to the Erebus of the Greeks.

Bel, also called *Enu*, and known as *Belus* by the Greeks, was the second of the first triad of gods. His name *Bil* or *Bel* signifies "Lord." He was called "the Supreme," "the Father of the gods," "the Procreator," "the Lord," "the King of all the spirits," "the Lord of the world," "the Lord of all the countries." When Nimrod, "the mighty hunter before the Lord," the legendary founder of the Chaldæan Empire, after his death was deified as Bel-Nimrod, or Bilu-Nipru, "the Hunter Lord," his attributes and titles were mingled with those of Bel. Calneh, or Nipur, the modern Niffer, was his sacred city and the seat of his worship, and here was the great temple consecrated to him. Many legends and traditions connect his name with this ancient city, which was also dedicated to his wife Beltis. Bel-Nimrod was called "Lord of Nipra," and his wife "Lady of Nipra." His temple at Nipur, called *Kharris-Nipra*, and famed for its wealth, magnificence and antiquity, was an object of intense veneration to the Assyrian monarchs. Temples were likewise dedicated to his worship at Calah (now Nimrud), and Dur-Kurri-galzu (now Akkerkuf). He is sometimes said to have had four "arks" or "tabernacles." Inscriptions are found on Assyrian tablets, in which his name is invoked as "the Lord of the world." This fact attests that his worship was general throughout Chaldæa and Assyria. In Assyria he was inferior only to Asshur, and in Chaldæa only to El and Ana. Thus Bel and Bel-Nimrod were virtually the same god. Beltis was his wife; and Nin, the Assyrian Hercules, was their son, and was frequently joined in their invocations. Sin, the Moon-god, is also said to be Bel-Nimrod's son, in some inscriptions. His title "Father of the gods" would indicate an almost infinite paternity. Bel-Nimrod was worshiped during the whole period of the monarchy. Urukh built him his temple at Calneh, or Nipur (now Niffer), and Kurri-galzu erected the one at Akkerkuf. Urukh often mentions him in the inscriptions in connection with Sin, or Hurki, the Moon-god, whom he calls Bel-Nimrod's "eldest son."

Beltis, or Mulita—the Mylitta of Herodotus—as the wife of Bel-Nimrod, presented a strong contrast to Anata, the wife of Ana. Beltis was not only a female power of Bel-Nimrod, but was really a distinct and important deity. Her common title was "the Great Goddess." Her Chaldæan name, Mulita, or Enuta, signifies "the Lady." Her Assyrian name, Bilta or Bilta-Nipruta, were the feminine forms of Bil and Bilu-Nipru. Her favorite title was "the Mother of the gods," or "Mother of the great gods," likewise "Queen-mother of the gods," "the Queen of the land," "the Great Lady," "the Goddess of war and battle," "the Goddess of birth." Though usually classed as the wife of Bel-Nimrod and the mother of his son Nin, she is sometimes called "the wife of Nin," and in one place "the wife of Asshur." She is likewise styled "the lady of Bit-Ana," "the lady of Nipur." Her worship was general, and her temples were numerous. At Erech (now Warka) she was worshiped on the same platform with Ana. At Calneh, or

Nipur (now Niffer), she shared fully in her husband's honors. She had a shrine at Ur (now Mugheir), another at Rubesi, and another outside the walls of Babylon. Some of these temples were very ancient, those at Erech and Nipur being built by Urukh, while that at Ur was either built or repaired by Ismi-Dagon. One record makes Beltis the daughter of Ana, and as "Queen of Nipur" she was "the wife of Nin." Beltis was "the Goddess of fertility and birth," "the Lady of offspring." The worship of Beltis was general throughout Chaldæa, and the magnificence of her temples prove the adoration of the Chaldæans and the Later Babylonians for her as the source of beauty and the dispenser of love.

Hea, or Hoa, the third of the first triad of deities, was the Sea-god, who, Berosus says, taught language and letters, art and science, and agriculture to the primitive Chaldees. Though he is represented as a fish-monster, Berosus calls him "the Great Giver of good gifts to man," and he also bears the title of "Lord of the abyss," and "Lord of the great deep." He was adored as the dispenser of life and knowledge, and as such his emblem was the serpent, which Eastern races generally employed as the symbol of more than human wisdom. Rawlinson considers the legend of Hea in the form of a serpent teaching men wisdom, as bearing some relation to the story of the serpent in the Garden of Eden, enticing Adam and Eve to eat the forbidden fruit of the tree of knowledge by promising them extended wisdom. The connection of Hoa with the introduction of letters is symbolized in the arrow-head in the cuneiform inscriptions. The Assyrian kings built him temples at Asshur and Calah. Davkina was the wife of Hoa, and her name signifies "the Chief Lady." Like Anata, Davkina had no distinctive titles or important position in the Pantheon, but took her husband's epithets with a simple distinction of gender. Merodach and Nebo were the sons of Hoa and Davkina.

Sin, or Hurki, the Moon-god, was the first deity of the second triad. He was called "the Powerful," "the Lord of the spirits," "He who dwells in the great heavens," "the Chief of the gods of heaven and earth," "the King of the gods," "the Bright," "the Shining," "the Lord of the month." As the patron and protector of buildings and architecture, he was styled "the Supporting Architect," "the Strengthener of fortifications," "the Lord of building." Bricks were under his protection, and the sign of the month under his special care was the one by which they were designated. His common symbol was the crescent, or new moon. The monuments represent him in the form of an aged bearded figure with illustrations of the different phases of the crescent near his head. The signet-cylinder of King Urukh, now in the British Museum, bears this representation of the Moon-god. In this figure he is represented as offering one hand in salutation in the presence of three worshipers standing before him. The Moon-god was the special object of kingly worship. Ur, or Hur, which derived its name from Hurki, was his sacred city, and here was the great temple built for his worship by King Urukh and his famous son and successor, Ilgi. This deity was likewise worshiped by the princes of Borsippa and Babylon, and one dynasty of Chaldæan monarchs bore the title of the *Sin* kings. The Moon-god was adored by the Chaldæans and Babylonians to the latest days of antiquity, through the period of Assyrian supremacy to the times of Nebuchadnezzar and Nabonadius, the last of whom restored his shrine at Ur and bestowed on him high-sounding titles, such as "the Chief of the gods of heaven and earth, the King of the gods, God of gods, He who dwells in the great heavens." In some inscriptions the Moon-god is called the eldest son of Bel-Nimrod. His wife, the Moon-goddess, called "the Great Lady," was often associated with him in the lists. Hurki and his wife were the tutelary deities of Ur, or Hur, and a part of the temple was dedicated to his wife. Her "ark" or "tabernacle," which was separate from that of her husband, was also deposited in this sanctuary.

It was called "the lesser light," while his ark was styled "the light."

San, or Sansi, the Sun-god—whose Semitic names were Samas, Shamas, and Shemesh—was the second deity of the second triad. He was regarded as the lord of the daylight, and was represented as lighting the universe. His emblem was the circle. He was called "the Lord of fire," "the Light of the gods," "the Ruler of the day," "He who illumines the expanse of heaven and earth," "the Regent of all things," "the Establisher of heaven and earth." The Sun-god inspired warlike thoughts in the minds of kings, and directed and favored their military expeditions. He caused the Chaldæan monarchs to assemble their chariots and warriors, and went forth with their armies and defeated their foes in battle. He extended their dominions, and brought them back to their own land as conquerors. He chased their enemies before them and crushed all opposition. He aided them to sway the kingly sceptre and to enforce their authority over their subjects. He was thus called "the Supreme Ruler who casts a favorable eye on expeditions," "the Vanquisher of the king's enemies," "the Breaker-up of opposition." As the sun diffused light and warmth throughout the realm of nature, so San lightened men's minds and hearts with wisdom and inspiration. The chief seats of the Sun-god's worship were at Larsa and Sippara. At Larsa was the great temple to San, called Bit-Parra, built by Urukh, and restored at times to as late a period as the age of Nebuchadnezzar. At Sippara the worship of this deity took precedence of all others, so that the Greeks called this place Heliopolis, or City of the Sun. The idolatry of the "Fire-king," Adrammelech, which the Second Book of Kings mentions as being set up in Samaria, was the worship of the Chaldæan Sun-god. At Sippara, called *Tsipar sha Shamas*, "Sippara of the Sun," in the inscriptions, was the large temple to the Sun-god which was repaired and adorned by many of the ancient Chaldæan kings, as well as by Nebuchadnezzar and Nabonadius.

Most of the signet-cylinders of the Chaldæan monarchs have the emblem of the sun among their symbols of divinity.

Ai, Gula, or Anunit, the wife of San, as the female power of the sun, was usually associated with the Sun-god in temples and invocations. Gula signifies "great." As a deity separate from her husband, she presided over life and birth. She was worshiped with her husband both at Larsa and Sippara, and her name appears on the inscriptions at both places. She is believed to have been the Anammelech whom the Sepharvites adored in combination with Adrammelech, the "Fire-king." In later times she had temples independent of her husband at Babylon and Borsippa, as well as at Calah and Asshur. Her emblem was the eight-rayed disk or orb, which is often associated with the four-rayed orb in the Babylonian representations, or sometimes an eight-rayed star, and frequently a star of only six rays.

Vul, or Iva, the Air-god—also variously translated as Bin, Yem, Ao or Hu—was the third god of the second triad. Like the Zeus of the Greeks and the Jupiter of the Romans, Vul wielded the thunderbolt and directed the storm and the tempest. The Chaldæan account of the great Flood represents Vul as thundering in heaven. He was considered the destroyer of crops, and consequently the author of famine, scarcity and pestilence. The "flaming sword" which he is said to have held in his hand is represented as his symbol on the tablets and cylinders, where it is figured as a thunderbolt. He was regarded as "the Prince of the power of the air." His usual titles were "the Minister of heaven and earth," "the Lord of the air," "He who makes the tempest to rage." He was the great destroyer in the realm of nature, but as the dispenser of rain he was adored as the source of the fertility of the nourishing earth. He was regarded as the protector of rivers, canals and aqueducts. Thus he was styled "the Careful and Beneficent Chief," "the Giver of abundance," "the Lord of canals," and "the Establisher of works of irrigation."

The name of King Shamus-Vul, son and successor of Ismi-Dagon, indicates that Vul must have been worshiped in early times, as that king set up his worship at Asshur, (now Kileh-Sherghat), in Assyria, where a temple was built to him and Ana conjointly. All through the period of Assyrian ascendency and to the end of the Later Babylonian Empire the Air-god was highly venerated. Shala, or Tala, was the wife of Vul, or Iva and her usual title is *sarrat* or *sharrat*, meaning "queen," the feminine of the word *sar*, which signifies "king," "chief," or "sovereign."

First among the deities who represented the five planets then known, was Nin, or Ninip, also called Bar, or Adar, who was the representative of Saturn. Bar, the Semitic name, and Nin, the Hamitic designation, signify "Lord" or "Master." Ninip signifies "Nin by name," or "He whose name is Nin." Barshen signifies "Bar by name," or "He whose name is Bar." In his character and attributes Nin most nearly corresponded to the Hercules of the Greeks, as he was adored as the god of strength and heroism, according to the testimony of the inscriptions. He boldly faced the foe in battle, and his name was invoked to encourage the warrior in the deadly conflict. He was styled "the Lord of the brave," "the Champion," "the Warrior who subdues foes," "He who strengthens the hearts of his followers," "the Destroyer of enemies," "the Reducer of the disobedient," "the Exterminator of rebels," "He whose sword is good." In character he thus very much resembled Bel-Nimrod and Nergal, and also the Greek Hera, the Roman Mars, and the Scandinavian Odin. The inscriptions call Nin, and not Hoa, the "Fish-god." His emblem was generally the fish; and on some reliefs he is represented as part man and part fish, and beneath are such titles as "the God of the sea," "He who dwells in the deep," "the Opener of aqueducts." On other tablets he is styled "the Powerful Chief," "the Supreme," "the First of the gods," "the Favorite of the gods," "the Chief of the spirits," and like titles. In his planetary character, he is called "the Light of heaven," "He who, like the sun, the light of the gods, irradiates the nations." In the sculptured courts of the Assyrian palaces, Nin is represented as a winged man-bull, the impersonation of strength and power. He guards the palaces of the Assyrian kings, who consider him their tutelary deity, and whose capital city, Nineveh, is named in his honor. Nin does not rank with the most ancient of the Chaldæan gods on the monuments; but as the Fish-god, whom Berosus represented as coming out of the sea to teach the Chaldæans letters and science, he must have been an object of veneration from primeval times. His oldest temples were the two at Calah (now Nimrud), and his temple at Nineveh was widely famed for its splendor, and is noticed in the "Annals" of Tacitus. His worship was very general throughout Chaldæa and Assyria, as is shown by the frequency with which his emblems are found among the inscriptions. As we have said, Nin was the son of Bel-Nimrod, and the inscriptions represent him as the husband and son of Beltis. One tablet calls Nin the father, instead of the son, of Bel-Nimrod. This contradiction is the result of the double character of Nin, who, as Saturn, was the father, but as Hercules, the son of Jupiter.

Merodach, or Bel-Merodach, represented the planet of Jupiter, and was called "the Old Man of the gods," "the King of the earth" "the Most Ancient," "Senior of the gods," "the Judge," and the like. He was regarded as the god of judgment, justice and right. He was believed to preside wherever justice was dispensed by kings sitting in the gates, the early seats of justice. He was considered the most spiritual of the Chaldæan deities, and in the Babylonian inscriptions he is classed as superior to all celestial and terrestrial divinities, under the title of Belrabu. The Tel Sifr tablets indicate that Merodach must have been worshiped in the early Chaldæan kingdom. He is believed to have been the tutelary deity of Babylon from the most remote antiquity, and as the city grew into importance his worship became more and more prominent.

The Assyrian kings always associated Babylon with Merodach, and in the Later Babylonian Empire his worship took precedence of that of the other gods. Herodotus minutely described his temple, and the prophet Daniel bore testimony to the devotion with which he was worshiped by the Babylonians. Nebuchadnezzar called him "the King of the heavens and the earth," "the Great Lord," "the Senior of the gods," "the Most Ancient," "the Supporter of sovereignty," "the Layer up of treasures," and the like; and attributed to this god all his glory and success. His emblem is not definitely known; but Diodorus states that the great statue of Merodach at Babylon was a figure "standing and walking," and such a form frequently appears upon the Babylonian cylinders. Merodach's wife, Zir-Banit, had a temple at Babylon, attached to her husband's, and is believed to have been the goddess whose worship was introduced into Samaria by the Babylonian colonists, and who is called Succoth-benoth in the Old Testament.

Nergal, the War-god, was the representative of the planet Mars, and his name, which is Hamitic, signifies "the Great Man" or "the Great Hero." In the Assyrian account of the Deluge, Nergal is alluded to as the destroyer; but he was chiefly celebrated for his power over the chase and the battle-field, thus partaking of the character and attributes of Bel-Nimrod, with which deity he is compared in the adoration bestowed upon him as the ancestor of the Assyrian monarchs. He was called "the King of battles," "the Champion of the gods," "the Storm ruler," "the Strong Begetter," "the Tutelary God of Babylonia," and "the God of the chase." He is usually coupled with Nin, who also presides over battles and hunting. The chief seats of Nergal's worship were the ancient cities of Cutha and Tarbissa. Cutha was the sacred city where he was said to "live," and in which was his famous shrine. The "men of Cuth," when transported as colonists to Samaria by the Assyrians, naturally "made Nergal their god," introducing his worship into the land of their forced adoption. Nergal's emblem was the famous winged man-lion, the impersonation of human intelligence and physical strength, as seen at the entrances of the great palaces of Susa and Nineveh. Of Nergal's wife, called Lax, only her name is known.

Ishtar, or Nana, was the representative of the planetary Venus, and in character and attributes she mainly corresponded with the classical goddess whose name the planet bears. Ishtar was her Assyrian name, and Nana was her Babylonian appellation. The Phœnicians called her Astarte, and the Hebrews Astoreth. Ishtar is styled in the inscriptions, "the Goddess who rejoices mankind," and her most common epithet is Asurah, "the Fortunate," or "the Happy." She is also called "the Mistress of heaven and earth," "the Great Goddess," "the Queen of all the gods;" and also "the Goddess of war and battle," "the Queen of victory," "She who arranges battles," and "She who defends from attacks." In the inscriptions of one monarch she is represented as "the Goddess of the chase." Her worship was general, and her shrines were numerous. She is often styled "the Queen of Babylon," and must have had a temple in that city. She likewise had temples at Asshur, Arbela and Nineveh. Her symbol, as represented on the cylinders, is the naked female form.

Ishtar, in her journey to the under-world, symbolized the disappearance in winter of the Life in nature as ushered in at spring. Ishtar is represented as going down to the House of Iskalla. Mr. Fox Talbot, the English Orientalist, gives the following translation of the descent of Ishtar to Hades, or the House of Iskalla:

"To the land of Hades, the land of her desire, Ishtar, daughter of the Moon-god Sin, turned her mind. The daughter of Sin fixed her mind to go to the House where all meet, the dwelling of the god Iskalla, to the house which men enter, but cannot depart from—the road which men travel, but never retrace—the abode of darkness and of famine, where earth is their food, their nourishment clay—where light is not seen, but in darkness they dwell—where ghosts, like birds, flutter their wings, and on the door and the door-posts the dust lies undisturbed.

"When Ishtar arrived at the gate of Hades, to the keeper of the gate a word she spake: 'O keeper of the entrance, open thy gate! Open thy gate, I say again, that I may enter in! If thou openest not thy gate, if I do not enter in, I will assault the door, the gate I will break down, I will attack the entrance, I will split open the portals. I will raise the dead, to be the devourers of the living! Upon the living the dead shall prey.' Then the porter opened his mouth and spake, and thus he said to great Ishtar: 'Stay, lady, do not shake down the door; I will go and inform Queen Nin-ki-gal.' So the porter went in and to Nin-ki-gal said: 'These curses thy sister Ishtar utters; yea, she blasphemes thee with fearful curses.' And Nin-ki-gal, hearing the words, grew pale, like a flower when cut from the step; like the stalk of a reed, she shook. And she said, 'I will cure her rage—I will speedily cure her fury. Her curses I will repay. Light up consuming flames! Light up a blaze of straw! Be her doom with the husbands who left their wives; be her doom with the wives who forsook their lords; be her doom with the youths of dishonored lives. Go, porter, and open the gate for her; but strip her, as some have been stripped ere now.' The porter went and opened the gate. 'Lady of Tiggaba, enter,' he said: 'Enter. It is permitted. The Queen of Hades to meet thee comes.' So the first gate let her in, but she was stopped, and there the great crown was taken from her head. 'Keeper, do not take off from me the crown that is on my head.' 'Excuse it, lady, the Queen of the Land insists upon its removal.' The next gate let her in, but she was stopped, and there the ear-rings were taken from her ears. 'Keeper, do not take off from me the ear-rings from my ears.' 'Excuse it, lady, the Queen of the Land insists upon their removal.' The third gate let her in, but she was stopped, and there the precious stones were taken from her head. 'Keeper, do not take off from me the gems that adorn my head.' 'Excuse it, lady, the Queen of the Land insists upon their removal.' The fourth gate let her in, but she was stopped, and there the small jewels were taken from her brow. 'Keeper, do not take off from me the small jewels that deck my brow.' 'Excuse it, lady, the Queen of the Land insists upon their removal.' The fifth gate let her in, but she was stopped, and there the girdle was taken from her waist. 'Keeper, do not take off from me the girdle that girds my waist.' 'Excuse it, lady, the Queen of the Land insists upon its removal.' The sixth gate let her in, but she was stopped, and there the gold rings were taken from her hands and feet. 'Keeper, do not take off from me the gold rings of my hands and feet.' 'Excuse it, lady, the Queen of the Land insists upon their removal.' The seventh gate let her in, but she was stopped, and there the last garment was taken from her body. 'Keeper, do not take off, I pray, the last garment from my body.' 'Excuse it, lady, the Queen of the Land insists upon its removal.'

"After that Mother Ishtar had descended into Hades, Nin-ki-gal saw and derided her to her face. Then Ishtar lost her reason, and heaped curses upon the other. Nin-ki-gal hereupon opened her mouth, and spake: 'Go, Namtar, * * * and bring her out for punishment, * * * afflict her with disease of the eye, the side, the feet, the heart, the head' (some lines effaced). * * *

"The Divine messenger of the gods lacerated his face before them. The assembly of the gods was full. * * * The Sun came, along with the Moon, his father, and weeping he spake thus unto Hea, the king: 'Ishtar has descended into the earth, and has not risen again; and ever since the time that Mother Ishtar descended into hell, * * * * the master has ceased from commanding; the slave has ceased from obeying.' Then the god Hea in the depth of his mind formed a design; he modeled, for her escape, the figure of a man of clay.

Go to save her, Phantom, present thyself at the portal of Hades; the seven gates of Hades will all open before thee; Nin-ki-gal will see thee, and take pleasure because of thee. When her mind has grown calm, and her anger has worn itself away, awe her with the names of the great gods! Then prepare thy frauds! Fix on deceitful tricks thy mind! Use the chiefest of thy tricks! Bring forth fish out of an empty vessel! That will astonish Nin-ki-gal, and to Ishtar she will restore her clothing. The reward—a great reward—for these things shall not fail. Go, Phantom, save her, and the great assembly of the people shall crown thee! Meats, the best in the city, shall be thy food! Wine, the most delicious in the city, shall be thy drink! A royal palace shall be thy dwelling, a throne of state shall be thy seat! Magician and conjuror shall kiss the hem of thy garment!'

"Nin-ki-gal opened her mouth and spake; to her messenger, Namtar, commands she gave: 'Go, Namtar, the Temple of Justice adorn! Deck the images! Deck the altars! Bring out Anunnak, and let him take his seat on a throne of gold! Pour out for Ishtar the water of life; from my realms let her depart.' Namtar obeyed; he adorned the Temple; decked the images, decked the altars; brought out Anunnak, and let him take his seat on a throne of gold; poured out for Ishtar the water of life, and suffered her to depart. Then the first gate let her out, and gave her back the garment of her form. The next gate let her out, and gave her back the jewels for her hands and feet. The third gate let her out, and gave her back the girdle for her waist. The fourth gate let her out, and gave her back the small gems she had worn upon her brow. The fifth gate let her out, and gave her back the precious stones that had been upon her head. The sixth gate let her out, and gave her back the ear-rings that were taken from her ears. And the seventh gate let her out, and gave her back the crown she had carried on her head."

Ishtar's return to earth symbolized the reappearance of spring.

The god Nebo represented the planet Mercury, and was the last of the five planetary deities. Nebo was the god of wisdom and intelligence, the patron and protector of knowledge and learning, and the teacher of mankind. His attributes were the same as those of the Greek Hermes. He was styled "the God who possesses intelligence," "He who hears from afar," "He who teaches," or "He who teaches and instructs." He thus somewhat resembled Hoa, whose son he is called in some inscriptions. Like Hoa, he had for his emblem the simple wedge or arrow-head, the primary element in the cuneiform writing, to signify his association with that god in the patronage of letters. Nebo's other titles were "the Lord of lords, who has no equal in power," "the Supreme Chief," "the Sustainer," "the Supporter," "the Ever-ready," "the Guardian over the heavens and the earth," "the Lord of the constellations," "the Holder of the sceptre of power," "He who grants to kings the sceptre of royalty for the government of their people." Sometimes he is classed with the inferior deities. His worship was more general in Chaldæa than in Assyria. In the later ages Borsippa was the chief seat of Nebo's worship, and there the great temple, called Birs-i-Nimrud, was consecrated to him. The ruins of one of his shrines are found on the site of the ancient Assyrian city of Calah, (now Nimrud), whence imposing statues of this god have been transferred to the British Museum. He was a favorite deity of the later Babylonian kings, many of whom were named after him, such as Nabonassar, Nabopolassar, Nebuchadnezzar and Nobanadius. Nebo's wife was Varamit, or Urmit, a name signifying "exalted," who was only a companion of her husband and had no special attributes. Besides the deities described, the Chaldæan Pantheon embraced a multitude of inferior divinities, of whom but very little is known.

It is thus seen that the Chaldæan religion was, from the most remote antiquity, an astronomical worship. The twelve constellations of the Zodiac were the sun's "twelve houses," and his proper abode was in the constellation of Leo. The planets likewise traversed twelve stages in their course, and each sign or "house" passed by any one of these celestial bodies was regarded as a seat of divine power, while the planets themselves were considered gods. Thirty of the fixed stars were associated with the planets as "counseling gods;" and twelve others in the northern heavens, and twelve in the southern firmament, were designated "the judges." The twelve "judges" above the horizon controlled the destinies of the living, while the twelve below were masters of the fate of the dead. Each of the twelve months of the year was assigned to one of the twelve great gods, beginning with Ana. The seven days of the week were controlled by the seven great heavenly bodies—the sun, the moon, and the five planets then known. The hours were assigned to certain stars.

Thus in the earliest twilight of Oriental history, more than four thousand years ago, the Wise Men of ancient Chaldæa—priests, bards, sages and prophets—by their observations of the heavens and their explorations of the paths of the celestial luminaries, became the great pioneers of astronomical science, and the founders of that semi-mythical and semi-scientific learning which became diffused throughout the whole West of Asia. The priests performed the task of watching the courses, positions and phases of the celestial orbs and luminaries, and estimating and calculating the influence of this ever-varying aspect upon the destinies of men and nations. The seer and the prophet endeavored to show how the good and evil fortune of the state was blended with conjunctions and oppositions in the starry firmament. Thus astrology became mingled with astronomy. In the Book of Daniel the Chaldæans are mentioned as interpreters of stars and signs. The following inscription has been deciphered from a tablet found at Nineveh: "If Jupiter is seen in the month of Tammuz, there will be corpses. If Venus comes opposite the star of the fish, there will be devastation. If the star of the great lion is gloomy, the heart of the people will not rejoice. If the moon is seen on the first day of the month, Accad will prosper." From that ancient period to the present there has prevailed among the superstitious, in all ages and nations, a belief that stars and astrological signs bear some relation to the fate of men and nations.

BIRS-I-NIMRUD.

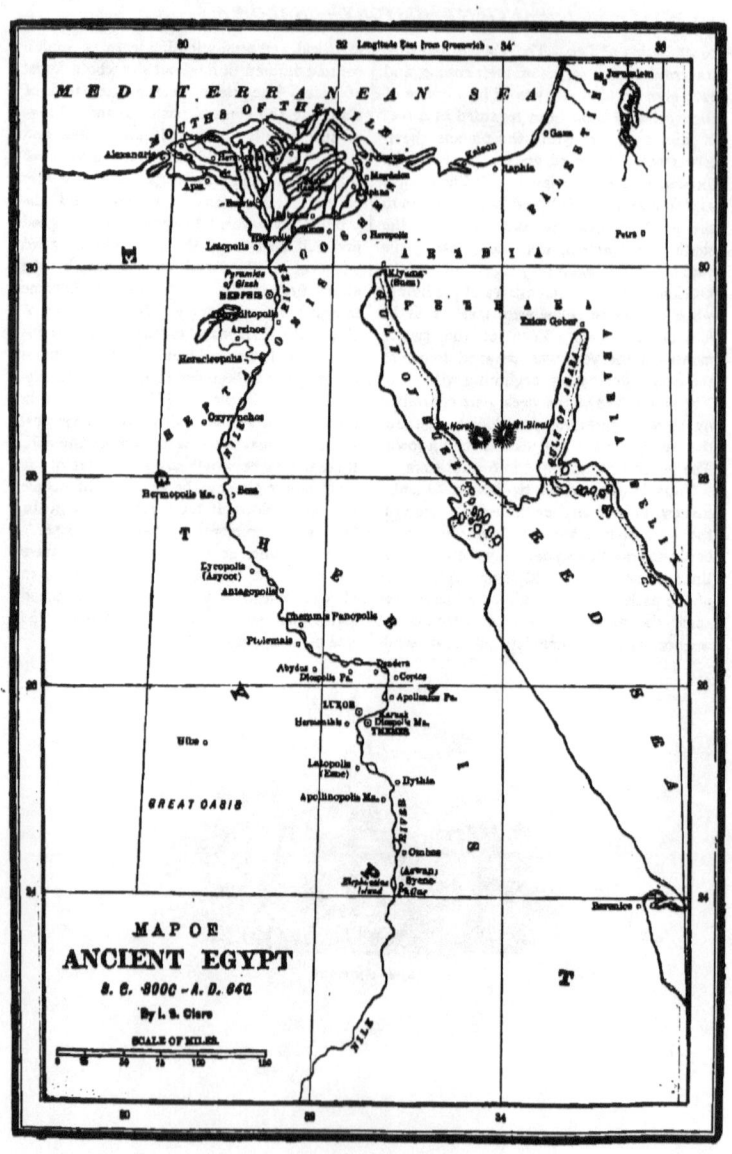

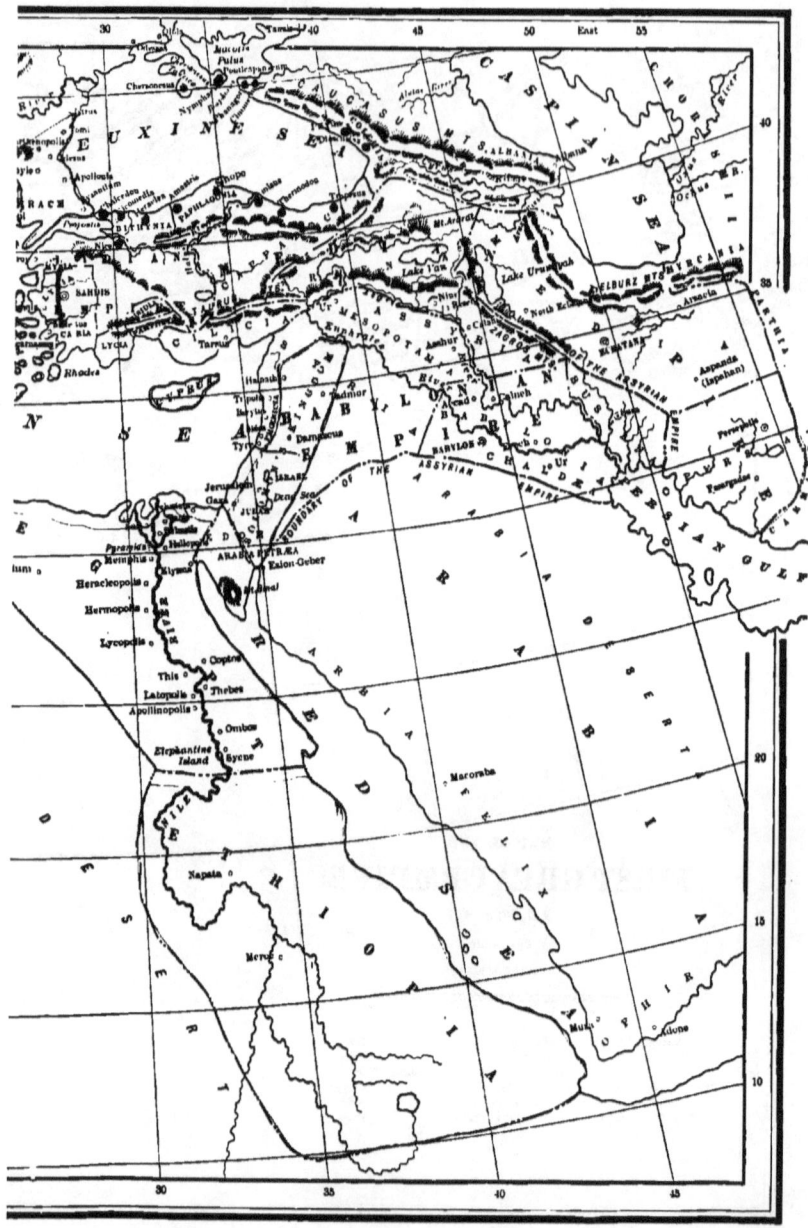

CHAPTER III.

THE ASSYRIAN EMPIRE.

SECTION I.—GEOGRAPHY OF ASSYRIA.

ASSYRIA, as we have seen, embraced the portion of the Tigris-Euphrates valley north of Chaldæa, or Babylonia—the region now known as Kurdistan. The soil of Assyria was not so fertile as that of Chaldæa, but was generally productive; and careful cultivation and irrigation brought luxuriant yields of various grains and vegetables; while such fruits as the citron, the orange, the lemon, the date-palm, the pomegranate, the olive, the vine, the fig and the apricot flourished in profusion, and the mulberry gave nourishment to an unusually large silk-worm found nowhere else; but ever since the fall of the Assyrian Empire the country has been exposed to the ravages of plundering nomad hordes and to the devastations of hostile armies, so that this region is now almost a wilderness.

Unlike Chaldæa, which, as we have observed, produced no stone or minerals of any kind, Assyria was supplied with an abundance of stone, iron, copper, lead, silver, antimony and other metals; while bitumen, naphtha, petroleum, sulphur, alum and salt were also yielded in sufficient quantities.

Assyria has a varied climate, but on the whole the summers are cooler and the winters more severe than in Chaldæa, because of mountain breezes from the Zagros and from Armenia; while there is also more moisture, and in portions of the country heavy rains, snows and dews fall during the winter and spring.

The wild animals of Assyria were the lion, the leopard, the lynx, the hyena, the jackal, the ibex, the gazelle, the jerboa, the bear, the deer, the wolf, the stag, the buffalo, the beaver, the fox, the hare, the badger, the porcupine, the wild cat, the wild boar, the wild sheep and the wild ass. The rivers abounded with fish, and the marshy thickets with wild fowl. The domestic animals were the camel, the horse, the ass, the mule, the ox, the cow, the sheep, the goat and the dog.

The true heart of Assyria was the country close along the Tigris between latitude thirty-five degrees and thirty-six degrees and thirty minutes north. Within these limits were the four great cities marked by the mounds of Khorsabad, Mosul, Nimrud and Kileh-Sherghat, besides a multitude of cities of minor importance. Three of the four great capitals of the Assyrian Empire were located on the east bank of the river; but the early capital, Asshur, now called Kileh-Sherghat, was on the west bank. The Assyrian ruins strew the country between the Tigris and the Khabour. Mounds exist along the Khabour's great western affluent, and even near Seruj, in the country between Harran and the Euphrates. But the remains on the east side of the Tigris are more extensive and more important. Nebbi-Yunus, Koyunjik and Nimrud—which have furnished by far the most valuable and interesting of the Assyrian monuments—are all situated on the east side of the Tigris, while the only places on the west side which have yielded striking relics are Arban and Kileh-Sherghat.

In Assyria, as in Chaldæa, four cities were in early times preëminent. The Book of

1—9.—U. H.   (137)

Genesis in speaking of the Assyrian emigration from Chaldæa, or the Land of Shinar, says: "Out of that land went forth Asshur, and builded Nineveh, and the city Rehoboth, and Calah and Resen." In the flourishing period of the Assyrian Empire we find four cities—Nineveh (or Ninua), Calah, Asshur and Dur-Sargina, (or City of Sargon)—all of which were cities of the first rank. Besides these four capitals, there were a vast number of minor cities and towns, so numerous that the whole country is strewn with their ruins. Among these minor places were Tarbisa, Arbil (or Arbela), Arapkha and Khazeh, in the region between the Tigris and the Zagros mountains, the ancient Assyria proper and the modern Kurdistan; and Harran, Tel-Apni, Razappa (or Rezeph) and Amida in the North-west; Nazibina, (or Nisibis) on the eastern branch of the Khabour; Sirki (or Circesium), at the confluence of the Khabour with the Euphrates; Anat on the Euphrates, a little below the junction; Tabiti, Margarisi, Sidikan, Katni, Beth-Khalupi, and others between the lower course of the Khabour and the Tigris.

On the east bank of the Tigris, opposite the present town of Mosul, are the ruins of the once-mighty city of Nineveh, the celebrated and magnificent capital of the Assyrian Empire when that monarchy was in the zenith of its greatness and splendor. The name Nineveh is read on the bricks, and a uniform tradition from the time of the Arab conquest gives the mound this title. These are the most extensive ruins of Assyria. As the city will be described in a subsequent part of this book, we will not enter into any minute description of the place in this connection. At the present town of Khorsabad, on the east bank of the Tigris, about nine miles north of Nineveh, are the ruins of Dur-Sargina (City of Sargon), chief of which are those of the magnificent palace erected there by the famous Sargon, one of the most celebrated of Assyrian monarchs. These ruins were brought to light in recent years by the excavations of that enterprising French explorer, M. Botta. The present town of Nimrud, on the east side of the Tigris, about twenty miles south of the ruins of Nineveh in a direct line, and about thirty miles by the course of the Tigris, occupies the site of the ancient Calah, the second great Assyrian capital city, whose ruins, among which are those of several royal palaces, cover an area of nearly one thousand English acres, which is little over half the area of the ruins of Nineveh. Forty miles south of Nimrud, at Kileh-Sherghat, on the west bank of the Tigris, are the remains of the ancient city of Asshur, the third great city and the early Asssyrian capital, whose ruins, marked by long lines of low mounds, are scarcely less in extent than those of Calah.

Four miles north-west from Khorsabad are the ruins of Tarbisa, among which are those of a royal palace and several temples. About twenty miles south-east of Khorsabad is the ruin of Keremles. About halfway between the ruins of Nineveh and Nimrud, or Calah, is Selamiyah, supposed by some to be the Resen of Scripture. About forty miles east of Nimrud was the famous city of Arabil, or Arbil, called Arbela by the Greeks, and still retaining its ancient designation. Besides these principal towns of Assyria proper, the inscriptions mention a large number of cities whose site is not known.

Considering the wonderful discoveries made in this field of ancient Oriental history within the last half century by the patience and diligence of such renowned explorers as Layard and Botta, the day may not be far distant when other ruins may be identified with undiscovered places recorded in ancient writings. Let us hope that the zeal of some future explorer may further add to our stock of knowledge of the ancient Oriental world.

SECTION II.—SOURCES OF ASSYRIAN HISTORY.

OUR sources of Assyrian history are the Greek historians, Herodotus and Ctesias, and the Assyrian monumental inscriptions. Little reliance can be placed upon exact dates relating to the annals of most of the very ancient nations. With Assyrian chronology, however, we can depend upon the accuracy of the two trustworthy documents already alluded to—the *Canon of Ptolemy*, a Babylonian record having important bearing upon Assyrian dates, and the *Assyrian Canon*, discovered and edited by Sir Henry Rawlinson in 1862, and which gives the succession of the Assyrian kings for 251 years, beginning with the year 911 B. C. and ending 660 B. C. These two documents not only harmonize remarkably with each other, but they agree admirably with statements of Berosus and Herodotus. According to Berosus, Assyria became independent of Chaldæa about 1300 B. C., and according to Herodotus half a century later, about the year 1250 B. C. From these sources, and from the inscriptions on Assyrian tablets, bricks and sculptures, we are able to fix the dates of Assyrian events with tolerable accuracy.

With respect to the duration and antiquity of the Assyrian monarchy, the two original authorities are the Greek historians alluded to at the beginning of the preceding paragraph, and between these two the judgment of the learned has since been divided. Ctesias maintained that the Assyrian monarchy had an existence of 1306 or 1360 years, and that it had almost as remote an antiquity as had the city of Babylon ; while Herodotus asserted that the Assyrian Empire had a duration of less than seven centuries, beginning about the year B. C. 1250, when a flourishing Empire had already existed in Chaldæa for more than a thousand years from the time of Nimrod. Ctesias was followed by such writers as Cephalion, Castor, Diodorus Siculus, Nicolas of Damascus, Trogus Pompeius, Agathias, Syncellus, Velleius Paterculus, Josephus, Eusebius, and Moses of Chorêné, among the ancients, and by Freret, Rollin and Clinton, among the moderns. Herodotus has been sustained by such modern writers as Volney, Heeren, B. G. Niebuhr, Brandis, the two Rawlinsons and many others. The English historians and Orientalists consider the Assyrian Empire as having ended in 625 B. C., while the French regard the year 606 B. C. as the date of that event.

Herodotus wrote within two centuries after the fall of the Assyrian Empire, and about thirty years before Ctesias. He had traveled extensively in the East, as well as in Egypt, and had availed himself of all the accessible sources of information, consulting the Chaldæans of Babylon and others. He was thoroughly honest and conscientious, and implicit reliance can be placed in the accuracy of his statements. He had especially endeavored to inform himself fully and correctly regarding Assyria, of which country he designed writing an elaborate work entirely distinct from his general history.

Ctesias also visited the East, spending seventeen years at the court of the Persian king. Being the court-physician to Artaxerxes Mnemon, he may have had access to the archives in the possession of the Persian monarchs. He was a man of such temper and spirit as to be disposed to differ with others. He flatly called Herodotus "a liar," and was therefore resolved to differ with him. He continually differs with Thucydides wherever they handle the same subject. He perpetually disagrees with Ptolemy on Babylonian chronology, and with Manetho on Egyptian dates. He is also constantly at variance with the cuneiform inscriptions, which generally confirm the statements of Herodotus. His Oriental history likewise contradicts the Old Testament, as he places the destruction of Nineveh at 875 B. C., long before the time of Jonah. The judgment of Aristotle, of Plutarch, of Arrian, among the ancients, and of Niebuhr, Bunsen and other modern historians and Orientalists, is all on the side of Herodotus, whose chronology is to be preferred, on every account, to that of Ctesias.

Herodotus assigns the year B. C. 1250 as the beginning of the Assyrian Empire, which, according to his account, lasted six and a half centuries. During the first five hundred and twenty years of this period, from B. C. 1250, to B. C. 730, the Assyrians maintained their supremacy over Western Asia, after which the Medes revolted and formed an independent kingdom east of the Zagros mountains. The Assyrian monarchy, thus reduced, lasted one hundred and thirty years longer, to the close of the seventh century before the Christian era, when the Medes took and destroyed Nineveh (B. C. 603). These dates, though nearer the truth than those of Ctesias, are not absolutely accepted by modern historians and Orientalists.

The chronology of Berosus coincides more nearly with that of Herodotus than with that of Ctesias. As his sixth Chaldæan, or Babylonian dynasty, which was Assyrian in race, began to reign about 1300 B. C., and as the Assyrian monarchy became independent when this dynasty was founded, it follows that the foundation of the Assyrian Empire dates from that year. As Berosus also placed the fall of the Assyrian Empire at 625 B. C., that empire must have existed six hundred and seventy-five years.

SECTION III.—POLITICAL HISTORY.

THE history of Assyria is divided into three periods—the period of its subjection to Chaldæa, from the time of the settlement of the Assyrians in the Tigris valley and Upper Mesopotamia to B. C. 1300; the Old Assyrian Empire (B. C. 1300-745); and the New or Lower Assyrian Empire (B. C. 745-625).

The origin of the Assyrians is shrouded in obscurity, although it is known that they were a Semitic tribe originally dwelling in Chaldæa, the Scriptural Shinar, and that they migrated to the middle Tigris valley during the general movement of Semitic and Hamitic tribes from "the land of Shinar," some time after Nimrod's death. Says the Mosaic account: "Out of that land went forth Asshur and builded Nineveh, and the city Rehoboth, and Calah, and Resen between Nineveh and Calah; the same is a great city."

It was before their settlement along the middle Tigris, and while they yet dwelt in the flat alluvial plain in the southern portion of the Tigris-Euphrates valley—that productive region where nature so readily supplied everything requisite for the support of man, with so little exertion on his part—it was there that the Assyrians had grown from a family into a tribe or nation, and had developed a religion and learned the most essential of the arts. The style and character of the Assyrian architecture indicates that it originated in the low flat alluvium where brick and bitumen were the only building materials. The cuneiform writing of the Assyrians also shows its Chaldæan origin; while their religion was very nearly identical with that of their southern neighbors, the only essential point of difference being that the chief Assyrian god, Asshur, was unknown in Chaldæa. The monumental and tablet inscriptions thus verify the statements of the Pentateuch, in representing the Assyrians as originally dwelling in Chaldæa, and at an early period migrating northward to the middle Tigris region.

It is not known whether the Semitic and Hamitic migrations from Chaldæa, their mother country, were voluntary removals on the part of the migrating tribes themselves, or compulsory colonizations inaugurated and carried out by the Chaldæan monarchs. One body led by Terah, Abraham's father, removed from Ur to Harran; another from the shores of the Persian Gulf to Syria, Canaan and Phœnicia; and a third, the Assyrian branch, larger than either of the other two, ascended the Tigris valley, occupied Adiabêné, with the neighboring districts, gave its own tribal name of Asshur to its chief city and territory, and was known to adjacent peoples first as a separate tribe, and afterwards as an independent and powerful nation. The date of their settlement in Assyria is uncertain, but it must have occurred before the reigns of the Chaldæan kings, Purna-puriyas and Kurri-galzu, in the fifteenth century before the Christian era. A temple to Anu and Vul was erected on the site of Asshur, as early as the nineteenth century before Christ, by Shamas-Vul, the son and viceroy of the Chaldæan king, Ismi-Dagon.

The Assyrians were likely at first governed in their new country by viceroys under the Chaldæan sovereigns. Bricks of a Babylonian description have been discovered at Kileh-Sherghat, the site of the ancient Asshur, the early Assyrian capital, which are believed to be older than any distinctly Assyrian remains, and which were in all probability stamped by these viceroys. Very soon, however, the Assyrians liberated themselves from the Chaldæan yoke and founded an independent kingdom of their own in their new abode, while the old Chaldæan Empire continued to flourish in the alluvial plain at the head of the Persian Gulf. The co-existence of these two kingdoms side by side is attested by a mutilated tablet of much later date, containing a synchronistic record of Assyrian and Chaldæan annals from a very remote antiquity. This tablet gives us the names of three of the most ancient Assyrian monarchs — ASSHUR-BIL-NISI-SU, BUZUR-ASSHUR and ASSHUR-UPALLIT—the first two of whom are recorded as having concluded treaties of peace with contemporary Chaldæan, or Babylonian sovereigns, while the third interfered in the domestic affairs of Chaldæa, deposing a usurper and restoring the rightful claimant, his own relative, to the throne. Intermarriages occurred between the royal families of Assyria and Chaldæa at this early period; and Asshur-upallit, the last of these three Assyrian kings, had given a daughter in marriage to the Chaldæan king, Purna-puriyas. On the death of the latter, his son, KARA-KHAR-DAS, became king of Chaldæa, but lost his life in attempting to put down a rebellion of his own subjects, and was succeeded by a usurper, Nazi-bugas. Thereupon Asshur-upallit marched an army into Chaldæa, defeated and killed the usurper, and placed Kurri-galzu, another son of Purna-puriyas, on the Chaldæan throne.

The tablet just referred to shows the power and influence of Assyria at this early day as fully equal to that of her more ancient southern neighbor. After the events just narrated Assyrian history is a blank for sixty years, only the names of the kings being known to us. The bricks of Kileh-Sherghat show us that Asshur-upallit was succeeded as king by his son, BEL-LUSH, or Bellikhus, who was followed in succession by his son PUDIL, his grandson VUL-LUSH I., and his great-grandson SHALMANESER I. All that is known of Bel-lush, Pudil and Vul-lush I. is that they erected at Asshur (now Kileh-Sherghat), which remained the capital of Assyria for several centuries later. This place, located on the west bank of the Tigris, was not favorably situated, the most fertile region of Assyria being on the east bank; but Calah and Nineveh were not yet built.

Shalmaneser I., who reigned from B. C. 1320 to B. C. 1300, is chiefly distinguished as the founder of Calah (now Nimrud), the second of those great cities which the Assyrian kings delighted to embellish with magnificent edifices, and which in the course of several centuries succeeded Asshur as the capital. Calah was advantageously situated on the east bank of the Tigris, forty miles north of Asshur, in a region of exceeding fertility and great natural strength, being protected on one side by the Tigris and on the other by the Shor-Derreh torrent, while it was defended on the south by the Greater Zab and on the north-east by the Khazr, or Ghazr-Su. The inscriptions of Asshur-izir-pal show us that Shalmaneser I. undertook expeditions against the tribes on the upper Tigris, and founded cities in that region, which he colonized with settlers brought from other distant quarters. Shalmaneser's extension of the Assyrian dominion to the northward ranks him as the first known Assyrian conqueror. With the death of Shalmaneser I. in B. C. 1300 ends the first period of Assyrian history—the period of its subjection to Chaldæa.

Shalmaneser I. was succeeded on the Assyrian throne by his son TIGLATHI-NIN I., the founder of the *Old Assyrian Empire*, which embraces the second period of Assyrian history (B. C. 1300-B. C. 745). The date of this monarch is seen to synchronize with the time given by Berosus as the beginning of the sixth Chaldæan, or Babylonian dynasty, and by Herodotus to the founding of the Assyrian Empire. The inscriptions mention Tiglathi-Nin as transferring to Assyria the supremacy hitherto claimed and exercised by Chaldæa, or Babylonia, in consequence of a successful war with the latter kingdom, which circumstance induced him to inscribe upon his signet-seal this title: "Tiglathi-Nin, King of Assyria, son of Shalmaneser, King of Assyria, and conqueror of Kar-Dunyas. Whoever injures my device or name, may Asshur and Vul destroy his name and country." This signet-seal, recovered six centuries later at Babylon by Sennacherib, shows that Tiglathi-Nin I. reigned personally for some time in that city, where he afterwards established an Assyrian dynasty of dependent kings—probably a branch of his own family. On a genealogical tablet he is called "King of Sumir and Accad," a title not bestowed on any of the other kings.

Chaldæa, or Babylonia, was not, however, from this time permanently subject to Assyria. Nearly a century after Tiglathi-Nin's conquest the Assyrian supremacy was shaken off, and Babylonian kings with Semitic names, and perhaps of Assyrian descent, were engaged in wars with the Assyrian monarchs. The Babylonian kingdom was not permanently subjected to the Assyrian dominion until the time of Sargon, in the latter part of the eighth century before Christ, and even under the dynasty of the Sargonidæ the Babylonians were constantly in revolt, and were only reconciled to Assyrian rule when Esar-haddon united the two crowns and reigned alternately at Babylon and Nineveh. Nevertheless, from the time of Tiglathi-Nin's conquest Assyria was recognized as the ruling power in the Tigris-Euphrates valley, as is fully shown by its conquest of, and its imposition of a dynasty upon, the southern kingdom. Its influence was therefore felt, even while its yoke was rejected; and from the time of Tiglathi-Nin's conquest, throughout the whole period of Assyrian ascendency in the Tigris-Euphrates valley, the process of Semitizing the Chaldæans went on; the names of the Babylonian kings during all this time being Semitic, whether those kings recognized the domination of Assyria or were at war with that power.

Tiglathi-Nin I., who was the eighth and last Assyrian king of the line founded by Asshur-bil-nisi-su, died about B. C. 1280. After an interval of half a century there followed another series of eight kings, known to us chiefly through the celebrated Tiglath-Pileser cylinder, which gives us the succession of five of them, but completed from the united testimony of several other documents, the most important of which are the Babylonian and Assyrian synchronistic tablet and the mutilated statue of the goddess Ishtar now in the British Museum, which bears an inscription giving the names and direct genealogical succession of the last three of these monarchs. The combined reigns of these eight sovereigns embraced about one hundred and sixty years, from about B. C. 1230 to B. C. 1070.

BEL-KUDUR-UZUR, the first king of this second series, is only known on account of his unsuccessful war with the contemporary king of Babylon. The Semitic line of kings established at Babylon by the Assyrians were dissatisfied with their state of vassalage; and during Bel-kudur-uzur's reign in Assyria, Vul-baladan, the Babylonian vassal ruler, attempted to throw off the yoke of his Assyrian suzerain, and the war which followed ended in the defeat and death of Bel-kudur-uzur in a great battle about B. C. 1210.

NIN-PALA-ZIRA was the second Assyrian monarch of this second series. It is not certain whether he was related to his predecessor, but he avenged his death. The inscriptions call him "the king who organized the country of Assyria, and established the troops of Assyria in authority." Soon after he ascended the throne, Vul-baladan of Babylon, encouraged by his triumph over Bel-kudur-uzur, invaded Assyria and attacked Asshur, its capital, but was completely defeated in a battle under the walls of the city and fled into his own dominions, leaving Assyria in peace during the remainder of Nin-pala-zira's reign.

ASSHUR-DAYAN I., the third king of the second series, enjoyed a long and prosperous reign, according to the inscription of Tiglath-Pileser I. He made a successful raid into Babylonia and returned to Assyria with valuable spoils. He also tore down the delapidated temple erected by Shamus-Vul, the son of Ismi-Dagon, at Asshur; and the structure was not rebuilt until sixty years later.

MUTAGGIL-NEBO, the son and successor of Asshur-dayan I., reigned from about B. C. 1170 to B. C. 1150. The Tiglath-Pileser inscription informs us that "Asshur, the great Lord, aided him according to the wishes of his heart, and established him in strength in the government of Assyria."

ASSHUR-RIS-ILIM, the son and successor of Mutaggil-Nebo, reigned between about B. C. 1150 and B. C. 1130; and the inscription of his son, Tiglath-Pileser I., calls him "the powerful king, the subduer of rebellious countries, he who has reduced all the accursed." The synchronistic tablet of Babylonian and Assyrian history informs us that he warred with Nebuchadnezzar I., or Nabu-kudur-uzur, of Babylon, who began the struggle by invading Assyria by way of the Zagros mountains, but was repulsed by Asshur-ris-ilim in person in this mountain region, and driven back. Nebuchadnezzar invaded Assyria a second time, directly from the south, but was defeated by Asshur-ris-ilim's general, and driven back, leaving to the victorious Assyrians forty chariots and a banner.

TIGLATH-PILESER I., the son and successor of Asshur-ris-ilim, who died about B. C. 1130, was the first Assyrian king of whose history we possess elaborate details. The discovery of his inscription on two duplicate cylinders, now in the British Museum, and which was translated in 1857 by Sir Henry Rawlinson, Mr. Fox Talbot, Dr. Hincks and M. Oppert, has given us the record of events during the first five years of his reign.

The Tiglath-Pileser inscription begins by naming and glorifying the "great gods" who "rule over heaven and earth," and who are "the guardians of the kingdom of Tiglath-Pileser." These deities are "Asshur, the great Lord, ruling supreme over the gods; Bel the lord, father of the gods, lord of the world; Sin, the leader, the lord of empire; Shamas, the establisher of heaven and earth; Vul, he who causes the tempest to rage over hostile lands; Nin, the champion who subdues evil spirits and enemies; and Ishtar, the source of the gods, the queen of victory, she who arranges battles." These gods, it is said in this inscription, have placed Tiglath-Pileser upon his throne, have "made him firm, have confided to him the supreme crown, have appointed him in might to the sovereignty of the people of Bel, and have granted him preëminence, exaltation and warlike power;" and are invoked to make the "duration of his empire continue forever to his royal posterity, lasting as the great temple of Kharris-Matira."

Then follows a self-glorification of the king with an enumeration of his titles, thus: "Tiglath-Pileser, the powerful king, king of the people of various tongues; king of the four regions; king of all kings; lord of lords; the supreme; monarch of monarchs; the illustrions chief, who, under the auspices of the Sun-god, being armed with the scepter and girt with the girdle of power over mankind, rules over all the people of Bel; the mighty prince, whose praise is blazoned forth among the kings; the exalted sovereign, whose servants Asshur has appointed to the government of the four regions, and whose name he has made celebrated to posterity; the conqueror of many plains and mountains of the Upper and Lower country; the victorious hero, the terror of whose name has overwhelmed all regions; the bright constellation who, as he wished, has warred against foreign countries, and under the auspices of Bel—there being no equal to him—has subdued the enemies of Asshur."

Tiglath-Pileser then recounts his conquests during his first five years as king. The first people he subdued were the Muskai, or Moschians—believed to be the Meshech of the Old Testament—who were governed by five kings and inhabited the countries of Alzi and Purukhuz, parts of Taurus or Niphates. The Moschians had neglected for fifty years to pay the tribute due from them to the Assyrians; and at this time, with a force of twenty thousand men, they had invaded the neighboring country of Qummukh (afterwards Commagêné), an Assyrian dependency, and had subdued it; but were there attacked and defeated by Tiglath-Pileser I., who then conquered Commagêné, burned its cities, plundered its temples, ravaged the country, and carried away cattle and treasure as booty or tribute.

The following is a passage from this inscription: "The country of Kasiyara, a difficult region, I passed through. With their twenty thousand men and their five kings, in the country of Qummukh I engaged. I defeated them. The ranks of their warriors in fighting the battle were beaten down as if by the tempest. Their carcasses covered the valleys and the tops of the mountains. I cut off their heads. Of the battlements of their cities I made heaps, like mounds of earth. Their movables, their wealth, and their valuables I plundered to a countless amount. Six thousand of their common soldiers, who fled before my servants, and accepted my yoke, I took and gave over to the men of my own territory as slaves."

The Moschians still refusing to pay tribute, Tiglath-Pileser conducted a second campaign in their country and again subdued them, completely overrunning Commagêné, which was annexed to the Assyrian Empire. He also attacked the neighboring tribes in their fastnesses, burned their cities and ravaged their territories. He likewise invaded the country of the Khatti (Hittites), because two of their tribes had committed an aggression on Assyrian territory, and completely chastising them, carried away one hundred and twenty chariots and much valuable booty. He also invaded the mountainous region of the Zagros, reduced its stronghold and seized much treasure.

Tiglath-Pileser's third campaign was against the Nairi tribes of the Euphrates valley in Northern Syria and Mesopotamia, the district subsequently known as Commagêné. These tribes were ruled by many petty kings. Those east of the Euphrates were easily conquered, but those west of the river were only subdued after a desperate and protracted struggle. The Assyrians gained a great victory, taking one hundred and twenty chariots, and pursued the Nairi and their allies to the Mediterranean. The country was frightfully ravaged, and the vanquished were required to pay a tribute of twelve hundred horses and two hundred cattle.

In his fourth campaign, Tiglath-Pileser attacked the Aramæans, or Syrians, who then occupied the narrow valley of the Euphrates for a distance of two hundred and fifty miles, from the territories of the Tsukhi, or Shuhites, between Anah and Hit on the south-east, to Carchemish, the capital and stronghold of the Khatti, or Hittites, on the north-west. Tiglath Pileser says in his inscription that he reduced this region "at one blow." He first plundered the east bank

ASSUR-BANI-PAL ENTHRONED. RELIEF FROM CALACH.

TIGLATH-PILESER STORMING A TOWN. PALACE OF NINEVEH.

of the river, and then crossed the stream in boats covered with skins, and burned six cities on the west bank and carried away a vast amount of booty.

Tiglath-Pileser's fifth and last campaign was against the land of Musr, or Muzr, in the upper part of the present Kurdistan, which was completely overrun, and its armies were defeated, its cities burned and its strongholds taken. Arin, the capital, was spared because of its submission, and a tribute was imposed upon the country. The Comani, who, though Assyrian subjects, had assisted the inhabitants of Musr, were punished for their defection by Tiglath-Pileser, who invaded their country, defeated their army of twenty thousand men, and took their towns and castles, some by storm and others without resistance, burning the former and sparing the latter, but destroying the fortifications of both; and the "far-spreading country of the Comani" was soon reduced to submission and an increased tribute exacted from it.

After this fifth campaign, Tiglath-Pileser's inscription sums up the result of his wars thus: "There fell into my hands altogether between the commencement of my reign and my fifth year, forty-two countries with their kings, from the banks of the river Zab to the banks of the river Euphrates, the country of the Khatti, and the upper ocean of the setting sun. I brought them under one government; I took hostages from them; and I imposed on them tribute and offerings."

The king next boasts of his hunting exploits. He says that he killed with his arrows in the country of the Hittites, "four wild bulls, strong and fierce;" and in the vicinity of Harran, on the banks of the river Khabour, he slew ten large wild buffaloes and took four alive. He took these captured animals, with the hides and horns of the killed beasts, to Asshur, his capital city. He also says that he slew nine hundred and twenty lions in his various journeys, and attributes all these exploits to the protection of the gods Nin and Nergal.

This great monarch then gives an account of the buildings which he had erected and of the improvements which he had introduced. Among these buildings are the temples to Ishtar, Martu, Bel, Il, and the presiding deities of the city of Asshur, his own royal palaces, and castles for the military defence of his dominions. Among his public improvements he mentions the construction of works of irrigation, the introduction of cattle and wild animals from other countries into Assyria, as well as of foreign vegetable productions, the increase in the number of chariots, the enlargement of his dominions, and the growth of the population.

Before speaking of the restoration of two old temples in the city of Asshur, Tiglath-Pileser gives an account of his descent from Nin-pala-zira, the founder of the dynasty, as follows: "Tiglath-Pileser, the illustrious prince, whom Asshur and Nin have exalted to the utmost wishes of his heart; who has pursued after the enemies of Asshur, and has subjugated all the earth—the son of Asshur-ris-ilim, the powerful king, the subduer of rebellious countries, he who has reduced all the accursed—the grandson of Mutaggil-Nebo, whom Asshur, the Great Lord, aided according to the wishes of his heart, and established in strength in the government of Assyria—the glorious offspring of Asshur-dayan, who held the scepter of dominion, and ruled over the people of Bel; who in all the works of his hands and the deeds of his life placed his reliance on the great gods, and thus obtained a long and prosperous life—the beloved child of Nin-pala-zira, the king who organized the country of Assyria, who purged his territories of the wicked, and established the troops of Assyria in authority."

The temple torn down by Asshur-dayan I., the great-grandfather of Tiglath-Pileser I., and which had stood for six hundred and forty-one years, was not rebuilt; and, after its site had remained vacant for sixty years, Tiglath-Pileser, soon after his accession, resolved upon the erection there of a new temple to the old gods, Anu and Vul, believed to be tutelary deities of the city of Asshur.

Tiglath-Pileser relates the circumstances

of the building and dedication of this new temple, as follows: "In the beginning of my reign, Anu and Vul, the Great Gods, my lords, guardians of my steps, gave me a command to repair this their shrine. So I made bricks; I leveled the earth; I took its dimensions; I laid down its foundations upon a mass of strong rock. This place, throughout its whole extent, I paved with bricks in set order; fifty feet deep I prepared the ground; and upon this substructure I laid the lower foundations of the temple of Anu and Vul. From its foundation to its roof I built it up better than it was before. I also built two lofty towers in honor of their noble godships, and the holy place, a spacious hall, I consecrated for the convenience of their worshipers, and to accommodate their votaries, who were numerous as the stars of heaven. I repaired, and built, and completed my work. Outside the temple I fashioned with the same care as inside. The mound of earth on which it was built I enlarged like the firmament of the rising stars, and I beautified the entire building. Its towers I raised up to heaven, and its roofs I built entirely of brick. An inviolable shrine for their noble godships I laid down near at hand. Anu and Vul, the Great Gods, I glorified inside the shrine. I set them up in their honored purity, and the hearts of their noble godships I delighted."

The other temple, which Tiglath-Pileser I. says he restored, was one to Anu only, which, like the one just mentioned, was originally built by Shamas-Vul, the son of Ismi-Dagon. This building had likewise fallen into decay, but had not been taken down like the other. Tiglath-Pileser says that he "leveled its site," and then rebuilt it "from its foundations to its roofs," enlarging and embellishing it. Inside the building he "sacrificed precious victims to his lord, Vul." In the temple he likewise deposited a collection of rare stones and marbles, which he had procured in the country of the Nairi during his wars there.

Tiglath-Pileser's inscription ends with the following lengthy invocation: "Since a holy place, a noble hall, I have thus consecrated for the use of the Great Gods, my lords, Anu and Vul, and have laid down an adytum for their special worship, and have finished it successfully, and have delighted the hearts of their noble godships, may Anu and Vul preserve me in power! May they support the men of my government! May they establish the authority of my officers! May they bring the rain, the joy of the year, on the cultivated land and the desert, during my time! In war and in battle may they preserve me victorious! Many foreign countries, turbulent nations, and hostile kings I have reduced under my yoke; to my children and my descendants, may they keep them in firm allegiance! I will lead my steps" (or, "may they establish my feet"), "firm as the mountains, to the last days, before Asshur and their noble godships! The list of my victories and the catalogue of my triumphs over foreigners hostile to Asshur, which Anu and Vul have granted to my arms, I have inscribed on my tablets and cylinders, and I have placed, [to remain] to the last days, in the temple of my lords, Anu and Vul. And I have made clean the tablets of Shamas-Vul, my ancestor; I have made sacrifices, and sacrificed victims before them, and have set them up in their places. In after times, and in the latter days * * * if the temples of the Great Gods, my lords Anu and Vul, and these shrines should become old and fall into decay, may the prince who comes after me repair the ruins! May he raise altars and sacrifice victims before my tablets and cylinders, and may he set them up again in their places, and may he inscribe his name on them together with my name! As Anu and Vul, the Great Gods, have ordained, may he worship honestly with a good heart and a full trust! Whoever shall abrade or injure my tablets and cylinders, or shall moisten them with water, or scorch them with fire, or expose them to the air, or in the holy place of God shall assign them a place where they cannot be seen or understood, or shall erase the writing and inscribe his own name, or shall divide the sculptures and break them off from my tablets, may Anu and Vul, the Great

POLITICAL HISTORY.   147

Gods, my lords, consign his name to perdition! May they curse him with an irrevocable curse! May they cause his sovereignty to perish! May they pluck out the stability of the throne of his empire! Let not his offspring survive him in the kingdom! Let his servants be broken! Let his troops be defeated! Let him fly vanquished before his enemies! May Vul in his fury tear up the produce of his land! May a scarcity of food and of the necessaries of life afflict his country! For one day may he not be called happy! May his name and his race perish!"

The document is then dated—"In the month Kuzalla (Chisleu), on the 29th day, in the year presided over by Ina-iliya-pallik, the Rabbi-Turi."

The most striking feature of Tiglath-Pileser's inscription is its religious tone. His wars are not only wars of conquest, but they are religious wars, designed to extend the worship of Asshur, as well as to enlarge the dominion of the Assyrian monarch. All the king's successes in war and hunting are ascribed to the aid and favor of Asshur. The wars were undertaken to chastise the enemies of Asshur, as the Hebrews fought to punish the enemies of Jehovah. The commanding position which religion occupied in the hearts of the Assyrian kings and people is proven by the long and solemn invocation of the Great Gods, the religious character and purposes of the wars, the account given of the building and renovation of the temples, the dedication of offerings, and the characteristic final prayer. The deep earnestness of this religious faith of the Assyrians, in its outward manifestations, displayed a zeal and fanaticism akin to that of the Israelites in their wars with the Canaanites, Philistines and other nations, or to that of the followers of Mohammed in their warfare against the foes of Islam. The Assyrian king glorifies himself much, but he glorifies the gods more. While fighting for his own credit and the extension of his own dominion, he likewise fights for the honor and glory of Asshur, the Great Lord, and the other Great Gods, whom the neighboring nations reject. His buildings are temples for the worship of the gods. His whole mind is deeply imbued with religious feeling, showing that the gods are "in all his thoughts." This religious feeling is highly exclusive and intolerant.

The king, while exalting himself, is still "the illustrious chief, who, under the auspices of the Sun-god, rules over the people of Bel," and "whose servants Asshur has appointed to the government of the four regions." If his enemies fly, "the fear of Asshur has overwhelmed them; if they refuse tribute, they withhold the offerings due to Asshur." The king himself feels inclined to make an expedition against a country; "his lord Asshur, invites him" to proceed thither; if he collects an army, "Asshur has committed the troops to his hand." When a country not previously subject to Assyria is attacked, it is because the people "do not acknowledge Asshur;" when its plunder is carried off, it is to adorn and enrich the temples of Asshur and the other gods; when it yields, the first thing is to "attach it to the worship of Asshur." The king hunts "under the auspices of Nin and Nergal," or of "Nin and Asshur;" he puts his tablets under the protection of Anu and Vul; he attributes the long life of one ancestor to his exceeding piety, and the prosperity of another to the protection which Asshur bestowed upon him. The name of Asshur occurs in the inscription almost forty times, or once in nearly every paragraph. Shamas, the Sun-god, and the gods Anu, Vul and Bel, are mentioned frequently; while Sin, the Moon-god, and the deities Nin, Nergal, Ishtar, Beltis, Martu and Il, are also acknowledged. All this is on an historical inscription.

The energetic character of Tiglath-Pileser I. is fully attested by his military exploits during the first five years of his reign, as displayed in the conquest of six neighboring nations and many petty tribes; the humbling of forty-two kings; the traversing of difficult mountain regions; the victories in battle; the sieges of towns; the storming and destruction of strongholds; the ravaging of countries; the incessant employment of the monarch; his pursuit of the chase; his contests with the wild bull and the lion, in which he rivaled "the mighty hunter before the Lord," counting his victims by the hundreds; while all this time he was concerned for the welfare of his dominions, as shown in the magnificent structures which he erected, the introduction of the animal and vegetable products of other regions and climes, the fertilizing of the land by works of irrigation, and his measures in general, "improving the condition of the people, and obtaining for them abundance and security."

Asshur was still the Assyrian capital, and no other native city is yet named, though mention is made of "fortified cities." In his inscription Tiglath-Pileser calls himself "king of the four regions," and also "the exalted sovereign whose servants Asshur has appointed to the government of the country of the four regions." The Assyrian territory seems at this time to have been bounded on the east by the Zagros mountains, on the north by the Niphates ranges, on the west by the Euphrates, and on the south by Chaldæa, or Babylonia. The plunder of other countries poured wealth into Assyria, the introduction of enslaved captives cheapened labor, irrigation was improved, new fruits and animals were introduced, fortifications were repaired, palaces were renovated, and temples were embellished or rebuilt.

The countries bordering upon Assyria on the north, east and west exhibited conditions of political weakness, and were divided into a multitude of petty nations and tribes, the most powerful of which could raise an army of only twenty thousand men. These nations lacked the essential elements of unity, being divided into many separate communities governed by their own kings, who in times of war united against the common foe, but who were too jealous of each other to even select a generalissimo. On the Euphrates, between Hit and Carchemish, were, first, the Tsukhi, or Shuhites; next above them, on both banks of the river, were the Aramæans, or Syrians, who possessed many cities; and above the Aramæans, also on both sides of the stream, were the Khatti, or Hittites, who were divided into tribes, and whose chief city was Carchemish. North and north-west of the Khatti were the Muskai, or Moschi, a warlike people, who endeavored to extend their dominion eastward into the territory of the Qummukh, or people of Commagêné. The Qummukh occupied and ruled the mountain region on both sides of the upper Tigris, and had many strongholds, most of which were on the west bank of the river. East of the Qummukh were the Kirkhi, while south of them were the Naïri, who occupied the region from Lake Van, along the line of the Tigris, to the district called Commagêné by the Romans. The Naïri had, at least, twenty-three kings, each of whom ruled his own tribe or city. South of the eastern Naïri was the country of Musr, or Muzr, a mountain region densely inhabited and abounding in strong castles. To the east and south-east of Muzr were the Comani, or Quwana, the most powerful of Assyria's neighbors, like the Moschi, able to raise an army of twenty thousand men. The Comani and the people of Muzr were at this time close allies. Across the lower Zab, skirting the Zagros, were the many petty tribes who offered little resistance to the Assyrian arms.

Thus, late in the twelfth century before Christ, Assyria was a compact and powerful kingdom, surrounded on her eastern, northern and western sides, by weak neighbors. Centralized therefore under one monarch, Assyria, with a single great capital, was easily able to triumph over foes, who, although united in confederations to resist their common enemy, were easily dispersed after suffering a defeat. Only on her southern border did Assyria have a powerful neighbor in the ancient and venerable monarchy of Chaldæa, or Babylonia, whose Semitic sovereigns, although established in that country by Assyrian influence, had renounced all dependence upon their old protectors. Chaldæa, almost equal in territorial extent and population to Assyria, and as much centralized and consolidated in her government, served as a check to her aggressive and vigorous northern neighbor, thus preserving some semblance of the balance of power in Western Asia.

In addition to the great cylinder inscription of Tiglath-Pileser I., five more years of his annals exist in fragments, which give us accounts of the continuance of his aggressive expeditions, principally in the direction of the north-west, during which he subdued the Lulumi in Northern Syria, attacked and took Carchemish, and pursued the fleeing inhabitants across the Euphrates in boats.

Near the end of his reign Tiglath-Pileser I. marched an army into Babylonia, and ravaged its northern territories with fire and sword for two years, taking the cities of Dur-Kurri-galzu (now Akkerkuf), Sippara of the Sun, and Sippara of Anunit (the Sepharvaim, or "two Sipparas" of the Hebrews), Hupa (or Opis), on the Tigris, and finally the great capital, Babylon, itself.

After the capture of Babylon, Tiglath-Pileser I. led an army up the Euphrates, and took several of the cities of the Tsukhi. But the Babylonian king, Merodach-iddin-akhi, captured some of Tiglath-Pileser's baggage during his retreat from Babylon. The images of the gods which Tiglath-Pileser had carried with him in his expedition against Babylonia, to secure him victory by their presence, were captured by Merodach-iddin-akhi, who carried them to Babylon, where they remained over four centuries as mementoes of victory. The Synchronistic Tablet, the chief authority for this war, says nothing of the capture of these idols, but this fact is mentioned in a rock inscription of Sennacherib's at Bavain, near Khorsabad.

Thenceforth a spirit of hostility and jealous rivalry marked the relations between Assyria and Babylonia, and no more intermarriages occurred between their royal families, while wars between them were almost constant, nearly every Assyrian king of whose history we possess detailed knowledge, leading one or more expeditions into Babylonia.

In a cavern from which rises the Tsupnat, or eastern branch of the Tigris, near the village of Korkhar, about fifty or sixty miles north of Diarbekr, is a bas-relief sculptured on rock smoothed for the purpose, consisting of a figure of Tiglath-Pileser I. in his priestly dress, with the right arm extended and the left hand grasping the sacrificial mace, with the following inscription: "By the grace of Asshur, Shamas and Vul, the Great Gods, I, Tiglath-Pileser, King of Assyria, son of Asshur-ris-ilim, King of Assyria, who was the son of Mutaggil-Nebo, King of Assyria, marching from the great sea of Akhiri" (the Mediterranean) "to the sea of Nairi" (Lake of Van), "for the third time have invaded the country of Nairi."

Tiglath-Pileser I. was succeeded on the Assyrian throne by his son ASSHUR-BIL-KALA, of whom very little is known besides his war with Merodach-shapik-ziri, king of Babylonia, the successor of Merodach-iddin-akhi. This war is recorded on the Synchronistic Tablet, along with the wars of Asshur-bil-kala's father and grandfather, but the injured condition of this portion of the tablet prevents us getting details from it. A monument of Asshur-bil-kala's time—one of the oldest Assyrian sculptures yet remaining—bears witness that he was actuated by the same religious spirit displayed by his father, and that he also adorned temples and set up images of the gods. A mutilated female figure, supposed to be the image of the goddess Ishtar, discovered by Mr. Loftus at Koyunjik, and now in the British Museum, bears a dedicatory inscription, almost illegible, from which it appears to have been set up by Asshur-bil-kala, the son of Tiglath-Pileser I. and grandson of Asshur-ris-ilim.

It is supposed that Asshur-bil-kala reigned from about B. C. 1110 to B. C. 1090. His successor seems to have been his younger brother, SHAMAS-VUL I., of whom nothing is known except his building or repairing a temple at Nineveh. He is thought to have reigned from B. C. 1090 to B. C. 1070; being thus contemporary with Samuel or Saul in

Israel. During the eleventh century before Christ, Assyria for a time passed under a cloud, and its ancient glories were then eclipsed by the imperial splendor of the Israelitish kingdom under David and Solomon. For two centuries, between the reigns of Shamas-Vul I. and Tiglathi-Nin II., who, according to the Assyrian Canon, ascended the throne of Assyria in B. C. 889, Assyrian history is a blank. The very names of the kings are almost entirely unknown to us for three-fourths of this period, from about B. C. 1070 to B. C. 930. The inscription of Shalmaneser II., the Black-Obelisk king, speaks of certain cities on the west bank of the Euphrates being taken from ASSHUR-MAZUR, whose reign has been assigned to this period.

While Assyria, from the absence of records, at this time had apparently sunk into insignificance, her influence seems to have extended into Egypt, whose kings of the Twenty-second Dynasty beginning with Sheshonk I., or Shishak, a contemporary of Solomon, married Assyrian women of royal or noble birth, who gave Assyrian names to their children, thus introducing Semitic names in Egyptian dynastic lists.

When Assyria again emerged from darkness with the accession of ASSHUR-DAYAN II. about B. C. 930, Asshur was still the capital of the kingdom. Asshur-dayan II. was the first of a series of kings who repaired and enlarged public edifices, which is recorded to their honor in the inscription of a subsequent sovereign. Asshur-dayan II. reigned from B. C. 930 to B. C. 911. His son and successor, VUL-LUSH II., occupied the throne from B. C. 911 to B. C. 889. Nothing is yet known of the history of these two kings, no historical inscriptions of their reigns being yet found, and no exploits being recorded of them in the inscriptions of later sovereigns.

TIGLATHI-NIN II., the successor of Vul-lush II., reigned only six years; but according to the inscriptions of his son and successor, Asshur-izir-pal, on the Nimrud monolith, he recorded his military exploits and also the fact that he set up his sculptures at the sources of the Tsupnat river beside the sculptures set up by his ancestors, Tiglath-Pileser I. and Tiglathi-Nin I. The Assyrian Canon assigns the reign of Tiglathi-Nin II. between the years B. C. 889 and B. C. 883.

ASSHUR-IZIR-PAL, the son and successor of Tiglathi-Nin II., reigned twenty-five years, from B. C. 883 to B. C. 858, which period is one of the most flourishing in the annals of the Assyrian Empire. Asshur-izir-pal was an active and energetic monarch, and did not allow himself any repose. The limits and influence of Assyria were expanded in every direction, and her progress in wealth and the arts was so rapid that she suddenly attained a point not previously reached by any people. The size, magnificence and excellent artistic embellishment of Asshur-izir-pal's architectural structures, the high skill in the practical arts which they exhibit, the pomp and splendor of this reign which they imply, have excited the wonder and admiration of modern Europe, which has seen that the Assyrians nine centuries before Christ, or nearly twenty-eight centuries ago, had reached a degree of advancement in the inventions and arts of practical life equal to the boasted achievements of the modern ages.

Asshur-izir-pal's first campaign was in the north, in portions of Armenia, where he says he penetrated a region "never approached by the kings his fathers." Here he easily subdued the mountaineers, the Numi, or Elami, and the Kirkhi, from whom has been derived the name of the modern Kurkh, as applied to some ruins on the west bank of the Tigris, about twenty miles below Diarbekr, some remains of which have been transferred to the British Museum. Asshur-izir-pal took and destroyed the fortresses of these mountain tribes, and one captive was taken to Arbela, where he was flayed and hung up on the town wall.

Asshur-izir-pal's second expedition occurred in the same year as the first, and was directed against the tribes to the west and north-west of Assyria. He first overran the countries of Qummukh, Serki and Sidikan, or Arban, and reduced them to tribute. Then he took the field against the Laki of Central Mesopotamia, where the people of the city of Assura had rebelled, killed their governor, and invited a foreigner to govern them. The rebels submitted on Asshur-izir-pal's approach and surrendered to him their city and their new ruler, who was carried in fetters to Nineveh. The rebellious inhabitants were cruelly punished by Asshur-izir-pal, who plundered the city, gave the houses of the rebel leaders to his own officers, placed an Assyrian governor over the city, crucified some of the inhabitants, burned others, and cut off the ears and noses of the remainder. The other kings of the Laki submitted, and sent in their tribute readily, though it was "a heavy and much-increased burden."

In the second year Asshur-izir-pal undertook a third expedition. Marching northward, he reduced to submission the kings of the Naïri, who had recovered their independence, and exacted from them a yearly tribute in gold, silver, horses, cattle and other commodities. Ascending the Tsupnat river, or Eastern Tigris, he set up his memorial beside monuments hitherto erected on the same site by Tiglath-Pileser I. and by the first or second Tiglathi-Nin. The inscriptions also give Asshur-izir-pal's own account of his severe treatment of the revolted city of Tela, upon retaking it, in the following words: "Their men, young and old, I took prisoners. Of some I cut off the feet and hands; of others I cut off the noses, ears and lips; of the young men's ears I made a heap; of the old men's heads I made a minaret. I exposed their heads as a trophy in front of their city. The male children and the female children I burnt in the flames. The city I destroyed, and consumed, and burnt with fire."

Asshur-izir-pal's fourth campaign was in the south-east, where he crossed the Lesser Zab and entered the Zagros range, ravaged the fruitful valleys with fire and sword, took many towns, and exacted tribute from a dozen petty kings. On his return, he built a city which the Babylonian king Tsibir had destroyed at an early period, and named it Dur-Asshur, in gratitude for the protection bestowed upon him by Asshur, "the Great Lord," "the chief of the gods."

Asshur-izir-pal's fifth campaign was directed to the north. Crossing the country of the Qummukh and receiving their tribute, the warlike king invaded the Mons Masius and took the cities of Matyat (now Mediyat) and Kapranisa. He then crossed the Tigris and warred along the Niphates ranges against the people of Kasiyara and other enemies. He next invaded the country of the Naïri, where he says he destroyed two hundred and fifty strong walled cities, and put to death many princes.

Asshur-izir-pal's sixth campaign was in the west. He started from Calah (now Nimrud), where he crossed the Tigris, marched through Central Mesopotamia, received tribute from many subject towns, among which were Sidikan (now Arban), Sirki and Anat (now Anah). He then entered the territories of the Tsukhi, or Shuhites, took their city Tsur, and compelled them to surrender, although they were aided by the Babylonians; after which he invaded Babylonia, or Chaldæa, and chastised its people.

His seventh campaign was likewise against the Shuhites, who had rebelled against the Assyrian yoke and invaded the Assyrian territories, being aided by their north-eastern neighbors, the Laki. The allied army numbered twenty-thousand men, including many warriors who fought in chariots. Asshur-izir-pal first reduced the cities on the east bank of the Euphrates, and, as he says, "made a desert" of the banks of the Khabour, and impaled thirty of the chief captives on stakes, in punishment for the rebellion. He then crossed the river on rafts and defeated the Tsukhi and their allies with great slaughter, many of them being drowned in their flight across the river. Six thousand five hundred of the rebels were killed in the battle, and the west bank of the river was frightfully ravaged with fire and sword; cities and castles were burned, men were massacred, and women, children and cattle were carried away. One king of the Laki escaped, but another was carried in captivity to Assyria. An increased rate of tribute was exacted of the conquered people, and two new cities were built by the Assyrian king, one on either bank of the Euphrates, the one on the east bank being named after the king, and the one on the west bank after the god Asshur.

Asshur-izir-pal's eighth campaign was higher up the Euphrates, where the Assyrian monarch invaded the country of the Beth-Adina, to punish its people for giving refuge to Hazilu, the king of the Laki who had escaped capture after his defeat in the previous war. Asshur-izir-pal besieged the people of Beth-Adina in their chief city, Kabrabi, which he soon took and burned. The part of Beth-Adina east of the Euphrates, in the vicinity of the modern Balis, was overrun and annexed to the Assyrian Empire, and two thousand five hundred captives were settled at Calah.

Asshur-izir-pal's ninth and most interesting campaign was the one against Syria. After marching across Northern Mesopotamia, and receiving tributes from various nations and tribes on the way, the Assyrian king crossed the Euphrates on rafts and entered the city of Carchemish, where he received the submission of the Hittite king, Sangara, whose capital was that city, and of many other princes, "who came reverently and kissed his scepter." Then he "gave command to advance toward Lebanon." He entered the country of the Patena, which embraced the region about Antioch and Aleppo, and took their capital, Kinalua, located between the Abri (or Afrin) and Orontes; whereupon the rebel king, Lubarna, in alarm, submitted and agreed to pay a tribute. The Assyrian monarch then crossed the Orontes and destroyed some of the cities of the Patena, and marched along the northern flank of Lebanon to the Mediterranean. In this region he built altars and offered sacrifices to the gods, and then received the submission of the leading Phœnician states, such as Tyre, Sidon, Byblus and Aradus. He then went inland, and cut timber, set up sculptured memorials, and offered sacrifice on the Amanus mountains. Among the plunder which he carried to Assyria were cedar beams for his public buildings at Nineveh.

Asshur-izir-pal's tenth campaign, and the last recorded, was in the region of the Upper Tigris, where he defeated his enemies and overcame all resistance, burned cities and carried away many captives. The chief "royal city" which he assailed was Amidi, now Diarbekr.

During all his ten campaigns, which were prosecuted during the first six years of his reign, Asshur-izir-pal indulged in the sports of the chase. He records among his inscriptions that on one occasion he killed fifty large wild bulls on the east bank of the Euphrates, and captured eight of the same kind of beasts; while at another time he slew twenty ostriches and captured as many. This monarch's sculptures bear testimony that hunting the wild bull was a favorite recreation with him. He had a menagerie park in the vicinity of Nineveh, in which he kept various strange animals. He received, as tribute from the Phœnicians, animals called *pagûts*, or *pagâts*—believed to be elephants—which were placed in this zoölogical enclosure, where he says they throve and bred. A certain King of Egypt sent him a present of curious animals when he was in Southern Syria. In an obelisk inscription, designed to commemorate a great hunting expedition, he says he took all sorts of antelopes to Asshur and killed lions, wild sheep, red deer, fallow deer, wild goats, or ibexes, leopards large and small, bears, wolves, jackals, wild boars, ostriches, foxes, hyenas, wild asses, and other animals not yet identified. An inscription of his at Nimrud informs us that in another hunting expedition he slew three hundred and sixty large lions, two hundred and fifty-seven large wild cattle, and thirty buffaloes; and that he sent to Calah fifteen full-grown lions, fifty young lions, some leopards, several pairs of wild buffaloes and wild cattle, along with ostriches, wolves, red deer, bears, cheetas and hyenas. Thus, like his distinguished ancestor, Tiglath-Pileser I., Asshur-izir-pal was renowned alike as a warrior and a hunter.

Asshur-izir-pal surpassed his predecessors in the grandeur of his public edifices, and the profusion of sculpture and painting in their embellishment. The structures of the earlier Assyrian kings at Asshur were far inferior to the buildings of Asshur-izir-pal and his successors at Calah, Nineveh and Dur-Sargina. The mounds of Kileh-Sherghat have not revealed bas-reliefs or traces of buildings which can be compared with those which excite the wonder of the traveler at Nimrud, Koyunjik and Khorsabad. Asshur-izir-pal's great palace was at Calah (now Nimrud), which he raised from the condition of a provincial town to that of a metropolis of his empire. This palace was three hundred and sixty feet long and three hundred feet wide, had seven or eight large halls, and many more small chambers grouped round a central court one hundred and thirty feet long and almost one hundred feet broad. The longest hall faced toward the north, was the first room entered upon coming from the city, and measured one hundred and fifty-four feet in length and thirty-three feet in breadth. The others were of different dimensions, some almost as spacious as the largest one, while the smallest room had a length of sixty-five feet with a breadth of less than twenty feet. The chambers were nearly or altogether square, and none of them were more than thirty feet in their greatest dimensions. The entire palace was raised upon a high platform, constructed of sun-dried bricks, but cased on the outside with hewn stone. Of the two grand façades, one faced the north, and on that side was an ascent to the platform from the town; the other, in the opinion of Mr. Layard, faced the Tigris, which in ancient times flowed at the foot of the platform toward the west. On the northern front were two or three great gateways flanked with andro-sphinxes, or sculptured figures representing the body of a winged lion with the head of a man. These gateways led to the principal hall or audience chamber, which was lined throughout with sculptured slabs illustrating the king's various deeds, and which contained at the eastern end a raised stone platform cut into steps or stages, which Layard believes was designed to support the monarch's carved throne. A grand portal in the southern wall of the chamber, guarded on either side by sculptured representations of winged man-headed bulls carved out of yellow limestone, opened the way into a second hall much smaller than the first, and with less variety of ornament. This second hall was about one hundred feet long by twenty-five broad, and all the slabs which adorned it were ornamented with colossal eagle-headed figures in pairs, facing one another and separated by the sacred tree. This second hall was connected with the central court by an elegant gateway towards the south, and communicated likewise with a third hall towards the east. This third hall was one of the most remarkable apartments of the palace, and was better proportioned than most of the others, being about ninety feet long by twenty-six wide. It ran along the eastern side of the great court, with which it was connected by two gateways, and on the inside it was ornamented with more elaborately-finished sculptures than any other apartment in the palace. Back of this eastern hall was another hall opening into it, somewhat longer, but only twelve feet broad; and this led to five small chambers, which here bounded the palace. South of the great court were also two halls communicating with each other, but these were smaller than those on the north and west, and were less profusely adorned. Mr. Layard believes that there were also two or three halls on the west side of the court toward the river. Nearly every hall had one or two small chambers adjoining it, which were generally at the ends of the halls, and communicated with them by large doorways. The grand halls of this palace, so narrow for their length, were decorated on all sides, first with sculptures as high as nine or ten feet, and then with enameled bricks or patterns painted in frescoes to the height of seven or eight feet more. The rooms were sixteen or eighteen feet high. The square chambers had no other embellishments than inscribed alabaster slabs.

Asshur-izir-pal's sculptures display great boldness, force and spirit, but are usually clumsily drawn and roughly executed. Assyrian mimetic art suddenly sprung up at this period, the only specimens more ancient than this monarch being the rock-tablet of Tiglath-Pileser I., already referred to, and the mutilated female statue brought from Koyunjik to the British Museum and inscribed with the name of Asshur-bil-kala, the son and successor of Tiglath-Pileser I. Asshur-izir-pal's ornamentation was his own invention. Not a solitary fragment of a sculptured slab has been found about the mounds of Kileh-Sherghat, while bricks have been found in abundance. This monarch was the first to use bas-reliefs on a large scale for architectural ornamentation, and to employ them to illustrate the history of the monarch. This king likewise adorned his edifices by means of enameled bricks and painted frescoes upon plaster.

Asshur-izir-pal's sculptures attest the surprising advance made in manufactures by the Assyrians at this early period. The metallurgy of the time is represented by swords, sword-sheaths, daggers, earrings, necklaces, armlets and bracelets. The chariots, the harness of the horses, and the embroidery which adorned the robes, further attest the mechanical skill of the Assyrians in the age of this famous king. The sculptures bear testimony to the fact that this ancient people at this early day already reveled in luxury, and that in the useful arts, in dress, furniture, jewelry, etc., they were not far behind the moderns.

Besides the splendid palace which he erected at Calah, Asshur-izir-pal built many temples, the most important of which have already been described. They occupied the northwestern corner of the Nimrud platform, and consisted of two structures; one precisely at the corner, embracing the higher tower, or *ziggurat*, which stood out as a corner buttress from the great mound, and a shrine with chambers at the tower's base; the other, a little farther to the east, comprising a shrine and chambers without a tower. The tower of the first structure was partly built by Asshur-izir-pal's son and successor, Shalmaneser II. These temples were highly adorned with embellishments, both internally and externally; and in front of the larger one was an erection indicating that the Assyrian kings received divine honors from their subjects. On a plain square pedestal two feet high was raised a solid limestone block cut in the form of an arched frame, within which was carved a figure of the king in sacerdotal costume, with the sacred collar encircling his neck, and the five chief divine symbols represented above his head. In front of this figure was a triangular altar with a circular top, resembling the Grecian tripod. A stele of Asshur-izir-pal, resembling the figure just described, has been brought to England from Kurkh, near Diarbekr, and is now in the British Museum.

Asshur-izir-pal built a temple at Nineveh, which was dedicated to the goddess Beltis. A white stone obelisk, set up as a memorial of his reign, is now in the British Museum. The sculptures and inscriptions which commemorated his military and hunting exploits, and which covered the four sides of this monument, are now almost obliterated. The obelisk is a monolith, twelve or thirteen feet high, and two feet wide on the broader side of the base and less than fourteen inches on the narrower side. It tapers slightly and is crowned at the top by three steps or gradines. Fragments of two other obelisks erected by this great monarch were discovered at Koyunjik by Mr. Loftus, and are likewise now in the British Museum. One of these, in white stone, had sculptures on one side only, being mostly covered by an inscription recording his hunting exploits in Syria and his repairs of the city of Asshur. The other, in black basalt, had sculptures on every side representing the great king receiving tribute-bearers.

Asshur-izir-pal constructed a tunnel and canal by which the water of the Greater Zab was brought to Calah. He records this fact in his annals, and Sennacherib, who repaired the tunnel two centuries later, set up therein a tablet with an inscription commemorating Asshur-izir-pal as its author.

Asshur-izir-pal's favorite capital was Calah, although he beautified Asshur, the old capital, and the rising city of Nineveh. The continual spread of the Assyrian dominion northward necessitated the removal of the capital to a more central point than Asshur; and for that reason Calah, which was forty miles farther north, on the opposite or east side of the Tigris, was selected for the seat of government. Calah, located in the fertile and healthy region of Adiabênê, near the junction of the Greater Zab with the Tigris, was strongly protected by nature, being defended on either side by a deep river. The new capital rapidly grew to greatness, and palace after palace rose on its high platform, profusely embellished with carved woodwork, gilding, painting, sculpture and enamel; while stone lions, sphinxes, obelisks, shrines and temple-towers also adorned the scene. The lofty *ziggurat* attached to the temple of Nin stood forth preëminent amid the varied mass of royal palaces and sacred temples, giving unity to the whole.

After his glorious reign of twenty-five years, Asshur-izir-pal—who styled himself "The conqueror from the upper passage of the Tigris to Lebanon and the Great Sea, who has reduced under his authority all countries from the rising of the sun to the going down of the same"—died at no advanced age, and was succeeded on the throne by his son, SHALMANESER II.

Shalmaneser II. inherited the warlike spirit and genius of his illustrious father; and during his reign of thirty-five years, from B. C. 858 to B. C. 823, he conducted twenty-three military expeditions in person, and entrusted four others to a favorite general. His twenty-three expeditions were undertaken during the first twenty-seven years of his reign, and were directed against the territories of neighboring peoples. Babylonia, Chaldæa, Media, the Zimri, Armenia, Upper Mesopotamia, the country of the Upper Tigris, the Hittites, the Patena, the Tibareni, the Hamathites, and the Syrians of Damascus, were attacked by the armies of Shalmaneser II., their hosts defeated, their cities besieged and taken, their kings reduced to submission and forced to pay tribute.

Shalmaneser II. took tribute from the Phœnician cities of Tyre, Sidon and Byblus; from the Tsukhi, or Shuhites; from the people of Muzr, or Musr; from the Bartsu, or Partsu (believed to be the Persians), and from the Israelites. He thus traversed the entire region from the Persian Gulf on the south to the Niphates mountains upon the north, and from the Zagros range on the east to the Mediterranean sea on the west. Over this whole vast domain he made his power felt, while his influence extended beyond its limits, where the nations feared and respected him and willingly sought his favor by placing themselves under his protection. In the closing years of his reign he deputed the command of his armies to his favorite general, Dayan-Asshur, in whom he reposed great confidence. Dayan-Asshur held an important office in the fifth year of Shalmaneser's reign; and in the twenty-seventh, twenty-eighth, thirtieth, and thirty-first he was sent with an army against the Armenians, the rebellious Patena, and the people of the region included in modern Kurdistan. In his twenty-ninth year the king himself led an expedition into Khirki, the Naphates district, where he "overturned, beat to pieces, and consumed with fire the towns, swept the country with his troops, and impressed on the inhabitants the fear of his presence."

Shalmaneser's most interesting campaigns are those of the sixth, eighth, ninth, eleventh, fourteenth, eighteenth and twenty-first years of his reign. Two of these campaigns were directed against Babylonia, three against Ben-hadad of Damascus, and two against Khazail (Hazael) of Damascus.

In his eighth year, while Babylonia was rent by a civil war between King Merodach-sum-adin and his younger brother, Merodach-bel-usati, Shalmaneser II. invaded that kingdom ostensibly to aid its legitimate sovereign, but really for his own aggrandizement. He at once seized several Babylonian towns, and in the following year he defeated and killed the pretender to the Babylonian crown, entered Babylon and invaded Chaldæa, the country along the Persian Gulf, then independent of Babylon, and compelled its kings to become his tributaries. He informs us in his inscriptions that "the power of his army struck terror as far as the sea."

The wars of Shalmaneser II. in Southern Syria began in the ninth year of his reign. He had extended his dominion in Northern Syria over the Patena and most of the Northern Hittites. Alarmed at the rapid growth of the Assyrian power, Ben-hadad, King of Damascus; Tsakhulena, King of Hamath; Ahab, King of Israel; the kings of the southern Hittites; the kings of the Phœnician cities upon the coast, and others, formed an alliance, but their combined forces were defeated by the King of Assyria, with the loss of twenty thousand men killed in battle, while many chariots and much war material fell into the hands of the victorious Assyrians.

Five years later, in the eleventh year of his reign, Shalmaneser II. again took the field against Hamath and the Southern Hittites. Suddenly invading their territories, he took many towns without resistance; but Ben-hadad of Damascus joined the Hittites, and though the allies were again defeated by the Assyrian monarch, the latter did not succeed in extending his sway over Southern Syria. Three years afterward, Shalmaneser II. again attempted the conquest of Southern Syria. Collecting his people "in multitudes that were not to be counted," he crossed the Euphrates with an army of more than a hundred thousand men and marched southwards. This time he gained a decisive victory over the allied armies of Ben-hadad of Damascus, the Hamathites and the Hittites, who fled in dismay, losing many chariots and implements of war. The coalition at once fell to pieces, and the Hamathites and Hittites submitted to the conqueror's yoke, Damascus being deserted by her allies.

The next year Shalmaneser II. advanced against the Syrians of Damascus, who were strongly posted in the Anti-Lebanon fastnesses, and were under the leadership of their new king, Hazael, who had treacherously murdered Ben-hadad. Hazael raised an immense army, including over eleven hundred chariots, and took a strong position in the mountain range dividing the kingdoms of Damascus and Hamath, where he was attacked and utterly defeated by the Assyrian king, losing sixteen thousand men, eleven hundred and twenty-one chariots, a large amount of war material and his camp. This blow completely broke the power of Damascus, and three years later Hazael made no resistance when Shalmaneser II. again invaded Syria and took and plundered his towns. In his inscription, Shalmaneser II. says: "I went to the towns of Hazael of Damascus, and took part of his provisions." He next says: "I received the tributes of Tyre, Sidon and Byblus." Jehu, King of Israel—"son of Omri," as he is called in the Assyrian inscription—sent a

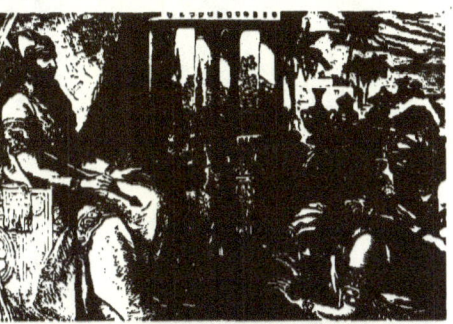

JEHU'S EMBASSY BEFORE SHALMANESER II.

quantity of gold and silver, in bullion and manufactured articles, as tributes to the Assyrian monarch. Sculptures at Nimrud represent the Israelitish ambassadors presenting this tribute to Shalmaneser II., the

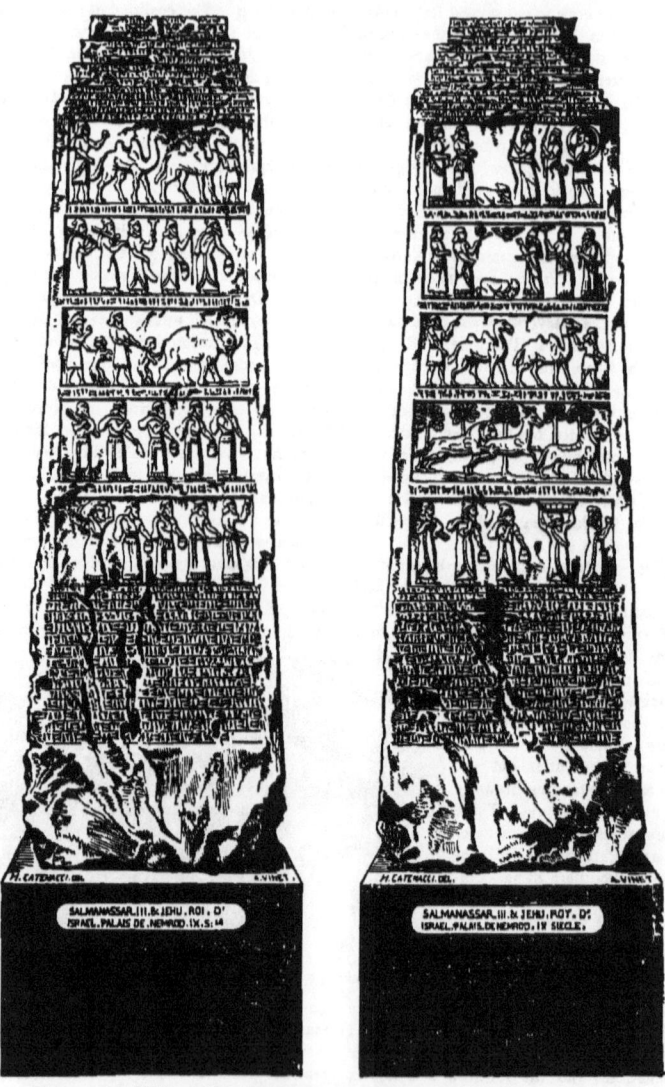

THE BLACK OBELISK OF SHALMANESER II.

articles appearing carried in the hands or on the shoulders of the envoys.

Like his distinguished father, Shalmaneser II. had great taste for architecture and the other arts. He completed the *ziggurat* of the great temple of Nin at Calah, which his father had commenced. He also built a more splendid palace than the one erected by his father on the same lofty platform of that city, about one hundred and fifty yards from the former palace. This is known as the "Central Palace" of the Nimrud platform, and was discovered by Mr. Layard on his first expedition. The ruined condition of this magnificent edifice rendered it impossible for its modern discoverer to obtain a clear idea of its ornamentation. Two massive winged man-headed bulls partially destroyed, in the grand portals of this great structure, and the sculptured fragments of bas-reliefs, which must have adorned its walls, illustrate its points of similarity to Asshur-izir-pal's great edifice. The sculptures of Shalmaneser's palace were on a grander scale and more mythological than those of his father's building.

A famous monument of Shalmaneser II. is an obelisk in black marble, in shape and general arrangement resembling that of his father already described, but of a handsomer and better material. This obelisk was discovered lying prostrate under the rubbish covering Shalmaneser's palace. It contained bas-reliefs in twenty compartments, five on each of its four sides, the space about them being covered with minute cuneiform inscriptions; the whole in an excellent state of preservation. It is somewhat smaller than Asshur-izir-pal's obelisk, being only seven feet high and twenty-two inches on its broad face. Its proportions make it more solid-looking and taper less than the former obelisk. The bas-reliefs represent Shalmaneser II., accompanied by his vizier and other chief officers, receiving tribute from five nations, whose envoys are ushered into the royal presence by officials of the court, and prostrate themselves at the feet of the Great King before they present their offerings. The gifts are mostly articles of gold, silver, copper bars and cubes, goblets, elephants' tusks, tissues, etc., and are carried in the hand; but there are also animals, such as horses, camels, monkeys and baboons of various types, stags, lions, wild bulls, antelopes, and the rhinoceros and elephant. As already related, the Israelites are one of the nations offering tribute. The others will now be noticed. The people of Kirzan, a country adjoining Armenia, present gold, silver, copper, horses and camels, and occupy the four highest compartments with nine envoys. The Muzri, or people of Muzr, or Musr, as we have observed, almost in the same region, bring various wild animals and fill the four central compartments with six envoys. The Tsukhi, or Shuhites, from the Euphrates, are represented by thirteen envoys, bringing two lions, a stag and various precious objects, such as metal bars, elephant tusks, and shawls or tissues; and are given four compartments below the Muzri. The Patena, from the Orontes, fill three of the lowest compartments, with a train of twelve envoys bearing gifts similar to those of the Israelites. A stele of Shalmaneser II., closely resembling those of his father, was brought to the British Museum from Kurkh in 1863.

Calah, where he and his father built their great palaces, was the usual capital of Shalmaneser II.; but he sometimes held his court in the new city of Nineveh, and also in the old capital, Asshur. At the latter place he left a monument in the shape of a stone statue representing a king seated, which was found by Mr. Layard in a mutilated condition. In his later years Shalmaneser II. was troubled by a dangerous rebellion of his eldest son, the heir apparent to the crown, Asshur-danin-pal. The rebellious prince had a powerful popular support, and was proclaimed king at Asshur, at Arbela in the Zab region, at Amidi on the Upper Tigris, at Tel-Apni near the site of Orfa, and in more than a score of other fortified places. The aged monarch called his second son, Shamas-Vul, to the command of the loyal troops, and this prince reduced the rebellious cities in succession and soon completely crushed the revolt. Asshur-danin-pal, the rebellious crown-prince, forfeited his claims to the crown by his treason, and is supposed to have been put to death; while his younger brother and conqueror, Shamas-Vul, became the heir to his father's kingdom, to which he shortly afterwards succeeded, upon Shalmaneser's death, in B. C. 823, after an active and glorious reign of thirty-five years.

SHAMAS-VUL II. reigned thirteen years, from B. C. 823 to B. C. 810. We will now briefly notice the extent of the Assyrian dominion at his accession. Since the time of Tiglath-Pileser I. the limits of the Assyrian Empire had been extended in different directions, but mainly toward the west and the north-west. In this direction the Assyrian limits had been pushed beyond the Euphrates over all Northern Syria, over Phœnicia, Hamath, and Samaria, or the Israelite kingdom. These countries were not, however, reduced to the condition of provinces; they still remained under their own native kings, and retained their administration and laws ; but they were virtually subject to Assyria, as they acknowledged the suzerainty of the Assyrian monarch, paid him an annual tribute, and allowed his armies a free passage through their territories. On the west the Assyrian Empire extended to the Mediterranean, from the Gulf of Iskanderun to Cape Carmel or to Joppa. The north-western boundary was the Taurus mountain range beyond Amanus, the region between the two belonging to the Tibareni (Tubal), who had submitted as tributaries. The northern limits were the Niphates range— "the high grounds over the affluents of the Tigris and the Euphrates"—where Shalmaneser II., set up "an image of his majesty." The eastern frontier was in the central Zagros region, the tract between the Lower Zab and Holwan, then called Hupuska. On the south the Assyrian kingdom was still bounded by the territories of the Babylonians and Chaldæans, who yet remained unconquered.

These conquests and changes, which converted Assyria's former enemies into subjects, brought the empire into contact with new enemies on her western, northern and eastern sides. In the west the Assyrians

ASSYRIANS GOING TO BATTLE.

came in collision with the Syrians of Damascus, and with the kingdom of Judah, through their tributary, Samaria, or Israel. In the north-west they found new foes in the Quin, or Coans, who occupied the farther side of Amanus, near the Tibareni, in a portion of what was subsequently called Cilicia, and the Cilicians also, who are now first mentioned. The Moschi had migrated from this section. On the north the Armenians were at this time Assyria's only neighbors. Toward the east were the Mannai, or Minni, about Lake Urumiyeh; the Kharkhar, in the Van region and in North-western

Kurdistan; the Bartsu, or Persians, then in South-eastern Armenia; the Mada, or Medes, east of the Zagros; and the Tsimri, or Zimri, in Upper Luristan. These new neighbors and enemies were all weak, and no powerfully-organized monarchy at this time existed to contest with Assyria the dominion of Western Asia. The Medes and Persians, afterwards so celebrated as powerful nations, at this period were no more important than the other insignificant tribes and nations upon the Assyrian borders. Neither of these kindred Aryan peoples had yet a capital city, neither was united under one sovereign, but each was divided into many tribes, headed by chiefs, and dispersed in scattered and defenseless towns and villages. They were thus in the same condition as the Nairi, the Qummukh, the Patena, the Hittites and other frontier nationalities whose comparative weakness Assyria had demonstrated to the world in a long course of wars in which she had uniformly triumphed.

Like his father, Shalmaneser II., Shamas-Vul II. resided principally at Calah, where he, like his father and grandfather, set up an obelisk, or rather a stele, to commemorate his exploits. This monument, covered on three sides with an inscription in the hieratic, or cursive character, contains an opening invocation to the god Nin, conceived in the usual terms, the king's genealogy and titles, an account of Asshur-danin-pal's rebellion and its suppression, and Shamas-Vul's own annals for the first four years of his reign. These inform us that he exhibited the same active and energetic spirit as his father and grandfather, conducting campaigns against the Nairi on the north, Media and Arazias on the east, and Babylonia on the south. The people of Hupuska, the Minni, and the Bartsu, or Persians, paid him tribute.

The fourth campaign of Shamas-Vul II. was against Babylonia, which country he entered from the north-east. He took a strongly-fortified position of the Babylonians after a vigorous siege, eighteen thousand of the garrison being slain, and three thousand made prisoners, while the city was plundered and burned, and the Assyrian monarch went in hot pursuit of the flying foe. Shamas-Vul II. next defeated the Babylonian king, Merodach-belatzu-ikbi, at the head of an allied host of Babylonians, Aramæans, or Syrians, and Zimri, on the river Daban; the allies losing five thousand killed, two thousand made prisoners, one hundred chariots, two hundred tents and the Babylonian royal standard and pavilion. The annals of Shamas-Vul II. here abruptly terminate; but it appears from other circumstances that from this time, for over half a century, Babylonia, which had for a long time been a separate and independent kingdom, was reduced to the condition of a tributary.

The stele of Shamas-Vul II. contains one allusion to a hunting exploit, stating that he killed several wild bulls at the foot of the Zagros, while leading his expedition against Babylonia. His stele consists of a single figure in relief, representing the king in his priestly dress, wearing the sacred symbols round his neck, standing with his right arm upraised, and enclosed in the usual arched frame. This figure is somewhat larger than life, and is cut on a single solid stone, and then set on a larger block serving for a pedestal. The figure closely resembles that of Asshur-izir-pal, already described.

Shamus-Vul II., upon his death, in B. C. 810, was succeeded on the Assyrian throne by his son VUL-LUSH III., who reigned twenty-nine years, from B. C. 810 to B. C. 781. The scanty memorials of this king consist of two slabs found at Nimrud, of a short dedicatory inscription on duplicate statues of the god Nebo, brought from the same place, of some brick inscriptions from the Nebbi-Yunus mound of Nineveh, and of short notices of the regions in which he conducted campaigns, contained in one copy of the Assyrian Canon.

Vul-lush III. was as warlike as any of his predecessors, and extended the Assyrian dominion in every direction. He led seven expeditions across the Zagros mountains into Media, two into the Van region, and three into Syria. He says that in one of his

POLITICAL HISTORY.

Syrian expeditions he reduced Damascus, whose kings had defied the repeated attacks of Shalmaneser II. He counts as his tributaries in this region, besides Damascus, the Phœnician cities of Tyre and Sidon, and the countries of Khuniri, or Samaria; Palestine, or Philistia; and Hudum (Edom, or Idumæa). On the north he received tokens of submission from the Nairi, the Minni, the Mada, or Medes, and the Bartsu, or Persians. On the south he ruled Babylonia like a sovereign, received homage from the Chaldæans, and in the great cities of Babylon, Borsippa and Cutha, or Tiggaba, he was permitted to sacrifice to the gods Bel, Nebo and Nergal. In one place he styles himself "the king to whose son Asshur, the chief of the gods, has granted the kingdom of Babylon;" from which it has been inferred that he appointed his own son viceroy of Babylon.

Thus, by the time of Vul-lush III., early in the eighth century before Christ, Assyria was master of Babylonia in the south, and of Philistia and Edom in the west. Her dominion thus skirted the Persian Gulf on the one hand and came into contact with Egypt on the other. At the same time she received the submission of some of the Median tribes on the east; and held Southern Armenia, from Lake Van to the sources of the Tigris, on the north. She was in possession of all Northren Syria, including Commagêné and Amanus, and had tributaries beyond that mountain range. She ruled supreme over the entire Syrian coast from Issus to Gaza; and her sway was acknowledged by all the tribes and kingdoms between the Mediterranean coast and the Syrian desert, such as the Phœnicians, the Hamathites, the Patena, the Hittites, the Syrians of Damascus, the Israelites, or Samarians, and the Edomites, or Idumæans. In the east she had subjugated nearly the whole region of the Zagros, and had tributaries in the highlands on the east side of that range. On the south she had either absorbed Babylonia, or made her influence supreme in that kingdom. Although she had not attained the highest pinnacle of her greatness until a century later, she was already, as described by the Hebrew prophet Ezekiel, "a cedar of Lebanon," whose "height was exalted above all the trees of the field; and his boughs were multiplied, and his branches became long," and "under his shadow dwelt great nations."

Vul-lush III. calls himself the "restorer of noble buildings which had gone to decay." On the Nimrud mound, between the north-western and south-western palaces, are chambers built by him, and on the Nebbi-Yunus mound of Nineveh are the ruins of a palace erected by him. The walls of the Nimrud chambers were plastered, and then painted in fresco with patterns of winged bulls, zigzags, squares, circles, etc. The superstitious regard of the natives for the supposed tomb of the prophet Jonah has thus far thwarted all efforts of Europeans to explore the Nebbi-Yunus palace.

Sir Henry Rawlinson discovered two rude statues of the god Nebo in a temple at Nimrud dedicated to that deity by Vul-lush III., along with four colossal statues of the same god, and two others resembling those now in the British Museum. These statues display no artistic merit, as Assyrian sculptors were trammeled by precedent and conventional rules in religious subjects, and in representations of kings and nobles, being thus limited by law or custom to certain ancient forms and modes of expression, which we see repeated with uniform monotony through all the periods of Assyrian history.

These statues are interesting as containing inscriptions showing that they were offered to Nebo by an officer who was governor of Calah, Khamida (Amadiyeh) and three other places for the life of Vul-lush III. and of his wife, Sammuramit, "that the god might lengthen the monarch's life, prolong his days, increase his years, and give peace to his house and people, and victory to his armies." This Sammuramit, wife of Vul-lush III., has been identified as the legendary Semiramis, whom the Greek historians represented as a woman of masculine qualities, the mightiest queen that ever reigned, and whose conquests rivaled or surpassed those of Cyrus the Great or Alexander the Great. This Sammuramit, or Semiramis, the Babylonian wife of Vul-lush III., gave that king his title to the Babylonian dominions, and reigned jointly with him both in Babylonia and Assyria. The exaggerated stories of this princess, as transmitted to modern times through the accounts of Herodotus and Ctesias, have been exploded in the present century; the renowned German historians, Heeren and Niebuhr, first pronouncing the story of her conquering career a myth, and patient explorers in the field of Assyrian antiquity substituting for the shadowy marvel of Ctesias a very prosaic Assyrian queen, a very common-place Babylonian princess, who never really executed great works or performed great exploits.

With the death of Vul-lush III., in B. C. 781, ended the brilliant Calah line of Assyrian sovereigns; and for a period of almost forty years Assyrian history is again involved in partial obscurity. The Assyrian Canon informs us that three monarchs reigned during this interval—SHALMANESER III. from B. C. 781 to B. C. 771, ASSHUR-DAYAN III. from B. C. 771 to B. C. 753, and ASSHUR-LUSH from B. C. 753 to B. C. 745. During this short period Assyrian conquests ceased, Assyrian glory for the time had passed away, and a general decline seems to have set in. None of these three kings left any important buildings, memorials or monumental records. The onward march of this great empire, which remained unchecked for over a century, was thus brought to a sudden halt.

At this point there is an apparent contradiction between the native Assyrian records and the incidental allusions to their history as found in the Second Book of Kings. The Scriptural Pul—the "King of Assyria" who came up against the land of Israel and received from Menahem a thousand talents of silver, "that his hand might be with him to confirm the kingdom in his hand"—is not mentioned in the Assyrian inscriptions, and is not named in the Assyrian Canon. The Scripture records would make Pul the immediate predecessor of Tiglath-Pileser II.; as his expedition against Menahem is followed, at most, thirty-two years later, by an expedition by Tiglath-Pileser II. against Pekah, King of Israel. Berosus represented Pul as a Chaldæan king, whom Polyhistor calls Pulus, and is believed to be the Porus mentioned in the Canon of Ptolemy.

During this interval of Assyrian darkness and decay, under the first three successors of Vul-lush III., the frontier kingdoms began to assert their power and independence. Babylon, which had remained under Assyrian sway since its conquest by Shamas-Vul II., the father and immediate predecessor of Vul-lush III., reëstablished its independence under Nabonassar in B. C. 747, from which point—thereafter known as the *Era of Nabonassar*—the Babylonians thereafter reckoned time. Enterprising Kings of Israel, such as Jeroboam II. and Menahem, also cast off the Assyrian yoke and extended their own dominions, as did the tribes of Armenia and the Zagros region. The reign of Asshur-dayan III. was disturbed by three formidable rebellions in the heart of Assyria itself—one at the city of Libzu, another at Arapkha, the chief town of Arrapachitis, and a third at Gozan, the chief city of Gauzanitis, or Mygdonia. The inscriptions do not inform us of the results of these revolts, but the degeneracy of the military spirit, and the voluptuous and luxurious disposition of the kings, give ground for the belief that the attempts made to subdue the rebels were failures. Asshur-dayan III. and Asshur-lush spent their reigns mostly in inaction and inglorious ease at their rich and luxurious capitals. At the close of this period of darkness and decline, Calah, the second city of the kingdom, revolted, and thus inaugurated the dynastic and political revolution which ushered in the brilliant period of the *New or Lower Assyrian Empire*, founded by the great Tiglath-Pileser II.

It has been supposed that it was during this period of general national weakness and decay, when an unwarlike sovereign was reveling in inglorious ease amid the luxuries and refinements of Nineveh, and when the Ninevites had abandoned themselves to vicious indulgences, that they were suddenly startled by a strange voice in their streets uttering the solemn warning: "Yet forty days, and Nineveh shall be overthrown!" A strange wild man clad in a rude garment of skin—a traveler unknown to the inhabitants, pale, emaciated, weary—proclaimed in every quarter of the great and luxurious city: "Yet forty days, and Nineveh shall be overthrown!" Coming as this cry did, when the glory of Assyria had departed, and when it had to defend its own existence against the foes it had subdued in the days of its former prosperity, the people were seized with consternation and alarm. This dismay invaded the royal palace, and his frightened servants "came and told the King of Nineveh," who then sat on his throne in the great audience-chamber, surrounded by all the wealth, luxury, pomp and magnificence of his court. The monarch at once "arose from his throne, and laid aside his robe from him, and covered himself with sackcloth and ashes." After having an edict framed, he "caused it to be proclaimed and published through Nineveh, by the decree of the king and his nobles, saying, Let neither man nor beast, herd nor flock, taste anything; let them not feed, nor drink water; but let man and beast be covered with sackcloth, and cry mightily unto God; yea, let them turn every one from his evil way, and from the violence that is in their hands." The fast thus commanded by royal authority was at once proclaimed, and the Ninevites, fearing the Divine wrath, clothed themselves in sackcloth "from the greatest of them even to the least of them." From joy and merriment, from revelry and feasting, the great city turned to lamentation and mourning. The people abandoned their vices and humbled themselves; they "turned from their evil way," and by a sincere repentance of their past sins they sought to avert their threatened doom. The haggard and travel-stained stranger who had alarmed the inhabitants of this great capital and metropolis to repentance, by announcing to them their threatened destruction, was the Jewish prophet Jonah. He sat in vain outside the eastern limits of the city, waiting to behold the destruction which he expected that the Lord Jehovah would visit upon the "great city," which then is said to have had "six score thousand persons that could not discern between their right hand and their left." The expected doom was not inflicted in forty days, and Nineveh was not overthrown until more than a century later.

With TIGLATH-PILESER II., who became King of Assyria in B. C. 745, began the *New or Lower Assyrian Empire* (B. C. 745-625) —the third and last, and the most brilliant, period of Assyrian history. Tiglath-Pileser II. was thus the restorer of Assyrian greatness. The circumstances of his accession are unknown to us, but he was the founder of a new dynasty, and Rawlinson thinks he was a usurper, and places no reliance upon the story of Bion and Polyhistor that this monarch rose from the humble station of a vine-dresser who had been employed in keeping in order the king's gardens. In his inscriptions Tiglath-Pileser II. is repeatedly represented as speaking of "the kings his fathers," and as calling the royal palaces at Calah "the palaces of his fathers," but he never gives the name of his actual father in any record that has come to the eye of modern archæologists and antiquarians. This circumstance gives ground for the conclusion that he owed his possession of the crown, not to the legitimate title of hereditary succession, but to the fortunes of a successful revolution which displaced the preceding dynasty.

Tiglath-Pileser II. undertook to effect the restoration of the Assyrian Empire by a series of wars upon his different frontiers, seeking by his unwearied activity and tireless energy to recover the losses occasioned by the imbecility of his predecessors. The chronological order of these wars, which was previously unknown, is now definitely determined by the Assyrian Canon. Among his many military expeditions only those undertaken into Babylonia and Syria are of any consequence. The expeditions of Tiglath-Pileser II. against Babylon occurred in the first and fifteenth years of his reign, B. C. 745 and 731. As soon as he was firmly seated upon his throne he led an army against Babylon, over which, according to the Canon of Ptolemy, Nabonassar then reigned, and against the other petty Chaldæan princes, among whom was Merodach-Baladan, who reigned in his father's city of Bit-Yakin. After attacking and defeating several of these princes, and taking the towns of Kurri-galzu (now Akkerkuf) and Sippara, or Sepharvaim, and other places in Chaldæa, Tiglath-Pileser II. compelled Merodach-Baladan to acknowledge him as suzerain and agree to pay an annual tribute, whereupon the Assyrian monarch assumed the title of "King of Babylon" and offered sacrifice to the Babylonian gods in all the chief cities (B. C. 729).

The first Syrian war of Tiglath-pileser II. began in the third year of his reign (B. C. 743), and lasted five years. During its progress he conquered Damascus, which had recovered its independence and was governed by Rezin. He also subdued Syria, where Menahem, Pul's old foe, was still reigning. He likewise reduced Tyre, whose reigning sovereign bore the common name of Hiram. The Assyrian monarch also subjected Hamath, Gebal and the Arabs bordering upon Egypt, who were ruled by a queen named Khabiba. He also defeated a large army under Azariah, or Uzziah, King of Judah, but failed to reduce him to submission. Tiglath-Pileser II. did not conquer Judæa, Idumæa, Philistia, Phœnicia, or the tribes of the Hauran, in his first war; and in B. C. 734 he renewed the struggle by an attack on Samaria, whose king at that time was Pekah, and taking " Ijon, and Abel-bethmaachah, and Janoah, and Kedesh, and Hazor, and Gilead, and Galilee, and all the land of Naphtali, and carrying them captive to Assyria," thus "lightly afflicting the land of Zebulun and the land of Naphtali," or the more northern part of the Holy Land, about Lake Merom, and thence to the Sea of Gennesareth.

Then followed the most important of the Syrian wars of Tiglath-Pileser II. The common danger united Pekah, King of Samaria, and Rezin, King of Damascus, in a close alliance; and when Ahaz, King of Judah, refused to unite with them they invaded his kingdom and attempted to dethrone him and put "the son of Tabeal" in his place. Ahaz applied to the King of Assyria for help, offering to be his "servant"— his vassal and tributary—if he came to his relief. Tiglath-Pileser II. gladly came to the rescue of Ahaz, and with a large army he entered Syria, defeated Rezin and besieged him in Damascus for two years, when he was taken captive and slain. The Assyrian king then invaded Samaria; and the tribes of Reuben and Gad, and the half tribe of Manasseh, who occupied the provinces east of the Jordan, were carried captive to Assyria and colonized in Upper Mesopotamia, on the affluents of the Bilikh and the Khabour, from about Harran to Nisibis. Some cities on the west bank of the Jordan, in the territory of Issachar, but belonging to Manasseh—among which were Megiddo, in the plain of Esdraelon, and Dur, or Dor, upon the coast—were also seized and occupied by the conquering Assyrians; and Assyrian governors were placed over Dur and the other leading cities of Southern Syria.

Tiglath-Pileser II. then marched southward and subdued the Philistines and the Arab tribes of the Sinaitic peninsula as far as the borders of Egypt. He deposed the native queen of these Arabs, and put an Assyrian governor in her place. Returning to Damascus, he there received the submission of the neighboring states and tribes; and before he left Syria he received submission and tribute from Ahaz, King of Judah; Mit'enna, King of Tyre; Pekah, King of Samaria; Khanun, King of Gaza; Mitinti, King of Ascalon; and from the Moabites, the Ammonites, the people of Arvad, or Aradus, and the Idumæans. Thus Tiglath-Pileser II. fully reëstablished the Assyrian power in Syria, and restored to his empire the territory from the Mediterranean on the west to the Syrian desert on the east, and from Mount Amanus on the north to the Red Sea and the frontiers of Egypt on the south.

Tiglath-Pileser II. afterwards sent another expedition into Syria, to quell the disorders occasioned by the revolt of Mit'enna, King of Tyre, and the assassination of Pekah, King of Israel, by Hoshea. The Tyrian king quickly submitted, and Hoshea agreed to govern his kingdom only as an Assyrian province; whereupon the Assyrian army retired beyond the Euphrates.

Calah was the chosen residence of Tiglath-Pileser II. Here he repaired and adorned the palace of Shalmaneser II., whose ruins are now in the center of the Nimrud mound. Here he also erected a new edifice, the most splendid of his structures. The sculptures which embellished Shalmaneser's palace were afterwards used by Esar-haddon to adorn his own palace. The new palace which Tiglath-Pileser II. built, was afterward ruined by some invader, and then built upon by the last Assyrian king. The excavations of this palace by Messrs. Layard and Loftus have revealed the ground-plan of the edifice, showing its arrangements of courts and halls and chambers, and the sculptures which ornamented the walls, representing animal forms, such as camels, oxen, sheep, goats, etc.

The Assyrian Canon gives Tiglath-Pileser II. a reign of eighteen years, from B. C. 745 to B. C. 727. He was succeeded by SHALMANESER IV. It is not known whether this monarch was related to his predecessor or not, but he is supposed to have been his son. Shalmaneser IV. reigned only between five and six years (B. C. 727-722). Soon after he became king he terrified Hoshea, King of Judah, into a renewal of his submission, so that "Hoshea became his servant and gave him presents," or "rendered him tribute." The arrears of tribute were rendered and the homage of the vassal king to his lord were paid. But soon afterward Hoshea, disregarding his engagements, was seeking the alliance of the King of Egypt. Says the Second Book of Kings: "And the King of Assyria found conspiracy in Hoshea; for he had sent messengers to So, King of Egypt, and brought no present to the King of Assyria, as he had done year by year." The native Pharaohs of Egypt had been friendly to Assyria, but the Ethiopian dynasty which had recently conquered Egypt was the natural foe of the Assyrians, and gladly accepted the proposals of Hoshea for an alliance against Shalmaneser IV. Hoshea then revolted against the Assyrian monarch, withheld his tribute and declared his independence. Shalmaneser at once invaded Judah a second time, and seized, bound and imprisoned Hoshea. A year or two later Shalmaneser led a third expedition into Syria and "came up throughout all the land," and laid siege to Samaria, B. C. 724. But the siege lasted two years, on account of the heroic resistance of the inhabitants, aided by the Egyptians; and the city was only taken after the reign of Shalmaneser IV. had been ended by a successful revolution.

While engaged in the siege of Samaria, Shalmaneser IV. was likewise prosecuting hostilities against the Phœnician cities, which had also revolted against Assyria after the death of Tiglath-Pileser II. Shalmaneser quickly overran Phœnicia in the first year of his reign, and forced all the revolted cities to submit to the Assyrian yoke. Insular Tyre soon again revolted; whereupon Shalmaneser reëntered Phœnicia, and collecting a fleet from the other Phœnician cities, Sidon, Palæ-Tyrus and Akko, he began the siege of Tyre. His sixty vessels were manned by eight hundred Phœnician rowers, coöperating with a smaller number of unskilled Assyrians. Shalmaneser's large fleet, however, was easily routed and dispersed, with the loss of five hundred prisoners, by a Tyrian fleet of only twelve vessels manned by skillful seamen. Shalmaneser thereupon abandoned active operations against the devoted city, but left a body of troops on the main-land to cut off the supplies of water which the Tyrians were in the habit of drawing from the river Litany, and from the aqueducts which conducted the water from springs in the mountains.

The Tyrians heroically held out against this pressure for five years, using rainwater, which they collected in reservoirs, to quench their thirst. It is not known whether they submitted, or whether the siege was abandoned, as the quotation from Menander, our only authority on this point, here breaks off abruptly.

Before either of the two great military enterprises of his reign were concluded, Shalmaneser IV. was hurled from his throne by a successful revolution, which put the usurper SARGON in his place. The monuments furnish us no knowledge of the circumstances concerning this usurpation, beyond the mere absence of Shalmaneser in Syria; but it is believed that discontent, caused by the distress in consequence of the king's long absence from the capital of his empire, and by his failure to speedily reduce Samaria and Tyre, encouraged Sargon in his usurpation. The usurper's station must previously have been obscure, or, at least, mediocre, as no inscription can be found in which he glories in his ancestry, or even names his father, as was the custom with the legitimate heirs and successors of Assyrian and Babylonian monarchs, but he only alludes to the Assyrian kings, in a general way, as his ancestors. Sargon, or Sargina, means "the firm" or "well-established king."

Sargon determined to confirm his doubtful title to the throne by the prestige of military success, and at once began a series of warlike expeditions. He conducted successive wars in Susiana, in Syria on the borders of Egypt, in the tract beyond Amanus, in Melitêné and Southern Armenia, in Media and in Chaldæa. His expeditions occupied the whole of the first fifteen years of his reign. Immediately upon his accession he invaded Susiana and defeated its king, Humbanigas, and Merodach-Baladan, the old enemy of Tiglath-Pileser II., who had revolted and made himself King of Babylonia. Though an important victory was thus gained, and many captives taken and transported to the country of the Hittites, the Susianian and Babylonian kings were not fully reduced to subjection. In the same year, B. C. 722, Samaria surrendered to Sargon's generals, after its two years' siege begun by Shalmaneser IV. Sargon punished the devoted city by deposing its native king and placing an Assyrian governor over it instead, and by carrying into slavery 27,280 of its inhabitants. On those who remained he re-imposed the rate of tribute to which the city had been subjected before its revolt. The next year, B. C. 721, Sargon was obliged to lead an expedition into Syria to quell a formidable revolt. The usurper, Yahu-bid, or Ilu-bid, King of Hamath, had headed a rebellion, in which the cities of Arpad, Zimira, Damascus and Samaria had participated; but the allied rebels were defeated by Sargon at Karkar, or Gargar, Yahu-bid and the other revolted leaders being taken prisoners and put to death.

Having crushed this revolt in Syria, Sargon marched southward against the Egyptians, who had extended their dominion over a part of Philistia. At Rapikh, on the Mediterranean coast, half-way between Gaza and Wady-el-Arish, or " River of Egypt "—the Raphia of the Greeks and Romans, and the modern Refah—the united forces of the Philistines under Khanun, King of Gaza, and those of Sabaco, or Shabak, the Ethiopian King of Egypt, were defeated by the Assyrian monarch ; Khanun being made prisoner, and Shabak seeking safety in flight, B. C. 720. Khanun was deprived of his crown and carried a captive to Assyria by his conqueror. The battle of Raphia is important as being the beginning of Egypt's subjection to the successive dominion of Asiatic and European nations—Assyrians, Babylonians, Medo-Persians, Greeks, Romans, Saracens and Turks.

After conducting unimportant wars toward the north and north-east, Sargon led another expedition towards the south-west in B. C. 715, five years after his victory at Raphia. He first chastised the Arab tribes who had made plundering raids into Syria, during which "he subdued the uncultivated plains of the remote Arabia, which had never before given tribute to Assyria," subjected the Thamudites and other Arab tribes, and settled a certain number of them in Samaria. The surrounding princes sought the conqueror's favor by sending him embassies and offering to become Assyrian tributaries. The King of Egypt, as well as It-hamar, King of the Sabæans, and Tsamsi, the Arab queen, thus became vassals to Sargon and sent him presents.

Four years afterward, B. C. 711, Sargon conducted a third expedition into this region to punish Azuri, King of Ashdod, who had revolted against the Assyrian monarch, withheld his tribute and incited rebellion among the neighboring princes. Sargon deposed Azuri and put his brother Akhimit on the throne of Ashdod in his stead; but the people of this Philistine city refused to recognize Sargon's creature as their king, and chose a certain Yaman, or Yavan, for their ruler, who, to secure himself, entered into alliances with the other Philistine cities, and with Judah and Edom. Thereupon Sargon led an army against Ashdod, but Yaman sought safety in flight, and "escaped to the dependencies of Egypt, which were under the rule of Ethiopia." The Assyrian king besieged and took Ashdod, and Yaman's wife and children, with most of the inhabitants, were transported to Assyria, while captives from other nations taken in Sargon's Eastern wars were colonized in Ashdod, over which an Assyrian governor was also placed. Shabak, or Sabaco, the Ethiopian king of Egypt, greatly terrified, sent an embassy imploring his favor, and surrendered the fugitive Yaman. In consequence of this suppliant attitude of the Ethiopian sovereign of Egypt, "the Assyrian monarch boasts that the King of Meroë, who dwelt in the desert, and had never sent ambassadors to any of the kings his predecessors, was led by the fear of his majesty to direct his steps towards Assyria and humbly bow down before him."

Sargon next led an expedition against Babylon, over which Merodach-Baladan had been quietly reigning for twelve years. Having established his court at Babylon, Merodach-Baladan formed alliances with Sutruk-Nakhunta, King of Susiana, and the Aramæan, or Syrian, tribes above Babylonia, to resist any attack by the Assyrian monarch. Nevertheless when Sargon advanced against Babylon, Merodach-Baladan fled to his own city, Beth-Yakin, leaving garrisons under his generals in the more important inland towns. At Beth-Yakin, which was situated on the Euphrates, near its mouth, the Babylonian king prepared for a stubborn resistance, summoning the Aramæans to his assistance. He posted himself in the plain in front of the city, and protected his front and left flank with a deep ditch, which he filled with water from the Euphrates. Sargon soon appeared at the head of his army, and defeated the Babylonian troops and drove them into their own dyke, where many of them were drowned, while the allies were also driven away in headlong flight. Merodach-Baladan shut himself up in Beth-Yakin, which was besieged and taken by Sargon. The Babylonian king himself became a prisoner, but his life was generously spared by his conqueror, who, however, plundered the palace and burned the city, and himself assumed the government of Babylonia, depriving Merodach-Baladan of his throne. In the Canon of Ptolemy, Sargon is called Arceanus.

Sargon then reduced the Aramæans and conquered a portion of Susiana, to which country he transported the Commukha from the Upper Tigris, placing an Assyrian governor over the mixed population, and making him dependent upon the Assyrian viceroy of Babylon. Thus the Assyrian dominion was firmly established over Chaldæa, or Babylonia, whose power was now completely broken. Thenceforth, with a few brief interruptions, Chaldæa remained an Assyrian dependency until the downfall of the Assyrian Empire in B. C. 625. Now and then, for a short interval, the unwilling subject kingdom cast off the conqueror's yoke only to be again reduced to a more humiliating state of vassalage, until it eventually submitted to the hand of fate and remained quiet. During the last half century of the Assyrian Empire, from B. C. 680 to B. C. 625, Babylonia was one of the most tranquil of its provinces.

While Sargon held his court at Babylon in B. C. 708 or 707, he received embassies from two opposite quarters, both from islanders dwelling "in the middle of the seas" that bordered on his dominions. One embassy was sent by Upir, King of Asmun, the ruler of the island of Khareg, or Bahrein, in the Persian Gulf; and the other by seven kings of Cyprus—princes of a country which was located "at the distance of seven days from the coast, in the sea of the setting sun"—who offered the great Oriental sovereign treasures of gold, silver, vases, logs of ebony, and the manufactures of their own country. By bestowing these presents the Cypriots acknowledged the suzerainty of the King of Assyria; and they carried home with them an effigy of their sovereign lord carved in the usual form, and bearing an inscription recording his name and titles, which they set up at Idalium, near the center of the island. This effigy of Sargon, found upon the sight of Idalium, is now in the Berlin Museum. In the inscriptions, "setting up the image of his majesty" is always a sign that a monarch has conquered a country. Such images are sometimes represented in the bas-reliefs.

Sargon's expeditions to the north and north-east also yielded successful results; and the mountain tribes of the Zagros, the Taurus and the Niphates—the Medes, the Armenians, the Tibarenians, the Moschians and others—were thus subdued. Ambris the Tibarenian, Mita the Moschian, and Urza the Armenian had become allies against their common foe, the King of Assyria; and their submission was only forced after a long and fierce contest. Ambris was deposed, and an Assyrian governor was placed over his country. Mita, after a resistance of many years, only agreed to pay tribute. Urza committed suicide, in despair at his defeat. But this region was only brought quietly under the Assyrian yoke when the King of Van was conciliated by the cession to him of a large extent of country which the Assyrians had wrested from Urza. Having rapidly overrun Media, Sargon seized a number of towns and "annexed them to Assyria," thus reducing a large part of that country to the condition of an Assyrian province. He erected a number of fortified posts in one part of the country, and imposed upon the Medes a tribute consisting wholly of horses.

After the fourteenth year of his reign, B. C. 708, Sargon resigned the leadership of his armies entirely into the hands of his generals. A disputed succession in Illib, a small country on the borders of Susiana, in B. C. 707, afforded him an occasion for interference in that quarter. Nibi, a pretender to the throne of Illib, had solicited the aid of Sutruk-Nakhunta, King of Elam, or Susiana, who held his court at Susa, from whom he received promises of support and protection. The other claimant, named Ispabara, thereupon sought and received the assistance of Sargon, who sent "seven captains with seven armies," and these defeated the troops of the King of Susiana and established Ispabara on the throne of Illib. The next year, however, Sutruk-Nakhunta invaded Assyria, and took some of its cities and annexed them to his kingdom.

In all his wars Sargon made use of the plan of wholesale deportation of populations. Israelites were thus transferred from Samaria to Gozan, or Mygdonia, and the cities of the Medes. Armenians were colonized in Hamath and Damascus. Tibarenians were settled in Assyria, and Assyrians were transported to the country of the Tibarenians. Mountaineers from the Zagros were likewise carried captive to Assyria. Chaldæans, Arabians and others were established in Samaria. Medes and other Eastern people were placed in Ashdod. The Commukha were removed from the extreme North to Susiana, and Chaldæans were brought from the far South to supply their place. In every quarter of his dominions Sargon "changed the abodes" of his subjects, with a view of weakening the more powerful nationalities by dispersion, and of smothering all patriotic impulses in the feebler races by severing at one stroke all the bonds of attachment to their native land. Although this system had been practised by former Assyrian kings, none had carried it out on so extensive and so grand a scale as Sargon. The splendid palace which this monarch had erected at Dur Sargina (City of Sargon), the modern Khorsabad, was the most striking of his great architectural works. It was not as large as the palaces built by previous or subsequent kings, but it surpassed all other royal residences by its magnificence and grandeur, with the solitary exception of the great palace of Asshur-bani-pal at Nineveh. Its ornamentation was resplendent beyond description. It was literally covered with sculptures, both inside and outside, generally arranged in two rows, one above the other, and illustrating the events in Sargon's wars, his battles and sieges, his captives, his treatment of prisoners, etc. Above this it was embellished with enameled bricks, fashioned in beautiful models. Leading to this magnificent edifice were noble flights of steps; and the structure stood by itself, so that its appearance was not marred by the proximity of other buildings. Its entrances and passages were guarded by colossal winged man-headed bulls and lions. It was in many particulars the most interesting of Assyrian works. The city where this palace was located was surrounded with strong walls, enclosing a square two thousand yards each way. Assigning fifty square yards to each person, this space could have accommodated eighty thousand people. The city, as well as the palace, was wholly built by Sargon, whose name it bore until after the Arab conquest in the seventh century after Christ.

Sargon's palace is the most complete of the Assyrian royal residences yet uncovered. It exhibits the architecture, the decorative art and sculpture of the Assyrians in their highest forms. Like all other Assyrian palaces, it stands on the summit of an immense mound constructed of bricks. The mound was arranged in two platforms of unequal height in the form of the letter T. The palace proper was built on the more elevated mound, and consisted of a series of structures ranged around immense courts. The main building occupied by the king was located at the bottom of the principal court, and had a perfectly regular façade, with a magnificently-ornamented gateway in the middle. Two-thirds of the northwest part of the palace was occupied by the grand reception hall and its large and magnificent galleries, with walls cased with bas-reliefs; one-third, to the south-east, by the inhabited apartments, with smaller and less decorated rooms. Passages led into two of the sides of the large court; one on the north-west to a square esplanade, or court, occupying the northern angle of the artificial mound of the palace, in front of a building joining the north-west face of the seraglio, with which it had no communication internally. This edifice was most profusely ornamented; it contained six immense halls decorated with sculpture, and some other smaller rooms. It was "a second palace grafted on to the first—a second selamnik, rivaling in splendor that of the seraglio." The passage leading into the south-east side of the reception hall of the seraglio opened to the lower platform, and to the great court of the offices. The lower platform of the artificial hill raised for the palace of Sargon was occupied by the khan and the harem. This part of the structure faced towards the city, and communicated directly with it. In the midst was the khan proper, an enormous square court, surrounded on every side by buildings, stables, lodgings for grooms and for most of the slaves. It was reached from the city by two immense flights of steps in the center of the south-east face of the terrace. As we have observed, an elaborately-decorated passage led from this court of the khan into the reception hall of the seraglio. Two small doors likewise communicated directly with the occupied rooms of the palace. To the right of the khan was the khazneh, or treasury, with its many courts and chambers, constituting some of the offices or common rooms of the palace. Here were the stores of provisions for the royal household, and places for the custody of the valuables which Sargon informs us, in his dedicatory inscription, that he had acquired by his conquests and stored in his palace. Adjoining the khazneh was the harem, containing three courts, the walls of one of them being covered with rich decorations in enameled bricks. Besides the three courts, the harem had many long galleries and many rooms for habitation. The harem was shut in in the closest possible manner; all communication with the outside world was intercepted, and the women were virtually imprisoned. A solitary vestibule, guarded by eunuchs, led to it by two issues; one connecting with the great court of the offices being from

SARGON'S PALACE (RESTORED), WESTERN FAÇADE.

the outside; the other opening to a long, narrow court leading to the inhabited apartments of the seraglio, through which passage the king found access to the harem without being exposed to the view of the public. Behind the harem was the Temple Court, consisting of an immense tower, or pyramid, in seven stages, nearly fifty yards high. The seven stages, equally high, and each one smaller in area than the one below it, were covered with stucco of various colors, thus exhibiting to view the colors consecrated to the seven great celestial bodies, the least important being at the base. This tower was the *ziggurat*, or observatory, on whose summit the priestly disciples of the Chaldæans endeavored to divine the future in the stars.

Before the construction of the great palace at Dur-Sargina, Sargon's residence was at Calah, where he repaired the decayed palace of Asshur-izir-pal. He also repaired the ruined walls of Nineveh, where he built a temple to Nebo and Merodach. He likewise improved the embankments at Babylon, thus controlling and directing the distribution of the waters. The number of Assyrian scientific tablets, shown by the dates upon them to have been written in his time, fully attest his patronage of science.

There was nothing significant in the progress of mimetic art during Sargon's reign, but several branches of industry showed signs of improvement, while there was better taste in design and ornamentation. At this time transparent glass was first brought into use, and intaglios were first cut upon hard stones. The furniture of this period is far superior in design to that of any former age represented, while the models of sword-hilts, maces, armlets and other ornaments are singularly tasteful and elegant. At this time the enameling of bricks had attained its highest degree of perfection; while the styles of vases, goblets and boats indicate a decided advance upon the same class of works of previous times. In sculpture the advance in animal forms in the times of Tiglath-Pileser II. still went on under Sargon; and the drawing of horses' heads, especially, shows very remarkable accuracy.

Sargon died in B. C. 705, after a glorious reign of seventeen years, and was succeeded on the throne by his son, SENNACHERIB, the most renowned of all the Assyrian kings, and of whom we have such long notices in the Old Testament. Sennacherib reigned twenty-four years, from B. C. 705 to B. C. 681. The sources which we have of the annals of his reign are the notices in the Hebrew Scriptures, some fragments of Polyhistor preserved by Eusebius, a passage from Herodotus mentioning his name, and two records written during his reign, giving descriptions of his military exploits and his buildings, and known respectively as the "Taylor Cylinder" and the "Bellino Cylinder."

The Canon of Ptolemy shows an interregnum of two years at Babylon, from B. C. 704 to B. C. 702, and Polyhistor mentions three pretenders to the throne of Babylonia during this brief interval. These were a brother of Sennacherib; a claimant named Hagisa; and Merodach-Baladan, who had escaped from captivity, murdered Hagisa and resumed the throne of which Sargon had deprived him six years before. In B. C. 703 Sennacherib led an army into Babylonia and defeated the troops of Merodach-Baladan and their Susianian auxiliaries, took Babylon and overran Chaldæa, plundering (according to his own account) seventy-six large towns and four hundred and twenty villages. Merodach-Baladan again escaped from the country, and his sons were afterwards found living as refugees in Susiana. Before leaving Babylon, Sennacherib appointed as tributary king an Assyrian named Belipni—the Belibus of Ptolemy's Canon, and the Elibus of Polyhistor. After returning from Babylon, Sennacherib ravaged the country of the Aramæans on the middle Euphrates, carrying into captivity more than two hundred thousand inhabitants, and seizing also large numbers of horses, camels, asses, oxen and sheep. The next year, B. C. 702, Sennacherib attacked the mountain tribes of the Zagros, driving from the country Ispabara, whom Sargon had elevated to power, and reducing to subjection many cities, over which he placed Assyrian governors.

In the fourth year of his reign, B. C. 701, Sennacherib engaged in the most important of all his military expeditions. This was his invasion of Syria, Phœnicia and Palestine, during which he attacked Luliya, King of Sidon, and also Hezekiah, King of Judah. With an immense host he first invaded Phœnicia, where Luliya—the Elulæus of Menander—had broken out into revolt during the early years of Sennacherib's reign. Luliya had made himself master of most of Phœnicia, including Tyre, Akko and many other leading cities. On the approach of the Assyrian king, the Sidonian chief fled from the main-land and found refuge in "an island in the middle of the sea," probably the island of Tyre, or perhaps Cyprus. Sennacherib received the submission of the Phœnician cities which Luliya had ruled, and placed over them a tributary prince named Tubal. The King of Assyria next marched southwards into Philistia, and put an end to the resistance of Sidka, King of Ascalon, who, with his wife, children and brothers, were made captives; while the city was also taken and another prince set up, the revolted chief being carried a prisoner to Assyria. The towns of Hazor, Joppa, Bene-berak, and Beth-Dagon—dependencies of Ascalon—were soon afterwards taken and plundered.

The conquering Sennacherib then took the field against Egypt, whose Ethiopian king—the Sevechus of Manetho, and the So of Scripture—had come to the support of the revolted Philistine city of Ekron, which had expelled its king, Padi, who had remained loyal to Assyria. The Egyptian army, consisting of chariots, horsemen and archers, was so large that Sennacherib called it "a host that could not be numbered." At Altaku—believed to be the Eltekeh of the Jews—was fought the second great battle between the Assyrians and the Egyptians. Again the power of Asia triumphed over that of Africa. The Egyptians and Ethiopians were defeated with frightful slaughter, many of their chariots, with their drivers, falling into the hands of the conquering Assyrians. In consequence of their great victory, the Assyrians immediately captured the towns of Altaku and Tamna. Rebellious Ekron also at once submitted to Sennacherib, opening its gates to the victorious monarch, who inflicted a terrible punishment upon the rebels, whose leaders were put to death, their bodies being exposed on stakes round the entire circuit of the city walls; while large numbers of inferior rank were sold into slavery. Padi, the expelled king who was friendly to Assyria, was restored to his authority as king, tributary to the Assyrian monarch.

Besides the Egyptians and Ethiopians, the revolted city of Ekron had Hezekiah, King of Judah, for an ally. When the Ekronites deposed Padi, they seized him, loaded him with chains, and sent him to Hezekiah for safe keeping. To punish the King of Judah for his complicity in the Ekronite revolt, " Sennacherib, King of Assyria, came up against all the fenced cities of Judah and took them. And Hezekiah, King of Judah, sent to the King of Assyria to Lachish, saying, I have offended: return from me; that which thou puttest on me will I bear. And the King of Assyria appointed unto Hezekiah, King of Judah, three hundred talents of silver and thirty talents of gold. And Hezekiah gave him all the silver that was found in the house of the Lord, and in the treasures of the king's house. At that time did Hezekiah cut off the doors of the house of the Lord, and the pillars which Hezekiah, King of Judah, had overlaid, and gave it to the King of Assyria." Such is the short account of this expedition of Sennacherib, as recorded in the Second Book of Kings.

We will now give the account recorded by Sennacherib himself in these words: "Because Hezekiah, King of Judah, would not submit to my yoke, I came up against him, and by force of arms and by the might of my power I took forty-six of his strong fenced cities; and of the smaller towns which were scattered about I took and plundered a countless number. And from

SENNACHERIB ATTACKING JERUSALEM.

these places I captured and carried off as spoil two hundred thousand and one hundred and fifty people, old and young, male and female, together with horses and mares, asses and camels, oxen and sheep, a countless multitude. And Hezekiah himself I shut up in Jerusalem, his capital city, like a bird in a cage, building towers round the city to hem him in, and raising banks of earth against the gates, so as to prevent escape. * * * Then upon this Hezekiah there fell the fear of the power of my arms, and he sent out to me the chiefs and the elders of Jerusalem with thirty talents of gold and eight hundred talents of silver, and divers treasures, a rich and immense booty. * * * All these things were brought to me at Nineveh, the seat of my government, Hezekiah having sent them by way of tribute, and as a token of his submission to my power."

After wreaking his vengeance upon the people of Ekron, Sennacherib invaded Judah, directing his march toward Jerusalem, taking many small towns and villages on the way, and carrying two hundred thousand of their inhabitants into slavery and captivity. Upon reaching Jerusalem he laid siege to the city in the usual way, erecting towers around it, from which stones and arrows were discharged against the defenders of the fortifications, and "casting banks" were hurled against the walls and gates. The fortifications of Jerusalem were weak, and there had recently been many "breaches of the city of David." The inhabitants had hastily fortified the city by pulling down the houses near the wall. Great alarm was felt for the safety of the holy places. Jerusalem was "full of stirs and tumult." The people rushed to the housetops, and saw "the choicest valleys full of chariots, and the horsemen set in array at the gates." Then followed "a day of trouble, and of treading down, and of perplexity"—a day of "breaking down the walls and of crying to the mountains." In the midst of this consternation some were made reckless by despair; so that there was a general "call to weeping, and to mourning, and to baldness, and to girding with sackcloth —beholding joy and gladness, slaying oxen and killing sheep, eating flesh and drinking wine—'Let us eat and drink, for to-morrow we shall die.'" Seeing the hopelessness of further resistance, Hezekiah offered to surrender upon terms which Sennacherib granted. It was agreed that Hezekiah should pay an annual tribute of thirty talents of gold and three hundred talents of silver, and that he should also give up the chief treasures of the city as a "present" to the Great King. To procure an adequate supply of gold, Hezekiah was obliged to strip the walls and pillars of the Temple of this precious metal, with which they were partly overlaid. He gave up all the silver from the royal treasury and from the treasury of the Temple, which amounted to five hundred talents more than the fixed rate of tribute. Besides these sacrifices the Jewish king was obliged to deliver up Padi, the Ekronite king whom he had held in captivity, and was forced to surrender certain parts of his territories to the neighboring Philistine kings.

After this triumph over Hezekiah, Sennacherib returned to Nineveh, and in the following year, B. C. 700, he led an expedition into Babylonia, where Merodach-Baladan, with the aid of Susub, a Chaldæan prince, had again risen in arms against the authority of the Assyrian monarch. After defeating Susub, Sennacherib marched upon Beth-Yakin, and compelled Merodach-Baladan to flee for refuge to one of the islands of the Persian Gulf, leaving his brothers and adherents to the conqueror's mercy. Upon returning to Babylon, Sennacherib removed the viceroy Belibus, whom he blamed for disloyalty or incompetency, appointing in his stead his own eldest son, Asshur-inadisu, the Asordanes of Polyhistor, and the Aparanadius, or Assaranadius, of Ptolemy's Canon.

The dates of the remaining events of Sennacherib's reign can not be fixed with certainty, Ptolemy's Canon taking no account of any subsequent event recorded in the inscriptions of this reign. It is believed that his second expedition into Palestine occurred

B. C. 699, Hezekiah having again revolted against the Assyrian king, and entered into an alliance with the Ethiopian King of Egypt, Tehrak, or Tirhakah. Sennacherib directed his expedition first against his more powerful foe, and marched his army through Palestine southwards to Libnah and Lachish, laying siege to the latter city, and sending a detachment of his army, under a Tartan, or general, supported by two high officers of his court—the Rabshakeh, or Chief Cupbearer, and the Rab-saris, or Chief Eunuch—to demand the surrender of Jerusalem. Hezekiah sent high dignitaries to treat with the Assyrians encamped outside the city walls, but the Assyrian envoys demanded the unconditional submission of the Jewish king and people. The Rabshakeh, or Chief Cupbearer, familiar with the Hebrew language, took the word and delivered the message in insolent phraseology, laughing at Hezekiah's simplicity in relying upon Egypt, and at his foolish superstition in depending upon a Divine deliverance, and defiantly asking the Jewish king to produce two thousand disciplined soldiers capable of serving as horsemen. Then the prophet "Isaiah said unto them, Thus shall ye say unto your master, Thus saith the Lord, 'Be not afraid of the words which thou hast heard, with which the servants of the King of Assyria have blasphemed me. Behold, I will send a blast upon him, and he shall hear a rumor, and shall return to his own land; and I will cause him to fall by the sword in his own land.'" When asked to speak in some other language rather than the Hebrew, for fear that the people upon the walls might hear, the intrepid envoy, in utter disregard of diplomatic courtesy, made a loud and direct appeal to the fears and hopes of the people. Seeing that they could make no impression upon the Jewish king or people, and regarding their military detachment as inadequate for a siege, the Assyrian ambassadors returned to their sovereign at Libnah and informed him of their failure. Thereupon Sennacherib sent other messengers with a letter to Hezekiah, reminding him of the fate of other kingdoms and nations which had the hardihood to resist the mighty Assyrian power, and again urging the Jewish king to submit. Hezekiah took this letter into the Temple, where he "spread it before the Lord," praying: "Lord, bow down thine ear, and hear; open, Lord, thine eyes, and see; and hear the words of Sennacherib, which hath sent him to reproach the living God." Thereupon the prophet Isaiah declared to his afflicted sovereign that Jehovah would "put his hook in Sennacherib's nose, and his bridle in his lips, and turn him back by the way by which he came." The prophet further declared: "Therefore thus saith the Lord concerning the King of Assyria, He shall not come into this city, nor shoot an arrow there, nor come before it with shield, nor cast a bank against it. By the way that he came, by the same shall he return, and shall not come into this city, saith the Lord. For I will defend this city, to save it, for mine own sake, and for my servant David's sake."

After receiving the submission of Libnah, Sennacherib advanced toward Egypt, and had come within sight of the Egyptian army at Pelusium when Hezekiah received his letter and made the prayer to which Isaiah delivered the response. The immense host of the Egyptians and Assyrians encamped opposite each other for the night, the Egyptians and their king full of anxious alarm, and Sennacherib and his Assyrians in proud confidence of a victory on the morrow as grand as those of Raphia and Altaku. But these bright hopes were destined to sad disappointment. Ere the morrow appeared the immense Assyrian host was destroyed in a night panic. Says the Hebrew record: "And it came to pass that night, that the angel of the Lord went out, and smote in the camp of the Assyrians an hundred fourscore and five thousand; and when they arose early in the morning, behold, they were all dead corpses." While the Hebrews ascribed this destruction of Sennacherib's army to the miraculous interposition of Jehovah, the Egyptians regarded their deliverance as the special intervention of their own gods, and pursued the fleeing Assyrian hosts, distressing their retreating columns and cutting off stragglers. The haughty Sennacherib returned to Nineveh with the shattered remnants of his mighty host, shorn of his glory. The proud capital of Assyria was plunged into such grief and despair as is beyond the power of the historian to describe. The Assyrian annals say nothing of this disastrous campaign.

According to Sennacherib's own annals, his fifth campaign was in a mountainous country called Nipur, or Nibur, supposed to be near Mount Ararat. He there took many towns, and then moving westward toward the Taurus range bordering on Cilicia, he warred with Maniya, King of Dayan, and, according to his own boast, plundered and ravaged the country, burned the towns and carried away the inhabitants, their flocks and herds, and their valuables.

His next contest was a fierce struggle of three years with the Babylonians and Susianians. The Chaldæans of Beth-Yakin, dissatisfied with the Assyrian yoke, migrated in a body from their own city to the territory of the King of Susiana. Carrying with them their gods and their treasures, they set sail in their ships, crossed "the Great Sea of the Rising Sun"—the Persian Gulf—and landed on the Elamite, or Susianian coast, where they were kindly received by the Susianian monarch, who allowed them to build a new city on his territory. This voluntary desertion of Beth-Yakin by its own people aroused the anger of the Assyrian king, who accordingly determined to bring back his deserting subjects to their native city, and to his dominion, by force.

The suzerainty of Assyria over Phœnicia had placed at the Assyrian king's disposal the most skilled shipwrights and the best sailors in the world, and Sennacherib resolved to invade Susiana by sea to reclaim his emigrant subjects. The shipwrights of Tyre and Sidon were therefore set to work at building a fleet of war-galleys on the Tigris. This fleet, manned by Phœnician sailors, descended the river to the Persian Gulf, astonishing the inhabitants on the shores with a spectacle never before seen in those waters. The Chaldæans, who had navigated those waters for many centuries, were far inferior as ship-builders and mariners to the Phœnicians, whose ships with their masts, sails, double tiers of oars and sharp beaks, were novelties to the nations in these parts.

Sennacherib, in his Phœnician ships, crossed from the mouth of the Tigris to the new settlement of the emigrant Chaldæans, destroyed their newly-built city, captured the deserters, ravaged the vicinity, burned many Susianian towns, and transported his captives, Chaldæan deserters and Susianians, across the gulf to Chaldæa, and thence took them to Assyria. The Susianians, not expecting an invasion by sea, had assembled an army near their north-western frontier, so that Sennacherib had found no force to oppose him when he landed on the Susianian coast.

Taking advantage of circumstances, the Babylonians now revolted and set up a king of their own called Susub; but the Babylonian army was defeated by the Assyrian troops upon their return from Susiana, Susub being captured; and the Susianian army which had come to the aid of the revolted Babylonians was routed. Susub and many other captives were carried to Nineveh.

Kudur-Nakhunta, who was still King of Susiana, held the cities of Beth-Kahiri and Raza, which Sennacherib regarded as part of his paternal inheritance. The Assyrian king now easily retook these towns, and leading his army into the heart of Susiana, took and burned thirty-four large cities and many small villages. After besieging and taking by storm Vadakat, or Badaca, the second city of Susiana, after it had been abandoned by Kudur-Nakhunta, Sennacherib returned to Nineveh with a large booty.

Susub, the Babylonian prince, having escaped from his captivity at Nineveh, returned to Babylon, where he was again hailed as king by the inhabitants. He secured the alliance of the new King of Susiana, Ummanminan, the younger brother and successor of Kudur-Nakhunta, by sending him as a present the gold and silver belonging to the great temple of Bel at Babylon. The Susianian monarch at once led an army to the Tigris, while many Aramæan, or Syrian, tribes on the middle Euphrates, which Sennacherib had subjugated in his third year, revolted, and their army joined that of Susub. Sennacherib defeated the allied host in a great battle at Khaluli, a town on the Lower Tigris, both Susub and the Susianian king escaping, but Nebosumiskun, a son of Merodach-Baladan, and many other chiefs, being made prisoners. Sennacherib entered Babylon in triumph, destroyed its fortifications, pillaged and burned its temples, and broke to pieces the images of the gods. Either Regibelus, or Mesesimordachus, whom the Canon of Ptolemy makes contemporary with the middle part of Sennacherib's reign, is believed to have been placed over the rebel city as viceroy by the conqueror.

Sennacherib is said to have also led an expedition against Cilicia, and, according to Abydenus, a Greek writer, a Grecian fleet was beaten by the Assyrian fleet on the Cilician shores; while according to Polyhistor, Sennacherib's army defeated a Greek land force in Cilicia itself; after which Sennacherib took possession of Cilicia, in which country he built the city of Tarsus, afterwards renowned as the birth-place of St. Paul. Among the inscriptions of Sennacherib's wars upon the Koyunjik bulls is one stating that he "triumphantly subdued the men of Cilicia inhabiting the inaccessible forests."

The Canon of Ptolemy marks an interregnum at Babylon for eight years, from B. C. 688 to B. C. 680, the year of Esar-haddon's accession; from which circumstance it is evident that Babylonia had again thrown off the Assyrian yoke and maintained her independence for eight years.

Thus the military glory of Sennacherib, the greatest and best-known of Assyrian kings, was tarnished by two great disasters—the destruction of his army at Pelusium by a night panic during his war with Hezekiah of Judah and Tirhakah of Egypt, and the successful revolt of Babylon just mentioned. Still he was the most illustrious and the most successful of Assyrian warrior kings. In his inscription, Sennacherib calls himself "the great king, the powerful king, the king of nations, the king of Assyria, the king of the four regions, the diligent ruler, the favorite of the great gods, the observer of sworn faith, the guardian of the law, the embellisher of public buildings, the noble hero, the strong warrior, the first of kings, the punisher of unbelievers, the destroyer of wicked men."

Sennacherib takes the first rank among Assyrian monarchs as an architect and patron of art, as well as that of a warrior. The gigantic palace erected by him at Nineveh surpassed in dimensions and grandeur all previously-built structures, and covered an area of more than eight acres. The grand halls and smaller chambers of this vast and magnificent edifice were arranged around at least three courts or quadrangles, which were respectively one hundred and fifty-four by one hundred and twenty-five feet, one hundred and twenty-four by ninety feet, and ninety-three by eighty-four feet. Small apartments were grouped around the smallest of these courts. A narrow passage leading out of a long gallery, two hundred and eighteen by twenty-five feet, opened the way to the king's seraglio. This gallery was entered through two other passages, one leading from each of the two main courts. The principal halls were immediately within the two chief entrances, one on the north-east, and the other on the south-west front of the palace. One of these seems to have been one hundred and sixty feet long, and the other one hundred and eighty feet, while each was a little over forty feet wide. The palace had about twenty other rooms, and from forty to fifty smaller chambers, about square, entered from some hall or large apartment. Mr. Layard says he explored seventy-one chambers, including the three courts, the long gallery and four passages.

Sennacherib's palace, like other Assyrian architectural works, was built on an artificial platform, eighty or ninety feet above the plain, and covered with a brick pavement. It is believed to have had three grand façades, respectively on the north-east, south-east and south-west sides. Its chief apartment was first entered by the visitor. All the walls ran in straight lines, and all the angles of the rooms were right angles. Although there were numerous passages, the apartments in many instances directly opened into one another, nearly half of the rooms being passage-rooms. The doorways were usually towards the corners of the apartments. In many cases a room was entered by two or three doorways from another room or from a court. There were also many square recesses in the sides of rooms. The walls were very thick. The apartments, never much over forty feet wide, were comparatively narrow for their length, but the courts were much better proportioned.

Sennacherib's royal building differed from others in the size and number of its rooms, in its use of passages and in its style of ornamentation. His principal state apartments were one-third wider, though very little longer, and thus were in better proportion. But one gallery, connecting the more public portion of the building with the harem, or private apartments, formed a corridor, two hundred and eighteen feet long by twenty-five feet wide, uniting the two parts of the palace. This corridor communicated by passages with the two public courts, which were also joined by a third passage. Timber from Lebanon and Amanus was used in the roofing of this palace.

Sennacherib's ornamentation was marked by the first general use of the back-ground in completing each scene, as it really existed at the time and place of its occurrence. Mountains, rocks, trees, roads, rivers and lakes were represented with the highest degree of perfection which the ability of the artist and the means and facilities at his command would permit. In Sennacherib's bas-reliefs the species of trees is distinguished; gardens, fields, ponds, reeds, etc., are portrayed with great exactness; wild animals, such as stags, boars and antelopes, are illustrated; birds are represented flying from one tree to another, or standing over their nests feeding their young as they stretch up to receive the food; fish swim in the water; fishermen, boatmen and agricultural laborers are depicted; the entire scene being striking and real in appearance.

On the walls of the passages of Sennacherib's palace are depicted ordinary scenes of every-day life. Trains of servants daily bring to the royal residence game and locusts for the monarch's dinner, and cakes and fruits for his dessert, just as they walked through the courts carrying the delicacies for which he displayed special fondness. In another place is exhibited the work of carving and transporting a gigantic bull of solid stone, from the removal of the material from the quarry, to its elevated position on a palace-mound as part of the great entrance-passage of the royal dwelling. The trackers are shown dragging the huge rough block, supported on a low flat-bottomed boat, along the course of a river, divided in gangs performing their work under taskmasters who ply their rods upon the most trifling provocation. The trackers, three hundred in number, in their national costumes, are each delineated with the utmost precision. We next see the stone block conveyed to land, and carved into the rough likeness of a bull, and in that shape it is set on a sledge and moved along level ground by gangs of laborers, arranged very much as before, to the base of the mound, at the top of which it must be located. The building of the mound is illustrated in detail. Brick-makers are represented moulding the bricks at the foot of the mound, and workmen are seen with baskets at their backs, filled with earth, bricks, stones or rubbish, climbing the ascent after the mound is partially raised, and emptying their burdens upon the top. The bull on the sledge is then drawn up an inclined plane to the summit by four gangs of laborers, before the eyes of the king and his attendants. The carving is then finished, and the gigantic figure is set into an upright position and dragged along the surface of the platform to the place assigned it.

Sennacherib also restored the old royal

palace at Nineveh. He built a brick embankment on the banks of the Tigris to confine the river to its channel, and supplied his capital with good water by constructing for that purpose a system of canals and aqueducts. He strengthened the defenses of Nineveh by the erection of colossal towers at some of the brick gateways. Lastly, he erected a temple to the god Nergal at Tarbisi (now Sherif Khan), on the Tigris, about three miles above Nineveh.

Sennacherib's conquering expeditions into other lands furnished him with a sufficient amount of forced labor, which he employed in the construction of his great works. The Bellino Cylinder tells us that he employed Chaldæans, Aramæans, or Syrians, Armenians, Cilicians, and Quhu, or Coans, in this way. A bull-inscription informs us that in one raid he carried into slavery two hundred and eight thousand Aramæans. By this means the colossal bulls of stone were transported and elevated, the vast mounds built, the bricks moulded, the walls of edifices erected, the canals excavated and embankments constructed. They were forced to labor in gangs, under the rods of brutal and exacting taskmasters, and in their respective national costumes. The work was directed by Assyrian foremen, and the forced laborers were frequently compelled to work in fetters, sometimes supported by a bar fastened to the waist, and sometimes consisting of shackles around the ankles. The king, standing in a chariot drawn by his attendants, often witnessed the laborers at their task.

Sennacherib's glorious reign of twenty-four years experienced a sad end. The great monarch fell a victim to a plot of assassination on the part of his sons, Adrammelech and Sharezer. He was slain while at worship in a temple; and his son Nergilus, who claimed the crown, was also soon murdered by his brothers, Adrammelech and Sharezer; but these were soon overthrown by their brother ESAR-HADDON, who, in command of the army on the Armenian frontier, marched to Nineveh and was recognized as the rightful successor to his father's throne.

The year of Sennacherib's assassination and Esar-haddon's accession was B. C. 681, according to the Assyrian Canon—the year just before his first year in Babylon on the authority of the Canon of Ptolemy. This is to be accounted for by the fact that a king was not entered on the Babylonian list until the Thoth which followed his accession, and the Thoth in this instance occurred in February. Thus the Babylonian dates are generally one year later than the Assyrian, and the two Canons are seen to harmonize with remarkable precision.

Esar-haddon held the throne for thirteen years, and reigned alternately at Nineveh and Babylon, thus placing the two great capitals on an equality, and reconciling the Babylonians to the Assyrian rule. Esar-haddon's inscriptions show that he was engaged for some time after the opening of his reign in a civil war with his half-brothers, who, at the head of large bodies of troops, contested his claims to the Assyrian crown. Esar-haddon, who, at the time of his father's death, was stationed on the Armenian frontier, at once marched upon Nineveh, defeated the army of his brothers in the country of Khanirabbat, north-west of Nineveh, and entered the capital, where he was universally acknowledged king. Abydenus says that Adrammelech fell in the battle, but better authorities state that both he and his brother Sharezer escaped into Armenia, where the ruling sovereign treated them with kindness, bestowing upon them lands, which long remained in the possession of their posterity.

Our information of Esar-haddon's reign is mainly derived from a cylinder inscription, existing in duplicate, which records nine campaigns. A memorial which he set up at the mouth of the Nahr-el-Kelb, and a cylinder of his son's, give us some additional knowledge concerning the closing portion of his reign. The Old Testament, in several instances, connects him with Jewish history; and Abydenus alludes to some of his foreign conquests. An incomplete cylinder inscription of Esar-haddon's reign contains accounts of his civil war with his brothers and also his Arabian and Syrian expeditions. Esar-haddon's first expedition was into Phœnicia. The civil dissensions resulting from Sennacherib's murder encouraged a revolt in that region on the part of Abdi-Milkut, King of Sidon, and Sandu-arra, King of the neighboring portion of Lebanon, who had entered into an alliance to cast off the Assyrian yoke. Esar-haddon first attacked Sidon and soon took the city, and Abdi-Milkut sought refuge in an island, either Aradus or Cyprus, but was pursued and made prisoner by Esar-haddon, who, it was said, traversed the sea "like a fish." Esar-haddon next attacked Sandu-arra in his mountain fastnesses, defeated his troops and took him prisoner. Both captive kings were executed in punishment for their rebellion; the walls of Sidon were destroyed, its inhabitants and those of the whole neighboring coast were carried off into Assyria, and thence dispersed among the provinces; while a new city was built and named after Esar-haddon, which was designed to succeed Sidon as the leading city in this region, and Chaldæan and Susianian captives were colonized in the new city and the adjacent country, over which an Assyrian governor was appointed.

Esar-haddon's second campaign was in Armenia, where he took a city named Arza, which, he says, was in the neighborhood of Muzr, and carried away its inhabitants, along with a number of mountain animals, settling the captives "beyond the eastern gate of Nineveh." At the same time he received the submission of Tiuspa, the Cimmerian.

Esar-haddon's third campaign was in Cilicia and the adjacent regions. The Cilicians, so recently subdued by Sennacherib, re-asserted their independence at his death, and formed an alliance with the Tibareni, or people of Tubal, who occupied the high mountain district about the junction of Amanus and Taurus. After defeating the Cilicians, Esar-haddon invaded the mountain region, where he took twenty-one towns and many villages, all of which he plundered and burned, carrying the inhabitants into captivity.

Esar-haddon next conducted a petty war in Northern Syria, and another in South-eastern Armenia against the Mannai, or Minni. He then made an expedition into Chaldæa, against Nebo-zirzi-sidi, Merodach-Baladan's son, who, aided by the Susianians, had regained a footing on the Chaldæan coast: while his brother Nahid-Marduk, sought the favor of the Assyrian king, quitting his refuge in Susiana to present himself before the Great King's foot-stool at Nineveh. After subduing Nebo-zirzi-sidi, Esar-haddon bestowed the entire coast district previously ruled by that prince on Nahid-Marduk. At the same time the Assyrian king deposed Shamas-ipni, a Chaldæan prince, who had extended his sway over a small town in the vicinity of Babylon, putting Nebo-sallim in his place. Esar-haddon next engaged in a war with Edom, where he took a city bearing the same name as the country—a city, which he says, had been previously taken by his father—transporting the inhabitants into Assyria, and carrying away certain of the Edomite gods. Thereupon the Edomite king, Hazael, sent an embassy to Nineveh, to offer submission and presents, while he also begged the Assyrian monarch to restore his gods and permit them to be returned to Edom. This humble request was granted by Esar-haddon, who restored the images to the envoy; but he increased the annual tribute by sixty-five camels, and appointed to the succession, or joint sovereignty of the throne of Edom, a woman named Tabua, who had been born and brought up in his own palace.

Esar-haddon's next expedition was into a country named Bazu, said to be "remote, on the extreme confines of the earth, on the other side of the desert." This country was reached by traversing a hundred and forty *farsakhs* (four hundred and ninety miles) of sandy desert, then twenty *farsakhs* (seventy miles) of fertile land, and beyond that a stony region. None of Esar-haddon's predecessors had ever penetrated so far "into the middle of Arabia." Bazu was located beyond Khazu, the stony tract, and its principal city was Yedih, which was ruled by a king named Lailé. The country here noticed is supposed to have been the region of the modern Arabian kingdom of Hira. Esar-haddon boasts that he marched into the middle of this region, that he slew eight of its kings, and carried their gods, their treasures and their subjects into Assyria; and that Lailé's gods were also conveyed to Nineveh, though Lailé himself escaped. Lailé, like the Edomite monarch went to Nineveh, and, prostrating himself at the foot-stool of the Assyrian king, humbly requested the return of the images of his gods. This request Esar-haddon granted, but only on the condition that Lailé became one of his tributaries. In this invasion of Arabia, Esar-haddon led an army across the deserts which enclose that country on the land side, and penetrated to the more fertile tracts beyond them, a region of cities and fixed settlements, where he took towns and carried off their plunder to Assyria. This invasion was a most remarkable success, taking in account the natural perils of the desert, and the warlike character of its inhabitants, who have never fully bowed to the yoke of any foreign conqueror. The dangers of the simoom and the aridity of the northern portion of Arabia, with the difficulty of carrying water and provisions for a large army, and the perils of plunging into the wilderness with a small one, have deterred most Oriental conquerors from even the thought of leading an expedition into this dreary and desolate region. Esar-haddon is the only monarch who ever ventured upon the hazardous undertaking of penetrating in person into this vast desert land.

Esar-haddon next invaded the marshy region on the Euphrates, where the Aramæan tribe of Gambulu dwelt, as he says, "like fish, in the midst of the waters." The sheikh of this tribe had revolted, but submitted on the approach of the Assyrian monarch, bringing in person the arrears of his tribute and a present of buffaloes, thereby seeking to propitiate his suzerain. Esar-haddon says that he forgave him, and strengthened his capital with fresh works of defense and garrisoned it, making it a stronghold to protect the country against the attacks of the Susianians.

Esar-haddon's last expedition recorded on his principal cylinder, which was not apparently led by the king personally, was against the country of Bikni, or Bikan, a remote part of Media, supposed to be Azerbijan. None of his predecessors ever penetrated this region, which was governed by many petty chiefs, each of whom ruled over his own town and its surrounding territory, and whose names illustrate their Aryan character. Esar-haddon carried two of these chiefs captive to Assyria, whereupon the others submitted, agreeing to pay tribute and to share their power with Assyrian officers.

The various expeditions of Esar-haddon already described have been made known to us from his cylinder inscriptions; but his conquest of Egypt and his punishment and pardon of Manasseh, King of Judah—the greatest and most interesting events of his reign—have been brought to our knowledge from other sources. All that we know of the circumstances of Esar-haddon's conquest of Egypt is derived from an imperfect transcript of the Nahr-el-Kelb tablet, and the brief annals of his son and successor, Asshur-bani-pal, who alludes to his father's proceedings in Egypt, for the purpose of making known the condition of affairs when he himself invaded that country.

It thus appears that Esar-haddon led a large army into Egypt about B. C. 670, won a great victory over the forces of Tirhakah, or Tehrak, the reigning Ethiopian sovereign of that country, took Memphis, his capital, and conquered the entire Nile valley as far southward as Thebes, taking Thebes itself. Tirhakah fled into Ethiopia, leaving Esar-haddon master of all Egypt as far as Thebes, the Diospolis of the Greeks and the No, or No-Amon, of the Old Testament. The conquering Assyrian king weakened Egypt by dividing the country into twenty governments, appointing a petty king in each town, but placing all the others under the rule of the prince reigning at Memphis. This Memphite prince was Neko, the father of Psammetichus, or Psamatik I., a native Egyptian mentioned both by Herodotus and Manetho; and the other petty kings were also native Egyptians, with a few exceptions where Assyrian officers were appointed governors. After thus arranging the government of Egypt, and setting up his tablet at the mouth of the Nahr-el-Kelb beside that of Rameses the Great, Esar-haddon returned to Assyria and began to introduce sphinxes into the ornamentation of his palaces, at the same time adding to his previous titles the following: "King of the kings of Egypt, and conqueror of Ethiopia." This title does not occur on the cylinders, but appears on the back of the slabs at the entrance of the south-west palace of Nimrud, where the sphinxes are found, and also on a bronze lion dug up at the Nebbi-Yunus mound of Nineveh, and on the slabs of Esar-haddon's palace at Sherif-Khan.

The revolt of Manasseh, King of Judah, occurring about the time of Esar-haddon's conquest of Egypt, was suppressed by the "captains of the host of the King of Assyria." These Assyrian generals invaded Judah to subdue Manasseh, and "took and bound him with chains, and carried him to Babylon," where Esar-haddon had erected a palace for himself and frequently held his court. The Great King at first treated his royal captive with severity, and Manasseh's affliction is said to have humbled his pride and to have led him to humiliate himself before Jehovah and to repent of his cruelties and idolatries. According to the Book of Chronicles, God "was entreated of him, and heard his supplication, and brought him back again to Jerusalem into his kingdom." Esar-haddon generously pardoned Manasseh for his defection, and sent him back to Jerusalem, restoring him to his throne, on the condition of paying an increased tribute.

To augment the Assyrian power in Palestine, Esar-haddon determined to strengthen the foreign element already introduced into the country by Sargon, who, as we have seen, colonized Samaria with foreign settlers from Babylon, Cutha, Sippara, Ava, Hamath and Arabia. Esar-haddon settled colonists in Palestine collected from Babylon, Erech, or Orchoë, Susa, Elymais, Persia, and other surrounding nations, and placing them under an officer of high rank—"the great and noble Asnapper."

When intelligence of Esar-haddon's illness reached Egypt in B. C. 669, Tirhakah, the Ethiopian king, whom Esar-haddon had driven out of Egypt the previous year, at once descended the Nile from Ethiopia, drove out the petty kings set over Egypt by the Assyrian monarch, and reëstablished his authority over all Egypt. Esar-haddon thereupon resigned the crown of Assyria to his son Asshur-bani-pal, but retained that of Babylonia, residing in Babylon until his death shortly afterward, B. C. 668, when Asshur-bani-pal succeeded to the sovereignty of the whole empire.

Esar-haddon was one of the most active of Assyria's royal builders and architects. During his short reign of thirteen years he erected four palaces and more than thirty temples. Three of his great palaces were located respectively at Babylon, Nineveh and Calah; but that at Calah, or Nimrud, is the only one which has been explored to any great extent, and even the ground-plan of that has been but imperfectly traced. This palace had never been finished, its ornamentation had hardly been commenced, and the small portion of this that was original had been so seriously injured by a destructive fire that it perished immediately upon its discovery. We must therefore rely for our knowledge of Esar-haddon's sculptures upon the report of persons who saw them before they were destroyed, and upon one or two drawings; and our only knowledge of the palace is derived from a half-explored fragment of a half-finished palace destroyed by the flames before its completion.

Esar-haddon's palace at Calah was built at the south-western corner of the Nimrud mound, abutting towards the west on the Tigris, and towards the valley formed by the Shor-Derreh torrent. It faced northward and was entered on this side from the open space of the platform, through a portal guarded by two winged man-headed bulls. The entrance led into a large court, two hundred and eighty by one hundred feet, bounded on the north side by a mere wall, but surrounded by buildings on the east, west and south sides. The chief building was opposite, and was entered from the court by two gateways, one directly facing the great northern portal of the court, and the other slightly to the left, the former being guarded by colossal winged man-headed bulls, and the latter only reveted with slabs. These gateways both opened into the same room, the design of which was on the most magnificent scale of all the Assyrian apartments, but it was so thoroughly broken up through the architect's inability to cover the wide space without sufficient supports, that this room virtually constituted four chambers of moderate size rather than one grand hall. As one apartment this room was one hundred and sixty-five feet long by sixty-two feet wide. Viewed as a suite of four chambers, the rooms appeared to be two long and narrow halls running parallel to each other, and connected by a grand doorway in the middle, with two smaller chambers located at the two ends, running at right angles with the principal ones. The smaller chambers were sixty-two feet long, and respectively nineteen feet and twenty-three feet wide. The larger ones were one hundred and ten feet long, and respectively twenty feet and twenty-eight feet wide.

Mr. Fergusson's account of the grand apartment of this palace is as follows: "Its general dimensions are one hundred and sixty-five feet in length, by sixty-two feet in width; and it consequently is the largest hall yet found in Assyria. The architects, however, do not seem to have been quite equal to roofing so large a space, even with the number of pillars with which they seem usually to have crowded their floors; and it is consequently divided down the center by a wall supporting dwarf columns, forming a center gallery, to which access was had by bridge galleries at both ends, a mode of arrangement capable of great variety and picturesqueness of effect, and of which I have little doubt that the builders availed themselves to the fullest extent."

The inner of the two long parallel chambers was connected by a grand doorway, guarded by sphinxes and colossal lions, either with a small court or with a large chamber extending to the southern edge of the mound; while the two end rooms were connected with smaller apartments in the same direction, but Mr. Layard's excavations here were incomplete. The buildings on the right and left sides of the great court appear to have been wholly separate from those at its southern end. Those on the left have not been explored, but on the right several long narrow apartments, with one or two passages, have been examined. Eastward the palace has not been explored, and its extent northward, southward and westward is not certain. Southward and westward the mound has been worn away by the Tigris and the Shor-Derreh torrent.

The walls of Esar-haddon's palace were built of sun-dried bricks, reveted with alabaster slabs, taken from the decayed palaces of his predecessors. Ere the new sculptures on these slabs were completed, Esar-haddon died, and the work ceased, or the palace was ruined by fire. The only sculptures finished were the winged man-headed bulls and lions at the various portals, a few bas-reliefs near them, and some sphinxes within the span of the two widest doorways. These sphinxes were Egyptian in idea, but had the horned cap like those on the bulls, the Assyrian arrangement of hair, Assyrian ear-rings, and wings like those of the bulls and lions. The figures near the lions were mythic, and according to Mr. Layard's representations, were more than ordinarily grotesque.

The inscriptions give us a full account of the character of Esar-haddon's buildings and their ornamentation. These inform us that the thirty-six temples which this king erected in Assyria and Babylonia were profusely adorned with plates of gold and silver, making them "as splendid as the day." His palace at Nineveh, located on the Neb-bi-Yunus mound, was said to have been built upon the site of a former palace of the Assyrian kings. The materials for its construction were procured from different coun-

POLITICAL HISTORY.

tries; the Phœnician, Syrian and Cyprian kings sending to Nineveh for this purpose great beams of cedar, cypress and ebony, stone statues, and various works in different kinds of metal. The size of this palace is said to have surpassed all the structures of former kings. Carved beams of cedar wood were used in roofing this edifice, which was partly supported by columns of cypress wood, ornamented with rings of silver and strengthened with iron bands. Winged man-headed bulls and lions guarded the portals; and the gates were made of ebony and cypress ornamented with iron, silver and ivory ; while the walls were adorned with sculptured slabs and enameled bricks.

The prejudice of the present Mohammedan inhabitants against disturbing their dead, and against violating the tomb of Jonah has thus far prevented satisfactory excavations of the Nebbi-Yunus mound. Mr. Layard stealthily made a slight excavation in this mound, thus discovering a few fragments bearing Esar-haddon's name. Turkish excavations soon afterwards uncovered a long line of wall of one of Sennacherib's palaces, and likewise a part of Esar-haddon's palace. On the outside surface of the former were winged man-headed bulls in high relief, sculptured seemingly after the wall was erected, each bull covering ten or twelve distinct stone blocks. A slab-inscription obtained from this palace was published in the British Museum Series. A bronze lion with legend was obtained from Esar-haddon's palace.

We know nothing of Esar-haddon's palace at Babylon, which now lies buried beneath the mounds at Hillah. Mr. Layard and Sir Henry Rawlinson have carefully examined the Sherif-Khan palace, which was found to be very much inferior to the ordinary Assyrian royal residences, being only a dwelling erected by Esar-haddon for his eldest son, and it also is believed to have been unfinished when the king died.

After a reign of thirteen years, Esarhaddon, "King of Assyria, Babylonia, Egypt, Meroë and Ethiopia," as he calls himself in his later inscriptions, died in B.

C. 668, and was succeeded on his throne by his eldest son, ASSHUR-BANI-PAL, whom he had already associated in the government. Asshur-bani-pal, upon his accession, appointed to the viceroyalty of Babylon his younger brother, Saül-Mugina, called Sammughes by Polyhistor, and Saosduchinus by the Canon of Ptolemy.

Upon his accession, Asshur-bani-pal found himself involved in a war with Egypt. Late in Esar-haddon's reign Tirhakah, the Ethiopian king, descended the Nile, recovered Thebes, Memphis and other Egyptian cities, and expelled the princes and governors appointed by Esar-haddon when he had conquered the country. Asshur-bani-pal, soon after his accession, led an expedition through Syria into Egypt, and defeated the Ethiopian and Egyptian army near the city of Kar-banit. Tirhakah at once fled from Memphis, sailing up the Nile to Thebes; and being pursued by the Assyrians to the latter place, the Ethiopian king continued his retreat up the Nile valley, leaving all Egypt north of Thebes in the possession of the Assyrian monarch. Asshur-bani-pal restored the princes and rulers whom his father had placed over Egypt, and whom Tirhakah had expelled; and, after a short rest at Thebes, returned in triumph by way of Syria to Nineveh.

No sooner had the Assyrian king left Egypt than intrigues to restore the Ethiopian power commenced. Neko and other Egyptian governors restored by Asshur-bani-pal deserted the Assyrian cause and sided with the Ethiopians. The governors who remained loyal to Assyria tried to suppress the revolt; Neko and several other rebel leaders were carried in chains to Assyria; and Sais, Tanis, Mendes and other revolted Egyptian cities were punished. The revolt was, however, successful, and Tirhakah having reëstablished himself at Thebes, threatened to again extend his sway over the entire Nile valley. But when Asshur-bani-pal forgave Neko and sent him back to Egypt with a large Assyrian army, Tirhakah again fled to Upper Egypt, where he died shortly afterwards. Tirhakah's stepson and successor, Urdamané—believed to be the Rud-Amun of the hieroglyphics—descended the Nile valley with an army, defeated the Assyrians near Memphis, forced them to seek refuge within its walls, besieged and took the city, and regained possession of Lower Egypt. Upon hearing of this, Asshur-bani-pal left Asshur, and leading an expedition personally against the new Ethiopian monarch, drove him from Memphis to Thebes, and thence to the city of Kipkip, far up the Nile. After entering Thebes in triumph and sacking the city, and again placing governors over the Egyptian cities and taking hostages to secure their loyalty, Asshur-bani-pal returned to Nineveh with his plunder of gold, silver, ebony, ivory, obelisks, precious stones, dyed garments, monkeys and elephants of the Theban palace, male and female captives.

Between his first and second expeditions into Egypt, Asshur-bani-pal attacked Tyre, whose king, Baäl, had incurred his displeasure, and, reducing him to submission, exacted from him a large tribute, which he sent to Nineveh. About the same time Asshur-bani-pal married a Cilician princess. Soon after his second expedition into Egypt, Asshur-bani-pal invaded Asia Minor, crossing the Taurus mountains and penetrating a region never before entered by an Assyrian king; and, after reducing a number of towns, he returned to Nineveh, where he received an embassy, of which he gives the following account: "Gyges, King of Lydia, a country on the sea-coast, a remote place, of which the kings my ancestors had never even heard the name, had formerly learned in a dream the fame of my empire, and had sent officers to my presence to perform homage on his behalf." The Lydian king now sent a second time to Asshur-bani-pal and told him that since his submission he defeated the Cimmerians, who had formerly ravaged his country, and he begged him to accept Cimmerian chiefs whom he had taken captive in battle, along with other presents, which the Assyrian monarch regarded as "tribute." About the same time Asshur-bani-pal repulsed an attack by the "King of Kharbat" on a district of Babylonia, and after taking Kharbat, transported its inhabitants to Egypt.

Asshur-bani-pal next invaded Minni, or Persarmenia, the mountain region about Lakes Van and Urumiyeh. Akhsheri, the King of Minni, having lost his capital, Izirtu, and several other cities, was murdered by his subjects; and his son, Vahalli, was forced to submit, and sent an embassy to Nineveh to do homage, with tribute, presents and hostages. Asshur-bani-pal received the envoys graciously, pardoned Vahalli and kept him on the throne of Minni, but compelled him to pay a heavy tribute. Asshur-bani-pal also conquered a region called Paddiri, which his predecessors had separated from Minni, but which he annexed to his own dominion, placing an Assyrian governor over it.

Asshur-bani-pal next engaged in a struggle of twelve years with Elam, or Susiana. Certain tribes, pressed by famine, had passed from Susiana into the Assyrian dominions, where they were permitted to settle; but when, after the famine had ceased, they wished to return to their former home, Asshur-bani-pal would not agree to their removal. Urtaki, King of Susiana, resented this by invading Babylonia, and was aided by Belu-bagar, King of the Gambulu, an important Aramæan tribe. Saül-Mugina, Asshur-bani-pal's brother and viceroy at Babylon, greatly alarmed, sent to Nineveh for aid. Thereupon an Assyrian army drove the Susianian monarch out of Babylonia, inflicting upon him a severe defeat before he escaped and returned to Susa, where he died within a year.

A dynastic revolution in Susiana now proved of great advantage to the Assyrians. Urtaki had wrested the Susianian throne from his elder brother, Umman-aldas. At his death, his younger brother, Temin-Umman, usurped the crown; and the sons of Umman-aldas and those of Urtaki, who claimed the Susianian crown, only saved their lives by fleeing to Nineveh with their relatives and adherents, and putting themselves under the protection of the Assyrian monarch. Thus

Asshur-bani-pal, in the expedition which he now undertook, had a party which favored him in Susiana itself; but Temin-Umman strengthened himself by alliances with two descendants of Merodach-Baladan, who had principalities upon the Persian Gulf coast, with two sons of Belu-bagar, sheikh of the Gambulu, with two mountain chiefs, one a blood relation of the Assyrian king, and with several inferior chieftains. Asshur-bani-pal defeated the allies, took Temin-Umman prisoner, executed him, and exposed his head over one of the gates of Nineveh. He then divided Susiana between Urtaki's sons, Umman-ibi and Tammarit, establishing the former at Susa, and the latter at a town called Khidal, in Eastern Susiana. A son of Temin-Umman was executed with his father. Several of Merodach-Baladan's grandsons suffered mutilation. A Chaldæan prince and a chieftain of the Gambulu had their tongues torn out by the roots. Another Gambulu chief was beheaded. Two of Temin-Umman's principal officers were chained and flayed. By these cruelties Asshur-bani-pal expected to strike terror into his enemies.

No sooner, however, had the Assyrians returned to Nineveh then fresh troubles broke out. Asshur-bani-pal's own brother, Saül-Mugina, dissatisfied with his subordinate position as viceroy of Babylon, rebelled, and, declaring himself King of Babylon, obtained a number of important allies. These were Umman-ibi, who, though he had received his crown from Asshur-bani-pal, had been bribed by gift of treasure from the Babylonian temples; Vaiteha, a powerful Arabian prince; and Nebo-bel-sumi, a surviving grandson of Merodach-Baladan. Saül-Mugina's fair prospects of success were blighted by domestic troubles in Susiana, where Umman-ibi was defeated and slain in a civil war with his brother Tammarit, who thus became King of all Susiana. Tammarit, however, entered into an alliance with Saül-Mugina; but while absent with his army in Babylonia, a mountain chief from Luristan named Inda-bibi, or Inda-bigas, excited a

1—12.-U. H.

revolt in Susiana and seized the throne; and Tammarit, deserted by his army, was obliged to flee and seek safety in concealment, while the Susianian army returned home. While Saül-Mugina thus lost the most important of his allies, Asshur-bani-pal had overrun the northern Babylonian provinces and besieged and took the Babylonian towns one after another. Saül-Mugina was taken prisoner by Asshur-bani-pal, who punished his rebel brother more terribly than any of his other captured enemies, burning him alive.

A lull of some years in actual hostilities between Assyria and Susiana followed. Inda-bibi having given refuge to Nebo-bel-sumi, and having repeatedly refused to surrender the fugitive prince as demanded by the Assyrian king, was killed by the commander of his archers, a second Umman-aldas, who then usurped the Susianian throne. At the same time many pretenders claimed the Susianian crown, and Asshur-bani-pal again demanded the surrender of Nebo-bel-sumi, who would have been given up had he not committed suicide. About B. C. 645 Asshur-bani-pal invaded Susiana, took the strongly-fortified town of Bit-Imbi by siege, drove Umman-aldas into the mountain region of Susiana, took Susa, Badaca and twenty-four other cities, and assigned the government of Western Susiana to Tammarit, who, after his flight from Babylonia, had become a fugitive at the court of Assyria. Umman-aldas was allowed to retain the sovereignty of Eastern Susiana.

Tammarit, in order to cast off his vassalage to the Assyrian monarch, plotted to massacre all the foreign garrisons in his dominions, but was carried a prisoner to Nineveh, and Western Susiana was put under military rule. Umman-aldas, in his mountain fastness, collected a new army, and took possession of Bit-Imbi the following spring; but unable to resist the Assyrian assaults, he soon evacuated the town, and defended himself in his entire retreat to Susa, holding the different strong towns and rivers in succession. But the Assyrians drove him from post to post, and finally took both Susa and Badaca, thus again placing Susiana at Asshur-bani-pal's mercy, all the towns making their submission, while Umman-aldas was carried a prisoner to Nineveh. Inflamed with rage on account of the revolt, Asshur-bani-pal plundered the Susianian capital of its treasures, among which were eighteen images of gods and goddesses, thirty-two statues of former Susianian kings, including those of Kudur-Nakhunta and Tammarit. He also gave the other Susianan cities to be pillaged by his soldiers for a period of almost two months. He then annexed Susiana to the Assyrian Empire, thus closing this Susianian war, after it had lasted, with short intervals, for twelve years.

While Asshur-bani-pal was thus engaged in Susiana and Babylonia, Psammetichus declared himself independent in Egypt and began a war against the petty Egyptian princes who remained steadfast in their loyalty to their Assyrian suzerain. In Asia Minor, Gyges, King of Lydia, who had so recently done homage to Assyria, sent aid to the Egyptian rebel. Egypt cast off the Assyrian yoke; but Gyges was slain in a terrible struggle with the Cimmerians, who had spread desolation throughout his dominions; and Ardys, his successor on the Lydian throne, renewed the homage to the Assyrian king which his father had relinquished.

Asshur-bani-pal next engaged in an important war with some Arab tribes of the desert who had aided Saül-Mugina in his revolt against his brother and suzerain. The Arab leader in this war was Vaiteha, whose allies were Natun, or Nathan, King of the Nabathæans, and Ammu-ladin, King of Kedar. The whole border of Arabia from the Persian Gulf to Syria, and thence southward by Damascus to Petra, was the scene of military operations in this war. Petra, Moab, Edom, Zoar and several other cities fell into the hands of the Assyrians. The Arabs were defeated with great slaughter in the final battle at Khukhuruna, in the mountains near Damascus; and the two Arab chiefs who had aided Saül-Mugina were carried captives to Nineveh, and there publicly executed.

Thus ended the annals of Asshur-bani-pal, who was the most enterprising and the most powerful of Assyrian warrior kings, and who extended the Assyrian Empire in every direction beyond its previous limits. In Egypt he completed the task begun by his father Esar-haddon, and established the Assyrian dominion for some years, not only at Sais and Memphis, but likewise at Thebes. In Asia Minor he subdued large sections never before invaded by any Assyrian king, and carried his renown to the western extremity of the Asiatic continent. In the north he held, not only the Minni, but the Urarda, or true Armenians, among his tributaries. On the south he formally annexed Susiana to the Assyrian Empire, and on the west he signally chastised the Arabs.

Thus in the middle part of Asshur-bani-pal's brilliant reign Assyria reached the culminating point of her greatness—the zenith of her power and the widest extent of her dominion—being at this time paramount over the portion of Western Asia from the Mediterranean and the Halys on the west to the Caspian Sea and the Persian desert on the east, and from Arabia and the Persian Gulf on the south to the northern frontier of Armenia and the center of Cappadocia on the north. In Africa the authority of Assyria was at this time acknowledged by Egypt as far south as Thebes. Thus the Assyrian influence extended over Susiana, Chaldæa, Babylonia, Media, Matiene, or the Zagros range, Mesopotamia; portions of Armenia, Cappadocia and Cilicia; Syria, Phœnicia, Palestine, Idumæa, part of Arabia and nearly all of Egypt. The island of Cyprus may also have been a dependency. But Persia proper, Bactria and Sogdiana, even Hyrcania, were beyond the eastern limit of Assyrian power, which on the north did not on this side extend farther than about the vicinity of Kasvin, and towards the south was confined within the Zagros mountain range; while on the west, Phrygia, Lydia, Lycia, even Pamphylia, were independent, the arms of Assyria having never been, as far as known, carried westward beyond Cilicia or across the river Halys.

Asshur-bani-pal was also noted for his love of hunting, especially lion-hunting. On the banks of streams, and in his pleasure-galley in mid-stream, he roused the king of beasts from his lair by means of hounds and beaters, and slew him with his arrows. In his own park of paradise large and ferocious beasts, brought from distant quarters, were placed in traps about the grounds, and when he approached they were released from confinement, while he drove among them in his chariot, letting fly his arrows at each, seldom missing the marks at which they were directed. With two or three attendants armed with spears, he often encountered the terrific spring of the bolder beasts, who rushed wild with rage at the royal marksman to tear him from the chariot. On some occasions he left the chariot-board and engaged in a close struggle single-handed with the brutes, without the protection of armor, in his usual dress, with only a fillet upon his head, and would pierce them through the heart with sword or spear. He often engaged in the chase of the wild ass, and hunted the stag, the hind and the ibex, or wild goat. His love of sport is also attested by the figures of his favorite hounds made in clay, and painted and inscribed with their respective names.

Asshur-bani-pal was the only Assyrian king who exhibited any taste for learning and literature. His predecessors only left to their posterity some records of the events of their reigns, inscribed on cylinders, tablets, slabs, winged man-headed bulls and lions, and a few dedicatory inscriptions, addresses to the deities whom they particularly worshiped. Asshur-bani-pal displayed far more varied and all-embracing literary tastes. He established a Royal Library, consisting of clay tablets, at Nineveh, from which the British Museum has derived its most valuable collection. Under the auspices of this monarch were prepared comparative vocabularies, lists of deities and their epithets, chronological lists of kings and eponyms, records of astronomical observations, grammars, histories and various kinds of scientific works. These treasures of learning were preserved in certain chambers of the palace of Asshur-bani-pal's grandfather, Sennacherib, where they were discovered by Mr. Layard. There are also a large number of religious documents, prayers, invocations, etc., besides many juridical treatises, the fines to be imposed for certain social offenses; and lastly, there are all the contents of the Registry office, such as deeds of sale and barter referring to land, houses, and all kinds of property, contracts, bonds for loans, benefactions and other different kinds of legal instruments. Selections from the tablets have been published in England, being prepared for that purpose by Sir Henry Rawlinson and others. The clay tablets on which they were inscribed lay here in such large numbers, sometimes whole, but generally in fragments, that they covered the floors of the chambers for more than a foot high. Mr. Layard truly says that "the documents thus discovered at Nineveh probably exceed all that has yet been afforded by the monuments of Egypt." Among the interesting and valuable results which these documents have recently yielded is the chronological scheme drawn from seven different tablets, and known as "the Assyrian Canon."

As a builder Asshur-bani-pal fully rivaled, if he did not surpass, the greatest of his predecessors. His magnificent palace at Nineveh, whose ruins are seen on the Koyunjik mound, within a few hundred yards of his illustrious grandfather's splendid royal edifice, was built on a plan different from those of former kings. The main building consisted of three arms branching from a common center, thus in its general form resembling the letter T. The central point was entered by a long ascending gallery lined with sculptures, leading from a gateway, with rooms attached, at a corner of the great court, first a distance of one hundred and ninety feet in a direction parallel to the top bar of the T, and then a distance of eighty feet in a direction at right angles to this, thus bringing it down precisely to the central point from which the arms extended. The whole structure was thus shaped like a cross, having one arm extending from the top towards the left or west. The principal apartments were in the lower limb of the cross, where a grand hall extended almost the entire length of the limb, no less than one hundred and forty-five feet long by twenty-eight and a half feet wide, opening towards the east on a great court, paved principally with patterned slabs, and communicating with a number of smaller rooms towards the west, and through these smaller rooms with a second court, facing towards the south-west and the south. The next largest apartment was in the right or eastern arm of the cross, and was a hall one hundred and eight feet long by twenty-four feet broad, divided by a wide doorway, in which were two pillar-bases, into a square ante-chamber twenty-four feet each way, and an inner apartment about eighty feet long. Neither arm of the cross was thoroughly explored, and it is not known whether they reached to the extreme edge of the eastern and western courts, dividing each into two, or whether they only extended into the courts a certain distance. Only one doorway has been discovered leading from the rest of the palace to the western rooms.

Asshur-bani-pal's great palace was especially remarkable for its beautiful and elaborate ornamentation. The courts were paved with large slabs covered with elegant patterns. Some of the doorways had arched tops highly adorned with rosettes, lotuses, etc. The chambers and passages were lined throughout with alabaster slabs, which bore reliefs designed with remarkable spirit, and executed with wonderful detail and fineness. Here were represented interesting hunting scenes, such as the wild ass, the stag, the hind, the dying wild ass, the lion about to spring, the wounded wild ass seized by hounds, the wounded lion, the lion biting a chariot-wheel, the king shooting a lion with his arrow, the lion-hunt on a river, the king killing lions, the lion let out of a trap, the hound held in leash, the wounded lioness, the hound chasing a wild ass, the hound chasing a doe, the stag taking the water, etc.

In this part of the palace were likewise illustrated the king's private life, the trees and flowers of the palace garden, the royal galley with its two banks of oars, the libation over four dead lions, the temple with pillars resting on lions, and different bands of musicians. A part of the ascending passage was adorned with various scenes, such as a long train, with game, nets and dogs returning from the chase. In combination with all the sculptures just enumerated were many scenes of sieges and battles, illustrating Asshur-bani-pal's wars. Reliefs resembling these last were discovered by Mr. Layard in certain chambers of Sennacherib's palace which had been embellished by Asshur-bani-pal. These reliefs were distinguished for the large number and small size of the figures, for the variety and spirit of the attitudes, and for the careful finish of all the minute details of the scenes illustrated upon them. These give us a good representation of an Assyrian battle, showing us at one view the battle, the flight and pursuit, the capture and treatment of prisoners, the gathering of the spoil and the beheading of the slain. These reliefs are now in the British Museum.

Asshur-bani-pal, as already observed, made additions to Sennacherib's great palace at Nineveh, and erected some other buildings at the same city, whose remains are seen on the Nebbi-Yunus mound, where have been discovered slabs inscribed with his name and an account of his wars. He also built a temple to Ishtar at Nineveh, whose ruins are seen on the Koyunjik mound, and repaired a shrine of the same goddess at Arbela. If he was the monarch called Sardanapalus by the Greeks, he was the founder of Tarsus, in Cilicia, and of the neighboring city of Anchialus, on the authority of some classical writers, though more reliable authors inform us that Tarsus was founded by Sennacherib. It was believed generally by the Greeks that the tomb of Sardanapalus was in this vicinity. They described this tomb as a monument of some height, having a statue of the king on the top, representing him as snapping his fingers.

The stone base bore an inscription in Assyrian characters, which they interpreted as follows: "Sardanapalus, son of Anacyndaraxes, built Tarsus and Anchialus in one day. Do thou, O stranger, eat, drink, and amuse thyself; for all the rest of human life is not worth so much as this"—"this" signifying the sound supposed to be made by the king with his fingers. Clearchus said that the inscription was simply the following: "Sardanapalus, son of Anacyndaraxes, built Tarsus and Anchiale in one day—yet now he is dead." Amyntas said that the tomb of Sardanapalus was at Nineveh, and gave a very different inscription. Rawlinson thinks that the so-called tomb of Sardanapalus was really the stele set up by Sennacherib on his conquest of Cilicia and founding of Tarsus, as related by Polyhistor.

The Greeks seem to have known more of this monarch than of any other Assyrian king. The account given by Ctesias of the voluptuous Assyrian monarch whom he called Sardanapalus, and repeated from him by subsequent authors, does not probably refer to Asshur-bani-pal, but rather alludes to his successor, the last Assyrian king. Asshur-bani-pal, the vanquisher of Tirhakah, the conqueror of the tribes beyond the Taurus, the great warrior king whom the wealthy and prosperous Gyges, King of Lydia, sought to propitiate by means of rich presents, was so unlike the mere voluptuary who never ventured outside the palace gates, but confined himself exclusively to the seraglio, performing woman's work and often attired in female apparel. He was one of the greatest of Assyria's kings. He conquered Egypt and Susiana, held Babylon in quiet subjection with the exception of the short revolt of Saül-Mugina, extended his conquests far into Armenia, led his armies beyond the Taurus, and subjugated the barbarous tribes of Asia Minor. During the intervals of peace he employed himself in hunting the lion, and in the erection and embellishment of palaces and temples. In one respect alone does Asshur-bani-pal's character, as disclosed to us by the monuments, exhibit the slightest likeness to that of the Sardanapalus of Ctesias. Asshur-bani-pal obtained for himself a multitude of wives. Always upon the suppression of a revolt, he required the conquered vassal to send to Nineveh, along with his tribute, one or more of his daughters. These princesses became inmates of his harem, or seraglio.

Asshur-bani-pal's glory was well known to the Greeks. He was doubtless one of the "two kings called Sardanapalus," celebrated by Hellanicus; and he must have been "the warlike Sardanapalus" of Callisthenes. Herodotus alluded to his great wealth, and Aristophanes employed his name as a byword for magnificence. In his reign the Assyrian Empire attained its greatest dimensions, Assyrian art reached its highest point, and the Assyrian dominion appeared likely to extend itself over the entire East. Then Assyria most fully answered the forcible description given her by the Jewish prophet Ezekiel in these words: "The Assyrian was a cedar in Lebanon, with fair branches, and with a shadowing shroud, and of high stature; and his top was among the thick boughs. The waters made him great; the deep set him up on high with her rivers running about his plants, and sent out her little rivers unto all the trees of the field. Therefore his height was exalted above all the trees of the field, and his boughs were multiplied, and his branches became long because of the multitude of waters, when he shot forth. All the fowls of the heaven made their nests in his boughs, and under his branches did all the beasts of the field bring forth their young, and under his shadow dwelt *all great nations*. Thus was he fair in his greatness, in the length of his branches; for his root was by great waters. The cedars in the garden of God could not hide him; the fir-trees were not like his boughs; and the chestnut-trees were not like his branches; *nor any tree in the garden of God was like unto him in his beauty*."

With all their advance in civilization, their progress in art and the practical inventions, their ever-increasing literature, the Assyrians still retained the cruel and vindictive spirit of the most barbarous ages and nations in conducting their wars. Through the whole period of their history their treatment of captured enemies continued to be of the most barbarous brutality, which all their advancing culture and their progress in the arts of civilized life did not tend to mitigate or soften. Sennacherib and Esarhaddon were more merciful than their predecessors, frequently sparing their captives, even when rebels; but Asshur-bani-pal restored the old practice of executions, mutilations and tortures, and was apparently the most cruel of all the Assyrian kings. On his bas-reliefs we see the unresisting enemy pierced through with the spear, the tongue torn from the mouth of the captive accused of blasphemy, the rebel king beheaded on the battle-field, and the prisoner led to execution with the head of a friend or brother hung round his neck. We see the scourgers preceding the king as his regular attendants, with their whips passed through their girdles. We observe living and dead men subjected to the operation of flaying. We behold scenes in which the executioner is represented as first striking in the face with his fist those about to be executed. Thus we have all the evidence of barbarous cruelty, such as had a brutalizing influence on those who inflicted it, and also on those who witnessed it. Nineveh was deservedly designated by the Jewish prophet Nahum as "a bloody city," or "a city of bloods;" and, in the language of the same prophet, "the lion did tear in pieces enough for his whelps, and strangled for his lionesses, and filled his holes with prey, and his dens with ravin." Asshur-bani-pal gloried in his vindictive and unsparing cruelties, transmitting the record of them to posterity by representing them in all their horrors upon his palace walls.

It has been generally supposed that Asshur-bani-pal died about B. C. 648 or 647, in which case his entire reign would have been a brilliant and prosperous one; but recent discoveries render it probable that he lived and reigned until B. C. 626, and that he was the Cinneladanus of the Canon of Ptolemy, who occupied the Babylonian throne from B. C. 647 to B. C. 626. Asshur-bani-pal distinctly asserts that when he subdued Babylon and put his brother Saül-Mugina to death he became King of Babylon himself; and many tablets remain, dated by his regnal years at Babylon, while the eponyms which can be assigned to his reign are at least twenty-six or twenty-seven. Polyhistor distinctly says that the successor of Sam-mughes, or Saül-Mugina, on the Babylonian throne was his brother, and that he reigned twenty-one years. Thus modern writers have identified Asshur-bani-pal with Cinneladanus, and have concluded that he reigned in all forty-two years, from B. C. 668 to B. C. 626. In this case Assyria's decline commenced during the later years of Asshur-bani-pal's reign, so that during this period she was obliged to exchange her former aggressive course toward other nations for a defensive attitude to maintain her own continued existence against the fierce assaults of the powerful neighboring kingdom of Media and the destructive inroads of the wild Scyths from the plains of Central Asia.

The centralized monarchy established in Media about B. C. 640 rapidly developed into a great military power. Setting aside the old system of separate government and village autonomy, the Medes had united themselves into a single consolidated monarchy, and about B. C. 634, when Asshur-bani-pal had reigned over Assyria thirty-four years, these people undertook an expedition against Nineveh, but failed in this first attack. Phraortes, or the actual leader of this army of invasion, was thoroughly defeated by the Assyrians, his host being cut to pieces, and himself being among the slain. Nevertheless the fact that the Medes had assumed the offensive was a potent cause for alarm, as it illustrated a new state of affairs in Western Asia, fully demonstrating that Assyria was no longer the arbitress of the destinies of nations. Cyaxares, the next Median king, led an army against Assyria about B. C. 632, defeated the Assyrians in battle, and at once laid siege to Nineveh, but was recalled to the defense of his own country against a devastating barbarian tor-

POLITICAL HISTORY.

rent which threatened to engulf the monarchy which had so suddenly grown up on the eastern borders of Assyria. This new danger was an irresistible inroad of the Scyths, or Scythians, from Central Asia, who swept with destructive force over both Media and Assyria, threatening the utter annihilation of the civilized nations of Western Asia.

Herodotus and Hippocrates described the Scythians as coarse and gross in their habits, with large fleshy bodies, loose joints, soft swollen bellies and scanty hair. They never washed themselves, only cleansing their persons with a vapor bath, their women applying to their bodies a paste which left them glossy after it had been removed. They dwelt in wagons, or in rude tents consisting of woolen felts arranged around three bent sticks inclined towards each other. They subsisted on mare's milk and cheese, adding at times boiled beef and horse-flesh as a delicacy. They drank the blood of their enemies slain in battle. They cut off the heads of these dead foes, and showed them to their kings to obtain each his respective share of the spoil. They also stripped the scalps from the skulls and suspended them on their bridle-reins as trophies. Occasionally they flayed the right arms and hands of their slain enemies, and used the skins as coverings for their quivers. The upper part of the skulls were usually converted into drinking-cups. They spent the larger portion of each day on horseback, attending on the vast herds of cattle which they pastured. They used the bow, their favorite weapon, while riding, shooting their arrows with unerring aim. They also each carried a short spear or javelin, and sometimes also a short sword or battle-ax.

The Scythian nation embraced many separate tribes. At the head of all was a royal tribe, corresponding to the "Golden Horde" of the Mongols, surpassing in numbers and bravery any of the others, and considering them all as slaves. The kings ruled by hereditary right, and their families belonged to the royal tribe. Several kings frequently ruled at the same time, but in great emergencies the supreme power was always virtually vested in one man.

The Scythian religion embraced the worship of the Sun and Moon, Fire, Air, Earth, Water, and a deity resembling the Greek Hercules; but the chief object of adoration was the naked sword. The country was divided into sections, in each of which was a vast pile of brushwood, serving as a temple to the vicinity, and having planted at its top an antique sword or cimeter. On a specified day of each year solemn sacrifices of human beings and animals were offered at these shrines, and the warm blood of the victims was poured upon the sword at the top. The human victims for sacrifice, who were captives taken in war, were hewn to pieces at the foot of the mound; their limbs were wildly tossed into the air by the votaries, and the bloody fragments were left where they had fallen. The Scythians had no priest caste, but they believed in divination, the diviners comprising a distinct class vested with important powers. When the king was ill he sent for these diviners, to inform him of the cause of his illness, which they generally ascribed to the circumstance that an individual, whom they named, had sworn falsely by the Royal Hearth. Those accused of this offense, if found guilty by several bodies of diviners, were beheaded in punishment, and their property was given to their original accusers.

Such were the chief characteristics of the Scythians, as described by Herodotus, who tells us that they were the ruling race over a great part of the steppe region extending from the river Ister (now Danube) and the Carpathian mountains on the west to the eastern limits of the region embraced by modern Turkestan on the east. Coarse and repulsive in appearance, ferocious in temper, savage in habits, and powerful on account of their vast numbers and a system of warfare not easy to withstand, and in which they had become expert, they could well strike consternation even into the strong and warlike Median nation. Successive hordes of Scyths swept through the passes of the Caucasus, and spread ruin and devastation over the rich plains to the south of them. Onward they pushed in swarms, overwhelming and irresistible, overrunning Iberia and Upper Media, reducing the rich cultivated country to a howling wilderness. They consumed the crops, carried off or destroyed the herds, burned the villages and homesteads, massacred or enslaved such of the inhabitants as did not escape to the lofty mountain summits or other strongholds, sparing neither age nor sex, and converted the whole country into a scene of desolation. The strongly-fortified towns which resisted the invading Scyths, when not starved into submission, escaped by consenting to pay a tribute. Herodotus informs us that these barbarians were masters of all Western Asia from the Caucasus to the frontiers of Egypt for a period of twenty-eight years; and their ravages spread over, not only Media, but Armenia, Assyria, Mesopotamia, Syria and Palestine.

The resistless tide of barbarian invasion continued to roll on, sweeping from one region to another, plundering and ravaging everywhere, settling nowhere. When the savage hordes had reached Southern Palestine, the course of invasion was stayed by the Egyptian king, Psammetichus, who was then engaged in the siege of Ashdod. Upon hearing of the approach of the Scythian host to Ascalon, Psammetichus sent an embassy to their leader and bribed him by means of valuable presents to abstain from an invasion of Egypt.

Thenceforth the power of the Scythian invaders declined, and the nations whose armies they had beaten, whose lands they had ravaged with fire and sword, began to recover themselves. Cyaxares, King of Media, and the sovereigns of other nations, drove them beyond their dominions, many of the barbarians returning across the Caucasus to their home-land, large numbers being slain in battle or massacred, and the remainder submitting and entering the service of the native Asian monarchs. The only vestiges of this destructive Scythic inroad were the names of the Armenian province thenceforth called Sacasēné and the Syrian town known thereafter as Scythopolis, a Greek name signifying City of the Scyths.

Weakened by the severity of the Scythian attack, Assyria rapidly declined from this time. The country had been ravaged and depopulated, the provinces had been plundered, many of the great towns had been pillaged, the palaces of the kings had been burned, and much of the gold and silver had been carried away. Assyria was but the shadow of her former self when the Scythians retired from the country. Enfeebled and exhausted, she was ready to fall before the arms of a conqueror. Babylonia and the other provinces of the empire, from the force of habit and because they too had been exhausted by the barbarian inundation, continued loyal to Assyria to the very last. Thus Asshur-bani-pal ruled over an extensive empire to the end of his life.

But Asshur-bani-pal died B. C. 626, after a reign of forty-two years, and was succeeded by his son, ASSHUR-EMID-ILIN, called Saracus by Abydenus. He was the last Assyrian king, and reigned but one year. We have very few native records of this monarch, and the only classical notices concerning him are the account given of him by Ctesias, and a few sentences in the writings of Abydenus and Polyhistor. A few legends on bricks inform us that he began the erection of a palace at Calah, whose remains are now seen at the south-east part of the Nimrud mound. The contrast between this unfinished edifice and those grand royal residences of former Assyrian kings clearly exhibited the waning glory of the mighty monarchy which had swayed the destinies of Western Asia for nearly seven centuries. Instead of the alabaster bas-reliefs which embellished the palaces of the predecessors of this last Assyrian monarch, his edifice was adorned with nothing better than coarse limestone slabs without sculptures or inscriptions; and in place of the enameled bricks of elegant patterns which ornamented the magnificent structures of Sargon, Sennacherib and Asshur-bani-pal, we find in this building a simple plaster above the slabs.

A series of small chambers, none of which was over forty-five feet long, nor more than twenty-five feet in its greatest width, was sufficient for the last Assyrian sovereign, whose diminished court could not now have filled the spacious halls of his predecessors. The Nimrud palace of Asshur-emid-ilin, or Saracus, appears to have occupied less than half the space covered by any other palace upon the mound. The decline of taste is clearly demonstrated by its lack of grand façades or magnificent gateways, its small and inconvenient rooms, running in suites which communicated with one another without any entrances from courts or passages, composed of sun-dried bricks faced with limestone and plaster, and roughly paved with limestone flags. The mere fact that Saracus should have entertained the thought of making his residence in a structure of so poor and mean a character is the most convincing evidence of Assyria's decadence and degeneracy on the eve of her overthrow. The rude condition of this palace, and its entire want of elegant ornamentation, is to be partially accounted for by the circumstance that Saracus perished, along with his capital and his empire, before he had time to complete the edifice.

While this building was undergoing erection Saracus held his court at Nineveh, where he prepared to defend himself against the enemy who, taking advantage of his powerless condition, lost no time in pressing forward the conquest of his rapidly-decaying and declining empire. The Medes, favored by nature in their land of rocky hills and inaccessible mountain chains, did not suffer as much from the ravages of the Scyths as did the Assyrians in their defenseless plains; and they were the first of the nations exposed to the barbarian inundation to recover from its destructive effects. Having repulsed the Scyths and expelled them from his country, Cyaxares, the warlike monarch who founded the great Median Empire, led a large army into Assyria from the east; while his allies, the Susianians, entered the country in force from the south.

To defend his country against this double invasion, Saracus, the last of the great dynasty founded by Sargon, divided his forces, retaining a portion under his own command to oppose the Medes, while he assigned the other part to his general, Nabopolassar, whom he ordered to Babylon to check the advance of the Susianians. But Nabopolassar, seeing his own opportunity in his sovereign's perilous dilemma, turned traitor, and, instead of fighting loyally against the foes of Assyria, he entered into secret negotiations with Cyaxares, agreeing to an alliance with him against the Assyrians, and obtaining the daughter of the Median king as a bride for his eldest son, Nebuchadnezzar. Uniting their forces, Cyaxares and Nabopolassar jointly attacked Nineveh; whereupon Saracus, or Asshur-emid-ilin, unable to defend his capital, and overcome by despair, set fire to his palace and perished in the flames. The once-proud city of Nineveh was plundered and destroyed by the conquering Medes and their allies.

The account of the downfall of Assyria as related by Ctesias is so fanciful that it is utterly discarded by the best modern historians. He says that the Medes were accompanied by the Persians, and the Babylonians by some Arab allies, and that the assailing army numbered four hundred thousand men. In the first engagement the Assyrians were victorious, and the attacking army was driven to the Zagros mountains. A second and a third attack likewise failed. The tide of battle turned in favor of the assailants upon the arrival of a strong reënforcement from Bactria, when a night attack upon the Assyrian camp was crowned with complete success. The Assyrian king sought refuge in his capital, leaving his army under the command of his brother-in-law, Salæmenes, who was soon defeated and slain. The siege of Nineveh then began, and lasted over two years without any result. An unusually wet season in the third year of the siege caused an extraordinary rise in the Tigris, destroying more than two miles of the city wall; whereupon the king, who had been told by an oracle to fear nothing until the river became his enemy, yielding to despair, made a funeral pile of all his richest furniture, and burnt himself with his concubines and his eunuchs in his palace. The Medes and their allies thereupon entering the city on the side laid open by the flood, plundered and destroyed it. This description of the last siege of Nineveh, as related by Ctesias, has been transmitted to posterity through the

WINGED MAN-HEADED BULL.
Now in British Museum.

writings of Diodorus Siculus, and, like most of his statements, is unworthy of credit.

Thus fell the mighty Assyrian Empire, not so much from any inherent weakness as by an unfortunate combination of circumstances—the invasion of the powerful and warlike Medes when the empire had been exhausted by the terrible inroad of the Scyths, and the treason and perfidy of its leading general. With the destruction of the empire the Assyrian race sank into oblivion, and Assyrian history ceased forever. Assyria upon its downfall was divided between its conquerors, the portion east of the Tigris falling to Media, and the part west of the river being absorbed by Babylonia. By the successive changes in this part of Asia, the country has continually changed masters, being successively under the Medo-Persian, Græco-Macedonian, Syrian, Parthian, New Persian, Saracen, Seljuk, Mongol, and for the last five centuries under the Ottoman Turkish, dominion. The country now forms part of the Turkish province of Kurdistan, and the half-savage modern Kurds are the direct descendants of the renowned ancient Assyrians. The palaces in which Sargon, Sennacherib, Esarhaddon and Asshur-bani-pal dwelt in luxury and splendor, after lying imbedded beneath the mounds and ruins of twenty-five centuries, have in our day, thanks to the enterprise and diligence of patient explorers like Layard and Botta, been brought out of their long concealment to the light of the modern world; and many wonderful sculptures from the great cities of ancient Assyria now adorn the museums of London, Paris and Berlin. The great cities of Asshur, Calah, Dur-Sargina and Nineveh, with their magnificent royal residences, their busy shops and factories teeming with the products of industry, their crowded thoroughfares in which victorious warrior-kings were greeted with the applause of their subjects and the triumphant shouts of their stalwart and invincible soldiery, now exist only in the records and memory of their past glory and greatness, and in the ruins on the mounds of Kileh-Sherghat, Nimrud, Khorsabad and Koyunjik, only tenanted by the wandering Kurds watching their herds

WINGED MAN-HEADED LION.
Now in British Museum.

and flocks, and resounding with the jackal's howl after the sun in its daily course has sunk to rest beneath the western horizon.

The independent kingdom of Assyria lasted about a thousand years, but the empire covered a little less than the last seven centuries of this period, from B. C. 1300 to B. C. 625, when it fell before the arms of the Medes, or more properly only about five centuries, from B. C. 1150. The power and extent of the empire culminated during the brilliant reign of Asshur-bani-pal, just before its rapid decline and sudden fall.

THE DEATH OF SARACUS.

KINGS OF ASSYRIA.

B. C. B. C.			
	BEL-SUMILI-KAPI	Called the founder of the kingdom on a genealogical tablet.	
* * * * * * *			
	IRBA-VUL	Mentioned by Tiglath-Pileser I. as a former king. A very archaic tablet in the British Museum is dated in his reign.	
* * * * * * *			
	ASSHUR-IDDIN-AKHI	Mentioned by Tiglath-Pileser I. as a former king,	
* * * * * * *			
About 1440 to 1420.	ASSHUR-BIL-NISI-SU	Mentioned on a synchronistic tablet, which connects them with the time of Purna-puriyas, the Chaldæan king. Asshur-upallit mentioned on Kileh-Sherghat bricks.	EARLY ASSYRIAN KINGDOM.
" 1420 to 1400.	BUZUR-ASSHUR (successor) . .		
" 1400 to 1380.	ASSHUR-UPALLIT (successor) .		
" 1380 to 1360.	BEL-LUSH (his son)	Names and succession found on Kileh-Sherghat bricks, vases, etc. Shalmaneser I. mentioned also on a genealogical slab and in the standard inscription of Nimrud.	
" 1360 to 1340.	PUD-IL (his son)		
" 1340 to 1320.	VUL-LUSH I. (his son) . . .		
" 1320 to 1300.	SHALMANESER I. (his son) . .		
" 1300 to 1280.	TIGLATHI-NIN I. (his son) . .	Mentioned on a genealogical tablet. Called "the conqueror of Babylon," and placed by Sennacherib 600 years before his own capture of Babylonia in B. C. 703.	
* * * * * *			
" 1230 to 1210.	BEL-KUDUR-UZUR	Mentioned on the synchronistic tablet as the predecessor of Nin-pala-zira.	
" 1210 to 1190.	NIN-PALA-ZIRA (successor) . .	Names and relationship given in cylinder of Tiglath-Pileser I.	THE OLD ASSYRIAN EMPIRE.
" 1190 to 1170.	ASSHUR-DAYAN I. (his son) . .		
" 1170 to 1150.	MUTAGGIL-NEBO (his son) . .		
" 1150 to 1130.	ASSHUR-RIS-ILIM (his son) . .	Mentioned on the synchronistic tablet above spoken of. Date of Tiglath-Pileser I. fixed by the Bavian inscription. Dates of the other kings calculated from his at twenty years to a generation.	
" 1130 to 1110.	TIGLATH-PILESER I. (his son) .		
" 1110 to 1090.	ASSHUR-BIL-KALA (his son) . .		
" 1090 to 1070.	SHAMAS-VUL I. (his brother) .		
* * * * * *			
	ASSHUR-MAZUR	Mentioned in an inscription of Shalmaneser II.	
* * * * * *			
" 930 to 911 . .	ASSHUR-DAYAN II, ...	The kings from Asshur-dayan II. to Vul-lush III. are proved to have been in direct succession by the Kileh-Sherghat and Nimrud monuments. The last nine reigns are given in the Assyrian Canon. The Canon is the sole authority for the last three. The dates of the whole series are determined from the Canon of Ptolemy by calculating back from B. C. 680, his date for the accession of Esar-haddon (Asaridanus). They might also be fixed from the year of the great eclipse.	
" 911 to 889 . .	VUL-LUSH II. (his son) . . .		
" 889 to 883 . .	TIGLATHI-NIN II. (his son) . .		
" 883 to 858 . .	ASSHUR-IZIR-PAL (his son) . .		
" 858 to 823 . .	SHALMANESER II. (his son) . .		
" 823 to 810 . .	SHAMAS-VUL II. (his son) . .		
" 810 to 781 . .	VUL-LUSH III. (his son) . . .		
" 781 to 771 . .	SHALMANESER III.		
" 771 to 753 . .	ASSHUR-DAYAN III.		
" 753 to 745 . .	ASSHUR-LUSH		
" 745 to 727 . .	TIGLATH-PILESER II.	The years of these kings, from Esar-haddon upwards, are taken from the Assyrian Canon. The dates accord strictly with the Canon of Ptolemy. The last year of Asshur-bani-pal is to some extent conjectural.	NEW OR LOWER ASSYRIAN EMPIRE.
" 727 to 722 . .	SHALMANESER IV.		
" 722 to 705 . .	SARGON		
" 705 to 681 . .	SENNACHERIB (his son)		
" 681 to 668 . .	ESAR-HADDON (his son) . . .		
" 668 to 626 . .	ASSHUR-BANI-PAL (his son) . .		
" 626 to 625 . .	ASSHUR-EMID-ILIN (his son) . .		

SECTION IV.—ASSYRIAN CIVILIZATION.

AYS Professor Rawlinson: "The nature of the dominion established by the great Mesopotamian monarchy over the countries included within the limits above indicated, will perhaps be best understood if we compare it with the empire of Solomon. Solomon 'reigned over *all the kingdoms* from the river (Euphrates) unto the land of the Philistines and unto the border of Egypt: they *brought presents* and *served* Solomon all the days of his life.' The first and most striking feature of the earliest empires is that they are a mere congeries of kingdoms; the countries over which the dominant state acquires an influence, not only retain their distinct individuality, as is the case in some modern empires, but remain in all respects such as they were before, with the simple addition of certain obligations contracted towards the paramount authority. They keep their old laws, their old religion, their line of kings, their law of succession, their whole internal organization and machinery; they only acknowledge an external suzerainty which binds them to the performance of certain duties towards the Head of the Empire. These duties, as understood in the earliest times, may be summed up in the two words 'homage' and 'tribute;' the subject kings 'serve' and 'bring presents.' They are bound to acts of submission; must attend the court of their suzerain when summoned, unless they have a reasonable excuse; must there salute him as a superior, and otherwise acknowledge his rank; above all, they must pay him regularly the fixed tribute which has been imposed upon them at the time of their submission or subjection, the unauthorized withholding of which is open and avowed rebellion. Finally, they must allow his troops free passage through their dominions, and must oppose any attempt at invasion by way of their country on the part of his enemies. Such are the earliest and most essential obligations on the part of the subject states in an empire of the primitive type, like that of Assyria; and these obligations, with the corresponding one on the part of the dominant power of the protection of its dependents against foreign foes, appear to have constituted the sole links which joined together in one the heterogeneous materials of which that empire consisted. * * *

"Such, in its broad and general outlines, was the empire of the Assyrians. It embodied the earliest, simplest and most crude conception which the human mind forms of a widely extended dominion. It was a 'kingdom-empire,' like the empires of Solomon, of Nebuchadnezzar, of Chedor-laomer, and probably of Cyaxares, and is the best specimen of its class, being the largest, the longest in duration, and the best known of all such governments that has existed. It exhibits in a marked way both the strength and weakness of this class of monarchies —their strength in the extraordinary magnificence, grandeur, wealth, and refinement of the capital; their weakness in the impoverishment, the exhaustion, and the consequent disaffection of the subject states. Ever falling to pieces, it was perpetually reconstructed by the genius and prowess of a long succession of warrior princes, seconded by the skill and bravery of the people. Fortunate in having for a long time no very powerful neighbors, it found little difficulty in extending itself throughout regions divided and subdivided among hundreds of petty chiefs, incapable of union, and singly quite unable to contend with the forces of a large and populous country. Frequently endangered by revolts, yet always triumphing over them, it maintained itself for five centuries, gradually advancing its influence, and was only overthrown after a fierce struggle by a new kingdom formed upon its borders, which, taking advantage of a time of exhaustion, and leagued with the most powerful of the subject states, was enabled to accomplish the destruction of the long-dominant people."

CIVILIZATION.

As in the case of the Chaldæans, it was formerly a subject of dispute as to what branch of the Caucasian race the Assyrians belonged; but it has now been definitely determined by the evidence of language, as well as the testimony of the Hebrew accounts, that the Chaldæans were mainly a Hamitic, or Cushite race, fused slightly with Semitic, Aryan and Turanian elements; while the Assyrians are found to have been pure Semites, and therefore a kindred people with the Hebrews, or Israelites, the Arabs, the Syrians, or Aramæans, and the Phœnicians. The Mosaic genealogies connected Asshur with Aram, Eber and Joktan, the progenitors respectively of the Aramæans, or Syrians, the Israelites, or Hebrews, and the Northern, or Joktanian, Arabs. The languages, physical types and moral characteristics of these races were well known, as they all belonged to a single family—to what ethnologists and philologists call the Semitic family. The manners and customs, particularly the religious customs, of the Assyrians were identical with those of the Syrians and Phœnicians. The modern Chaldæans of Kurdistan, who consider themselves descendants of the ancient inhabitants of the neighboring Assyria, still speak a Semitic dialect— a fact discovered and reported by the elder Niebuhr, and confirmed by Mr. Ainsworth. These three circumstances are sufficient evidence that the Assyrians were Semites, being closely allied in race with the Syrians, the Later Babylonians, the Phœnicians, the Israelites and the Northern Arabs; and recent linguistic discoveries have fully confirmed this view. We now have in the engraved slabs, the clay tablets, the cylinders and the bricks, excavated from the ruins of the great Assyrian cities, abundant documentary testimony of the character of the Assyrian language, and of the ethnic character of the people. All who have examined this evidence have arrived at the conclusion that the language of these records is Semitic, and that it is closely connected with the Hebrew, the Syriac, the Later Babylonian and the Arabic.

The physical characteristics of the Assyrians, as disclosed to us by their sculptures, also confirm this view. Their sculptured effigies bear the most striking resemblance to the Jewish physiognomy. The low and straight forehead, the full brow, the large and almond-shaped eye, the aquiline nose a little coarse at the end and unduly depressed, the strong and firm mouth with over-thick lips, the well-formed chin—best observed in the representation of eunuchs—the thick hair and heavy beard, both of black color—all these, as exhibited by the Assyrian sculptures, display a remarkable likeness to the striking peculiarities of the Jewish head and face, and also bear somewhat of a resemblance to the physiognomy of the Arabs, and to all branches of the Semitic race. These traits are now common to the Jew, the Arab and the Kurd, while in ancient times they characterized the Assyrians, Syrians, Phœnicians, Hebrews and the minor Semitic nations. The Egyptian sculptures of Amunoph III., as representing the Patena, or people of Bashan; the Asuru, or Assyrians; and the Karukamishi, or people of Carchemish, show us the same type of physiognomy, which the Egyptians regarded as common to all the nations of Western Asia. In shape the Assyrians are most truly represented by their descendants, the modern Chaldæans of Kurdistan. Like the modern Kurd, the Assyrian was robust and stalwart in bodily frame, with broad shoulders and large limbs. The monuments of no other people show us so strong a race in muscular development as the ancient Assyrian. The large brawny limbs of this resolute and sturdy people, whom Rawlinson fitly calls "the Romans of Asia," indicate a physical power belonging to no other nation.

The mental and moral characteristics of the Jews and the Assyrians also bore the closest analogy. In each the religious sentiment was peculiarly predominant. The inscriptions of Assyrian kings begin and end with praises, invocations and prayers to their chief deities. All the king's victories and conquests, his successful feats in the chase of the lion and the wild bull, are ascribed to the protection and favor of the gods. Thus Tiglath-Pileser I. says in his cylinder: "Under the auspices of Ninip, my guardian deity, I killed four wild bulls strong and fierce;" and "Under the auspices of Ninip, one hundred and twenty lions fell before me." One of Asshur-bani-pal's sculptured inscriptions says: "I, Asshur-bani-pal, king of the nations, king of Assyria, in my great courage fighting on foot with a lion, terrible for his size, seized him by the ear, and in the name of Asshur and Ishtar, Goddess of War, with the spear that was in my hand I terminated his life." Wherever the Assyrian monarch led his conquering hosts, he "set up the emblems of Asshur," or of "the great gods;" and compelled the vanquished to render them homage. The most precious of the spoils of conquest were dedicated as thank-offerings in the temples. The temples themselves were adorned, repaired, beautified, enlarged and multiplied numerically by most of the Assyrian sovereigns. The kings worshiped in these temples in person and offered sacrifices. They embellished their palaces with religious figures, such as emblems of chief deities and illustrations of acts of adoration, as well as with representations of their victories in war and their exploits in hunting. Their signets, and those of the Assyrians generally, are religious in character. In every respect religion occupies an important place among the Assyrians, who fight more for the honor of their gods than for their king, and aspire as much toward extending their religion as their dominion.

As in the Jewish religion, we perceive in the Assyrian system a sensuousness contending with a higher and purer element, which in this case reigns uncontrolled, giving a gross, material and voluptuous character to its religion. This practical people cared very little for the spiritual and the ideal, and, not being satisfied with symbols, made idols, or images, of wood and stone to represent their gods; and their intricate mythological system, with its priestly hierarchy, its magnificent ceremonial and lascivious ceremonies, resembled that of Egypt, and thus differed from that of the Jews.

The Hebrew Scriptures represent the Assyrians as "a fierce people." Their personal valor and courage, and their skill and superiority over all other nations in the art of war, gave them their victories over their less-civilized neighbors and enemies. The valor and courage of the Assyrians, like that of the Romans, was kept up by constant wars, and by the cultivation of their manly characteristics, developed in the pursuit and slaying of ferocious beasts. The lion and other fierce and dangerous animals infested Assyria; and, unlike other Asiatics, who tremble with fear before the great beasts of prey and avoid an encounter with them by flight if possible, the ancient Assyrians hunted the strongest and fiercest animals, provoked them to a collision and engaged with them in close combat. The spirit of Nimrod, "the mighty hunter before the Lord," which animated his own people, the Chaldæans, inspired to even a greater extent their northern neighbors, the Assyrians, according to the evidence afforded us by the monuments. The Assyrians, from the sovereign to the lowest subject, delighted especially in hunting the lion and the wild bull, noted for their strength and courage, and to attack either of which was to incur extreme peril.

The Assyrians were not only a brave and hardy people, but also very fierce and ferocious in their nature. In the language of the Hebrew prophet Isaiah, the Assyrian nation was "a mighty and a strong one, which, as a tempest of hail and a destroying storm, as a flood of mighty waters overflowing, cast down to the earth with the hand." The Israelitish prophet Nahum could well describe Nineveh as "a bloody city," or "a city of bloods." In this fierce disposition the Assyrians were not unlike other conquering races, few of which have been tender-hearted, or inclined to spare a vanquished foe. Carnage, ruin and desolation marked the course of an Assyrian army, and excited feelings of fear and animosity among their enemies. Assyrian fierceness was, however, often tempered with clemency. The slain foe was mutilated not by way of insult, but as a proof of the slayer's prowess, perhaps to obtain a reward given for heads, as has frequently been the case with Orientals. Scribes are often represented on the sculptures taking an account of the heads cut off. Otherwise the Assyrians had no actually cruel customs. They readily gave quarter when asked for, and chose rather to take prisoners than to massacre. They were very terrible foes to encounter in battle and to withstand in an attack, but in the hour of triumph they forgave and spared the fallen foe. The exceptions to this general clemency were in the cases of the subjugation of rebellious towns, wherein the most guilty of the rebellion were impaled on stakes, and in several instances prisoners are represented on the sculptures as being led before the king by a rope fastened to a ring passing through the under lip, while occasionally one appears as being flayed with a knife. But usually captives were either released, or transferred, without unnecessary suffering, from their own country to another part of the Assyrian Empire; there being some exceptional cases, where the captives were urged onwards by blows, like tired cattle, and where they were heavily fettered. Captive women were never manacled, but were treated with real tenderness, being frequently permitted to ride on mules or in carts.

The greatest vice of the Assyrians seems to have been their treachery. Says the Hebrew prophet Isaiah: "Woe to thee that spoilest, though thou wast not spoiled, and dealest treacherously, though they dealt not treacherously with thee!" The prophet Nahum declared Nineveh to be "full of lies and robbery." Isaiah further declared, in alluding to the Assyrian king: "He hath broken the covenant, he hath despised the cities, he regardeth no man." But the denunciations of the Assyrians for cruelty or treachery by Jewish prophets and writers would carry more weight if the Hebrew history did not abound with tales of barbarous cruelty, bloodshed, treachery and crime.

Another failing in the character of the Assyrians was their pride, which is especially denounced in the Hebrew Scriptures, where it is expressly declared to have called forth the Divine judgments upon the nation. Says the prophet Ezekiel: "Because thou hast lifted up thyself in height, and he hath shot his top among the thick boughs, and his heart is lifted up in his height; I have therefore delivered him into the hand of the mighty one of the heathen; he shall surely deal with him; I have driven him out for his wickedness." The prophets Isaiah, Ezekiel and Zephaniah alike denounce Assyrian pride. This characteristic everywhere pervades the Assyrian inscriptions. The Assyrians considered themselves greatly superior to all other nations. They alone were favored by the gods. They only were really wise or actually brave. The armed hosts of their foes were chased before them like chaff before the wind. Their enemies were afraid to fight, or were at once defeated with ease. They carried their arms in triumph wherever they pleased, and never acknowledged that they had experienced a reverse. The only merit that they admitted other people to possess was some skill in the mechanical and mimetic arts, and this acknowledgment was only tacitly made by employing foreign artists to ornament their edifices.

The Greek accounts as given by Ctesias, and transmitted therefrom to the Romans and through them to the moderns, represented luxurious living and sensuality as the predominant vice of Assyrian monarchs, from Ninyas to Sardanapalus, from the origin to the overthrow of the Assyrian Empire. The entire race of Assyrian sovereigns are thus represented as voluptuaries, who carried into practice the principle that human happiness consisted in freedom from all cares or troubles, and in unrestrained indulgence in every kind of sensual pleasure. This account is directly contradicted by the authentic records which the Assyrian monuments and sculptures furnish us concerning the warlike character and manly pursuits of so large a number of the monarchs. Nevertheless in so flourishing a monarchy as Assyria luxury did gradually advance; and when the Empire fell before the combined attack of two powerful neighboring kingdoms, it had lost much of its old-time vigor. There is only one passage in the Old Testament ascribing luxury and sensuality as a cause of the downfall of Assyria. The usual faults for which Jewish prophets generally denounced the Assyrians are their violence, treachery and pride. When Nineveh repented in Jonah's time it was by each man having "turned from his evil way and from the violence which was in their hands." When Nahum announced the final overthrow, it was "the bloody city, full of lies and robbery." In the figurative language of the prophet, the lion was selected as the symbol of Assyria, even at the close of her history. Thus Assyria is still represented as "the lion that did tear in pieces enough for his whelps, and strangled for his lionesses, and filled his holes with prey, and his dens with ravin." The chosen national emblem of Assyria is thus accepted as the true type of her people; and blood, ravin and robbery are the Assyrian qualities in the view of the Jewish prophet.

The Assyrians were among the foremost Asiatic nations in mental power. Though they derived the elements of their civilization originally from their mother country, Chaldæa, they excelled their instructors in many particulars, and rendered the old arts more valuable by continual improvements. Their language, arts and government attest their native genius, and are advances upon what had previously prevailed in Mesopotamia and in the world. The Assyrians were the superiors of the highly-lauded Egyptians in many essential particulars. The progressive character and spirit of Assyrian art contrasts most strongly with the stiff, lifeless and fixed conventionalism of the Egyptian. The Assyrian language and alphabet are an advance upon the Egyptian. The Assyrian religion is more earnest and less degraded than that of the Nile land. The courage and military genius of the Assyrians were also superior to the same qualities in the Egyptians, who were on the whole an unwarlike nation. But in the grandeur and durability of her architecture Egypt surpassed Assyria. The Assyrian palaces, with all their splendor, were inferior to the colossal structures of Thebes. Neither Assyria, Rome or any other nation, has rivaled Egypt in the vastness and the solemn grandeur of its edifices. But with this solitary exception, the great kingdom of Africa was decidedly the inferior of her powerful Asiatic rival, which was truly described by the Hebrew prophet Ezekiel as "a cedar in Lebanon, exalted above all the trees of the field —fair in his greatness, in the length of his branches—so that all the trees of Eden, that were in the garden of God, envied him—and not one was like unto him in his beauty."

The material and physical vigor of the Assyrians outran their intellectual progress and development. The elements of their science and literature, their cuneiform writing, their architecture and other arts, they brought with them from their mother country, Chaldæa. Even the Hamitic, or Cushite, dialect of the Chaldees became the language of the Assyrian priests and scholars, and in this dead language were preserved the records of the old Chaldæan kingdom and the early history of the Assyrian monarchy. It was not until the culminating period of Assyrian greatness and glory, during the brilliant reign of Asshur-bani-pal, just before the rapid decay and decline of Assyrian power, that the works written in the Chaldee classic tongue were translated into the Assyrian vernacular. The Assyrian race manifested its greatness in art and manufactures, and not in science and literature.

As we have before noticed, the same system of cuneiform, or wedge-shaped, characters used in Chaldæan writing was employed in the written language of Assyria. The mounds of Assyria and Mesopotamia have yielded a mass of documents in the Assyrian language. Some of these are stone slabs bearing long historic inscriptions with which the walls of palaces were paneled, and which are wonderfully preserved to this day. Other memorials are the hollow cylinders, or, more properly,

CIVILIZATION.

hexagonal or octagonal prisms, made of extremely thin terra-cotta, and which the Assyrian kings inscribed with the records of their actions and with many religious invocations, and deposited at the corners of temples. These cylinders are from a half yard to a yard high, and the inscriptions covering the outside face are arranged in columns, one of which occupies each side, reading from top to bottom. This writing was so wonderfully fine as to often require a good magnifying-glass to decipher it. The cylinder of Tiglath-Pileser I. contains thirty lines in a space of six inches, or five lines to an inch, which is almost as close as the type of this book. The cylinder of Asshurbani-pal has six lines to the inch. The durability of these cylinders is attested by the fact that many of them still remain, and give us most of our knowledge of the annals of this great people, as recorded by themselves twenty-five and thirty centuries ago.

Besides slabs and cylinders, the written records of Assyria were inscribed upon the stone bulls and lions, stone obelisks, engraved seals, bricks and clay tablets. Both the sun-dried and kiln-burned bricks are stamped with legends, to preserve them from the two great dangers of flood and fire, to which Assyria was subject. Fire would only harden the sun-dried bricks, and water could not affect those burned in kilns. The clay tablets are numerous, and of sizes varying from nine by six and a half inches, to an inch and a

SLAB WITH CUNEIFORM INSCRIPTION.
Now in British Museum.

1—13.—U. H.

half by an inch. In some cases they are wholly covered with writing, while in other instances a portion of their surface is stamped with seals, mythological emblems, etc. Thousands of these tablets have been found, many being historical, many mythological, some linguistic, some geographic, some astronomical. Such are the treasures of Assyrian literature.

The few stone obelisks are in a fragmentary condition, the only perfect one being the one in black basalt, discovered by Mr. Layard at Nimrud, and which has now been ten clearly cut lines. It is one of the most important of the remaining Assyrian memorials, and contains a record of the victories won and the tribute brought to Shalmaneser II., who set it up.

The many inscribed lions and bulls guarding the portals of palaces are raised in a bold relief on alabaster slabs; the inscriptions generally covering only the portions of the slabs not occupied by the animal, and usually giving a detailed account of some important campaign. Clay tablets were used in ordinary business affairs, and for lit-

EXHUMING A WINGED MAN-HEADED BULL AT NIMRUD.

for many years in the British Museum. This monument is about seven feet high, two feet broad at the base, tapering slightly towards the top, which is crowned with three low steps, or gradines. The inscription occupies the upper and lower portions of each side, and is carried along the spaces between the bas-reliefs, consisting of two hundred and erary and scientific writings; and, when wanted for instruction or evidence, were carefully baked. That they exist to this day, in as legible a condition, with letters as clear and sharp, as any Greek or Roman legend on stone, marble or metal, proves that the best clay, properly baked, is as durable as stone or metal.

Says Professor Rawlinson: "Of all the Assyrian works of art which have come down to us, by far the most important are the bas-reliefs. It is here especially, if not solely, that we can trace progress in style; and it is here alone that we see the real artistic genius of the people. What sculpture in its full form, or in the slightly modified form of very high relief, was to the Greeks, what painting has been to modern European nations since the time of Cimabue, that low relief was to the Assyrians—the practical mode in which artistic power found vent among them. They used it for almost every purpose to which mimetic art is applicable; to express their religious feelings and ideas, to glorify their kings, to hand down to posterity the nation's history and its deeds of prowess, to depict home scenes and domestic occupations, to represent landscape and architecture, to imitate animal and vegetable forms, even to illustrate the mechanical methods which they employed in the construction of those vast architectural works of which the reliefs were the principal ornamentation. It is not too much to say that we know the Assyrians, not merely artistically, but historically and ethnologically, *chiefly* through their bas-reliefs, which seem to represent to us almost the entire life of the people."

The bas-reliefs were sculptured on stone slabs, which were set in the lower part of the walls of the palaces which they adorned. These reliefs were of five different classes— 1. War scenes, such as battles, sieges, devastations of an enemy's country, naval expeditions and triumphant returns from foreign wars, with the trophies and fruits of victory; 2. Religious scenes, mythical and real; 3. Processions, mostly of tribute-bearers, carrying the products of their respective countries to the Assyrian king; 4. Hunting and sporting scenes, such as the chase of ferocious animals, and of animals hunted for food, the spreading of nets, the shooting of birds, etc.; 5. Scenes of everyday life, such as the transportation and erection of colossal bulls, and landscapes, temples, interiors, gardens, etc.

Assyrian mimetic art is in the form of statues, bas-reliefs, metal castings, ivory carvings, clay statuettes, brick enamelings, and intaglios on stones and gems. Assyrian statues are rare and imperfect. The best specimens are two royal statues now in the British Museum; also two statues of the god Nebo, one of the goddess Ishtar, and one of Sargon—all of which are now also in the British Museum. The Assyrian clay statuettes, mostly images of deities, possess even less artistic excellence than the statues. Small animal figures, mostly dogs and ducks, in terra-cotta, have likewise been discovered.

In painting, as well as in sculpture, the Assyrians made great progress, and many of the drawings on the prominent sculptures are elegant. Everything indicates a taste for display. In architectural designs, and in the grouping of flowers and animals for the purposes of embellishment, great richness and variety of fancy are exhibited. The dresses of the kings display gorgeous robes, elegantly and profusely embroidered, fringed and tasseled. Sandals made of wood or leather were used for the feet, while caps and tiaras of silk were worn on the head. Many articles of furniture likewise displayed great elegance. Tables constructed of wood or metal, inlaid with ivory and having legs gracefully carved, were in the dwellings of the wealthy. Elegant baskets seem to have been in use. Ornaments, such as tassels, fringes, necklaces, armlets, bracelets, anklets, ear-rings of various forms and elegant workmanship, clasps, etc., were worn in profusion. There were drinking-cups of gold and silver. Everywhere was manifested a love of elaborate and gaudy decoration.

The excavations within the last half century at Khorsabad, Koyunjik, Nimrud and Kileh-Sherghat have revealed to us the fact that truly did Assyria rank next to Egypt in monumental grandeur. The remains of Assyrian art and architecture exhumed from these mounds give a very considerable knowledge of their stupendous palaces in the days of their splendor and glory. We can, by looking at the remains of the sculptured and painted walls of their vast edifices, read the records of Assyria—its battles, its sieges, its conquests and its triumphs. We see around the colossal images of the Assyrian gods, by which, in monstrous yet striking emblems, the Assyrians endeavored to express their conceptions of divinity. We are here introduced to the semblances of monarchs who flourished from twenty-five to thirty centuries ago. We see these in their costumes of state, in all the pomp and circumstance of war, in the pursuit of the chase, and in the solemn ceremonials of religion. We are also enabled from these sculptures to inform ourselves of many of the domestic customs of the Assyrians, of their household furniture, their mechanical tools and implements, their methods of agriculture, the crops of the husbandman, and in fact, the occupations and amusements of this renowned Asiatic people in the days of their preëminence.

Layard and Botta, the fortunate discoverers of these famous ruins, have given us glowing descriptions of the massive dimensions, the magnificence and grandeur, of the Assyrian palaces, whose ruins they uncovered from the Khorsabad, Koyunjik and Nimrud mounds. The stranger who visited these splendid palaces in the flourishing periods of the Assyrian Empire was ushered in through the portal, guarded by colossal winged man-headed lions and bulls of white alabaster. In the first hall he saw all around him the sculptured records of the empire—battles, sieges, triumphs, hunting exploits, religious ceremonies—all portrayed on the palace walls, sculptured in alabaster, and painted in gorgeous colors. Under each picture he saw engraved, in characters filled up with bright copper, inscriptions descriptive of the scenes thus illustrated.

Above the sculptures he observed paintings representing other events—the Assyrian king, attended by his eunuchs and his warriors, receiving his captives, negotiating alliances with other monarchs, or performing some sacred duty; these representations being surrounded by colored borders, of elaborate and elegant designs. He saw the emblematic tree, also winged man-headed bulls and lions, occupying conspicuous places among the ornaments. At the upper end of the hall was a gigantic figure of the king, in adoration before Asshur, "the Great Lord," or receiving from his eunuch the holy cup. He was attended by warriors bearing his arms, and by the priests, or presiding divinities. His robes and those of his followers were adorned with groups of figures, animals and flowers, all painted with brilliant colors.

The visitor trod upon alabaster slabs, each bearing an inscription, recording the titles, the genealogy and the achievements of the Great King. Several doorways, guarded by gigantic winged man-headed lions and bulls, or by the figures of guardian deities, led into other apartments, which likewise opened into more remote halls. In each of these apartments and halls were sculptures. On the walls of some were processions of colossal figures—armed men and eunuchs following the king, or warriors laden with spoil, conducting captives or bearing presents and offerings to the gods. On the walls of others were portrayed the winged priests, or presiding divinities, standing before the sacred trees.

The ceilings above the visitor were divided into square compartments, painted with flowers or with figures of animals. Some were inlaid with ivory, each compartment being surrounded with elegant borders and mouldings. The beams, as well as the sides of the chambers, may have been gilded, or even plated with gold and silver; and the most highly prized species of wood, prominent among which was the cedar, were used in the wood-work. The palaces were lighted from the roofs, which were of wood, the light being admitted through square openings into the ceilings of the chambers. A pleasing light was thus cast over the sculptured walls, and gave a majestic expression to the human features of the colossal figures guarding the entrances. The azure hue of the eastern sky was seen through these apertures, which were enclosed in frames, whereon were painted in vivid colors the winged circle, in the midst of elegant ornaments and the graceful figures of ideal animals.

These vast edifices were the great Assyrian monuments, upon whose walls were represented in sculpture, or inscribed in cuneiform characters, the chronicles of the Assyrian Empire. The visitor who entered these splendid structures might here read the annals and learn all about the glory and triumphs of this great people. These memorials served also to constantly remind those who assembled within the palace on festive occasions, or for celebrating religious ceremonies, of the deeds and prowess of their ancestors, and the power and majesty of the Assyrian gods. The palaces seem to have been of one story, but of vast extent. Under the floor of each room was a drain, consisting of a clay pipe. No traces of the dwellings of the common people remain. The sculptures inform us that the Assyrians used the arch in building. Assyrian pillars in the temples and palaces rested on circular or globular bases, or on animal figures. The temple towers, or *ziggurats*, were erected in the form of steps or stages around their four sides, thus gradually becoming narrower at the top. Such were the royal residences of Assyria—each of which was at the same time a temple and a palace—the dwelling of him who was at once the sovereign, the priest and the prophet of his people.

The Assyrian ruins exhibit no tombs like those of Egypt, whose painted interiors, protected from the ravages of the elements, have transmitted to succeeding ages the thoughts, feelings and opinions of their ancient builders. All that remains of Assyrian architecture are scattered bricks, usually marked with inscriptions and with sculptures and reliefs. The most interesting and valuable are the stone slabs facing the inside walls of the temples. The Assyrian structures were generally built of brick, which was preferred as a building material, although stone was abundant in the country. The temples constructed of stone have partly remained, though buried in heaps of rubbish for twenty-five centuries. Marble, alabaster and basalt were used in the palaces. The ancient Assyrian edifices, like the palaces, had no windows, but were lighted through their wooden roofs.

So thoroughly was Nineveh destroyed that when Xenophon, about two hundred and twenty-five years afterward, passed over its ruins the very name of the place was unknown to the inhabitants; and in the time of Alexander the Great, nearly a century later, the city was forgotten; so that for over two thousand years the very site of the renowned capital and metropolis of Assyria was unknown. But the wonderful discoveries of Layard in recent times have identified its locality as the ruins opposite the present town of Mosul, on the Tigris, consisting of two principal mounds, known respectively by their present Arab names of Nebbi-Yunus and Koyunjik. The Koyunjik mound is the larger of the two, and is located about nine hundred yards, or a little over half a mile, north-west of the Nebbi-Yunus. Its shape is an irregular oval, elongated to a point towards the north-east, in the line of its greater axis. The surface is almost flat, and the sides slope at a steep angle, being furrowed with many ravines, worn in the soft material by the rains of twenty-five centuries. The mound rises to its greatest height above the plain towards the south-eastern extremity, there overhanging the small stream of the Khosr-su, where the height is about ninety-five feet. The mound covers about a hundred acres. On this artificial mound the Assyrian palaces and temples, now buried beneath heaps of earth and rubbish, were erected in ancient times.

The Nebbi-Yunus mound is almost triangular at its base and covers about forty acres. It is more elevated, and its sides are more precipitous than Koyunjik, particularly on the west, where it abutted upon the wall of the city. The surface is mostly flat, but is divided into an eastern and a western portion by a deep ravine running nearly from north to south. The supposed tomb of Jonah occupies a conspicuous place on the

EXCAVATIONS AT MOSUL.

northern edge of the western portion of the mound, and the cottages of Kurds and Turkomans are grouped about it. The eastern portion forms a general Mohammedan burial-ground for the surrounding country.

Palaces and temples were raised on these two great mounds, both of which are in the same line and abutted on the western wall of the city. On this side Nineveh was thirteen thousand six hundred feet, or over two and a half miles long, and in ancient times overhung the Tigris, which is now a mile farther to the west, leaving a plain of that impends over a deep ravine formed by a winter torrent, thus running in a direct line about a thousand yards, when it is joined with the eastern wall, with which it forms a slightly acute angle.

The eastern wall is the longest and the most irregular of the four ramparts, and skirts the edge of a rocky ridge, there rising above the level of the plain and presenting a slightly convex course to the north-east. This wall is sixteen thousand feet, or over three miles long, and is divided a little north of the middle into two portions, by the

THE GREAT MOUND OF KOYUNJIK, ON THE SITE OF NINEVEH.

width between the river and the old rampart of the city. This rampart followed the natural course of the river bank. At its northern extremity the western wall approaches the present course of the Tigris, and is there connected, at exactly right angles, with the northern or north-western rampart, which runs in a direct line to the north-eastern angle of the city and measures exactly seven thousand feet. At one third of the distance from the north-west angle this wall is broken by a road, and adjoining this is a remarkable mound, which covers one of the principal gates of the city. At its other end the western wall forms an obtuse angle with the southern wall, which Khosr-su, which flows through the city ruins, running across the low plains to the Tigris.

Thus the entire enceinte of Nineveh forms an irregular trapezium. Its greatest width, which is in its northern portion, is four-ninths of its length, thus giving the city an oblong shape, as Diodorus described it, though he greatly exaggerated its size. The circuit of the walls is not quite eight miles, instead of being over fifty; and the area thus embraced is eighteen hundred English acres, and not one hundred and twelve thousand.

It has been estimated that populous Oriental cities have a hundred inhabitants to the acre, or one to fifty square yards, thus

208 ANCIENT HISTORY.—ASSYRIA.

NEBBI-YUNUS (THE TRADITIONAL TOMB OF JONAH), NINEVEH.

giving ancient Nineveh one hundred and seventy-five thousand souls, a population exceeding that of any city of Western Asia at the present time.

Diodorus described the wall with which Ninus surrounded his capital as being one hundred feet high, and so wide that three chariots could be driven abreast along the top. Xenophon, who passed near the ruins while conducting the Retreat of the Ten Thousand, says that the walls were one hundred and fifty feet high and fifty feet broad. The greatest height at present appears to be forty-six feet; but the great amount of rubbish at the foot of the walls, and their ruined condition, have led Mr. Layard to say: "The remains still existing of these fortifications almost confirm the statement of Diodorus Siculus, that the walls were a hundred feet high." The walls in their present condition are from one hundred to two hundred feet broad.

Xenophon says that the walls up to fifty feet were constructed of a fossiliferous limestone, smoothed and polished on the outside, and that above that height sun-dried bricks were used. The stone masonry, in Mr. Layard's opinion, was ornamented along its top by a continuous series of battlements, or gradines, of the same material, and it is probable that a like ornamentation crowned the upper brick structure. The wall was pierced at irregular intervals by gates, above which rose high towers; and lower towers occurred in the parts of the wall between the different gates. A gate in the north-western rampart, cleared by excavation, seems to have consisted of three gateways, the inner and outer being ornamented with colossal winged man-headed bulls and other figures, while the middle one was only paneled with alabaster slabs. Between the gateways were two large chambers, seventy feet long by twenty-three feet wide, being thus capable of holding a considerable body of soldiers. The chambers and gateways are believed to have been arched over, similar to the castles' gates on the bas-reliefs. The gates themselves have entirely ceased to exist, but the rubbish which filled both the chambers and the passages contained so much charcoal as to give rise to the belief that they were constructed of bronze. The ground within the gateway was paved with large limestone slabs, which still bear the marks of chariot-wheels.

Besides its ramparts, Nineveh was protected on all sides by water barriers, the west and south being defended by natural streams, and the north and east by artificial canals beginning at the Khosr-su. Skirting the northern and eastern walls was a deep moat, into which the waters of the Khosr-su were turned by occupying its natural channel with a strong dam, carried across it in the line of the eastern wall, and at the point where the stream now flows into the enclosure. On coming in contact with this obstruction, of which some vestiges yet remain, the waters separated into two parts, one flowing to the south-east into the Tigris by the ravine immediately to the south of the city, which is a natural water-course, and the other turning at an acute angle to the north-west, washing the remainder of the eastern and the entire northern wall, and emptying into the Tigris at the north-west angle of the city, where a second dam kept it at a sufficient height. On the eastern side, which seems to have been the weakest and the most exposed, a series of outer defenses were constructed for the further protection of the city. North of the Khosr-su, between the city wall and that stream, which there flows parallel to the wall and forms a second or outer moat, are the remains of a detached fort which, from its size, evidently added considerable strength to the city's defenses in that quarter. The works are yet more elaborate to the south and south-east of the Khosr-su. From a point where the stream leaves the hills and reaches low ground, a deep ditch, two hundred feet wide, was extended for two miles, until it connected with the ravine forming the natural defense of the city on the south. On each side of the ditch, which could be easily filled with water from the Khosr-su at its northern extremity, was erected a high and wide wall; the eastern one forming the outermost defense, and rising even yet a hundred feet above the bottom of the ditch on which it adjoins. Between this outer barrier and the city moat was a kind of demi-lune, defended by a double wall and a broad ditch, and joined by a covered way with the city itself. Thus Nineveh was protected on its most vulnerable side, towards the centre, by five walls and three broad and deep moats; towards the north by a wall, a moat, the Khosr-su and a strong outpost; towards the south by two moats and three lines of rampart. The entire fortification on the eastern side is two thousand two hundred feet, or nearly a half mile wide.

The accounts of Ctesias and Diodorus respecting the immense size of Nineveh are highly exaggerated, and it is known that these writers regarded the ruins of Nimrud, Keremles, Khorsabad and Koyunjik as all being the remains of that renowned Assyrian capital. The Book of Jonah also bears testimony to the immense size of this great city. Unlike Ctesias, who only saw the ruins of Nineveh, Jonah saw the city itself in its splendor. This Hebrew prophet tells us that Nineveh was "an exceeding great city, of three days' journey," and also that in it were "more than sixscore thousand persons that could not discern between their right hand and their left." Though these passages are very vague, they yet convey some idea of the vastness of the city. It has been supposed that the one hundred and twenty thousand persons "that could not discern between their right hand and their left" were children, which would thus indicate a population of about six hundred thousand. It has also been believed that the phrase "six score thousand persons that could not discern between their right hand and their left" alluded to the dense ignorance of the inhabitants, in which case the number here mentioned included the entire population of the city.

The sculptures of the Assyrians furnish us with very complete representations of their system of warfare. The Assyrians, like other ancient nations, fought in chariots, on horseback and on foot. Like the Egyptians, the early Greeks, the Canaanites, the Syrians, the Jews and Israelites, the Philistines, the Hittites, the Lydians, the Elamites, or Susianians, the Medes and Persians, the Hindoos, the Gauls, the Britons, and other peoples of antiquity, the Assyrians looked upon the chariot as most honorable. Their king invariably went to war and battle riding in a chariot, only dismounting and shooting his arrows on foot while besieging a town. The leading officers of state, and other dignitaries of high rank, followed the same custom. The cavalry and infantry were composed of persons of the lower classes.

The Jewish prophet Isaiah, in warning his countrymen of the miseries in store for them, described the Assyrians as a people "whose arrows were sharp, and all their bows bent, whose horses' hoofs should be counted like flint, and their *wheels* like a whirlwind." The same prophet, in afterwards announcing Jehovah's displeasure with Sennacherib on account of his pride, speaks of that king's reliance upon "the multitude of his chariots." The prophet Nahum, in announcing the coming overthrow of the haughty nation, declares that Jehovah is "against her, and will burn her *chariots* in the smoke." In the fabulous Assyrian history by Ctesias the war-chariots of the mythical king Ninus are represented as amounting to nearly eleven thousand, and those of his wife and successor, Semiramis, are estimated at the extravagant number of one hundred thousand.

The Assyrian war-chariot is believed to have been made of wood. Like that of the Greeks and Egyptians, it seems to have been mounted from behind, being there completely open, or only closed by means of a shield, which could be hung across the aperture. It was richly ornamented, and completely paneled at the sides. The two wheels were placed at the extreme hind end of the body, as in the Egyptian war-chariot. The chariot-wheels of the early period had six spokes; those of the middle and later periods had eight. The felloes of the wheels usually consisted of three distinct circles, the

ASSYRIAN PALACES AT NINEVEH (RESTORED).

middle one being the thinnest, and the outer one the thickest of the three. Sometimes there was a fourth circle. These circles were fastened together with bands of iron. The wheels were attached to an axle-tree fastened to the body without any springs between them. They were furnished with bows, quivers of arrows, spears, or javelins, hatchets, battle-axes and shields.

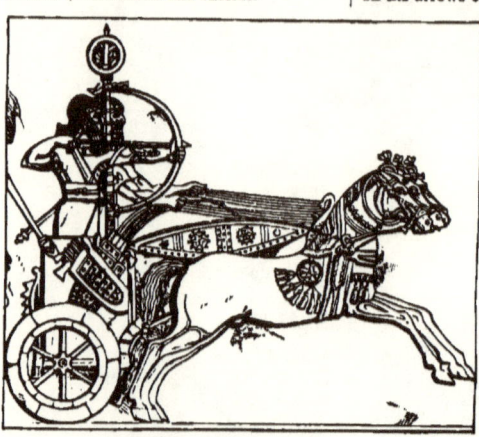

ASSYRIAN WAR-CHARIOT.

The chariots were drawn by two or three horses, two being yoked together in front, while the third was hitched before the others by means of a rope, and was designed as a supply in case of loss. The harness and trappings of the horses were extremely rich and elegant; ribbons, tassels, fringes and rosettes, of gay colors, profusely decorating the head, neck and sides. The bits and ornaments of the bridles were of gold and silver. Embroidered robes were sometimes thrown over the backs of the chariot-horses.

The chariots contained two persons at least, the driver, or charioteer, and the warrior. Sometimes they contained in addition an attendant who protected the warrior with a shield while he discharged his arrows at the foe. In rare instances there was a second attendant with a shield to protect the archer from behind, thus making four persons occupying the chariot. The bow was the usual weapon of the chariot warrior, as well as of the cavalry and infantry soldiers. The chariot warrior was sometimes dressed in a long tunic confined at the waist by a girdle, and sometimes in a coat of mail, like the Egyptian chariot warrior. Sometimes he descended from the chariot to shoot off his arrows on foot.

The Assyrian cavalry rank in importance almost equally with the war-chariots. Ctesias made the number of horsemen in Assyrian armies always greater than the chariots. The writer of the Apochryphal Book of Judith assigns Holofernes twelve thousand horse-archers, and the prophet Ezekiel alludes apparently to all the "desirable young men" as "horsemen riding upon horses." The Assyrian sculptures represent the cavalry as far exceeding in number the chariots. In the early period of Assyrian history cavalry was but little used, but in the times of Sargon and Sennacherib the cavalry came to be prominent in all battle scenes, the chariot being only used by the king and high dignitaries.

The Assyrian cavalry were divided, according to their weapons, into mounted archers, or bowmen, and mounted spearmen. In the early period each cavalry archer was accompanied by an unarmed attendant, who managed his steed, while the archer discharged his arrows.

Assyrian armies, like others, consisted mainly of infantry. Ctesias gives Ninus 1,700,000 footmen, 210,000 horsemen and 10,600 chariots. Xenophon showed the wide contrast between the immense host of infantry and the scanty numbers of the cavalry and the chariots. Herodotus says that the Assyrians in the great army of Xerxes were all footmen. The Book of Judith assigns to Holofernes ten times as many footmen as horsemen. The Assyrian monuments show the same proportion of infantry to cavalry, and represent a hundred footmen to each chariot soldier. For their military successes the Assyrians were chiefly indebted to the valor, discipline, solidity and equipment of their infantry, which consisted mainly of foot archers, or bowmen, and foot spearmen. Besides these the foot soldiers embraced swordsmen, mace-bearers, ax-bearers, and from Sennacherib's time, slingers. Pioneers accompanied the army to clear away trees with their axes. In Sargon's time the foot soldiers consisted of those of the light equipment, those of the intermediate equipment, and those of the heavy equipment. Sennacherib's foot archers embraced four classes, two heavy-armed and two light-armed.

The offensive weapons were the bow and arrow, the spear, pike, or javelin, the sword, the mace, the battle-ax and the sling. The defensive armor consisted of a shield of metal or wicker-work; a crested or pointed helmet of metal; and a coat of mail, consisting of successive rows of iron scales in the early period and reaching to the feet or

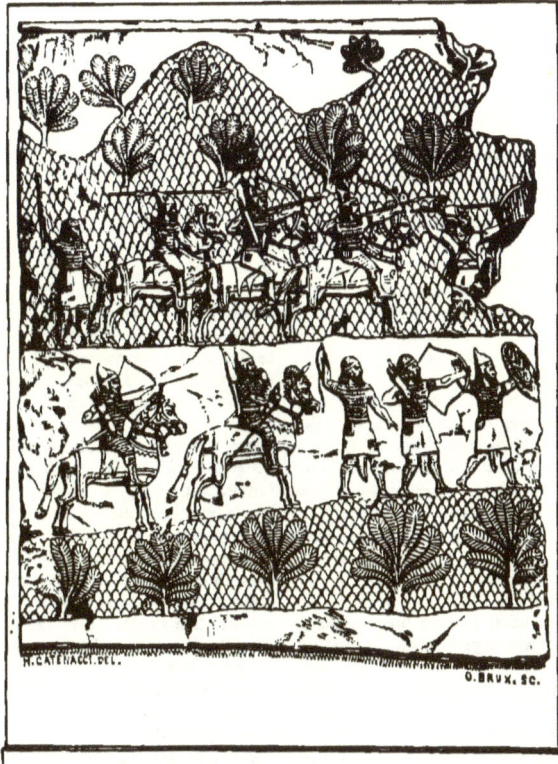

BATTLE PIECE; FROM NINEVEH.

CIVILIZATION.

knees, and in later times composed of larger metal plates and bands fastened together and reaching only as low as the waist.

The warriors were variously costumed, those of the lighter equipment only wearing a short tunic reaching from the waist to half-way down the thigh, the rest of the person being bare; those of the intermediate equipment wearing a coat of mail to the waist and a tunic thence to half-way down the thigh; and those of the heavy equipment wearing a coat of mail above the waist, and a robe thence down to the feet. Both these latter classes wore helmets over the head, and sandals on the feet. The arms were bare. When not covered by the robe the legs were also sometimes bare, and sometimes covered by close-fitting trousers and short greaves, or boots. The hilts of swords and daggers were ornamented with gold chasings of elegant forms, and the points of sheaths with the beaks of birds. The bow was the chief weapon of war, alike among chariot, cavalry and infantry soldiers, and was richly mounted.

The barbarous custom of rewarding those who carried back to camp the heads of foemen, caused the heads of the dead, and even of the wounded, the disarmed and the unresisting, of the enemy, to be carried back to camp, in proof of the slayer's prowess. Quarter was generally only given to generals and dignitaries of rank whom it was desirable to spare. Scribes were always present to take an account of the spoil at the close of the battle. The usual practice upon taking a city or town was to plunder it of everything of value.

The strongly-fortified towns of an enemy were besieged and assailed in three principal ways. The attack by escalade was by means of ladders placed against the city walls. These ladders were mounted by the spearmen, followed by the archers, while the bowmen and slingers kept up a constant discharge of arrows and stones. The assailants protected themselves with their shields. The besieged endeavored to dislodge and break the ladders, and defended themselves by discharging their arrows and stones, or meeting their assailants spear to spear and shield to shield.

If the escalade failed, or was impracticable, the battering-ram, an engine mounted on four or six wheels, and having either a pointed or blunt head, was driven with force against the walls to effect a breach. In connection with the battering-ram a movable tower containing soldiers was sometimes employed, the besiegers being thus enabled to meet the besieged on a level and protect the engine from attacks. The besieged often tried to fire the battering-ram by casting upon it torches, burning tow or other inflammable substances. To thwart these attempts the soldiers in the battering-ram were furnished with a supply of water which they directed through leather or metal pipes against the combustibles. Sometimes they suspended a curtain of cloth or leather from a pole in front of the battering-ram to protect themselves. Sometimes the besieged attempted to catch the point of the battering-ram by means of a chain suspended from the walls, but the besiegers in turn tried to catch the chain by means of strong metal hooks. The Assyrians in their sieges also used a catapult, a large engine designed for throwing stones against fortified walls, the besiegers working the engine from a mound or inclined plane, and the besieged endeavoring to destroy it by fire. The besiegers also endeavored to mine the foundations of the walls by means of crowbars and pickaxes, protecting themselves by holding their shields above them. Sometimes the besiegers would try to break open the gates with axes, or fire them with the torch. When a city or town was taken it was fired, its walls demolished and its treasures carried off.

The Assyrians had three modes of executing captives—impaling them on stakes in the ground, beating in their skulls with a mace, and beheading them. Several bas-reliefs represent them flaying prisoners with a knife. This may have been after death, as was the custom of the Persians and the barbarous Scythians. Sometimes prisoners were punished by mutilation instead of

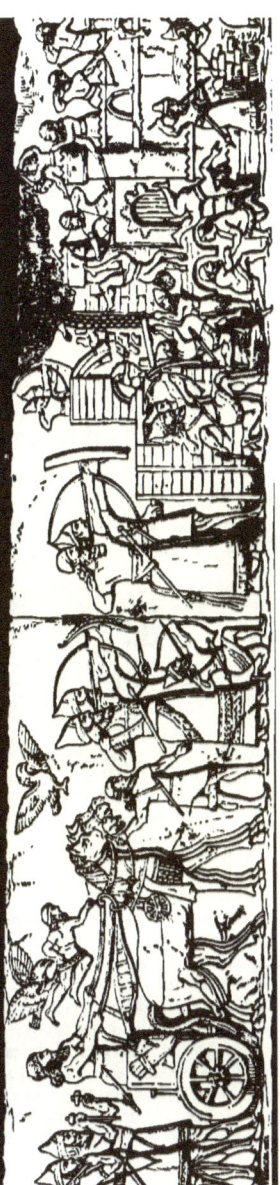

death. Cutting off the ears, blinding the eyes with hot irons, cutting off the nose, and tearing out the tongue by the roots, have always been favorite Asiatic punishments. Asshur-izir-pal says in his great inscription that he frequently cut off the noses and ears of captives; and a slab of Asshur-bani-pal represents a captive in the hands of torturers, one holding the prisoner's head, and another thrusting his hand into his mouth to tear out the tongue. The captives consisted of men, women and children. The men were driven in bands under the conduct of brutal officers, who hurried them on by blows to the Assyrian capital, where the kings employed them in labor. The skilled workmen were required to aid in ornamenting palaces and shrines. The great mass of the unskilled laborers were set to work, under brutal taskmasters, in quarrying and transporting stone, in raising mounds, making bricks, etc. Sometimes the captives were only colonized in new regions, to prevent rebellion in their own native lands, and to keep down malcontents in their new abodes.

Besides captives, the Assyrians carried off great numbers of domesticated animals, such as oxen, sheep, goats, horses, asses, mules and camels. Sennacherib, in his inscriptions, says that in one foray he carried away from the tribes on the Euphrates "7,200 horses and mares, 5,230 camels, 11,000 mules, 120,000 oxen and 800,000 sheep." Other Assyrian monarchs mention the captured animals as "too numerous to be counted," or "countless as the stars of heaven." Precious metals were often among the spoils carried off.

As in all other Asiatic monarchies from time immemorial, the severest form of des-

CAPTIVES OF WAR; FROM ASSHUR-BANI-PAL'S PALACE.

potism existed in Assyria. The sovereign's will was law, and no code was in existence to restrict his judgments, even the ancient customs and usages being set aside at his pleasure. The king was the head of the church, as well as of the state, and claimed divine worship. His palace was filled with as many wives and concubines as he chose to collect, and these were placed under the guardianship of eunuchs, an unfortunate class, first brought into use in Assyria. The portion of the royal palace assigned to the king's women was his harem, or seraglio.

A rigid etiquette separated the king from

his subjects, no one being allowed access to him except through the proper court officials, who always accompanied him. No one but the vizier and the chief eunuch were permitted to begin conversation with the king, who was seated on his throne when he received them, they standing before him. As a rule, the Assyrian kings led hardy and active lives. In times of peace they superin-

ASSYRIAN KING; FROM NIMRUD.

tended the public works, administered justice, and found recreation in the dangerous pastime of hunting the lion and the wild bull. In war the king generally rode in his chariot, though he occasionally marched on foot, going into battle in the same manner. The sovereign showed himself freely to his subjects, but maintained his haughty dignity in everything, and was very seldom the effeminate voluptuary that the Greeks supposed him to be. The Assyrian court ceremonial was most elaborate and imposing. The monarch's dress in peace and war was of the most exceeding magnificence, and while engaged in the religious ceremonies prescribed for him he was clothed in a special dress.

The musical instruments of the Assyrians were the harp, the lyre, the guitar, the pipe, the tambourine, the cymbal, the drum, the dulcimer and the trumpet. Bands of musicians are represented in some of the bas-reliefs, showing their employment on the occasions of public ceremonials.

The usual apparel of the common people was a plain tunic, reaching from the neck almost down to the knee, and held to the waist by a wide belt or girdle. The sleeves were very short. The head and feet were entirely bare. The king and his great officers wore head-dresses and shoes. Laborers above the lowest grade wore sandals. The better class of laborers wore close-fitting trousers and leather boots. The lower classes wore no ornaments; armlets and bracelets being worn only by persons of rank, and ear-rings by soldiers and musicians. Men of rank wore long fringed robes extending almost down to the feet, the sleeves being short and barely covering the shoulders. This robe fitted closely down to the waist, where it was confined to the body with a belt or girdle, being loose below the waist. The jewelry of the higher classes consisted of fillets, ear-rings, armlets and bracelets. Women of the upper ranks were dressed in long fringed gowns, looser than those of the men, the sleeves being long. Over this dress they frequently wore a short cloak of a similar pattern, open in front and falling over the arms, which they covered as far down as the elbows. Their hair was arranged in short crisp curls, or carried back in waves to the ears, from which it was in part twisted into long pendant ringlets, and in part curled, like that of the men, in three or four rows at the back of the neck. A fillet frequently encircled the head. They also wore girdles around the waist. Their feet were either bare or protected by sandals. Women of the lower classes wore only a gown extending down to the ankles, and a hood to cover the head. The ornaments and toilet articles of the upper ranks of Assyrian women exhibited the high degree of luxury in their manner of living.

The Assyrians excelled in the arts of weaving and dyeing. They decorated their stuffs by introducing colored threads and tissues of gold in the woof. They had indigo, cotton and silk in abundance. The chief dignitaries wore richly-figured robes. The men seem to have prized their beards, which they dressed in long artificial curls.

Assyrian plows have been found. Irrigation was common. Sesame, millet and corn were the chief articles of food.

The Assyrians were fond of entertainments, and these were conducted with great pomp and luxury. Drinking scenes are represented on the sculptures. They had vessels of gold and silver. Wine flowed freely; while delicious fruits, rich viands, honey, incense, conserves of dates, etc., were among the delicacies of the repast. Women, even wives, danced naked before the guests; while the music of stringed instruments heightened the festivity of the occasion.

The Assyrians carried on an extensive commerce, principally by land and by means of caravans. At a later period their maritime traffic was likewise considerable. They imitated the Phœnician ships, which are also represented in the later sculptures. The first Assyrian ships seem to have been round, with ribs of willow boughs covered with skins. They had neither stem nor stern. They were used chiefly on rivers, though large and strong enough to transport cattle.

The genius and greatness of the Assyrian people are displayed in their art and manu-

MUSICAL PROCESSION, NINEVEH.

factures, and not in the field of literature and science. The works of their sculptors, and the products of their shops and factories, bear testimony to the patience, diligence and care which they exhibited in every field of material and practical activity. The characteristics of their sculptures, and their manifest appreciation of works of general utility, show their preference for the practical over the theoretical, for the useful over the ideal, for the real over the imaginary.

Architecture, the only one of the fine arts actually useful, constitutes their greatest glory. Unlike the Egyptians, whose chief works were their temples and tombs, the interest attaching to which is spiritual and ideal, the Assyrians bestowed most attention on their palaces and dwellings, the more useful structures. Assyrian sculptures aimed to illustrate the real, the historically true; the only departure from this rule being the representations of dragons fighting, and the colossal winged man-headed bulls and lions guarding the entrances and passages of palaces, which are the symbols of strengh combined with intelligence. With the exception of the few emblematic figures relating to the Assyrian religion, the Assyrian bas-reliefs are closely copied from nature. The imitation is always laborious but in

1—14.-U. H.

most cases very accurate. Even where the laws of representation are apparently departed from, it is always done to impress correct ideas upon the beholder. Thus the gigantic stone bulls and lions have five legs, so that they may appear from every point of view as having four. The ladders are set edgeways against the walls of besieged cities, to show that they are really ladders. The disproportionate smallness of city walls, as represented in these sculptures, is designed to convey a full and correct idea of the real fact. The spirit of faithfulness and honesty pervading these sculptures is fully illustrated by the pains-taking finish, the minute detail, the elaboration of every hair in a beard, and every stitch in the embroidery of a dress. The Assyrian sculptures have a grandeur and a dignity, a boldness, a strength, and a life-like appearance, which render them intrinsically valuable as works of art, and which excite our wonder and admiration; though in conception, in grace, and in freedom and perfection of outline, they are surpassed by the wonderful productions of the Greek sculptors. Egyptian art was confined to a lifeless religious conventionalism which checked progress; Assyrian art aimed to represent vividly the highest scenes of human activity. All phases of war—the march of the army, the battle-field, the pursuit of the flying foe, the siege of cities, the passage of rivers and marshes, the submission and treatment of captives, and the "mimic war" of hunting—the chase of the lion, the stag, the antelope, the wild bull and the wild ass—constitute the chief subjects of Assyrian sculpture; and here all conventionality is utterly discarded. Fresh scenes, new groupings, bold and strange attitudes, are continually seen; and the animal representations particularly exhibit an unceasing advance with the progress of time, gradually becoming more and more spirited, more varied, more true to nature, though proportionately losing in the qualities of grandeur and majesty. This disposition to depict things in their reality continues to develop in perfection; and the progress in grace and delicacy of execution fully testify to the progressive character of Assyrian art, which only culminated in the closing years of the empire, during the brilliant reign of Asshur-bani-pal. The art of Assyria was thoroughly national, and developed by the inherent genius of the race.

In manufactures and the useful arts the Assyrians displayed a preëminence over all other ancient Oriental nations. The native industrial skill of this great people produced in abundance what was required for their comfort and happiness; while the multitudes of skilled workmen brought to Nineveh from the conquered nations by every war, in accordance with the policy of the Assyrian monarchs, led to the introduction of foreign fabrics and manufactures in the great Assyrian cities, and thus contributed to the industrial development of this active and practical race. The plunder, tribute and commerce of the subject states united to enrich Assyria with the products of all civilized lands. The vases, jars, bronzes, glass bottles, carved ornaments of ivory and mother-of-pearl, engraved gems, bells, dishes, ear-rings, arms, working implements, musical instruments, etc., found in recent years at Koyunjik, Nimrud and Khorsabad, were the products of Assyrian skill and industry. Most of the weapons of warfare, offensive and defensive, used by the stalwart warriors of Assyria, were forged in abundance in the armories of this great military nation.

ASSYRIAN LION HUNT.

Most of the ornaments, utensils, etc., are of elegant forms, and display much knowledge of metallurgy and other arts, as well as a refined taste; and some of these anticipate inventions supposed until recently to have been modern. One of these was transparent glass, and glass-blowing was one of the industries of Assyria, as it had been of ancient Egypt. A lens discovered at Nimrud, together with the fact that many of the Assyrian inscriptions are so minute that they can not be read without the use of magnifying-glasses, proves that they must have used such glasses in making these inscriptions.

The ornamental metallurgy of the Assyrians displayed wonderful skill; and consisted of entire figures or parts of figures cast solid, castings in low relief, and embossed work wrought principally with the hammer "but finished by a sparing use of the graving tool." The solid figures, most of which were small, comprised animal forms, chiefly lions. Castings in low relief were principally used in the ornamentation of thrones and chariots, and embraced animal and human figures, winged deities, griffins, etc. The embossed work was curious and elegant, as displayed in weapons, ornaments for the person, household implements and numerous other objects. The ornamental metallurgy of the Assyrians was mostly in bronze, consisting of one part of tin to ten parts of copper, which is yet regarded as the best proportion.

The Assyrians also understood other practical arts. Their buildings show that they were acquainted with the principle of the arch. They constructed tunnels, aqueducts and drains. They knew the use of the pulley, the lever and the roller; and constantly used the inclined plane in attacking fortified towns. They understood the arts of inlaying, enameling and overlaying with metals; and they cut and engraved gems with a degree of skill and finish not excelled by the French in our own day. Assyrian civilization did not fall far behind the boasted achievements of the moderns.

Says Rawlinson concerning the civilization of this wonderful ancient people: "With much that was barbaric still attaching to them, with a rude and inartificial government, savage passions, a debasing religion, and a general tendency to materialism, they were, towards the close of their empire, in all the ordinary arts and appliances of life, very nearly on a par with ourselves; and thus their history furnishes a warning—which the records of nations constantly repeat—that the greatest material prosperity may co-exist with the decline—and herald the downfall—of a kingdom."

Thus it will be seen that the inherent genius of the Assyrian people displayed itself in centuries of continued conquest and in material greatness. The glory of their arms and the grandeur of their art gave them the ascendency over the nations of Western Asia for almost seven hundred years. Their almost uninterrupted course of conquests poured wealth into their great capitals, developed luxury, and made them haughty and domineering. The mingled civilization and barbarism exhibited in the case of this mighty ancient Asiatic people has ever been the distinguishing characteristic of all the great Oriental empires which have successively risen, flourished, decayed, and crumbled to pieces.

SECTION V.—ASSYRIAN RELIGION.

HE Assyrian religion was almost identical with the Chaldæan, the only essential point of difference being that the supreme national deity of Assyria, Asshur, "the Great Lord," was unknown in Chaldæa, where Il was the chief god. With this solitary exception, the gods of Chaldæa were also the gods of Assyria. The minor points of difference were that certain deities prominent in the Chaldæan pantheon occupied a subordinate position in the pantheon of Assyria, and *vice versa*. Each pantheon began with the preëminence of a single god followed by the same groupings of identically the same divinities, and, after that, by a multitude of local deities. Each country had almost the same worship—temples, altars and ceremonies of a similar character—the same religious institutions—the same religious ideas. But Assyria furnishes us with a clearer knowledge of the material aspects of the religious system so nearly common to the two nations.

Asshur, the head of the Assyrian pantheon, is usually called "the Great Lord," "the King of all the Gods," "He who rules supreme over the Gods." He is also called "the Father of the Gods," though that title is more properly assigned to Bel. Asshur always has the first place in invocations. The testimony of the Assyrian inscriptions shows that Asshur was considered the special tutelary deity of the Assyrian monarchs and of the nation. He put kings on the throne, firmly established them in authority, prolonged their reigns, maintained their power, protected their fortresses and armies, made their names famous, and the like. They turned to him for victory in war, to give them all they desire, and to permit their thrones to be occupied by their dynasty to the latest posterity. They usually spoke of him as "Asshur, my Lord." They represented themselves as devoting their lives to his service. They prosecuted their wars to extend his worship. In his name they fought their battles and carried ruin and destruction among their enemies. When they conquered a country they "set up the emblems of Asshur," and spread a knowledge of his laws and his worship.

The tutelage of Asshur over Assyria is significantly indicated by the identity of his name with that of their country. The god Asshur, the country Asshur, and the city Asshur, and "an Assyrian" are all represented by the same term, which is written both *Ashur* and *Asshur*. This tutelage is likewise shown by the circumstance that Asshur had no famous temple or shrine in any particular Assyrian city like the other deities, and that his worship was general throughout Assyria. The early Assyrian capital was named after this supreme national deity; and all the local temples and shrines in the land were open to his worship, in addition to that of the divinities to whom they were dedicated. The inscriptions continually describe the Assyrians as "the servants of Asshur," and allude to their foes as "the enemies of Asshur." No phrases of a like character have been employed in referring to any other deity of the Assyrian pantheon.

It is therefore certain that the ancestor and founder of the Assyrian nation, Asshur, the son of Shem, had been deified after his death, as Nimrod had been; and that he was thenceforth "the Great Lord" of the Assyrians—the supreme ruler over heaven and earth—the chief object of Assyrian adoration.

The favorite emblem of Asshur was the winged circle or globe, from which is frequently seen issuing a figure in a horned cap, sometimes holding a bow only, sometimes discharging arrows from a bow against the enemies of Assyria. It has been conjectured that the circle symbolizes eternity, that the wings signify omnipotence, and that the human figure typifies wisdom or intelligence. There are numerous varieties of this emblem. Sometimes the human figure has no bow, and only extends the right hand. Sometimes both hands are extended, and a ring or chaplet is held in the left. In one instance there is no full human figure, but a pair of hands are seen issuing from behind the winged disk, the right hand showing the palm, and the left holding a bow. In many cases the winged circle appears alone, with the disk either plain or ornamented. Sennacherib's signet-cylinder bears an emblem of Asshur having three human heads, that on the entire human figure, and one on each side of it, resting on the feathers of the wing.

The sculptures represent the winged circle in close connection with the king, who has it embroidered upon his robes, engraved upon his cylinder, represented over his head in the rock tablets on which his image is carved; and who stands or kneels in adoration before it, fights under its shadow, returns in triumph under its protection, and assigns it a prominent place in the scenes in which he himself is represented on his obelisks. It is when the king is engaged in battle that Asshur is represented as drawing the bow and aiming the arrow towards the king's enemies. It is when he is returning in triumph from the field of conquest that Asshur is represented as only carrying the bow in his left hand, and holding out his right. In peaceful scenes Asshur is represented without a bow. In representations of the king at worship Asshur extends his hand in aid. Where the monarch is represented as engaged in secular matters Asshur's presence is indicated by the winged circle without the human figure.

The sacred tree is an emblem frequently seen, under various forms, in connection with the symbol of Asshur. The simplest form consists of a short pillar springing from a solitary pair of ram's horns, upon which is mounted a capital consisting of two pairs of rams' horns, with one, two or three horizontal bands between them; while above this capital is a scroll like that usually surmounting the winged circle, and above the scroll is a flower like the Greek "honeysuckle ornaments." In some cases the pillar is elongated, with a capital in the middle as well as one at the top; the blossom above the upper capital, and usually the stem also, throwing out many smaller blossoms of the same kind, or fir-cones, or pomegranates. Sometimes there is likewise an intricate network of branches forming an arch surrounding the tree. This Assyrian sacred tree has been compared with the Scriptural "tree of life."

In early times the Assyrians ranked Anu and Vul next to Asshur; but later they accorded this honor to Bel, Sin, Shamas, Vul, Nin and Nergal. Gula, Ishtar and Beltis were favorite goddesses. Hoa, Nebo and Merodach were less worshiped in Assyria than in Chaldæa, or Babylonia, though they were more esteemed in the later period of Assyrian history. As the characteristics of these deities have been described in our account of the religion of Chaldæa, we will here simply refer to their worship in Assyria, and to the temples dedicated to them.

The worship of Anu was introduced into Assyria from Babylonia during the period of Chaldæan supremacy before Assyria had become an independent kingdom. Shamas-Vul, the son of Ismi-Dagon, King of Chaldæa, erected a temple to Anu and Vul at Asshur, the early Assyrian capital, about B. C. 1820. The Inscription of Tiglath-Pileser I. says that this temple lasted six hundred and twenty-one years, when, on account of its decayed condition, it was torn down by Asshur-dayan I., the great-grandfather of Tiglath-Pileser I. Its site remained vacant for sixty years, after which Tiglath-Pileser I. rebuilt the temple more splendidly than before, and thenceforth it was one of the principal shrines of Assyria. A tradition relating to this ancient temple was the source from which the site of the city of Asshur in later times derived the name of Telané, or "the Mound of Asshur," a title it bears in Stephen.

Anu's name is no element in the names of monarchs or of other prominent characters, and is not found in many solemn invocations; but where his name occurs it is always placed next to that of Asshur, and Tiglath-

Pileser I. mentions him in his great Inscription, as his lord and protector, in the place next to Asshur. Asshur-izir-pal calls himself "him who honors Anu," or "him who honors Anu and Dagon." Asshur-izir-pal's son and successor, Shalmaneser II., gives Anu the second place in the invocation of thirteen gods with which he begins his record. The monarchs of the New or Lower Assyrian Empire did not usually esteem Anu very highly, with the exception of Sargon, who glorified him, coupled him with Asshur, and made him the tutelary god of one of the gates of his new city, Dur-Sargina (now Khorsabad), uniting him in this capacity with the goddess Ishtar. Anu did not have many temples in Assyria, having none at Nineveh or Calah, the only important one being at Asshur.

Bel, or Bel-Nimrod, according to the testimony of the Assyrian monuments, was worshiped as extensively in Assyria as in Chaldæa, or Babylonia. From the time of Tiglath-Pileser I. to the fall of the Assyrian Empire, the Assyrians, as a nation, were specifically denominated "the people of Bel;" and a certain part of Nineveh was designated "the city of Bel." The word Bel was an element in the names of three Assyrian kings. In the invocation of the gods Bel's place is next to Asshur's when Anu's name is omitted; but when Anu occupies his proper place next to Asshur, Bel ranks third. In several places, however, where Anu is omitted, Shamas, the Sun-god, is second, and Bel ranks third.

Bel was worshiped in early Assyrian times, as indicated by the royal names of Bel-sumili-kapi and Bel-lush, as borne by two of the earliest Assyrian monarchs. Bel had a temple at Asshur in connection with Il, and its antiquity is proven by the fact that as early as the time of Tiglath-Pileser I., B. C. 1130, it had fallen into decay and was rebuilt by that famous king. Bel had also a temple at Calah, and four "arks" or "tabernacles," whose sites are not identified. Sargon accorded high honor to Bel, coupling him with Anu in his royal titles, and dedicating to him, in conjunction with his wife, Beltis, one of the gates of his city. In this dedication Bel is called "the establisher of the foundations of his city;" and in many passages Sargon attributes his royal authority to the favor of Bel and Merodach.

It is believed that the horned cap, the general emblem of divinity, was the special symbol of Bel. Esar-haddon says that he set up over "the image of his majesty the emblems of Asshur, the Sun, Bel, Nin and Ishtar." The other kings invariably mention Bel as one of the chief objects of their worship.

Hoa was not prominently worshiped in Assyria. Asshur-izir-pal says that Hoa allotted the senses of hearing, seeing and understanding to the four thousand deities of heaven and earth; and then, mentioning that the four thousand deities had transferred these senses to himself, he assumes Hoa's titles and identifies himself with this god. Asshur-izir-pal's son and successor, Shalmaneser II., the Black Obelisk king, in his opening invocation, assigned Hoa his proper place, between Bel and Sin. Sargon placed one of the gates of his new city under Hoa's protection, in conjunction with Bilat-Ili, "the Mistress of the Gods," believed to be Gula, the Sun-goddess. Sennacherib, after his successful expedition across the Persian Gulf, offered sacrifice to Hoa on the sea-shore, presenting him with a golden boat, a golden fish and a golden coffer. Hoa's emblem, the serpent, was found on the black stones on which were recorded benefactions, and on the Babylonian cylinder-seals, but was not adopted by the Assyrian monarchs among the divine symbols worn by them, nor among those inscribed by them above their effigies. Hoa's name seldom occurs among the royal invocations. His only two known temples in Assyria were the one at Asshur (now Kileh-Sherghat) and the one at Calah (now Nimrud). The Assyrian devotion to Nin, the tutelary god of the Assyrian monarchs and of their capital, caused Nin's worship gradually to supersede that of Hoa.

Beltis, "the Great Mother," the wife of

Bel, ranked in Assyria next to the triad embracing Anu, Bel and Hoa. She is usually mentioned in the Assyrian inscriptions in close relation with her husband. The Assyrians particularly considered Beltis "the Queen of fertility," thus resembling the Greek Demeter, the Roman Ceres, who was also known as "the Great Mother." Sargon put one of the gates of his new city under the protection of Beltis, along with her husband, Bel; and Sargon's great-grandson, Asshur-bani-pal, repaired and re-dedicated to this goddess a temple at Nineveh, originally erected by Asshur-izir-pal. She also had a temple at Asshur; and at Calah was a temple dedicated either to Beltis or to Ishtar, the epithets used applying to either goddess. The goddess, though known in Assyria as Beltis, was called Mylitta in Babylonia.

Sin, the Moon-god, occupied the next place to Beltis in the Assyrian pantheon, the sixth place among the gods where Beltis was inserted, and the fifth place wherever her name did not occur. His worship in the early period of the Assyrian Empire is indicated by the invocation of Tiglath-Pileser I., where he is mentioned in the third place among the gods, between Bel and Shamas. Sin's emblem, the crescent, was worn by Asshur-izir-pal, and is always seen among the divine symbols which the Assyrian monarchs inscribed over their effigies. Sin was one of the most highly esteemed of the Assyrian deities, and his sign is found as often as any other among both Assyrian and Babylonian cylinder-seals. His name is sometimes seen in the appellation of kings and princes; as in that of Sennacherib, signifying "Sin multiplies brethren." Sargon was particularly devoted to the worship of Sin, after whom he named one of his sons, and to whom, in connection with Shamas, the Sun-god, he erected a temple at his new city, assigning to him the second place among the tutelary deities of the city.

The Assyrians seem to have regarded Sin as a very ancient god, and when they desired to mark a very old period they would say: "From the origin of the god Sin." This was a vestige of the old connection of Assyria with Chaldæa, whose primitive capital, Ur, was under the special protection of the Moon-god, and where the most ancient temple was dedicated to his worship. The only two temples known to have been erected to Sin in Assyria were the one dedicated to him, along with Shamas, by Sargon at his new city, and the other to Sin alone at Calah.

Shamas, the Sun-god, ranked next below Sin, but was more popular and far more generally worshiped in Assyria. Many passages would seem to indicate that the Assyrian kings esteemed him next to Asshur, as they really ranked him above Bel in some of their lists. The emblem of the Sun-god, the four-rayed orb, was worn upon the neck of the Assyrian king, and is seen more generally than most others upon the cylinder-seals. In some cases the emblem of Shamas is even united with Asshur's emblem, the central circle of which is marked by the fourfold rays of Shamas.

The worship of Shamas in Assyria extended to a very remote antiquity. Tiglath-Pileser I. mentions him in his invocation, and represents himself as ruling specially under his auspices. Asshur-izir-pal names Asshur and Shamas as the tutelary gods under whose influence he conducted his wars. Asshur-izir-pal's son and successor, Shalmaneser II., the Black Obelisk king, gives Shamas his proper place among the gods whom he invokes at the beginning of his long Inscription. The kings of the New or Lower Assyrian Empire rendered him more devotion than their predecessors. Sargon dedicated the north gate of his new city to Shamas, along with Vul, the Air-god; and erected a temple to both Shamas and Sin at the same city, assigning the Sun-god the third place among the tutelary gods of the new city. Sennacherib and Esar-haddon named Shamas next to Asshur in passages when mentioning the gods whom they considered their chief protectors.

The only special temple dedicated to the worship of Shamas was the one assigned to him and Sin jointly at Sargon's new city; but his images are frequently seen among the lists of idols, so that he may have been worshiped in temples consecrated to other deities. His emblem is usually seen united with that of the Moon-god, either beside or above it.

Vul, the Air-god, was known in Assyria from the earliest times; a temple having been erected at Asshur, during the period of Assyria's subjection to Chaldæa, by Shamas-Vul, the son of Ismi-Dagon, King of Chaldæa; as well as the temple which the same king dedicated to both Anu and Vul. As these edifices had fallen to ruin by the time of Tiglath-Pileser I., that monarch rebuilt them from their base; and Vul, being regarded as one of the special "guardian deities," was worshiped in both temples. In Shalmeneser II.'s Black Obelisk invocation the intermediate place between Sin and Shamas is assigned to Vul, and on that obelisk is recorded the fact that Shalmaneser II. held a festival in honor of both Asshur and Vul. Sargon gave Vul the fourth place among the tutelary deities of his new city, and dedicated to him the north gate in connection with Shamas, the Sungod. Sennacherib spoke of hurling thunder on his enemies like Vul, and other Assyrian monarchs say they "rush on the enemy like the whirlwind of Vul," or "sweep a country as with the whirlwind of Vul." The Tiglath-Pileser Inscription mentions Vul as "he who causes the tempest to rage over hostile lands." The name Vul often occurred as an element in the names of kings and other personages, as in Vullush, Shamas-Vul, etc. The symbol of Vul, the double or triple bolt, is often seen among the emblems worn by the Assyrian monarchs, and engraved above their heads on the rock tablets. Besides his two temples at Asshur, Vul had a temple at Calah dedicated to him and his wife, the goddess Shala.

Gula, the Sun-goddess, the wife of Shamas, was not very highly ranked among the Assyrian deities. It is true, her emblem, the eight-rayed disk, was borne by the Assyrian kings, along with her husband's symbol, and is often inscribed on the rock tablets, on the stones on which benefactions are recorded, and on the cylinder-seals. But her name is not often found in the inscriptions, and, where it does occur, it is seen low down in the lists. Gula is the next to the last among the thirteen deities named in the Black Obelisk invocation. The only other places where she is mentioned is in inscriptions of a distinctly-religious nature. At Asshur was a temple dedicated to Gula, Ishtar and ten inferior deities. Gula's other Assyrian temple was at Calah, where her husband likewise had a temple. Gula has been identified with Bilat-Ili, "the Mistress of the Gods," to whom, together with Hoa, Sargon dedicated one of the gates of his new city.

Nin was one of the most devotedly worshiped in Assyria among the second order of gods. The oldest traditions mention Nin as the founder of the Assyrian royal race, and the mighty city which finally became the capital and metropolis of the Assyrian Empire derived its name from this god. As far back as the thirteenth century before Christ, Nin became an element in royal names. The Ninus of the Greek writers has been regarded by moderns as the Nin of the Assyrian inscriptions. Herodotus and Ctesias both considered Ninus as the founder of the Assyrian dynasty. Tiglath-Pileser I., the first Assyrian king who has left us an historical inscription, and who considered himself under Nin's guardianship, is called "the illustrious prince whom Asshur and Nin have exalted to the utmost wishes of his heart." This monarch mentions Nin sometimes alone, and sometimes along with Asshur, as his "guardian deity." Nin and Nergal are spoken of as sharpening weapons for Tiglath-Pileser, and it is further said that under the auspices of Nin the most ferocious animals fall beneath these weapons. Asshur-izir-pal erected a splendid temple to Nin at Calah. Asshur-izir-pal's grandson, Shamas-Vul I., dedicated to Nin the obelisk which he set up at Calah to commemorate his victories. Sargon put the new city which he founded under Nin's protection, and invoked this god spe-

RELIGION.

cially to guard his gorgeous palace. Sargon's veneration for Nin was strikingly indicated by the ornamentation of that magnificent structure; and Nin's emblem, the winged man-headed bull, stood guard at all its principal gateways. The figure strangling a lion, occupying so prominent a place on the harem portal facing the great court, represented this god. Sargon attributed his victories in war to the favor of Nin, and for this reason he placed Nin's emblems on the sculptures representing his military expeditions. Sennacherib, Sargon's son and successor, had the same reverence for Nin, as he also placed the winged man-headed bull at most of the doorways of his magnificent palace at Nineveh, and assigned the figure strangling the lion a prominent place on the grand façade of the same splendid edifice. Esar-haddon states that he continued in the worship of Nin, and that he set up the emblem of that god over his own royal effigy, in connection with the symbols of Asshur, Shamas, Bel and Ishtar.

Nin's name entered as an element into the names of three Assyrian kings—Nin-pala-zira and the two Tiglathi-Nins. The principal temples dedicated to Nin were at Calah. The vast edifice at the north-western corner of the great Nimrud mound, including the pyramidal elevation constituting the most conspicuous feature of the ruins, was a temple dedicated to Nin by Asshur-izir-pal, who erected the north-west palace. It has been supposed that this edifice was the "busta Nini" of the Greek writers, where Ninus, whom the Greeks considered the hero-founder of the Assyrian nation, was interred and specially worshiped. This great temple was named Bit-zira, or Beth-zira, and from its fane Nin had the title *Pal-zira*, "the son of Zira." Nin's other temple at Calah was named Bit-kura, or Beth-kura, from the fane of which Nin was called *Pal-kura*, "the son of Kura."

Merodach was a god mentioned by most of the early Assyrian kings in their opening invocations, and an allusion in their inscriptions indicates that he was regarded as a very powerful god. Shalmaneser II., the Black Obelisk king, says in one place that "the fear of Asshur and Merodach fell upon his enemies." But Merodach was not a popular deity in Assyria until the later times of the empire, Vul-lush III. being the first monarch who assigned him a prominent place in the Assyrian pantheon. Sargon and his successors continued the worship of Merodach. Sargon constantly ascribed his power to the united favor of Asshur and Merodach, and Esar-haddon sculptured the emblems of these two gods over the images of foreign gods presented to him by a suppliant prince. But Merodach had no temple in Assyria.

Nergal was a god highly reverenced, being regarded by the Assyrian monarchs as their divine ancestor, Sargon having traced the line of descent through three hundred and fifty generations. Nergal's symbol was the winged man-headed lion, or the national lion, whose figure enters largely into Assyrian architecture. The confident reliance of the Assyrians on Nergal's protection is proven by the conspicuous place his emblems everywhere occupied in their palaces. Nin and Nergal, as the gods of war and hunting, in which occupations the Assyrian kings spent their lives, were tutelary gods of these monarchs; and these two deities are found equally associated in the royal inscriptions and sculptures. Sennacherib dedicated a temple to Nergal at Tarbisi (now Sherif-Khan); and he may have had one at Calah, as a smaller temple with the lion entrance is found in the ruins on the northwest corner of the Nimrud mound, and as he was mentioned as one of the "resident gods" of Calah.

Ishtar was a favorite goddess of the Assyrian kings, who styled her "their lady," and sometimes coupled her with Asshur, "the Great Lord," in their invocations. Ishtar had a very old temple at Asshur, the primitive Assyrian capital, and this temple Tiglath-Pileser I. repaired and beautified. Asshur-izir-pal erected a second temple to her at Nineveh, and she had a third at Arbela, which Asshur-bani-pal says he restored. Sargon put the western gate of his new city under the united protection of Ishtar and Anu. Sargon's son and successor, Sennacherib, spoke of Asshur and Ishtar as about to "call the kings his sons to their sovereignty over Assyria," and implored Asshur and Ishtar to "hear their prayers." Sennacherib's grandson, Asshur-bani-pal, the royal hunter, was devoted to Ishtar, whom he considered the special patron of his favorite pastime, the chase of the lion and the wild bull. Ishtar appears as one goddess divided into many; as the Ishtar of Nineveh, the Ishtar of Arbela, and the Ishtar of Babylon are all distinguished from each other, a separate address being made to each of them in the same invocation, as in that of Sennacherib and in that of Esar-haddon. Thus though Ishtar was a general object of worship throughout Assyria, she had a distinctly local character in the various Assyrian and Babylonian cities.

Nebo was one of the most ancient of Assyrian gods, and his name enters as an element into a king's name in the twelfth century before Christ, namely that of Mutaggil-Nebo. But he was not extensively worshiped until Vul-lush III. had given him a prominent place in the Assyrian pantheon after leading an expedition into Babylonia, where Nebo had always been highly honored. Vul-lush III. set up two statues to Nebo at Calah, and perhaps erected to him the temple there called Bit-Saggil, or Beth-Saggil, from which Nebo derived his name of *Pal-Bit-Saggil*. Sennacherib and Esar-haddon held this god in high veneration, the latter putting him above Merodach in an important invocation. Asshur-bani-pal also paid Nebo much reverence, alluding to him and his wife, Warmita, as the deities under whose auspices he engaged in some literary work.

After these chief deities, the Assyrians recognized and adored a multitude of inferior divinities. Beltis, the wife of Bel; and Gula, the wife of Shamas; also Ishtar, who is sometimes alluded to as the wife of Nebo, were all goddesses of exalted rank and importance. But Sheruba, the wife of Asshur; Anata, or Anuta, the wife of Anu; Davkina, the wife of Hoa; Shala, the wife of Vul; Zirbanit, the wife of Merodach; Laz, the wife of Nergal; and Warmita, usually called the wife of Nebo, did not occupy a place in the Assyrian pantheon at all in comparison with the dignity and rank of their husbands. Nin, the Assyrian Hercules, and Sin, the Moon-god, had wives also; but their proper names are not known, Nin's wife being called "the Queen of the Land," and Sin's wife "the Great Lady."

Thus the Assyrians usually combined in the same temple the worship of the male and the female principle; the female deities— with the exception of Beltis, the wife of Bel; Gula, the wife of Shamas; and Ishtar, either as an independent goddess or as the wife of Nebo, who are as strong and distinct as their husbands—are in most cases only the reflection of their husbands, thus having an unsubstantial character, and occupying a very insignificant position in the pantheon. Some minor goddesses, among whom was Telita, the goddess of the great marshes near Babylon, stood alone, unassociated with any male deity. Most of the minor male divinities likewise had no female companions, the notable exceptions to this rule being Martu, whose wife was called "the Lady of Tigganna," and Idak, God of the Tigris, whose wife was Belat-Muk.

Prominent among the minor male divinities were Martu, called a son of Anu and "the Minister of the deep," and corresponding to the Greek Erebus; Sargana, also ranked as a son of Anu, and from whom Sargon is supposed to have derived his name; Idak, God of the Tigris; Supulat, Lord of the Euphrates; and Il, who, though the Babylonian chief god, occupied an humble position in the Assyrian pantheon. Tiglath-Pileser I. repaired a temple to Il at Asshur about B. C. 1150. Besides these just mentioned, there were a multitude of minor Assyrian divinities, of whom but very little is yet known.

The Assyrians are supposed to have believed in the existence of genii, some of whom they considered powers of good, others powers of evil. The winged figure wearing the horned cap, usually represented as waiting upon the king when he is engaged in any sacred capacity, is believed to be his tutelary genius, the spirit carefully watching over him and protecting him from the spirits of darkness. This figure generally carries a pomegranate or a pine-cone in the right hand, and sometimes holds a plaited bag or basket in the left, while at other times this hand is free. The pine-cone, when carried, is always pointed towards the king, as if signifying the means of communication between the protector and the protected, the instrument conveying grace and strength from the genius to the human being whom he had taken under his care. The sacred basket is often very elegantly and elaborately ornamented, sometimes with winged figures in adoration before the sacred tree, and they themselves holding baskets. The hawk-headed figure, also found attending upon the king and watching his actions, is likewise believed to represent a good genius.

NISROCH BEFORE THE SYMBOLIC TREE.
As Seen in Sargon's Great Palace.

Few representations of evil genii have been discovered. Among these is the monster—half lion, half eagle, driven into retreat by Vul's thunderbolts—found among the sculptures at Nimrud, the ancient Calah. Certain grotesque statuettes found at Khorsabad, representing a human figure having a lion's head with the ears of an ass, have likewise been classed with these evil genii. In one case we see two monsters with heads like the one just described, placed on human bodies whose legs end in eagle's claws, both armed with daggers and maces, and struggling with each other. This sculpture—found in the ruins of Asshur-bani-pal's great palace at Nineveh, and now in the British Museum—is believed to be a symbolical illustration of the tendency of evil to turn upon itself and waste its strength by internal contention and turmoil. Instances are abundant in which a human figure with the head of a hawk or an eagle threatens a winged man-headed lion, the emblem of Nergal, with a strap or a mace; thus typifying the spirit of evil attacking a god, or the hawk-headed genius driving Nergal out of Assyria—an emblematic representation of war.

The Assyrian religion had a strongly-idolatrous character in its mode of worship. The different images of the same deity came to be regarded as separate objects of worship in their different temples; and thus we find the Ishtar of Arbela, the Ishtar of Nineveh, and the Ishtar of Babylon invoked by the same monarch in the same inscription as separate divinities. The identification of the god with the image is exemplified in the great Inscription of Tiglath-Pileser I., where the king boasts that he set up Anu and Vul in their places, and where he constantly identifies the images which he carries off from foreign lands with their gods. In the same spirit Sennacherib inquires, through Rabshakeh: "*Where are the gods* of Hamath and of Arpad? *Where are the gods* of Sepharvaim, Hena and Ivah?" The meaning of these interrogatory expressions is that the gods of those foreign lands had been carried captive to Assyria when their idols were conveyed there. When Hezekiah, King of Judah, had destroyed all the images throughout his dominions Sennacherib thought that monarch had deprived his subjects of all divine protection. The usual Assyrian custom of carrying off the idols of foreign countries was designed to weaken the enemies of Assyria by depriving them of their divine protectors. These idols were not removed in an irreverent or sacrilegious manner, and were deposited in the chief Assyrian temples, so that these gods would thereafter be among the celestial guardians of the Assyrians.

Assyrian idols were made from stone, baked clay or metal. Some images of Nebo and of Ishtar have been found among the ruins. Those of Nebo are standing figures somewhat larger than the human size. They show the marks of the ravages of time, and, like many of the winged man-headed lions and bulls, are disfigured by several lines of cuneiform inscriptions, stating the fact that the statues represent Nebo, and relating the circumstances of their dedication.

The few clay idols found are usually of good material and of different sizes, smaller than the full human stature, but are commonly mere statuettes less than a foot high. These statuettes are believed to have been mostly intended for private use among the people in general, while the stone idols were designed for public worship in the shrines and temples. Idols in metal have not been found among the Assyrian remains, but a passage from the Hebrew prophet Nahum indicates that the Assyrians had images made of that material in their temples. In alluding to Nineveh, Nahum says: "And the Lord hath given a commandment concerning thee, that no more of thy name be sown; out of the house of thy gods will I cut off the graven image and the *molten* image."

The Assyrian method of worship consisted mainly of sacrifices and offerings. Tiglath-Pileser I. states in his long Inscription that he offered sacrifices to Anu and Vul when he had finished repairing their temple. Asshur-izir-pal states that he sacrificed to the gods after having embarked on the Mediterranean. Vul-lush III. sacrificed to Merodach, Nebo and Nergal in their respective temples at Babylon, Borsippa and Cutha. Sennacherib offered sacrifices to Hoa on the seashore after his expedition in the Persian Gulf against Susiana. Esar-haddon "slew great and costly sacrifices" at Nineveh when he had finished his great palace in that city. The Assyrian monarchs in general considered sacrifice a duty, and this was the usual method by which they propitiated the favor of the national deities.

The bas-reliefs give us scant information concerning the manner of the Assyrian sacrifices, but they show that the animal specially sacrificed was the bull. The inscriptions inform us that sheep and goats were likewise used for sacrifice, and there is a representation of a ram or wild goat being led to the altar. On Lord Aberdeen's Black Stone, a monument of Esar-haddon's reign, a bull is represented as brought up to a temple by the king. On a mutilated obelisk of Asshur-bani-pal's time, now in the British Museum, the whole sacrificial scene is presented to our view. The king and six priests, one of whom carries a cup, while the other five are employed about the sacrificial animal, advance in procession towards the front of the temple, where the god with the horned cap on his head occupies a throne, while a beardless attendant priest is paying adoration to him. The king pours a libation over a large bowl, fixed in a stand, just in front of a tall fire-altar, from which flames arise. The priest stands close behind with a cup in his hand. The bull's advance is stayed by a bearded priest just in front of the animal. Two priests walk behind the bull and hold him with a rope fastened to one of his front legs near the hoof. These two priests and two others behind them appear, from the position of their heads and arms, to be engaged in a solemn chant. The flame on the altar indicates that the sacrifice is to be burned upon that altar, which is only large enough to burn a part of the animal at a time.

Assyrian altars differed in form and size. Some were square and not high, with the top ornamented with gradines, below which the sides were plain or fluted. Others about the same height were triangular, with a round top consisting of a plain flat stone, sometimes inscribed round the edge. An altar of this form was discovered by M. Botta at Khorsabad. Another of almost the same shape was found by Mr. Layard at Nimrud, and is now in the British Museum. A third kind of altar resembled a portable

RELIGION.

stand, narrow but reaching up to a man's head. These kinds of altars the Assyrians carried about in their expeditions, and in the entrenched camps priests are sometimes seen officiating at them in their sacerdotal costume.

The Assyrian kings deposited in the temples of their gods, as thank-offerings, many precious products from the countries which they invaded with their armies. Various kinds of stones or marbles, rare metals and images of foreign deities, are specially named in the Tiglath-Pileser Inscription as among such offerings. Silver and gold—so largely employed in the adornment of temples that they were said to have been sometimes "as splendid as the sun"—were thus dedicated to the gods.

The sculptures, mostly monuments erected by the kings, represent their own religious performances, but not those of the people. The Assyrian kings thus exercised priestly functions, and in the religious scenes which illustrate their acts of worship no priest is represented as intervening between the king and the god, but all priests occupy a very unimportant position. The king himself stands and worships near the holy tree, pours out libations with his own hands, and may himself have slain victims for sacrifice. As the Babylonians and all other Oriental nations had their priesthoods, it is likewise probable that the religious affairs of the Assyrian people were conducted under the auspices of their priests, whom the cylinders represent as introducing worshipers to the gods, and who are attired in long robes and wearing mitres upon their heads. The worshiper is usually represented as carrying an antelope or a young goat, intended to propitiate the deity. The Assyrian sculptures generally represent the priests without beards.

At the Assyrian festivals great multitudes, particularly of the chief men, assembled; many sacrifices were offered, and the festivities continued several days. Many of the worshipers were afforded accommodations in the royal palace, to which the temple was commonly only an addition, and were fed at the monarch's expense and given lodging in the halls and other apartments. The Assyrian religion also embraced fasting, as attested exclusively by the Book of Jonah. When a fast was proclaimed, the king, the nobles and the people attired themselves in sackcloth, sprinkled ashes upon their heads, and abstained from eating and drinking

THE KING DRINKING OR DIVINING IN THE PRESENCE OF THE GODS OF ASSYRIA.

until the fast was ended. The animals within the walls of the city where the fast was ordered were also robed in sackcloth, and were likewise denied food and drink. Business was suspended, and the entire populace united in prayer to Asshur, "the Great Lord," thus imploring his pardon and seeking to propitiate his favor. These were not simply formal ceremonies. On the occasion alluded to in the Book of Jonah, the repentance of the Ninevites appears to have been sincere. Says this authority: "God saw their works, that they turned from their evil way; and God repented of the evil that he said he would do unto them; and he did it not."

Altogether the Assyrians were a strongly-religious people, although not as intensely so as the Egyptians. Their temples, however, were subordinated to their palaces, and the most imposing emblems of their gods, such as the winged man-headed bulls and lions, symbolizing respectively Nin and Nergal, were degraded to mere architectural ornaments. Their religion was very gross and sensuous in its nature, and its intensely-materialistic character is attested by the practice of image-worship. The Assyrians worshiped more by means of sacrifices and offerings than by prayer, though in times of distress and misfortune they could offer prayers of the deepest sincerity, which goes to prove that they were actuated by honest motives and purposes concerning their numerous solemn addresses and invocations, as read in their public and private documents. The devotion of the learned to religious subjects is shown by the many mythological tablets; and the piety of the masses is indicated by the general character of their names, and by the almost universal custom of inscribing sacred figures and symbols upon their signets.

The sensuous nature of the religion consequently led to an ostentatious ceremonial, a taste for pompous processions, and the use of gorgeous vestments; the last being very elaborately represented in the Nimrud sculptures. The costume of the priests was magnificent, their robes being elegantly embroidered, mostly with religious figures and emblems, such as the winged circle, the pine-cone, the pomegranate, the sacred tree, the winged man-headed lion, etc. The officiating priests wore armlets, bracelets, necklaces and ear-rings; and their heads were encircled with an elegantly-adorned fillet, or covered with a mitre or a showy cap. In the religious processions the musicians performed an imposing part.

CHIEF DEITIES OF THE ASSYRIANS.

	GODS.	CORRESPONDING GODDESSES.	CHIEF SEAT OF WORSHIP.
	ASSHUR	SHERUHA	Throughout the Empire.
FIRST TRIAD.	ANU	ANUTA	Asshur.
	BEL	BELTIS (MYLITTA)	Asshur and Calah.
	HOA	DAV-KINA	Asshur and Calah.
SECOND TRIAD.	SIN	"THE GREAT LADY"	Calah and Dur-Sargina.
	SHAMAS	GULA	Dur-Sargina.
	VUL	SHALA	Asshur and Calah.
	NIN	"THE QUEEN OF THE LAND."	Calah and Nineveh.
	MERODACH	ZIR-BANIT	
	NERGAL	LAZ	Tarbisi.
	NEBO	WARMITA AND ISHTAR	Calah.

CHAPTER IV.

THE MEDIAN EMPIRE.

SECTION I.—GEOGRAPHY OF MEDIA.

EDIA occupied an extensive region south and south-west of the Caspian Sea, east of Armenia and Assyria, north of Persia proper, and west of the great salt desert and Parthia. It was about six hundred miles in extent from north to south, and about two hundred and fifty miles from east to west; thus having an area of nearly one hundred and fifty thousand square miles, a greater extent than Assyria and Chaldæa combined. It occupied a tract in one solid mass, "with no straggling or outlying portions; and it is strongly defended on almost every side by natural barriers offering great difficulties to an invader."

The Median territory comprises two regions—the northern and western portion being a mountain district embracing a series of lofty ridges; and the southern and eastern section forming a part of the great plateau of Iran, extending southward to the Indian Ocean, embracing all of ancient Persia and Carmania, the latter being the modern Kerman, while eastward this extensive table-land is bounded by the modern Afghanistan. The average elevation of the territory occupied by ancient Media is about three thousand feet above the level of the sea.

The western part of the mountain region of Media was anciently called the Zagros, and is part of the modern Kurdistan and Luristan. It is thus spoken of: "Full of torrents, of deep ravines, of rocky summits, abrupt and almost inaccessible; containing but few passes, and those narrow and easily defensible; secure, moreover, owing to the rigor of its climate, from hostile invasion for more than half the year, it has defied all attempts to effect its permanent subjugation, whether made by the Assyrians, Persians, Greeks, Parthians, or Turks, and remains to this day as independent of the great powers in its neighborhood, as it was when the Assyrian armies first penetrated its recesses. Nature seems to have constructed it to be a nursery of hardy and vigorous men, a stumbling-block to conquerors, a thorn in the side of every powerful empire which arises in this part of the great Eastern continent."

The northern part of the mountain region is called Elburz, and contains the lofty, snow-covered peak of Demavend, which overlooks Teheran, the present capital of Persia, and is the highest portion of Asia west of the great Himalaya mountain chain. The Elburz region is not as well watered as the Zagros district, its streams being small, frequently dry in summer, and absorbed by the Caspian Sea, which bounds the region on the north.

"The elevated plateau which stretches from the foot of these two mountain regions to the south and east, is for the most part a flat, sandy desert, incapable of sustaining more than a sparse and scanty population. The northern and western portions are, however, less arid than the east and south, being watered for some distance by the streams that descend from Zagros and Elburz, and deriving fertility also from the spring rains. Some of the rivers which flow from Zagros on this side are large and strong. One, the Kizil-Uzen, reaches the Caspian. Another, the Zenderud, fertilizes a large district near Isfahan. A third, the Bendamir, flows by Persepolis and terminates in a sheet of water of some size—Lake Bakhtigan. A tract thus intervenes between the mountain regions and the desert, which, though it cannot be called fertile, is fairly productive, and can support a large settled population. This forms the chief portion of the region which the ancients called Media."

Media was mainly a sterile country, and had an attractive appearance only in spring. In the mountain region the climate is severe. On the plateau it is more temperate, but the thermometer does not often reach ninety degrees in the shade. All in all, the climate is considered healthy. With the aid of irrigation the great table-land yields "good crops of grain, rice, wheat, barley, Indian corn, *doura*, millet and sesame. It will likewise produce cotton, tobacco, saffron, rhubarb, madder, poppies which give a good opium, senna and asafœtida. Its garden vegetables are excellent, and include potatoes, cabbages, lentils, kidney-beans, peas, turnips, carrots, spinnach, beet-root and cucumbers."

Media produced various valuable minerals. Many different kinds of stone are yet found throughout the country, chief of which is the beautiful Tabriz marble. Iron, copper and native steel are still mined. Gold and silver were found in the mountains in ancient times. Sulphur, alum and gypsum are found in different portions of the country, and salt likewise exists in abundant quantities.

The wild animals of Media were the lion, the tiger, the leopard, the bear, the beaver, the jackal, the wolf, the wild ass, the ibex, or wild goat, the wild sheep, the stag, the antelope, the wild boar, the fox, the hare, the rabbit, the ferret, the rat, the jerboa, the porcupine, the mole and the marmot. The domestic animals were the camel, the horse, the mule, the ass, the cow, the goat, the sheep, the buffalo, the dog and the cat.

The southern part of Media, or Media proper, was called Media Magna ; while the northern, or mountainous, portion was known as Media Atropatênê. The capital and metropolis of each of these divisions was a city called Ecbatana. Next to the two Ecbatanas were Rhages, Bagistan, Adrapan, Aspadan and a few other cities.

The southern Ecbatana, or Agbatana—the capital and metropolis of Media Magna—was called Hagmatán by the Medes and Persians themselves; and, according to Polyhistor and Diodorus, was situated on a plain at the foot of Mount Orontes, a little west of the Zagros range. The notices of these writers and those of Eratosthenes, Isidore, Pliny, Arrian and others, would imply that the site of this famous city was that of the modern town of Hamadan, the name of which is a slight corruption of the ancient name as known by the Medes and Persians. Mount Orontes has been identified as the modern Elwend, or Erwend, a long and lofty mountain connected with the Zagros range, and surrounded with fertile plains famed for their rich and abundant vegetation and their dense groves of forest trees with their luxuriant foliage. Hamadan lies at the foot of this mountain.

Ecbatana was mainly renowned for its magnificent royal palace, which Diodorus ascribed to Semiramis; Polybius assigned the edifice a circumference of seven stadia, or 1,420 yards, a little over four-fifths of an English mile. The latter writer also spoke of two classes of pillars, those of the main buildings and those which skirted the courts, thus implying that the courts were surrounded with colonnades. These wooden pillars, either of cedar or cypress, supported beams of the same wood crossing each other at right angles, leaving square spaces between, which were then filled in with woodwork. Above the whole was a roof sloping at an angle and composed of silver plates in the shape of tiles. The pillars, beams and the other wood-work were also lined with a thin coating of gold and other precious metals. Herodotus described an edifice which he called "the palace of Deioces," but this is believed to apply to the northern Ecbatana. Polybius says that Ecbatana was an unwalled city in his time, which was in the second century before Christ. The Medes and Persians did not generally surround their cities with walls, being satisfied with establishing in each town a fortified citadel or stronghold, around which the houses were clustered. Ecbatana therefore never withstood a siege, and always submitted to a conquering foe without resistance. The description in the Apocryphal Book of Judith—which, contradicted by every other evidence, is purely mythical—represents Ecbatana as having walls of hewn stone nine feet long and four and a half feet wide; the walls being one hundred and five feet high and seventy-five feet wide, the gates of the same altitude, and the towers over the gates one hundred and fifty feet high.

The chief city of Media Atropatênê was the northern Ecbatana, which the Greeks sometimes mistook for the southern metropolis and the real capital of Media, and which in later times was known as Gaza, Gazaca, Canzaca, or Vera. The description of Ecbatana accords with the remains of a city in Azerbijan, and not with the local features of the site of Hamadan; and a city in this region was called by Moses of Chorênê "the second Ecbatana, the seven-walled town." This city was located on and about a conical hill sloping gently down from its summit to its base, interposed by seven circuits of wall between the plain and the crest of the hill. The royal palace and the treasuries were at the top of the hill, within the innermost circle of the defenses; while the fortifications were on the sides, and the dwellings and other edifices of the city were at the base of the hill, outside the circuit of the outermost wall. Herodotus states that the battlements crowning the walls were differently colored; those of the outer being white, the next black, the third scarlet, the fourth blue, the fifth orange, the sixth silver, and the seventh gold. This gave the citadel towering above the town seven distinct rows of colors. The city thus described by Herodotus coincides with the ruins at the modern town of Takht-i-Suleïman, in the upper valley of the Saruk, a tributary of the Jaghetu; and this is believed to be the site of the ancient northern Ecbatana, though only one wall can now be traced.

Rhages, the Median city next in importance to the two Ecbatanas, was situated near the Caspian Gates, near the eastern extremity of the Median territory. It is mentioned in the Zend-Avesta among the primitive Aryan settlements, and in the Books of Tobit and Judith. In the Behistun Inscription, Darius Hystaspes, the great Persian king, mentioned it as the scene of the closing struggle of the great Median revolt. Darius Codomannus, the last Persian king, sent thither his heavy baggage and the ladies of his court when he determined to leave Ecbatana and flee eastward after his final defeat by Alexander the Great. The site of this ancient city has sometimes been identified with the ruins of a town called Rhei, or Rhey, though this is uncertain. In the same vicinity, perhaps on the site of the present ruins known as Uewanukif, was the Median city of Charax. The cities of Bagistan, Adrapan, Concobar and Aspadan, were in the western part of Media. Bagistan is described by Isidore as "a city situated on a hill, where there was a pillar and a statue of Semiramis." Diodorus gives an account of the arrival of Semiramis at the place; of a royal park being established by her in the plain below the mountain, which was watered by an abundant spring; of the face of the rock of the lofty precipice on the side of the mountain, and of her carving her own effigy on the surface of this rock with an Assyrian cuneiform inscription. This ancient city has been identified with the celebrated Behistun, where the plain, the fountain, the precipitous rock and the scraped surface are yet to be seen; though the supposed figure of Semiramis, her pillar and her inscription are not visible. The Assyrian, Persian and Parthian monarchs made this rock renowned by giving it the sculptures and inscriptions which showed them to have been the successive lords of Western Asia during a period of a thousand years. The great inscription of Darius Hystaspes at this place has already been alluded to. The Parthian Gotarzes inscribed on this famous rock a record of his victory over his rival Meherdates.

Adrapan was mentioned by Isidore as being situated between Bagistan and Ecbatana, at the distance of twelve schœni—thirty-six Roman, or thirty-four English miles—from the latter city. He described it as the site of an ancient city destroyed by Tigranes the Armenian. This place has been identified with the modern village of Arteman, on the southern face of Elwend, near its base. Sir Henry Rawlinson says of this place that "during the severest winter, when Hamadan and the surrounding country are buried in snow, a warm and sunny climate is to be found; whilst in the summer a thousand rills descending from Elwend diffuse around fertility and fragrance." Professor George Rawlinson, in describing the same place, says: "Groves of trees grow up in rich luxuriance from the well-irrigated soil, whose thick foliage affords a welcome shelter from the heat of the noonday sun. The climate, the gardens, and the manifold blessings of the place are proverbial throughout Persia, and naturally caused the choice of the site for a retired palace, to which the court of Ecbatana might adjourn when either the summer heat and dust, or the winter cold, made residence in the capital irksome."

Concobar was in the vicinity of Adrapan, on the road leading to Bagistan, and is believed to be the modern Kungawar. It is also supposed to be the place called Chavon by Diodorus, where he says that Semiramis built a palace and laid out a paradise. Isidore says that a famous temple to Artemis was at this place. Colossal ruins crown the summit of the acclivity on which Kungawar is situated.

The Median town of Aspadan—mentioned by Ptolemy—has been identified as the famous modern Persian city of Isfahan, the great capital of the Suffee Kings of Persia several centuries ago.

SECTION II.—POLITICAL HISTORY.

HE origin of the Medes is involved in impenetrable obscurity. They were of Aryan descent, and were a kindred people with their southern neighbors, the Persians, from whom they differed but little in race, language, institutions and religion. From the little that we know of their primitive history it appears that they were an important tribe in very early times. The Book of Genesis mentions them under the name of Madai, and Berosus states that they furnished a dynasty to Babylon at a period anterior to B. C. 2000. These circumstances would seem to show that the Medes were a powerful primeval race, and actually constituted a ruling power in Western Asia as early as the twenty-third century before Christ—long before Abraham migrated from Ur to Harran.

Recent linguistic research has satisfactorily shown that the *Arba Lisun*, or "Four Tongues," of ancient Chaldæa, so frequently mentioned on the ancient monuments, included an Aryan formation, thus confirming Berosus's account of an Aryan conquest of Chaldæa B. C. 2286. There are other evidences of the early spread of the Median race, thus implying that they were a great nation in Western Asia long prior to the date of the Aryan, or Iranic, movements in Bactria and adjacent regions. Scattered remnants of a great migratory host, which issued from the mountains east of the Tigris and dispersed itself over the regions to the north and north-west in prehistoric times, are plainly visible in such races as the Matieni of Zagros and Cappadocia, the Sauromatæ (or Northern Medes) of the country between the Palus Mæotis and the Caspian Sea, the Mætæor Mæotæ of the tract about the mouth of the Don, and the Mædi of

Thrace. A tribe mentioned by Herodotus—the Sigynnæ in the region between the Danube and the Adriatic—claimed to be of Median descent, and this claim was substantiated by the resemblance of their national dress to that of the Medes. Herodotus, in relating these facts, remarks that "nothing is impossible in the long lapse of ages."

Two Greek legends designated the Medes under the two eponyms of Media and Andromeda, and refer to a period anterior to the age of Homer—no later than B. C. 1000. These legends connect the Medes with Syria and Colchis—two countries remote from each other—thus showing that the fame of the Medes was great in that part of Asia known to the Greeks. From these observations it would seem that the Medes must have been as great and powerful a people in primitive times as they became in the period of the decline and fall of Assyria. We possess no distinct historical knowledge of the first period of Median greatness, the only traces of early Median preponderance being found in ethnological names and mythological speculations. Recent discoveries show that the Median dynasty which governed Chaldæa from B. C. 2286 to B. C. 2052 was a Susianian, or Elamite, race of kings.

The history of the Medes as a nation begins in the latter half of the ninth century before Christ. The Assyrian monarch, Shalmaneser II., the Black Obelisk king, states that in the twenty-fourth year of his reign, B. C. 835, after conquering the Zimri of the Zagros mountain region and reducing the Persians to tribute, he invaded Media Magna, which he plundered after ravaging the country with fire and sword. The Medes were then divided into many tribes ruled by petty chieftains, and were thus a weak and insignificant people.

The time of this first Assyrian attack on Media, when Assyria was in her prime, and Media was only emerging from weakness and obscurity, was the period which Ctesias assigned to the fall of Assyria and the rise of Media. The account of Ctesias regarding this fact was accepted until the recent discoveries of the native Assyrian records showed the untrustworthiness of his chronology.

The Assyrian king, Shamas-Vul II., the son and successor of Shalmaneser II., also invaded Media and devastated the country with fire and sword. Shamas-Vul's son and successor, Vul-lush III., reduced the Medes to tribute. Towards the end of the ninth century before Christ the Medes agreed to pay an annual tribute to exempt their country from ravage.

A century later, about B. C. 710, the great Assyrian king, Sargon, invaded Media with a large army, overran the country, seized several towns and "annexed them to Assyria," and also established a number of fortified posts in portions of the country. A standing army was stationed in these posts to overawe the inhabitants and to prevent them from making an effectual resistance to the arms of the Assyrians. With the same end in view wholesale deportations were resorted to, many of the Medes being colonized in other portions of the Assyrian Empire, while Samaritan captives were settled in the Median cities. By way of tribute the Medes were required to furnish annually a number of horses to the Assyrian royal stud.

As Ctesias's account of the Median revolt under Arbaces and the conquest of Nineveh synchronizes almost with the first known Assyrian ravages in Media, so Herodotus's account of the revolt of the Medes under Deïoces corresponds with the date assigned by the Assyrian records for the complete Assyrian subjugation of Media.

After Sargon's conquest of Media Magna the Medes of that region quietly submitted to Assyrian domination for almost three-fourths of a century. During this period the Assyrian supremacy was extended over the more remote Median tribes, particularly those of Azerbijan. Sennacherib boasted that in the beginning of his reign (B. C. 702) he received an embassy from the more distant portions of Media—"parts of which the kings his fathers had not even heard"—which brought him presents in token of submission, and willingly accepted his yoke. Sennacherib's son, Esar-haddon, stated that about his tenth year (B. C. 671) he invaded Bikni, or Bikan, a remote Median province—"whereof the kings his fathers had never heard the name"—and compelled the cities of this region to acknowledge his dominion. The numerous petty independent chiefs who ruled the cities of this territory, according to Esar-haddon's account, submitted to his arms and agreed to pay tribute, after he had carried two of them captive to Assyria, and Assyrian officers were admitted into their cities.

The Median kings according to Ctesias, beginning with Arbaces, are regarded by modern writers as fictitious personages, as is also the Deïoces at the head of the list according to Herodotus. The following is a table of the Median kings according to these two Greek writers:

MEDIAN KINGS ACCORDING TO CTESIAS.	
ARBACES	28 years
MAUDACES	50 "
SOSARMUS	30 "
ARTYCAS	50 "
ARBIANES	22 "
ARTÆUS	40 "
ARTYNES	22 "
ASTIBARAS	40 "

MEDIAN KINGS ACCORDING TO HERODOTUS.	
INTERREGNUM	
DEÏOCES	53 years
INTERREGNUM	
DEÏOCES	53 "
PHRAORTES	22 "
CYAXARES	40 "
PHRAORTES	22 "
CYAXARES	40 "

As the time assigned by Herodotus to the reign of Deïoces, whom he represents as the founder of a centralized monarchy in Media, is the very period during which Sargon of Assyria was establishing fortified posts in the country and settling his Israelite captives in the "cities of the Medes"—and as the alleged reign of Deïoces according to Herodotus synchronizes with the brilliant Assyrian reigns of Sargon, Sennacherib, Esar-haddon and Asshur-bani-pal—it is evident that the whole story of Deïoces is purely mythical, as his name is not mentioned in the contemporary annals of Assyria, according to which the Medes were still a weak, disorganized and divided people. Even as late as B. C. 671 Esar-haddon is said to have subdued the more distant Medes, whom he still found under the government of many petty chiefs. According to the evidence furnished us by modern investigation and discovery, a consolidated monarchy could not have been organized in Media before B. C. 660, almost a half century subsequent to the time assigned by Herodotus.

The sudden development of national power and the rise of a centralized monarchy in Media were owing to the recent Aryan migrations from the regions east and southeast of the Caspian sea. CYAXARES, who about B. C. 632 conducted a Median expedition against Nineveh, was known to the Aryan tribes of the North-east, and in the reign of the great Persian king, Darius Hystaspes, a Sagartian headed a revolt in that region, claiming the Sagartian throne as a descendant from Cyaxares. It is supposed that Cyaxares and his father, the Phraortes of Herodotus, conducted fresh Aryan migrations from Bactria and Sagartia to Media, thus augmenting the strength of the Aryan race in the region just east of the Zagros range, and laying the foundations of a powerful consolidated kingdom in that mountain land. Accepted by the Aryan Medes as their chief, Cyaxares reduced the scattered Scythic tribes who occupied the high mountain region, and subdued the Zimri, the Minni, the Hupuska and other small nations occupying the territory between Media Magna and Assyria.

Thus Cyaxares is generally regarded as the founder of the great Median Empire; and Phraortes, whom Herodotus represents as the second King of Media and as the father of Cyaxares, is believed to be a fabulous personage. The testimony of Æschylus and the Behistun Inscription both make Cyaxares the founder of the Median monarchy.

No sooner did Cyaxares find himself at the head of a powerful centralized monarchy, and free from all danger of Assyrian conquest, than he meditated the bold enterprise of attacking the colossal power which had for almost seven centuries swayed the destinies of Western Asia. The last great Assyrian king, Asshur-bani-pal, was now in his old age, and his declining vigor and energy afforded encouragement to the ambitious designs of the warlike Median monarch. Therefore about B. C. 634, when Cyaxares had reigned thirty-four years, the Medes suddenly issued from the passes of the Zagros and overran the fertile plains of Assyria at the base of the mountains. The Assyrian monarch, in great alarm, placed himself at the head of his troops and took the field against the invaders. The Medes were thoroughly defeated in a great battle, their army being entirely cut to pieces, and the father of Cyaxares being among the slain.

Thus the first Median attack on Asssyria ended in complete disaster. The Medes had overrated their military strength. Although they had already proven themselves a match for the Assyrians while acting on the defensive in their mountain fastnesses, they could not withstand their enemy in the open plain while assuming the aggressive. Cyaxares abandoned the struggle until his troops could be properly disciplined to prevail against the armed hosts of Assyria. He at once set about organizing his army into several distinct corps, consisting respectively of infantry and cavalry, of archers, slingers and lancers. Feeling himself able to cope with the Assyrians, Cyaxares renewed the war and led a large army into Assyria, signally defeating the troops of Asshur-bani-pal and forcing them to seek refuge behind the defenses of Nineveh. The victorious Median king pursued the fleeing Assyrian hosts to the very walls of their capital, which he at once besieged, but he was soon recalled to the defense of his own land by the terrible Scythian inundation which swept ruin and devastation over both Assyria and Media.

The Scythians, as we have noticed in the history of Assyria, occupied the vast plains north of the Euxine (now Black Sea), the Caucasus mountains, the Caspian sea, and the Jaxartes, or Sihon river. Their characteristics have been described in our account of their invasion of Assyria. After pouring over the Caucasus, the Scyths attacked the Medes under Cyaxares as they were returning from the siege of Nineveh to defend their own country from the barbarous hordes of the North. The Medes and the Scyths were fully matched, each being hardy, warlike, active and energetic, and each having the cavalry as its chief arm and the bow as its chief weapon. The Medes were doubtless the better disciplined. They had more of a variety of weapons and soldiers, and were personally the more powerful. But the Scythians were by far the more numerous, besides being recklessly brave and masters of tactics which made them well-nigh irresistible. The Scyths had overrun Western Asia to plunder and ravage. Madyes, the Scythian leader, defeated Cyaxares and forced him to accept the suzerainty of the Scyths and to pay an annual tribute. The Scythian invaders continued to levy contributions upon the conquered people and oppressed them with repeated exactions. Spreading over all Western Asia the Scythic invaders carried plunder, devastation and massacre wherever they went.

The brave and patriotic Medes, with the love of independence so characteristic of mountaineers, and inspired with pride by their sudden rise and their great success in Assyria, took advantage of the gradual weakening of the barbarians, who were constantly dispersing their hosts over Assyria, Mesopotamia, Syria, Palestine, Armenia and Cappadocia, plundering and marauding everywhere and settling nowhere, conducting sieges and fighting battles, while their numbers were by degrees reduced by the sword, by sickness and excesses. Still fearing to encounter the Scyths in open battle, the Median king and his court invited the Scythian chiefs to a grand banquet, and, after making them helplessly intoxicated, remorselessly massacred them.

The Medes at once flew to arms and attacked their Scythian oppressors with a fury intensified by years of repression. Nothing is known of the duration and circumstances of the war which ensued, and the stories of Ctesias concerning it are utterly without credit. He says that the Parthians united with their Scythian kinsmen, and that the war continued many years, numerous battles being fought with heavy losses on both sides, and the struggle ending without any decisive result. This fanciful writer also states that the Scyths were led by a queen of great beauty and bravery named Zarina, or Zarinæa, who won the hearts of her foes when unable to withstand their arms.

A singularly-romantic love story is related concerning this beautiful Amazon. She was said to be the wife of Marmareus, the Scythian king, and to have gone with him to the field, participating in all his battles. Being at one time wounded she was in danger of being taken prisoner by Stryangæus, son-in-law of the Median king, and only escaped by earnestly imploring Stryangæus to permit her to go. When Stryangæus was shortly afterwards made prisoner by Marmareus and threatened with death by his captor, Zarina interceded for him, and when her entreaties failed she murdered her husband in order to save her preserver's life. By this time Stryangæus and Zarina were in love with each other; and peace having been arranged between the Scyths and the Medes, Stryangæus visited Zarina at her court and was received with hospitality; but when he revealed the secret of his love Zarina repulsed him, reminding him of his wife, Rhætæa, who was famed as being more beautiful than herself, and entreating him to exhibit sufficient manhood by conquering an improper passion. Thereupon Stryangæus retired to his chamber and committed suicide, after having written to reproach Zarina with being the cause of his death.

Ctesias mentions Zarina's capital as a town named Roxanacé, which is unknown to any other historian or geographer. The same writer mentions Zarina as having founded other towns. He says that the tomb of Zarina was a triangular pyramid, six hundred feet high and more than a mile around the base, crowned with a gigantic figure of the queen constructed from solid gold. This structure is represented as being the principal architectural monument of Zarina's capital.

But, casting aside these fabulous stories by Ctesias, we only know that the war ended in the utter discomfiture of the Scythians, who were driven from Media and the neighboring countries across the Caucasus into their own homeland. The only vestiges which they left behind were the names of the Palestinian city of Scythopolis and the Armenian province of Sacassêné.

Herodotus assigned the duration of the Scythian supremacy over Western Asia a period of twenty-eight years from their defeat of Cyaxares to his treacherous massacre of their chiefs. But the chronology of Herodotus is disputed by modern writers, many of whom give the year B. C. 625 as the date of the fall of Nineveh. According to Herodotus that event would have occurred B. C. 602. The belief that 625 is the proper date rests upon the statement of Abydenus and Polyhistor, who connect the fall of Nineveh with the accession of Nabopolassar at Babylon, which event the Canon of Ptolemy fixes at B. C. 625. Besides, the Lydian war of Cyaxares, which took place between B. C. 615 and 610, must have occurred after the fall of Nineveh. Eusebius gives B. C. 618 as the year of the destruction of Nineveh, and assigns a much shorter period to the Scythian domination over Western Asia than twenty-eight years; and his view is to be preferred to that of Herodotus. It is more likely that the twenty-eight years covered the entire period from the time of this first Scythian attack on Media to the final expulsion of the Scyths from Western Asia. The weakness of Assyria and the exhaustion of her resources after the Scythian inroad encouraged Cyaxares to renew his attack on Nineveh, which lay apparently at the mercy of any bold enemy ready to assail her. The gigantic power which had so long dominated Western Asia had thus fallen into decay; her prestige was gone, her glory had departed, her army had lost its spirit and organization, her defenses had been weakened, her haughty spirit had been broken.

While Cyaxares and his Medes were marching against Nineveh from the east, the Susianians rose in revolt and advanced against Assyria from the south. The last Assyrian king, Asshur-emid-ilin, or Saracus, with a portion of his army prepared to defend his capital against the Medes, and sent another portion under his general, Nabopolassar, to check the advance of the Susianians from the south. But Nabopolassar, as already related, betrayed his master and led a revolt of the Babylonians against the Assyrian king. He at once sent an embassy to the Median king, and the result was the close alliance between Cyaxares and Nabopolassar, cemented by the marriage of the daughter of Cyaxares with Nabopolassar's son Nebuchadnezzar, as also before noted. The united armies of the Medes and the Babylonians besieged Nineveh, which they finally took and destroyed. The fabulous account of this siege as narrated by Ctesias has been given in our account of Assyria, to which the reader is referred for its details. Ctesias called the Assyrian king Sardanapalus, the Median commander Arbaces, and the Babylonian Belesis. The self-immolation of the last Assyrian king, as related by Ctesias, is, however, confirmed by Abydenus and Berosus; and the story of Saracus perishing in his palace in a funeral pyre lighted with his own hand may therefore be accepted without question.

The conquerors divided the Assyrian Empire between them, Cyaxares obtaining Assyria proper and all the provinces to the north and north-west, while Nabopolassar obtained Babylonia, Susiana, Upper Mesopotamia, Syria, Phœnicia and Palestine. Thus two great empires—the Median and the Babylonian—arose out of the ashes of the Assyrian. These empires were founded by mutual consent, and were united in friendship and alliance by treaties and by a royal intermarriage. In all emergencies they were ready to give each other important aid. Thus once in the history of the ancient world two powerful monarchies stood beside each other in peace, and without jealousy or hatred. Media and Babylonia were content with sharing the dominion of Western Asia between them, and, considering the world large enough for both, they remained fast friends and allies for more than half a century.

The overthrow of Assyria did not bring repose to the Median king. Roving bands of Scyths still ravaged Western Asia; while the vassal states of Assyria, released from her yoke by her downfall, made use of the occasion to assert their independence; but they were soon reminded that a new master, as powerful and aggressive as the one from which they had been freed, had arisen to claim as her inheritance the suzerainty of the vassal states of the fallen Assyrian Empire. Cyaxares, encouraged by his successes, was stimulated to fresh conquests. Herodotus briefly tells us that Cyaxares "subdued to himself all Asia above the Halys." This would imply the conquest of the countries between Media and Assyria on the east and the river Halys on the west, which would include Armenia and Cappadocia. For centuries had Armenia, strong in its lofty mountains, its deep gorges and its many rapid rivers—the sources of the Tigris, the Euphrates, the Kur and the Aras —withstood all efforts at conquest by the Assyrian kings, and had only agreed to a nominal dependence upon Assyria during the reign of the last great Assyrian king. Cappadocia had not even been subject to Assyria in name, and had not thus far come into collision with any great Asiatic power. Other tribes of this region—neighbors of the Armenians and Cappadocians, but more remote from Media—were the Iberians, the Colchians, the Moschians, the Tibarenians, the Mares, the Macrones and the Mosynœcians; and were, according to Herodotus, conquered by Cyaxares, who thus extended his dominions to the Caucasus and the Euxine, or Black Sea, upon the north, and to the Halys river upon the west. But it is likely that the terrible Scythian ravages in Armenia and Cappadocia had made the inhabitants of those countries willing to accept the suzerainty of the powerful and civilized Medes, as the various tribes and nations of Asia Minor accepted the yoke of the powerful Kings of Lydia.

Contemporaneously with the great Aryan migration from the East under Cyaxares, or his father, Phraortes, an Aryan wave swept over Armenia and Cappadocia, which had previously been under the supremacy of Turanian tribes. In Armenia the present Aryan language supplanted the former Turanian in the seventh century before Christ, as shown by the cuneiform inscriptions of Van and its vicinity. In Cappadocia the Moschians and Tibarenians were forced to yield their habitations to a Medo-Persian tribe called Katapatuka. This spread of Aryan nations into the region between the Caspian Sea and the Halys prepared the way for Media's supremacy over this part of Western Asia, as Cyaxares was welcomed by the Aryan immigrants, who joined his standard in the wars against the barbarous Scyths and the old Turanian aborigines of these countries. The last remnants of the Scyths were expelled; and within less than ten years from the overthrow of Assyria, Cyaxares enlarged the Median Empire with the addition of the fertile and valuable tracts of Armenia and Cappadocia—countries never really subject to Assyria—and also the entire region between Armenia and the Caucasus, and between the Caspian and Euxine seas.

The advance of the Median Empire westward to the Halys, involving the absorption of Cappadocia, brought the Medes in collision with Lydia, a new power in Asia Minor, which, like Media, had suddenly risen to greatness. Lydia headed a confederacy of all the nations of Asia Minor west of the Halys to resist the further progress of the Median power westward. Cyaxares obtained assistance from his old ally, Nabopolassar of Babylon, against the Lydians. With a large army the Median king invaded Asia Minor, and, according to Herodotus, fought many battles with the Lydians with various success. After the war had continued six years it was brought to an end by a rémarkable circumstance. On a certain occasion, as the Median and Lydian armies were engaged in battle, a sudden darkness enveloped the combatants and filled them with superstitious awe. The sun was eclipsed, and the two armies, ceasing from the struggle, gazed with dread upon the celestial phenomenon. Amid the general alarm, we are told, a desire for peace seized both armies. Two chiefs, the foremost allies on their respective sides, improved the occasion to induce the warring monarchs—Cyaxares of Media and Alyattes of Lydia—to sheathe their swords. Herodotus says that Syennesis, King of Cilicia, as the ally of the Lydian king, and Labynetus of Babylon, probably either Nabopolassar or Nebuchadnezzar, as the ally of the Median monarch, came to propose an immediate suspension of hostilities; and when this proposal was accepted a treaty of peace was arranged, B. C. 610. Both parties retained the territories they had respectively held before the war, so that the treaty left everything in *status quo.* The Kings of Media and Lydia agreed to swear a friendship, and to cement the alliance Alyattes agreed to give his daughter in marriage to Astyages, the son of Cyaxares. In accordance with the barbarous customs of the time and place, the two kings, having met and repeated the words of the formula, punctured their own arms, and then sealed their contract by each sucking a part of the blood from the other's wound.

By this peace the three great Asiatic empires of the time—Media, Lydia and Babylonia—became fast friends and allies, and stood side by side in peace for fifty years, until each was in turn absorbed in the great Medo-Persian Empire, which for several centuries held sway over all Western Asia and Egypt. The crown-princes of Media, Lydia and Babylonia were placed on terms of blood relationship, and "had become brothers." Thus all Western Asia, from the shores of the Ægean on the west to the Persian Gulf on the east, was now ruled by dynasties united by intermarriages, bound to respect each other's rights and animated by a spirit of mutual friendliness and genuine attachment. After more than five centuries of perpetual war and ravage, after fifty years of strife and bloodshed, during which the venerable monarchy of Assyria, which for seven centuries had ruled Western Asia at her will, had gone to pieces, and the new Median and Babylonian Empires had taken her place, that quarter of the globe entered upon a period of repose which contrasted strongly with the previous long period of almost constant struggle. Media, Lydia and Babylonia, as fast friends and allies, pursued their separate courses without quarrel or collision, thus allowing the nations under their respective dominions a repose which they greatly needed and desired.

According to Herodotus, Cyaxares, the founder of the great Median Empire, died B. C. 593, after a reign of forty years, and was succeeded by his son, ASTYAGES, who, as we have observed, had received as a bride the daughter of Alyattes, King of Lydia. Cyaxares, as a great warrior and the founder of an empire, was a conqueror after the Asiatic model. He possessed ability, perseverance, energy, ambition, and force of character, and these qualities made him a successful leader. He was faithful to his friends, but considered treachery permissible to his foes. He did not, however, possess the ability to organize the empire his conquests had built up; and his establishment of Magianism as the state religion was the only one of his institutions that appeared to be laid on deep and stable foundations. The empire which he founded was the shortest-lived of all the great ancient Oriental monarchies, having risen and fallen within the short space of threescore years and ten—the period allotted by the Psalmist as the natural lifetime of an individual.

Astyages lacked his father's ability and energy. Born to the inheritance of a great empire, and bred in the luxury of a magnificent Oriental court, he was apparently content with the lot which fortune seemed to have assigned him, and had no further ambition. He was said to have been handsome, cautious, and of an easy and generous temper; but the anecdotes of his manner of living at Ecbatana, as related by Herodotus, Xenophon and Nicolas of Damascus, are mainly legendary and therefore unreliable as material for history. Still the united testimony of these three writers gives us some idea of the court of Astyages, which resembled that of the Assyrian kings in its main features. The Median monarch led a secluded life, and could only be seen by those who asked and obtained an audience. He was surrounded by guards and eunuchs, the latter holding most of the offices about the royal person. The court of Ecbatana was celebrated for the magnificence of its apparel, for its banquets and for the number and organization of its attendants. The courtiers wore long flowing robes of various colors, red and purple predominating, and adorned their necks with gold chains or collars, and their wrists with bracelets of the same costly material. Their horses frequently had golden bits to their bridles. One royal officer was called "the King's Eye;" another was assigned the privilege of introducing strangers to the sovereign; a third was his cupbearer; a fourth his messenger. Guards, torch-bearers, serving-men, ushers and sweepers were among the lower attendants. "The king's table-companions" were a privileged class of courtiers of the highest rank. Hunting was the chief pastime in which the court indulged. This usually took place in a park, or "paradise," near the capital; but sometimes the king and court went out on a grand hunt in the open country, where lions, leopards, bears, wild boars, wild asses, antelopes, stags and wild sheep abounded, and when the beaters had driven the beasts into a confined space, the hunting parties dispatched them with arrows and spears.

Herodotus tells us that the priestly caste of the Magi, who were held in the highest esteem by both king and people, were in constant attendance at the Median court, ready to expound dreams and omens, and to give advice on all matters of state policy. They had charge of the religious ceremonial, and often held high offices of state. They were the only class who possessed any real influence over the monarch.

The long reign of Astyages was mainly peaceful until near its close. Eusebius contradicts Herodotus by saying that Astyages, and not Cyaxares, conducted the great war with Alyattes of Lydia; and Moses of Chorênê alone states that Astyages carried on a long struggle with Tigranes, an Armenian king—neither of which statements deserve any credit. The Greeks evidently regarded Astyages as an unwarlike king. On the north-eastern frontier of his empire, Astyages extended his dominion by the acquisition of the low country now called Talish and Ghilan, where the powerful tribe of the Cadusians had thus far maintained its independence. Diodorus alone states that they were able to bring two hundred thousand men into the field—a statement unsupported by any other writer and unworthy of credit. At this time the Cadusian king, Aphernes, or Ornaphernes, uncertain of his position, surrendered his sovereignty to Astyages by a secret treaty, and the Cadusians peacefully passed under the sway of the Median king.

Astyages was unhappy in his domestic relations. His "mariage de convenance" with the Lydian princess, Aryênis, brought him no son, and the want of an heir led him to contract those marriages mentioned by Moses of Chorênê in his History of Armenia—one with Anusia, and another with the beautiful Tigrania, sister of the Armenian king, Tigranes. Still he had no male offspring. Herodotus and Xenophon assigned him a daughter named Mandané, whom they considered the mother of Cyrus the Great; but Ctesias denied this, and gave him a daughter named Amytis, whom he regarded as the wife, first of Spitaces the Mede, and afterwards of Cyrus the Persian. These stories, designed to gratify the vanity of the Persians and to flatter the Medes, are entitled to no credit. It is therefore doubtful if the second and last Median king had any child at all.

In his old age, B. C. 558, occurred the event which ended the reign of Astyages and the empire of Media. The Persians—the Aryan kinsmen of the Medes—had become settled in the region south and southeast of Media, between the 32nd parallel and the Persian Gulf, and had acknowledged the suzerainty of the Median kings during the period of their greatness. But dwelling in their rugged mountains and high upland plains, the Persians had retained the primitive simplicity of their manners, and had intermingled but slightly with the Medes, being governed directly by their own native kings of the Achæmenian dynasty, whose founder was said to have been the legendary Achæmenes. These princes were related by marriage with the Cappadocian kings, and their royal house was considered one of the noblest in Western Asia. Herodotus regarded Persia as absorbed into Media at this time, and the Achæmenidæ as simply a noble Persian family. Nicolas of Damascus considered Persia a Median satrapy, Atradates, the father of Cyrus, being satrap. Xenophon and Moses of Chorênê gave the Achæmenidæ their royal rank, and considered Persia as completely independent of Media, while they regarded Cyrus as a great and powerful sovereign during the reign of Astyages; and this view is sustained by the native Persian records. In the Behistun Inscription, Darius declares: "There are eight of my race who have been kings before me. I am the ninth." In an inscription found on a brick brought from Senkereh, Cyrus the Great calls himself "the son of Cambyses, *the powerful king.*" The residence of Cyrus at the Median court at Ecbatana—which is asserted in almost every narrative of his life before he became king—would seem to imply at least an acknowledgment of nominal Median supremacy over Persia.

During his residence at the Median court Cyrus observed the unwarlike disposition of that generation of Medes, who had not seen any actual military service. He had a contempt for the personal character of Astyages, who spent his life in luxury, mainly at Ecbatana, amid eunuchs, concubines and dancing-girls. The Persian crown-prince resolved to raise the standard of rebellion, to free his country from Median supremacy, and to vindicate the pure Zoroastrian religion, which the Achæmenians championed, and which the Magi, aided and upheld by the Median monarchs, had corrupted.

Cyrus asked permission from Astyages to visit his father, who was in poor health, but this request was refused by the Median king on the plea that he was too much attached to the Persian crown-prince to miss his presence for a single day. But on the application of a favorite eunuch, Cyrus was allowed a leave of absence for five months, and with several attendants he left Echatana by night, taking the road leading to his native Persia.

The next evening, enjoying himself over his wine as usual, in the company of his concubines, singing-girls and dancing-girls, Astyages asked one of them to sing. The girl took her lyre and sang as follows: "The lion had the wild-boar in his power, but let him depart to his own lair; in his lair he will wax in strength, and will cause the lion a world of toil; till at length, although the weaker, he will overcome the stronger." The words of this song caused the king extreme anxiety, as he had already learned of a Chaldæan prophecy designating Cyrus as a future king of the Persians. Astyages at once ordered an officer with a body of horsemen to pursue the Persian crown-prince and bring him back dead or alive. The officer overtook Cyrus and announced his errand, whereupon Cyrus expressed his willingness to return to the Median court, but proposed that, as it was late, they should rest for the night. The Medes agreed to this; and Cyrus, feasting them, made them all intoxicated, after which he mounted his horse and rode off at full speed with his attendants, until he arrived at a Persian outpost, where he had arranged with his father to meet a body of Persian troops. After having slept off their drunkenness and discovering that their prisoners had fled, the Medes pursued, and again overtaking Cyrus, who was backed by an armed force, they attacked him, but were defeated with great loss and driven into retreat; and Cyrus escaped into Persia.

Upon hearing of the escape of the Persian crown-prince, Astyages was greatly chagrined, and, smiting his thigh, he exclaimed: "Ah! fool, thou knewest well that it boots not to heap favors on the vile; yet didst thou suffer thyself to be gulled by smooth words; and so thou hast brought upon thyself this mischief. But even now he shall not get off scotfree." Instantly the Median king, in his rage, sent for his generals, who, in pursuance of the royal orders, soon collected an army of three thousand chariots, two hundred thousand horse, and a million footmen, to reduce Persia to obedience. With this immense host Astyages invaded the revolted province, and engaged the army which Cyrus and his father, Cambyses, had assembled for defense. The Persian army consisted of a hundred chariots, fifty thousand horsemen, and three hundred thousand light-armed foot, who were drawn up in front of a fortified town near the frontier. The first day's battle was sanguinary but indecisive; but on the second day Astyages, by a skillful use of his superior numbers, won a decided victory.

After detaching one hundred thousand men with orders to make a circuit and get into the rear of the town, the Median king renewed the attack; and when the Persians had their whole attention directed to the battle in their front, the detached Median troops fell on the city and took it, before the garrison was aware. Cambyses, who commanded the garrison, was mortally wounded and taken prisoner. The Persian army in the open field, finding itself attacked in front and rear, broke and fled towards the interior, to defend Pasargadæ, the Persian capital. After giving Cambyses an honorable burial, Astyages hotly pursued the fleeing Persian host.

Between the battle-field and Pasargadæ was a barrier of lofty and precipitous hills, penetrated only by a single narrow pass, guarded by ten thousand Persians. Seeing that the pass could not be forced, Astyages sent a detachment along the foot of the range till they found a place where they could ascend the mountain, when they climbed the rugged declivity and seized the heights directly above the defile. Thereupon the Persians were obliged to evacuate their strong position and to fall back to a lower range of hills near Pasargadæ, where another conflict of two days occurred. On the first day the Medes failed in all their efforts to ascend the low but steep hills, the Persians hurling heavy masses of stone upon their ascending columns. On the second day Astyages had placed a body of troops at the foot of the hills below his attacking columns, with orders to kill all who refused to ascend, or who, after ascending, endeavored to descend the heights. Thus forced to advance, the Medes fought with desperation, driving the Persians before them up the slopes of the hill to its summit, where the Persian women and children had been placed for safety. The courage of the Persians was aroused by the taunts and reproaches of their mothers and wives, and, by a sudden furious charge, they overbore the astonished Medes, driving them in headlong flight down the declivity in such confusion that the Persians slew sixty thousand of them.

Astyages still persevered, but was decisively defeated by Cyrus in a fifth battle near Pasargadæ, his army being routed and his camp taken. All the Median royal insignia fell into the hands of the victorious Persian king, who assumed them amid the enthusiastic shouts of his troops, who saluted him as "King of Media and Persia." Astyages sought safety in flight, his army dispersed, and most of his followers deserted him. He was hotly pursued by his triumphant foe, who, forcing him to an engagement, again defeated him and took him prisoner.

The Median Empire had now received its death-blow. Media and all its dependencies at once submitted to Cyrus, who thus became the founder of the great Medo-Persian Empire, which for two centuries swayed the destinies of all Western Asia and Northeastern Africa, after the conquest and absorption of the great Oriental empires contemporary with Media—namely, Lydia, Babylonia and Egypt. Thus the supremacy of the Aryan race in Asia was transferred from the Medes to their near kinsmen, the Persians; and pure Zoroastrianism was restored on the ruins of the corrupt Magian system which the Median kings had allowed to take the place of the primitive faith of the Bactrian prophet. The law of the new empire was still "the law of the Medes and Persians." Official employments were open to the people of both these kindred Aryan nations.

The Median Empire, in its extent and fertility of territory, was not inferior to the Assyrian. It reached from Rhagas and the Carmanian desert on the east to the river Halys on the west—a distance of about thirteen hundred miles. From its northern confines along the Euxine (now Black Sea), the Caucasus and the Caspian, to its southern limits along the Euphrates and the Persian Gulf, its width was about five hundred and forty miles in its eastern portion and about two hundred and forty miles in its western portion. It thus had an area of about half a million square miles; being as large as Great Britain, France, Spain and Portugal combined.

SECTION III.—MEDIAN CIVILIZATION.

ALL sacred and profane history classes the Medes and Persians as kindred nations—a fact sustained by recent linguistic research, which proves them to have been a people similar in race and language, as well as in institutions and religion. This fact, along with the express statements of Herodotus and Strabo, shows that the Medes and Persians, the leading Iranic nations, belonged to the great Aryan, or Indo-European branch of the Caucasian race. In ancient times all the leading tribes and nations of the great plateau of Iran and even beyond it in a northerly direction to the Jaxartes (now Sihon) river, and eastward to the Hyphasis (now Sutlej)—Medes, Persians, Sagartians, Chorasmians, Bactrians, Sogdians, Hyrcanians, Sarangians, Gandarians and Sanskritic, or Brahmanic Indians—all belonged to a single stock, united by the tie of a common language, common manners and customs, and mainly a common religious faith. The Medes and Persians—the two leading Aryan nations of Asia—were scarcely distinguishable from each other in any ethnic features.

The sculptures of the Achæmenian Kings of Persia represent the Medes and Persians as a noble variety of the human species—with a tall, graceful and stately physical form; a handsome and attractive physiognomy, frequently bearing some resemblance to the Greek; a high and straight forehead; the nose nearly in the same line, long and well-formed, sometimes markedly aquiline; the upper lip short, usually shaded by a mustache; the chin rounded and commonly covered with a curly beard. The race was proud of their hair, which grew plentifully. On the top of the head the hair was worn smooth, but was drawn back from the forehead and twisted into a row or two of crisp curls, being also arranged into a large mass of similar small close ringlets at the back of the head over the ears.

Xenophon tells us that the Median women were remarkable for their stature and beauty. Plutarch, Ammianus Marcellinus and others say the same of the Persian women. The ancient Aryan nations appear to have treated women with a spirit of chivalry, allowing them the full development of their physical powers, and rendering them specially attractive to their own husbands and to men of other nations.

Says Rawlinson: "The modern Persian is a very degenerate representative of the ancient Aryan stock. Slight and supple in person, with quick, glancing eyes, delicate features and a vivacious manner, he lacks the dignity and strength, the calm repose and simple grace of the race from which he is sprung. Fourteen centuries of subjection to despotic sway have left their stamp upon his countenance and his frame, which, though still retaining some traces of the original type, have been sadly weakened and lowered by so long a term of subservience. Probably the wild Kurd or Lur of the present day more nearly corresponds in physique to the ancient Mede than do the softer inhabitants of the great plateau."

The ancient Medes were noted for their bravery. Originally equal, and perhaps superior to their Persian kinsmen, they were during the entire period of Persian supremacy only second to them in courage and warlike characteristics. When allowed to take his choice out of the vast host of Xerxes during the war with Greece, Mardonius selected the Median troops next to the Persians. When the battle opened he kept the Medes near himself, assigning them their place in the line near that of the Persian contingent. Diodorus states that the Medes were chosen to make the first attack upon the Greek position at Thermopylæ, where they showed their valor, though unsuccessful. In the earlier periods of their history, before they had been corrupted by wealth and luxury, their courage and military prowess fully earned them the titles applied to them by the Hebrew prophet Ezekiel:

"the mighty one of the heathen—the terrible of the nations."

Median valor was utterly merciless. Median armies, we are told, did "dash to pieces" the fighting-men of other nations, giving them no quarter; and inflicted indignities and cruelties upon the women and children of their enemies. The worst atrocities which lust and hate inspired accompanied the Median conquests, neither the virtue of women nor the innocence of children being any protection to them. The infant was slain before its parents' eyes, and the sanctity of the domestic hearth was invaded. Insult and vengeance were allowed full scope, and the brutal Median soldiery freely indulged their tiger-like thirst for the blood of their foes.

The habits of the Medes were at first simple and manly; but, as with all conquering Oriental nations, success was at once followed by degeneracy, and the Medes in due time became corrupted and enervated by the luxuries of conquest. After their conquests they relaxed the stringency of their former habits and indulged in the pleasures of soft and luxurious living. Xenophon contrasted in vivid colors the primitive simplicity of Persia proper, where the old Aryan habits, once common to both nations, were still maintained in all their original stringency, with the luxury and magnificence prevailing at Ecbatana. Herodotus and Strabo alluded to the luxury of the Median dress. Thus it appears that the Medes in the later days of their empire were a luxurious people, displaying a pomp and magnificence unknown to their ancestors, affecting splendor in their dress, grandeur and elegant ornamentation in their buildings, variety in their banquets, and reaching a degree of civilization almost equal to that of the Assyrians, though vastly inferior to them in taste and refinement. Their ornamentation displayed a barbaric magnificence, distinguished by richness of material. Literature and letters received little attention. A stately dress and a new style of architecture are the only Median inventions. Professor Rawlinson says of the Medes:

"They were brave, energetic, enterprising, fond of display, capable of appreciating to some extent the advantages of civilized life; but they had little genius, and the world is scarcely indebted to them for a single important addition to the general stock of its ideas."

Herodotus says that in the army of Xerxes the Medes were armed exactly like the Persians, and that they wore a soft felt cap on the head, a sleeved tunic on the body, and trousers on the legs. He tells us that their offensive arms were the spear, the bow and the dagger. They had large wicker shields, and carried their quivers suspended at their backs. The tunic was sometimes made into a coat of mail by adding to it on the outside a number of small iron plates arranged so as to overlap each other like the scales of a fish. They served alike on horseback and on foot, with like equipments in both cases. Strabo and Xenophon, as well as Isaiah and Jeremiah, describe the Median armies as originally simpler in character. The primitive Medes were a nation of horse-archers. Trained from early boyhood to a variety of equestrian exercises, and skillful in the use of the bow, they dashed upon their enemies with swarms of horse, like the Scythians, and won their victories mainly by the skillful discharge of their arrows as they advanced, retreated, or manœuvred about their foe. The prophet Jeremiah spoke of the sword and the spear being used by the Medes and Persians.

The sculptures of Persepolis represent the bow used by the Medes and Persians as short, and curved like that of the Assyrians. It was generally carried in a bow-case, either suspended at the back or from the girdle. The arrows, carried in a quiver suspended behind the right shoulder, were not over three feet long. The quiver was round, covered at the top and fastened by means of a flap and strap, the last passed over a button. The Median spear, or lance, was six or seven feet long. The sword was short, and was suspended at the right thigh by means of a belt encircling the waist, and was also held by a strap fastened to the bottom of the sheath and passing around the right leg just above the knee. Median shields were either round or oval.

The sculptures show us the favorite dress of the Medes in peace. The Persian bas-reliefs represent the long flowing robe, with its graceful folds, as the garb of the kings, the chief nobles and the chief officers of the court. This dress is also seen upon the darics and the gems, and is believed to be the celebrated "Median garment" mentioned by Herodotus, Xenophon and Strabo. This garment fitted closely to the chest and shoulders, but hung over the arms in two large loose sleeves open at the bottom. It was fastened at the waist by a cincture. Below it drooped in two clusters of perpendicular folds at both sides, and hung between these in festoons like a curtain. It reached to the ankles. The Median robes were of many colors, some being purple, some scarlet, and others a dark gray or a deep crimson. Procopius says that they were made of silk. Xenophon says that the Medes wore undergarments, such as a sleeved shirt, or tunic, of a purple color, and embroidered trousers. The feet were covered with high shoes or low boots, opening in front and fastened with buttons. The Medes wore felt caps like the Persians, or high-crowned hats, made of felt or cloth, and dyed in different hues.

Xenophon tells us that the Medes used cosmetics, rubbing them into the skin to improve the complexion. They also used false hair in abundance. Like other Oriental nations, ancient and modern, they used dyes to improve the brilliancy of the eyes and make them appear larger and softer. They also wore golden ornaments, such as chains or collars around the neck, bracelets around the wrists, and ear-rings fastened into the ears. The bits and other parts of the harness of their horses were also frequently of gold.

Xenophon also tells us that the Medes were extremely luxurious at their banquets. Not only plain meat and various kinds of game, with bread and wine, but many side-dishes and different kinds of sauces, were set before their guests. They ate with the hand, as Orientals still do, and used napkins. Each guest had his own dishes. Wine was drunk at the meal and afterwards, and the feast often ended in turmoil and confusion. At court the king received his wine at the hands of the cupbearer, who first tasted it, so that the king might be certain that it was not poisoned, and then handed it to his master with much pomp and ceremony.

The court ceremonial was imposing. Herodotus tells us that the monarch was ordinarily kept secluded, and that no person could be admitted to his presence without formally requesting an audience and without being led before the sovereign by the proper officer. Strabo says that when he was admitted he prostrated himself with the same signs of adoration as when he entered a temple. The king, surrounded by his attendants, eunuchs and others, maintained a haughty reserve, and the visitor only saw him from a distance. Business was mainly transacted by writing. The monarch seldom left his palace, and was informed of the state of his empire through the reports of his officers.

The chief court amusement was hunting, but the king himself seldom participated in this pastime. Beasts of the chase were always abundant in Media; and the Median nobles are mentioned by Xenophon as hunting lions, bears, leopards, wild boars, stags, gazelles, wild sheep and wild asses. The first four of these were considered dangerous, the others harmless. These animals were usually pursued on horseback, and aimed at with the bow or the spear.

The Median monarch, like other Oriental sovereigns, maintained a seraglio, or harem, of wives and concubines; and polygamy was a common custom among the wealthy. Strabo tells us of a peculiar law among some Median tribes which required every man to have at least five wives. The eunuchs, who swarmed at court, were mostly foreigners purchased in their infancy. This despised class were all-powerful with their royal master near the close of the Median Empire.

Thus corruption gradually sapped the vitality of the empire; and both the court and people had abandoned the hardy and simple customs of their ancestors, and had become enervated through luxury when the revolt of the Persians under Cyrus brought the Median Empire to a speedy end.

Median architecture was characterized by a barbaric magnificence. It is believed that the Medes had learned sculpture from the Assyrians and that they taught it to the Persians; as everywhere among the remains of the Achæmenian kings are seen modifications of Assyrian types, such as the carving of winged genii, of colossal figures of bulls and lions, of grotesque monsters, and of clumsy representations of actual life, in imitation from Assyrian bas-reliefs. The only remnant of sculpture remaining that can be assigned to the Medes is a portion of a colossal stone lion yet to be seen at Hamadan, greatly injured by time, and consisting of the head and body of the lion, measuring about twelve feet, the tail and the forelegs being broken off. Its posture indicates some originality in Median art.

SECTION IV.—ZOROASTRIANISM AND MAGISM.

THE great Iranic religion—the faith of the Bactrians, and of the Medes and Persians for many centuries—was founded by the ancient Bactrian sage and prophet, Zoroaster, or Zarathustra; and its sacred book was the Zend-Avesta. Zoroaster claimed divine inspiration and professed to have occasional revelations from the Supreme Being, delivering them to his people in a mythical form and securing their acceptance as divine by the Bactrian people, after which his religion gradually spread among the other Iranic nations. It was the religion of the Persians until driven out by the intolerance of Mohammedanism in the seventh century after Christ. It now exists in Guzerat and Bombay in Hindoostan, as the creed of the Parsees, descendants of Persians who sought refuge there after the Mohammedan conquest of Persia. The Median and Persian kings, as servants of Ormazd, worshiped the fire and the sun—symbols of the god; and resisted the impure griffin—the creature of Ahriman. The Zend-Avesta teaches that every created being has its Fereuer, or Fravashis, its ideal essence, first created by the thought of Ormazd. Ormazd himself has his Fravashis, and the angelic essences are objects of adoration everywhere to the disciples of Zoroaster.

Plato mentioned Zoroaster about four centuries before Christ. In speaking of the education of a Persian prince, Plato says that "one teacher instructs him in the magic of Zoroaster, the son (or priest) of Ormazd (or Oramazes), in which is comprehended all the worship of the gods." Zoroaster is also spoken of by Diodorus, Plutarch, the elder Pliny, and many writers of the first centuries after Christ. The worship of the Magi, the Median and Persian priesthood, is described by Herodotus before Plato. Herodotus gives full accounts of the ritual, the priests, the sacrifices, the purifications, and the mode of burial employed by the Magi in his day, about four and a half centuries before Christ; and his account closely corresponds with the practices of the Parsees, or fire-worshipers, yet remaining in a few places in Persia and India. He says: "The Persians have no altars, no temples nor images; they worship on the tops of the mountains. They adore the heavens, and sacrifice to the sun, moon, earth, fire, water and winds." "They do not erect altars, nor use libations, fillets or cakes. One of the Magi sings an ode concerning the origin of the gods, over the sacrifice, which is laid on a bed of tender grass." "They pay great reverence to all rivers, and must do nothing to defile them; in burying they never put the body in the ground till it has been torn by some bird or dog; they cover the body with wax, and then put it in the ground." "The Magi think they do a meritorious act when they kill ants, snakes, reptiles."

Plutarch gives the following account of Zoroaster and his precepts:

"Some believe that there are two Gods—as it were, two rival workmen; the one whereof they make to be the maker of good things, and the other bad. And some call the better of these God, and the other, Dæmon; as doth Zoroastres, the Magee, whom they report to be five thousand years elder than the Trojan times. This Zoroastres therefore called the one of these Oromazes, and the other Arimanius; and affirmed, moreover, that the one of them did, of anything sensible, the most resemble light, and the other darkness and ignorance; but that Mithras was in the middle betwixt them. For which cause, the Persians called Mithras the mediator. And they tell us that he first taught mankind to make vows and offerings of thanksgiving to the one, and to offer averting and feral sacrifice to the other. For they beat a certain plant called homomy in a mortar, and call upon Pluto and the dark; and then mix it with the blood of a sacrificed wolf, and convey it to a certain place where the sun never shines, and there cast it away. For of plants they believe, that some pertain to the good God, and others again to the evil Dæmon; and likewise they think that such animals as dogs, fowls, and urchins belong to the good; but water animals to the bad, for which reason they account him happy that kills most of them. These men, moreover, tell us a great many romantic things about these gods, whereof these are some: They say that Oromazes, springing from purest light, and Arimanius, on the other hand, from pitchy darkness, these two are therefore at war with one another. And that Oromazes made six gods, whereof the first was the author of benevolence, the second of truth, the third of justice, and the rest, one of wisdom, one of wealth, and a third of that pleasure which accrues from good actions; and that Arimanius likewise made the like number of contrary operations to confront them. After this, Oromazes, having first trebled his own magnitude, mounted up aloft, so far above the sun as the sun itself above the earth, and so bespangled the heavens with stars. But one star (called Sirius or the Dog) he set as a kind of sentinel or scout before all the rest. And after he had made four-and-twenty gods more, he placed them all in an egg-shell. But those that were made by Arimanius (being themselves also of the like number) breaking a hole in this beauteous and glazed egg-shell, bad things came by this means to be intermixed with good. But the fatal time is now approaching, in which Arimanius, who by means of this brings plagues and famines upon the earth, must of necessity be himself utterly extinguished and destroyed; at which time, the earth, being made plain and level, there will be one life, and one society of mankind, made all happy, and one speech. But Theopompus saith, that, according to the opinion of the Magees, each of these gods subdues, and is subdued by turns, for the space of three thousand years apiece, and that for three thousand years more they quarrel and fight and destroy each other's works; but that at last Pluto shall fail, and mankind shall be happy, and neither need food, nor yield a shadow. And that the god who projects these things doth, for some time, take his repose and rest; but yet this time is not so much to him although it seems so to man, whose sleep is but short. Such, then, is the mythology of the Magees."

This description of the ancient Median and Persian religion, by Plutarch, corresponds with the religion of the modern Parsees, as it was developed out of the primitive doctrine taught by Zoroaster.

A little over a century ago an enterprising, energetic and enthusiastic young Frenchman, Anquetil du Perron—who had learned the Zend language, in which the Zend-Avesta was written, from the Parsees at Surat, in India—brought one hundred and eighty manuscripts of that sacred book to Europe and published them in French in

1—16.—U. H.

1771, thus giving us a new and clear idea of the religious system and faith of the ancient Medes and Persians. For the last half century eminent Orientalists — the Frenchman Burnouf, and the Germans Westergaard, Brockhaus, Spiegel, Haug, Windischmann, Hübschmann — have analyzed the Zend-Avesta, and have found that its different parts belong to different dates. The Gâthâs, or rhythmical hymns, are found to be very ancient.

Modern Orientalists and antiquarians differ widely as to the age of the books of the Zend-Avesta, and as to the period at which Zoroaster lived. Plato spoke of "the magic (or religious doctrines) of Zoroaster the Ormazdian." Plato spoke of his religion as Magism, or the Median system, in Western Iran; while the Zend-Avesta originated in Bactria, or Eastern Iran, at least no later than the sixth or seventh century before Christ. When the Zend-Avesta was written Bactria was an independent kingdom, and Zoroaster is represented as teaching under King Vistaçpa. Bunsen says that "the date of Zoroaster, as fixed by Aristotle, cannot be said to be very irrational. He and Eudoxus, according to Pliny, place him six thousand years before the death of Plato; Hermippus, five thousand years before the Trojan war," which would be about B. C. 6300, or B. C. 6350. Bunsen, however, further says: "At the present stage of the inquiry the question whether this date is set too high cannot be answered either in the negative or affirmative." Spiegel regards Zoroaster as a neighbor and contemporary of Abraham, and thus living about B. C. 2000. Döllinger believes that he may have flourished "somewhat later than Moses, perhaps about B. C. 1300;" but says that "it is impossible to fix precisely" when he did live. Rawlinson alludes only to the fact that Berosus placed him anterior to B. C. 2234. Haug believes the Gâthâs, the oldest songs of the Zend-Avesta, to have been composed as early as the time of Moses. Duncker and Rapp think Zoroaster lived about B. C. 1200 or 1300; and their view agrees with the period assigned to him by Xanthus of Sardis, a Greek writer of the sixth century before Christ, and by Cephalion in the second century after Christ.

The place where Zoroaster lived, and the events of his life, are not known with certainty. Most writers think that he lived in Bactria. Haug holds that the language of the Zend-Avesta is Bactrian. A highly fabulous and mythical life of Zoroaster, translated by Anquetil du Perron, called the Zartusht-Namah, represents him as going to Iran in his thirtieth year, passing twenty years in the desert, performing miracles during ten years, and teaching philosophical lessons in Babylon, Pythagoras being one of his pupils; but this account is proven to be false. Says Professor Max Müller: "The language of the Avesta is so much more primitive than the inscriptions of Darius, that many centuries must have passed between the two periods represented by these two strata of language." The Behistun Inscriptions of Darius are in the Achæmenian dialect, a later linguistic development of the Zend.

Though nothing is known of the events of his life, Zoroaster, by his essentially moral religion, influenced various Aryan races over wide regions for many centuries. His religion was in the interest of morality, human freedom, and the progress of mankind. Zoroaster based his law on the eternal distinction between right and wrong. His law was therefore the law of justice, according to which the supreme good consists in truth, duty and right. Zoroaster taught providence, aimed at holiness, and emphasized creation. He maintained that salvation was only wrought out by an eternal battle between good and evil.

The whole religion of the Zend-Avesta revolves around the person of Zoroaster, or Zarathustra. In the Gâthâs of the Yaçna, the oldest of the second books, he is designated "the pure Zarathustra, good in thought, speech and work." Zarathustra only is said to know the precepts of Ahura-Mazda (Ormazd), and that he shall be made skillful in speech. In one of the Gâthâs he asserts his wish to bring knowledge to the pure, in the power of Ormazd, to give them happiness, as Spiegel translates it. Haug translates the same passage thus: "I will swear hostility to the liars, but be a strong help to the truthful." He prays for truth, declaring himself the most faithful servant in the world of Ormazd the Wise One, and for this reason implores for a knowledge of what is most desirable to do. Says Zoroaster, according to Spiegel: "When it came to me through your prayer, I thought that the spreading abroad of your law through men was something difficult."

Zoroaster was oppressed with the sight of evil. Spiritual evil—the evil having its origin in a depraved heart and a will turned from goodness—tormented him most. His meditations convinced him that all the woe of the world had its origin in sin, and that the root of sin was in the demonic world. He maintained that the principles of good struggle with the principles of evil, rulers of darkness, spirits of wickedness in the supernatural world. Firmly believing that a great conflict was perpetually in progress between the powers of Light and Darkness, he urged all good men to take part in the war, and battle for Ahura-Mazda, (Ormazd), the good God, against Angra-Mainyus (Ahriman), the dark and evil tempter.

Great natural misfortunes intensified Zoroaster's conviction. In his time some geological convulsion changed the climate of Northern Asia, and suddenly caused bitter cold where there had previously been a tropical heat. Both Spiegel and Haug have in recent years translated the first Fargard of the Vendidad, which commences by describing a good country, Aryana-Vaêjo, which Ahura-Mazda had created as a region of delight. Thereupon the "evil being, Angra-Mainyus, full of death, created a mighty serpent, and winter, the work of the Daêvas. Ten months of winter are there, two months of summer." It is next stated in the original document: "Seven months of summer are (were) there; five months of winter were there. The latter are cold as to water, cold as to earth, cold as to trees. There is the heart of winter; there all around falls deep snow. There is the worst of evils." Spiegel and Haug both consider this passage an interpolation, but it doubtless referred to a great climatic change, by which the primeval home of the Aryans, Aryana-Vaêjo, became suddenly very much colder than it had hitherto been. Such a change may have induced the migration of the Aryans from Aryana-Vaêjo (Old Iran) to Media and Persia (New Iran). Bunsen and Haug believed such a history of migration to be related in the first Fargard (chapter) of the Vendidad. This would carry us back to the oldest part of the Veda, and show the movement of the Aryan stream southward from its primitive home in Central Asia, until it divided into two branches, one spreading over Media and Persia, and the other over India. The first verse of this old document represents Ormazd as declaring that he had created new regions, desirable as homes; thus preventing Aryana-Vaêjo becoming over-populated. Thus the very first verse of the Vendidad contains the pleasant remembrance of the migratory races from their Central Asian fatherland, and the Zoroastrian faith in a creative and protective Providence. The terrible convulsion which changed their summer climate into the present Siberian winter of ten months was a portion of the divine arrangement. The previous attractiveness of Old Iran would have over-crowded that Eden with the whole human race. Thus the evil Ahriman was allowed to enter it, as "a new serpent of destruction," changing its seven months of summer and five of winter into ten of winter and two of summer. Says the first Fargard of the Vendidad: "Therefore Angra-Mainyus, the death-dealing, created a mighty serpent and snow." The serpent entering the Iranic Eden is one of the curious coincidences of the Iranic and Hebrew traditions. Bunsen and Haug believe Aryana-Vaêjo, or Old Iran —the original seat of the great Aryan, or Indo-European race—to have been located on the elevated plains north-east of Samarcand, between the thirty-seventh and fortieth parallels of north latitude, and between the eighty-sixth and ninetieth meridians of east longitude. This region has precisely the climate described—ten months of winter and two of summer. The same is the case with Western Thibet and the greater portion of Central Siberia. Malte-Brun says: "The winter is nine or ten months long through almost the whole of Siberia." The only months free from snow are June and July.

Sir Charles Lyell says that "great oscillations of climate have occurred in times immediately antecedent to the peopling of the earth by man." During the present century frozen elephants, or mammoths, have been found in Siberia, in vast numbers and in a perfect condition. For this reason Lyell considers it "reasonable to believe that a large region in Central Asia, including perhaps the southern half of Siberia, enjoyed at no very remote period in the earth's history a temperate climate, sufficiently mild to afford food for numerous herds of elephants and rhinoceroses."

In the midst of these awful convulsions of nature—these antagonistic forces of external good and evil—Zoroaster evolved his belief in the dualism of all things. He believed that the Supreme Being had set all things in opposition to each other, two and two. He did not believe that, "whatever is, is right." Some things appeared woefully wrong. The world was a scene of war and turmoil, not one of peace and quiet. Life was battle to the good man, not sleep. He believed that the good God watching over all was constantly opposed by a powerful evil spirit, with whom we are to battle constantly and to whom we are never to yield. In the remote future he perceived the triumph of good; but that triumph could only be attained by fighting the good fight now, not, however, with carnal weapons. The whole duty of man was to have "pure thoughts" entering into "true words" and ending in "right actions."

The Zend-Avesta is a liturgy—a collection of hymns, prayers, invocations and thanksgivings. It contains prayers to numerous deities, the supreme one of whom is Ormazd, the others being only his servants.

Says Zarathustra: "I worship and adore the Creator of all things, Ahura-Mazda (Ormazd), full of light ! I worship the Amĕsha-Spentas (Amshaspands, the seven archangels, or protecting spirits)! I worship the body of the primal Bull, the soul of the Bull! I invoke thee, O Fire, thou son of Ormazd, most rapid of the Immortals! I invoke Mithra, the lofty, the immortal, the pure, the sun, the ruler, the quick Horse, the eye of Ormazd! I invoke the holy Sraosha, gifted with holiness, and Raçnu (spirit of justice), and Arstat (spirit of truth)! I invoke the Fravashi of good men, the Fravashi of Ormazd, the Fravashi of my own soul! I praise the good men and women of the whole world of purity! I praise the Haŏma, health-bringing, golden, with moist stalks! I praise Sraosha, whom four horses carry, spotless, bright-shining, swifter than the storms, who, without sleeping, protects the world in darkness!"

The Zend-Avesta, as a holy book, was to be read in private by the laity, or to be recited in public by the priests. This sacred book of the ancient Medes and Persians consists of the Vendidad, of which twenty-two Fargards, or chapters, have been preserved: the Vispered, in twenty-seven; the Yaçna, in seventy; and the Khordah-Avesta, or Little-Avesta, containing the Yashts, the Patets, and other prayers for the use of the laity. Spiegel regards the Gâthâs of the Yaçna as the oldest of these, the Vendidad next, and lastly the first part of the Yaçna and the Khordah-Avesta.

The Bundehesch is a book later than those just mentioned, but, in its contents, it goes back to primitive times. Windischmann, who, in 1863, made a new translation of this book, says: "In regard to the Bundehesch, I am confident that closer study of this remarkable book, and a more exact comparison of it with the original texts, will change the unfavorable opinion hitherto held concerning it into one of great confidence. I am justified in believing that its author has given us mainly only the ancient doctrine, taken by him from original texts, most of which are now lost. The more thoroughly it is examined the more trustworthy it will be found to be."

Only the germs of the Parsee system are found in the elder books of the Zend-Avesta. It has been doubted if the doctrine of Zerâna-Akerana, or the Monad behind the Duad, is to be found in the Zend-Avesta, though important texts in the Vendidad seem to imply a Supreme and Infinite Being, who created both Ormazd and Ahriman. The following is an outline of the Parsee system, as derived from the Bundehesch and the later Parsee writings:

In the beginning the Eternal or Absolute Being (Zerâna-Akerana) produced two other great divine beings. The first of these, called Ahura-Mazda, or Ormazd, remained true to him and was the King of Light. The other, called Angra-Mainyus, or Ahriman, was the King of Darkness. Ormazd being in a world of light and Ahriman in a world of darkness, the two became antagonists. The Infinite Being (Zerâna-Akerana) thereupon resolved to create the visible by Ormazd, for the purpose of exterminating the evil which Ahriman had caused; fixing its duration at twelve thousand years, which he divided into four periods of three thousand years each. Ormazd was to rule alone during the first period. Ahriman was to begin his operations during the second period, still, however, occupying a subordinate position. Both were to rule together during the third period. Ahriman was to have the ascendency during the fourth period.

Ormazd produced the Fereuers, or Fravashi, thus beginning the creation. Everything, either already created or to be created, has its Fravashi, containing the reason and basis of its existence. Ormazd himself has his Fravashi relating to Zerâna-Akerana, the Infinite. A spiritual, invisible world therefore existed before this visible world of matter.

In the creation of the material world, which was simply an incorporation of the spiritual world of Fravashis, Ormazd first made the firm vault of heaven and the earth on which that vault rests. On the earth he created the lofty mountain Albordj, the modern Elburz, which soared upward through all the spheres of the heaven, till it reached the primal light, and Ormazd established his abode on this summit. From this summit the bridge Chinevat extends to the vault of heaven and to Gorodman, which is the opening in the vault above Albordj. Gorodman is the abode of Fravashis and of the blessed, and the bridge leading to it is directly above the abyss Duzahk, the awful gulf beneath the earth, the dwelling-place of Ahriman.

Ormazd, knowing that his battle with Ahriman would commence after his first period, armed himself, and for his aid created the shining heavenly host—the sun, the moon and the stars—the mighty beings of light which were entirely subservient to him. He first created "the heroic runner, who never dies, the sun," and made him king and ruler of the material world. From Albordj he starts on his course in the morning, circling the earth in the highest spheres of the heaven, and returns at evening. Ormazd next created the moon, which "has its own light," which, leaving Albordj, circles the earth in a lower sphere and returns. He then created the five planets then known; also the entire host of fixed stars, in the lowest circle of the heavens. The space between the earth and the firm vault of the heavens is consequently divided into three spheres—that of the sun, that of the moon, and that of the stars.

The host of stars were common soldiers in the war with Ahriman, and were divided into four troops, each having its appointed leader. Twelve companies were arranged in the twelve signs of the Zodiac. These were all grouped into four great divisions, in the east, west, north and south; the planet Tistrya (Jupiter) presiding over the eastern division and named "Prince of the Stars," Sitavisa (Saturn) watching over the western division, Vanant (Mercury) over the southern, and Hapto-iringa (Mars) over the northern. The great star Mesch, or Meschgah (Venus), is in the middle of the firmament, and leads the heavenly host of stars in the struggle against Ahriman.

The dog Sirius (Sura) is also a watchman of the heavens, but is fixed to one place, at the bridge Chinevat, standing guard over the abyss out of which Ahriman comes.

After these preparations in the heavens had been finished by Ormazd, the first of the four periods of three thousand years each reached its end, and Ahriman saw from his gloomy abode what Ormazd had done. To antagonize Ormazd, Ahriman created a world of Darkness, a terrible host, as numerous and powerful as the beings of Light. Ormazd, knowing all the misery and woe that Ahriman would produce, yet knowing that he himself would triumph in the struggle, offered Ahriman peace; but Ahriman chose war. But, blinded by the majesty of Ormazd, and terror-stricken at the sight of the pure Fravashis of holy men, Ahriman was conquered by the strong word of Ormazd, and fell back into the abyss of Darkness, lying fettered there during the three thousand years of the second period.

Ormazd now finished his creation upon the earth. Sapandomad was guardian spirit of the earth. The earth, as Hethra, was mother of the living. Khordad was chief of the seasons, years, months and days, as well as protector of the water, which flowed from the fountain Anduisur, from Albordj. The planet Tistrya was appointed to raise the water in vapor, gather it in clouds, and let it fall in rain, with the aid of the planet Sitavisa. These "cloud-compellers" were regarded with the highest reverence. Amerdad was the god of vegetation, but the great Mithra was the lord of fructification and reproduction in the entire organic world, his duty being to lead the Fravashis to the bodies which they were to occupy.

Everything earthly in Ormazd's world of Light had its protecting divinity, or guardian spirit. These spirits were divided into series and groups, and had their captains and their associated assistants. The seven Amshaspands (in Zend, Amĕsha-Spentas) were the principal ones of these series, of whom Ormazd was the first. The other six were Bahman, King of Heaven; Ardibehescht, King of Fire; Schariver, King of the Metals; Sapandomad, Queen of the Earth; Amerdad, King of the Vegetables; and Khordad, King of Water.

Thus ended the second period of three thousand years; during which Ormazd had likewise produced the great primitive Bull, which, being the representative of the animal world, contained the seeds of all living creatures.

While Ormazd was thus finishing his creation of Light, Ahriman, in his gloomy abyss, was ending his antagonistic creation of Darkness—making a corresponding evil being for every good being that Ormazd created. These spirits of Darkness stood in their ranks and orders, with their seven presiding evil spirits, or Daêvas, corresponding to the seven Amshaspands of the world of Light.

The vast preparations for the great war between Ormazd and Ahriman being finished, and the end of the second period of three thousand years now approaching, Ahriman was urged by one of his Daêvas to commence the struggle. Having counted his host, and found nothing therein to oppose to the Fravashis of good men, he fell back dejected. When the second period ended, Ahriman sprang aloft fearlessly, knowing that his time had arrived. He was followed by his host, but he only reached the heavens, his troops remaining behind. Seized with a shudder, he sprang from heaven upon the earth in the form of a serpent, penetrating to the earth's center, and entering into everything which he found upon the earth. Passing into the primal Bull, and even into fire, the visible symbol of Ormazd, he defiled it with smoke and vapor. He then assailed the heavens; and a portion of the stars were already in his power, and enveloped in smoke and mist, when he was attacked by Ormazd, aided by the Fravashis of holy men. After ninety days and ninety nights he was thoroughly defeated, and driven back with his troops into the abyss of Duzahk.

He did not, however, stay there. He made a way for himself and his companions through the middle of the earth, and is now living on the earth with Ormazd, in accordance with the decree of the Infinite.

He had produced terrible destruction in the world; but the more evil he attempted to do, the more he unknowingly fulfilled the counsels of the Infinite, and hastened the development of good. He thus entered the Bull, the original animal, and so injured him that he died. But then Kaiomarts, the first man, came out of his right shoulder, and from his left shoulder proceeded Goshurun, the soul of the Bull, who now became the guardian spirit of the animal creation. The entire realm of clean animals and plants came from the Bull's body. Overwhelmed with rage and fury, Ahriman now created the unclean animals—for every clean beast an unclean one. Ormazd having created the dog, Ahriman produced the wolf. Ormazd having made all useful animals, Ahriman made all noxious ones; and likewise of plants.

Having nothing to oppose to Kaiomarts, the original man, Ahriman resolved to kill him. Kaiomarts was both man and woman, and after his death a tree grew from his body, bearing ten pair of men and women, Meschia and Meschiane being the first. They were at first pure and innocent and made for heaven, worshiping Ormazd as their creator; but Ahriman tempting them, they drank milk from a goat, thus injuring themselves; and by eating the fruit which Ahriman brought them, they lost a hundred parts of their happiness, only one part remaining. The woman was the first that sacrificed to the Daêvas. After fifty years they had two children, Siamak and Veschak. They died at the age of one hundred years. They remain in hell until the resurrection, in punishment for their sins.

Thus the human race became mortal by the sin of its first parents. Man stands between the worlds of Light and Darkness, left to his own free will. Being a creature of Ormazd he is able to and should honor him, and aid him in the war with Ahriman; but Ahriman and his Daêvas surround him night and day, trying to mislead, so that they must thus be able to increase the power of Darkness. He was only able to resist these temptations, to which his first parents yielded, because Ormazd had taken pity on him and given him a revelation of his will in the law of Zoroaster. If he obeys these precepts he is beyond harm from the Daêvas, being directly protected by Ormazd. The essence of the law is the command: "Think purely, speak purely, act purely." From Ormazd comes all that is pure; from Ahriman all that is impure. Bodily purity is no less worthy than moral purity. This is the reason for the many minute precepts regarding bodily cleanliness. The entire liturgic worship hinges vastly on this point.

The Fravashis of men originally created by Ormazd are preserved in heaven, in Ormazd's world of Light. But they must come from heaven, to be joined to a human body, and to enter upon a path of probation in this world, called the "Way of the Two Destinies." At death the souls of those who have chosen the good in this world are received by the good spirits, and guided, under the protection of the dog Sura, to the bridge of Chinevat, where the narrow road conducts to heaven, or paradise. The souls of the wicked are dragged to the bridge by the Daêvas. Ormazd here holds a tribunal and decides the fate of the human souls. The righteous safely pass the bridge into the abode of the blessed, being there welcomed with rejoicing by the Amshaspands. The pious soul is aided in crossing the bridge by the angel Serosh, "the happy, well-formed, swift, tall Serosh," who greets the new comer in his happy journey to the abode of the blessed, where he is greeted by the angel Vohu-mano, who, rising from his throne, exclaims: "How happy art thou, who hast come here to us, exchanging mortality for immortality!" The good soul then proceeds to the golden throne in paradise. The wicked fall over the bridge of Chinevat, into the abyss of Duzahk, where they find themselves in the realm of Angra-Mainyus, the world of Darkness, where they are forced to remain in misery and woe, tormented by the Daêvas.

Ormazd fixes the duration of the punishment, and some are redeemed sooner by means of the prayers and intercessions of their friends, but many must stay until the resurrection of the dead.

Ahriman himself effects this consummation, after having exercised great power over men during the last period of three thousand years. He made seven comets to antagonize the seven great luminaries created by Ormazd—the sun, moon and five planets then known. These comets went on their destructive course through the heavens, filling everything with danger and every human being with terror. But Ormazd put them under the control of his planets to restrain them. The planets will exercise this power until, by the decree of the Infinite at the close of the last period, one of the comets will break away from his watchman, the moon, and dash upon the earth, causing a general conflagration. Before this, however, Ormazd will send his Prophet, Sosioch, and cause the conversion of mankind, to be followed by the general resurrection.

Ormazd will clothe the bones of men with new flesh, and friends and relatives will again recognize each other. Then comes the great division of the just from the wicked.

When Ahriman causes the comet to fall upon the earth to gratify his destructive inclinations he will be really serving the Infinite Being against his own will; as the conflagration caused by this comet will change the whole earth into a stream like melted iron, which will pour down with fury into the abode of Ahriman. All beings must now pass through this stream. It will feel like warm milk to the righteous, who will pass through to the realm of the just; but the sinners shall be carried along by the stream into the abyss of Duzahk, where they will burn three days and nights, after which, being purified, they will invoke Ormazd and be received into heaven.

Ahriman himself and all in the abyss of Duzahk shall afterwards be purified by this fire; all evil will be consumed and all darkness will be banished. A more beautiful earth, pure and perfect, and destined to be eternal, will come from the extinct fire.

Ahura-Mazda (Ormazd) was the "all bountiful, the all-wise, living being" or "spirit" who was at the head of all that was good and lovely, of all that was beautiful and delightful. Angra-Mainyus (Ahriman) was the "dark and gloomy intelligence," that had ever been Ahura-Mazda's enemy, and was resolved on foiling and tormenting him. Ahura-Mazda was "the creator of life, the earthly and the spiritual." He had made "the celestial bodies," "earth, water, and trees," "all good creatures," and "all good things." He was "good," "holy," "pure," "true," "the holy god," "the holiest," "the essence of truth," "the father of truth," "the best being of all," "the master of purity." He was supremely happy and possessed every blessing—"health, wealth, virtue, wisdom, immortality." From Ahura-Mazda proceeded all good to mankind. He rewarded the good by granting them everlasting happiness, and punished the bad.

Angra-Mainyus was the author of all that was evil, and had been engaged in constant warfare with Ahura-Mazda. He corrupted and ruined the good things created by Ahura-Mazda. He was the dispenser of moral and physical evils. He blasted the earth with barrenness, made it produce thorns, thistles and poisonous plants. He sent the earthquake, the tempest, the hail, the thunder-bolt. He caused disease and death, famine and pestilence, wars and tumults. He was the inventor of witchraft, murder, unbelief, cannibalism, etc. He created ferocious wild beasts, serpents, toads, mice, hornets, mosquitoes, etc. He continually incited the bad against the good, and sought by every device to give vice the victory over virtue. Ahura-Mazda could not always defeat or baffle him.

Zoroaster's religion was strictly free from idolatry. The only emblems were a winged circle with a human figure, robed and wearing a tiara—a symbol of Ahura-Mazda; and a four-winged figure at Murgab, the ancient

Pasargadæ, the early capital of Persia, representing Sraosha, or Serosh—"the good, tall, fair Serosh"—who in the Zoroastrian system corresponds with the Archangel Michael in the Christian. The great Persian king, Darius Hystaspes, placed the emblems of Ahura-Mazda and Mithra in prominent places on the sculptured tablet above his tomb, as did all the later monarchs of his race whose sepulchers are yet to be seen. Artaxerxes Mnemon put the image of Mithra in the temple attached to the royal palace at Susa, and in his inscriptions unites Mithra and Ahura-Mazda, praying for their joint protection. Artaxerxes Ochus does the same a little later. The portions of the Zend-Avesta composed at this period observed the same practice. Ahura-Mazda and Mithra are called "the two great ones," "the two great, imperishable and pure."

Man was in duty bound to implicitly obey his creator, the Good Being, Ahura-Mazda, and to battle earnestly against Angra-Mainyus and his evil creatures. He was to be pious, pure, truthful and industrious. He was to acknowledge Ahura-Mazda as the One True God, and to reverence the Amĕsha-Spentas and the Izeds, or lower angels. He was to worship by prayers, praises, thanksgivings, singing of hymns, sacrifices of animals, and the occasional ceremony of the Haŏma, or Homa. This was the extraction of the juice of the Homa plant by the priests while reciting prayers, the formal presentation of the liquid extracted to the sacrificial fire, the consumption of a small part of it by the officiating priests, and the division of the most of it among the worshipers. The horse was considered the best sacrificial victim, but oxen, sheep and goats were also offered. The animal being brought before an altar on which the sacred fire was burning, believed to have been originally kindled from heaven, was there killed by a priest, who showed some of the flesh to the sacrificial fire, after which the victim was cooked and eaten by the priests and worshipers at a solemn meal.

Outward purity was enforced by numerous external observances. All impure acts, impure words and impure thoughts were to be abstained from. Ahura-Mazda, "the pure, the master of purity," would not tolerate impurity in his votaries. Man was placed on earth to preserve Ahura-Mazda's "good creation," which could only be done by carefully tilling the soil, eradicating the thorns and weeds sent by Angra-Mainyus, and reclaiming the tracts which that Evil Being had cursed with barrenness. The cultivation of the soil was thus a religious duty, and all were required to perform agricultural labors; and either as proprietor, farmer or laborer, each Zoroastrian was obliged to "further the works of life" by tillage of the soil.

Truth was another duty inculcated earnestly by the Zoroastrian creed. Herodotus tells us that "the Persian youth are taught three things only; to ride the horse, to draw the bow, and to speak the truth." Ahura-Mazda was the "*true* spirit," and the chief of the Amĕsha-Spentas was Asha-vahista, "the best *truth*." The Zend-Avesta and the Persian cuneiform inscriptions hold up Druj, "falsehood," to detestation, "as the basest, the most contemptible and the most pernicious of vices."

After a time the early Iranian religion became corrupted by the admixture of foreign superstitions. The followers of Zoroaster, spreading themselves from their primeval seat on the Oxus over the regions to the south and south-west of the Caspian Sea, came into contact with a religious system vastly different from that which they had previously professed, yet capable of being easily fused with it. This was Magism, or the worship of the elements. The primitive inhabitants of Armenia, Cappadocia and the Zagros mountain-range, had, under circumstances to us unknown, developed this system of religion, associating with its tenets a priest-caste claiming prophetic powers and a highly sacerdotal character. The essentials of Magism were the four elements of Fire, Air, Earth and Water, which were regarded as the only proper objects of human adoration. Personal gods, temples, shrines and images were rejected. The worshipers reverenced not the powers presiding over the elements of nature, but the elements themselves. Fire, the great ethereal principle and the most powerful agent, was specially regarded; and on the Magian fire-altars the sacred flame, usually considered to have been kindled from heaven, was kept constantly burning year in and year out by bands of priests, whose special duty it was to see that the sacred spark was never permitted to die out. It was a capital offense to defile the altar by blowing the fire with one's breath, and it was just as odious to burn a corpse. Only a small part of the fat of the victims for sacrifice was consumed in the flames. Water was reverenced next to fire. Sacrifice was offered to rivers, lakes and fountains, the victim being brought near to them and then killed, the greatest care being taken that not a drop of blood should touch the water and pollute it. No refuse was permitted to be thrown into a river, nor was it lawful to wash one's hands in one. The earth was reverenced by means of sacrifice, and by abstaining from the common manner of burying the dead. Herodotus and Strabo are our main authorities for this account of Magism.

The Magian priest-caste held a high rank. A priest always mediated between the Deity and the worshiper, and intervened in every rite of religion. The Magus prepared the sacrificial victim and slew it, chanted the mystic strain giving the sacrifice all its force, poured the propitiatory libation of oil, milk and honey on the ground, and held the bundle of thin tamarisk twigs, the barsom (*baresma*) of the later books of the Zend-Avesta, the use of which was necessary to all sacrificial ceremonies. "Claiming supernatural powers, they explained omens, expounded dreams, and by means of a certain mysterious manipulation of the barsom, or bundle of tamarisk twigs, arrived at a knowledge of future events, which they would sometimes condescend to communicate to the pious inquirer."

With all these pretensions, it is not surprising that the Magi assumed a lofty demeanor, a stately dress, and surroundings of ceremonial splendor. Attired in white robes, and wearing upon their heads tall felt caps, with long lappets at the sides, which are said to have hidden the jaw and the lips, the Magi, with a barsom in their hands, marched in procession to the fire-altars, around which they performed their magical incantations for an hour at a time. The credulous masses, impressed by such scenes and imposed upon by the claims of the Magi to supernatural powers, paid the priest-caste willing homage. The kings and chiefs consulted them; and when the Iranians, in their westward migrations, came into contact with the nations professing Magism, they found the Magian priesthood all-powerful among most of the Western Asian races.

The followers of Zoroaster had at first been intolerant and exclusive, and regarded the faith of their Aryan kinsmen, the Sanskritic Hindoos, with aversion and contempt. They had fiercely opposed idolatry, and hated with deep animosity every religion but their own. But in the course of ages these feelings had become lax, and the early religious fervor gradually died away; and in its stead "an impressible and imitative spirit had developed itself."

Thus Zoroastrianism, in its contact with Magism, was impressed favorably, and the result was the development of a new system by the fusion of the two. The chief tenets of the two systems harmonized and were thoroughly compatible. Thus the Iranians, though holding fast to their original creed, adopted the main points of the Magian faith and all the more remarkable practices and customs of Magism. This fusion of Zoroastrianism and Magism occurred in Media. The Magi became a Median tribe and the priest-caste of the Medes. Worship of the elements, divination by means of the barsom, expounding of dreams, incantations at fire-altars, sacrifices at which a Magus officiated, were made a part of the Zoroastrian creed. Thus a mixed religious system was developed, which finally triumphed over pure Zoroastrianism after a long struggle. The Persians, sometime after their conquest of the Medes, adopted the new faith, accepted the Magian priesthood, and attended the ceremonies at the fire-altars. The introduction of the Magian creed by the Zoroastrians led to a singular practice regarding the disposition of the dead. It became unlawful to burn dead bodies, because that would pollute fire; or to bury them, as that would pollute the earth; or to cast them into a river, as that would pollute water; or to place them in a tomb, or in a sarcophagus, as that would pollute the air. The dead were therefore removed to a solitary place to be devoured by beasts and birds of prey—wolves, jackals, foxes, crows, ravens and vultures. This, as the orthodox practice, was employed by the Magi in the disposal of their own dead, and was urgently recommended to others. Those who would not adopt this custom were allowed to coat the dead bodies of their friends with wax and then bury them, thus avoiding the pollution of the earth by preventing direct contact between it and the corpse.

Says Rawlinson, concerning the fusion of Zoroastrianism with Magism:

"The mixed religion thus constituted, though less elevated and less pure than the original Zoroastrian creed, must be pronounced to have possessed a certain loftiness and picturesqueness which suited it to become the religion of a great and splendid monarchy. The mysterious fire-altars upon the mountain-tops, with their prestige of a remote antiquity—the ever-burning flame believed to have been kindled from on high—the worship in the open air under the blue canopy of heaven—the long troops of Magians in their white robes, with their strange caps, and their mystic wands—the frequent prayers, the abundant sacrifices, the low incantations—the supposed prophetic powers of the priest-caste—all this together constituted an imposing whole at once to the eye and to the mind, and was calculated to give additional grandeur to the civil system that should be allied with it. Pure Zoroastrianism was too spiritual to coalesce readily with Oriental luxury and magnificence, or to lend strength to a government based on the principles of Asiatic despotism. Magism furnished a hierarchy to support the throne and add splendor and dignity to the court, while it overawed the subject class by its supposed possession of supernatural powers and of the right of mediating between man and God. It supplied a picturesque worship, which at once gratified the senses and excited the fancy. It gave scope to man's passion for the marvelous by its incantations, its divining-rods, its omen-reading, and its dream-expounding. It gratified the religious scrupulosity which finds a pleasure in making to itself difficulties, by the disallowance of a thousand natural acts, and the imposition of numberless rules for external purity. At the same time it gave no offense to the anti-idolatrous spirit in which the Iranians had always gloried, but upheld and encouraged the iconoclasm which they had previously practiced. It thus blended easily with the previous creed of the Iranian people, and produced an amalgam that has shown a surprising vitality, having lasted above two thousand years—from the time of Xerxes, the son of Darius Hystaspes (B. C. 485-465) to the present day."

The following passages are from the oldest part of the Avesta, the Gâthâs:

"Good is the thought, good the speech, good the work of the pure Zarathustra."

"I desire by my prayer with uplifted hands this joy—the pure works of the Holy Spirit, Mazda . . . a disposition to perform good actions . . . and pure gifts for both worlds, the bodily and spiritual."

"I have intrusted my soul to Heaven . . . and I will teach what is pure so long as I can."

"I keep forever purity and good-mindedness. Teach thou me, Ahura-Mazda, out of thyself; from heaven; by thy mouth, whereby the world first arose."

"Thee have I thought, O Mazda, as the first, to praise with the soul . . . active Creator . . . Lord of the worlds . . . Lord of good things . . . the first fashioner . . . who made the pure creation . . . who upholds the best soul with his understanding."

"I praise Ahura-Mazda, who has created

cattle, created the water and good trees, the splendor of light, the earth and all good. We praise the Fravashis of the pure men and women—whatever is fairest, purest, immortal."

"We honor the good spirit, the good kingdom, the good law—all that is good."

"Here we praise the soul and body of the Bull, then our own souls, the souls of the cattle which desire to maintain us in life . . . the good men and women . . . the abode of the water . . . the meeting and parting of the ways . . . the mountains which make the waters flow . . . the strong wind created by Ahura-Mazda . . . the Haôma, giver of increase, far from death."

"Now give ear to me, and hear! the Wise Ones have created all. Evil doctrine shall not again destroy the world."

"In the beginning, the two heavenly Ones spoke—the Good to the Evil—thus: 'Our souls, doctrines, words, works, do not unite together.'"

"How shall I satisfy thee, O Mazda, I, who have little wealth, few men? How may I exalt thee according to my wish! . . . I will be contented with your desires; this is the decision of my understanding and of my soul."

The following is from the Khordah-Avesta:

"In the name of God, the giver, forgiver, rich in love, praise be to the name of Ormazd, the God with the name, 'Who always was, always is, and always will be'; the heavenly amongst the heavenly, with the name 'From whom alone is derived rule.' Ormazd is the greatest ruler, mighty, wise, creator, supporter, refuge, defender, completer of good works, overseer, pure, good, and just.

"With all strength (bring I) thanks; to the great among beings, who created and destroyed, and through his own determination of time, strength, wisdom, is higher than the six Amshaspands, the circumference of heaven, the shining sun, the brilliant moon, the wind, the water, the fire, the earth, the trees, the cattle, the metals, mankind.

"Offering and praise to that Lord, the completer of good works, who made men greater than all earthly beings, and through the gift of speech created them to rule the creatures as warriors against the Daêvas.

"Praise the omniscience of God, who hath sent through the holy Zarathustra peace for the creatures, the wisdom of the law—the enlightening derived from the heavenly understanding, and heard with the ears—wisdom and guidance for all beings who are, were, and will be, (and) the wisdom of wisdoms; which effects freedom from hell for the soul at the bridge, and leads it over to that Paradise, the brilliant, sweet-smelling of the pure.

"All good do I accept at thy command, O God, and think, speak, and do it. I believe in the pure law; by every good work seek I forgiveness for all sins. I keep pure for myself the serviceable work and abstinence from the unprofitable. I keep pure the six powers—thought, speech, work, memory, mind, and understanding. According to thy will am I able to accomplish, O accomplisher of good, thy honor, with good thoughts, good words, good works.

"I enter on the shining way to Paradise; may the fearful terror of hell not overcome me! May I step over the bridge Chinevat, may I attain Paradise, with much perfume, and all enjoyments, and all brightness.

"Praise to the Overseer, the Lord, who rewards those who accomplish good deeds according to his own wish, purifies at last the obedient, and at last purifies even the wicked one of hell. All praise be to the creator, Ormazd, the all-wise, mighty, rich in might; to the seven Amshaspands; to Ized Bahrâm, the victorious annihilator of foes."

The following is a Confession or Patet:

"I repent of all sins. All wicked thoughts, words, and works which I have meditated in the world, corporeal, spiritual, earthly, and heavenly, I repent of, in your presence, ye believers. O Lord, pardon through the three words.

"I confess myself a Mazdayaçnian, a Zarathustrian, an opponent of the Daêvas, devoted to belief in Ahura, for praise, adoration, satisfaction, and laud. As it is the will of God, let the Zaôta say to me, Thus announces the Lord, the Pure out of Holiness, let the wise speak.

"I praise all good thoughts, words, and works, through thought, word, and deed. I curse all evil thoughts, words, and works away from thought, word, and deed. I lay hold on all good thoughts, words, and works, with thoughts, words, and works, *i. e.*, I perform good actions, I dismiss all evil thoughts, words, and works, from thoughts, words, and works, *i. e.*, I commit no sins.

"I give to you, ye who are Amshaspands, offering and praise, with the heart, with the body, with my own vital powers, body and soul. The whole powers which I possess, I possess in dependence on the Yazatas. To possess in dependence upon the Yazatas means (as much as) this: if anything happen so that it behoves to give the body for the sake of the soul, I give it to them.

"I praise the best purity, I hunt away the Dévs, I am thankful for the good of the Creator Ormazd, with the opposition and unrighteousness which come from Ganâmainyo, am I contented and agreed in the hope of the resurrection. The Zarathustrian law created by Ormazd I take as a plummet. For the sake of this way I repent of all sins.

"I repent of the sins which can lay hold of the character of men, or which have laid hold of my character, small and great which are committed amongst men, the meanest sins as much as is (and) can be, yet more than this, namely, all evil thoughts, words, and works which (I have committed) for the sake of others, or others for my sake, or if the hard sin has seized the character of an evil-doer on my account—such sins, thoughts, words, and works, corporeal, mental, earthly, heavenly, I repent of with the three words: pardon, O Lord, I repent of the sins with Patet.

"The sins against father, mother, sister, brother, wife, child, against spouses, against the superiors, against my own relations, against those living with me, against those who possess equal property, against the neighbors, against the inhabitants of the same town, against servants, every unrighteousness through which I have been amongst sinners—of these sins repent I with thoughts, words, and works, corporeal as spiritual, earthly as heavenly, with the three words: pardon, O Lord, I repent of sins.

"The defilement with dirt and corpses, the bringing of dirt and corpses to the water and fire, or the bringing of fire and water to dirt and corpses; the omission of reciting the Avesta in mind, of strewing about hair, nails and toothpicks, of not washing the hands, all the rest which belongs to the category of dirt and corpses, if I have thereby come among the sinners, so repent I of all these sins with thoughts, words, and works, corporeal as spiritual, earthly as heavenly, with the three words: pardon, O Lord, I repent of sin.

"That which was the wish of Ormazd the Creator, and I ought to have thought, and have not thought, what I ought to have spoken and have not spoken, what I ought to have done and have not done; of these sins repent I with thoughts, words, and works," etc.

"That which was the wish of Ahriman, and I ought not to have thought and yet have thought, what I ought not to have spoken and yet have spoken, what I ought not to have done and yet have done; of these sins I repent," etc.

"Of all and every kind of sin which I committed against the creatures of Ormazd, as stars, moon, sun, and the red burning fire, the dog, the birds, the five kinds of animals, the other good creatures which are the property of Ormazd, between earth and heaven, if I have become a sinner against any of these, I repent," etc.

"Of pride, haughtiness, covetousness, slandering the dead, anger, envy, the evil eye, shamelessness, looking at with evil intent, looking at with evil concupiscence, stiff-neckedness, discontent with the godly arrangements, self-willedness, sloth, despising others, mixing in strange matters, unbelief, opposing the Divine powers, false witness, false judgment, idol-worship, running naked, running with one shoe, the breaking of the low (midday) prayer, the omission of the (midday) prayer, theft, robbery, whoredom, witchcraft, worshiping with sorcerers, unchastity, tearing the hair, as well as all other kinds of sin which are enumerated in this Patet, or not enumerated, which I am aware of, or not aware of, which are appointed or not appointed, which I should have bewailed with obedience before the Lord, and have not bewailed—of these sins repent I with thoughts, words, and works, corporeal as spiritual, earthly as heavenly. O Lord, pardon, I repent with the three words, with Patet.

"If I have taken on myself the Patet for any one and have not performed it, and misfortune has thereby come upon his soul or his descendants, I repent of the sin for every one with thoughts," etc.

"With all good deeds am I in agreement, with all sins am I not in agreement, for the good am I thankful, with iniquity am I contented. With the punishment at the bridge, with the bonds and tormentings and chastisements of the mighty of the law, with the punishment of the three nights (after) the fifty-seven years am I contented and satisfied."

The following is a hymn to a star:

"The star Tistrya praise we, the shining, majestic, with pleasant good dwelling, light, shining conspicuous, going around, healthful, bestowing joy, great, going round about from afar, with shining beams, the pure, and the water which makes broad seas, good, far-famed, the name of the bull created by Mazda, the strong kingly majesty, and the Fravashi of the holy pure, Zarathustra.

"For his brightness, for his majesty, will I praise him, the star Tistrya, with audible praise. We praise the star Tistrya, the brilliant, majestic, with offerings, with Haôma bound with flesh, with Maúthra which gives wisdom to the tongue, with word and deed, with offerings with right-spoken speech."

"The star Tistrya, the brilliant, majestic, we praise, who glides so softly to the sea like an arrow, who follows the heavenly will, who is a terrible pliant arrow, a very pliant arrow, worthy of honor among those worthy of honor, who comes from the damp mountain to the shining mountain."

The following is a hymn to Mithra:

"Mithra, whose long arms grasp forwards here with Mithra strength; that which is in Eastern India he seizes, and that which [is] in the western he smites, and what is on the steppes of Raúha, and what is at the ends of this earth.

"Thou, O Mithra, dost seize these, reaching out thy arms. The unrighteous destroyed through the just is gloomy in soul. Thus thinks the unrighteous: Mithra, the artless, does not see all these evil deeds, all these lies.

"But I think in my soul: No earthly man with a hundred-fold strength thinks so much evil as Mithra with heavenly strength thinks good. No earthly man with a hundred-fold strength speaks so much evil as Mithra with heavenly strength speaks good. No earthly man with a hundred-fold strength does so much evil as Mithra with heavenly strength does good.

"With no earthly man is the hundred-fold greater heavenly understanding allied as the heavenly understanding allies itself to the heavenly Mithra, the heavenly. No earthly man with a hundred-fold strength hears with the ears as the heavenly Mithra, who possesses a hundred strengths, sees every liar. Mightily goes forward Mithra, powerful in rule marches he onwards; fair visual power, shining from afar, gives he to the eyes."

The following are inscriptions at Persepolis, the Persian capital:

"Darius, the King, King of Kings, son of Hystaspes, successor of the Ruler of the World, Djemchid."

"Ahura-Mazda (Ormazd) is a mighty God; who has created the earth, the heaven, and men; who has given glory to men; who has made Xerxes king, the ruler of many. I, Xerxes, King of Kings, king of the earth near and far, son of Darius, an Achæmenid. What I have done here, and what I have done elsewhere, I have done by the grace of Ahura-Mazda."

The following is one of the Gâthâs, and is by some assigned to Zoroaster himself:

"Now will I speak and proclaim to all who have come to listen
Thy praise, Ahura-Mazda, and thine, O Vohu-mano.
Asha! I ask that thy grace may appear in the lights of heaven.

Hear with your ears what is best, perceive with your mind what is purest,
So that each man for himself may, before the great doom cometh,
Choose the creed he prefers. May the wise ones be on our side.

These two spirits are twins; they made known in times that are bygone
That good and evil, in thought, and word, and action.
Rightly decided between them the good; not so the evil.

When these Two came together, first of all they created
Life and death, that at last there might be for such as are evil
Wretchedness, but for the good a happy blest existence.

Of these Two the One who was evil chose what was evil;
He who was kind and good, whose robe was the changeless Heaven,
Chose what was right; those, too, whose works pleased Ahura-Mazda.

They could not rightly discern who erred and worshipped the Devas;
They the Bad Spirit chose, and, having held counsel together,
Turned to Rapine, that so they might make man's life an affliction.

But to the good came might; and with might came wisdom and virtue;
Armaiti herself, the eternal, gave to their bodies
Vigor; e'en thou wert enriched by the gifts she scattered, O Mazda.

Mazda, the time will come when the crimes of the bad shall be punished;
Then shall thy power be displayed in fitly rewarding the righteous—
Them that have bound and delivered up falsehood to Asha the Truth-God.

Let us then be of those who advance this world and improve it,
O Ahura-Mazda, O Truth-God bliss conferring!
Let our minds be ever there where wisdom abideth!

Then indeed shall be seen the fall of pernicious falsehood;
But in the house where dwell Vohu-mano Mazda, and Asha—
Beautiful house—shall be gathered forever such as are worthy.

O men, if you but cling to the precepts Mazda has given,
Precepts, which to the bad are a torment, but joy to the righteous,
Then shall you one day find yourselves victorious through them."

Another specimen is from the "Yaçna," or "Book on Sacrifice," and is probably some centuries later than the great bulk of the Gâthâs:

"We worship Ahura-Mazda, the pure, the master of purity:
We worship the Amêsha-Spentas, possessors and givers of blessings:

We worship the whole creation of Him who is True, the heavenly,
With the terrestrial, all that supports the good creation,
All that favors the spread of the good Mazd-Yaçna religion.

We praise whatever is good in thought, in word, or in action,
Past or future; we also keep clean whatever is excellent.

O Ahura-Mazda, thou true and happy being!
We strive both to think, and to speak, and to do whatever is fittest
Both our lives to preserve, and bring them both to perfection.

Holy spirit of earth, for our best works' sake, we entreat thee,
Grant us beautiful fertile fields—aye, grant them to all men,
Believers and unbelievers, the wealthy and those that have nothing."

CHAPTER V.

THE BABYLONIAN EMPIRE.

SECTION I.—EXTENT AND PRODUCTIONS.

ABYLONIA proper being almost identical in its situation and territorial extent with the old kingdom of Chaldæa, it need not be described here. It was located wholly west of the Tigris, and consisted of two "vast plains, or flats, one situated between the two rivers (the Tigris and the Euphrates), and thus forming the lower portion of the Mesopotamia of the Greeks and Romans—the other interposed between the Euphrates and Arabia, a long but narrow strip along the right bank of that abounding river." In area it was smaller than Scotland or Ireland. The country east of the Tigris constituted no portion of Babylonia proper, but was Cissia, or Susiana—a separate country called Elam by the Jews—and was occupied by an Aryan people. The cities of Babylonia have been mentioned in connection with Chaldæa.

The small kingdom of Babylonia suddenly became the mistress of an extensive empire in the latter half of the seventh century before Christ. When Media and Babylonia overthrew Assyria in B. C. 625, they divided the Assyrian Empire between them, as already related. Babylonia obtained all that part of the Assyrian dominions west of the Tigris and south of Armenia, along with Elam, or Susiana, east of the Lower Tigris. Thus the countries included within the Later Babylonian Empire, besides Babylonia proper, the heart of the empire, were Elam (Elymais), or Susiana (Cissia), Mesopotamia proper, Cilicia, Syria, Phœnicia, Palestine, Edom, Northern Arabia and part of Egypt. There was a great variety of climate and productions in this vast domain. The climate, products and animals of Babylonia have been mentioned and described in our account of Chaldæa. The exceeding fertility of its soil, which so richly rewarded the labors of the husbandman, have there been noted. The testimony of Herodotus in that particular was sustained by Theophrastus, Strabo and Pliny, and also by Berosus, who said: "The land of the Babylonians produces wheat as an indigenous plant, and has also barley, and lentils, and vetches, and sesame; the banks of the streams and the marshes supply edible roots, called *gongæ*, which have the taste of barley cakes. Palms, too, grow in the country, and apples, and fruit-trees of various kinds." The chief article of food for the great mass of the people in Babylonia, as in Egypt, was the date-palm, which flourished in luxuriant abundance.

The products of Susiana were mainly the same as those of Babylonia proper; the date-palm, wheat and barley growing in abundance. The palm-tree also furnished building timber. The modern Khusistan, the ancient Susiana, produces all the fruits which thrive in Persia. In Northern Mesopotamia are found the walnut, the vine and pistachio-nut, while good crops of grain, oranges, pomegranates, and the ordinary fruits are grown. In Northern Syria all kinds of trees and shrubs grow in luxuriance, while the pasture is excellent, and much of the land is adapted to the growth of cotton. Here the Assyrian kings frequently obtained timber for build-

EXTENT AND PRODUCTIONS.

ing purposes, and here are yet found dense forests of oak, pine, ilex, walnuts, willows, poplars, ash-trees, birches, larches and locust-trees. Such wild shrubs as the oleander, the myrtle, the bay, the arbutus, the clematis, the juniper, and the honeysuckle abound; and such cultivated fruit-trees as the orange, the pomegranate, the pistachio-nut, the vine, the olive and the mulberry also thrive. The *adis*, an excellent pea, and the *Lycoperdon*, or wild potato, grow in the vicinty of Aleppo. The castor-oil plant is cultivated in the plain of Edib. Melons, cucumbers and most of the common vegetables flourish in abundance all over Syria.

In Southern Syria and Palestine most of the same vegetable productions occur. The date-palm flourishes in Syria as far as Beyreut, and formerly thrived in Palestine. The banana is also found on the Syrian coast. The fig-mulberry, or true sycamore, also thrives in Southern Syria, as do the jujube, the tamarisk, the wild olive, the gum-styrax plant, the egg-plant, the Egyptian papyrus, the sugar-cane, the scarlet mistletoe, the liquorice plant, the yellow-flowered acacia, and the solanum that produces the "Dead Sea apple." Here also flourishes the celebrated cedar of Lebanon, several oaks and junipers, the maple, the mulberry, the berberry, the jessamine, the ivy, the butcher's broom, a rhododendron, and the gum-tragacanth plant. The same fruits flourish in Southern Syria that thrive in the North, with the addition of dates, lemons, almonds, shaddocks and limes.

The principal mineral products of the Babylonian Empire were bitumen, with its concomitants, naphtha and petroleum, salt, sulpher, nitre, copper, iron, perhaps silver, and several kinds of precious stones. The springs of Hit, or Is, were famous in the time of Herodotus for their great abundance of bitumen, which was likewise procured from Ardericca (now Kir-Ab), and probably from Ram Ormuz, in Susiana, and also from the Dead Sea, in Palestine. Salt was procured from the various lakes without outlets, especially from the Sabakhah, the Bahr-el-Melak, the Dead Sea, and a small lake near Tadmor, or Palmyra. The Dead Sea perhaps also furnished sulphur and nitre. The hills of Palestine yielded copper and iron. Silver was probably found in Anti-Lebanon. Gems and precious stones were most probably procured from Susiana, and from Syria and Phœnicia. Among these precious stones were agates from Susiana, amethysts from Petra, alabaster from near Damascus, cyanus from Phœnicia, and gems found in the cylinder-seals, such as cornelian, rock-crystal, chalcedony, onyx, jasper, quartz, serpentine, syenite, hæmatite, green felspar, pyrites, loadstone and amazon-stone, from the various provinces.

Building stone did not exist in Babylonia and the alluvial districts of Susiana; but abounded in other parts of the empire, being plentiful in the Euphrates valley above Hit, in the mountain regions of Susiana, and in Syria, Palestine and Phœnicia. Near to Babylonia was limestone. In the vicinity of Haddisah, on the Euphrates, was a silicious rock alternating with iron-stone, and in the Arabian desert were sandstone and granite. The stone used in the Babylonian cities was conveyed down the Euphrates, or transported by canals from the neighboring districts of Arabia. But the inexhaustible supply of clay furnished by their own country caused the Babylonians to prefer brick almost exclusively for building purposes.

The principal wild animals of the Babylonian Empire were the lion, the panther, or large leopard, the hunting leopard, the bear, the hyena, the wild ox, the buffalo, the wild ass, the stag, the antelope, the ibex, or wild goat, the wild sheep, the wild boar, the wolf, the jackal, the fox, the hare and the rabbit. Other wild animals were the lynx, the wild cat, the ratel, the sable, the genet, the badger, the otter, the beaver, the polecat, the jerboa, the rat, the mouse, the marmot, the porcupine, the squirrel and the alligator. Great varieties of birds, including eagles, vultures, falcons, owls, hawks, crows, and many kinds of small birds, abounded. Reptiles of many varieties prevailed. Fish abounded in the Chaldæan marshes and in most of the fresh-water lakes

1—17.-U. H.

and rivers. The domestic animals were the camel, the horse, the mule, the ass, the cow, the ox, the goat, the sheep and the dog.

The summer heat in Babylonia proper, or Chaldæa, in Susiana, or Elam, in Philistia and in Edom was intense, but the winters here were short and mild. In Susiana the cool breezes from the Zagros mountains somewhat modified the heat; while in Babylonia the sirocco, or hot wind, from the Arabian desert was at times oppressive. In Central Mesopotamia, in the Euphrates valley, in Syria, Palestine and Phœnicia, the winters were longer and colder, but the summer heat was less oppressive. In the northern portion of the empire, along the flanks of the Masius, the Taurus and the Amanus, the climate was like that of Media, the summers being milder, but the winters intensely severe. Thus a variety of climate existed in the Babylonian Empire; although the region as a whole was the hottest and dryest outside the tropics, because of the close proximity of the great Arabian desert, the smallness of the neighboring seas, the absence of mountains, and the scarcity of timber.

On the east and north the Babylonian Empire was bounded by the territories of the great Median Empire, including Persia and Media on the east, and Armenia and Cappadocia on the north. On the south lay the desert land of Arabia, and on the west was the Mediterranean sea.

The great cities of the empire outside of Babylonia itself were Jerusalem and Samaria in Palestine; Tyre and Sidon in Phœnicia; Damascus and Tadmor in Syria; Carchemish, in the land of the Hittites, on the Euphrates; Ashdod, Ascalon, Ekron and Gaza in Philistia; and Susa in Susiana, or Elam.

SECTION II.—POLITICAL HISTORY.

THE history of the Babylonian Empire begins with Nabopolassar, who ascended the throne of Babylon in B. C. 625. We have observed in the history of Assyria, that from the time of Tiglathi-Nin's conquest of Chaldæa, in B. C. 1300, that country sunk into a state of comparative insignificance, and remained, during the whole period of Assyrian ascendency in Western Asia, subject to Assyria, or occupied a secondary position among the Oriental nations. The Assyrians at first governed Chaldæa from their own capital, but they soon placed the country under an Assyrian dynasty, over which they claimed and exercised a sort of suzerainty, but which was practically independent and ruled its kingdom without interference.

The first monarch of the Assyrian dynasty in Chaldæa was NEBUCHADNEZZAR I., a contemporary of Asshur-ris-ilim, King of Assyria. Nebuchadnezzar twice attacked Nineveh; first by way of the Diyaleh and the outlying Zagros hills, the route of the great Persian military road in subsequent times; and secondly by crossing directly the Mesopotamian plain. The Assyrian records say that both these attacks were repulsed, and that after his second failure the Babylonian king retreated hastily back into his own dominions. Tiglath-Pileser I., King of Assyria, the son and successor of Asshus-ris-ilim, led an expedition into Babylonia, then ruled by MERODACH-IDDIN-AKHI, the successor of Nebuchadnezzar I. After a struggle of two years, and taking Kurri-galzu (now Akkerkuf), the two Sipparas, Opis, and even Babylon itself, Tiglath-Pileser returned to Assyria, harassed on his retreat by the Babylonian monarch, who captured the Assyrian baggage, along with certain Assyrian idols, which were carried as trophies to Babylon. Babylonia and Assyria continued at war during the following reigns of MERODACH-SHAPIK-ZIRI in the former country and Asshur-bil-kala in the latter, without any important result.

The period of these Assyro-Babylonian wars synchronizes with the epoch of the Judges in Israel, and was succeeded by an interval of obscurity in the history of both Assyria and Babylonia. Assyria had sunk into a declining condition; while Babylonia was prosperous, and according to the testimony of Asshur-izir-pal, the great Assyrian monarch of the ninth century before Christ, conquered some of the Assyrian territories, and according to Macrobius held communication with Egypt.

But after remaining for two centuries in a state of comparative weakness and unimportance, Assyria entered upon another period of prosperity and greatness, and made Babylonia feel the effects of her vengeance. The Assyrian king, Asshur-izir-pal, invaded Babylonia about B. C. 880, and recovered the territories which the Babylonians had held during the period of Assyria's depression. Asshur-izir-pal's son and successor, Shalmaneser II., the Black Obelisk king, led an expedition into Babylonia while that country was distracted by a civil war between its legitimate sovereign, MERODACH-SUM-ADIN, and his younger brother. Shalmaneser took a number of Babylonian towns, and was allowed to enter Babylon itself after defeating and slaying the pretender to the Babylonian throne; after which he overran Chaldæa, or the district upon the coast, which seems to have been then independent of Babylon and governed by a number of petty kings. The Chaldæan chiefs were forced to pay tribute; and, having "struck terror as far as the sea," the Assyrian king returned to his capital. Thus all of Babylonia and Chaldæa was again under Assyrian influence; and Babylonia was once more a secondary power, dependent on Assyria.

About B. C. 821 the Assyrian king, Shamas-Vul II., the son and successor of Shalmaneser II., invaded Babylonia, defeated its king, MERODACH-BELATZU-IKBI, in two pitched battles, and forced him to submit to Assyrian suzerainty; though in the last battle he had been aided by the Zimri of Mount Zagros, the Aramæans of the Euphrates, and the Chaldæans of the South. Babylon remained under Assyrian supremacy until the middle of the eighth century before Christ, when it is supposed that PUL, seeing his opportunity in Assyria's weakness under Asshur-dayan III., about B. C. 770, shook off the hated yoke of Assyria and extended the Babylonian dominion over the Euphrates valley and Western Mesopotamia, whence he proceeded to extend his conquests into Syria and Palestine. But such obscurity rests upon Pul that it is not positively known whether he was a Babylonian king. The Jewish Scriptures call him "king of Assyria," and Berosus represents him as "Chaldæorum rex."

Soon after regaining its independence, Babylonia was disintegrated into a number of independent sovereignties—Nabonassar governing Babylon; Yakin, the father of Merodach-Baladan, ruling the Chaldæan coast region; and Nadina, Zakiru and other princes holding sway in petty districts in Northern Babylonia. NABONASSAR, who became King of Babylon in B. C. 747, is regarded as the restorer of Babylonian independence; and the year of his accession, known as the "Era of Nabonassar," was the point from which the Babylonians thereafter reckoned dates of events. According to Berosus, Nabonassar sought to obliterate the memory of the previous epoch of Babylonian subjection to Assyria by having "destroyed the acts of the kings who had preceded him."

Nabonassar lived at peace with the contemporary King of Assyria, Tiglath-Pileser II., who early in his reign invaded the other portions of Babylonia and Chaldæa, forcing Merodach-Baladan, the son and successor of Yakin, to become his tributary. Nabonassar reigned over Babylon fourteen years, from B. C. 747 to B. C. 733. It has been generally believed that the time of Nabonassar's reign was the same as that assigned by Herodotus to the reign of Semiramis, who, as the wife or as the mother of Nabonassar, governed Babylon on behalf of her husband or her son. But this is a mere conjecture, contradicted by the native records. We have observed in the history of Assyria that Semiramis was a Babylonian princess married to the Assyrian king, Vul-lush III., who reigned from B. C. 810 to B. C. 781. Nobonassar was followed on the Babylonian throne by NADIUS, who reigned only two years, from B. C. 733 to B. C. 731. Nadius is supposed to have been one of the independent Babylonian princes reduced to subjection by Tiglath-Pileser I. in his expedition into Babylonia. Nadius was succeeded by CHINZINUS and PORUS, who jointly reigned from B. C. 731 to B. C. 726. Their successor was ELULÆUS, identified with the prince of that name called King of Tyre by Menander—the Luliya of the cuneiform inscriptions; but Rawlinson considers this theory a mere conjecture and highly improbable.

MERODACH-BALADAN—the successor of Elulæus, and the son of Yakin, the prince who established himself in authority over Southern Babylonia, the ancient Chaldæa, and founded a capital city, naming it after himself Beth-Yakin, or Bit-Yakin—inherited the dominion of Yakin upon the death of the latter. Being forced to become tributary to the Assyrian king, Tiglath-Pileser II., he remained in comparative obscurity and quiet during the reigns of Tiglath-Pileser II. and Shalmaneser IV. of Assyria; but when Sargon usurped the Assyrian throne, B. C. 721, Merodach-Baladan established his sway over Babylonia, of which he was recognized as king. It was some time during his twelve years' reign over Babylon that Merodach-Baladan sent ambassadors to Hezekiah at Jerusalem to ascertain the particulars of the strange astronomical marvel, or miracle, accompanying the sickness and recovery of that king. Hezekiah exhibited all his treasures to these ambassadors. A coalition appears to have been formed against Assyria by Babylon, Susiana, the Aramæan tribes, Judah and Egypt. In B. C. 711 Sargon, King of Assyria, invaded Egypt and compelled its Ethiopian king, Sabaco, to sue for peace. In the following year, B. C. 710, Sargon led an army into Babylonia, defeated Merodach-Baladan and his Aramæan and Susianian allies in a great battle, and took Bit-Yakin, making Merodach-Baladan prisoner and gaining possession of all his treasures; whereupon Babylonia submitted to Sargon, who carried Merodach-Baladan captive to Assyria, and himself assumed the title of "King of Babylon."

But when Sargon died, B. C. 704, the Babylonians cast off the Assyrian yoke. A number of pretenders claimed the Babylonian crown. A son of Sargon and a brother of Sennacherib restored Assyrian supremacy for a short time, but the Babylonians again revolted. HAGISA reigned over Babylon about a month. Merodach-Baladan, escaping from his Assyrian captivity, murdered Hagisa and seized the Babylonian throne, of which he had been deprived seven years before. But Sennacherib, King of Assyria, Sargon's son and successor, led an army into Babylonia in B. C. 703, defeated Merodach-Baladan and drove him into exile, after a reign of six months, and annexed Babylonia to the Assyrian kingdom. Thenceforth, for seventy-eight years, until the revolt of Nabopolassar, B. C. 625, Babylonia, with a few short intervals, remained an Assyrian dependency. During this period the Assyrian monarchs governed Babylonia by means of viceroys, such as Belibus, Regibelus, Mesesimordachus, and Saos-duchinus, or directly and personally, as by Esar-haddon and by Asshur-bani-pal in his later years. During Sennacherib's reign there were two Babylonian revolts against Assyria, one headed by Merodach-Baladan in Chaldæa, and the other by Susub at Babylon. These were soon suppressed by Sennacherib, as related in the Assyrian history. While Asshurbani-pal was King of Assyria, his brother, Saül-Mugina, also called Sammughes, or Saos-duchinus, attempted to make himself independent, but was subdued and burned alive, as also stated in the history of Assyria. Thus ended the second period of Chaldæan. or Babylonian history—the period of Babylonian and Chaldæan subjection to Assyria. from Tiglathi-Nin's conquest in B. C. 1300 to Nabopolassar's successful revolt in B. C. 625.

We will now proceed to the history of the Babylonian Empire, first relating the circumstances of its foundation. When the Medes under their valiant king, Cyaxares, a second time crossed the Zagros range and attacked Nineveh from the east, the Susianians menaced the great capital from the south. In this extremity the last Assyrian king, Assshur-emid-ilin, or Saracus, divided his forces, retaining a portion under his own command for the defense of his capital against the Medes, and sending a portion under his general, Nabopolassar, or Nabupal-uzur, to Babylon to oppose the advance of the Susianians from the south. Taking advantage of the perilous straits of his sovereign, Nabopolassar resolved to betray him in order to obtain for himself an independent kingdom. He therefore negotiated an alliance with Cyaxares, the Median king, and obtained that king's daughter as a bride for his own son, Nebuchadnezzar. The united Median and Babylonian armies then besieged Nineveh, which was finally taken and destroyed, B. C. 625, as already related in the histories of Assyria and Media. In the division of the Assyrian Empire, which followed the fall of Nineveh, Cyaxares obtained Assyria proper and all Assyria's dependencies towards the north and north-west; while the traitor Nabopolassar received Babylonia, Chaldæa, Susiana, Upper Mesopotamia, Syria and Palestine. Thus arose the Babylonian Empire.

We know very little about the reign of NABOPOLASSAR. The Canon of Ptolemy informs us that he dated his accession from the year B. C. 625, and that his reign lasted twenty-one years, ending in B. C. 604. During most of this time Babylonian history is a blank. Babylon had no inclination to jeopardize her position at the head of an empire by aggression, and her peaceful attitude of course provoked no hostility from her neighbors. Media, bound by dynastic interests and by formal treaty, could be depended upon as a firm friend. Persia was too feeble, and Lydia too distant, to be formidable. Egypt, though hostile and powerful, was ruled by a sovereign whom misfortune and age prevented engaging in any distant military enterprise; so that as long as Psammetichus was living Babylon had comparatively nothing to fear from any quarter, and, in the language of the Jewish prophet Isaiah, could "give herself to pleasure and dwell carelessly."

It was only as the ally of Media that Babylon was obliged to exert herself during the first eighteen years of her empire, being bound by treaty to aid Cyaxares in his wars and conquests after the capture and destruction of Nineveh, the Babylonian contingents on these occasions being led either by Nabopolassar or by his son, the crown-prince Nebuchadnezzar. In a war between Media and Lydia, as the armies of these two hostile nations were about to engage in battle, an eclipse of the sun excited the superstitious fears of both, so that they were disposed to reconciliation. Thereupon the Babylonian monarch acted as peacemaker. Having discovered that Syennesis of Cilicia, the leading man of the Lydian side, was disposed to second his friendly offices, Nabopolassar proposed the holding of a peace conference. The result was that a treaty of peace and friendship, cemented by a royal intermarriage, was concluded between Media and Lydia; thus giving Western Asia almost half a century of peace, after almost perpetual warfare and devastation.

After this successful attempt at mediation, Nabopolassar returned to Babylon. He was prevented from ending his last years in peace by the warlike attitude of Neko, King of Egypt, the son and successor of Psammetichus, who sought to wrest Syria and Palestine from the Babylonian Empire. In B. C. 608 the Egyptian king led an army into Palestine, where the Jewish king Josiah, in fulfillment of his duty as vassal monarch to the King of Babylon, had assembled an army at Megiddo to oppose his further advance in the territories of Nabopolassar. Thereupon Neko sent an embassy to persuade Josiah that he had no hostile feelings toward the Jews, and claiming divine approval of his enterprise. But Josiah, loyal to his suzerain, remained firm in his opposition to the advance of the invaders; whereupon he was attacked and defeated at Megiddo, and fled mortally wounded to Jerusalem, where he died. Neko followed up his victory by advancing through Syria to the Euphrates, and extended his authority over the whole region from Egypt on the south-west to the "Great River" on the north-east. Returning three months later, Neko dethroned Jehoahaz, a younger son of Josiah, whom the Jewish people had made king, and bestowed the Jewish crown on Jehoiakim, his elder brother. During this time Neko besieged and took the Philistine city of Gaza.

Three years later, in B. C. 605, Nabopolassar, now venerable for his age, sent an army under his son, the crown-prince Nebuchadnezzar, against the conquering hosts of the Egyptian king. The Hittite city of Carchemish, on the right bank of the Euphrates, was then the key of Syria; and at this place Nebuchadnezzar thoroughly defeated and routed the Egyptians, who fled in dismay. Nebuchadnezzar rapidly reëstablished the Babylonian sway over Syria and Palestine, received the submission of Jehoiakim, King of Judah, restored the frontier line, and according to Berosus invaded Egypt itself. But upon receiving news from Babylon of his father's death, Nebuchadnezzar hastily concluded a peace with Neko, and speedily returned to his capital, in fear of a disputed succession.

NEBUCHADNEZZAR had no cause for his fears, as the priests had assumed control of affairs in his absence, and the Chief Priest, or Head of the Order, had kept the throne vacant for him until his return, while no pretender disputed his claims. Nebuchadnezzar was the great monarch of the Babylonian Empire, which continued but eighty-seven years, from B. C. 625 to B. C. 538, and which for almost half that period was ruled by him. The military glory of this empire is mostly attributable to this renowned king, whose character and genius gave it the constructive enterprise which was its essential characteristic. To Nebuchadnezzar the prominent place of the Babylonians in history is almost wholly due. Besides being an able general, Nebuchadnezzar was one of the greatest builders of antiquity.

Our knowledge of Nebuchadnezzar's wars is almost entirely derived from the Old Testament. Therefore we are only informed of his wars in Palestine and its immediate vicinity, as related by the Jewish writers. We only possess a full account of his wars with the Jews, and some knowledge of his campaigns against Egypt and Phœnicia, though Berosus says he warred against the Arabs and conquered a part of their country.

A few years after Nebuchadnezzar's victory over Neko, King of Egypt, troubles once more distracted Syria. Tyre headed a rebellion in Phœnicia, while Jehoiakim, the Jewish king, relying upon the promised aid of the Egyptian monarch, renounced his allegiance to his Babylonian suzerain. Thereupon Nebuchadnezzar, in his seventh year, B. C. 598, led into Palestine an expedition, consisting of his own subjects and his Median allies. Polyhistor says this army numbered 10,000 chariots, 120,000 cavalry, and 180,000 infantry. Having invested Tyre and found that city too strong to assail with success, Nebuchadnezzar left a part to continue the siege, while he himself marched against Jerusalem. On the approach of the Babylonian king, Jehoiakim submitted, as he was not supported by his Egyptian allies; but Nebuchadnezzar put him to death, in punishment for his rebellion, and treated his body with indignity. Says the prophet Jeremiah: "He shall be buried with the burial of an ass, drawn and cast forth beyond the gates of Jerusalem," and again, "His dead body shall be cast out in the day to the heat and in the night to the frost."

Nebuchadnezzar first placed Jehoiachin, the son of the unfortunate Jehoiakim, upon the Jewish throne. The new Jewish king, a mere youth, was deposed three months later by the suspicious Nebuchadnezzar, and carried a captive to Babylon; while his uncle, Zedekiah, a brother of Jehoiakim and Jehoahaz, was placed upon the Jewish throne. The island city of Tyre, in the meantime, withstood a siege of thirteen years against the forces of Nebuchadnezzar; during which Jerusalem perished in a final effort for independence.

Zedekiah, King of Judah, remained a faithful vassal of the Babylonian king for eight years, after which he sought an alliance with Uaphris, King of Egypt,—the Apries of Herodotus—in order to strike for independence. Says the prophet Ezekiel, in speaking of Zedekiah on this occasion: "He rebelled against him in sending his ambassadors into Egypt, that they might give him horses and much people." The Egyptian king looked with favor upon the overture of Zedekiah, who at once revolted from Babylon, and prepared to defend himself with vigor. As this was the fourth time the feeble Jewish kingdom revolted against him, Nebuchadnezzar resolved to crush it by a decisive blow. "He and all his host" came against Jerusalem, and, after conquering and pillaging the open country, "built forts" and laid siege to the city. Uaphris led an army from Egypt to the relief of his beleaguered ally, whereupon the Babylonian army raised the siege and took the field against this new foe. Josephus says that the Egyptians were defeated in battle, but according to the prophet Jeremiah they avoided an engagement by retreating to their own land. In either case the attempted relief of the Jewish capital failed. After a short interval the siege was renewed, the city was completely blockaded, and after a siege and investment of eighteen months Jerusalem was taken by the Babylonians, B. C. 586. Before the city fell, Nebuchadnezzar withdrew in person to press the siege of Tyre, which, if it fell after its thirteen years' siege, must have fallen the year after the capture of Jerusalem, B. C. 585.

By the capture of Jerusalem and Tyre, the Babylonian king secured the quiet possession of Palestine and Phœnicia. Four years after the fall of Tyre, according to Josephus, Nebuchadnezzar invaded Egypt, put its king, Uaphris, the friend and ally of Zedekiah, to death, and bestowed the Egyptian crown upon a creature of his own, B. C. 581. Herodotus, however, says that Uaphris was put to death by a rebellious subject, and he is known to have reigned as late as B. C. 569. But Nebuchadnezzar's second invasion of Egypt, B. C. 570, ended in the deposition of Uaphris, whose successor, Amasis, was a mere vassal of the Babylonian king.

Thus Nebuchadnezzar defeated Neko, recovered Syria, suppressed the revolt of Judah, reduced Tyre and humbled Egypt. Megasthenes says that he conquered North Africa, from which he invaded Spain and subdued the Iberians, colonizing his Iberian captives on the shores of the Euxine sea in the region between Armenia and the Caucasus. Nebuchadnezzar was thus represented as reigning over an empire extending from the Atlantic ocean on the west to the Caspian sea on the east, and from the Caucasus on the north-east to the great Sahara on the south-west.

Nebuchadnezzar's military successes gave him that great command of "naked human strength" by which he was enabled to prosecute his great projects for beautifying and benefiting his kingdom without unnecessarily oppressing his own people. From the start he carried out the Assyrian system of forcible deportation of the entire populations of conquered lands, and colonized them in remote portions of his dominions. Multitudes of captives taken in his wars—Jews, Egyptians, Phœnicians, Syrians, Ammonites, Moabites and others—were settled in different parts of Mesopotamia, principally about Babylon. By the forced labor of these captives the great works of Nebuchadnezzar, which were the chief glory of the Babylonian Empire, were erected.

Abydenus and Eusebius say that Nebuchadnezzar built the great wall of Babylon, seventy-five feet high, and thirty-two feet wide, with a circumference of three hundred and sixty-five stadia. This wall was of solid brick masonry, the Babylonian bricks being about a foot square and from three to four inches thick. Nebuchadnezzar, in the Standard Inscription, only claims to have repaired the old wall of the city. He erected a splendid new palace in the vicinity of the old royal residence. He constructed the famous "Hanging Gardens" to delight his Median wife, Amyitis, the daughter of Cyaxares. He repaired and beautified the great temple of Bel at Babylon; and all the inscribed bricks thus far discovered in the Babil mound bear Nebuchadnezzar's legend. He dug the immense reservoir at Sippara, which was said to have been one hundred and forty miles in circumference, and one hundred and eighty feet deep, providing it with flood-gates, through which its waters might be drawn off for purposes of irrigation. He constructed many canals, among which was the *Nahr Malcha*, or "Royal River," a wide and deep channel connecting the Euphrates and the Tigris. He built quays and breakwaters along the shores of the Persian Gulf, and founded the city of Diridotis, or Teredon, near that gulf.

According to Nebuchadnezzar's own inscriptions, or to existing remains, this renowned Babylonian monarch erected the Birs-i-Nimrud, or great temple of Nebo, at Borsippa; constructed a vast reservoir in Babylon itself, called the *Yapur-Shapu*, and a brick embankment along the course of the Tigris, near Bagdad, the bricks of which bear his name and have remained undisturbed; and built many temples, walls and other public buildings at Cutha, Sippara, Borsippa, Babylon, Chilmad, Bit-Digla and other places. This indefatigable king either rebuilt or repaired nearly all the Babylonian cities and temples. No less than a hundred sites in the vicinity of Babylon testify, by inscribed bricks bearing his legend, to his wonderful activity and energy.

Nebuchadnezzar is also believed to have constructed the canal called by the Arabs the *Kerek Saideh*, or canal of Saideh, and ascribed by them to a wife of Nebuchadnezzar. This canal, four hundred miles long, extended from Hit, on the Euphrates, along the extreme western edge of the alluvium close to the Arabian frontier, to the head of the Bubian creek, about twenty miles west of the Shat-el-Arab. Traces of this canal yet remaining attest the magnitude of this great work. The Pallacopas, or canal of Opa, (Palga Opa), which flowed from the Euphrates at Sippara (now Mosaib) to a great lake in the vicinity of Borsippa, whence the neighboring lands were irrigated, is also believed to have been constructed by this great monarch. It was an old canal, out of repair, in the time of Alexander the Great; and is called the *Nahr Abba* by the Arabs, who consider it the oldest canal in the country.

The Old Testament gives us some knowledge of Nebuchadnezzar's private life and personal character. The Book of Daniel represents the great monarch at the head of a most magnificent court; surrounded with "princes, governors, captains, judges, treasurers, councilors, and sheriffs;" waited upon by carefully-chosen eunuchs, "well-favored" and educated with care; attended, at his desire, by a host of astrologers and other "wise men," who sought to reveal to him the divine will. He was an absolute monarch, having the lives and properties of his subjects, from the highest to the lowest, at his disposal; and dispensing all offices at his pleasure. He could elevate a foreigner to a second place in the kingdom, and even place him over the whole priesthood. His immense wealth is proven by the fact that he made an image or obelisk of pure gold, ninety feet high and nine feet wide. He wavered in his religion, sometimes acknowledging the Jehovah of the Jews as the only real deity, sometimes relapsing into the idolatrous Babylonian polytheism, and forcing his subjects to do the same. But his polytheism was characterized by a special devotion to a particular deity, whom he designates emphatically as "his god." Nebuchadnezzar's inscriptions clearly show that his favorite god was Merodach.

Nebuchadnezzar was hasty and violent in temper, but not obstinate. His fierce resolves were taken suddenly and repented of quickly. He could occasionally give way to outbursts of gratitude and devotion. He was as vainglorious as Orientals generally, but could bow in humiliation before the divine castigation. He often showed a spirit of sincere piety, self-condemnation and self-abasement, as the following from the Book of Daniel clearly proves: "I blessed the Most High, and I praised and honored Him that liveth forever, Whose dominion is an everlasting dominion, and His kingdom is from generation to generation; and all the inhabitants of the earth are reputed as nothing, and He doeth according to His will in the army of heaven, and among the inhabitants of the earth; and none can stay His hand, or say unto Him, What doest Thou? Now I, Nebuchadnezzar, praise and extol and honor the King of heaven, Whose works are truth, and His ways judgment; and those that walk in pride He is able to abase."

Another Jewish prophet, Jeremiah, gives a darker shade to the character of the illustrious Babylonian monarch. This writer tells us that Nebuchadnezzar executed Jehoiakim and treated his body with indignity, murdered Zedekiah's sons before his eyes, put out the eyes of Zedekiah himself, and kept Zedekiah and Jehoiachin in prolonged imprisonment. These acts of barbarous cruelty imply in the great Babylonian king a disposition as ferocious as that of Sargon or Asshur-bani-pal.

Berosus informs us that Nebuchadnezzar was devotedly attached to his Median wife, Amyitis, whom his father had selected for him for reasons of state. Solely to please her, he erected the celebrated "Hanging Gardens" at Babylon. The rocks and trees of this delightful artificial Paradise, where art strove to rival nature, were designed to imitate the beautiful mountain scenery of Media.

In his later days Nebuchadnezzar dreamed a strange dream, the meaning of which was interpreted to him by the Jewish prophet Daniel, who, though carried into the Babylonian captivity with his nation, had arrived at high honors under the Babylonian king. Daniel told the king that his dream portended that he would for seven years be a victim to a strange and rare kind of madness. A victim to this malady, called *Lycanthropy*, imagines himself a beast, does not talk, rejects the usual human food, and sometimes loses the erect attitude and walks on hands and feet. Within a year of the warning, Nebuchadnezzar was stricken in the very hour in which he had exclaimed in his pride: "Is not this great Babylon, that I have built for the house of the kingdom by the might of my power, and for the honor of my majesty!" The great monarch became a helpless and wretched madman. He lived in the open air day and night, "and did eat grass as oxen," and went naked "till his hairs were grown like eagles' feathers, and his nails like birds' claws." After suffering thus for seven years, Nebuchadnezzar regained his reason, and his recovery was hailed with rejoicing by his court. His councilors and lords greeted his presence. He again resumed the government of his empire, issued his proclamations, and discharged all his royal duties. He had now reached old age, "but 'the glory of his kingdom,' his 'honor and brightness' returned;" "his last days were as brilliant as his first; his sun set in an unclouded sky, shorn of none of the rays that had given splendor to its noonday." Nebuchadnezzar died in B. C. 561, in the forty-fourth year of his reign, when almost eighty years old.

Nebuchadnezzar was succeeded by his son EVIL-MERODACH, of whose short reign of two years but very little is known. He seemed disposed to favor the Jews. Upon his accession, he released Jehoiachin from his thirty-five years' imprisonment, and treated him with kindness and respect, recognizing his royal rank and giving him precedence over all the captive kings residing at Babylon. Josephus says that he actually accepted Jehoiachin as one of his most intimate friends. After Evil-Merodach had occupied the Babylonian throne but two years he was accused of lawlessness and intemperance, a conspiracy was formed against him, his own brother-in-law, Neriglissar, heading the malcontents; and Evil-Merodach lost both crown and life, B. C. 559.

NERIGLISSAR was at once recognized as King of Babylon. His real name, as seen on his bricks, was Nergal-sar-uzur; and he is believed to have been the "Nergal-sharezer, Rag-Mag," mentioned by the Jewish prophet Jeremiah, and who held an important office among the Babylonian nobles left to press the siege of Jerusalem when Nebuchadnezzar retired to Riblah. It is known that the king bore the office of Rag-Mag, and that title is also upon his bricks. Neriglissar styled himself the son of Bel-sumiskun, "king of Babylon"—a sovereign whose name is not mentioned by the Canon of Ptolemy, but who was perhaps a chieftain who took the royal title during the troubles preceding the fall of the Assyrian Empire. Neriglissar reigned only three years and four months, and was engaged chiefly in the erection of the Western Palace at Babylon, an immense edifice at one corner of the fortified enclosure, directly opposite the old palace, and abutting on the Euphrates. Diodorus described this structure as most magnificent, being elaborately ornamented with painting and sculpture in the best style of Babylonian art, though it may have been smaller than the ancient royal residence on the opposite side of the river.

Neriglissar died B. C. 556, after the short reign mentioned, and was succeeded by his son, LABOROSOARCHOD, so called by Berosus and the Canon of Ptolemy. This monarch, a mere youth, only wore the Babylonian crown a few months, when he was accused of showing many signs of a bad disposition, and was deposed and put to death, B. C. 555; and with him ended the dynasty of Nabopolassar, which had occupied the Babylonian throne seventy years, from B. C. 625 to B. C. 555.

NABONADIUS, so called by the Canon of Ptolemy, and whom the conspirators chose from among their own number to succeed Laborosoarchod, was not related to his predecessor. He was called Nabonnedus by Berosus. Thus Nabonadius, like Neriglissar, was a usurper; and, like his father, held the important office of Rag-Mag, as on his bricks and cylinders he styled himself "Nabonidus, the son of Nabu- * * -dirba, the Rag-Mag." To secure his usurped throne, Nabonadius married a princess of the royal house of Nabopolassar.

Soon after his accession, in B. C. 555, Nabonadius received an embassy from the remote North-west. Three years before, in B. C. 558—during the reign of Neriglissar at Babylon—Cyrus the Great founded the Medo-Persian Empire by deposing the Median king Astyages and transferring the supremacy of the Aryan race from the Medes to the Persians. Cyrus at once entered upon a career of conquest which eventually brought all of Western Asia under the Medo-Persian dominion.

Fearing the rising power of Persia in the East, Lydian ambassadors were sent to Babylon in B. C. 555, the very year in which Nabonadius ascended the Babylonian throne, proposing an alliance against the new power which threatened the existence of the other Oriental monarchies of the time. Nabonadius decided to unite in the proposed offensive and defensive alliance with Lydia and Egypt to check the growing power of his new eastern neighbor.

Aware that he thus provoked the hostility of a powerful foe by this decisive course, and not knowing how soon he might be obliged to defend his kingdom against the whole force of Persia, Nabonadius at once began to strengthen Babylon. Herodotus ascribed these defensive works to Nitocris, a queen whom he calls the mother of Nabonadius; but Berosus says that they were erected by Nabonadius himself. These works consisted partly of defenses within the city, intended to secure it against an enemy who should enter it by the river, partly of hydraulic works designed to obstruct the advance of an army by the usual route. The river had thus far flowed in its natural channel through the middle of the city; but Nabonadius confined the stream by a brick embankment extended the whole way along both banks, after which he erected on the top of the embankment a high wall, pierced at intervals by gateways, in which were set gates of bronze. He also con-

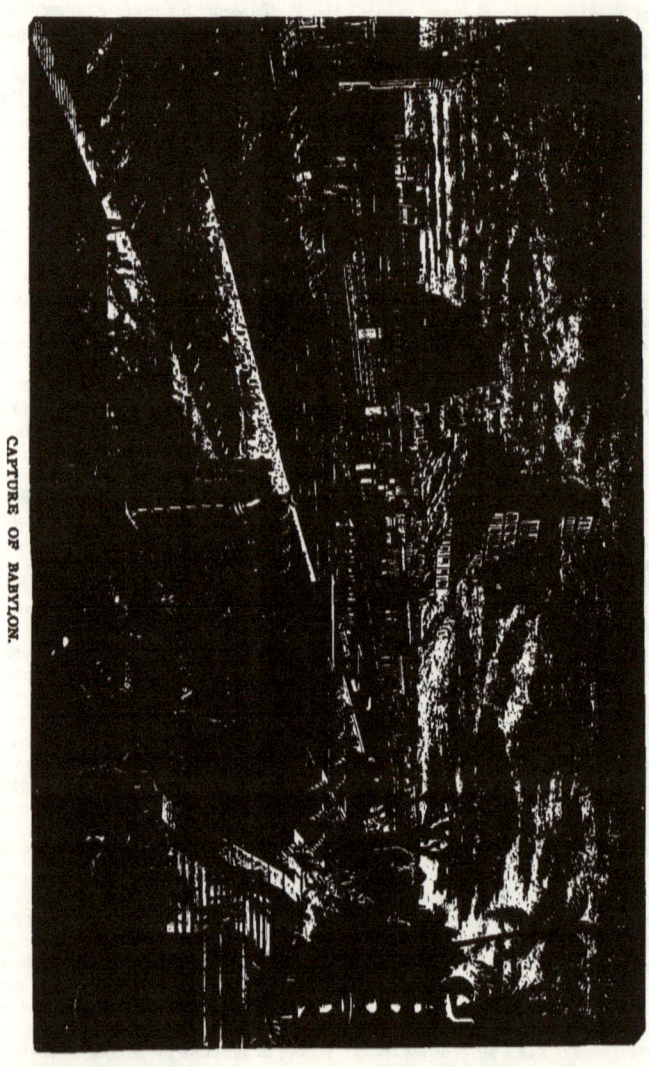

CAPTURE OF BABYLON.

structed cuttings, reservoirs and sluices at some distance from Babylon towards the north, designed to obstruct the march of a hostile army. Xenophon likewise spoke of a rampart—known as the "Median Wall"—extending across the tract between the two rivers—a vast barrier a hundred feet high and twenty feet thick—intended to be insurmountable by an unskillful enemy, but this is doubted by modern writers.

Nabonadius was permitted to complete his fortification of Babylon unmolested; but his rash ally, Crœsus, the wealthy King of Lydia, rushed impetuously into a war with Persia without asking the assistance of the Babylonian monarch. Cyrus promptly attacked Crœsus by invading Lydia, defeated him in the battle of Pteria, and besieged and captured Sardis, the Lydian capital, before Nabonadius could render his impulsive ally any aid. For fourteen years Babylon remained unmenaced by the Persian king.

Finally, in B. C. 559, Nabonadius received tidings that Cyrus the Great was marching from Ecbatana, the Median capital, in the direction of Babylon; but as his defenses were completed and the city amply provisioned, the Babylonian monarch felt perfectly secure behind the walls of his capital. Herodotus says that the Persian invader paused half-way between Ecbatana and Babylon, because one of the sacred white horses which drew the chariot of Ormazd had been drowned in crossing a river. Declaring that he would punish the insolent stream, Cyrus employed his soldiers during the whole summer and autumn of B. C. 539 in dispersing the waters of the stream into three hundred and sixty channels.

Cyrus renewed his march upon Babylon in the spring of B. C. 538, crossing the Tigris without opposition and soon appearing before Babylon. The Babylonian army under Nabonadius himself was here drawn up to oppose him. In the battle which ensued the Babylonian king was thoroughly defeated, the greater part of his army seeking refuge inside the walls of the capital, while he himself with a small body of troops fled for safety into the important city of Borsippa, a short distance south-west from Babylon.

In the meantime, the Babylonian crown-prince, Belshazzar, or Bel-shar-uzur, the son of Nabonadius, and the grandson of the illustrious Nebuchadnezzar—supported by the counsels of his mother and the officers of the court—for a time successfully resisted all the Persian assaults, so that Cyrus, almost reduced to despair, resorted to a stratagem whose failure might have cost him dear. Leaving a corps of observation behind him, Cyrus, with the bulk of his army, marched up the course of the Euphrates for some distance, and dug a new channel, or channels, from the river, by means of which a part of its water could be drawn off. Cyrus awaited the arrival of a certain festival at Babylon, when the entire Babylonian population would be engaged in drinking and revelry. The festival on this occasion was held with more than usual pomp and magnificence, and Belshazzar gave himself up entirely to the delights of the season, entertaining a thousand dignitaries in his palace. The rest of the population was occupied in feasting and dancing; and in the midst of drunken riot and mad excitement the siege of the city was wholly forgotten, and the usual precautions were neglected. The Babylonians abandoned themselves for the night to orgies characterized by a strange mingling of religious frenzy and drunken excess.

While this was going on inside the city during this eventful night, the Persians were silently watching outside at the two points where the Euphrates entered and left the walls. They anxiously and cautiously watched the gradual sinking of the river-bed, to discover if their silent movements would be observed and cause alarm. Had they entered the river channel to find the river-walls manned and the river-gates locked fast they would have been caught in a trap. Flanked on both sides by an enemy they could neither see nor reach they would have been caught at a terrible disadvantage. In such a case they would have been entirely cut to pieces without being able to make any effectual resistance, or to escape from their perilous position. But as they observed no signs of alarm, but only the shouts of riotous revelry, on the part of the unsuspecting populace, the Persians grew bolder, and, when the revelry was at its height, emerged from the deep river-bed and seized the two undefended gateways. The frightened Babylonians at once raised a war-shout and spread the alarm. Swift runners hurried off to "show the King of Babylon that his city was taken at one end;" so says the Book of Jeremiah. In the darkness and confusion of the night a frightful massacre occurred, says Xenophon. The drunken revelers were unable to resist. Belshazzar, completely surprised and utterly helpless "at the awful handwriting upon the wall," which appeared at this time, was warned of his danger when too late, and could offer no check to the progress of the assailants, who had the paralyzed populace completely at their mercy. A band of Persians forced their way into the royal palace and slew the astonished Belshazzar on the scene of his sacrilegious revelry. Such is the testimony of Herodotus and Xenophon, of Daniel and Jeremiah. Says the Book of Daniel: "In that night was Belshazzar slain." The triumphant Persians destroyed right and left with fire and sword. The dawn found Cyrus undisputed master of the mighty Babylon.

After ordering the fortifications of Babylon to be dismantled, Cyrus marched against Nabonadius at Borsippa; but, seeing the folly of resistance, the unfortunate Nabonadius surrendered himself upon the approach of his triumphant foe. Cyrus kindly treated the captive king, sparing his life, and, according to Abydenus, conferring on him the government of the important province of Carmania.

Thus fell the mighty Babylonian Empire, after an existence of eighty-seven years, from B. C. 625 to B. C. 538. For half a century did Babylon, along with Media and Lydia, control the destinies of Western Asia. The Babylonian dominions then became a part of the great Medo-Persian Empire, and the great city which had played so important a part in Oriental history for centuries became the winter capital of the Medo-Persian kings.

THE KASR, BABYLON.

ANCIENT HISTORY.—BABYLONIA.

KINGS OF BABYLON.

B. C.	KINGS.	CONTEMPORARY KINGS OF ASSYRIA.	REMARKABLE EVENTS.
1300	Assyrian Dynasty	Tiglathi-Nin I.	The Assyrians conquer Babylon.
	* * *	Bel-kudur-uzur. Nin-pala-zira. Asshur-dayan I. Mutaggil-Nebo.	
1150	NEBUCHADNEZZAR I.	Asshur-ris-ilim	Wars between Assyria and Babylon.
1130	MERODACH-IDDIN-AKHI	Tiglath-Pileser I.	
1110	MERODACH-SHAPIK-ZIRI	Asshur-bil-kala	
	* * *	Shamas-Vul I.	
	TSIBIR (Deboras)	Asshur-Mazur	Babylon in alliance with Egypt. Takes territory from Assyria.
	* * *	Asshur-dayan II. Vul-lush II. Tiglathi-Nin II.	
880		Asshur-izir-pal	Assyria recovers her lost territory.
850	MERODACH-SUM-ADIN	Shalmaneser II.	Civil war in Babylon. Assyria helps the legitimate king.
820	MERODACH-BELATZU-IKBI	Shamas-Vul II. Vul-lush III. Shalmaneser III. Asshur-dayan III.	Babylon conquered. Passes under Assyria.
775	PUL (?)		
752		Asshur-lush.	
747	NABONASSAR		Babylon reëstablishes her independence.
745		Tiglath-Pileser II.	
733	NADIUS		
731	CHINZINUS and PORUS		
726	ELULÆUS	Shalmaneser IV.	
721	MERODACH-BALADAN	Sargon.	
713(?)			Embassy of Merodach-Baladan to Hezekiah.
709	ARCEANUS (Sargon)		Babylou conquered by Sargon.
704	Interregnum	Sennacherib	Babylon revolts.
703	{ HAGISA { MERODACH-BALADAN (restored) }		Sennacherib conquers Babylon.
702	BELIBUS (viceroy)		
699	ASSARANADIUS (viceroy)		Babylon revolts. Revolt put down.
696(?)	SUSUB		
694(?)			Ditto.
693	REGIBELUS (viceroy)		
692	MESESIMORDACHUS (viceroy)		Troubles in Babylon. Interregnum of eight years, coinciding with last eight years of Sennacherib.
688	Interregnum		
680	ESAR-HADDON	Esar-haddon	Babylon recovered by Esar-haddon.
667	SAOS-DUCHINUS (viceroy)	Asshur-bani-pal	Babylon revolts and again returns to allegiance.
647	CINNELADANUS (or Asshur-bani-pal)		
626	NEBO-SUM-ISKUN (?)	Asshur-emid-ilin.	
625	NABOPOLASSAR		Assyrian Empire destroyed.
605	NEBUCHADNEZZAR		Nebuchadnezzar carries the Jews into captivity.
561	EVIL-MERODACH		
559	NERIGLISSAR		
556	LABOROSOARCHOD		
555	NABONADIUS		
538	{ Conquest of Babylon by Cyrus { the Great of Persia. }		Babylon taken by Cyrus the Great of Persia.

SECTION III.—BABYLONIAN CIVILIZATION.

AYS Professor Rawlinson: "In its general character the Babylonian Empire was little more than a reproduction of the Assyrian. The same loose organization of the provinces under native kings rather than satraps almost universally prevailed, with the same duties on the part of suzerain and subjects, and the same results of ever-recurring revolt and re-conquest. Similar means were employed under both empires to check and discourage rebellion—mutilations and executions of chiefs, pillage of the rebellious region, and wholesale deportation of its population. Babylon, equally with Assyria, failed to win the affections of the subject nations, and, as a natural result, received no help from them in her hour of need. Her system was to exhaust and oppress the conquered races for the supposed benefit of the conquerors, and to impoverish the provinces for the adornment and enrichment of the capital. The wisest of her monarchs thought it enough to construct works of public utility in Babylonia proper, leaving the dependent countries to themselves, and doing nothing to develop their resources. This selfish system was, like most selfishness, short-sighted; it alienated those whom it would have been true policy to conciliate and win. When the time of peril came, the subject nations were no source of strength to the menaced empire. On the contrary, it would seem that some even turned against her and made common cause with the assailants.

"Babylonian civilization differed in many respects from Assyrian, to which however it approached more nearly than to any other known type. Its advantages over Assyrian were in its greater originality, its superior literary character, and its comparative width and flexibility. Babylonia seems to have been the source from which Assyria drew her learning, such as it was, her architecture, the main ideas of her mimetic art, her religious notions, her legal forms, and a vast number of her customs and usages. But Babylonia herself, so far as we know, drew her stores from no foreign country. Hers was apparently the genius which excogitated an alphabet—worked out the simpler problems of arithmetic—invented implements for measuring the lapse of time—conceived the idea of raising enormous structures with the poorest of all materials, clay—discovered the art of polishing, boring, and engraving gems—reproduced with truthfulness the outlines of human and animal forms—attained to high perfection in textile fabrics—studied with success the motions of the heavenly bodies —conceived of grammar as a science—elaborated a system of law—saw the value of an exact chronology—in almost every branch of science made a beginning, thus rendering it comparatively easy for other nations to proceed with the superstructure. To Babylonia, far more than to Egypt, we owe the art and learning of the Greeks. It was from the East, not from Egypt, that Greece derived her architecture, her sculpture, her science, her philosophy, her mathematical knowledge—in a word, her intellectual life. And Babylon was the source to which the entire stream of Eastern civilization may be traced. It is scarcely too much to say that, but for Babylon, real civilization might not even yet have dawned upon the earth. Mankind might never have advanced beyond that spurious and false form of it which in Egypt, India, China, Japan, Mexico, and Peru, contented the aspirations of the species."

The later Babylonians were a mixed race, as were the early Chaldæans, from whom they were mainly descended. The Chaldæans of the First Empire were chiefly a mixed Hamitic, or Cushite, and Turanian race, with a slight intermingling of Semitic and Aryan elements. But the Babylonians of the later period—called Chaldæans by the Hebrew prophets—were still more of a composite race, on account of the colonization of foreigners in Babylonia in accordance with the policy of the Assyrian kings, and because of the influence exerted upon them by their Assyrian conquerors. The conquest of Chaldæa by the Arabian dynasty B. C. 1546, and the Assyrian conquest of the same country B. C. 1300, establishing an Assyrian royal race upon the Chaldæan throne, tended to the fusion of new Semitic elements with the old Chaldæan population, as both the Arabs and the Assyrians were prominent branches of the Semitic race.

Semitic dynasties reigning in Chaldæa would naturally tend to the introduction of new Semitic blood into that old land, and bring along Semitic customs and ideas, and causing the old Turano-Cushite language of ancient Chaldæa to give way to a Semitic tongue. The original Chaldæan population gradually became intermingled with the new Semitic settlers, thus tending to the production of a nation composed about equally of Semitic, Turanian and Cushite, or Hamitic elements. The colonizations of the Sargonid dynasty brought, in addition, small proportions of other foreign elements, so that the later Babylonians could more appropriately be called a "mingled people" than any other ancient nation of Western Asia. By the time of the Later Empire the Babylonians had become thoroughly Semitized, as the vitality and energy of the Semitic elements fused in the population predominated over the original Cushite and Turanian elements; so that the later Babylonians were scarcely distinguishable from their northern neighbors, the Assyrians. The Greek writers seem to have regarded the Assyrians and Babylonians as one and the same race of people, and as having a common civilization.

The Babylonian cylinders and three or four representations by Babylonian artists give us some scant idea of the physical characteristics of this renowned ancient people. Among these remains is the representation of a Babylonian king, believed to be Merodach-iddin-ahki, on a black stone in the British Museum; also representations of the warrior and the priest in the tablet from Sir-Pal-i-Zohab, the man accompanying the Babylonian hound, and some imperfect figures on a frieze. A few Assyrian bas-reliefs represent Assyrian campaigns in Babylonia. The Babylonian cylinders represent the Babylonians as of far slighter and sparer physical frames than the Assyrians; but the Assyrian sculptures show the Babylonians as having bodily forms as brawny and massive as their northern neighbors, while the features of the two peoples were very nearly alike. The Assyrian sculptures represent the physiognomy of the Babylonians as distinguished by a low and straight but somewhat depressed forehead, full lips, and a well-marked, rounded chin. The few remaining Babylonian sculptures sustain the correctness of the Assyrian, but represent the eye as larger and less almond-shaped, the nose as shorter and more depressed, and the general expression of the countenance as more common-place. These differences are to be ascribed to the influence exerted upon the physical form of the race by the primitive Cushite Chaldæan element. Herodotus states that the Babylonians wore their hair long, and this statement is sustained by the Babylonian sculptures. These sculptures commonly represent the hair as forming a single stiff and heavy curl at the back of the head, but sometimes they give it the form of long flowing locks depending over the back, or over the back and shoulders, extending almost to the waist. Sometimes we find types closely resembling the Assyrian, the hair forming a round mass behind the head, on which there appears to have been sometimes a slight wave. The style mentioned by Herodotus was the national fashion, and is represented by the three usual modes. The round mass was an Assyrian style, aped by the Babylonians during their subjection to Assyria. The Assyrian sculptures represent the hair of the Babylonians as reaching below the shoulders, and as worn smooth on the top of the head and

CIVILIZATION.

depending from the ears to the shoulders in many large, smooth, heavy curls.

The Babylonians are likewise often represented with a large beard, usually longer than the Assyrian, and reaching almost down to the waist. Sometimes it curls crisply upon the face, but below the chin it depends over the breast in long straight locks, while in other cases it droops perpendicularly from the cheeks and the lower lip; but here the Assyrian sculptures represent the Babylonian beard as little longer than the Assyrian. Often there is no beard, as in the case of the priests.

The Assyrian sculptures also represent the Babylonian women as tall and large-limbed, with the Assyrian physiognomy, and with not very abundant hair; but the Babylonian cylinders make the hair appear long and prominent, while the physical forms are as spare and meagre as those of the male sex.

It is evident that altogether the physical types of the Assyrians and Babylonians were very nearly alike, though the Babylonians had a somewhat sparer form, longer and more flowing hair, less strong and stern features, and a darker complexion. The last characteristic is to be attributed partly to the infusion of Ethiopian elements in the population, and partly to their more tropical location, Babylonia being four degrees farther south than Assyria. The Cha'ab Arabs, who now occupy the southern parts of the ancient Babylonia, are almost black; while the "black Syrians," mentioned by Strabo, were probably the Babylonians.

The Babylonians were distinguished for their intellectual ability. They inherited the scientific lore of their predecessors, the early Chaldæans, whose astronomical and mathematical knowledge they not only retained, but advanced and enlarged by their exertions. The fame of their "wisdom and learning" is recorded by the Jewish prophets. In alluding to them, Isaiah said: "Thy wisdom and thy knowledge, it hath perverted thee." Says Jeremiah: "A sword is upon the Chaldæans, saith the Lord, and upon the inhabitants of Babylon, and upon her princes, and upon her wise men." Daniel alludes to "the learning and the tongue of the Chaldæans." Herodotus mentions their useful inventions, and Aristotle was indebted to them for scientific data. They were celebrated for their observations of astronomical phenomena, and their careful records of these observations. They were also famed as mathematicians. But unfortunately their astronomy was corrupted by astrology; and they professed to cast nativities, interpret dreams, and foretell future occurrences by means of the stars, thus tinging their astronomy with a mystic and unscientific element; though there were always some who confined themselves to pure science and repudiated all astrological pretensions.

The Babylonians were also a very enterprising people. Their active spirit led them to engage extensively in manufactures and commerce by sea and land. The same commercial spirit which so distinguished the ancient Phœnicians, and which has made the modern Jews such successful merchants, characterized the Semitized Babylonians, whose land the Jewish prophet Ezekiel called "a land of traffic," and whose chief city Isaiah described as "a city of merchants." The trading spirit of the Babylonians developed in them the opposite vices of avarice and fondness for luxury. They "coveted with an evil covetousness," as we are informed by the Jewish writers Habakkuk and Jeremiah. The "shameful custom" which Herodotus relates, requiring of every Babylonian woman, rich or poor, high-born or humble, prostitution as a religious duty in the great temple of Beltis at Babylon once in her life, was probably dictated by this spirit of greed, for the purpose of attracting strangers to the capital; as was also the custom of selling the marriageable virgins at public auction, which Herodotus also mentions. Quintus Curtius, the Roman writer, also says that the avarice of husbands and parents induced them to sell the virtue of their wives and daughters to strangers.

Both sacred and profane writers continu-

1—18.—U. H.

ally dwell upon the luxury of the Babylonians. We are informed by Isaiah that the "daughter of the Chaldæans" was "tender and delicate," "given to pleasures," disposed to "dwell carelessly." Ezekiel tells us that her young men made themselves "as princes to look at—exceeding in dyed attire upon their heads." Nicolas of Damascus relates that these young men painted their faces, wore ear-rings, and dressed in robes of rich and soft material. Polygamy prevailed extensively. The pleasures of the table were indulged in to excess, and drunkenness was a general vice. Rich unguents, so celebrated by Posidonius, were likewise invented. The tables were loaded with gold and silver plate, according to Nicolas of Damascus. In short, the Babylonians utterly abandoned themselves to self-indulgence and luxurious living.

They nevertheless were always brave and skillful in war, and in the height of their glory they were one of the most formidable of the Oriental nations. The Jewish prophet Habakkuk speaks of them as "the Chaldæans, that bitter and hasty nation," and also as "terrible and dreadful—their horses' hoofs swifter than the leopard's, and more fierce than the evening wolves." Isaiah says that they "smote the people in wrath with a continual stroke," and that they "made the earth to tremble, and did shake kingdoms." In their great enterprises they swept everything before them with irresistible force, in spite of all opposition, and unmoved by the calls of mercy. Centuries of warfare with the well-armed and well-disciplined Assyrians made the Babylonians worthy successors of the nation which had so long held them in subjection, so far as the warlike virtues of energy, valor and military skill are concerned. They extended their conquests from the Persian Gulf on the east to the Nile on the west. Their invincible hosts of sturdy warriors speedily crushed all resistance and rapidly established the Babylonian dominion, fully deserving the title of "the hammer of the whole earth," given them by the prophet Jeremiah.

The Babylonians stained their triumphs in war with useless violence and with the usual Oriental outrages. The Assyrian policy of wholesale deportation of conquered nations was practiced by them, regardless of the sufferings which resulted in consequence. Such needless and inexcusable atrocities as the mutilation of captives, the long imprisonments, the massacre of non-combatants, the execution of children before the eyes of their fathers, disgraced the military annals of the Babylonians, and exasperated more than they terrified the subjugated nations, thus weakening instead of strengthening the empire. These barbarous punishments indicate the general Asiatic temper—a temper inhuman and savage. The tiger-like thirst for blood which characterized the Babylonians led them to sacrifice their national self-interest and the peace of the empire to the promptings of a spirit of vengeance.

The Babylonian nobles stood in danger of losing their own heads if by the most trifling fault they aroused the sovereign's displeasure. The venerable "Chaldæans," so famed for their "wisdom and learning," were at one time threatened with extermination because they failed to interpret a dream forgotten by the king. If a monarch incurred the displeasure of his court, and was considered as showing a bad disposition, he was put to death by torture. Such punishments as cutting to pieces and casting into a fiery furnace prevailed, as related by the prophet Daniel, who also informs us that the houses of offenders were torn down and turned into dung-hills. These harsh practices indicate the height of Eastern cruelty. When the prophet Habakkuk denounced the final judgment against Babylon, it was announced as being inflicted "because of men's blood, and for the violence of the land—of the city, and all that dwelt therein."

Pride was another fault of the Babylonians, as it has ever been the accompaniment of military success in a nation. The sudden transfer of supremacy in the Mesopotamian region from Assyria to Babylonia awakened a haughty spirit in the hitherto subject kingdom. The Babylonians in the zenith of their power and glory quite naturally regarded themselves as the greatest nation on earth; and this spirit was distinctly manifested by Nebuchadnezzar, who, when walking in his palace and viewing the splendid edifices which he had erected on all sides from the plunder of his conquests, and by tne forced labor of his captives, exclaimed: "Is not this great Babylon, that I have built for the house of the kingdom by the might of my power, and for the honor of my majesty!" The arrogance of the Babylonians was as intense and as deep-seated as that of the Assyrians, if not so offensive. Truly did Isaiah say, in alluding to this people: "Thou that art given to pleasure, that dwellest carelessly, that sayest in thine heart, I am, and none else besides me."

The Babylonians, in spite of their pride, cruelty, covetousness, and fondness for luxury, were a very religious people. In Babylonia the temple held nearly the same preëminence over other edifices which it possessed in Egypt. The immense ruins of the Birs-i-Nimrud show the degree of labor expended in the construction of sacred buildings, and the costly ornamentation of these structures is more wonderful than their vast dimensions. Immense sums were expended on the idols, and the entire appendages of worship displayed indescribable pomp and magnificence. The kings devoutly worshiped the various deities, and devoted considerable attention to building and repairing temples, erecting images of the gods, etc. The names given their children showed their religious feeling and their actual faith in the power of the gods to protect their devotees. Thus Nabu-kuduri-izzir means "Nebo is the protector of landmarks;" Bel-shar-izzir means "Bel protects the king;" and Evil-Merodach implies "Merodach is a god." The people in general used names of the same kind, containing in nearly every case the name of a god as an element, such as Belibus, Belesis, Nergal-shar-ezer, Shamgar-nebo, Nebu-zar-adan, Nabonidus, etc. The seals and signets worn by each man were almost universally of a religious character. Even in banquets and entertainments, while drinking, they uttered praises of the deities. Says the prophet Daniel: "They drank wine, and praised the gods of gold, and of silver, of brass, of iron, of wood and of stone."

Nicolas of Damascus tells us that the Babylonians specially cultivated the virtues of honesty and calmness. The fact that their trade was flourishing, that their products were everywhere in demand, sufficiently proves their commercial honesty.

Babylon was perhaps the largest and most splendid city of the ancient Eastern world. On its site great masses of ruins cover a space much larger than those of Nineveh. Beyond this space in all directions are seen detached mounds, showing that there existed in past times vast edifices, while spaces between the mounds indicate that there also were buildings in former ages. Modern investigation and exploration give us no definite idea of the size of Babylon.

Herodotus says that the enceinte of Babylon was a square, one hundred and twenty stadia (about fourteen miles) each way, so that the whole circuit of the walls was fifty-six miles, and the area enclosed within them less than two hundred square miles. Ctesias, who, like Herodotus, saw the city itself, gave the circuit of the walls an extent of three hundred and sixty stadia, or forty-one miles, thus representing the area as little more than one hundred square miles. Clitarchus gave the circumference as three hundred and sixty-five stadia; Quintus Curtius as three hundred and sixty-eight stadia; Strabo as three hundred and eighty-five stadia. Quintus Curtius tells us that there was a clear space of a quarter of a mile between the city and the wall. The walls of the city were pierced with a hundred gates, and the streets or roads led directly to these portals. The houses were usually three or four stories high, and are said to have had vaulted roofs, unprotected on the outside with any tiling, because the dryness of the climate rendered such protection unnecessary. The beams of the houses were of palm-wood, the only plentiful timber in the country. The pillars were posts of palm-wood with twisted wisps of rushes around them, covered with plaster and colored.

The Euphrates flowed through the city, dividing it into two almost equal parts. Its banks were lined all the way with quays of brick laid in bitumen, and were also guarded by two brick walls skirting them along their entire extent. Each of these walls had twenty-five gates, corresponding to the number of streets extending upon the river. Outside each gate there was an inclined landing-place, by which the water's edge could be reached. Boats kept at these landing-places conveyed passengers across the river. The river was also crossed by a bridge consisting of a number of stone piers erected in the channel, firmly held together with fastenings of iron and lead, and connected only during the day by wooden drawbridges, on which people passed over, and which were removed at night to prevent the use of the bridge in the dark. Diodorus gives this bridge a length of five stadia (about one thousand yards) and a width of thirty feet. He also says that there was a tunnel under the river, connecting its two sides, and that it was fifteen feet broad and twelve feet high to the spring of its arched roof.

The most remarkable edifices of Babylon were its two palaces, one on each side of the river, and the great temple of Bel. Herodotus describes the great temple as surrounded by a square enclosure, two stadia (almost a quarter of a mile) long, and as wide. Its main feature was the *ziggurat*, or tower, a gigantic solid mass of brick-work, built in the same manner as all other Babylonian temple-towers, in stages, with square upon square, thus forming a rude pyramid, with a shrine of the god at the top. The basement platform of this temple-tower, Herodotus says, was a stadium, or a little over two hundred yards, each way. This tower had eight stages, and the ascent to the highest, which contained the shrine of the god, was on the outside, and consisted of a series of steps, or of an inclined plane, carried round the four sides of the structure, and leading to the top in this way. Strabo says that the tower was a stadium (six hundred and six feet and nine inches) high, but this is evidently an exaggeration. About midway up there was a resting-place provided with seats. The shrine on the summit of the structure was large and elegant. It had no image in the time of Herodotus, but only a golden table and a large couch, covered with an elegant drapery; but Diodorus says that before the Persian conquest of Babylon the shrine contained gigantic golden images of Bel, Beltis and Ishtar respectively. Two golden lions were in front of the images of Beltis, and near these were two colossal serpents of silver, each weighing thirty talents. The golden table was forty feet long and fifteen feet wide, and was in front of the statues. Two immense drinking-cups, as heavy as the serpents, were upon the golden table. The shrine likewise had two vast censors and three golden bowls for the three deities respectively.

There was a second shrine, or chapel, at the base of the tower. In the time of Herodotus this shrine contained a sitting image of Bel, consisting of gold. There was a golden table before the image, and a golden stand for the image itself. The Babylonian priests informed Herodotus that the gold of the image, table and stand together weighed eight hundred talents. Before the Persian conquest this second shrine had a human figure of solid gold twelve cubits high. The shrine was also well supplied with private offerings. Within the sacred enclosure outside the structure were two altars, the smaller one of gold on which to offer sucklings, and the larger one of stone on which full-grown victims were sacrificed, and whereon a thousand talents' weight of frankincense was offered yearly at the festival of the god.

The great palace was larger than the great temple. Diodorus says that it was located within a triple enclosure, and that the innermost wall was twenty stadia, the middle forty stadia, and the outermost sixty stadia (almost seven miles) in circumference.

RUINS OF BABYLON.

The outer wall was entirely built of plain baked brick. The other two walls were built of the same kind of brick fronted with enameled bricks representing hunting scenes. Quintus Curtius only knew of one enclosure, and this corresponded to the inner wall of Diodorus, having a circuit of twenty stadia. Curtius represented this wall as eighty feet high, and its foundations as lying thirty feet below the surface of the ground. Diodorus says that the figures in the hunting scenes were larger than life-size, and that they embraced a large variety of animal forms, and likewise of human forms, one of a man thrusting his spear through a lion, and another of a woman on horseback aiming a javelin at a leopard. These last the later Greeks supposed to represent the mythical Ninus and Semiramis. The palace was said to have had three gates, two of bronze, which had to be opened and closed by a machine.

The "Hanging Gardens"—regarded by the Greeks as one of the "Seven Wonders of the World"—were the chief glory of the great palace, and constituted its pleasure-ground. This remarkable construction was a square, each side measuring four hundred Greek feet, according to Diodorus. It rested upon several tiers of open arches, built one over the other, and bearing at each stage, or story, a solid platform, from which arose the next tier of arches. The structure was seventy-five feet high, and at the top it was covered with a vast mass of earth, in which were grown flowers and shrubs, and even the largest trees. Quintus Curtius says that the trunks of some of these trees were twelve feet in diameter, and Strabo states that some of the piers were hollowed and filled with earth to afford nourishment for the roots of the trees. Water, conveyed from the Euphrates through pipes, was said by Strabo to have been raised by a screw working on the principle of Archimedes. There was a layer of reeds mixed with bitumen, next a double layer of burnt brick cemented with gypsum, and then a coating of sheet-lead, between the bricks and the mass of soil, to protect the building against gradual decay by the moisture penetrating the brick-work. The garden was reached by steps. Stately apartments were among the arches on which rested the structure, on the ascent to the garden. The machinery which raised the water was in a chamber within the structure. The object of the structure was to produce an artificial mountain.

The smaller palace, on the side of the river opposite the larger one, was also surrounded by a triple enclosure, the whole circuit, according to Diodorus, measuring thirty stadia. This palace contained some bronze statues, believed by the Greeks to represent the god Bel and the legendary king and queen, Ninus and Semiramis, along with their officers. Painted and enameled bricks representing war and hunting scenes covered the walls.

The walls of Babylon, in connection with the "Hanging Gardens," were among the "Seven Wonders of the World." Herodotus says that they were fifty royal cubits (about eighty-five English feet) wide. Strabo and Quintus Curtius gave the width as thirty-two feet. Herodotus assigned the walls a height of two hundred royal cubits, or three hundred royal feet (about three hundred and thirty-five English feet). Ctesias gave the height as fifty fathoms, or three hundred ordinary Greek feet. Pliny and Solinus made the altitude two hundred and thirty-five feet. Philostratus and Quintus Curtius assigned the walls a height of one hundred and fifty feet. Clitarchus, according to Diodorus Siculus, and Strabo gave the height as seventy-five feet.

The walls were made of bricks cemented with bitumen, with occasional layers of reeds between the courses. Outside the walls were protected by a wide and deep moat. Low towers, two hundred and fifty in number according to Diodorus Siculus, and rising about ten or fifteen feet above the walls according to Quintus Curtius and Strabo, served as guard-rooms for the defenders. Herodotus says the space between the towers was wide "enough for a four-horse chariot to turn in." The height and thickness of the walls gave them their strength and rendered scaling and mining utterly hopeless.

Such was the mighty Babylon in the day of its glory—a great city, irregularly built, surrounded by populous suburbs interspersed among fields and gardens, the whole included within a large square strongly-fortified *enceinte*, or wall of brick. There are at present few vestiges of this vast and magnificent metropolis of the ancient Oriental world. As Jeremiah foretold, "the broad walls of Babylon" are "utterly broken." As Isaiah predicted, "the golden city ceased;" truly is "it a possession for the bittern, and pools of walls;" it has been swept "with the besom of destruction;" and "Babylon, the glory of kingdoms, the beauty of the Chaldees' excellency," has become "as when God overthrew Sodom and Gomorrah." As Jeremiah prophesied, Babylon has "become heaps," "an astonishment," and "without an inhabitant." There are great "heaps" of shapeless and formless mounds scattered at intervals over the whole region where ancient Babylon was located, and the soil between the "heaps" is in many instances composed of remnants of broken pottery and bricks, and deeply impregnated with nitre, which indisputably proves that the site was at one time occupied by an immense mass of buildings. On going southward from Bagdad these remains gradually increase, and between Mohawil and the Euphrates they are continuous, forming a region of immense mounds.

These mounds commence about five miles above the modern town of Hillah, extending more than three miles along the river from north to south, and are located chiefly on the eastern bank. On the eastern side the ruins consist mainly of three vast masses of ruined buildings. The modern Arabs call the most northern of these mounds BABIL, which was the real native name of the great ancient city, meaning "the Gate of Il," or "the Gate of God." The Babil mound is an immense heap of brick-work shaped like an irregular quadrilateral, having precipitous sides with ravines, and being flat on the top. The southern side of the ruin is the most perfect, and extends about two hundred yards directly east and west. At its eastern end it forms a right angle with the eastern side, which extends almost due north in a direct line for about one hundred and eighty yards. The western and northern sides appear to be much worn away, and here are the principal ravines. The Babil mound, whose greatest height is about one hundred and thirty or one hundred and forty feet, consists chiefly of sun-dried bricks, but appears to have been faced with fire-burned bricks skillfully cemented with an excellent white mortar. Nebuchadnezzar's name and titles are on the bricks of this outer facing. The little of the building uncovered shows that the lines of the structure were perpendicular, and that the side walls were supported by buttresses at intervals.

This great structure was situated within a square enclosure, the northern and southern sides of which are yet clearly marked. A low line of rampart extends four hundred yards parallel to the eastern side of the building, about one hundred and twenty or one hundred and thirty yards distant from it, and a line of mound a little longer runs parallel to the northern side, but more distant from it. A third line on the western side traced early in the present century is now obliterated. On the western and southern sides are the remains of an ancient canal.

The Babil mound stands isolated from the other ruins, and below it are two mounds, the more northern of which the Arabs call EL KASR, meaning "the Palace," and the more southern "the mound of Amran," from the tomb of a prophet called Amran-ibn-Ali, crowning its summit. The Kasr mound is an oblong square, about seven hundred yards from north to south, and about six hundred yards from east to west, the sides facing the cardinal points of the compass. The height of this mound above the plain is seventy feet. The rubbish uncovered by exploration is composed of loose bricks, tiles, and fragments of stone. An underground passage, seven feet high, with floor and walls of baked brick, and arched at the top with huge sandstone blocks, has been discovered, and is believed to have been an immense drain. The Kasr, or "palace" proper, is another important relic, and from it the mound has received its name. This consists of excellent brick masonry, remarkably preserved, in the form of walls, piers and buttresses, and in certain places ornamented with pilasters. The bricks are of a pale yellow color and of excellent quality, and every one is stamped with the name and titles of Nebuchadnezzar. The mortar in which they are laid appears like a fine lime cement, which so closely adheres to the bricks that it is not easy to get a specimen whole. Many fragments of brick, painted, and covered with a thick glaze or enamel, are seen in the dust at the foot of the walls. Here, also, have been discovered a few fragments of sculptured stone, among which is the frieze discovered by Layard; and slabs giving an account of the erection of Nebuchadnezzar's palace have likewise been found. Near the northern edge of the mound, and half-way in its width, is a gigantic figure of a lion, rudely carved in black basalt, standing over the prostrate figure of a man with extended arms. A solitary tree has grown out of the great ruin, which the Arabs say is of a species not found elsewhere, and which they consider a remnant of the hanging garden of Bokht-i-nazar. This tree is a tamarisk, with a strange growth and foliage, on account of its great age and its exposed situation.

The mound of Amran, or Jumjuma, about eight hundred yards south of the Kasr mound, has an irregular and ill-defined triangular shape, with its three sides respectively a little east of north, a little south of east, and a little south of west. The south-western side, which runs almost parallel with the Euphrates, appears to have been at one time washed by the river, and is over a thousand yards long; while the south-eastern side is about eight hundred yards long, and the north-western about seven hundred yards. Countless ravines traverse the mound on all sides, extending almost to its center, while the surface is altogether undulating. Sculpture or masonry can nowhere be seen, but only a mass of rubbish; no clear outlines of buildings being thus far discovered. Bricks bearing the names and titles of some of the earlier Babylonian kings are sometimes found, but not the slightest vestige of a wall has been brought to light.

Among other remarkable remains are some long lines of rampart on both sides of the Euphrates, outside of the other ruins, enclosing all of them, excepting the Babil mound. On the east bank of the river are traces of a double line of wall, or rampart, running almost directly north and south, and situated about a thousand yards east of the Kasr and Amran mounds. Beyond this rampart is a single line of wall to the north-east, which can be traced for about two miles, running in a direction almost from north-west to south-east, and a double line of rampart to the south-east, which can be traced for a mile and a half, extending in a direction from north-east to south-west. The two lines of this last rampart are between six hundred and seven hundred yards apart, and diverge from each other as they extend out to the north-east. The inner line connects with the north-eastern rampart almost at a right angle, and is a part of the same work.

A low line of mounds can be traced between the western side of the Amran and Kasr mounds and the present eastern bank of the Euphrates, enclosing a narrow valley, in which the main stream, or a branch of it, appears to have flowed in ancient times.

On the west bank of the river are ruins of the same kind. A rampart twenty feet high extends for almost a mile parallel with the general line of the Amran mound, about a thousand yards from the ancient course of the stream. Each end of the line of rampart turns at a right angle, extending down towards the river, and can be traced towards the north for four hundred yards and towards the south for fifty or sixty. There are evidences that before the Euphrates flowed in its present channel there was a rectangular enclosure, a mile long and a thousand yards wide, opposite to the Amran mound; and at the south-east angle of this enclosure appears to have been an important edifice, the bricks here bearing the name of Neriglissar.

There are likewise many scattered and irregular heaps, or hillocks, on both banks of the Euphrates; most of them on the east bank, among which is the mound called by the Arabs *El Homeira*, "the Red." This mound is located about eight hundred yards due east of the Kasr mound, and is about three hundred yards long and one hundred wide, and sixty or seventy feet high. It consists of baked bricks of a bright red color, which are inscribed along their edges, and not, as the others, on their lower face.

The remains of a brick embankment are also traceable on the east bank of the river between the Babil and Kasr mounds, extending about a thousand yards in a slightly-curved line and a general direction of south by south-west. The bricks of this embankment are very hard, of a bright red color, and are wholly laid in bitumen. They bear a legend showing that the quay was constructed by Nabonidus.

All the ruins of Babylon now traceable are found in a space not much over three miles long and a mile and three-fourths wide. These remains are surrounded on all sides by nitrous soil and low mounds which have not been excavated, but which are believed to mark the locations of smaller temples and other public edifices of the renowned ancient city. Such masses are most general to the north and east, and often extend for miles. The mass of Babylonian ruins reaching from Babil to Amran covers an area about as large as the Koyunjik mound on the sight of Nineveh. These Babylonian ruins appear to have been "the heart of the city," "the royal quarter." Says Layard: "Southward of Babil for the distance of three miles there is almost an uninterrupted line of mounds, the ruins of vast edifices, collected together as in the heart of a great city."

Thus Babylon vastly exceeded Nineveh in its dimensions. The Kasr mound indicates that it was the site of the great palace of Nebuchadnezzar. Tradition has given the name of Kasr, or "Palace," to this mound, and this is confirmed by the inscriptions upon slabs found here, in which Nebuchadnezzar calls the structure his "Grand Palace;" while all the bricks of that portion of the ruin remaining uncovered bear that great king's name. Diodorus says that the walls were ornamented with sculptured representations of hunting scenes; and modern exploration has brought to light from the soil of the mound vast masses of fragments of enameled bricks with various hues and containing portions of human and animal forms, such as portions of a lion, of a horse, and of a human face.

The Amran mound is believed to be the site of the old palace to which Nebuchadnezzar's structure was an addition. Berosus says that Nebuchadnezzar's edifice adjoined upon the old palace. On the Amran mound monuments of the times previous to Nebuchadnezzar's day have been found; and as the early Babylonian kings only left memorials in the old palace, it is reasonable to infer that this mound is the site of the ancient royal residence. The oblong-square enclosure with an important building at its south-east angle is believed to have been the second or smaller palace of Ctesias.

The ruin now known as the Birs-i-Nimrud, about eleven or twelve miles from the Babil mound, has been supposed by some to be the site of the old temple of Bel; but the cylinders found by Sir Henry Rawlinson in the Birs-i-Nimrud call the structure "the wonder of Borsippa," and all the ancient authorities say that Borsippa was a city by itself—a town wholly distinct from Babylon. It has also been believed that the Babil mound itself is the site of the old temple of Bel—the spot on which was built the Tower of Babel. The great difficulty in identifying this site with the old temple is the statement of Herodotus expressly asserting that the temple of Bel and the great palace were upon opposite sides of the river, whereas the Babil and Kasr mounds are both on the eastern side of the Euphrates.

The Babylonians were among the most ingenious of all ancient nations, and made great progress in the arts and sciences. The classical writers usually rank them with the Egyptians in this respect. The Babylonians especially excelled in architecture and astronomy. The primitive Chaldæans, the ancestors of the later Babylonians, first appear in history as great builders; and Nebuchadnezzar, the great king of the Later Babylonian Empire, specially prided himself upon his architectural works. Herodotus, upon visiting Babylon, was mainly impressed with its wonderful edifices; and the glowing descriptions of these structures by the Greek writers have mainly given to the Babylonians their fame and their high rank among the great nations of ancient Asia.

Their architecture appears to have culminated in the temple. The temple in Babylonia occupied the same rank which it held in Egypt and in Greece, and unlike in Assyria, where the temple was a mere appendage of the palace. The temple was the great edifice of a city, or a portion of a city, being higher and more conspicuous than any other building. It rivaled the palace in every respect, being magnificently adorned, and having offerings of enormous value deposited in it. It inspired awe by its religious associations, and was not only a place of worship, but a refuge to many on perilous occasions.

The Babylonian temple was usually surrounded by a walled enclosure, a square of two stadia each way, or an area of thirty acres. The temple commonly consisted of two parts. The *ziggurat*, or tower, was either square or rectangular, and built in stages, as high as seven, or as low as two, in number. A shrine or chapel containing altars and images was at the top of the tower. The towers were ascended on the outside by means of winding steps or an inclined plane. Either the sides or the angles of the tower faced the cardinal points of the compass. Diodorus Siculus said that the towers were used not only for worship, but also as observatories. There was a second shrine or chapel at the base of the tower, in which the images and furniture were of gold and silver. In the vicinity of this lower shrine was a golden altar, on which were sacrificed various kinds of victims.

The most remarkable of Babylonian ruins is that of the Birs-i-Nimrud, or ancient temple of Nebo at Borsippa. Upon a crude brick platform, a few feet above the level of the alluvial plain, was erected the basement stage of the vast stucture, an exact square, two hundred and seventy-two feet each way, and twenty-six feet high. The second stage was just as high, and a square of only two hundred and thirty feet, twelve feet from the south-western edge of the first stage, and thirty feet from the north-eastern edge. The third stage was placed the same way upon the second, and was also twenty-six feet high, and a square of one hundred and eighty-eight feet. The fourth stage was fifteen feet high, and was a square of one hundred and forty-six feet, and was placed upon the third in the same way as the others had been upon those below them. The fifth stage was a square of one hundred and four feet, the sixth a square of sixty-two feet, and the seventh a square of twenty feet. These stages were each fifteen feet high. The shrine or tabernacle was on the seventh and highest stage, which was fifteen feet high and square. The entire structure was thus one hundred and fifty-six feet high.

This temple was chiefly ornamented by means of color. The seven stages represented the Seven Spheres in which the seven planets were believed to move. Each planet was given a special hue or tint. The sun was golden, the moon silver, the planet Saturn black, Jupiter orange, Mars red, Venus a pale yellow, Mercury a deep blue. The basement stage, assigned to Saturn, was blackened with bitumen. The second stage, that of Jupiter, was faced with burned bricks of an orange hue. The third stage, that of Mars, was made red with burned bricks of a bright red clay. The fourth stage, that of the sun, was covered with plates of gold.

CIVILIZATION.

The fifth stage, that of Venus, was faced with bricks of a pale yellow tint. The sixth stage, that of Mercury, was given an azure tint by vitrifaction, the entire stage having been subjected to a great heat after it was erected, which gave the bricks a blue color. The seventh stage, that of the moon, was coated with silver plates. The basement stage had a number of square recesses. The third stage was supported by a number of low buttresses. The shrine was of brick, and is believed to have been richly ornamented. The tower is believed to have fronted to the north-east, on which side was the ascent, believed to have been a broad staircase extending along the entire front of the structure. The side platforms, towards the south-east and north-west, were occupied by a series of chambers abutting upon the perpendicular wall. The side chambers communicated with vaulted apartments within the solid mass of the edifice.

The Babylonian palace stood upon a high mound or platform, like the Assyrian and the Susianian palace. The palace mound was usually square, elevated about fifty or sixty feet. It was built chiefly of sun-dried bricks, enclosed on the outside by burnt bricks, and also on the inside. The whole was carefully drained, and the waters were conveyed through underground channels to the level of the plain at the base of the mound. The Babylonian palaces are so completely ruined that no full description of them can be given with certainty. The lines of the edifice were straight, the walls arose to a considerable height without windows, and numbers of pilasters and buttresses broke the flatness of the straight line. The palace was often ornamented with sculptured stone slabs, on which were carefully-wrought figures of a small size. Diodorus states that the general ornamentation consisted of colored representations of war-scenes and hunting-scenes on brick. Many such representations have been found on the Kasr mound. They are alternated with cuneiform inscriptions, in white and on a blue ground, or with a patterning of rosettes in the same colors. The "Hanging Gardens" of Babylon have already been described.

The Babylonian domestic architecture was of a poor and coarse style, and displayed little taste. The houses were three or four stories high, but were of a rude construction; the pillars were palm posts surrounded with wisps of rushes, and then plastered and painted.

The only Babylonian building material was brick, consisting of two kinds, sun-dried and kiln-burned, as was the case in ancient Chaldæa and in Assyria. The Babylonians, however, only applied the sun-dried bricks to the platforms, and to the interior of palace mounds and of very thick walls, and never made that kind the only building material. In all cases there was at least a *revêtement* of kiln-dried brick, while the more splendid edifices were entirely built of that kind. The baked bricks were of several kinds and sizes. The finest kind were yellow, another kind were blackish-blue, while the ordinary and coarser kind were pink or red. The bricks were always shaped square, and were twelve or fourteen inches long and wide, and from three to four inches thick. Half-bricks were used in alternate rows at the corners of buildings. They were always made with a mold, and were usually stamped on one face with an inscription. They were commonly laid horizontally, though sometimes vertically, separated from one another by single horizontal layers.

The Babylonians used three kinds of cement in their buildings. One kind was a crude clay, or mud, mixed with chopped straw. A better material was bitumen; but the most common kind was mortar, or lime cement.

There are few remaining specimens of Babylonian mimetic art, and these are mainly fragmentary, and worn by time and exposure. Besides the quaint and grotesque intaglios on seals and gems, there are less than a half-dozen specimens of their mimetic art remaining. There is a sculpture of a lion standing over the prostrate figure of a man, yet seen on the Kasr mound. There are a few modeled clay figures. One is a statuette of a mother with a child seated on a rough square pedestal. The mother is naked, except a hood on the head, and a narrow apron in front. The child sleeping on her left arm wears a short tunic, gathered into plaits. The statuette is about three and a half inches high. There is a figure of a king, principally remarkable for the elaborate ornamentation of the head-dress and the robes engraved on a large black stone. This figure, supposed to represent Merodach-iddin-akhi, is now in the British Museum. There are engraved animal forms on black stones, such as the figure of a dog sitting and the figure of a bird. The engravings on gems and cylinders are grotesque figures of men and animals, and men and monsters. The most elaborate and artistic of the Babylonian works of art were the enamelings on brick. According to the prophet Ezekiel "the images of the Chaldæans, portrayed upon the wall, were vermilion." Other colors were used in the adornment of palaces and public edifices, such as white, blue, yellow, red, brown and black.

The Babylonians also made considerable progress in the mechanical arts, such as cutting, boring and engraving hard stones, and the arts of agriculture, metallurgy, pottery, weaving, embroidery, etc. Besides the softer stones, such as alabaster, serpentine, and lapis-lazuli, the Babylonian artisans worked the harder kinds, such as agate, quartz, jasper, syenite, cornelian, lodestone, and green felspar, or amazon-stone. The minuteness of the work in some of the Babylonian seals and gems indicates that they must have been engraved with the aid of a powerful magnifying-glass. The art of cutting glass was well understood.

The Babylonians used gold and silver for statues, furniture and utensils, bronze for gates and images, and iron also for the latter. They used lead and iron in building. The golden images were sometimes solid, and sometimes only plated. The silver images, ornamental figures and utensils are also believed to have been solid. The city and palace gates were of bronze. The metal-work of personal ornaments, such as bracelets, armlets and dagger-handles, resembled the work of the Assyrians. Small bronze figures of dogs, monsters and grotesque figures of men, were cast as ornaments for houses, furniture, etc.

The Babylonian pottery was excellent, and the bricks were superior to the Assyrian. The earthenware is of fine terra-cotta, usually of a light red color, and slightly baked, but sometimes of a yellow hue, tinged with green; and consists of cups, jars, vases and other vessels, which appear to have been made upon the wheel. The Babylonians had small glass bottles, several of which were found by Mr. Layard in the Babil mound. Broken glass is found generally in the rubbish of the mounds.

The textile fabrics of the Babylonians were the most celebrated of all their productions. Their carpets had acquired a wide fame and were largely exported to foreign lands. They were dyed in various colors, and represented griffins and other monsters. They ranked above all others in the ancient world, as those of the Turks and Persians do in the modern. The Babylonian muslins were almost as celebrated as the carpets, and were formed of the finest cotton and dyed with the most brilliant colors. The Orientals regarded them as the best material for dress, and the Persian monarchs preferred them to their own wear. Borsippa was the chief seat of the Babylonian linen manufacture. Long linen robes were generally worn by this people.

In astronomy the Babylonians far excelled all other ancient nations, as their Chaldæan ancestors were the great pioneers in this sublime science. The first Greeks who made any advance in this science acknowledged themselves the disciples of Babylonian teachers. Hipparchus, the first great Greek astronomer, mentioned the Babylonians as astronomical observers from a dimly-remote antiquity. Aristotle confessed that the Greeks were vastly indebted for astronomical information to the Babylonians and Egyptians. Ptolemy made much use of the Babylonian observations of eclipses. Sir Cornwall Lewis says that "the Greeks were in the habit of

CIVILIZATION.

attributing the invention and original cultivation of astronomy either to the Babylonians or to the Egyptians, and represented the earliest scientific Greek astronomers as having derived their knowledge from Babylonian or from Egyptian priests."

We have alluded to the progress of the early Chaldæans in astronomy. On the broad, flat plains of Chaldæa the clear sky, the dry atmosphere, and the level horizon, afforded facilities for observation and naturally first turned man's attention to the celestial hemisphere. At a very early date the fixed stars were distinguished from five larger luminaries which the Greeks called "planets," which are the only movable stars that can be seen without the aid of a telescope of high magnifying power. They also soon discovered that the moon was a wandering luminary, and observed that the sun rose and set in the vicinity of different constellations in different parts of the year.

They arranged the stars in groups, or "constellations," to mark out the courses of the sun and moon among the stars. The names of these constellations were derived from some real or fancied resemblance of the groups to objects with which the early observers were familiar. This department of astronomy is called *uranography*. Though these groupings of the fixed stars is mainly fanciful, its utility is inestimable, for by its means only are we enabled to point out individual stars and retain in the memory a knowledge of their general arrangement and relative positions.

This old Chaldæan, or Babylonian, uranography is to this day recognized by scientific astronomers, and is represented on our globes and maps. The zodiacal constellations, especially those through which the sun's course lies, originated, as we have said, with the Chaldæans, and many of them are represented on Babylonian monuments of a stellar character. A Babylonian conical black stone now in the British Museum, and belonging to the twelfth century before Christ, is an arrangement of constellations according to the forms assigned them in Babylonian uranography. On this stone are recognized the Ram, the Bull, the Scorpion, the Serpent, the Dog, the Arrow, the Eagle or Vulture. There are similar forms on other monuments of a like character.

The Babylonians called the zodiacal constellations the "Houses of the Sun," and distinguished them from another set of asterisms, which they designated the "Houses of the Moon." They observed and calculated eclipses, but their knowledge was empirical. We have noted of the early Chaldæans that they discovered the period of two hundred and twenty-three lunations, or eighteen years and ten days, after which eclipses, particularly those of the moon, recur again in the same order. Their knowledge of this cycle enabled them to foretell lunar eclipses accurately for ages, and solar eclipses with little inaccuracy for the next few cycles.

The Babylonians carefully noted and recorded eclipses. Ptolemy had access to a continuous series of such observations dating back from his own time to B. C. 747. From Babylonian sources Hipparchus described eclipses of the moon for the years B. C. 721, 720, 621 and 523, the first of which was total at Babylon, the others only partial. These observations are seen to answer every purpose of modern science. We have knowledge of Babylonian observations as far back as Nabonassar, B. C. 747, as that king, according to the account by Berosus, destroyed the previously-existing observations, so that exact chronology might begin with his own reign.

The Babylonians arranged a catalogue of the fixed stars, which were employed by the Greeks in compiling their stellar tables. They recorded their observations upon occultations of the planets by the sun and the moon. They invented two kinds of sundials, the *gnomon* and the *polos*, by means of which they could measure time during the day, and accurately establish the exact length of the solar day. They discovered the length of the synodic revolution of the moon within a small fraction. The exact length of the Chaldæan year was three hundred and sixty-five days, six hours and eleven minutes; which is only two seconds longer than the true sidereal year. They observed comets, and believed them to be permanent bodies, revolving in orbits like those of the planets. They believed eclipses of the sun to be due to the interposition of the moon between the sun and the earth. They knew very nearly the relative distances of the sun, the moon and the planets from the earth. Naturally adopting a geocentric system, they decided that the moon was nearest to the earth; that Mercury was beyond the moon, Venus beyond Mercury, Mars beyond Venus, Jupiter beyond Mars, and Saturn beyond Jupiter. From the difference in the periodic times of these luminaries the Babylonians inferred a corresponding difference in the size of the orbits, and therefore their relative distances from the common center.

The astronomical achievements of the Babylonians thus far described rest upon the authority of the ancient Greek and Roman writers. There are many Chaldæan and Babylonian astronomical tablets in the British Museum, which are not yet thoroughly understood. It is said that there is clear evidence that the Babylonians observed the four satellites of Jupiter, and good reason for believing that they had a knowledge of the seven satellites of Saturn. They so well understood the general laws of the movements of the celestial bodies that they could foretell the positions of the different planets throughout the year.

They must have employed some instruments to acquire the knowledge which they possessed. We have observed that they invented sun-dials to measure time during the day. The clepsydra, or water-clock, commonly used by the Greeks as early as the fifth century before Christ, is believed to have been a Babylonian invention. The astrolobe, an instrument used to measure the altitude of the stars above the horizon, and which was known to Ptolemy, is likewise believed to have been invented by this people. If, as believed, the satellites of Saturn are mentioned upon the tablets, the Babylonians must have had optical instruments like the telescope; as it is impossible, even in the clear and vaporless sky of Chaldæa, to see the moons of that remote planet without the aid of lenses. As we have said, a lens has been discovered among the Assyrian ruins. A people with sufficient ingenuity to discover the magnifying-glass would naturally be able to invent its opposite. The existence of two opposite kinds of lenses would furnish the elements of a telescope.

Though a class of pure astronomers existed among the Babylonians, most of those engaged in the study of astronomy followed it because they believed that the heavenly bodies had some mysterious influence upon the seasons, and also upon the lives and fortunes of individuals, and that this influence could be discovered and foretold by long and careful observation. The ancient Jewish and Greek writers bear witness to this fact, and their testimony is confirmed by existing astronomical remains. Most of the Babylonian tablets are of an astrological character, recording the supposed influence of the celestial bodies, singly, in conjunction, or in opposition, upon all earthly affairs, from the fate of kingdoms and empires to the washing of hands or the paring of nails. Says Rawlinson: "The modern prophetical almanac is the legitimate descendant and the sufficient representative of the ancient Chaldee Ephemeris, which was just as silly, just as pretentious, and just as worthless."

Chaldee astrology was chiefly genethlialogical, inquiring under what aspect of the heavens individuals were born or conceived, and pretending to ascertain the entire life and fortunes of men from the position of the heavenly bodies at one or the other of these moments. Diodorus says that it was believed that a particular star or constellation watched over the birth of each individual, and thereafter exercised a special malign or benignant influence over his life. His fortunes depended on the whole aspect of the heavens, as well as upon this one star. Casting the horoscope was reproducing this aspect, and then reading by its means the destiny of the individual.

The Chaldæans also pretended to predict changes of the weather, high winds and storms, great heats, the appearance of comets, eclipses, earthquakes, etc., from the stars. They published lists of lucky and unlucky days, and tables indicating what aspect of the heavens portended good or evil to particular nations. Sir Henry Rawlinson has discovered both lists among the tablets. They considered their art as confined to the countries occupied by themselves and their kinsmen; they being able to foretell storm, tempest, good or poor crops, war, famine, etc., for Syria, Babylonia and Susiana; but unable to prophesy concerning Media, Persia, Armenia or other countries. Like our almanacs, their calendars predicted the weather for stated days.

The Chaldæans also possessed considerable mathematical learning, and their methods seem to have been geometrical. The Greek mathematicians are said to have quoted the works of such Chaldæans as Cidên, Naburianus and Sudinus.

Herodotus, Diodorus, Strabo and Nicolas of Damascus have given accounts of the Babylonian manners and customs. Herodotus tells us that this people wore a long linen gown extending down to the feet, a woolen gown or tunic over this, a short cloak or cape of a white color, and shoes like those of the Bœotians. Their hair grew long, but was confined to the head by a head-band or a turban, and they always carried a walking-stick with some kind of a carving on the handle. This description doubtless applies to the higher and wealthier classes. The prophet Ezekiel thus alludes to these people: "Girded with girdles upon their loins, exceeding in dyed attire upon their heads, all of them princes to look to, after the manner of the Babylonians of Chaldæa, the land of their nativity."

The cylinders represent the poor worshiper bringing an offering to a god as dressed in a tunic reaching from the shoulder to the knee, ornamented with a diagonal fringe and confined to the waist by a belt. Rich worshipers usually present a goat, and are attired in a tunic, with a long robe without sleeves over it, and wear a fillet, or head-band. Figures of hunters attacking a lion, a man accompanying a dog, and a warrior conducting six captives, are represented on cylinders as dressed in short tunics. These tunics had no sleeves, and were seldom patterned. Rich worshipers are sometimes represented dressed in coats without sleeves, fringed down both sides, and extending only a little below the knees. They have also a fillet around the head.

The Babylonians are, with few exceptions, represented with bare feet, though the soldiers wore low boots, and the king had a kind of check-work patterned shoe. Herodotus, however, mentions them in his time as wearing a "peculiar shoe." Herodotus states that every Babylonian man carried a seal and a walking-stick.

The king wore a long gown, reaching to the feet, and elaborately patterned and fringed. Over this he had a close-fitting sleeved vest, reaching to the knees, and ending in a set of heavy tassels. The girdle was worn outside the outer vest, and in war the king carried besides two cross-belts. Both the upper and under vests were elegantly embroidered. From the girdle depended in front a heavy tassel fastened by a cord.

The Babylonian monarch wore a remarkable tiara, it being exceedingly high, almost cylindrical, slightly tending to swell out toward the crown, which was adorned with a row of feathers around its whole circumference. The space below was patterned with rosettes, sacred trees and mythological figures. A projection of feathers rose from the middle of the crown, rounded at the top. This head-dress was worn low on the brow, and covered most of the back part of the head.

The Babylonian king also wore bracelets. Nicolas of Damascus says that a Babylonian governor wore necklaces and ear-rings. The priests wore a long robe or gown with flounces and stripes, over which they wore an open jacket. A long riband or scarf hung down their backs. They wore an elaborate crown or mitre on their heads, which was likewise assigned to many of the gods. Sometimes a horned cap was worn instead of the mitre. The priests wore their heads uncovered in all sacrificial and ceremonial acts.

The Babylonian soldiers were armed with bows and arrows, spears, daggers, maces or clubs, and battle-axes, for weapons of offense; while their defensive armor consisted of bronze helmets, linen breast-plates and shields. The prophet Ezekiel mentions the shields and helmets of the Babylonians, and also their battle-axes; while Jeremiah mentions their spears and swords, and their breast-plates. The favorite weapon of the Babylonians was the bow, as attested by the Old Testament and the native monuments. The figure of a king is represented as carrying a bow; while the soldier conducting captives has a bow, an arrow and a quiver. An old Chaldæan monument represents a king with a bow and arrow, a club and a dagger. There is a cylinder representing a lion disturbed in the act of feasting off an ox by two rustics, one of whom attacks him in front with a spear, while the other, seizing his tail, assails him from behind with an ax.

The Babylonian armies consisted of chariots, cavalry and infantry. The cylinders sometimes represent a curious four-wheeled car, drawn by four horses, with a raised platform in front and a seat behind for the driver. The Jewish prophet Habakkuk, in speaking of the Babylonian cavalry, said: "They are terrible and dreadful." He also said: "Their horses also are swifter than the leopards, and are more fierce than the evening wolves; and their horsemen shall spread themselves, and their horsemen shall come from far; they shall fly as the eagle that hasteth to eat." Ezekiel, alluding to "the Babylonians and all of the Chaldæans," referred to the "desirable young men, captains and rulers, great lords and renowned; all of them riding upon horses." Jeremiah spoke of the Babylonian chariots and cavalry thus: "Behold, he shall come up as clouds, and his chariots shall be as a whirlwind; his horses are swifter than eagles. Woe unto us! for we are spoiled."

In the army of Xerxes the Babylonians were infantry, but Darius, in the Behistun Inscription, alludes to Babylonian horsemen; and the Babylonian armies which overran Syria, Palestine and Egypt consisted chiefly of cavalry. The Babylonian armies, like the Persian, consisted of immense hosts, poorly disciplined, comprising, besides native Babylonian troops, contingents from the subject nations, such as Susianians, Shuhites, Assyrians and others. They marched with great noise and tumult, scattering over the country invaded, plundering and destroying on every side. They assailed the weaker towns with battering-rams, and raised mounds before the stronger to the top of the walls, which they then easily scaled or broke down. They were noted for their determined persistence and unyielding perseverance in sieges, only taking Jerusalem in the third year, and Tyre in the fourteenth. Omens often decided which country was to be next attacked.

Diodorus described the Babylonian priests as a caste devoted to the service of their gods and to the study of philosophy. He says that they were highly esteemed by the people. They guarded the temples and served at the altars of the gods, to interpret dreams and prodigies, to understand omens, to read the warnings of the stars, and to inform men how to escape the perils with which they were thus menaced, by purifications, incantations and sacrifices. No one questioned their traditional knowledge transmitted from father to son. The people considered them as in possession of a wisdom of the highest importance to the human race.

The Book of Daniel describes a class of "wise men" at Babylon, chief of which were the Chaldæans, who are noted for a particular "learning" and a particular "tongue," and who expounded dreams and prodigies. They were in high favor with the king, who frequently consulted them. These "wise men" were of four classes, according to their occupations—"Chaldæans, magicians, astrologers and soothsayers." Jews were enrolled among these "wise men," and the prophet Daniel was made chief of the whole order by King Nebuchadnezzar. As a distinct order, these "wise men" had considerable power in the state. They had direct communication with the king, and were believed to be endowed with a supernatural power to foretell future events, as well as in possession of human learning; and some of them held high civil offices.

Herodotus mentions the Chaldæans as "priests;" and Strabo says that they were "philosophers," employed chiefly in astronomy. Strabo also states that they were divided into sects, differing from each other in their doctrines. The Babylonian priests were an order, not a caste; and, as in Egypt and Persia, they were an esteemed and important class. Priests may have brought up their sons to their own occupation, but other persons, even foreigners, were admitted to the order and to its highest privileges. The Babylonian priesthood was a sacerdotal and learned body, having a literature written in a peculiar language, which its members were obliged to study. This language and literature were inherited from the times of the early Chaldæan Empire, and were thus transmitted to Assyria and later Babylonia.

They professed especially a knowledge of astronomy, astrology and mythology, and may have also studied history, chronology, grammar, law and natural science. They were dispersed over the country, but had special seats of learning at Erech, or Orchoë (now Warka), at Borsippa (the site of the present Birs-i-Nimrud), and at other places. They were diligent and ingenious students, divided into sects with different doctrines, and given to speculation. They particularly cultivated astronomy with success, and the value of their knowledge in this science was afterwards acknowledged by the Greeks.

The priests stood high socially, having access to the king, and being feared and respected by the people. They were made wealthy by the offerings of the faithful, and their occupation as interpreters of the will of the gods secured them influence. The civil offices frequently conferred upon them added to their wealth and to the esteem in which they were held.

The Babylonians were a great manufacturing and commercial people. Their commerce was both foreign and domestic. Many were engaged in manufacturing the textile fabrics for which the Babylonians were so famous, especially carpets and muslins. Many were engaged as engravers on hard stone, with which the seal carried by every Babylonian was adorned. The trades and handicrafts commonly practiced in the East also flourished in Babylonia. An active and constant import and export trade was kept up. The Jewish prophet Ezekiel called Babylonia "a land of traffic," and Babylon "a city of merchants." Isaiah said that "the cry of the Chaldæans" was "in their ships." The monuments show that the primitive Chaldæans navigated the Persian Gulf, and Æschylus calls the Babylonians in the army of Xerxes "navigators of ships."

The Babylonians imported frankincense from Arabia; pearls, cotton, and wood for walking-sticks from the Persian Gulf; dogs and gems from India. Strabo says that they had a colony called Gerra, on the Arabian coast of the Persian Gulf, and this colony was a great emporium through which the Babylonian trade to the north and the south was conducted. The products of Western Asia were carried down into Babylonia by the courses of the Tigris and Euphrates. Wine, gems, emery and building stone were imported from Armenia and Upper Mesopotamia; tin and copper from Phœnicia; and fine wool, *lapis-lazuli*, silk, gold and ivory from Media and the distant East. But these articles were brought to Babylon mainly by foreign merchants. The Armenians and Phœnicians, and perhaps also the Greeks, used the route of the Euphrates for the transportation of goods. The Assyrians, the Medes and the Paretaceni floated their goods down the Tigris and its tributaries.

A great portion of the Babylonian people were engaged in agriculture. Babylonia was chiefly a grain-producing country, the wonderful fertility of whose soil has been noted in our account of ancient Chaldæa.

The deep and rich alluvium was cultivated with the greatest care. As before mentioned wheat, barley, millet and sesame flourished in luxuriant abundance. By means of canals the country was irrigated. Groves of date-palm furnished the chief article of food. Little beyond a proper water supply was needed for the cultivation of the date. The female palm-tree can only produce fruit by the pollen of the male palm coming in contact with its blossoms. Herodotus states that the Babylonians tied the branches of the male to those of the female palm.

Artificial means increased the yield of the date-palm in Babylonia. The seeds and cuttings were planted in a sandy soil, to which salt was applied if necessary. Abundant watering was required, and transplantation was resorted to at the close of the first and second year. The ground was broken with a plow drawn by two oxen.

Dates were the chief food of the Babylonians, and on this fruit and goat's milk the poorer class mainly subsisted. Palm-wine was an occasional beverage. In the marshy regions of the South fish was the principal food of some tribes of Chaldæans. The wealthy indulged in luxuries, such as wheat bread, meats, luscious fruits, fish, game and imported wine. The rich also drank to excess. They had magnificent banquets, which usually ended in drunkenness. Bands of musicians entertained the guests. The display of gold and silver plate, the magnificent dresses of the guests, the beautiful carpets and hangings, the many attendants, all contributed to the splendor of the scene.

The Babylonians and Susianians were both fond of music. Ctesias and Daniel testify to the musical taste of the Babylonians. Ctesias states that Annarus, or Nannarus, a Babylonian noble, enlivened a banquet with the music of a band of one hundred and fifty women, some singing and others playing on the pipe, the harp and the psaltery. The prophet Daniel assigns the same instruments to the Babylonians, along with the horn, the *sambuca* and the *symphonia*, or "symphony." The Babylonians also used music in their religious ceremonies. Daniel mentions their musical instruments in connection with Nebuchadnezzar's dedication of a gigantic idol of gold, when the worshipers were obliged to prostrate themselves before the idol upon hearing the music begin.

Women were not kept in the same seclusion in Babylonia as in other Oriental countries, as is apparent from the two curious customs mentioned by Herodotus—the sale of the marriageable maidens at public auction to the highest bidder, and the religious prostitution enjoined in the worship of Beltis. On the Babylonian cylinders are frequently found images of a goddess suckling a child, and also many representations of women engaged in different employments. Sometimes they are represented in a procession visiting the shrine of a goddess, and sometimes they are seen among birds and flowers in a garden, plucking the fruit from dwarf palms and handing it to one another. They are dressed in a long but scanty robe extending to the feet, and wear a fillet, or band, round the head, confining the hair, which is turned back behind the head, and tied by a riband, or held up by the fillet. The modeled clay image represents bracelets and ear-rings as worn by the women. A single representation of a priestess exhibits that class as wearing petticoats only, thus exposing the entire body above the waist.

A few Babylonian cylinders have been found representing saws and hatchets, stools, chairs, tables, and stands for water-jars. The Babylonian furniture was made from the wood of the palm-tree.

SECTION IV.—BABYLONIAN RELIGION.

HE later Babylonian religion being almost identical with the old Chaldæan, it will not be necessary to go into detail upon the subject in this connection. The early Chaldæans, and their successors in the same country, the later Babylonians, worshiped the same gods in the same temples and with the same rites, and had the same cosmogony, the same religious symbols, and the same priestly costume. If Urukh or Chedorlaomer could have risen from their graves, and again visited the shrines in which they had offered sacrifices fourteen centuries before, they would have seen little difference between the ceremonies of their own times and those of the ages of Nabopolassar and Nebuchadnezzar. In the later times the temples and the idols were more magnificent, music was more extensively employed in the ceremonial, and corruption concerning priestly impostures and popular religious customs made some advance; but in other respects the religion of Nabonadius and Belshazzar was like that of Urukh and Ilgi, the religion of both periods being the same in the objects and the mode of worship, in the theological ideas entertained and the ceremonial observances and practices.

The repair and restoration of the ancient temples by Nebuchadnezzar, and their re-dedication to the same deities, attests at once the identity of the gods and goddesses worshiped, as do likewise the old appellations of the gods as elements in the names of the later kings and nobles. But with all this general uniformity, there was a fluctuation of rank and place among the gods at various times, and distinct deities were often confounded with each other. Nebuchadnezzar showed special devotion to Merodach, bestowing upon him titles of honor signifying his supremacy over all the other gods, and identifying him with Bel, the ancient tutelary god of Babylon.

Among the titles which Nebuchadnezzar assigned to Merodach were the following: "The great lord," "the first-born of the gods," "the most ancient," "the supporter of sovereignty," "the king of the heavens and the earth." Nabonadius, however, restored Bel to his former place among the gods, as distinct from and above Merodach, and showed particular devotion to the former. This is proven by the fact that in his day the great temple at Babylon was known as the temple of Bel, and by the additional circumstance that Nabonadius named his eldest son Belshazzar, meaning "Bel protects my son."

In the same way the goddesses Beltis and Ishtar, or Nana, are often confounded, though the same was the case in this instance in the old Chaldæan monarchy. The basis of this confusion of deities was the esoteric doctrine known by the priests and taught by them to the kings, showing the actual identity of the several gods and goddesses, whom the more intelligent and better informed may have considered various phases of the Divine Nature and not as separate and distinct deities. The ancient polytheisms apparently had this origin among all nations, the various names and titles of the Supreme Being designating His different attributes or His different spheres of action gradually coming to be misapprehended by the ignorant masses, who regarded this seeming difference as appellations of a number of deities.

Bel, Merodach and Nebo were the deities chiefly worshiped by the later Babylonians, as attested by the native monuments, and confirmed by the Jewish writers. Nebo, the special deity of Borsippa, was considered a kind of powerful patron-saint, under whose protection it was regarded important to place individuals. Nebo's name is the most common divine element in the names of the kings and courtiers of the later Babylonian monarchy. Three of the seven monarchs of the kingdom had names composed with Nebo's—Nabopolassar, Nebuchadnezzar and Nabonadius. Among courtiers we find such names as Nebu-zar-adan, Samgar-Nebo and Nebu-shazban. It is also believed that Nebuchadnezzar's Master of the Eunuchs named one of the young Jewish princes whom he was educating Abed-Nebo, "the servant of Nebo"—a name which the Jews afterwards corrupted into Abed-nego.

Nergal was also highly reverenced by the Babylonians. He was worshiped at Cutha as the tutelary divinity of the city, and was also greatly esteemed by the nation in general. His name is often found on cylinder seals; and is sometimes an element in the names of men, as in "Nergal-shar-ezer, the Rag-Mag," and in Neriglissar, the king.

The Babylonian religion had a strong local character. Bel and Merodach were the special gods of Babylon; Nebo of Borsippa; Nergal of Cutha; the Moon-god of Ur, or Hur; Beltis of Niffer; Hea, or Hoa, of Hit; Ana of Erech, or Huruk; the Sun-god of Sippara, etc. These deities were particularly honored at their respective places, though all were recognized in a general way throughout the land. Each god was specially worshiped in his own city, where was located his most magnificent shrine. A god was only respected to any account out of his own city by such as considered him their special personal protector.

The Babylonians worshiped their deities directly through their images, thus giving their religion the same idolatrous character bestowed upon it by the Assyrians. Each shrine had one idol at least, and this idol was most impiously reverenced by the ignorant, who identified it in some way with the god whom it represented. Some of them appear to have believed that the idol ate and drank the offerings; while others regarded the idol as a mere symbol of the god, who was supposed to pay an occasional visit to the shrine where he was worshiped. Those who held the last doctrine nevertheless entertained gross anthropomorphic views, as they regarded the god as coming from heaven to earth to pass the night with the chief priestess in the inner shrine of the temple of Bel, which was furnished by the priests with a magnificent couch and a golden table.

Some of the idols were of wood, others of stone, and others again of metal, either solid or plated. The metals used were gold, silver, brass or bronze, and iron. Sometimes the metal was laid over a clay model. In some instances images of one metal were overlaid with plates of another, as in the case of one of the great images of Bel, originally of silver, but coated with gold by Nebuchadnezzar.

The Babylonian worship was conducted with great pomp and magnificence. A body of priests in each temple conducted the ceremonies and held custody of the treasures. The priests were married, and lived with their families in the temple itself or in its immediate vicinity. They were supported by lands belonging to the temple or by the offerings of the faithful. These offerings were usually animals, mostly oxen and goats, which are sacrificial animals represented on the cylinders. The priest always intervened between the worshiper and the deities, introducing him to them and making intercession in his behalf with upraised hands.

In the temple of Bel at Babylon, and perhaps in most of the temples throughout Babylonia, a great festival was celebrated once a year. Many victims were sacrificed on such occasions, and on the great altar in the precinct of Bel at Babylon it was the custom to burn a thousand talents' weight of frankincense. There were processions accompanied by music and dancing. The priests were magnificently costumed. The people were in holiday attire. Banquets were held, and the city was given up to merry-making. The king entertained his lords in his palace. There was dancing and revelry in private dwellings. Wine was drunk freely, passion was aroused, and the day often ended in wild orgies, in which the grossest sensual appetites were allowed free indulgence under the sanction of religion.

In the temples of one deity such excesses occurred daily. Every Babylonian woman

RELIGION.

was obliged once in her lifetime to visit a shrine of Beltis, and stay there until some stranger cast money into her lap and took her along with him. Herodotus witnessed this scene, which he described as follows: "Many women of the wealthier sort, who are too proud to mix with the others, drive in covered carriages to the precinct, followed by a goodly train of attendants, and there take their station. But the larger number seat themselves within the holy enclosure, with wreaths of string about their heads—and here there is always a great crowd, some coming and others going. Lines of cord mark out paths in all directions among the women; and the strangers pass along them to make their choice. A woman who has once taken her seat is not allowed to return home till one of the strangers throws a silver coin into her lap, and takes her with him beyond the holy ground. When he throws the coin, he says these words: 'The goddess Mylitta (Beltis) prosper thee.' The silver coin may be of any size; it cannot be refused, for that is forbidden by the law, since once thrown it is sacred. The woman goes with the first man who throws her money, and rejects no one. When she has gone with him, and so satisfied the goddess, she returns home; and from that time forth no gift, however great, will prevail with her. Such of the women as are tall and beautiful are soon released; but others, who are ugly, have to stay a long time before they can fulfill the law. Some have even waited three or four years in the precinct." Thus prostitution was enjoined as a religious duty, and its demoralizing tendency could not well be exaggerated. The statement of Herodotus, that "from that time forth no gift, however great, will prevail with a Babylonian woman," is not repeated by Strabo, and is bluntly contradicted by Quintus Curtius.

The Babylonian religious system had notions concerning legal cleanliness and uncleanliness similar to those prevailing among the Jews. They believed that both man and woman were made impure by the consummation of the marriage rite, and also by every subsequent act of the same kind. Every vessel touched by either was contaminated with this impurity. In order to cleanse themselves of this impurity, the pair were obliged first to sit down before a censer of burning incense, and then to wash themselves thoroughly. Only by these means were they able to again enter a condition of legal cleanliness. A like impurity affected such as came into contact with a human corpse.

The Babylonian symbolism in religion was quite extensive. First they assigned to each god a special mystic number, which was used as his emblem and might also stand for his name in an inscription. To Anu, Bel, and Hea, or Hoa—the gods of the First Triad—were given respectively the numbers 60, 50 and 40. To the Moon-god, the Sun-god and the Air-god—the gods of the Second Triad—were assigned the numbers 30, 20 and 10. To Beltis was attached the number 15, to Nergal 12, to Bar, or Nin, 40, as to Hea, or Hoa, but this last is uncertain. Other numerical emblems remain undiscovered.

There were likewise pictorial symbols of the various gods, as represented on the cylinders, many of these forms filling every vacant space where room could be found for them. A certain number may be given definitely to particular divinities. A circle, either plain or crossed, symbolized San, or Shamas, the Sun-god; a six-rayed or eight-rayed star the Sun-goddess, Gula, or Anunit; a double or triple thunderbolt the Air-god, Vul; a serpent probably Hea, or Hoa; a naked female form Ishtar, or Nana; a fish Bar, or Nin. There is a multitude of other symbols, whose meaning is obscure; such as a double cross, a jar or bottle, an altar, a double lozenge, one or more birds, an animal between a monkey and a jerboa, a dog, a double horn, a sacred tree, an ox, a bee, a spear-head. The inscribed cylinders inform us that these emblems do not refer to the god or goddess mentioned in the inscription upon them. Each seemingly represents a distinct deity, and their appearance upon a cylinder implies the devotion of the man whose seal it is to other deities besides those whose particular servant he regards himself. In some instances one cylinder has eight or ten such emblems.

The principal Babylonian temples had special sacred names transmitted from the old Chaldæan times, and belonged to the Turanian form of speech. The great temple of Bel at Babylon was known as Bit-Saggath; that of the same god at Niffer as Kharris-Nipra; that of Beltis at Erech (now Warka) as Bit-Ana; that of the Sun-god at Sippara as Bit-Parra; that of Anunit at the same place as Bit-Ulmis; that of Nebo at Borsippa as Bit-Tsida. These names seldom admit of explanation.

A SYRIAN SHEPHERD.

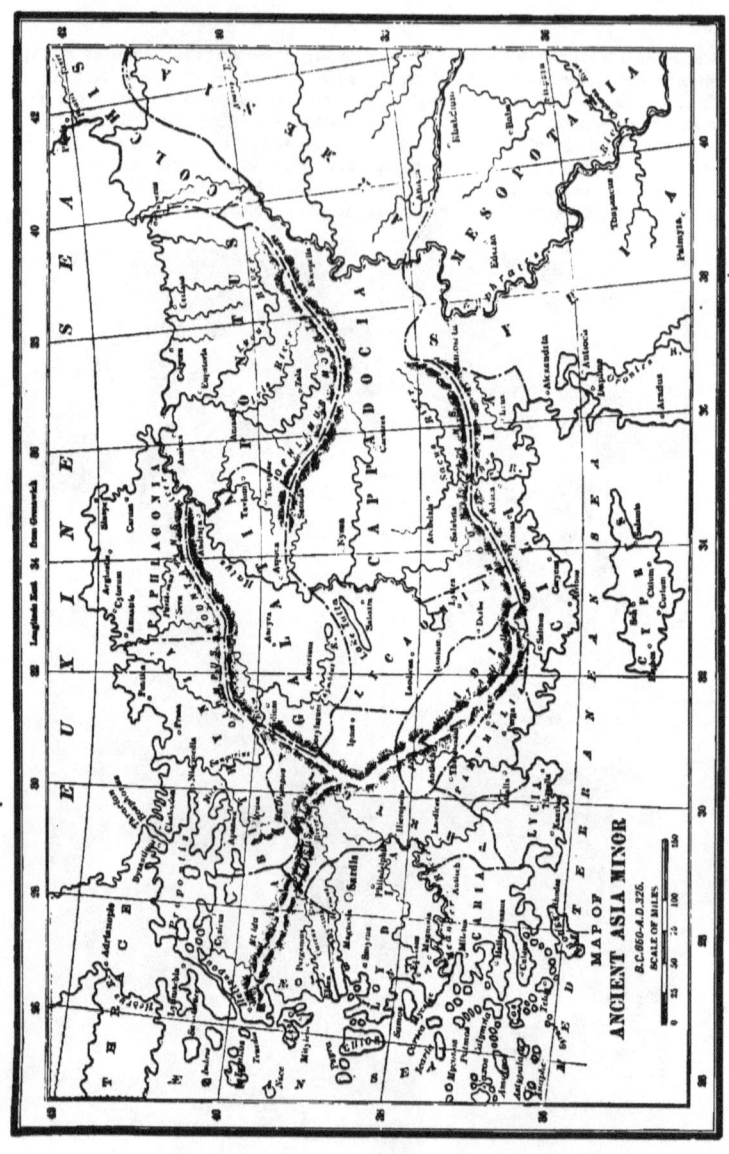

CHAPTER VI.
KINGDOMS OF ASIA MINOR.

SECTION I.—GEOGRAPHY OF ASIA MINOR.

ASIA MINOR is a large peninsula, forming the western extremity of Asia, and is now a part of the Ottoman, or Turkish Empire. It is bounded on the north by the Euxine, or Black Sea; on the east by Armenia; on the south by the Mediterranean; and on the west by the Ægean Sea (Grecian Archipelago), the Hellespont (Dardanelles), the Propontis (Sea of Marmora), and the Bosphorus.

The term *Asia Minor*, or *Lesser Asia*, was given to this peninsula in the middle ages. The region is now called *Anatolia*, or *Natolia*, meaning *the East*, or the place where the sun rises; being thus equivalent to the French term *Levant*, as often applied to the shores along the eastern portion of the Mediterranean.

Asia Minor is five hundred miles in extent from east to west, and two hundred and sixty from north to south, having an area of about one hundred thousand square miles, or about half that of France. It is in the same latitude as the Middle States of our Union, but has a warmer climate. In the North, along the Black Sea, ice and snow are somtimes seen in winter. In the elevated central regions the winters are very severe. In the South the seasons are mild; and here such fruits as figs, oranges, lemons, citrons and olives are yielded in large quantities. Corn, wine, oil, honey, coffee, myrrh and frankincense are produced in abundance in Asia Minor. The country has varied soil, climate and productions, and many portions of it are extremely fertile. The coasts of the Black Sea are considered the finest portions of Asia Minor. The western shores, along the Ægean, are likewise productive, and have always been noted for their delightful climate.

The rivers of Asia Minor, though small, are celebrated in history. The Halys (now Kizil-Ermak) anciently divided Paphlagonia and Pontus, and is the largest river of Asia Minor, being about three hundred and fifty miles long. The Iris (Yeshil-Ermak) is a considerable river. The Thermodas (Tarmeh) flowed through Themiscyra, the home of the fabled Amazons. The Sangarius (Sakaria) is the second river in length. All these and numerous smaller streams rise in the Anti-Taurus mountain range, and flow north into the Black Sea. The rivers in the South are small. The Granicus (Ousvola)—famed for the first great victory of Alexander the Great over the Persians—flows north into the Propontis. The Hermus and its tributary, the Pactolus, were celebrated for the gold found in their sands. The Meander was remarkable for its windings, and thence was derived the term *meandering*, as used in describing a crooked stream. These and other small rivers flowed west into the Ægean.

Two mountain ranges traverse Asia Minor from east to west, the southern range being the Taurus, and the northern the Anti-Taurus. Some of their summits are twelve thousand feet high, and are perpetually covered with snow. Many peaks of these mountains are renowned in history. Mount Cragus was the supposed abode of the fabled Chimera. Mount Ida was the place where Paris adjudged to Venus the prize of beauty. Mount Sipylus was the residence of Niobe. The sides of these mountains produce rich forests of oak, ash, elm, beech, etc. Here the plane-tree reaches its perfection. These forests yield a never-failing supply of timber for the Turkish navy.

Asia Minor has many fresh and salt water lakes. The mountains divide the surface into long valleys and deep gorges, with many plateaus. In the more elevated tablelands of the center, the South and the South-east are still lakes. The fresh water lakes are in the North-west, in the ancient Bithynia, five being of considerable size. Of these, the Ascanius is celebrated for its beauty, and on its eastern shore is the city of Nice (now Isnek), famous for the ecclesiastical council held there in A. D. 325, which established Christianity as the state religion of the Roman Empire.

Asia Minor abounds in mineral wealth. The Chalybes, in the North-east, were early celebrated as metal-workers. Copper is found near Trebizond, the ancient Trapezus, and other places along the Black Sea. There are likewise mines of lead, cinnabar and rock-alum. The gold of the Pactolus filled the treasury of the Lydian kings. Volcanic convulsions have made deserts of certain spots in Asia Minor. Many of the old Roman roads in the country yet remain.

Along the southern coast of Asia Minor, in the Mediterranean, are the beautiful islands of Cyprus and Rhodes. On the western shores, in the Ægean, are the fine islands of Cos, Icaria, Samos, Chios and Lesbos; all of whose history is closely connected with that of the adjacent territory upon the mainland.

Asia Minor played a considerable part in the drama of the world's history, and was the theater of many important events. Though never the seat of any very great empire—the ancient Lydian being the most powerful—its soil witnessed many struggles for dominion in ancient and mediæval times. It has been rendered famous by the personal prowess and the martial deeds of Achilles, Darius, Xerxes, Alexander the Great, Mithridates, Pompey, Cæsar, Tamerlane, Bajazet and Mohammed II.

There is very little unity in the history of Asia Minor. Only three of its ancient independent kingdoms are of any importance—Cilicia, Phrygia and Lydia—the last of which was the most powerful, and was contemporary with the great empires of Media and Babylonia. Since the fall of the last of these, Asia Minor has been under the successive dominion of the Persians, the Macedonian Greeks, the Romans, the Seljuk Turks, the Mongol Tartars, and for the last five centuries under the Ottoman Turks, under whose pernicious rule the country has everywhere fallen into decay.

The petty states or divisions of ancient Asia Minor varied in their respective boundaries at different times, and some of them were only geographical divisions or dependent provinces of other states, while others were independent kingdoms at various periods. In the northern part of the peninsula, bordering on the Euxine, beginning from the west, were Bithynia, Paphlagonia and Pontus. In the western portion, bordering on the Ægean, beginning from the north, were Mysia, Lydia and Caria. In the southern part, bordering on the Mediterranean, commencing from the west, were Lycia, Pamphylia and Cilicia. In the interior, beginning from the west, were Phrygia, Galatia, Lycaonia, Pisidia, Isauria and Cappadocia.

The western part of Mysia, on the coast, was called Lesser Phrygia, Troas, or the Troad. It was famous for the Trojan plains and the city of Troy, immortalized by Homer.

Bithynia, Paphlagonia and Pontus were skirted with Greek colonies on the Euxine coast, during the period of Grecian commerce. The Halys and Sangarius, the principal rivers of Asia Minor, which flow north into the Euxine, were in this section.

The whole western or Ægean coast of the peninsula, in Mysia, Lydia and Caria, were colonized by the Greeks, whose commercial cities in Ionia, Æolia and Doris were the most flourishing free states of antiquity, prior to their conquest by the Persians. The chief Greek cities of Asia Minor were Ephesus, Smyrna, Miletus and Halicarnassus.

Lydia—at first called Mæónia—was the richest and most fertile, and ultimately the most famous and the most powerful, country of Asia Minor. Its renowned capital and metropolis, Sardis, was situated on the river Pactolus at the foot of Mount Tmolus, famous for its rich veins of gold. Magnesia and Philadelphia were other leading cities of Lydia.

The limits of Phrygia were constantly changing. Its chief cities were Gordium, the capital, and Celænæ in ancient times; but many others were erected when the Macedonian Greeks became masters of the country, the chief of which were Apaméa, Laodicéa and Colossé.

Galatia was so called from a horde of Gauls who entered the country in the third century before the Christian era. Isauria and Lycaonia were intersected by the Taurus mountain chain. Cappadocia lay between the rivers Halys and Euphrates, and its chief town was Mazaca.

Caria was chiefly celebrated for the prosperous Greek colonies on its coast. Lycia, Pisidia and Pamphylia were mountainous regions in the South. Cilicia was in the South-east, and was separated from Syria by the Amanus mountains; its chief cities being Tarsus and Anchíale, both founded by Sennacherib, the renowned Assyrian monarch.

SECTION II.—PHRYGIA AND CILICIA.

N EARLY times Asia Minor was occupied by various Aryan nations — Phrygians, Cilicians, Lydians, Carians, Paphlagonians and Cappadocians—who migrated into the country from the East in primitive times, and were almost equal in power. This equality, along with the natural division of the country by mountain ranges, prevented the growth of a powerful empire in Asia Minor, and favored the development of a number of parallel, independent kingdoms. Herodotus states that the country contained thirty nations in his time.

The Phrygians are said to have been the first Aryan immigrants into Asia Minor, and they probably at one time occupied the whole peninsula, but successive migrations of other tribes from the east and the west pressed them in from the coast, except in the region just south of the Hellespont, and caused them to settle in the center of the peninsula, where they occupied a large and fertile country, abounding in rich pastures and containing a number of salt lakes. The Phrygians were a brave, but brutal race, engaged chiefly in agriculture, particularly in the culture of the vine. They migrated from the mountains of Armenia, bringing with them a tradition of the Deluge and of the resting of the ark on Mount Ararat. In primitive times they lived in caves or habitations which they hollowed out of the rocks on the sides of the hills, and many of these rock-cities can yet be found in every portion of Asia Minor. Before the time of Homer, however, the Phrygians had well-built towns and a flourishing commerce. Their religion consisted of many dark and mysterious rites, some of which were subsequently adopted by the Greeks. The worship of Cybele, and of Sabazius, the god of the vine, was accompanied by the wildest music and dancing.

The Phrygians appear to have had a well-organized monarchy about B. C. 750, or probably earlier, their capital being Gordium, on the Sangarius river. Their kings were alternately named GORDIAS and MIDAS, but we have no chronological list of these. Phrygia declined as Lydia grew powerful, and was conquered by Lydia and became a province of that monarchy about B. C. 560.

Cilicia occupied the south-eastern part of Asia Minor, and was a rich and fertile country, whose inhabitants were employed in agriculture. It was an independent monarchy during the early period of the Assyrian kingdom. It was subdued by Sargon, who, about B. C. 711 bestowed the country on Ambris, King of Tubal, as a dowry for his daughter, thus making it tributary to Assyria. Having revolted from Assyria, Cilicia was invaded and ravaged by Sennacherib about B. C. 701. That great Assyrian king founded in Cilicia the city of Tarsus, about B. C. 685—afterwards so renowned as the birth-place of St. Paul. Cilicia having again revolted against Assyrian rule, Esar-haddon invaded and ravaged the country about B. C. 677. A king named TYENNESIS ascended the throne of Cilicia about B. C. 616, and thereafter all the Cilician monarchs bore that name. Cilicia maintained her independence against Lydia, but was conquered by the Persians and became a province of the vast Medo-Persian Empire during the reign of Cambyses, the son and successor of Cyrus the Great.

SECTION III.—KINGDOM OF LYDIA.

THE most famous, and ultimately the most powerful, of all the kingdoms of Asia Minor was Lydia, at first called Mæonia. Its territory varied in geographical extent at different times. Lydia proper was bounded on the north by Mysia, on the east by Phrygia, on the south by Caria, and on the west by the Ægean sea. It ultimately embraced the whole peninsula, except Lycia, Cilicia and Cappadocia. Sardis, its renowned capital and metropolis, was situated on the Pactolus, at the foot of Mount Tmolus, with its strong citadel on the side of a lofty hill with a perpendicular precipice on one side. The other cities of Lydia were Magnesia, at the foot of Mount Sipylus; Thyatira and Philadelphia. Ephesus was the chief of the Greek cities on the coast of Lydia. The original territory of Lydia was noted for its wonderful fertility and for its mineral wealth. The Pactolus, a branch of the Hermus, carried a rich supply of gold from the sides of Mount Tmolus, and this precious metal was washed into the streets of Sardis. Mounts Tmolus and Sipylus contained rich veins of gold. The Lydians were celebrated for their wealth and culture, and were the first people who coined money. They "were one of the earliest commercial people on the Mediterranean, and their scented ointments, rich carpets, and skilled laborers or slaves were highly celebrated. The Greeks received from them the Lydian flute, and subsequently the cithara of three and of twenty strings, and imitated their harmony. The Homeric poems describe the Lydians, or Mæones, as men on horseback, clad in armor, and speak of their commerce and wealth. It seems that the worship of the Lydians resembled that of the Syrians, and was polluted with its immoral practices. The ancient writers often mention the depravity of the Lydians, while admitting their skill and courage in war. When subdued they submitted quietly to their conquerors."

According to Josephus, the Lydians were named from Lud, a son of Shem. Herodotus, however, derives the name from LYDUS, an ancient king of the country. An absolute hereditary monarchy was early established in Lydia. Three successive dynasties governed the country—the *Atyada*, so called from ATYS, the son of MANES, the first of the kings regarding whom no distinct account is given; the *Heraclidæ*, or descendants of Hercules: and the *Mermnadæ*, under whom Lydia ultimately became a powerful kingdom.

Herodotus tells us that the Lydian traditions represented Ninus and Belus as going from Lydia to found the cities of Nineveh and Babylon. We also learn from Herodotus of other Lydian traditions. It is said that in the reign of Atys, the son and successor of Manes, the pressure of a severe famine caused the king to compel a portion of the nation to emigrate to the distant Hesperia, under the command of Tyrrhenus, the king's son. After building a fleet at Smyrna, they sailed westward for their new country, which proved to be Etruria, in Italy; and thus was founded the Etruscan nation. At another time the Lydians pushed their conquests beyond the limits of Asia Minor to the very southern extremity of Syria, where their general, Ascalus, is said to have founded the famous city of Ascalon, in the land of the Philistines. Little confidence is to be placed in any of these early Lydian traditions concerning the remote period of the nation.

The real history of Lydia extends only as far back as the ninth century before Christ. The ruling dynasty of the Heraclidæ grew jealous of the Mermnadæ and treated them with injustice, whereupon the Mermnadæ sought safety in flight; but when they return themselves strong enough they returned, murdered the Heraclide king, and placed their leader, GYGES, upon the throne of Lydia, about B. C. 700. The prosperity of Lydia greatly increased under Gyges, and the nation assumed an aggressive attitude toward its neighbors. The great amount of his revenue made the name of Gyges proverbial, and he spread abroad his fame by sending to the temple of Delphi, in Greece, presents of such magnificence that they were the admiration of after times. The predecessors of Gyges had been on friendly terms with the Greek colonists on the western coast of Asia Minor. But Gyges changed this peaceful policy for the purpose of extending his sea-board, and thus made war on the Greek maritime cities, attacking Miletus and Smyrna unsuccess-

fully, but capturing the Ionic city of Colophon. Herodotus, Eusebius, Nicolas of Damascus, and Xanthus are our main authorities for the history of Lydia thus far related. Some tell us that Gyges also quarreled with the inland city of Magnesia, and reduced it to submission after many invasions of its territory; but Herodotus says nothing about this event. Strabo says that Gyges conquered the whole of the Troad, and that the Milesians could only establish their colony of Abydos on the Hellespont after obtaining his permission. The Greeks of Asia Minor and the islands of the Ægean evidently considered Gyges a rich and powerful monarch, and constantly celebrated his wealth, his conquests and his romantic history.

At the end of the long reign of Gyges a great calamity fell upon Lydia. The Cimmerians, from the peninsula now known as the Crimea, and the adjacent region of the present Southern Russia, pressed on by the Scythians from the steppe region, crossed the Caucasus and entered Asia Minor by way of Cappadocia, spreading terror and desolation all around. Alarmed at this barbarian invasion, Gyges placed himself under the protection of Assyria, and defeated the Cimmerians, taking several of their chiefs prisoners. Grateful for the Assyrian alliance, Gyges sent an embassy to Asshurbani-pal and courted his favor by rich gifts and by sending him Cimmerian chiefs. These the Assyrian monarch looked upon as tribute. Gyges, however, afterwards broke with Assyria, and aided the Egyptian rebel, Psammetichus, in reëstablishing his independence. Assyria thereupon withdrew her protection from Lydia, and Gyges was left to his own resources, which were totally inadequate when the great crisis came. Sweeping everything before them, the fierce Cimmerian hordes swarmed resistlessly into the western portions of Asia Minor; overrunning Paphlagonia, Phrygia, Bithynia, Lydia and Ionia. Gyges was defeated and killed in battle with them. The inhabitants shut themselves up in their walled towns, where they were often besieged by the barbarians.

Sardis itself, except its citadel, was taken, and a terrible massacre of its inhabitants ensued. Within a generation Lydia recovered from this terrible blow and renewed her attacks on the Greek colonies upon the coast.

Gyges was succeeded on the Lydian throne by his son, ARDYS, who made war on Miletus. SADYATTES, the son and successor of Ardys, continued this war. ALYATTES, the son and successor of Sadyattes, pursued the same aggressive policy toward Miletus, and besieged and took Smyrna and ravaged the territory of Clazomenæ. Herodotus, Nicolas of Damascus, Strabo and Eusebius are our main authorities for the events of these reigns.

The great task of the reign of Alyattes was the expulsion of the Cimmerians from Asia Minor. The barbarian hordes, greatly exhausted by time, by their losses in battle, and by their excesses, had long ceased to be dangerous, but were still able to menace the peace of the country. According to Herodotus, Alyattes is said to have "driven them out of Asia." This would imply that they were expelled from Paphlagonia, Bithynia, Lydia, Phrygia and Cilicia; a result which the Lydian king achieved by placing himself at the head of a league embracing the states of Asia Minor west of the Halys. Thus Alyattes, by freeing Asia Minor of the presence of the Cimmerian hordes, proved his great military capacity, and laid the foundations of the great Lydian Empire.

The conquest of Cappadocia by Cyaxares the Mede, who thus extended the western frontier of the Median Empire to the Halys, brought the Median and Lydian monarchs into collision. Coveting the great fertile plains west of the Halys, Cyaxares soon found a pretext for attacking the dominions of Alyattes. Herodotus tells us that a body of nomad Scyths had served under the Median king, serving him faithfully for some time, chiefly as hunters; but disliking their position or distrusting the intentions of their Median masters, they finally abandoned Media, and proceeding to Asia Minor, were welcomed by Alyattes. Cyaxares sent an embassy to Sardis demanding of the Lydian king the surrender of the fugitive Scyths; a demand which Alyattes answered with a refusal and immediate preparations for war. The numerous other princes of Asia Minor, alarmed at the rapid advance of the Median dominion westward, willingly placed themselves under the protection of the King of Lydia, to prevent the absorption of their respective territories into the powerful Median Empire, as they had previously put themselves under his leadership in the struggle which resulted in the expulsion of the Cimmerians.

Lydia herself had considerable resources. She was the most fertile country of Asia Minor, which was one of the richest regions of the ancient world. At this time Lydia was producing large quantities of gold, which was found in great quantities in the Pactolus, and perhaps in other small streams flowing from Mount Tmolus. The Lydian people were warlike and ingenious. They had invented the art of coining money, say Xenophon, Herodotus and others. They exhibited much taste in their devices. They also claimed to have invented many games familiar to the Greeks. Herodotus also informs us that they were the first who earned a living by shop-keeping. They were skillful in the use of musical instruments, and their own peculiar musical style was much favored by the Greeks, though condemned as effeminate by some of the Grecian philosophers. The Lydians were also brave and manly. They fought mostly on horseback, and were good riders, carrying long spears, which they employed very skillfully. Nicolas of Damascus says that, even as early as the time of the Heraclide dynasty, they were able to muster thirty thousand cavalry. They found recreation in the chase of the wild-boar.

Thus Lydia was no contemptible enemy, and, with the aid of her allies, she proved herself fully a match for the great Median Empire. For six years, Herodotus tells us, did the war go on between Media and Lydia with various success, until, as we have seen in the history of Media, it was terminated by the sudden eclipse of the sun in the midst of a battle, which excited the superstitious fears of both parties and led to the negotiation of a peace. Syennesis, King of Cilicia, the ally of the King of Lydia, and Labynetus of Babylon, the ally of the King of Media, proposed an armistice, which being agreed on, a treaty of peace was at once concluded, which left everything in *status quo*. The Kings of Media and Lydia swore a friendship, which was to be cemented by the marriage of Aryênis, the daughter of Alyattes, with Astyages, the son of Cyaxares. By this peace the three great empires of the time—Lydia, Media and Babylonia—became firm friends and allies, and stood side by side in peace for fifty years, pursuing their separate courses without jealousy or collision. The crown-princes of the three empires had become brothers, and all Western Asia, from the shores of the Ægean on the west to the Persian Gulf on the east, was ruled by interconnected dynasties, bound by treaties to respect each other's rights, and to assist each other in certain important emergencies; and this quarter of the globe entered upon an era of tranquillity which it had never before known.

Relieved from the fear of Median conquest by the treaty just mentioned, Alyattes renewed the war against the Greek colonists on the western coast of Asia Minor during the last years of his reign. He captured Smyrna and gained other important successes.

On the death of Alyattes in B. C. 568, his son, CRŒSUS, became his successor. Crœsus was the most famous, as well as the last, of the Kings of Lydia. He continued the wars begun by his father against the Asiatic Greeks, and conquered the Ionian, Æolian and Dorian Greeks, and all Asia Minor west of the Halys, excepting Lycia and Cilicia; thus enlarging his dominion by the acquisition of Phrygia, Mysia, Paphlagonia, Bithynia, Pamphylia and Caria. Herodotus remarks that he was the first conqueror of the Greeks of Asia Minor, who had hitherto never been subject to any foreign power. Under him Lydia attained the highest pinnacle of her glory and prosperity; but no sooner had she reached this position among the nations of the time than she was overthrown by a power which made itself master of all the then-known world outside of Europe—the great Medo-Persian Empire, founded by Cyrus the Great on the ruins of the Median Empire, and which absorbed Babylonia and Egypt along with Media and Lydia.

The kingdom of Lydia was now one of the great powers of the world and was far more extensive than at any previous period, and may truly be called an empire. Its capital, Sardis, advantageously situated at the foot of Mount Tmolus, on the river Pactolus, famous for its golden sands, now became famed among the great cities of Asia. Xenophon regarded it as second only to Babylon in riches. Herodotus observes that it was a place of great resort, and was frequented by all Grecians distinguished for their talents and wisdom.

Crœsus was renowned throughout the ancient world for his wealth, and his name became proverbial for great riches. His story has furnished a subject for moralists of every subsequent age to illustrate the uncertainty of earthly prosperity and the vicissitudes of human life. Crœsus considered himself the most fortunate of men. When only crown-prince his father had associated him in the government of the kingdom, and while holding this station, he was visited by Solon, the great sage and lawgiver of Athens, and one of the "Seven Wise Men of Greece." Crœsus entertained his distinguished guest with great hospitality in his palace; but the sage viewed the magnificence of the court with calm indifference, which mortified Crœsus. Solon was conducted to the royal treasury to view and admire the riches contained therein. Crœsus then asked him whom he considered the happiest man in the world, expecting to hear himself named. Solon replied: "Tellus, an Athenian, who, under the protection of an excellent form of government, had many virtuous and amiable children. He saw their offspring, and they all survived him. At the close of an honorable and prosperous life, on the field of victory, he was rewarded by a public funeral by the city."

Crœsus, disappointed with this reply, then asked Solon whom he regarded as the next happiest person. The sage mentioned two brothers of Argos, who had won the admiration of their countrymen by their devotion to their mother, and who had been rewarded by the gods with a pleasant and painless death. Crœsus, in astonishment, asked: "Man of Athens, think you so meanly of my prosperity as to rank me below private persons of low condition?" Solon, not willing either to flatter or disappoint Crœsus, replied: "King of Lydia, the Greeks have no taste for the splendors of royalty. Moreover, the vicissitudes of life suffer us not to be elated by any present good fortune, or to admire that felicity which is liable to change. He, therefore, whom Heaven smiles upon to the last, is, in our estimation, the happy man!" After giving this answer, the Athenian sage took his departure, leaving Crœsus chagrined, but none the wiser. Æsop, the celebrated fabulist, is also said to have visited Crœsus at Sardis, and is said to have observed to Solon: "You see that we must either not come near kings, or say only what is agreeable to them." To which the sage replied: "We should either say what is useful, or say nothing."

The vicissitudes of fortune, which Solon desired Crœsus to ponder upon, were soon exemplified in his own case. Crœsus had two sons, one of whom was dumb, the other, named Atys, was endowed with superior accomplishments. Crœsus is said to have had a vision warning him that this son would die by the point of an iron spear. The frightened father resolved to settle him in marriage and devote him to a peaceful life. He took away his command in the army, and removed every military weapon from those about his person. About this time a certain Adrastus, who had accidentally killed his brother, sought refuge in Sardis, having been banished from home by his father; and, in accordance with ancient pagan custom, sought expiation of a neighboring prince. Belonging to the royal family of Phrygia, he was received in a friendly manner by Crœsus, who allowed him an asylum at his court. Shortly afterward a wild-boar of remarkable size made his appearance near Olympus, in Mysia. The frightened inhabitants requested Crœsus to send his son with hunters and dogs to destroy the beast. The king, who had not forgotten the vision, kept back his son, but offered them a select band of dogs and hunters. The young man, mortified by his father's resolution, remonstrated, until he was permitted to go to the chase, under the protection of Adrastus. They attacked the boar, and the king's son was killed by an accidental thrust from the spear of the Phrygian refugee. The unhappy monarch pardoned Adrastus, thinking that he was the instrument of an inevitable fatality; but the killer, in the deepest anguish for what he had done, retired, in the darkness of night, to the grave of Atys, confessing himself the most miserable of mankind, and there committing suicide. Crœsus mourned for two years the loss of his son, who was his heir to the throne of Lydia.

Alarmed at the rapid growth of the new Medo-Persian Empire, which had recently been founded by Cyrus the Great on the ruins of the great Median power, and seeing that a struggle for the dominion of Asia Minor was inevitable, Crœsus entered into an alliance with Egypt and Babylonia against the new Persian power. Before entering upon the struggle, the King of Lydia, who was very superstitious and would never begin any important undertaking without consulting the ministers of the various deities worshiped in those countries, inquired of various oracles as to the result of his enterprise. But to assure himself of the truth of the answers of the oracles he consulted, he sent messengers to all the most famous oracles of Greece and Egypt, with orders to inquire, every one at his respective oracle, what Crœsus was doing at such a day and such an hour, before agreed upon. The replies are said to have been unsatisfactory to the monarch. But it is said that as soon as

CROESUS ON THE FUNERAL PYRE.

the messengers entered the temple of Delphi, the oracle there gave this answer:

"I count the sand; I measure out the sea;
The silent and the dumb are heard by me;
Even now the odors to my sense that rise,
A tortoise boiling with a lamb supplies,
Where brass below and brass above it lies."

When Crœsus heard of this reply, he declared that the oracle of Delphi was the only true one; because, on the day mentioned, resolving to do what would be difficult to discover or explain, he had cut a lamb and a tortoise in pieces and boiled them together in a covered brass vessel. This story is given us by Herodotus. There is no doubt about Crœsus consulting the oracle, but the marvelous part of the tale was likely an invention of the priests of Delphi to raise the reputation of their oracle.

Crœsus is represented as being satisfied of the divine character of the responses of the Delphic oracle, and as therefore resolved to make a magnificent gift to the oracle. Collecting three thousand chosen victims, a vast number of couches overlaid with gold and silver, along with goblets of gold and purple vests of immense value, he cast all these into a sacrificial pile and burned them. The melted gold ran into a mass, and he made of this a vast number of large tablets, and likewise a lion; and these and a number of vessels of gold and silver he sent to the Delphic oracle. The Lydians conveying these presents were instructed to inquire whether Crœsus could successfully undertake an expedition against the Persians, and whether he should strengthen himself by forming any new alliances. The response of the oracle was, that if Crœsus made war on the Persians he would ruin a great empire, and that he would do well by making alliances with the most powerful of the Grecian states.

The Lydian king, regarding this ambiguous answer as fully satisfactory, was exceedingly elated with the hope of conquering Cyrus the Great. He consulted the Delphic oracle a third time, wishing to know if his power would be permanent. He obtained the following reply:

"When o'er the Medes a mule shall sit on high,
O'er pebbly Hermus, then soft Lydian fly;
Fly with all haste; for safety scorn thy fame,
Nor scruple to deserve a coward's name."

Fully satisfied with this new answer, Crœsus advanced against Cyrus, crossing the Halys and marching through Cappadocia into Syria, and laying waste the country as he advanced. After some minor engagements, Crœsus was decisively defeated in the great battle of Thymbra, in which the army of Crœsus is said to have amounted to four hundred thousand men, and that of Cyrus to one hundred and ninety-six thousand. This is the first pitched battle of which the ancient writers give us any details. The mercenaries in the Lydian army dispersed, returning to their respective homes. Crœsus, with the remainder, retreated to Sardis, whither he was pursued by the triumphant Persians, who gained a second great victory, this time before the walls of the Lydian capital itself. The hopes of Crœsus now completely vanished, and his capital was taken by storm, B. C. 546.

Crœsus was taken prisoner by his conqueror, who condemned him to be burned alive. After the captive monarch had been led to execution on the funeral pile, and as the torch was about to be applied, Crœsus remembered the admonitions given him by the sage of Athens. Struck with the truth of Solon's words, and overwhelmed with grief and despair, the unhappy monarch exclaimed: "Solon! Solon! Solon!" Cyrus, who was present at the scene, demanded the reason for this exclamation, and the entire story was related to him. Greatly affected by the wisdom of Solon's words, and pondering on the vicissitudes of human affairs, the victorious Persian king was moved to compassion for his unfortunate captive, and therefore ordered the fire to be extinguished and Crœsus to be given his liberty.

Upon being restored to freedom, Crœsus at once sent to Delphi the fetters by which he had been confined, with the design of thus reproaching the oracle for deceiving him with false promises of victory for his arms. The Delphian priests explained the story of the mule as designating Cyrus, who had a double nationality, being born both a Persian and a Mede. It was explained that the great empire of which Crœsus was informed that he would ruin if he made war on Persia was his own, as that empire had been great, but was now ruined; but Crœsus was not comforted by this explanation of the Delphian priests.

In consequence of the overthrow of Crœsus, Lydia ceased to be an independent nation, and became a province of the great Medo-Persian Empire; and Sardis, the Lydian capital, became one of the chief cities of that vast empire. Cyrus ever afterward treated Crœsus as a friend, and Xenophon tells us that he took him along with him wherever he went.

KINGS OF LYDIA.

DYNASTIES.	KINGS.	TIME OF REIGNS, ETC.	
Atyadæ	Manes Atys Lydus Meles	Known Kings Before B. C. 1229, According to Herodotus.	
Heraclidæ		From B. C. 1229 to B. C. 724 or 698.	
	Adyattes I. Ardys Adyattes II. Meles Myrsus Candaules	Last Six Heraclide Kings, According to Xanthus and Nicolas of Damascus.	
		TIME ACCORDING TO	
		HERODOTUS.	EUSEBIUS.
Mermnadæ	Gyges Ardys Sadyattes Alyattes Crœsus	B. C. 724–686. " 686–637. " 637–625. " 625–568. " 568–554.	B. C. 698–662. " 662–624. " 624–609. " 609–560. " 560–546.

CHAPTER VII.

PHŒNICIA AND SYRIA.

SECTION I.—PHŒNICIA AND ITS PEOPLE.

HŒNICIA was the name anciently applied to a narrow strip of territory bordered on the east by the mountains of Lebanon, and on the west by the Mediterranean sea, being only about twenty miles wide from east to west, and about one hundred and twenty miles long from north to south. Near Sidon the Lebanon mountains are only two miles from the sea, and at Tyre the Phœnician plain is only five miles wide. The entire Phœnician plain was exceedingly fertile, being abundantly watered. The coast abounded with good harbors, and the cedars of Lebanon furnished material in great abundance for ship-building. The most important and renowned cities upon the Phœnician coast were Tyre and Sidon. Tyre—"the daughter of Sidon"—was the most southern city, and the only one whose political history can be traced. Sidon, the most ancient city of Phœnicia, was twenty miles north of Tyre, and its modern name is Saide. Berytus, now Beyreut, was sixteen miles north of Sidon, and is now the principal seaport of Syria. North of Berytus was Byblus, the Gebal of the Bible, inhabited by seamen and caulkers. North of Byblus was Tripolis, now called Tarabulus; and the most northern of all Phœnician cities was Aradus, the Arvad of Genesis and Ezekiel.

The Phœnicians were a branch of the Semitic race, being therefore a kindred people with the Hebrews, the Arabs, the Syrians, the Assyrians and the later Babylonians.

They have sometimes, however, been considered as the Canaanites of the coast and descendants of Canaan, a son of Ham; in which case they would belong to the Hamitic nations, but their Semitic language seems to identify them with the other nations classed as descended from Shem. The Phœnicians migrated from the plains of Chaldæa soon after the death of Nimrod. They were never united under one government, being divided into a number of petty states, or kingdoms, each Phœnician city with its adjacent territory constituting a small independent state with an hereditary sovereign at its head, the political power being shared with the priests and the nobles. In certain emergencies the Phœnician cities would unite in a confederacy, one of the cities being usually recognized as the leader of the confederation. This supremacy was only exercised in war, when a common danger threatened the existence of the separate cities, or when a common interest demanded unity. Each city was at all times allowed to manage its domestic affairs in its own way.

Sidon—whose name is the same as the oldest son of Canaan, a son of Ham—was the oldest of the Phœnician cities, and the first which became wealthy and powerful. It early engaged in commercial enterprises with other nations, by land and sea, and was the first to found colonies, a system which afterwards became a distinctive feature of Phœnician policy. Tyre was the first of Sidon's colonies. Sidon enjoyed the supremacy over the other Phœnician cities

CEDARS OF LEBANON.

until about B. C. 1050, when the city was taken and destroyed by the Philistines from the South of Palestine. The inhabitants found refuge in Tyre, which became the leading city of Phœnicia, and so remained for seven centuries.

It is not known exactly when Tyre was founded. The city originally was situated on the mainland, but in after years a new city was erected on an island about half a mile from the shore. This insular city soon eclipsed the old Tyre in wealth and splendor, and its name became a byword for commercial greatness.

SECTION II.—HISTORY OF TYRE.

OWING to its geographical situation and its sources of wealth, Phœnicia was a prey to all the great conquerors who made Syria their battle-ground in ancient times. For these reasons Phœnician independence was of short duration, and only in their national infancy were this renowned commercial people free from the yoke of foreign masters. At an early period Phœnicia was forced to acknowledge the supremacy of Egypt, and was successively reduced to subjection under the Assyrians, the Babylonians, the Medo-Persians and the Græco-Macedonians.

In the eleventh century before Christ, Tyre rapidly grew to be the leading city and kingdom of Phœnicia. Under the government of its own kings it advanced very fast in commercial wealth and internal magnificence. The first known King of Tyre was ABIBAAL, who was partly contemporary with King David. On his death, about B. C. 1025, he was succeeded on the Tyrian throne by his son HIRAM, who reigned during the remainder of that century. Hiram was a great friend of the illustrious Hebrew monarchs, David and Solomon, with both of whom he entered into commercial alliances. He furnished Solomon with a great part of the materials used in the construction of the great Jewish Temple at Jerusalem, and with the workmen by whom that grand edifice was erected. Hiram's reign of thirty-four years was a period of wonderful prosperity for the great Phœnician cities, Tyre's su-

VIEW OF MOUNT LEBANON.

premacy being acknowledged throughout the whole of Phœnicia. The other Phœnician kings, profiting by previous experience, entered into a close confederation and recognized the suzerainty of the King of Tyre, "the true and only monarch of the nation," who, in consequence, was called "King of the Sidonians." This title was not to be confounded with that of the King of Sidon, who was the local sovereign of the early Phœnician metropolis. The King of Tyre regulated the general interests of Phœnicia, its commerce and its colonies, concluded treaties with other nations, and directed the fleets and armies of the confederation. He was aided by deputies from the other Phœnician cities.

On the death of Hiram, in B. C. 991, his son, BAALEAZAR, became King of Tyre. He died after a reign of seven years, and was succeeded by his son ABDASTARTUS (or Abdastoreth), who, after reigning nine years, fell a victim to a plot of assassination. A long period of civil wars then distracted Tyre, in consequence of the claims of a number of pretenders who disputed the throne in quick succession. Order was restored about B. C. 941 when ETH-BAAL (or Ithobalus), the High-Priest of Astarte, slew the last pretender, Phales, and seated himself on the throne of Tyre as King of the Sidonians. He gave his daughter Jezebel in marriage to Ahab, King of Israel. By her force of character, Jezebel controlled her imbecile husband and rendered Phœnician influence predominant in Israel during Ahab's reign. Eth-baal died about B. C. 909, and was succeeded by his son BADEZOR, who reigned six years, dying in B. C. 903, when his son, MATGEN, became his successor.

Matgen died in B. C. 871, after a reign of thirty-two years, leaving a son named Pygmalion and a daughter named Elissar, or Elissa, but better known as Dido; the daughter being then thirteen and the son eleven years old. Matgen desired that his children should reign jointly. The people wanting a change in the aristocratic form of government, revolted and proclaimed PYGMALION king, excluding his sister, who married Zicharbaal, the Sichæus of Virgil. Zicharbaal was High-Priest of Melkarth, next in rank to the monarch among the Phœnicians, and the head of the aristocratic party. Shortly afterward he was assassinated by order of Pygmalion, whereupon Elissar organized a conspiracy of the Phœnician nobles to avenge her husband's death and to dethrone her brother, but she was foiled in her design by the vigilance of the popular party. Thereupon the conspirators, several thousand in number, seized a number of ships in the harbor of Tyre and sailed away under the leadership of Elissar, who was thereafter called Dido, "the fugitive." They landed on the northern coast of Africa and founded Carthage, a city whose greatness, glory and prosperity eventually eclipsed that of the mother country.

In consequence of the migration of the aristocratic party from Tyre the Tyrian king was thereafter an absolute monarch. During Pygmalion's reign the Assyrians under Asshur-izir-pal first appeared on the Mediterranean coast. The Phœnician cities submitted to the invaders and agreed to pay tribute—a condition of dependence which lasted almost a century. Pygmalion's reign ended in B. C. 824, but we have no record of any Phœnician king until the middle of the next century. The Phœnician cities were governed by native sovereigns tributary to Assyria, but this vassalage did not apparently retard the prosperity of Phœnicia, or weaken its maritime power.

The Phœnicians quietly bore the yoke of Assyrian supremacy until the middle of the eighth century before Christ, when they became restive. About B. C. 743, another HIRAM, King of Tyre, headed a Phœnician revolt against the Assyrian king, Tiglath-Pileser II., but the Phœnicians were again reduced to submission and tribute when the Assyrians advanced into Palestine. In B. C. 727, Phœnicia, under the leadership of ELULÆUS, revolted against Shalmaneser IV., King of Assyria; whereupon the Assyrian monarch led an army into the country, occupied Old Tyre, on the mainland, which made no opposition, but the Island Tyre withstood a siege. Shalmaneser was unable to assail the insular city from the land without the aid of a fleet, and was obliged to content himself with a simple blockade of the city, the most important feature being the cutting off of the water of the island city which had been supplied by means of aqueducts from the mainland. The besieged are said to have drunk rain-water during the five years that they held out against the besiegers. While the siege was in progress Shalmaneser IV. was hurled from the Assyrian throne by the usurper Sargon, who continued the siege. The other Phœnician cities had in the meantime submitted to the Assyrians, and Sargon collected a fleet of sixty ships from these cities and attempted to attack insular Tyre from the sea, but the Tyrians sallied out with twelve ships and defeated and destroyed Sargon's fleet. Finally, after the siege had lasted five years, the Assyrians relinquished it and retired.

Notwithstanding its successful resistance to the Assyrians, Tyre emerged from the siege greatly exhausted. Its supremacy had been shaken off by the other Phœnician cities, which had become tributary to Sargon; and finally, in B. C. 708, its flourishing colony of Cyprus submitted to the Assyrians. In B. C. 704, just after Sennacherib had ascended the Assyrian throne, Elulæus reëstablished Tyre's supremacy over Phœnicia and proclaimed the independence of the country. In B. C. 700 Sennacherib led a large Assyrian army into Phœnicia, whereupon the Phœnician cities forsook Tyre and submitted

SIEGE OF TYRE BY THE BABYLONIANS.

to the Assyrian king. Elulæus retired to the Island Tyre, relying upon his usual good fortune, which, however, deserted him on this occasion. Tyre was taken and Elulæus was obliged to flee for safety. Sennacherib spared the city, and made Tubal (or Ethbaal) king, as his vassal and tributary.

The capture of Tyre by Sennacherib put an end to the supremacy which that city had for some time exercised so oppressively over the other Phœnician cities. Tyre had retained most of the profits of Phœnician commerce for herself, and the other cities willingly aided Sennacherib in reducing her to submission. All the cities of Phœnicia were now placed on an equality as tributaries of Assyria. Upon the assassination of Sennacherib, Sidon rebelled against Assyria, and endeavored to acquire the supremacy over Phœnicia formerly exercised by Tyre. The revolt was mercilessly punished by Esarhaddon, who destroyed Sidon about B. C. 681 and reduced its inhabitants to slavery. At Esar-haddon's death the Phœnician cities cast off the Assyrian yoke, and allied themselves with Egypt, the enemy of Assyria. But the next Assyrian king, Asshurbani-pal, after reëstablishing the Assyrian dominion over Egypt, suppressed the Phœnician revolt. About B. C. 630, or B. C. 629, Phœnicia fell a prey to the ferocious Scythian invaders, who devastated the open country, but did not take any of the fortified cities. The overthrow of the Assyrian Empire in B. C. 625 gave the Phœnicians a temporary relief; but about B. C. 608 they submitted to the yoke of Neko, King of Egypt. The Egyptian sway over Phœnicia was ended by the defeat of Neko by Nebuchadnezzar of Babylon at Carchemish in B. C. 605; and after a short respite from foreign domination, the Phœnician cities found a new master in the Babylonian king In B. C. 598 Nebuchadnezzar led an army into Phœnicia, quickly reducing the country, and besieging Tyre, which resisted him for thirteen years, at the end of which he took the city and reduced it to a heap of ruins. Most of the inhabitants fled to their fleet and sailed to Carthage, carrying with them their wealth and industry, but a miserable remnant of the population remained in the city under a king named BAAL, whom the conquering Babylonian monarch had set up as his vassal. Some years afterward Uaphris, King of Egypt, attempted to wrest Phœnicia from the dominion of Babylon; but the Phœnicians remained loyal to Nebuchadnezzar, and, aided by Cyprus, defeated the Egyptian fleet, which was manned by Greek and Carian mercenaries. Uaphris was checked in his career by this reverse, and after having taken and sacked Sidon and ravaged the Phœnician coast, he returned to Egypt with a vast amount of spoils.

Upon the subversion of the Babylonian Empire, in B. C. 538, Phœnicia passed under the dominion of the Medo-Persian kings. The greater portion of the naval forces in the expedition of Cambyses, King of Persia, into Egypt consisted mainly of Phœnician ships and seamen. Phœnicia remained a province of the great Medo-Persian Empire for two centuries; and in B. C. 332 Tyre was taken after a vigorous siege and destroyed by Alexander the Great, who thus put an end to the national existence of Phœnicia, and inflicted the death-blow upon the Medo-Persian Empire in the memorable battle of Arbela the following year. Phœnicia then became a part of Alexander's vast empire and was absorbed in the dominions of his successors, sometimes falling under the dominion of the Ptolemies of Egypt and sometimes under the Seleucidæ of Syria. In the first century before Christ it shared the fortunes of Syria in being swallowed up by the overshadowing power of Rome. It has ever since shared the fortunes of Syria and Palestine, and has been under the Turkish dominion for almost four centuries.

ALEXANDER BEFORE TYRE.

SECTION III.—PHŒNICIAN COMMERCE AND COLONIES.

ARGELY because of the physical condition of their country and other circumstances, the Phœnicians devoted their entire attention to manufactures, commerce and colonization; and at a very early period they became the greatest manufacturing, commercial, colonizing and maritime people of antiquity.

The rapid growth of their commerce placed the carrying trade of antiquity almost exclusively in the hands of the Phœnicians. They extended their trade by establishing colonies and trading stations in distant lands, and many of these became important cities in later times. The location of these colonies indicates to some degree the extent of Phœnician commerce, and the colonies were centers from which ventures were made into more remote regions. The Phœnician colonies proceeded from east to west along the Mediterranean coasts, occupying the chief islands. The island of Cyprus—called Kittim, or Chittim, in Scripture—was a province, as well as a colony, of the Tyrians; and vestiges of their establishments on the island may yet be seen. Their principal settlements on Cyprus were Paphos, Amathus, Tamisus and Ammochosta. In the island of Rhodes were Ialyssus and Camarius. In the Ægean sea the Phœnicians had stations on the islands of Thera and most of the Cyclades, and also on Thasos. In the island of Sicily were the flourishing Phœnician colonies of Lilybæum and Panormus (Mahaneth). Their establishments in Sicily and Sardinia were only naval stations for vessels employed in the trade with Western Europe, especially with Spain, "the Mexico or Peru of the ancient world." Spain—called Tarshish in Scripture—was the country from which the Tyrians had the most lucrative trade; and in that country they established on the Mediterranean the colonies of Carteia and Malaca (now Malaga), and beyond the Pillars of Hercules (now Straits of Gibraltar) several flourishing colonies, such as Tartessus, on the Bœtis (now Guadalquivir), and Gades (now Cadiz), on an island near the Spanish coast; the latter of which is said to be the oldest town in Europe. These colonies soon became independent states, Tyre preferring a close alliance with them to retaining a political supremacy over them. From Gades and Tartessus voyages were made to the west coast of Africa for apes, to the mines of Cornwall in Britain for tin, and to the coasts of the North Sea and the Baltic for amber. The principal Phœnician colonies on the Mediterranean coast in North Africa, in the modern land of Tunis, were Leptis, Hadrumetum, Utica and Carthage; which attained a degree of splendor not reached by any other Phœnician cities, and eventually rivaled Tyre itself in wealth and magnificence. The Phœnicians formed commercial stations along the coasts of Asia Minor and the shores of the Euxine, or Black Sea, before the Greeks; thus establishing intercourse with Thrace, Colchis and Scythia. In the Persian Gulf the Phœnicians had trading stations on the islands of Tylos and Aradus (perhaps Bahrein), from which their vessels descended the Persian Gulf and traded with India and Ceylon, bringing diamonds and pearls from those Eastern lands. At the head of the Red Sea they had a station at Elath, or Ezion-géber, which was the starting-point for voyages to Ophir, a rich country in the distant South or East, believed by some to have been in the South-west of Arabia, or Arabia Felix (now Yemen), by others to have been on the Eastern coast of South Africa, in the modern Sofala, and by others still to have been on the peninsula of Malacca, in the Southern part of Farther India. Ophir was famed for its gold, which the Phœnicians brought from there in large quantities.

The land-trade of the Phœnicians was divided into three great branches—the Egyptian and Arabian; the Babylonian to

Central Asia and the far East; and the Armenian and Scythian. From Arabia Felix (Arabia the Happy)—now called Yemen—caravans brought through the desert such articles as frankincense, myrrh, cassia, gold and precious stones. Before the Phœnicians had a port on the Red Sea they brought by way of Arabia the products of Southern India and Africa, particularly cinnamon, ivory and ebony. The Hebrew prophet Ezekiel described this trade. The Arabian trade was mainly carried by caravans. The Northern Arabs, especially the princes of Kedar and the Midianites, were great traveling merchants; and the Kingdom of Edom, afterwards Idumæa, in the North of Arabia, reached a high degree of commercial prosperity. On the sea-coast the Edomites were in possession of the ports of Elath and Ezion-géber (now Akaba), at the head of the Red Sea; in the interior they had the metropolis of Pétra, whose magnificent remains were discovered in the present century. As is characteristic of the immutable civilization of Asia, the commercial caravans of antiquity resembled those of the present day. Merchants traveled in bands organized like an army, conveying their merchandise on the backs of camels, "the ships of the desert." They were escorted by armed forces, sometimes furnished from home, but more frequently consisting of some plundering tribe, hired at a great price, to secure the caravan from the exactions and attacks of other like marauding tribes. Most of the Phœnician trade with Egypt was overland, at least so long as Thebes was the capital and metropolis of Egypt; and when Memphis rose to preëminence an entire quarter of the city was assigned to the Phœnician merchants, and the trade by sea to the Delta became important.

PHŒNICIAN SHIPS.

The first branch of the Phœnician trade

in the East was with Judæa and Syria. The Phœnicians depended on Palestine for their grain, and this explains the cause of their close alliance and friendship with the Hebrew nation in the days of David and Solomon. The most important branch of Eastern trade was through Babylon with Central Asia. A considerable portion of the route lay through the Syrian desert; and, to facilitate the passage of the caravans, two of the most remarkable cities of antiquity—Baalath (afterwards Baalbec, or Heliopolis) and Tadmor (afterwards Palmyra) were founded in the Syrian desert by King Solomon, who desired to procure for his subjects a share in this lucrative traffic.

The Northern land-trade of the Phœnicians is thus described by the Hebrew prophet Ezekiel: "Javan, Tubal and Méshech, they were thy merchants; they traded the persons of men and vessels of brass in thy markets. They of the house of Togarmah, traded in thy fairs with horses and horsemen and mules."

But the Mediterranean sea was the great commercial highway of the Phœnicians. Spain was the richest country of the ancient world in the precious metals. The Phœnician colonies reduced the natives to slavery, and forced them to work in the mines. Says the prophet Ezekiel: "Tarshish was thy merchant by reason of the multitude of all kind of riches; with silver, iron, tin and lead, they traded in thy fairs." From Spain the Phœnicians entered the Atlantic Ocean and proceeded to the British Isles, where they obtained tin from the mines of Cornwall; and probably from the coasts of the Baltic they procured amber, which was considered more precious than gold in ancient times. From their trading stations on the Red Sea and the Persian Gulf, the Phœnicians traded with the coasts of India and the island of Ceylon, and with Africa. During the reign of Neko, King of Egypt, a Phœnician fleet, in a three years' voyage, discovered the passage around the Cape of Good Hope, returning home by way of the Atlantic and the Mediterranean, as we have seen in the history of Egypt.

Concerning the ancient Phœnicians, a certain writer says: "Though their voyages did not equal in daring those of modern times, yet, when we consider that they were ignorant of the mariner's compass, and of the art of taking accurate astronomical observations, it is wonderful to reflect on the commercial enterprise of a people whose ships were to be seen in the harbors of Britain and Ceylon."

SECTION IV.—PHŒNICIAN ARTS AND CIVILIZATION.

ESIDES their carrying trade the Phœnicians derived great wealth from their manufactures. The textile fabrics of the Sidonians, and the purple cloths of the Tyrians, were celebrated from the most remote antiquity. The "Tyrian purple," the chief product of the Phœnicians, was a famous dye, obtained in minute drops from two shell-fish, the *buccinum* and the *murex*. This purple was of a dark red-violet, of various shades, according to the species of mussel employed. Cotton, linen and silk fabrics were dyed with this hue, but the most beautiful effects were obtained from woolen goods. The dye being very costly, it was used only for stuffs of the best quality. The manufacture and use of this dye prevailed in all the Phœnician cities. Homer represents his heroes as clad in Sidonian robes dyed with Tyrian purple.

Vegetable dyes of exceeding beauty and variety were also in use, the dyeing being always performed in the raw materials; and the art of producing shot colors by using threads of various tints was only understood by the Phœnicians. The Phœnicians claimed to be the inventors of glass-blowing; and, though the Egyptians have as good a claim to the discovery, the Phœnicians were the first to attain the highest skill in the art. Sidon and Sarepta were the chief seats of the glass-manufacture. The sand used was procured from the banks of the little river Belus, near the promontory of Carmel. Numerous specimens of Phœnician glass-ware yet remain, and bear witness to the skillful workmanship of this renowned ancient people. The Phœnicians were likewise skilled in pottery; and the Greeks acquired from them the art of making painted vases, which they afterwards carried to remarkable perfection. They largely exported pottery in exchange for tin in their voyages to Cornwall and the Scilly Isles. The Phœnicians likewise achieved great skill in bronze-work and in jewelry. The specimens of their jewelry found by modern explorers testify to the wonderful skill and taste exhibited by these ancient people in this branch of industry. They were also celebrated for their beautiful carvings in ivory.

The Phœnicians also displayed some skill in agriculture. Excellent wines were produced in the vicinity of Tyre, Berytus and Gebal, and also in the Lebanon mountain region. Silk, then as at present, was an important product. The fruits of this region were famed for their excellence and abundance.

It was once thought that the Phœnicians invented letters, but recent investigations and discoveries throw considerable doubt upon this claim. But, while other ancient Oriental nations had ideographic systems of writing—as for example, the Egyptians—the Phœnicians had an alphabet of twenty-two letters apparently selected from the characters of the Egyptian hieratic writing. Each letter of this alphabet invariably represented one articulation, and the Phœnicians seem to have been the first people to use such a system. It is believed that the Phœnician alphabet was invented about the time of Avaris, one of the Shepherd Kings of Egypt, several centuries prior to the exodus of the Israelites from that country. It is the first real alphabet which has been thus far discovered; and whether the Phœnicians invented letters or not, they were the first people to use them in their proper manner, as a system different from hieroglyphic or ideographic writing. The Phœnicians established their alphabet wherever they carried their commercial enterprises, and thus they instructed other nations in the use of letters. As M. Renan truly asserts, the alphabet was a Phœnician export.

According to the evidence furnished us by the Hebrew Scriptures, the Phœnicians were descended from Canaan, a son of Ham, thus implying that they were a Hamitic people; but they spoke a purely Semitic language—a language akin to that of the Hebrews, the Syrians, the Assyrians and the Semitic Babylonians. Says a certain writer: "It is certain that the Phœnician idiom differed but slightly, and in no important point, from that of the Hebrews. The identity of grammatical forms and of the vocabulary are so complete between the Hebrew and the Phœnician, that they cannot be considered as two distinct languages, but merely as two slightly differing dialects of the same language."

The Phœnicians were a literary people at a very early day. Their written law embraced the principles of their religion and their social and political systems. They had books treating on religion, agriculture and the practical arts; and the different Phœnician cities had regular archives or records in writing, going back to very early times, and preserved with wonderful care. They made remarkable progress in the sciences. The Sidonian architects were regarded as the best in Syria. In Phœnicia, particularly in Sidon, did astronomy, arithmetic, geometry, navigation and philosophy flourish; and the Sidonians endeavored to atone for the loss of their political and commercial supremacy among the Phœnician cities by their intellectual glory. The eminent characters of ancient Phœnicia were the historian, Sanchoniathon, of Tyre, and the philosopher, Moschus, of Sidon; both of whom are said to have flourished about the time of the Trojan war, in the twelfth century before Christ.

The character of Phœnician architecture is shown by a few remaining buildings. Its prominent characteristic, in the words of M. Renan, "is its massive and imposing strength—a want, indeed, of finish in details, but a general effect of power and grandeur. In short it is a monolithic art." The Phœnician buildings were constructed of enormous stones, similar to those yet to be seen in the lower walls of the temple at Jerusalem, which were built by Phœnician architects and masons, and like those still to be seen in the sea-wall of the ruins of Tyre. The Phœnician tombs were original in design and grand in construction. All their edifices seemed intended to last; and so durable have they been, that, notwithstanding the hard fate to which they have been subjected, many monuments of the days of Phœnician glory remain to give us some light on the antiquities of this famous race of merchants and colonizers.

Phœnician statuary seems to be a mingling of the styles of Egypt and Assyria, the general form being Egyptian, while the execution is Assyrian. There were few large statues, but many small statuettes, some of which display remarkable artistic skill, and are made of stone, while others are constructed of baked clay and bronze, exhibiting neither taste in design nor elegance in execution. Both kinds of statuettes were designed as idols, of which one or more were in every Phœnician dwelling. The first class were those belonging to the wealthy; while the rougher and coarser sort, made hastily and cheaply, were those found in the possession of the poor.

The ancient Egyptian paintings represent the Phœnicians as having dark, florid complexions, and well-formed, regular features, approaching the European cast. They are also represented with blue eyes and flaxen hair. The hair, when dressed for ornament, was powdered white and covered with a network of blue beads, or a close cap wound around by a fillet of scarlet leather, with two long ends hanging down behind, in the Egyptian style.

The Phœnician dress was usually a short cloak or cape thrown over the shoulders and extending to the elbows, and fastened at the waist by a golden girdle, which, in some cases, encircled the body many times, and was tied in front with a large bow-knot. The inner garment was of fine linen, confined to the waist and extending almost down to the feet. The Phœnicians also wore woolen mantles and tunics, of fine texture and edged with gold lace.

The Egyptian paintings represent the Sidonians as allies of the Pharaohs in their wars with the Canaanites. The statesmen and merchants are represented as having long hair and beards, and with a fillet around the head. The soldiers are depicted with short hair and beard. The arms and accouterments of the Sidonians were very elegant. The helmet was of silver, with a peculiar ornament at the crest, consisting of a disk and two horns of a heifer, or of a crescent. The breast-plate was also of silver, quilted upon a white linen garment, which was laced in front and extended to the armpits, being held by shoulder-straps. The shield was large and round, and made of iron, rimmed and studded with gold. The sword was two-edged and made of bronze. The spear was remarkably long.

It is believed that the Hebrews obtained their ornaments of dress and their articles of domestic luxury from their Phœnician neighbors. Says the Jewish prophet Isaiah: "In that day the Lord will take away the bravery of their tinkling ornaments about their feet, and their cauls, and their round tires like the moon; the chains, and the bracelets, and the mufflers; the bonnets, and the ornaments of the legs, and the head-bands, and the tablets, and the ear-rings; the rings, and nose-jewels; the changeable suits of apparel, and the mantles, and the wimples, and the crisping-pins; the glasses, and the fine linen, and the hoods, and the veils."

SECTION V.—PHŒNICIAN RELIGION.

THE Phœnician religion was a gross polytheism, and is but imperfectly understood, as there is no sacred book, like the Old Testament of the Hebrews, or like the Zend-Avesta of the Medes and Persians, or the Vedas of the Sanskritic Hindoos, or the Ritual of the Dead of the Egyptians, to spread before us a view of the system. Neither is there any extensive range of sculptures or paintings to give us an idea of the outward aspect of the worship, as in Egypt, Assyria and Greece. Neither has any ancient writer given us any account of this religion excepting Philo Byblius, a Greek writer of the first or second century after Christ, and who was a native of Byblus. This author is quoted by Eusebius in his "Evangelical Preparation" several centuries later. But the work of Philo Byblius deals exclusively with Phœnician cosmogony and mythology, and thus gives us no light upon the real character of the religion. We are obliged to rely mainly upon the notices of the Phœnician religion by the writers of portions of the Old Testament, upon incidental allusions by classical authors, upon inscriptions, upon the etymology of names, and upon occasional representations accompanying inscriptions upon stones or coins. These are, however, so disconnected and vague as to give us but scanty and unsatisfactory knowledge of the inner nature of the Phœnician religious system.

The Phœnician religion evidently was derived from the same source from which the religions of Chaldæa and Assyria took their origin. It was based on the conception of one Supreme and Universal Divine Being, "whose person was hardly to be distinguished from the material world, which had emanated from his substance without any distinct act of creation." The Universal Supreme Being was usually termed Baal, meaning "the Lord." He represented the sun, which was regarded as the great agent of creative power. He was divided into a number of secondary divinities, named Baalim, who emanated from his substance and were simply personifications of his various attributes. "The supreme god, considered as the progenitor of different beings, became Baal-Thammuz, called also Adon, 'the Lord,' whence the Grecian Adonis. As a preserver, he was Baal-Chon; as a destroyer, Baal-Moloch; as presiding over the decomposition of those destroyed beings whence new life was again to spring, Baal-Zebub." Other gods were El, Elium, Sadyk, Adonis, Melkarth, Dagon, Eshmun, Shamas and Kabiri.

Each divinity had his female principle, or wife. Each secondary Baal had a corresponding Baalath, representing the same god under a different aspect. The female principle of the great god Baal at Sidon was Ashtoreth, or Astarte, the representative of the moon, therefore corresponding to the Grecian goddess Artemis, or Diana. The planets were worshiped under the generic title of Cabirim, the "powerful ones." Fire was likewise reverenced, and the sun and star deities were emphatically "fire gods." Movers describes the Phœnician religion as "an apotheosis of the forces and laws of nature; an adoration of the objects in which these forces were seen, and where they appeared most active."

The most cruel and licentious ceremonies accompanied the worship of the Phœnician deities. Children were burnt alive to appease the wrath of Baal-Moloch; a custom carried to great excess in Carthage. There was a systematic offering of human victims as expiatory sacrifices to El and other gods. The reason for this shocking superstitious custom is to be found in the words addressed by Balak to Balaam, as follows: "Wherewith shall I come before the Lord, and bow myself before the high God? Shall I come before Him with burnt offerings, with calves of a year old? Will the Lord be pleased with thousands of rams, or with ten thousands of rivers of oil? Shall I give my first-born for my transgression, the fruit of my body for the sin of my soul?" Philo Byblius says: "It was customary among the ancients, in times of great calamity and danger, that the rulers of the city or nation should offer up the best beloved of their children, as an expiatory sacrifice to the avenging deities; and these victims were slaughtered mystically." The Phœnicians were instructed that at one time the god El himself, under the pressure of extreme peril, had taken his only son, clad him in kingly attire, set him as a victim upon an altar, and killed him with his own hand. Thereafter it was the duty of rulers to follow this divine example, and private persons, when surrounded by difficulties, might offer up their children to appease the divine anger. Porphyry says that "the Phœnician history was full of instances, in which that people, when suffering under great calamity from war, or pestilence, or drought, chose by public vote one of those most dear to them, and sacrificed him to Saturn."

The worship of Ashtoreth in Phœnicia and Syria was accompanied with licentious rites. The worship of the great Nature-goddess "tended to encourage dissoluteness in the relations between the sexes, and even to sanctify impurities of the most abominable description." "This religion silenced all the best feelings of human nature, degraded men's minds by a superstition alternately cruel and profligate, and we may seek in vain for any influence for good it could have exercised on the nation." The religion well illustrated the moral character of the Phœnicians, who were generally insubordinate, but also servile, gloomy and cruel, corrupt and fierce, covetous and selfish, vindictive and treacherous. Being traders in everything they were devoid of every kindly feeling and lofty impulse.

The Phœnicians did not worship images of their deities, and were therefore not idolaters, in the usual acceptation of the term. In the temple of Melkarth at Gades there was no material emblem of the god whatever, exceping a constantly-burning fire. In other places conical stones, called *bætyli*, were dedicated to the different deities, and were honored with a limited adoration, being considered as possessing a certain mystic virtue. These stones were sometimes replaced by pillars, which were erected in front of the temples and had sacrifices offered to them. The pillars were mostly of wood, though sometimes of stone or metal, and were called *asherahs*, "uprights," by the Jews. On festive occasions they were adorned with boughs of trees, flowers and ribbons, and constituted the chief object of a worship of a sensual and debasing nature. An emblem in the Assyrian sculptures is regarded as conveying a correct idea of the usual appearance of these *asherahs* at such times.

Phœnician worship was conducted publicly, and included praise, prayer and sacrifice. Animals were generally sacrificed, though, as we have observed, there were frequently human sacrifices. The victims were usually consumed entirely upon the altars. Libations of wine were lavishly poured out in honor of the principal deities, and incense was burnt in extravagant profusion. Sometimes an endeavor was made to influence the deity by vociferous and prolonged cries, and even by self-inflicted wounds and mutilation. Festivals were frequently held, particularly one at the vernal equinox, on which occasion sacrifices on a large scale were made, and vast multitudes of people assembled at the leading temples.

Says Rawlinson: "Altogether the religion of the Phœnicians, while possessing some redeeming points, as the absence of images and deep sense of sin which led them to sacrifice what was nearest and dearest to them to appease the divine anger, must be regarded as one of the lowest and most debasing of the forms of belief and worship prevalent in the ancient world, combining as it did impurity with cruelty, the sanction of licentiousness with the requirement of bloody rites, revolting to the conscience, and destructive of any right apprehension of the true idea of God."

SECTION VI.—GEOGRAPHY OF SYRIA.

YRIA—at present a province of the Turkish Empire—now embraces ancient Syria, Palestine and Phœnicia; thus having an area of about seventy thousand square miles and a population of two millions. It is located between the Arabian desert on the east and the Mediterranean sea on the west. The Greeks regarded Syria as including Palestine and Phœnicia, but the Jews always considered these three countries as distinct from each other. Aram was the Jewish name for Syria. Ancient Syria proper was bounded on the west by the Mediterranean, on the north by Mount Amanus, on the east by the Euphrates and Arabia, and on the south by Arabia. Its principal geographical divisions in the time of the Romans were Syria proper; Cœle-Syria, or Hollow-Syria; and Commagéné, in the North.

The chief mountains of Syria were Amanus, now Al Lucan; Casius, now Cas; Libanus and Anti-Libanus, the Mount Lebanon of Scripture, whose summit is said to be perpetually capped with snow. The principal rivers of Syria are the Euphrates, the Orontes and the Leontes. The small river called Eleutherus was anciently said to be haunted by a dragon, whose immense jaws could receive a mounted horseman. The Sabbatum was represented as ceasing to flow on the Sabbath. The Adonis, tinged with reddish sand in the rainy season, was believed to flow with blood on the anniversary of the death of Adonis, who was said to have been killed on its banks by a wild boar. The palm, the plane-tree and the cypress are

PUBLIC GARDEN, DAMASCUS.

among the forest trees of Syria. Grapes are produced in abundance, as are also the different kinds of grain, and millet. The climate is delightful. The animals of Syria are those usually found in South-western Asia. The Syrian goat is remarkable for its long hair and its pendulous ears, the hair having been a valued article of commerce for many centuries. The wolf, the jackal and the fox are seen in the mountains.

Damascus—the chief city of ancient, as of modern, Syria—is believed by its people to be the original seat of paradise. Antioch, the Greek capital of Syria, was celebrated for its beauty and magnificence. In the famous grove of Daphne, near Antioch, Venus was worshiped with licentious ceremonies. Hieropolis was renowned for its temple of Venus, which was so rich that the Roman general Crassus was engaged for several days in weighing the spoils when he captured the city. Emessa had a temple to the sun. Other famous cities of ancient Syria were Tadmor, in the desert, later

PALMYRA. TRIUMPHAL ARCH.

known as Palmyra, and Baalbec, the Greek Heliopolis, or City of the Sun.

The earliest inhabitants are believed to have been the Aramites, or Aramæans, the descendants of Aram, Shem's youngest son. Some of the posterity of Hamath, a son of Canaan, is also said to have dwelt there in primitive times. The Hebrew Scriptures

The history of Syria, like that of Asia Minor, has little political unity. Since its petty ancient states have lost their independence the country has been under the successive sway of the Assyrians, the Babylonians, the Medo-Persians, the Græco-Macedonians, the Romans, the Saracens, the Seljuk Turks, the Mongol Tartars, and for the

PALMYRA; MIDDLE CROSSING OF GRAND COLONNADE; GRANITE MONOLITH.

represent primeval Syria as divided into a number of small kingdoms, among which were Damascus, Hamath, Zobah and Geshur. Syria is believed to be one of the earliest inhabited regions of the globe, and the modern Syrians still have traditions representing their country as the oldest in the world.

The Syrians were at first governed by numerous petty chiefs, called kings, a title which the ancient writers applied to every ruler or leader, or chief, of a community.

last four centuries under the Ottoman Turks. Under its present masters the country has everywhere fallen into decay, and can scarcely be said to have any history; though in ancient and mediæval times it was the theater of many important events, having witnessed the prowess and martial deeds of Sennacherib, Nebuchadnezzar, Pompey, Abu-bekir and Omar, Godfrey of Bouillon, Saladin and Richard the Lionhearted, Zingis-Khan and Tamerlane.

SECTION VII.—HISTORY OF DAMASCUS.

REVIOUS to its organization into a satrapy of the Medo-Persian Empire, Syria had never been united under one government. During the period of Assyrian supremacy the country was divided into no less than five leading states, some of which were mere loose confederacies. The five states were the Northern Hittites, whose capital was Carchemish, on the Euphrates; the Patena, on the Lower Orontes, whose capital was Kinalua; the Hamathites, on the Upper Orontes, whose capital was Hamath (now Hamah); the Southern Hittites, in the region south of Hamath; and the Syrians of Damascus, whose capital was Damascus.

Of all these pretty states, the most powerful and the best-known was Syria of Damascus. The city of Damascus is the oldest

ARAB TEMPLE AT BAALBEC.

known city of the world, its existence dating as far back as the time of Abraham, about four thousand years ago. The kingdom of Damascus arose in the twelfth century before Christ, after the Hebrew king Saul had vanquished the King of Zobah, one of the

1—21.-U. H.

ANCIENT HISTORY.—PHŒNICIA AND SYRIA.

GREAT STONE AT BAALBEC.

most ancient Syrian kingdoms. HADAD, King of Damascus, assisted Hadadezar, King of Zobah, against the great Hebrew king David, but was defeated in a great battle by David, who captured Damascus, Belah and Berothai; and Hadad submitted to the supremacy of his Hebrew conqueror. Near the close of the reign of Solomon, David's illustrious successor, REZON, King of Damascus, who had originally been a slave, revolted against the Hebrew rule and reëstablished the independence of the kingdom of Damascus. TAB-RIMMON, King of Damascus, was contemporary with Abijah, King of Judah, from about B. C. 960 to B. C. 950. BEN-HADAD I., his son and successor, was contemporary with Baasha in Israel and Asa in Judah, about from B. C. 950 to B. C. 920, and warred with Baasha and his successor, Omri. BEN-HADAD II., son and successor of Ben-hadad I., was contemporary with Ahab, King of Israel, about B. C. 900, and warred with that monarch. He was a powerful monarch, and had thirty-two vassal kings in his army. He adorned Damascus with splendid edifices, and did much to advance the glory of his kingdom. He was finally murdered treacherously by his servant HAZAEL, who then usurped the throne of Damascus. Hazael was a great warrior and an able monarch, and reigned contemporaneously with Jehu, King of Israel, and Shalmaneser II., the Black Obelisk King of Assyria, about B. C. 850. He won several great victories over the armies of Israel and Judah, wresting important territories from the kings of both of those nations, and forcing them to pay him tribute. He also seized Elath, on the Red Sea, and largely advanced the commercial prosperity of his dominions. After his death the Syrians deified him, and thus rendered him an object of worship. Hazael's son and successor, BEN-HADAD III., contemporary with Jehoahaz and Joash of Israel, about B. C. 840, oppressed the Israelites, but was three times defeated by Joash, and lost the provinces which his father had wrested from the Israelites. The Syrians of Damascus were now for some time tributary to Jeroboam II., King of Israel. They, however, recovered their independence amid the dissensions which prevailed in Israel upon Jeroboam's death. REZIN, the last King of Damascus, became the ally of Pekah, King of Israel, against Ahaz, King of Judah, for the purpose of dethroning the latter, and putting a stranger named Tabael on the throne of David. The allied kings besieged Jerusalem, but without success. They, however, carried on a predatory war during the following year, and the Syrians returned to Damascus with much valuable booty and many captives. Ahaz, in revenge, sent valuable presents to Tiglath-Pileser II., King of Assyria, for the purpose of securing his aid againgst Damascus. The Assyrian king at once led an army into Syria, took Damascus and put Rezin to death. Most of the Damascenes were carried captive to Kir, in Media, and the ancient kingdom of Damascus came to an inglorious end, about B. C. 732.

KINGS OF DAMASCUS.

KNOWN KINGS.	TIME OF REIGN.	CONTEMPORARY KINGS.
HADAD	About B. C. 1040	David in Israel.
REZON	" " 1000	Solomon in Israel.
TAB-RIMMON	" " 960–950	Abijah in Judah.
BEN-HADAD I.	" " 950–920	Baasha in Israel and Asa in Judah.
BEN-HADAD II.	" " 900	Ahab in Israel.
HAZAEL	" " 850	Jehu in Israel and Shalmaneser II. in Assyria.
BEN-HADAD III.	" " 840	Jehoahaz in Israel.
REZIN	" " 745–732	Ahaz in Judah and Pekah in Israel.

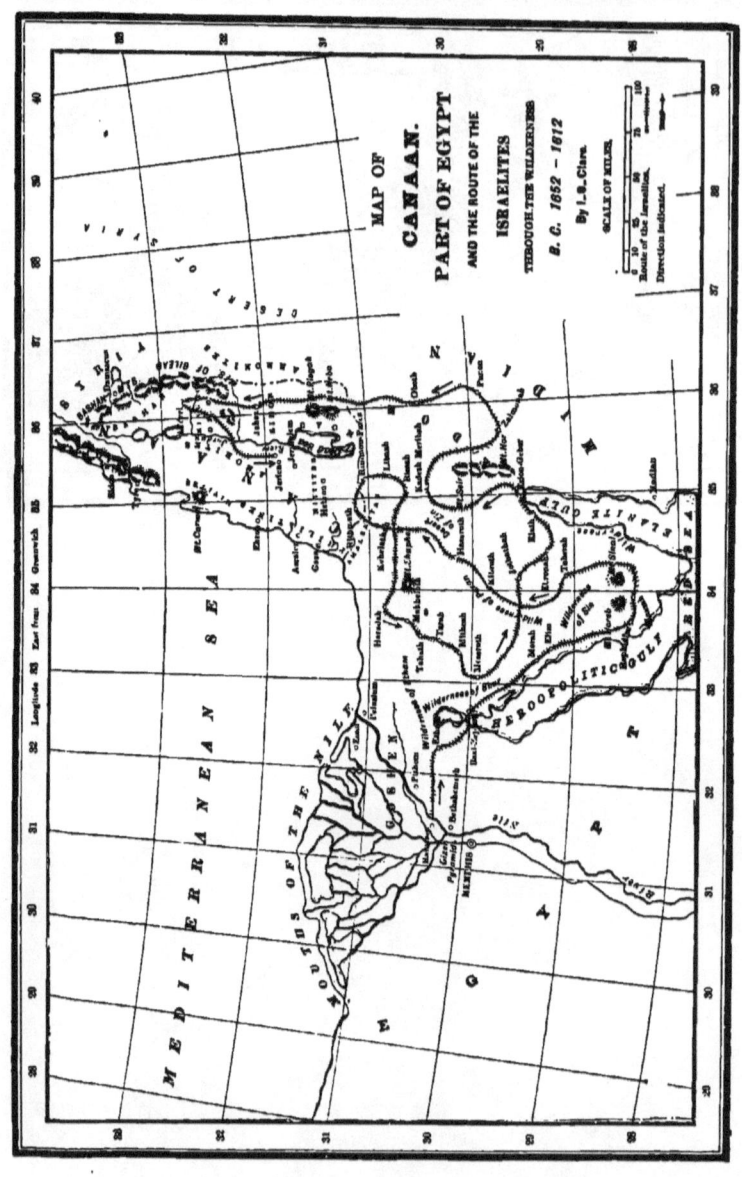

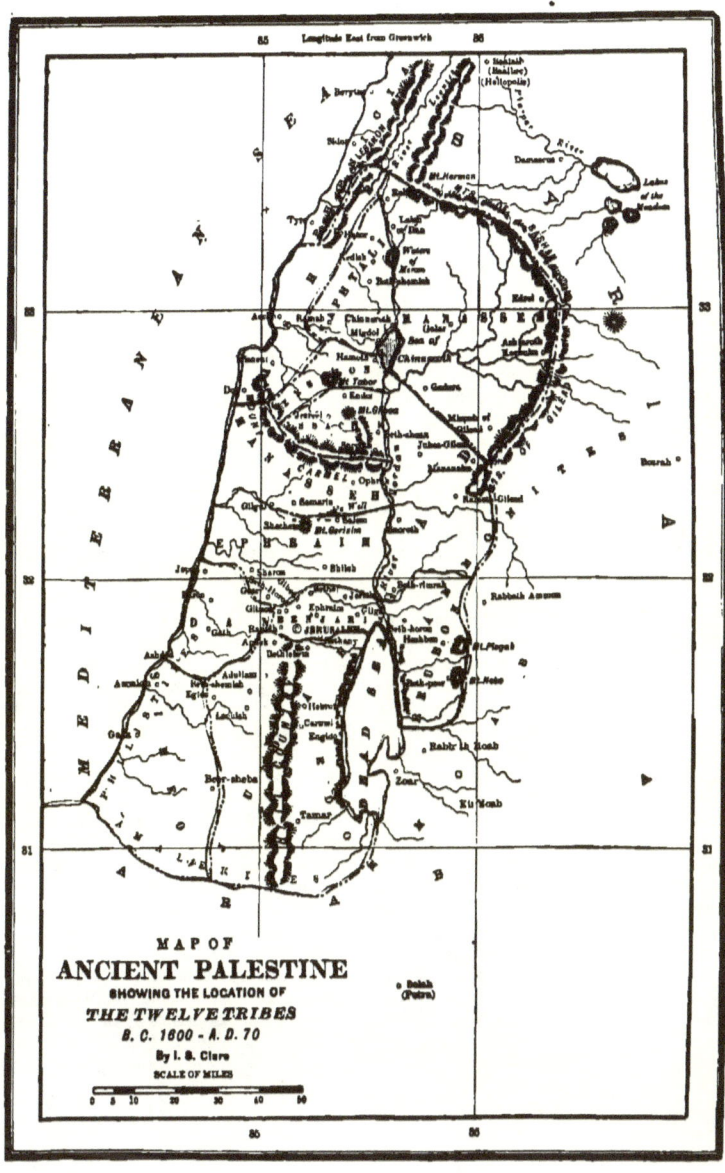

MAP OF
ANCIENT PALESTINE
SHOWING THE LOCATION OF
THE TWELVE TRIBES
B. C. 1600 - A. D. 70
By I. S. Clare
SCALE OF MILES

CHAPTER VIII.

THE HEBREW NATION.

SECTION I.—THE HEBREW PATRIARCHS.

HILE the great mass of the population of ancient Chaldæa about two thousand years before Christ were polytheists, worshiping the multitudinous deities of the Chaldæan pantheon, there was a small Semitic band of nomads who were pure monotheists, recognizing Jehovah (or Elohim) as the only God. At this time the leader of this small band was the famous patriarch Abram, the son of Terah, and a native of "Ur of the Chaldees." This patriarch has become celebrated as the founder of several Semitic nations, among them the Hebrews, or Israelites, and the Arabs. During the general migration of Semitic and Hamitic tribes from Chaldæa after the death of Nimrod, Abram with his father, Terah, and his flocks and herds, removed from Ur to Haran up the Euphrates.

Says the Book of Genesis: "And Terah took Abram his son, and Lot the son of Haran his son's son, and Sarai his daughter-in-law, his son Abram's wife; and they went forth with them from Ur of the Chaldees, to go into the land of Canaan; and they came unto Haran, and dwelt there." After alluding to Terah's death in Haran, the Mosaic narrative further says: "Now the Lord had said unto Abram, Get thee out of thy country, and from thy kindred, and from thy father's house, unto a land that I will show thee. And I will make thee a great nation, and I will bless thee, and make thy name great; and thou shalt be a blessing. And I will bless them that bless thee, and curse them that curse thee; and in thee shall all families of the earth be blessed."

Abram's brother, Nahor, delighted with the beauty and fertility of the Mesopotamian plain, remained at Haran; while Abram, after the burial of his father, migrated with his flocks and herds, and with his wife, Sarai, and his brother's son, Lot, "and all the souls they had gotten in Haran," to the "promised land of Canaan," where the new emigrants from Mesopotamia received from the inhabitants the name "Hebrews," meaning "strangers from the other side," "the men who had crossed the river," "the emigrants from Mesopotamia." Journeying through the Syrian desert he tarried for some time at Damascus, which was then an old city. At Damascus he met his faithful servant Eliezer, whom he created "steward of his house." Thence he passed on to the south, crossing the Jordan and entering the "Promised Land," halting in the valley of Sichem, or Shechem. The Hebrew record goes on to say: "And the Lord appeared unto Abram, and said, Unto thy seed will I give this land; and there builded he an altar unto the Lord, who appeared unto him." Abram proceeded "unto a mountain on the east of Bethel, and pitched his tent, having Bethel on the west, and Hai on the east; and there he builded an altar unto the Lord, and called upon the name of the Lord."

This country—then called Canaan, from one of Ham's sons, whose descendants had peopled it, and afterwards known as Judæa, and now called Palestine—was inhabited by many idolatrous tribes. Abram settled in the mountain region, where he was secure from the Canaanites, who dwelt in the more fertile plains below, but where he had but scant pasturage for his cattle. He pushed on further southward, but was driven by a famine into Egypt. Fearing that the Pharaoh who then reigned over Egypt would be tempted by Sarai's beauty to kill him to get her in his possession, Abram passed her off as his sister. Thinking that she was an unmarried woman, the Egyptian monarch took her to his house, and bestowed wealth and honors upon Abram with a lavish hand. But says the Mosaic account: "The Lord plagued Pharaoh and his house with great plagues because of Sarai, Abram's wife. And Pharoah called Abram, and said, What is this that thou hast done unto me? why didst thou not tell me that she was thy wife? Why saidst thou, She is my sister? so I might have taken her to me to wife; now therefore behold thy wife, take her, and go thy way. And Pharaoh commanded his men concerning him; and they sent him away, and his wife, and all that he had."

Thereupon Abram left Egypt, with his wife and with Lot, "and all that he had," and returned to Canaan. "And Abram was very rich in cattle, in silver, and in gold." Returning to Bethel, near which he had before erected his tent, "Abram called on the name of the Lord." "And Lot also, which went with Abram, had flocks, and herds, and tents." The land was not rich enough for their sustenance; and Abram and Lot here separated, because "there was strife between the herdmen of Abram's cattle and the herdmen of Lot's cattle." Abram at first remained on the mountains, while Lot descended to the fertile plain of the Jordan, near Sodom. Abram then removed southward to the "oaks of Mamre," near Hebron, and that place thereafter remained his usual abode.

Shortly afterward, Chedorlaomer, King of Chaldæa, who had built up the first great empire in Western Asia, invaded the South of Canaan, and conquered the five cities of Sodom, Gomorrah, Admah, Zeboiim and Bela (afterwards called Zoar), which had risen in revolt against him. In this war Lot and all his cattle were captured and carried away by the victorious Chaldæans. But Abram, with a band of three hundred and eighteen of his own people and a body of Amorite allies, pursued the hosts of Chedorlaomer, and routed them near Damascus, rescuing Lot and recovering all the booty that they had taken from the five Canaanite cities.

Says the Hebrew record: "After these things the word of the Lord came unto Abram in a vision, saying, Fear not Abram; I am thy shield, and thy exceeding great reward. And Abram said, Lord God, what wilt thou give me, seeing I go childless, and the steward of my house is this Eliezer of Damascus. And Abram said, Behold, to me thou hast given no seed; and, lo, one born in my house is mine heir. And, behold, the word of the Lord came unto him, saying, This shall not be thine heir; but he that shall come forth out of thine own bowels shall be thine heir. And he brought him forth abroad, and said, Look now toward heaven, and tell the stars if thou be able to number them; and he said unto him, So shall thy seed be. And he believed in the Lord and counted it for righteousness. And he said unto him, I am the Lord that brought thee out of Ur of the Chaldees, to give thee this land to inherit it. * * * * And when the sun was going down, a deep sleep fell upon Abram; and, lo, an horror of great darkness fell upon him. And he said unto Abram, know of a surety that thy seed shall be a stranger in a land that is not theirs, and shall serve them; and they shall afflict them four hundred years. And also that nation, whom they shall serve, will I judge; and afterwards shall they come out with great substance. And thou shalt go to thy fathers in peace; thou shalt be buried in a good old age. But in the fourth generation they shall come hither again: for the iniquity of the Amorites is not yet full. And it came to pass, that, when the sun went down, and it was dark, behold a

THE GARDEN OF GETHSEMANE, PALESTINE.

smoking furnace, and a burning lamp that passed between those pieces. In that same day the Lord made a covenant with Abram, saying, Unto thy seed have I given this land, from the river of Egypt unto the great river, the river Euphrates.''

After sojourning ten years in the land of Canaan, Sarai began to despair of becoming the mother of Abram's heir and advised Abram to take to wife her servant Hagar, an Egyptian woman, by whom Abram had a son. Before the birth of the child, Hagar, puffed up with pride, treated her mistress with such insolence that Sarai felt constrained to punish her. Thereupon Hagar fled into the wilderness of Kadesh, southeast of Abram's abode. "And the angel of the Lord said unto her, I will multiply thy seed exceedingly, that it shall not be numbered for multitude. And the angel of the Lord said unto her, Behold, thou art with child, and shalt bear a son, and shalt call his name Ishmael; because the lord hath heard thy affliction. And he will be a wild man; his hand will be against every man, and every man's hand against him; he shall dwell in the presence of all his brethren.'' Hagar returned to her mistress before the child was born, and Abram named the child Ishmael. He is regarded as the progenitor of the Bedouin Arabs, who have always lived in a wild state. Regarding Ishmael as the heir promised him by Jehovah, Abram treated him with fatherly affection.

We are further told that "when Abram was ninety years old and nine, the Lord appeared to Abram, and said unto him, I am the Almighty God; walk before me, and be thou perfect. And I will make my covenant between me and thee, and will multiply thee exceedingly. And Abram fell on his face; and God talked with him, saying, As for me, behold my covenant is with thee, and thou shalt be a father of many nations. Neither shall thy name any more be called Abram, but thy name shall be Abraham; for a father of many nations have I made thee. And I will make thee exceeding fruitful, and I will make nations of thee, and kings shall come out of thee. And I will establish my covenant between me and thee and thy seed after thee in their generations for an everlasting covenant, to be a God unto thee, and to thy seed after thee. And I will give unto thee, and to thy seed after thee, the land wherein thou art a stranger, all the land of Canaan, for an everlasting possession; and I will be their God. And God said unto Abraham, Thou shalt keep my covenant therefore, thou and thy seed after thee in their generations. This is my covenant, which ye shall keep, between me and you and thy seed after thee; every man-child among you shall be circumcised. * * * * And God said unto Abraham, As for Sarai thy wife, thou shalt not call her name Sarai, but Sarah shall her name be. And I will bless her, and give thee a son also of her; yea, I will bless her and she shall be a mother of nations; kings of people shall be of her. * * * * * And God said, Sarah thy wife shall bear thee a son indeed; and thou shalt call his name Isaac; and I will establish my covenant with him for an everlasting covenant, and with his seed after him. And as for Ishmael, I have heard thee; Behold, I have blessed him, and will make him fruitful, and will multiply him exceedingly; twelve princes shall he beget, and I will make him a great nation. But my covnant I will establish with Isaac, which Sarah shall bear unto thee at this set time in the next year. And he left off talking with him, and God went up from Abraham.'' Abraham and Ishmael and all the males of his household were then circumcised.

We are told that some time after this, when Abraham was sitting at the door of his tent, he saw three men approaching. He at once arose and greeted them with a hearty welcome, and urged them to remain for the night. They accepted his invitation, and when they had partaken of the meal placed before them they revealed themselves to him, one as the angel Jehovah and the other two as attendant angels. It is said that the angels renewed to Abraham the Lord's promise that Sarah should bear him a son within a year; and that Sarah, who was within the tent, hearing them, and being ninety years old, laughed at this prediction; whereupon the angel reproved her for her skepticism, and reassured Abraham of the Divine promise. The angels, we are then told, went toward Sodom, accompanied part of the way by Abraham. In consideration of the favor with which the Lord Jehovah regarded Abraham as the founder of his chosen people, the angels informed him of the Divine purpose to destroy Sodom and Gomorrah and the cities of the plain as a punishment for their extreme wickedness, and told him that they were on their way to warn Lot and his family to save themselves by flight from the doomed cities. After the departure of the angels, we are told that Abraham vainly interceded for the cities; and that the Lord, in response to the patriarch's prayer, promised that if ten righteous men could be found in the cities he would spare them, but that even so small a number could not be found. Lot and his family, in obedience to the angels' warning, fled from Sodom; but his wife, in disregard of the warning, looked back, and, says the Scriptural record, "became a pillar of salt." Sodom, Gomorrah, Admah and Zeboiim were destroyed by a dreadful convulsion of nature, not a single individual escaping the terrible doom. Says the Hebrew account: "And the Lord rained upon Sodom and upon Gomorrah brimstone and fire from the Lord out of heaven; and he overthrew all those cities, and all the plain, and all the inhabitants of the cities, and that which grew upon the ground." Lot and his daughters sought refuge in Zoar, which was spared, we are told, in answer to his prayer; but fearing to remain there, Lot fled to the hill country, and found refuge in a cave east of the Dead Sea. There occurred the incestuous birth of Moab and Ammon, the respective ancestors of the Moabites and the Ammonites, whom Moses and Joshua found settled in the region east of the Jordan and the Dead Sea.

Soon after the destruction of the cities of the plain, Abraham proceeded to the south, establishing his abode in the tract between Egypt and Canaan. He concluded a treaty with the king of the country, named Abimelech, beside a well, which he named Beersheba (the Well of the Oath), in memory of the event. During his residence at Beersheba, his wife, Sarah, gave birth to the long-promised heir, who was circumcised and called Isaac. When Isaac was weaned the patriarch celebrated the occasion by a feast, during which Sarah observed Ishmael taunting Isaac, thus exciting her anger. She asked her husband to send Hagar and Ishmael away, so that Isaac might have no rival in his father's house. Abraham hesitated, as he had a paternal affection for Ishmael. "And God said unto Abraham, Let it not be grievous in thy sight because of the lad, and because of thy bond-woman; in all that Sarah hath said unto thee, harken unto her voice; for in Isaac shall thy seed be called. And also of the son of the bond-woman will I make a nation, because he is thy seed." The next morning Hagar and her son were furnished with provisions and sent away. Wandering in the wilderness of Beer-sheba, they were in danger of perishing from thirst, when, it is said, they were rescued by an angel. After growing up in the wilderness, Ishmael became a skillful archer. His mother obtained for him a wife from her own people, the Egyptians, and from him are descended the Bedouin Arabs. The Koreish tribe, which inhabited Mecca, regarded themselves as the direct descendants of Ishmael. The chief sanctuary of this tribe was the Caaba, believed by them to have been built by Ishmael and Abraham. Among the descendants of this tribe was Mohammed, the great prophet and founder of Islam.

Abraham seems to have lived at Beersheba many years. During his residence there, we are told, his faith in Jehovah was put to its severest test. Says the Scriptural account: "And it came to pass after these things that God did tempt Abraham, and said unto him, Abraham; and he said, Behold, here I am. And he said, Take thy son Isaac, whom thou lovest, and get thee

THE PATRIARCHS.

into the land of Moriah; and offer him for a burnt offering upon one of the mountains which I will tell thee of." With a sad heart, we are told that Abraham obeyed the Divine command, and taking Isaac with him to the land of Moriah, which is believed to be the hill on which the great temple at Jerusalem afterwards was built, he there built an altar and prepared to offer up Isaac as a sacrifice, when, says the narrative, "the angel of the Lord called unto him out of heaven, and said, Abraham, Abraham; and he said, Here am I. And he said, Lay not thine hand upon the lad, neither do thou anything unto him; for now, I know that thou fearest God, seeing thou hast not withheld thy son, thine only son, from me." The patriarch, seeing a ram caught by its horns in the bushes, offered it as a sacrifice instead of his son. "And the angel of the Lord called unto Abraham out of heaven the second time, and said, By myself have I sworn, saith the Lord; for because thou hast done this thing, and hast not withheld thy son, thine only son; That in blessing I will bless thee, and in multiplying I will multiply thy seed as the stars of the heaven, and as the sand which is upon the sea shore; and thy seed shall possess the gate of his enemies; and in thy seed shall all the nations of the earth be blessed; because thou hast obeyed my voice."

Some time after this Abraham returned to his old home at Mamre, near Hebron, where Sarah died. After purchasing the cave of Machpelah from the Hittites of Hebron, then called Kirjath-Arba, Abraham buried Sarah there; and the cave became his family sepulcher. After Sarah's burial Abraham returned to Beer-sheba. As he felt his end approaching, he determined to secure a wife for his son Isaac; and, in order that Isaac's posterity might be a pure race, he resolved to secure one of his kindred as a bride for his son. For this reason he sent his steward, Eliezer, to Mesopotamia, binding him by a solemn oath to select from his own family a wife for Isaac. Reaching Haran, Eliezer met the family of Bethuel, the son of Nahor, Abraham's brother. He chose Rebekah, the youngest and most beautiful daughter of the house, who, upon hearing of his mission, agreed to leave her own family and become her cousin Isaac's wife. Going with Eliezer to Canaan, she was greeted with joy by Isaac and his father. Isaac was said to have been forty years old when he married. After a marriage of twenty years Rebekah gave birth to twin sons—one called Esau and also Edom (the Red), on account of his ruddy complexion; the other name Jacob (the Supplanter).

After Isaac's marriage, Abraham took another wife, named Keturah, by whom he had six sons, one of whom was Midian, the ancestor of the Midianites, who occupied the region between the Dead Sea and the Elanitic gulf of the Red Sea, to the east of the Nabætheans. Abraham lavished gifts upon these sons, but sent them out of Canaan, which was reserved exclusively as the inheritance of Isaac, to whom the patriarch bequeathed all his vast wealth. Abraham died at Beer-sheba "in a good old age, and full of years." His sons, Isaac and Ishmael, buried him in the family tomb in the cave of Machpelah. Thus ended the career of the renowned patriarch who was the ancestor of the Israelites, the Bedouin Arabs, the Edomites and the Midianites.

After Abraham's death Isaac continued to dwell by the well of Lahai-roi, in the extreme South of Canaan, or Palestine, where his sons grew to manhood. Esau was a reckless man, an expert hunter, and his father's favorite. He was rough and hairy in appearance, and caused his parents much trouble. When forty years old he married two Hittite wives, contrary to his father's wish; thus introducing heathen alliances into the chosen family. Jacob was peaceful and prudent—ready to obtain by cunning and intrigue what Esau sought to procure by violent means. He was smooth-skinned, and fond of the peaceful occupation of the shepherd and the quiet life of the tent. Jacob was his mother's favorite.

As Esau came in one day, tired and hungry from the chase, he saw Jacob preparing a mess of red lentils, and asked him for "some of that red." Jacob asked Esau's birth-right in payment for the mess; and Esau, simply to gratify his appetite for the moment, agreed to the demand, thus "selling his birth-right for a mess of pottage." For this proceeding St Paul calls him "a *profane* person, who for one morsel of food sold his birth-right." Jacob, by his craft, became the head of the chosen family, and the progenitor of the chosen race.

When, in his old age, Isaac felt that his end was near, he informed Esau of his design of transmitting to him the patriarchal authority, and ordered him to prepare a feast for the occasion. Esau started to obtain venison, of which his father was very fond, whereupon Rebekah informed Jacob of her husband's intention. With her help Jacob craftily passed himself off upon his father as Esau, thus securing the patriarchal blessing, which made him the head of his family, and which, when once given, was irrevocable. Esau now returned from the chase, and was apprised of the trick by which he had been defrauded of his inheritance. His anger and grief were great. "He cried with a great and exceeding bitter cry, and said unto his father, Bless me, even me also, O my father." The spiritual blessing, having passed to Jacob, could not be recalled, but Isaac blessed Esau by promising him great earthly prosperity, qualified by submisson to his brother, whose yoke he should eventually break. Concerning this promise, Dr. William Smith, in his History of the Bible, says: "The prophecy was fulfilled in the prosperity of the Idumæans, their martial prowess, and their constant conflicts with the Israelites, by whom they were subdued under David, over whom they triumphed at the Babylonian captivity, and to whom they at last gave a king in the person of Herod the Great."

Thenceforth Esau was resolved to kill Jacob, delaying his design until after Isaac's death. Becoming aware of this, Rebekah induced her husband to send Jacob to her kindred for safety. Isaac was glad to do this, to procure a wife of pure blood for Jacob. Taking his staff Jacob started for Mesopotamia, taking the route by which Abraham had entered Canaan. Upon arriving at Abraham's old encampment at Bethel, he remained there all night, taking a stone for a pillow. "And he dreamed, and behold! a ladder set up on the earth, and the top of it reached to heaven; and behold the angels of God ascending and descending on it. And behold! the Lord stood above it, and said, I am the Lord God of Abraham thy father, and the God of Isaac; the land whereon thou liest, to thee will I give it, and to thy seed. And thy seed shall be as the dust of the earth; and thou shalt spread abroad to the west, and to the east, and to the north, and to the south; and in thee and in thy seed shall all the families of the earth be blessed. And behold I am with thee, and will keep thee in all places whither thou goest, and will bring thee again into this land; for I will not leave thee, until I have done that which I have spoken to thee of." When Jacob awoke he acknowledged the Divine presence by erecting an altar on the spot, which he named Bethel (the House of God), and solemnly dedicated himself and all that Jehovah should give him to the service of the Almighty. This was the turning point in Jacob's religious life, and occurred when he had reached a good age.

Proceeding on his journey, Jacob at length reached the home of his uncle Laban, his mother's brother, at Padan-Aram. There he was heartily welcomed, and fell in love with his beautiful cousin Rachel, the youngest daughter of Laban. Entering his uncle's service as a shepherd for wages, he asked of Laban the hand of Rachel, offering to serve him seven years for her. Laban, more crafty than Jacob, accepted this offer, but, taking advantage of the marriage customs of the country, gave his eldest daughter, Leah, who suffered with sore eyes, and could not easily be disposed of, in marriage to his nephew. Jacob was indignant at the fraud practiced upon him, but was obliged to submit, and consented to serve Laban seven years longer for his beloved Rachel. In the progress of these years eleven sons and a daughter were born to Jacob. Leah's sons were Reuben, Simeon, Levi, Judah, Issachar and Zebulun. Rachael bore Jacob one son, named Joseph. Leah bore him a daughter, named Dinah. Jacob had four sons with two concubines. Rachael's handmaid, Bilhah, bore him Dan and Naphtali; and Leah's handmaid, Zilpah, bore him Gad and Asher.

After the birth of Joseph, Jacob's youngest and favorite child, the son of Rachel, Jacob desired to return to his own country, but Laban prevailed upon him to serve him longer for a part of his flocks, Jacob's portion to be distinguished by certain marks. Laban endeavored to defeat this arrangement by trickery; but Jacob, more expert in cattle-breeding, foiled him and obtained most of the produce of the flocks. At length Jacob became rich in "cattle, and maidservants and manservants, and camels and asses."

After sojourning twenty years with Laban the Scriptural record says, "the Lord said unto Jacob, Return unto the land of thy fathers, and to thy kindred; and I will be with thee." Fearing that Laban would detain him, Jacob secretly set out on his return to Canaan; and after crossing the Euphrates, he passed through the desert by the great fountain of Palmyra, traveled across the eastern portion of the plain of Damascus and the plateau of Bashan, and entered the mountain land of Gilead, east of the Jordan, which constitutes the frontier between Palestine and the Syrian desert. There Laban with a considerable force overtook him. Rachel had taken along her father's household effects, and now, by an ingenious device, succeeded in concealing them. "And God came to Laban the Syrian in a dream by night, and said unto him, Take heed that thou speak not to Jacob either good or bad." Not finding his idols, Laban made a treaty with Jacob and set up a pile of stones as a witness of it. "And Jacob went on his way, and the angels of God met him. And when Jacob saw them, he said, This is God's host; and he called the name of that place Mahanaim."

Approaching Mount Seir, of which his brother Esau had become the powerful chieftain, Jacob was seriously alarmed, fearing that Esau might kill him in revenge for the loss of his birthright, and seize his family and flocks. He sent him a conciliatory message, and Esau came to him at the head of four hundred warriors. Jacob, in great alarm, prepared to meet the peril which menaced him, dividing his people and his flocks into two portions. Then he prayed to Jehovah, after which he sent rich presents to his brother, and then rested for the night. He arose before day the next morning, and sent his wives and children over the Jabbok, remaining behind to prepare by solitary meditation for the day's trials. While he tarried "a man" made his appearance and wrestled with him until the break of day. And when "the man" observed "that he prevailed not against him, he touched the hollow of his thigh; and the hollow of Jacob's thigh was out of joint as he wrestled with him. And he said, Let me go, for the day breaketh. And he said, I will not let thee go, except thou bless me. And he said unto him, What is thy name? And he said, Jacob. And he said, Thy name shall be called no more Jacob, but Israel; for as a prince hast thou power with God and with men, and hast prevailed. And Jacob asked him and said, Tell me, I pray thee, thy name. And he said, Wherefore is it that thou dost ask after my name? And he blessed him there. And Jacob called the name of the place Peniel; for I have seen God face to face, and my life is preserved."

It is said that Jacob never recovered from the lameness caused by the angel's touch, and in memory of this the Israelites, in after times, would not eat of the sinew in the hollow of the thigh.

Descending into the valley of the Jabbok, Jacob met Esau, who gave him a brotherly welcome. He had long before forgiven his brother for defrauding him of the spiritual blessing which his father had designed for him, and was satisfied with the earthly prosperity which he had achieved. After a pleasant interview between the brothers, Esau returned to Mount Seir, and Jacob proceeded on his journey to the Jordan, crossing the stream at Succoth. Entering Canaan, he moved on to Shechem, which was then a considerable town of the Amorites. He bought a piece of land from these people, and this was the first possession of the chosen family in the "Promised Land." There Jacob erected an altar to the "God of Israel," and renewed his promise to serve Him. He likewise dug a well, which is yet shown there, and known as "Jacob's well."

Jacob was now to experience the greatest trials of his life. Shechem, son of Hamor, prince of the Shechemites, carried off and outraged his daughter, Dinah, and notwithstanding he subsequently demanded her in marriage, Jacob's sons resolved to avenge the wrong done to their sister. They agreed to the marriage, and, throwing the Shechemites off their guard, treacherously attacked them, killed all the males, pillaged the city, and carried off the women and children, and likewise the flocks and herds. Jacob was intensely indignant at this treacherous act; and, in fear that the Canaanites would endeavor to avenge the massacre of their brethren, removed with his family and possessions to Bethel, whence he proceeded southward towards Mamre, where his father, Isaac, was yet living. In the vicinity of Bethlehem his beloved wife, Rachel, died in giving birth to Benjamin, and was buried at that place. Her tomb is preserved to this day. Jacob then proceeded to Mamre where he rejoined his father. It was some years after this that Isaac died, when his sons, Esau and Jacob, buried him in the cave of Machpelah. He died about thirteen years after Joseph had been sold by his brethren.

Joseph, Rachel's eldest son, was Jacob's favorite, upon whom his father bestowed such repeated and distinguishing marks of his affection as to excite the envy of his other sons. By playing the part of a spy upon his brothers, and informing their father of their misdeeds, Joseph won the implacable hatred of his brethren. When yet a mere lad he dreamed several remarkable dreams, which he regarded as portending his future greatness at the expense of his brethren, and he very indiscreetly apprised them of these dreams. They at once resolved to put him out of the way; and when Joseph had been sent by his father to visit his brethren, who were feeding their flocks at Shechem, they determined to assassinate him. Reuben, the eldest son, prevailed upon his brothers not to kill Joseph outright, but to cast him into a dry well, where he would perish from hunger; intending to rescue him afterwards. They agreed to this; but while Reuben was temporarily absent, they sold Joseph to a caravan of Midianitish merchants, who were on their journey to Egypt. Returning to their father, they made him believe that Joseph had been killed by some wild beast.

Joseph was carried to Egypt by his purchasers, who sold him as a bond-slave to Potiphar, or Petephra, an officer of the Egyptian army. Winning the favor of his master, Joseph was made superintendent of his house. Potiphar's wife conceiving an unlawful passion for Joseph and being repulsed by him, in revenge, brought an infamous accusation against him, causing him to be cast into prison by his master. His good behavior won for him the favor of the prison officials, who conferred upon him important duties.

Among the prisoners were the chief cup-bearer and the chief cook of the reigning Pharaoh, who had been imprisoned for complicity in a conspiracy at the court of the king. Each of these prisoners dreamed a dream prophesying his fate. Relating their dreams to Joseph, the latter interpreted them. His interpretation was verified, the chief cupbearer being pardoned and restored to office, and the chief cook being executed, as he had predicted. The fortunate man promised to intercede for Joseph, but forgot him for two years, when the king, having had two dreams which caused him much trouble, and which the wise men of Egypt could not explain, the chief cupbearer remembered Joseph and informed the Pharaoh of the Hebrew prisoner's interpretation of his own dream and its fulfillment. The Pharaoh thereupon sent for Joseph and told

THE PATRIARCHS.

him of his dreams. Joseph told him that his dreams were prophetic, and were sent by God to warn him that Egypt would be blessed by seven years of rich harvests, which would be followed by seven years of dreadful famine. He urged the monarch to prepare for the famine by gathering stores of grain at certain points in the country during the years of abundance.

Egypt was then divided into two kingdoms, Upper Egypt being governed by a native Egyptian dynasty of Theban princes, and Lower Egypt being ruled by those Canaanite or Hittite conquerors known in Egyptian history as the Hyksos, or Shepherd Kings. These latter had adopted the Egyptian customs and language. The Pharaoh who sent for Joseph was one of this dynasty, and was called Apophis, or Apepi. As he was himself of foreign origin, this monarch did not indulge in the native Egyptian dislike of foreigners. Impressed with Joseph's interpretations of his dreams, Apepi at once declared that Joseph was the best man in the land to make the provision he had suggested against the famine. He therefore made the stranger his prime-minister, giving him his signet-ring in proof of the royal favor. Joseph was clothed in magnificent apparel, and received the Egyptian name of Zaph-n-to, the "Nourisher of the Country;" while all subjects were commanded to render him implicit obedience. He also received a bride in the person of Asenath, daughter of Petephra, the High Priest of On (afterwards Heliopolis), by whom he had two sons, Manasseh and Ephraim.

Joseph collected vast stores of grain from the abundant harvest in public granaries, which he constructed for the purpose. This he accomplished by doubling the usual royal impost of one-tenth of the grain. When the period of famine commenced he had stores of grain sufficient to supply the Egyptian population, and to sell to the neighboring nations which suffered from the famine. He sold to the Egyptian people on very hard conditions, requiring them to surrender, in return for the food which saved them from starvation, the fee simple of their lands, and to pay a quitrent of one-fifth of the produce for the right of occupation. The priests were exempt from this arrangement, and had the right to draw supplies from the public stores.

As the famine reached that portion of Canaan in which Jacob was living, he sent his sons to Egypt to purchase grain. They did not know Joseph, although he recognized them at once. He subjected them to a series of trials, partly as a punishment for their conduct towards him, and partly to subject their affection for their father and for their brother Benjamin to a test; after which he made himself known to them, forgave them for the wrongs which they had inflicted upon him, and brought them and their father into Egypt, where he would be able to provide for them. The Pharaoh willingly allowed them to settle in that portion of Lower Egypt east of the Delta known as "the land of Goshen." In this proceeding the Pharaoh was only carrying out a leading policy of the Shepherd Kings, encouraging the development in Egypt of a non-Egyptian element to support them in case of a formidable revolt of the native Egyptian population.

Jacob died seventeen years later, blessing his sons and declaring that the posterity of Judah should inherit the Divine promises to Abraham and should rank as the head of the chosen family; Reuben, Simeon and Levi—the three elder sons of Jacob—having forfeited their succession by their crimes. Jacob's body was embalmed in the usual Egyptian style, and was carried in great state by Joseph and his brethren, with a formidable escort of Egyptian troops, back to Canaan, and was interred in Abraham's tomb at Hebron. Joseph reached a venerable age, enjoying high honors, and continuing to be the protector of his family. On his death-bed he exacted a solemn oath from his brethren that his embalmed body should be conveyed to the land of Canaan when his Hebrew countrymen should leave Egypt.

SECTION II.—THE EXODUS AND WANDERINGS.

HE real history of the Hebrew nation, now called Israelites, only commences with their exodus from Egypt. The three great patriarchs—Abraham, Isaac and Jacob—and their posterity, were simply wandering nomads, roaming over the Promised Land of Canaan, but not possessing any portion of it.

The Hebrews, or Israelites, remained in the fertile land of Goshen for over two centuries, and multiplied so rapidly that the family of seventy persons which had entered Egypt with Jacob grew to be a nation of almost three million people. They constituted a people distinct from the Egyptians, having their own language, manners, religion and patriarchal government. Although they had somewhat departed from the pure monotheism of Abraham, Isaac and Jacob, they never adopted the Egyptian polytheism. They were governed directly by their own patriarchal chiefs, who were responsible to the Egyptian king for the collection of the taxes imposed upon the Hebrew colony.

During this period the native Egyptian dynasty reigning at Thebes expelled the Shepherd Kings from Lower Egypt, and united all Egypt into one great kingdom. This native dynasty was one of the greatest that ever occupied the throne of Egypt, and its monarchs appear to have favored the Hebrew colony in the land of Goshen.

But when the Eighteenth Dynasty, which had driven out the Shepherd Kings, was succeeded by the Nineteenth Dynasty, the Egyptian policy toward the Hebrews changed. This new dynasty of Pharaohs considered the Hebrews very dangerous on account of their rapid increase and their location, and inflicted upon them a series of cruel persecutions, with the design of weakening their power and destroying them as a nation. This oppressive policy was inaugurated by Rameses the Great, the most renowned of Egyptian kings, who was a great conqueror and a heartless tyrant. He oppressed the Israelites with overwork, and forced them to labor under brutal taskmasters in building the treasure cities of Pithom and Ramses. In spite of his cruelty and oppression—in spite of the heavy burdens which he imposed upon the Hebrews—their numbers continued to increase rapidly. Alarmed and enraged at this, the despotic monarch ordered all the Hebrew male children to be cast into the Nile as soon as they were born. The female children were spared to furnish wives for the Egyptians. By this means the great Pharaoh expected to wholly exterminate the race of Israel.

Amram, a man of the tribe of Levi, had married Jochebed, a woman of the same tribe. They had two children—a son named Aaron and a daughter named Miriam. Soon after the Pharaoh had issued his cruel edict, Jochebed gave birth to a second son, and concealed him for three months from the king's officers. Not being able to hide him any longer, she put him in a basket, or ark, of bulrushes, covered with pitch, and placed him among the flags on the bank of the Nile, where the infant was discovered by the daughter of the Pharaoh, who had gone down to the river to bathe. Touched with pity, the princess had the child brought to her. She gave it to Jochebed, who offered herself as nurse, and commanded her to rear the boy as "the son of Pharaoh's daughter." She gave the child the name Moses, meaning "drawn out of the water." When the boy had grown to manhood his mother took him to the princess, who had him educated as one of the royal family, and he became learned "in all the wisdom of the Egyptians," and was instructed in military science. A tradition represents him when reaching manhood as holding an important command in the Egyptian army in an expedition sent against Ethiopia.

Notwithstanding his fortunate lot, and the high favor he enjoyed at court, Moses

MOSES.

felt deeply the wrongs inflicted upon his Hebrew countrymen. He reflected upon their sufferings, and often went among them to cheer them. On one occasion, when he was forty years of age, he killed an Egyptian whom he had seen cruelly beating a Hebrew. For this homicide Moses was obliged to flee from Egypt for his life. He sought refuge in the peninsula of Sinai, and at length found himself in the land of Midian, where there was a tribe ruled by a chief and priest named Jethro. By defending Jethro's daughters from the violence of some shepherds who endeavored to drive them away from a well where they were watering their flocks, Moses was invited by the chief to come to his home and was urged to remain with him. Moses accepted Jethro's invitation and received the chief's daughter, Zipporah, as a wife. Moses remained with Jethro many years, during which Rameses the Great died, and the Pharaoh Menepta ascended the throne of Egypt. Menepta pursued his predecessor's oppressive policy toward the Hebrews. In their bitter distress the Hebrews prayed for the aid of the Lord Jehovah, the God of their fathers.

At length, when Moses had led his flock to a remote portion of Mount Horeb, we are told that he was startled by what appeared to be a burning bush. The Hebrew record says: "And the angel of the Lord appeared unto him in a flame of fire out of the midst of a bush; and he looked, and behold, the bush burned with fire, and the bush was not consumed. And Moses said, I will now turn aside and see this great sight, why the bush is not burnt. And when the Lord saw that he turned aside to see, God called unto him out of the midst of the bush, and said, Moses, Moses. And he said, Here am I. And he said, Draw not nigh thither; put off thy shoes from off thy feet, for the place whereon thou standest is holy ground. Moreover he said, I am the God of thy father, the God of Abraham, the God of Isaac, and the God of Jacob. And Moses hid his face; for he was afraid to look upon God.

"And the Lord said, I have surely seen the affliction of my people, which are in Egypt, and have heard their cry by reason of their taskmasters; for I know their sorrows; and I am come down to deliver them out of the hand of the Egyptians, and to bring them up out of that land unto a good land and a large, unto a land flowing with milk and honey; unto the place of the Canaanites, and the Hittites, and the Amorites, and the Perizzites, and the Hivites, and the Jebusites. Now therefore, behold, the cry of the children of Israel is come unto me; and I have also seen the oppression wherewith the Egyptians oppress them. Come now therefore, and I will send thee unto Pharaoh, that thou mayest bring forth my people the children of Israel out of Egypt."

It is further related that Jehovah revealed to Moses his design of making him the leader and the divine mouthpiece in this great movement. Moses timidly shrank from this position, but it is said that Jehovah reassured him and associated with him his brother, Aaron, who was to be his spokesman to the Egyptian king and to the Hebrews. The whole project of Jehovah is said to have been revealed to Moses, who was commanded to make it known to the Elders of the tribes. Jehovah, we are further told, directed Moses to return to Egypt, assemble the Elders of his people, disclose his mission to them, and, after securing their obedience, to go before the Pharaoh and demand permission for the Israelites to depart from Egypt. Jehovah, it is also said, told Moses that the Pharaoh would not grant this demand, but that He would display His power over Egypt and avenge the suffering of His "chosen people" by a series of punishments in the nature of plagues such as Egypt had never endured at any other period of its history.

Moses thereupon started on his return to Egypt, meeting on the way his brother Aaron, who is also said to have been divinely directed to look for him. The two brothers returned to Egypt, and, summoning the Elders of the Israelites, submitted to them the message from Jehovah. The people consented to obey the Divine will, and promised to faithfully execute all the commands of Jehovah.

We are told that the Pharaoh not only contemptuously refused to permit the Israelites to depart, but increased their burdens. Moses, it is said, complained to Jehovah that his effort for their release only brought sorrow and affliction upon his Hebrew countrymen; but was encouraged by the prediction that, although the Pharaoh would steadily refuse for some time to release the Israelites, and that he would steadily increase their hard tasks, yet Jehovah would break the obstinate pride of the Egyptian king and force him to agree to allow the Hebrews to depart. Moses and Aaron again asked repeatedly the Pharaoh Menepta to consent to the departure of the Israelites, but were as often refused. We are further told that Jehovah punished the king's refusals by inflicting upon Egypt ten violent plagues. These are enumerated as follows: 1. The waters of the Nile, the sacred river of Egypt, and the main support of its water supply, became red like blood and offensively putrid. As they were not able to use these waters, the Egyptians were obliged to sink wells along the banks of the river to obtain water to drink. 2. Frogs increased to such an extent as to become a dreadful pest to the Egyptians. 3. Swarms of lice covered the land, producing great suffering alike to man and beast. These increased and were a dreadful annoyance to the scrupulously-cleanly Egyptians, and were likewise a religious defilement. 4. Clouds of flies, or beetles, covered the country, swarmed in the houses, and devoured the harvest and shrubbery. The beetle being an object of worship to the Egyptians, they were thus scourged through their own gods. 5. An epizootic disease appeared among the cattle, carrying off great numbers of them. 6. A grievous affliction of boils and blains broke out on the bodies of the Egyptians and their beasts. Dr. Smith says: "This plague seems to have been the black leprosy, a fearful kind of elephantiasis, which was long remembered as the 'blotch of Egypt.' It also rendered the Egyptians religiously unclean." 7. A fearful hail storm, accompanied with thunder and lightning, devastated the country, destroying the crops and killing men and beasts. 8. Swarms of locusts overspread the land, devouring what the hail had left. 9. A remarkable darkness enveloped the country, and for three days the people could not see each other, or follow their daily pursuits. None of these visitations afflicted the land of Goshen, the dwelling-place of the Hebrews. It is said that the Pharaoh, terrified and humbled by these sufferings, more than once sent for Moses and Aaron, and implored them to induce Jehovah to release the Egyptians from these sufferings; but as soon as one plague ceased, the king's obstinate pride returned, and he refused to allow the Israelites to depart from Egypt.

The Mosaic record now tells us that the tenth and most dreadful plague was sent upon the land. It is said that Jehovah ordered Moses to institute the Feast of the Passover, which, marking the commencement of the Hebrew national history, was made the beginning of the Jewish year. Minute directions were given concerning the manner of celebrating the feast, no deviation being permitted from it, and the feast being made an annual celebration—a perpetual memorial of the deliverance of the Hebrew nation from the Egyptian bondage. Then says the Mosaic account: "And it came to pass that at midnight the Lord smote all the first-born in the land of Egypt, from the first-born of Pharaoh that sat on his throne unto the first-born of the captive that was in the dungeon; and all the first-born of cattle. And Pharaoh rose up in the night, he and all his servants, and all the Egyptians; and there was a great cry in Egypt; for there was not a house where there was not one dead."

Completely subdued in his haughty spirit by this last terrible visitation upon his subjects, the Pharaoh Menepta sent for Moses and Aaron and urged them to lead their countrymen out of Egypt at once. By order of Moses, the Hebrews asked the Egyptians for jewels of silver and gold and rai-

THE EXODUS AND WANDERINGS.

ment, which demands were immediately complied with. The Egyptians were glad to have the Israelites out of the country, fearing that any further delay would cause further suffering.

Under the leadership of Moses, the Hebrews started upon their march, taking the embalmed body of Joseph along with them. They numbered six hundred thousand men on foot, besides women and children. These, with the multitude following them, and consisting probably of other Semitic races, nomadic in their habits, who were doubtless glad of this opportunity to escape from Egypt, swelled the Israelite host to almost three millions of people. The Mosaic narrative says: "And the Lord went before them by day in a pillar of a cloud, to lead them the way; and by night in a pillar of fire, to give them light, to go by day and night; He took not away the pillar of the cloud by day, nor the pillar of fire by night, from before the people." After a march of three days the Israelites reached the head of the Red Sea, or Gulf of Suez, which then extended much farther north than at present.

Meanwhile the Pharaoh Menepta, regretting that he had allowed the Israelites to depart from Egypt, pursued them with a vast host, and came up with them as they were encamped near the Red Sea. Says the Mosaic account: "And Moses stretched out his hand over the sea; and the Lord caused the sea to go back by a strong east wind all that night, and made the sea dry land, and the waters were divided. And the children of Israel went into the midst of the sea upon the dry ground; and the waters were a wall unto them on their right hand, and on their left. And the Egyptians pursued, and went in after them to the midst of the sea, even all Pharaoh's horses, his chariots and his horsemen. And it came to pass, that in the morning watch the Lord looked unto the host of the Egyptians, through the pillar of fire and of the cloud, and troubled the host of the Egyptians. And took off their chariot wheels, that they drave them heavily; so that the Egyptians said, Let us flee from the face of Israel; for the Lord fighteth for them against the Egyptians. And the Lord said unto Moses, Stretch out thine hand over the sea, that the waters may come again upon the Egyptians, upon their chariots, and upon their horsemen. And Moses stretched forth his hand over the sea, and the sea returned to his strength when the morning appeared; and the Egyptians fled against it; and the Lord overthrew the Egyptians in the midst of the sea. And the waters returned, and covered the chariots, and the horsemen, and all the host of Pharaoh that came into the sea after them; there remained not so much as one of them. But the children of Israel walked upon dry land in the midst of the sea; and the waters were a wall unto them on their right hand, and on their left. Thus the Lord saved Israel that day out of the hands of the Egyptians; and Israel saw the Egyptians dead upon the seashore. And Israel saw that great work which the Lord did upon the Egyptians; and the people feared the Lord, and believed the Lord and his servant Moses."

In accordance with the chronology fixed upon by English Egyptologists the Exodus must have occurred about B. C. 1320. Among the various dates assigned to this great event in Jewish national history are the years B. C. 1652 and B. C. 1491.

After reaching the eastern shore of the Red Sea, the Israelites proceeded down the peninsula of Sinai towards the mountain peak of the same name, instead of going directly to the Promised Land. For forty years, we are told in the Mosaic account, did the Israelites wander in the "Wilderness" in the desert region of North-western Arabia. We are also told that Jehovah provided for the temporal wants of his chosen people, sweetening the bitter waters of the region through which they passed, making water gush forth from a rock to appease their thirst, and sending them food, first in the shape of quails, and afterward in the form of manna, the latter falling with the dew every morning in the camp. Only a day's supply of manna is said to have been allowed to be gathered, except on the sixth day, when a sufficient quantity was gathered to last two days, so that the people could scrupulously observe the Sabbath. This heavenly supply is said to have continued every day during the forty years' "Wanderings in the Wilderness."

When they arrived at Rephidim, believed to be the Wady-Feiran of the present day, the Israelites were attacked by the Amalekites, who endeavored to stay their advance into the Sinaitic peninsula. The Hebrew army led by Joshua, the future conqueror of Canaan, gained the victory. The Israelites then moved on to Mount Sinai, and encamped in the plain and in the ravines in the vicinity of that consecrated mountain.

We are now told that Jehovah descended upon Mount Sinai, and amid thunder and lightning delivered the law to the Hebrew nation. The Mosaic account says that Moses was called up into the mountain by Jehovah, and that the people promised obedience to His Ten Commandments. Says the narrative: "Then went up Moses, and Aaron, and Nadab, and Abihu, and seventy of the Elders of Israel; and they saw the God of Israel. * * * * And the Lord said unto Moses, Come up to me into the mount, and be there; and I will give thee tables of stone, and a law, and commandments which I have written; that thou mayest teach them. And Moses rose up, and his minister Joshua; and Moses went up into the mount of God. * * * * And Moses went up into the mount, and a cloud covered the mount. And the glory of the Lord abode upon Mount Sinai, and the cloud covered it six days; and the seventh day he called unto Moses out of the midst of the cloud. And the sight of the glory of the Lord was like devouring fire on the top of the mount in the eyes of the children of Israel. And Moses went into the midst of the cloud, and gat him up into the mount; and Moses was in the mount forty days and forty nights." During this time we are informed that Jehovah revealed to Moses minute directions afterwards embodied in the "Laws of Moses," which constituted the civil and religious systems of the Hebrew nation. The Mosaic record says that the Ten Commandments were engraven on tablets of stone by the hand of Jehovah himself.

The Decalogue, or Ten Commandments, and the other Laws of Moses were preserved in the Ark of the Covenant. The affairs of religion were conducted by the High Priest and Levites. Sacrifices of animals, and the feasts of the Passover, the Pentecost and the Tabernacles, formed the bond between Jehovah and His "chosen people." Every fiftieth year—the year of Jubilee—a new and equal distribution of the lands was made. The civil government established by Moses for the Hebrew nation was a theocratic system, and the Elders of the Twelve Tribes of Israel conducted the government in Jehovah's name.

During the long absence of Moses on Mount Sinai the Israelites, in disregard of their covenant with Jehovah, we are told, compelled Aaron to make a golden calf, in imitation of the Egyptian bull-deity Apis. They abandoned themselves to the worship of this idol; and Moses, upon returning to them from the mountain, found them thus occupied. Overcome with anger, he rallied the tribe of Levi, and attacked the idolaters with the sword, killing three thousand of them and destroying the idol. The people acknowledged the justice of their punishment, and promised to shun idolatry in the future. In consequence of their loyalty to Jehovah on this occasion, the Levites were constituted the sacerdotal class of the Israelitish nation.

The Israelites sojourned on Mount Sinai eleven months and twenty days, during which the second celebration of the Passover was held. This long halt was a busy season in the life of the nation. The Hebrews had arrived at Sinai without discipline, without institutions, without laws, almost ignorant of their God, and with no established form of religious worship. During the stay at Sinai this disorganized mob was converted into a compact and powerful nation, with a code of laws which has ever since won the admiration of all ages and of all nations, and which remained in force among the Hebrews until the end of their national career.

The Tabernacle, or sacred tent, was constructed in accordance with the mode prescribed by God, and all the particulars of the religious ceremonial were minutely arranged. The priesthood was organized, and the succession to the sacred offices were definitely provided for. The principle at the basis of the whole civil and religious system was the supreme authority of Jehovah over the Hebrew nation. "He was, in a literal sense of the word, their sovereign, and all other authority, both in political and civil affairs, was subordinate to the continual acknowledgment of His own. The other powers were instituted by God to administer affairs in accordance with His laws, but were not ordinarily chosen among the priests, descendants of Aaron, nor from the tribe of Levi, consecrated to the various functions of public worship. Each tribe had its civil authorities, although certain causes were reserved for the supreme central tribunal; but the unity of the nation was, above all, founded on unity in faith and worship, on the mighty recollections recalled each year by the solemn feasts; the Passover, or Feast of Unleavened Bread (commemorating the Exodus from Egypt); Pentecost (the promulgation of the law), and the Feast of the Tabernacles, or tents (the sojourn in the desert). The one tabernacle, where the solemn sacrifices were offered, and where was deposited the ark, the symbol and covenant made between God and His people, was equally the political and religious center of the nation. The Mosaic law presents the spectacle, unique in the history of the world, of a legislation which was complete from the origin of a nation, and subsisted for long ages. In spite of frequent infractions, it was always restored, even although in its very sublimity it was in direct opposition to the coarse inclinations of the people whom it governed. He alone could impose it on the Israelites, who could say: 'I am the Lord thy God,' and confirm the words by forty years of miracles."

We are further told that when everything was arranged, Moses, at the command of Jehovah, took a census of the males of the nation, from and over the age of twenty years, capable of bearing arms. The census was taken on the first day of the second month from the epoch of the Exodus (Jyar —May, 1490, or 1319, B. C.), and fixed the number of fighting men at 603,550. This great host was divided into four camps, one being placed on each of the four sides of the tabernacle, which stood in the center of the camp.

Being thus organized as a nation and an army, the Israelites broke up their camp at Sinai on the twentieth day of their second year—about May 20, B. C. 1490, or 1319— and continued their advance, and, we are informed, were again led by the "pillar of cloud" which was said to have guided them since the memorable night of the Exodus, and which was to lead them to the "Promised Land." Thus guided, the Israelites were conducted into the Wilderness of Paran.

After several halts, the Israelites arrived at Kadesh Barnea, near the frontiers of Canaan, whence Moses sent twelve spies, one from each tribe of the Hebrew nation, into Canaan to examine the country and to report the character, condition, strength and number of its inhabitants and its cities. These spies were absent fourteen days, and during that time they explored the country from the Dead Sea to the slopes of Mount Hermon. On their return to Kadesh Barnea they reported to Moses and the subordinate leaders that the land was extremely fertile, but that the Israelites would not be able to conquer it, because its inhabitants were men of immense size and lived in strongly-fortified cities. This report had a discouraging effect upon the Israelites; and Joshua and Caleb, who were two of the spies, vainly endeavored to persuade their countrymen that the other spies had exaggerated the impediments in the way of the conquest of Canaan, and tried to raise their courage by means of a more favorable report. The people, panic-stricken, broke out into open mutiny the following morning, declaring that they intended to choose a chief who would lead them back into Egypt. Moses and Aaron vainly fell on their faces before their countrymen. Joshua and Caleb vainly sought to assure them of victory and conquest, and to dissuade them from rebellion against Jehovah. The enraged people were on the point of stoning Moses, Aaron, Joshua and Caleb to death, when, we are again told, "the glory of the Lord filled the tabernacle" and the people were induced to repent of their rebellious conduct. Jehovah, it is said, threatened to disinherit the rebellious nation and select as his chosen people the posterity of Moses; but when Moses interceded for his ungrateful countrymen they were pardoned, but the rebels were threatened with the displeasure of Jehovah, who is said to have informed Moses that, excepting Joshua and Caleb, not a man of the nation from and over twenty years of age should enter the "Promised Land," that they should all die in the wilderness, in which the nation was condemned to wander thirty-eight years longer, and that their children should enter upon the promised inheritance of the Hebrew race.

The Israelites, stricken with anguish upon hearing of this doom, were anxious to be led into Canaan, but, we are told, the Divine decree would not be revoked. The people, it is said, were persistent in their resolve, and despite the warnings of Moses, who refused to lead them, they attempted to force their way through a mountain pass defended by the united armies of the Canaanites and the Amalekites. They met with a bloody repulse, and were driven back into the desert. The Israelites led a nomadic life for thirty-eight years, roaming over the desert north of the peninsula of Sinai, which the Arabs have named *Et Tih*, or *Tih Beni Israel* (the wanderings of the Children of Israel). Their range occupied the region from Kadesh Barnea on the north to the head of the Elanitic gulf (now Gulf of Akaba) on the south. They were not apparently disturbed by any of the neighboring tribes. In the meantime the males of the nation over twenty years of age died,

and the succeeding generation consisted of men trained to fatigue and war—men who were hardy and brave, and accustomed to freedom—a generation superior to their predecessors, who had been reared in the Egyptian bondage, and had suffered from the taint of that oppressive servitude.

At the commencement of the fortieth year after the Exodus, Aaron, the brother of Moses and the High Priest of the Hebrew nation, died at Masera at a ripe old age, and was buried there. Mount Hor was on the border of the territory of the Edomites, the descendants of Esau. Moses requested a free passage for his countrymen through the Edomite territory, offering to respect the property of the inhabitants, and to pay for even the water used by the people of Israel. But the Edomites refused this request, and it is said that the Hebrews were forbidden by Jehovah to attack their kindred, whereupon they turned towards the south, marching toward the head of the Elanitic gulf, and, rounding the mountain range, advanced again northward, east of the territory of Edom. The Canaanites of Arad endeavored to obstruct the passage of the hosts of Israel, but suffered a defeat. The Edomites permitted the Israelites to march past their territory without disturbing them. We are told that Jehovah forbade Moses attacking the Moabites and Ammonites, descendants of Lot.

The Hebrews had now arrived at the Arnon, a small stream flowing into the eastern side of the Dead Sea, and forming the southern boundary of a new kingdom, founded by Sihon, an Amorite adventurer, who had conquered it from the Moabites and Ammonites. The Jabbok formed the northern boundary of this kingdom, and Sihon established his capital at Heshbon. Moses sent a peaceful embassy to Sihon, requesting a free passage through his territory, promising to keep his countrymen to the highway on their march, and to pay for everything used by them. This request was refused by Sihon with extreme insolence, and that prince lead his army against the Israelites, but was totally routed, his capital was taken by storm, and his kingdom fell into the hands of the Hebrews. Og, the gigantic King of Bashan, whose dominions extended from the Jabbok to Mount Hermon, and who was a fortunate Amorite adventurer, attempted to avenge the overthrow of Sihon, but was defeated and killed, and his kingdom was likewise conquered by the Israelites. These two conquests made the Israelites masters of all the territory east of the Jordan, from Mount Hermon to the Dead Sea.

The hosts of Israel now encamped on the fertile plains opposite Jericho. Balak, King of Moab, in great alarm because of the appearance of so powerful a nation on his borders, entered into an alliance with the Midianites against the Hebrews. Feeling sufficiently strong to assail the strangers, Balak sought to induce Balaam, a noted diviner from the country of the Ammonites, to pronounce a curse against the Israelites and devote them to destruction. We are told, however, that Balaam was obliged to bless the "chosen people," and to prophesy to Balak their future triumphs. The Moabites and Midianites then endeavored to seduce the Israelites from their religion by inducing them to participate in their immoral and voluptuous worship of their god Baal-Peor. This scheme was so successful that Moses had to resort to severe measures to check the evil. All the Hebrews guilty of this apostasy from the worship of Jehovah were put to death; and twenty-four thousand men were carried off, by a plague which broke out in the camp. The Israelites then engaged in a war of extermination against the Midianites, defeated their armies, ravaged their country and carried off a vast booty.

A new census taken at this time showed that there were 601,730 fighting men in the Israelitish host. The country conquered on the east side of the Jordan was exceedingly fertile and was well adapted to grazing. Delighted with this section the tribes of Reuben and Gad and the half-tribe of Manasseh requested Moses the possession of this region for their inheritance, as they had many cattle. Moses sternly rebuked them for sowing dissensions in the nation; but agreed to the arrangement upon obtaining the promise of these tribes that they would only leave their families and their cattle in their new homes, while their fighting men would cross the Jordan with the other tribes and aid them in conquering the "Promised Land." The tribe of Reuben was assigned the southern portion of the country east of the Jordan, from the Arnon to Mount Gilead; the tribe of Gad was given the tract north of the former, including Mount Gilead, to the southern extremity of the Sea of Chinneroth (the Sea of Galilee); and the half-tribe of Manasseh was allotted the district north of Gad as far as Mount Hermon. The two tribes and a half faithfully observed their pledges to their brethren and rendered them valuable service in the conquest of the country west of the Jordan.

The great work of Moses was now finished. He had led the children of Israel to the borders of the "Promised Land" at a point where it could be easily entered, and he is said to have been warned by Jehovah that his end was near. The Scripture record says that both Moses and his brother Aaron had been denied permission to enter the "Promised Land," because their faith had failed when Jehovah had commanded them to speak to the rock in Kadesh to give water to his people. We are likewise told that Moses assembled the whole Hebrew nation, recited the law in their presence, prophesied for them a blessing, predicting for them a glorious future, named Joshua as his successor, and exhorted the people to continue faithful to Jehovah. He then bid his countrymen an affecting farewell, and we are told went up into Mount Nebo at the command of Jehovah, who there showed the great Hebrew lawgiver the land which was to be the inheritance of his people, after which he disappeared from among the living.

"And Moses went up from the plains of Moab unto the mountain of Nebo, to the top of Pisgah, that is over against Jericho. And the Lord showed him all the land of Gilead, unto Dan. And all Naphtali, and the land of Ephraim, and Manasseh, and all

MOUNT NEBO

the land of Judah, unto the utmost sea. And the south, and the plain of the valley of Jericho, the city of palm trees, unto Zoar. And the Lord said unto him, This is the land which I sware unto Abraham, unto Isaac, and unto Jacob, saying, I will give it unto thy seed; I have caused thee to see it with thine eyes, but thou shalt not go over thither. So Moses the servant of the Lord died there in the land of Moab, according to the word of the Lord. And he buried him in a valley in the land of Moab, over against Beth-peor; but no man knoweth of his sepulcher unto this day. * * * * And the children of Israel wept for Moses in the plains of Moab thirty days; so the days of weeping and mourning for Moses were ended. * * * * And there arose not a prophet since in Israel like unto Moses, whom the Lord knew face to face, In all the signs and the wonders which the Lord sent him to do in the land of Egypt to Pharaoh, and to all his servants, and to all his land, And in all that mighty land, and in all the great terror which Moses showed in the sight of all Israel."

SECTION III.—CONQUEST OF CANAAN—THE JUDGES.

FTER the thirty days of mourning for Moses—exactly forty years from the time that they departed from Egypt—the Israelites broke up their camp on the plains of Moab, and advanced toward the Jordan under the leadership of Joshua. The column was led by the priests carrying the Ark of the Covenant. The Jordan was swollen with the spring freshets, and was too high to be forded. As the priests stepped into the stream, carrying the sacred ark, the waters, we are told, were miraculously divided, as had been the Red Sea, and a wide path was opened, along which the Hebrew host passed to the western side of the stream, and entered Canaan (B. C. 1451 or B. C. 1280). The Israelites encamped at Gilgal, on the plains of Jericho, for the night. The supply of manna is said to have ceased here, and thenceforth the Israelites subsisted upon the products of the country which they had come to conquer.

We will now give an account of the character of the Canaanitish tribes, or nations, with whom the Israelites were now to wrestle for the possession of the "Promised Land."

During the patriarchial period, Canaan, or Palestine, was occupied by numerous tribes of Canaanites, descendants of Canaan, the fourth son of Ham. The name Canaanites was sometimes assigned to a particular tribe occupying a certain part of Palestine, but was more generally applied to all the inhabitants of that country, and embraced seven distinct nations, as follows, according to Dr. William Smith:

"I. The *Canaanites*, the 'lowlanders,' who inhabited the plain on the lower Jordan, and that on the sea-shore. These plains were the richest and most important part of the country.

"II. The *Perizzites* seem, next to the Canaanites, to have been the most important tribe. * * * * *' In Judges I. 4, 5, they are placed in the southern part of the Holy Land, and in Joshua XVI. 15-18, they occupy, with the Rephaim, or giants, the 'forest country' in the western flanks of Mount Carmel.

"III. The *Hittites*, or children of Heth, were a small tribe at Hebron, of whom Abraham purchased the cave of Machpelah. They are represented as a peaceful people.

"IV. The *Amorites*, 'mountaineers,' a warlike tribe, occupied first the barrier heights west of the Dead Sea, at the same place which afterwards bore the name of En-gedi, stretching westward towards Hebron. At the time of the conquest they had crossed the Jordan and occupied the rich tract bounded by the Jabbok on the north and the Arnon on the south, the Jordan on the west and the wilderness on the east.

"V. The *Hivites* are first named at the time of Jacob's return to the Holy Land, where they occupied Shechem. At the time of the conquest by Joshua, they were living on the northern confines of Western Palestine.

"VI. The *Jebusites*, a mountain tribe, occupying Jebus (Jerusalem), where they continued to dwell with the children of Judah and Benjamin to a late date.

"VII. The *Girgasites*, whose position is quite uncertain."

During the period when the Israelites were sojourning in Egypt several important changes occurred in the character and location of the nations occupying the land of Canaan. The maritime people of Phœnicia, situated immediately north of Palestine, had risen quietly and suddenly, and had become the most enlightened and the wealthiest community of antiquity. Phœnicia, however, did not attain its highest pinnacle of greatness and prosperity until several centuries later, about B. C. 1050. At the time when the Israelites entered Canaan, the Phœnicians, who occupied a narrow strip around the sea-coast, and whose territory was embraced in the region assigned as a heritage to the Hebrews, had established themselves firmly in the country, and were sufficiently powerful to hold it against the strangers.

The sea-coast of the Holy Land proper, on the coast south of Phœnicia, was occupied by the Philistines, a warlike and powerful nation, whom some authorities consider a Semitic people, while others regard them as a Hamitic race. Those who believe them to be Semites maintain that they crossed over from the island of Crete, while those who hold that they were Hamites suppose that they came into Canaan from Egypt. Their territory was called Philistia, from which the name Palestine has been derived. The Philistines are believed to have migrated to Canaan before the time of Abraham, and during their sojourn in that land they were a pastoral tribe in the vicinity of Gerar. During the patriarchal period, and the epoch of the sojourn of the Israelites in Egypt, the Philistines renounced their nomadic life and developed into a settled and powerful nation. They established themselves in the fertile plain bordering upon the sea-coast, which was therefore called the Plain of Philistia. The great fertility of this plain was the basis of their wealth and prosperity. In times of scarcity and famine all the neighboring nations depended upon them for bread. The low tract which they occupied favored their development as a formidable military people, as it enabled them to transport their troops with ease and rapidity, and admitted of the maneuvering of war-chariots, "the artillery of the ancients," in which these people were always very formidable. It is believed that the Philistines had a navy, as historians several times allude to them in accounts of naval expeditions and naval battles. Gaza and Ascalon were Philistine sea-ports. Many well-fortified cities were built by the Philistines in the plain, its undulating character affording numerous excellent sites for such strongholds. The most important Philistine cities besides its seaports, Gaza and Ascalon, were Ashdod, Ekron and Gath.

Thus the two most important nations in Palestine when the Israelites conquered the country were the Phœnicians on the north and the Philistines on the south. We have seen that the "Promised Land" embraced the territory extending from the Arabian desert to the Mediterranean, and from the desert of Sinai to "the entering in of Hamath," the name applied in Scripture to the low range of hills forming the water-sheds between the Orontes and the Litany. Phœnicia, the northern part of Canaan, was never occupied by the Israelites. The Philistine plain was constantly contested, and was seldom a safe and peaceful possession of the Hebrews. The "Land of Possession" lay only between Dan on the north and Beersheba on the south; hence the frequency of the allusion in the Old Testament in speaking of the northern and southern limits of the Hebrew state: "From Dan to Beersheeba."

The country itself—known variously as the Promised Land, Canaan, Palestine, Judæa, or the Holy Land—was in many particulars a remarkable region. Its importance in the history of mankind vastly overshadows its small territorial extent. Palestine is a very small country—about the size of the principality of Wales or the State of New Jersey. Its entire length from north to south is about one hundred and eighty miles, and its average breadth from east to west about forty-five miles, thus giving the country an area of eight thousand square miles. It lies between latitude thirty degrees forty minutes and thirty-three degrees forty-two minutes north, and between longitude thirty-three degrees forty-two minutes and thirty-five degrees forty-eight minutes east. It is bounded on the north by Syria, on the east by the Jordan and the country now known as the Haurân, on the south by the Desert of Et Tîk, and on the west by the Mediterranean. It is located in Western Asia, to the north of Egypt, and to the north and west of Arabia.

It is practically a mountainous region. It has no independent mountain chains, and other countries surpass it in the height and grandeur of its mountains; "but every part of the highland is in greater or less undulation." The mountain region occupies the center of the country, and lowlands border it on both the east and the west, extending from the foot of the uplands to the boundaries of Palestine. This lowland spreads out on the west into the two great plains of Philistia and Sharon, which extend from the foot of the mountains to the sea. The mountains are bordered on the east by the remarkable depression of the Jordan valley, still continued by the yet more remarkable depression of the Dead Sea and by the Ghor. "The slopes, or cliffs, which form, as it were, the retaining walls of this depression are furrowed and cleft by the torrent beds which discharge the waters of the hills, and form the means of communication between the upper and lower levels. These three features—the mountains, the plains and the torrent beds—make up the principal physical characteristics of the Holy Land."

Little over midway up the coast, the plain is suddenly broken by a bold spur of the mountain chain, leaving the middle mass and running abruptly north-west to the sea, there ending in the beautiful promontory of Mount Carmel, which is also the name of the entire spur or ridge. North of Carmel the plain again commences, and there pushes back the mountains and reaches entirely across Palestine to the Jordan valley. This is the famous plain of Esdraelon, or Jezreel. North of this plain the mountains are again seen, first in the low hills of Galilee, and rising higher until Mount Hermon and the Lebanons are reached. The mountains again push their way out to the sea, and end in the white headland of Ras Nakhûra, north of which is the ancient Phœnicia.

The height of the mountainous region is usually uniform along its whole course, with an average of from fifteen hundred to eighteen hundred feet above the level of the Mediterranean sea. Says Dr. William Smith: "It can hardly be denominated a plateau, yet so evenly is the general level preserved, and so thickly do the hills stand behind and between one another, that when seen from the coast or the western part of the maritime plain, it has quite the appearance of a wall." This seeming monotony is broken at intervals by greater elevations, and these constitute the most conspicuous features of the landscape. The water-shed of the country lies between these highest points, and on each side the many torrent beds descend to the Jordan valley on the east, and to the Mediterranean on the west. The valleys on the east are very steep and rugged, particularly in the middle and southern parts of the country; but those on the west slope more gradually. As the level of the maritime plain is higher than that of the Jordan valley, it gives them a more gradual descent, which is rendered easier by the greater distance intervening between the mountains and the sea than between the mountains and the Jordan. Upon the western side, as upon the eastern, the valleys, or wâdies, form the only means of communication between the mountains and the plains. All the roads from the borders to the interior are located along these valleys. These mountain passes constitute a singular feature of Palestine, and were very important to it in ancient times. Being difficult, they presented very great obstacles to an army burdened with a camp train or baggage. The western passes, though easier than the eastern, were still difficult, and made it no easy task for an enemy to enter the territory of the Israelites. Secure in their mountain fastnesses, the Israelites were frequently undisturbed, while the cities of the plain below them were captured and recaptured by the struggling armies of Egypt and Asia. The plain of Esdraelon was the great battle-field of Palestine, but the mountains were comparatively free from warlike operations.

The river Jordan constituted the eastern boundary of the "Promised Land," and is one of the most remarkable rivers of the world. It rises on the slope of Mount Hermon and flows through an extraordinary depression, known as the Jordan valley, passing through Lake Huleh and the Lake of Tiberias, or Sea of Galilee, and emptying into the Dead Sea. Its source is 1700 feet above the level of the Mediterranean; its mouth is 1317 feet below the sea level, making the entire descent of the river 3017 feet. The river is two hundred miles long; the distance in a straight line is sixty miles. The Jordan was never a navigable stream, and was passed only by fords in ancient times. No bridges were thrown over it until after the Roman conquest of Palestine. No cities were located on its banks. Jericho and the other towns were situated some distance away from the river.

The first exploit of the Israelites after entering Palestine was the capture of the strong city of Jericho, which stood immediately in front of the place where they had crossed the river Jordan, and which commanded the Jordan valley. The Israelites having no means of conducting a siege, it is said that Jehovah came to their aid. The walls are said to have been thrown down in a miraculous manner; and when the Israelites entered the city over its ruined fortifications they put the people to the sword and destroyed the city. The only family which escaped the general massacre was that of "Rahab the harlot," who had received and befriended the spies sent by Joshua into the city before it fell, and who had consequently been promised protection to her household. She afterward became the wife of one of the spies, and was the ancestress of David. Proceeding up the Jordan valley Joshua turned to the left and took the stronghold of Ai, near Bethel, by stratagem, and, advancing rapidly to Shechem, captured the city without striking a blow, and established himself in the heart of the country.

The Canaanitish tribes now recovered from the surprise and dismay into which they had been thrown by the quick and successful operations of the Israelites, and united in a general coalition against the Hebrew invaders of their country. Joshua defeated the allied forces of the Canaanitish kings in the great battle of Beth-horon, in which we are told that the day was miraculously lengthened to enable the Israelites to complete their victory. The kings of the five Canaanitish tribes were taken prisoners, and were hanged. After this victory the Israelites captured successively the cities of Makkedah, Libnah, Lachish, Eglon, Hebron and Debir, and exterminated their inhabitants. These successes completed the conquest of Southern Palestine by the Israelites.

A second coalition was now formed against the Hebrews, and embraced all the tribes of Northern Palestine. The leader of this coalition was Jabin, King of Hazor. Joshua routed the allied army on the banks of Lake Merom (now Lake Huleh), and Jabin was taken prisoner and put to death. Many cities of Northern Palestine then fell into the possession of the Israelites, and their inhabitants were massacred. The Anakin

CONQUEST OF CANAAN—THE JUDGES.

of Southern Palestine were then attacked and exterminated. The Israelites were occupied six or seven years in making these conquests, and were finally in possession of all the "Promised Land" from the foot of Mount Hermon to the borders of Edom. The Canaanites still held many of their strongest cities in the midst of the Hebrew conquests. The Philistines held the seacoast of Southern Palestine, and the Phœnicians that of Northern Palestine.

Joshua had now reached an advanced age, and concluded to suspend his conquests and devote his remaining years to establishing the Israelites firmly in the lands which their arms had won. It is said that he was commanded by Jehovah to divide the "Promised Land" by lot among the nine and a half tribes now located west of the Jordan; the other two and a half tribes having received their allotment east of the Jordan from Moses, and the Levites having no special territory bestowed on them. The division of the tribe of Joseph into the two tribes of Ephraim and Manasseh made up for the withdrawal of the Levites from the number of the twelve tribes to devote themselves especially to the service of Jehovah. The territory divided among the Hebrew tribes included many places yet held by the Canaanites and the Philistines, and Joshua resigned to each tribe the duty of reducing the strongholds and possessions of these people within the territory allotted to the twelve tribes.

The tribe of Judah obtained the South Country. Its southern boundary reached the territory of the Edomites and the Arabian desert, while its northern limit was a line drawn from the mouth of the Jordan westward to the Mediterranean sea. A considerable portion of the Philistine plain was embraced in this allotment. The children of Joseph were assigned the central part of the country, from the Jordan to the Mediterranean. The tribe of Ephraim obtained the southern part of this tract, and its southern limit "was drawn from the Jordan along the north side of the plain of Jericho to Bethel, whence it took a bend southward to Beth-horon, and thence up again to the sea near Joppa. The northern border passed west from the Jordan opposite the mouth of the Jabbok, past Michmethah to the mouth of the river Kanah." It included the sacred valley of Shechem and the maritime plain of Sharon. The half-tribe of Manasseh occupied the district north of Ephraim as far as the range of Mount Carmel and the plain of Esdraelon, from the Jordan westward to the Mediterranean. To Benjamin was assigned the hill country north of Judah and south of Ephraim, from the Jordan west as far as Jerusalem. Dan received the tract between Ephraim on the north, Judah on the south, Benjamin on the east, and the Mediterranean on the west. The greater part of this region was occupied by the Philistines. For this reason, and because their territory was too small for them, a portion of the people of Dan migrated northward, and took the city of Leshem, or Laish, at the source of the Jordan. They named the city Dan, and acquired a considerable tract around it. This city became the great northern landmark of the Promised Land, as Beersheba was the southern. Hence the phrase "from Dan even to Beer-sheba," so frequently used in alluding to the whole extent of the Hebrew country from north to south. The tribe of Simeon was allotted an inheritance out of Judah's portion, and was seated in the south-western portion of the maritime plain. Their frontier bordered on the desert from Beer-sheba westward to Gaza, and their sea-coast extended north to Ascalon. Issachar was given the great and fertile valley of Jezreel, known also as the plain of Esdraelon. Zebulun received the mountain range bordering the plain of Esdraelon on the north, and which in after times constituted the upper part of Lower Galilee. He possessed a small strip of sea-coast north of Mount Carmel, and his eastern border included the Sea of Chinneroth (Sea of Galilee). Asher obtained the plain along the Mediterranean from Mount Carmel, in a northerly direction, including a considerable portion of Phœnicia. The Israelites never made any attempt to secure the Phœnician portion of their inheritance, and Asher's northern boundary was actually the Phœnician border south of Tyre. His territory extended to the east about midway across Palestine. Naphtali was assigned the country north of Zebulun to Mount Hermon and between the Jordan and the territory of Asher. The two tribes and a half east of the Jordan were allowed to rest contented with their share of the spoils of conquest, and were dismissed with blessings, after which they returned to their homes beyond the river.

Feeling his end approaching, Joshua assembled the representatives of the entire Hebrew nation at Shechem, and after reminding them of the Divine goodness to the nation, exhorted them to remain faithful to the worship of Jehovah and the laws of Moses, and to continue the war against the Canaanites until they had ultimately expelled them from the whole of the Promised Land. Joshua, who was said to have been divinely commissioned to exterminate the Canaanitish race, because of its crimes, reminded his people of their duty, and predicted great misfortunes for them if they renounced their religion, or neglected to execute Jehovah's purposes regarding the Canaanites, or mingled with them. The people solemnly vowed to obey him and renewed their covenant with Jehovah. Thereupon Joshua set up in the place of the assembly a monumental stone as a witness of this vow of the Hebrew nation. Soon afterward Joshua died at a venerable age, after conducting the affairs of Israel for twenty-five years, and was greatly mourned by the whole Hebrew nation.

Joshua unfortunately failed to appoint a successor, and the nation was thus left without a legitimate head. During the lives of the Elders who had been his contemporaries, the Israelites reverenced the laws of Moses and held fast to the worship of Jehovah; but when these Elders died dissensions and divisions distracted the nation, alienating the different tribes from each other. No earnest effort was made to conquer the cities still held by the Canaanites. The northern tribes began to appear indifferent concerning the national ties, and secured the best terms possible for themselves from the Canaanites in their midst. The Israelites were repulsed in their efforts to conquer the land of the Philistines, and the coast cities mostly remained in the possession of that powerful and warlike people. The intercourse which arose between the Israelites and the Canaanites soon led to evil results. The great religious center of the Hebrew nation was Shiloh, where the Tabernacle and the Ark of the Covenant had been set up. At this time the Altar of God began constantly to become more and more neglected, and the idolatrous worship of the Canaanites was introduced among the Hebrews. Civil wars broke out among the tribes of Israel, and in one of these the tribe of Benjamin was almost exterminated by the other tribes. The Book of Judges describes this condition of affairs in the following words: "There was no king in Israel; every man did that which was right in his own eyes." There was no central or general government to hold the nation together or to enforce civil order; and although, according to the theocracy established by Moses, Jehovah was the King of the Hebrews, idolatry spread so rapidly and obtained so firm a hold on the nation that the moral restraints which had held the Israelites in loyalty to their Divine Ruler were utterly disregarded. The result was division and weakness. The Canaanites and Philistines were not slow to discover this, and sought to avenge their past grievances by subjecting the Israelites to their yoke. We are told that, as a punishment for their repeated apostasy from the worship of Jehovah, the Israelites were as repeatedly abandoned to their enemies, who cruelly oppressed them, and thus were blind instruments to execute the Divine judgments upon the faithless and rebellious nation. When the sufferings of the Israelites became unendurable, they realized the enormity of their sins and their ingratitude to Jehovah, and in sorrow and humiliation they became penitent and implored Jehovah for aid against their enemies. We are told

CONQUEST OF CANAAN—THE JUDGES. 361

that their prayers were heard and answered by Jehovah, who raised up valiant and heroic leaders to deliver His "chosen people" from the cruel yoke of their oppressors. These leaders delivered Israel by defeating its oppressors and reëstablishing the independence of the Hebrew nation. No sooner, however, were the Israelites liberated from the despotic sway of foreign kings and peoples, than they again apostatized to idolatry, and were again chastised by fresh defeats and subjugation.

The deliverers thus said to have been raised up by Jehovah to free His people from the oppressive yoke of their enemies were called *Judges*. By rescuing the people from their enemies they became their governors or rulers, performing their duties as representatives or agents of Jehovah, Whose desire was ascertained in a prescribed manner. These Judges were not only the civil chiefs of the Hebrews, but were their military commanders and led their armies in battle. The Judge did not rank with a king in power or dignity. His station was but little above that of the mass of the nation, and was not hereditary. The Judge was believed to be supernaturally directed by revelations from Jehovah, either to himself or to others. The consent of the people was necessary for the exercise of his functions, and his authority was not always recognized by the entire nation. He was appointed for life, but his successor was not always selected after his death. There were sometimes long interregnums between the administration of one Judge and that of another. During these interregnums the Hebrew nation was either without a civil head, or was subject to the dominion of some foreign conqueror. The Old Testament gives us the names of fifteen Judges altogether. The period of the Judges covered several centuries, and its chronology is very uncertain. The dates usually assigned for the events of this period are unreliable.

During the lifetime of the generation of Hebrews following the conquest of Canaan, a King of Western Mesopotamia, called Chushan-rishathaim, extended his dominions from the Euphrates to the borders of Canaan, reduced the Israelites to a condition of subjection, and held them tributary for eight years, during which he grievously oppressed them. At length Jehovah, we are informed, raised up Othniel, the nephew of Caleb, the contemporary of Moses and Joshua. Othniel, as Judge, defeated the invaders and recovered the independence of his countrymen, who remained undisturbed for forty years.

At the end of this period of forty years, Eglon, King of Moab, who had formed an alliance with the Ammonites and the Amalekites, crossed the Jordan, defeated the Israelites, and established himself near the site of Jericho. He held the Israelites in bondage for eighteen years, after which he was assassinated by Ehud, a Benjamite, as the latter was presenting to the king the tribute required of his tribe. Ehud escaped, rallied the Israelites, and drove the Moabites beyond the Jordan, inflicting a loss of ten thousand men upon them. This victory secured tranquillity for portions of Palestine for twenty-four years, but this state of peace did not embrace the whole country.

The Old Testament names Shamgar as the third of the Judges. He is said to have led a body of laborers armed only with agricultural implements, and to have defeated a Philistine army, himself slaying six hundred of the enemy with an ox-goad.

After the death of Ehud the Israelites again apostatized to idolatry, for which sin Jehovah is said to have delivered them into the power of the Canaanite Jabin, King of Hazor, a descendant of the king whom Joshua had defeated, and like him the chief of a powerful confederacy in the North of Palestine. This monarch had nine hundred iron chariots in his army, which was under the command of a great general named Sisera. Jabin overran the North of Palestine, reducing its inhabitants to slavery. This bondage lasted twenty years.

At this time the prophetess Deborah administered justice to the Israelites under a palm grove between Ramah and Bethel, in Mount Ephraim. Excited by the wrongs of her people, she summoned Barak, the son of Abinoam, of Kadesh, in Naphtali, to lead in an effort to free the Hebrew nation, promising him that Jehovah would give him victory. Barak agreed to do so on condition that Deborah should accompany him. She consented, but warned him that he would win no honor from the victory, as Jehovah would sell Sisera into the hands of a woman. Barak gathered the forces of Naphtali, Zebulun and Issachar, with a few men from Ephraim, Manasseh and Benjamin, altogether about ten thousand men, and took position on Mount Tabor. Sisera advanced to meet him without delay at the head of Jabin's army. Barak attacked him on the banks of the Kishon, and, with the aid of a severe storm which overflowed the stream and destroyed a portion of the army of the Canaanites, routed him with frightful loss. Sisera fled on foot and found shelter in the tent of Heber the Kenite, in the North of Palestine. Jael, Heber's wife, killed him in his sleep, thus fulfilling Deborah's prophecy. Barak took the city of Harosheth, Sisera's home, afterwards Hazor, Jabin's capital, and killed Jabin himself. Aided by the other tribes, Barak continued the war until he had liberated the whole Hebrew nation. These triumphs were followed by forty years of peace for the tribes that had participated in the war.

The Israelites were next chastised for lapsing into idolatry by being delivered into the power of the Midianites, who, aided by the Amalekites and the Bedouin Arab tribes, made repeated raids into Palestine, ravaging the country as far as Gaza, carrying off everything they could transport, and destroying everything that they could not take along. The Israelites were obliged to conceal their cattle and crops in caves in the ground, and to live in fortified cities. This condition of things lasted seven years, and finally the Hebrews, in humiliation and penitence, implored Jehovah for deliverance. Jehovah, it is said, summoned Gideon, the son of Joash, of the tribe of Manasseh, to head the movement for the liberation of the Israelites, and promised success to the enterprise. Gideon overthrew the altar of Baal and collected an army of thirty-two thousand Israelites. The Midianites and their allies, commanded by famous leaders, immediately took the field to subdue the rebellious Hebrews. Gideon took his position on Mount Gilboa, while the Arab tribes occupied the valley of Jezreel below. Assured of victory, Gideon allowed all of his men to depart who desired to do so, and twenty-two thousand immediately retired, leaving only ten thousand to face the foe. The Hebrew account states that Jehovah ordered Gideon to select three hundred warriors by a given test, and to hold the remainder of his army in reserve. Gideon divided the three hundred chosen men into three bands, with which he made a night attack on the camp of the Midianites. He armed his band with trumpets, and torches enclosed in earthenware pitchers. At a given signal each of his men blew his trumpet, broke his pitcher, and displayed his torch, shouting: "The Sword of the Lord and of Gideon!" The Midianites, aroused from their sleep, and utterly surprised and panic-stricken, turned their swords upon each other, and fled toward the Jordan, leaving their camp in possession of the Israelites. They were pursued by the remainder of Gideon's army, and were utterly exterminated, scarcely a man escaping across the Jordan. This great and decisive victory utterly broke up the power of the Midianites and liberated Israel from their oppressive yoke. The Israelites, in gratitude for this brilliant victory, offered to make Gideon king, but he refused the proffered dignity, saying: "Not I, nor my son, but Jehovah shall reign over you." Gideon ruled his countrymen for many years afterward as Judge. His rule was not fully beneficial to the nation, as he almost openly encouraged idolatry. After his death one of his sons, named Abimelech, made himself King of Shechem and the neighboring territory, but he only reigned three years, when he was killed by a woman while engaged in the siege of a town that had refused to acknowledge his authority.

The next Judge was Tola, who adminis

tered the government for twenty-three years, and was succeeded by Jair, the Gileadite, who ruled for twenty-two years. These two administrations were uneventful; but the Israelites again plunged so deeply into idolatry that Jehovah again, it is said, delivered them into the power of their enemies. The two and a half Hebrew tribes east of the Jordan were subdued by the Ammonites, who held them in bondage for eighteen years. During this period the Ammonites often crossed the Jordan and ravaged the lands of Judah, Benjamin and Ephraim. The tribes east of the Jordan selected for their leader a man named Jephthah, the chief of a band of outlaws occupying Mount Gilead. Jephthah defeated the Ammonites in a great battle, and liberated the country. He vowed at the beginning of his campaign that, if Jehovah would give him the victory, he would sacrifice to Him the first living being that he should meet at the door of his house when he returned home. The first who met him on his return home was his daughter, whom Jephthah, feeling himself bound by his vow, sacrificed after allowing her the respite of two months which she requested. This sacrifice, directly opposed to the laws of Moses, shows how far the Hebrew tribes east of the Jordan had departed from the teachings of the great lawgiver. Jephthah judged Israel for six years after his great victory over the Ammonites, and was buried on Mount Gilead.

Ibzan, the Zebulunite, who was the next Judge, encourage more extensive intercourse with the neighboring nations by marrying his children to foreigners. After judging Israel seven years, Ibzan was succeeded by Elon, also a Zebulunite, whose judgeship lasted ten years and was uneventful. Hillel, the Pirathonite, the next Judge, had an uneventful term of eight years, and is identified by some writers with Bedan, whom Samuel names among the Judges.

The great military triumphs of the Judges so completely broke the power of the Canaanites that they are no more heard of. Still the Israelites again offended Jehovah by relapsing into idolatry, for which we are informed He gave them over into the hands of the Philistines, a far more warlike and more powerful enemy than any they had hitherto encountered. As we have seen, these people occupied the strip of country along the sea-coast of the South of Palestine. At this time they conquered the whole South of Palestine, reducing the Hebrew tribes of Simeon, Judah, Benjamin and Dan to subjection, and held them in the severest bondage for forty years.

At this time Eli, of the house of Ithamar, Aaron's youngest son, was Judge of Israel. Eli, who was a man of sincere piety, resided at Shiloh, with the tabernacle; and his authority was generally acknowleged by the Hebrew nation. The crimes of his vicious and profligate sons disgraced the priesthood, but he passed them over, allowing his sons to retain their sacred offices. A prophet warned Eli that Jehovah would punish him for his indulgence to his sons, that they would be killed for their wickedness, and that the sacred office would be transferred to another family; but Eli simply remonstrated with his sons, permitting them to continue in their wickedness.

During Eli's judgeship, we are informed, Jehovah raised up two great champions for Israel—Samson and Samuel. Samson belonged to that portion of the tribe of Dan which dwelt to the westward of Judah. It is said that his birth had been foretold by the angel of Jehovah to his parents, and that they had been commanded to rear the child as a Nazarite, to keep him from all unclean food and strong drink, and not to allow a razor to be applied to his head. This child, it was predicted, was to accomplish wonders for his countrymen against the Philistines when he grew to manhood. Samson was the Hercules of the Israelites, who constantly warred with their oppressors; the sturdy warriors of the tribe of Dan living in a fortified camp near Kirjath-jearim, where, we are told, "the spirit of Jehovah began to move Samson at times." Samson is represented to us as possessing more than human strength, and as fearless and incapable of fatigue. For the purpose of provoking the Philistines, he asked the hand of a woman of Timnath, and on his way to seize her, it is said that he killed a lion by seizing it by its mouth and tearing its jaws apart. He left the dead lion by the wayside, and told no one of his exploit. Shortly afterward returning that way, he observed that a swarm of bees had made their abode in the dead lion's carcass. He ate the honey found there, but told no one. At his marriage feast he propounded a riddle to his thirty young groomsmen, the riddle to be solved during the week of the marriage feast, for the stake of thirty tunics and thirty changes of raiment. The young men induced Samson's wife to ask her husband the answer to the riddle, by threatening to burn her and her family if she refused. Samson, always subject to her wiles, told his wife, and she disclosed it to her kinsmen, the Philistines, who solved the riddle properly on the appointed day. Samson, at once seeing through the trick, and openly charging the Philistines with their treachery, proceeded to the Philistine city of Ascalon, where he killed thirty men, sent their clothing to their fellow-countrymen who had given the answer to the riddle, and returned to his people. His wife was given to one of his groomsmen, and he was refused permission to see her. In revenge for this wrong, Samson burned the standing harvests of the Philistines; whereupon they retaliated by burning his wife and her father. He avenged this cruelty by attacking them and slaying many of them, after which he took refuge in the territory of Judah. Thenceforth Samson was continually at war with the Philistines, and he is represented as repeatedly demonstrating his wonderful strength by a series of remarkable exploits. We are told that on one occasion "he slew a thousand Philistines with the jaw-bone of an ass."

As long as Samson remained true to his Nazarite's vow he escaped all the snares set for him, but he ultimately yielded to temptation, and this brought on his ruin. Falling in love with a Philistine woman, named Delilah, living in the valley of Sorek, her countrymen bribed her to betray her lover, and Samson finally yielded to her entreaties and informed her of the source of his strength as being in his long hair. As he lay asleep in her arms, the Philistines stole in upon him, cut off his hair, took him prisoner, put out his eyes, bound him in fetters, and took him to Gaza, where they compelled him to grind the prison-mill. When Samson's hair grew long again he recovered his former strength. Soon after this the lords and chief people of the Philistines held a great feast in the temple of Dagon, at Gaza, and brought out Samson to entertain them with feats of his strength. It is said that they then allowed him to rest between two pillars supporting the roof of the court, which, like the court itself, was filled with people, altogether about three thousand in number. Wildly praying to Jehovah for strength to avenge himself upon his enemies, the blind champion of the Israelites seized the two pillars in his arms and bore upon them with all his strength. The account says that the pillars gave way, whereupon the house fell, killing Samson and the whole concourse of people. "So the dead which he slew at his death were more than they which he slew in his life." His Israelite kinsmen took his body and interred it with the remains of his fathers. Samson is generally considered the thirteenth of the Judges, but his authority apparently only extended over his own tribe, that of Dan.

Samuel was the fifteenth and the last Judge of Israel. Like Samson, we are told, he was a child of promise. His father, Elkanah, was a descendant of Korah, and belonged to the tribe of Levi. He resided at Ramathaim-zophim. He had two wives, Peninnah and Hannah. The first of these was the mother of several children. The family attended regularly the national religious festivals at Shiloh. While they were feasting upon the free-will offering, Elkanah bestowed upon Hannah a mark of his affection, thus arousing the jealousy of Peninnah, who reproached Hannah so bitterly that she retired from the feast weeping.

CONQUEST OF CANAAN—THE JUDGES.

Hannah went to the door of the tabernacle and prayed silently for a son, whom she vowed to devote to Jehovah as a Nazarite. The High Priest, Eli, saw her lips in motion, and thinking that she had drunken at the feast rebuked her sharply. She assured him that she was stricken with sorrow, and was bewailing her griefs before Jehovah. Thereupon Eli spoke more mildly to her, bestowed upon her his blessing, and implored Jehovah to grant her prayer. She returned home in a happier state of feeling, and in due time gave birth to a son who was named Samuel. His mother kept him until he had reached a proper age to be separated from his family, after which she took him to Shiloh, where she solemnly dedicated him to the service of Jehovah, leaving him with the High Priest. Hannah afterwards bore her husband three sons and two daughters. Samuel grew up in the service of the tabernacle, gaining the favor of Jehovah and his Hebrew countrymen. We are told that when Samuel was still quite a youth, Jehovah spoke to him in the night, telling him of His design to destroy the house of Eli, and to deprive it of the office of High Priest in punishment for the sins of Eli's sons and for his own indulgence toward them. Thenceforth Samuel was a prophet of Jehovah. All his predictions are said to have been verified, and his renown and his influence over his countrymen increased as he grew up.

The favor bestowed upon Samuel by Jehovah inspired the Israelites with the belief that their God would aid them to cast off the Philistine yoke. They consequently arose in arms, but suffered a defeat in the hill country of Benjamin, a little north of Jerusalem. Eli's sons, Hophni and Phinehas, brought the Ark of the Covenant from Shiloh to the camp of the Israelites, thinking that such sacrilegious use of the Ark would give them victory. We are informed that Jehovah punished this sacrilege by permitting the Philistines to defeat the Hebrews with a loss of thirty thousand men. Hophni and Phinehas were both among the slain, and the Ark of the Covenant fell into the hands of the Philistines. Upon hearing of this misfortune, Eli, who was then sitting at the gates of the tabernacle, fell backward from his seat, broke his neck and died.

The Philistines carried the Ark in triumph into their own country, but the Hebrew record tells us that Jehovah chastised them so severely by means of a severe plague that they sent the sacred Ark to Bethshemesh. Excited by curiosity the men of Bethshemesh opened the Ark and looked into it, but Jehovah put 50,070 of them to death in punishment for this sacrilege. Appalled at this judgment, those who survived sent for the men of Kirjath-jearim to take the Ark away. These people took it to their own city, where it was kept in the house of Aminidab, a Levite, until David had it conveyed to Jerusalem.

Samuel was Eli's successor as Judge of Israel, and his authority was generally acknowledged by the Hebrew nation. For twenty years after the loss of the Ark, the Israelites were sorely oppressed by the Philistines. At the end of this time Samuel summoned the nation to make a bold strike for their deliverance from the Philistine yoke; and to prepare them for it he convened a solemn assembly at Mizpeh, where the Israelites renewed the broken covenant with Jehovah, amid fasting and repentance for their past transgressions. Upon hearing of this assembly the Philistines sent an army to disperse it. Samuel incited his countrymen to attack this Philistine force, and it is said that the Israelites were aided by a violent storm from heaven, which destroyed a great portion of the hostile army. The Philistines fled in dismay, and were pursued by the Israelites, who slaughtered a vast number of them.

This great Hebrew victory shattered the power of the Philistines in Palestine, and firmly established Samuel's authority over the Israelites. He made circuits of the country to administer justice, and appointed his sons, Joel and Abiah, as his assistants in the government of the nation. Under Samuel's administration, the Israelites enjoyed a period of peace and prosperity which they had never before known. But still

1—23.-U. H.

they were dissatisfied, and longed for a king who should govern them in peace and lead their armies to victory in war. They ascribed their past misfortunes to their want of union under a strong central government, and feared that the same cause might subject them to similar calamities in the future. Samuel vainly remonstrated with them, and tried to dissuade them from their determination to have an earthly sovereign to govern them, reminding them that Jehovah was their King. But they were deaf to all his arguments and entreaties, replying: "We *will* have a king over us." We are told that Jehovah therefore authorized Samuel to comply with the demand of his people; and in accordance with the Divine directions, Samuel anointed SAUL, the son of Kish, a Benjamite, as the first King over Israel, B. C. 1095.

SECTION IV.—THE UNITED KINGDOM OF ISRAEL.

SAUL, the first King of Israel, was about forty years old when he ascended the throne. The Book of Kings describes him as "taller than any of the people," and so kingly in bearing that when Samuel presented him to the people as their monarch, they hailed him with rapturous shouts of "God save the king." He possessed all the vigor of his race and tribe, all their courage and energy, but was impulsive and vacillating, and possessed a temper so utterly uncontrollable that opposition aroused him to a condition approaching madness.

The choice of a sovereign from the smallest of the Hebrew tribes greatly offended a considerable portion of the nation, and Samuel thought it prudent to postpone the solemn public installation of Saul until this opposition could be allayed. At this juncture, Gilead, the Israelitish territories east of the Jordan, suffered an invasion from Nahash, King of the Ammonites. Saul speedily collected the forces of Israel, crossed the Jordan, annihilated the Ammonites, and rescued Gilead. The valor and military ability displayed by Saul in this campagn utterly silenced the opposition to him, and his authority was acknowledged with enthusiasm by the whole Hebrew nation.

Samuel continued to exercise a great influence over the affairs of the Israelites. He considered the king simply a military chief, destitute of power to interfere with the old constitution and laws bequeathed to the nation by Moses, and entirely unlike the sovereigns of the neighboring nations. For some time Saul accepted Samuel's view of the powers of royalty, and submitted to the prophet's influence; but his ferocious temper could not long permit him to endure this control, and Saul began to resent the restraint exercised over him by Samuel, and desired to be king in fact as well as in name.

Saul's solemn installation as King of Israel occurred at Gilgal on his return from his triumphant campaign against the Ammonites; after which he dismissed the Israelites to their homes, and kept a force of only three thousand men in the field, retaining two thousand under his own command, and placing the remaining thousand under his son Jonathan, a very worthy young man. Jonathan surprised and took the Philistine stronghold of Gibeah, in the land of Benjamin, relieving that tribe of a constant annoyance. Thereupon the Philistines set a powerful army in motion, and Saul summoned the forces of Israel to assemble at Gilgal, where Samuel was to join him and offer a solemn sacrifice to Jehovah as the opening act of the campaign. The Israelites assembled at the appointed time, but Samuel did not appear. Saul waited for him seven days, when, seeing that the people were impatient, he seized the opportunity to throw off entirely the control of

Samuel and usurped the sacerdotal power belonging to the High Priest. He offered the sacrifice himself, thus claiming priestly as well as kingly authority. Soon afterward Samuel arrived, and immediately perceived that Saul's action was directed at putting the Hebrew monarchy on the same level as those of the neighboring nations, giving the king the supreme spiritual power, as well as the chief civil authority, over the Hebrew nation. The prophet rebuked Saul sharply for his sacrilegious proceeding; and in the name of Jehovah told him that the Divine favor would thenceforth be withdrawn from him, and that at his death the royal dignity would be transferred to another family. The bondage of the Philistines bore heavily upon the Southern Hebrew tribes, whose smiths were forbidden to pursue their occupation, in consequence of which weapons were so scarce that Saul found only six hundred armed men in the entire assembly of people. Notwithstanding this drawback, he advanced northward to Michmash to confront the foe; while Jonathan, accompanied only by his armor-bearer, surprised the camp of the Philistines, who, seized by a panic, turned their arms against each other, and fled. Saul immediately pursued the flying foe, and was joined by all the Israelites who could obtain arms. He soon found himself at the head of ten thousand men, and pursued the retreating Philistines to Beth-aven, inflicting frightful losses upon them.

The Philistines retired into their own territory, and did not molest the Israelites again for some years. During this time Saul repulsed the attacks of the Ammonites, the Moabites, the Edomites, and the Syrians of Zobah, who in succession endeavored to invade the Hebrew dominions. About the same time the Hebrew tribes east of the Jordan conquered the nomadic Arab tribe of the Hagareens and extended their territory in the direction of Damascus. Conscious that the security of his kingdom depended upon its defensive power against invasion, he made great exertions to organize a standing army, which, though not large, consisted of veterans and was kept in a high state of discipline and thorough efficiency. He assigned the command of this army to his cousin Abner, the son of Ner.

The High Priest Samuel, now venerable for his years, came to Saul and ordered him to undertake a war against the Amalekites, the earliest and most implacable foes of Israel. Saul immediately took the field against them and defeated them, but disobeyed the prophet's command to destroy everything he captured, carrying away a vast booty and sparing Agag, the Amalekite king, with the design of receiving a ransom for him.

Samuel met Saul at Gilgal when he returned from the campaign, and severely reproached him for his disobedience of the Divine command. In Jehovah's name, the prophet pronounced a curse upon the disobedient monarch, telling him that Jehovah had rejected him from that day. At the same time Samuel slew Agag with his own hand.

Samuel then departed from Saul, and the breach between the king and the High Priest of the nation was complete. The Divine protection, it is said, was withdrawn from Saul thenceforth; and Samuel, we are told, was commanded by Jehovah to go to Bethlehem to anoint the future King of Israel.

Samuel obeyed the Divine command, according to the Hebrew account, and going to Bethlehem he solenmly anointed, with sacred oil, DAVID, the youngest and most gifted son of Jesse, of the tribe of Judah. The newly-anointed King of Israel was descended from Nahshon, who had been the chief, or prince, of the tribe of Judah, in the Wilderness, and also from Rahab the harlot of Jericho and from the beautiful Ruth. David had already arrived at man's estate, and had proved his courage by his many successful defenses of his father's flock against the bandits and the wild beasts of that region.

After the breach with Samuel, Saul fell into a state of deep melancholy, amounting sometimes to madness, and which only the music of David's harp could alleviate; David having been introduced into Saul's palace through the secret influence of Samuel. Saul cherished a warm affection for David, conferring honors upon him and making him his armor-bearer.

The war with the Philistines had been renewed in the meantime, and the armies of Israel and Philistia confronted each other in the South of Palestine. The Philistines brought forward a champion in the person of the giant Goliath, of Gath. No Israelite had courage to meet him, until David, after joining the army, offered to fight him. Saul sought to prevail upon David not to venture upon so dangerous a proceeding, but finding him determined and depending upon Jehovah for victory, agreed to the encounter. It is said that David was armed only with his shepherd's sling, in the use of which he had become an expert, and that he killed the giant with a stone from this sling, the stone striking him on the forehead. After killing the giant, it is also said that David cut off his victim's head with his own sword. Appalled at the death of their champion, the Philistine army fled in dismay, and was pursued by Saul's forces to the gates of Gath and Ekron, suffering frightful slaughter during the retreat.

Saul, highly delighted with the prowess of David, gave him his daughter Michal in marriage. Saul's son, Jonathan, entertained a deep and permanent affection for the youthful hero. But soon afterward the vacillating Saul suddenly displayed a deadly jealousy of his young son-in-law, upon hearing the praises which were lavished upon him on account of his great feat in slaying the giant champion of the Philistines. Thenceforth Saul sought the life of David, who was at length obliged to flee from the court of Saul, and to seek refuge from his father-in-law's anger by fleeing to the court of the King of Gath, where he feigned madness, in order to escape the vengeance of the Philistines. Soon afterward he became the leader of a band of outlaws, living for some time in Moab, and then establishing himself in the dens and caves of the mountains in the region of the wilderness of Judæa, in the territory of Judah.

Samuel died about this time at Ramah, at an advanced age, and was deeply mourned by all Israel. After Samuel's death Saul gave full vent to his furious temper. He violently persecuted all who supported the laws of Moses, and massacred the High Priest Abimelech, eighty-five priests, and all the inhabitants of the city of Nob, the residence of the High Priest. Abiathar, the son of Abimelech and the heir to the office of High Priest, escaped the massacre by fleeing to David for protection.

Saul now turned his arms against David, and hunted him through the South of Palestine. On two occasions David had the king within his power, but magnanimously spared his life. He was finally obliged to take refuge with Achish, King of Gath, who assigned him the city of Ziklag, where he resided for some years, leading many expeditions against the Amalekites, the enemies of both Israel and Philistia.

The war between the Israelites and the Philistines was again resumed, and Achish, King of Gath, ordered David to join the Philistine army and advance against Saul. David was forced to obey, but the Philistine leaders, suspicious of the young Israelite refugee, induced the king to order him to return to Ziklag. The Philistines invaded the Hebrew territory; and in a great battle on Mount Gilboa the Israelites were routed, and Jonathan and two others of Saul's sons were slain, and Saul himself, being severely wounded, killed himself by falling on his own sword, in order to avoid being made prisoner by the victorious Philistines, B. C. 1055. Saul had reigned forty years (B. C. 1095-1055).

Upon hearing of the death of Saul and Jonathan, David returned to his own country, and was acknowledged as king by his own tribe of Judah; while all the other tribes adhered to Ishbosheth, the only surviving son of Saul, whom Abner had caused to be crowned at Mahanaim. For the next seven years the Hebrew kingdom was rent by a sanguinary civil war. When Abner deserted to the side of David, and Ishbosheth was assassinated by two of his guards, the whole Hebrew nation acknowledged David as its sovereign, and the civil war was brought to a close. David was solemnly anointed King of Israel at Hebron, his capital, B. C. 1095.

DAVID was almost thirty-eight years of age when he began to reign over the entire kingdom of Israel. He soon proved himself a great warrior and conqueror. His first great military exploit was the capture of Jebus, or Jerusalem, with its strong fortress, Mount Zion, from the Jebusites. He made this city the capital of his kingdom, and likewise the center of the Hebrew worship by bringing thither the Ark of the Covenant. He organized a standing army, set up a splendid court at his capital, provided himself with a large harem, or seraglio, after the usual fashion of Oriental monarchs, and introduced a royal magnificence hitherto unknown in Israel. He is ranked as a faithful servant of Jehovah, whom he delighted to honor and worship. The prophets Gad and Nathan were intimate associates of David, who always heard them with deference, even when they reproached him with the faults of his public and private life.

David was the greatest and most powerful monarch that ever reigned over the Hebrew nation. He extended his kingdom in every direction by successful wars. He broke the power of the Philistines by conquering their country as far south as Gaza. He subdued Moab, exterminating two-thirds of its population, and compelling the remaining third to pay tribute. He conquered the Ammonites and the various Syrian kingdoms between the Jordan and the Euphrates, including that of Damascus, thus extending his dominions eastward to the Euphrates. He also subdued Edom, and extended the Hebrew territory to the Red Sea and the frontier of Egypt. Thus David founded an empire extending from the Red Sea to the Euphrates, and from Phœnicia and the Mediterranean to the Arabian and Syrian deserts. He secured an important and powerful ally in Hiram, King of Tyre, who furnished him with cedars of Lebanon and with workmen and artificers for the construction of the splendid palace which he erected at Jerusalem.

David proved himself a wise and beneficent sovereign. He thoroughly organized the Israelitish army, personally superintended the civil administration, inaugurated an admirable internal service for the despatch of public business, and revised and settled the religious institutions upon a permanent basis. David was a great poet, as well as a successful king and warrior, as is proven by the *Psalms*, or hymns, which he composed, and which have ever since been ranked among the most soul-stirring productions of lyric poetry.

Says a certain writer concerning David's poetry: "Great as was the military glory of David, his fame with later times is derived from his psalms and songs. He was the first great poet of Israel, and perhaps the earliest in the world. The freshness of the pastures and mountain-sides among which his youth was passed, the assurance of Divine protection amid the singular and romantic incidents of his varied career, the enlargement of his horizon of thought with the magnificent dominion which was added to him in later life, all gave a richness and depth to his experience, which were reproduced in sacred melody, and found their fitting place in the temple service; and every form of Jewish and Christian worship since his time has been enriched by the poetry of David."

David had designed building a gorgeous temple to Jehovah at Jerusalem, but is said to have been forbidden to do so by Divine command, because his hands had been stained by blood. The temple was to be built by a man of peace, and was therefore to be deferred until the reign of his son and successor. David merely confined his efforts to securing a location and the collection of materials for the grand sacred edifice.

David sometimes yielded to temptation and gave way to the baser passions of his nature. During the siege of Rabbah, the

Ammonite capital, David offended Jehovah by seducing the beautiful Bathsheba, the wife of Uriah, the Hittite, one of his captains, and taking her to himself, giving her husband a dangerous command in which he was treacherously slain. For this crime David was severely reproved by the prophet Nathan, and we are told that he humbly confessed his sin and that his remorse and repentance obtained for him the pardon of Jehovah. He took Bathsheba to his harem, but the child which she bore him died in accordance with the prediction of the prophet Nathan. Another child born to Bathsheba was the illustrious successor of David.

The prosperity of David's reign was interrupted by domestic calamities, due directly to the evil of polygamy, which David had introduced into the kingdom. His sons by different wives tormented his later years by their jealousies and crimes. Ammon, his eldest son, was slain by Absalom in revenge for a gross insult offered to his sister. As soon as Absalom was pardoned and received into favor he conspired to dethrone his indulgent father, and raising the standard of rebellion, forced the king to flee from Jerusalem and take refuge in the country east of the Jordan; but a large army under Joab and his brothers took the field against Absalom and utterly routed his forces in the forests of Ephraim, and the unfortunate prince, in his endeavors to escape, was entangled by his long hair in the branches of an oak, being slain in that situation by Joab, contrary to the express command of David, who was fondly attached to this rebellious son. Adonijah also plotted to dethrone his father and rose in rebellion, but atoned for this crime with his life. David thereupon gave orders that Solomon, his son with Bathsheba, should be proclaimed king. The northern tribes revolted under a leader named Sheba, but were soon subdued, and the leader was punished with death. After a glorious but troubled reign of forty years, of which thirty-three were spent in Jerusalem, David died B. C. 1015, at the age of seventy-eight years, leaving to his people the proudest name in their history, and to his successor a flourishing empire.

SOLOMON—David's son with Bathsheba, and the favorite of his father—succeeded the illustrious warrior and psalmist on the throne of Israel. He began his reign by putting Adonijah, his rebel half-brother, to death. It is said that Jehovah appeared to him in a dream and promised to give him whatever he should ask, and that Solomon chose wisdom, and not only was this granted, but also riches, honor and length of days, on condition of his continued obedience to the Divine command. Solomon's reign was the most splendid period of Jewish history. He began his reign in peace, and all the neighboring nations acknowledged his dignity; and the reigning Pharaoh of Egypt gave him his daughter in marriage, and she received as her dowry a part of Canaan which had been conquered by that king. The Israelites were now the ruling people in Syria. Many kings were tributary to the Hebrew monarch, and the court of Jerusalem rivaled those of Nineveh and Memphis in its glory and magnificence. The fame and wisdom of Solomon secured for him the alliances of the most powerful Eastern monarchs; and thus tranquillity was established, and his entire reign was one of peace and prosperity.

Solomon's enterprise and luxury gave a wonderful impulse to commerce. Hiram, King of Tyre, was as warm a friend of Solomon as he had been of his father, David; and cedars were brought from Lebanon for the construction of the great Temple and a palace at Jerusalem. Through his alliance with Hiram, Solomon was allowed to participate in the Tyrian trade; and to facilitate commercial intercourse between Central and Western Asia, he founded two cities in the Syrian desert which became great emporiums for the caravan trade—Tadmor, (afterwards Palmyra), and Baalath (afterwards Baalbec, or Heliopolis). Says the Book of Kings: "He founded Baalath and Tadmor in the desert." Solomon also opened a lucrative trade with Egypt, and by the influence of the reigning Pharaoh, his father-in-law, he

PHOENICIAN EMBASSY AT THE COURT OF SOLOMON.

SOLOMON'S TEMPLE.

obtained from the Edomites the port of Ezion-géber (now Akaba), a convenient harbor on the Gulf of Akaba, at the northern end of the Red Sea, where he constructed a great fleet of merchant vessels, and whence his subjects, with the aid of the experienced mariners of Tyre, carried on a lucrative traffic with the rich countries of Southern Asia and Africa. Through these various channels of commerce, the rarest products of Europe, Asia and Africa were poured into Jerusalem. Gold and precious stones, sandals and spices from India, silver from Spain, ivory from Africa, and gold from Ophir, increased the wealth and luxury of the court of the great Hebrew monarch. Horses from Egypt, now first introduced into Palestine, filled the royal stables; and by tribute from the dependent monarchs, as well as by commerce, a constant stream of gold and silver flowed into Palestine. Solomon was the first to introduce horses and war-chariots into Israel, and these were procured from Egypt, from which linen-yarn and cotton manufactures were likewise brought into his kingdom.

Solomon's greatest work was the grand Temple to Jehovah, which he erected on Mount Moriah at Jerusalem, in which the Ark of the Covenant was thenceforth kept, and which has become famous as the sacred spot towards which the prayers of Israelites, though for many centuries dispersed in every portion of the world, have ever since been directed. The precincts of the Temple included apartments for the priests and towers for defense; and it has been said that the different purposes of forum, fortress, university and sanctuary were united in this immense and magnificent national edifice. Solomon enlisted the superior skill of the Phœnicians in wood and metal work in his service in the erection of the Temple. His warm, royal friend and ally, Hiram, King of Tyre—who was half Tyrian and half Israelite—was the chief architect and sculptor, and furnished the Hebrew monarch with cedars from Lebanon for the wood-work and with skilled workmen to build the grand structure. Seven and a half years were occupied in the erection of the splendid edifice, and the costliness of its materials was only surpassed by the beauty of its workmanship, all the resources of wealth and ingenuity being expended on the magnificent structure. When the work was completed it was solemnly dedicated to Jehovah; and the Feast of the Dedication brought to Jerusalem an immense multitude from both ends of the Hebrew dominions—"from Hamath to the river of Egypt." It is said that on this occasion the Shekinah, or cloud of glory hovering over the splendid edifice, announced the visible presence of Jehovah. This event is of such importance as a turning point in Jewish history as to mark the commencement of their connected record of months and years. Solomon also built a magnificent palace opposite Mount Moriah, on which the Temple was erected, and furnished it with unrivaled splendor.

Solomon's early years were marked by all the virtues which could adorn a prince. Humbly conscious of the great duties assigned him, and of the insufficiency of his powers, he preferred wisdom to long life or wealth or kingly dominion, and was rewarded with the possession of even what he had not asked for. His wisdom exceeded that of all the philosophers and learned men of the East, and his *Proverbs* are classed among the wisest maxims of antiquity. His knowledge of natural history, improved by the collections of rare plants and strange animals, which he obtained from every quarter of the world, was regarded as miraculous. All monarchs sought Solomon's alliance and friendship; and the Queen of Sheba, whose dominion is supposed to have been in the modern Abyssinia, or Southwestern Arabia, and who had heard of his fame and wisdom, came to visit him from a far country.

But Solomon's character was corrupted by prosperity. He had introduced the licentious luxury of an Oriental court into the Holy City of David, and his harem, or seraglio, was vastly augmented, so that it reached a point which has no parallel, as we are told that Solomon had seven hundred wives and three hundred concubines. His commerce was a monopoly of the government and did not benefit the people. His enormous and expensive court was maintained by taxes so excessive as to impoverish the nation and arouse general discontent. His great public works withdrew large numbers of men from the tillage of the soil, and from the proper channels of industry, thus lessening the resources of the nation. The luxury and sensuality of the court had a corrupting influence upon the nation, and the people were estranged from the ancient faith by the encouragement given heathen religions by their luxurious and sensual monarch. Seduced by his many "strange wives," who were taken from all the surrounding nations, Solomon not only permitted them their idolatrous worship, but even participated in the rites of their impious and licentious idolatry, and forsook Jehovah to whose glory he had erected the magnificent sanctuary on Mount Moriah. Then we are told enemies arose against him on all sides, and the subject kingdoms arose in revolt. Rezon, King of Damascus, threw off the Hebrew yoke. Hadad endeavored to restore the independence of Edom, but was defeated and compelled to flee to Egypt. The tribes of Ephraim and Manasseh almost broke out into open rebellion; but the attempt was discovered, and Jeroboam, the leader in the conspiracy, was obliged to flee to Egypt, where he found refuge at the court of King Shishak. Solomon died in B. C. 975, after a reign of forty years, like those of Saul and David.

The glory of Solomon's reign dazzled the Hebrew nation and silenced all discontent, but when he was succeeded on the throne by his son REHOBOAM, the smothered dissatisfaction assumed the form of open rebellion. Rehoboam, instead of quieting his subjects by necessary reforms, exasperated them by his haughty refusal to lessen their burdens. Ten of the twelve tribes therefore at once revolted, under the leadership of JEROBOAM; and the Hebrew kingdom, which had cut such a grand figure under David and Solomon, was rent in twain, B. C. 975. This secession and successful revolution is known as the "Revolt of the Ten Tribes." Thenceforth there were two Hebrew states —the *Kingdom of Judah*, embracing the two tribes of Judah and Benjamin, which remained true to the House of David represented by Rehoboam and his successors, whose capital was Jerusalem; and the *Kingdom of Israel*, comprising the ten revolted tribes governed by Jeroboam and his successors, who were idolaters, and whose capital at first was Shechem.

SECTION V.—THE KINGDOM OF ISRAEL.

THE Kingdom of Israel, established by the Northern tribes under Jeroboam, extended from the borders of Damascus to within ten miles of Jerusalem, including all the Hebrew territory east of the Jordan, and held Moab as a tributary. It had far the more extensive and fertile territory, and twice the population of Judah; but its capital was far inferior to Jerusalem, alike in strength, beauty or sacred association. Its successive capitals were Shechem, Tirzah and Samaria.

Jeroboam, the first monarch of the new Kingdom of Israel, in order to sever the most powerful tie binding the people to the House of David, made golden calves for idols, setting up two national sanctuaries, one at Dan and the other at Bethel, with idolatrous emblems, saying: "It is too much for you to go to Jerusalem; behold thy gods, O Israel, which brought thee up out of the land of Egypt!" A new priesthood was instituted in opposition to that of the Levites, whereupon many Levites and other faithful adherents of the religion of Jehovah migrated into the Kingdom of Judah. The people of the Northern kingdom fell into the snare set for them by their sovereign. A succession of prophets, some of them the greatest in Hebrew history, strove to keep the people faithful to Jehovah, but the taint of idolatry had become so deeply rooted into the national life that it could not be eradicated. In the time of Elijah only seven thousand were left who had not "bowed the knee unto Baal;" and even these were not known by the prophet, being forced by persecution to hide their religion.

The Kings of Israel belonged to nine different dynasties, only two of which, those of Omri and Jehu, occupied the throne for any considerable time. All but a few of the nineteen kings had short reigns, and eight met with violent deaths. The kingdom was repeatedly at war with Judah, Damascus and Assyria. Jeroboam was aided in his war with Judah by his friend and protector in his exile, Shishak, King of Egypt. Jeroboam's reign of twenty-two years was passed in almost constant war with Judah. He died in B. C. 953; and his son and successor NADAB, after a reign of two years, was murdered by BAASHA, the commander of the army, who then usurped the throne. Baasha removed the capital to Tirzah. He was grossly addicted to idolatry. The remnant of the worshipers of Jehovah retired from Israel and settled in Judah, being attracted thither by the piety of its king, Asa. To check this defection, Baasha made war upon Judah, and built the fortress of Ramah, by which he designed holding the Jewish frontier, but was forced to desist by Ben-hadad of Damascus, whose alliance had been bought by Asa.

Baasha died in B. C. 930, and was succeeded by his son, ELAH, who, while intoxicated, was murdered by ZIMRI, who usurped the throne, but was not acknowledged by the army, which set up its commander, OMRI. A civil war of seven years ensued, and Zimri, being defeated, shut himself up in his palace, which he set on fire, himself perishing in the flames. Omri began to reign B. C. 929. At first he had a rival named Tibni, whose claim was supported by half the people, but Omri overcame him and reigned until B. C. 918. Omri built the strong city of Samaria and made it his capital. He made war on Damascus, but was obliged to conclude a humiliating peace.

The next king was AHAB, who strengthened himself by marrying Jezebel, the daughter of Ethbaal, King of Tyre and High Priest of Astarte; and the result of this alliance was the introduction of the Phœnician religion into Israel. Near the end of this century the prophet Elijah came to denounce upon the king and people of Israel the Divine punishment for their sins, and a famine for three years devastated the kingdom. At its close Elijah offered sacrifice on Mount Carmel, and the priests of Baal were slaughtered, which was regarded as a vindication of Jehovah's power. In the latter part of his reign Ahab waged a successful war with Damascus and reëstablished the independence of Israel. Three years of peace followed. About B. C. 897 Ahab renewed the war with Damascus, by uniting with Jehoshaphat, King of Judah, in an effort to seize the strong frontier of Ramoth-Gilead, but in the battle which followed the allied army was routed and Ahab was killed.

AHAZIAH, the son of Ahab, became his successor, and reigned a little more than a year, during which Moab revolted. JEHORAM, Ahaziah's brother and successor, continued the alliance with Judah. He abolished the worship of Baal, though he adhered to the idolatry of Jeroboam. He waged war with Moab, and was joined in the struggle by Jehoshaphat and by the King of Edom, the vassal of the King of Judah. We are told that the allied army was miraculously supplied with water, and that the Moabites met with a decisive defeat, after which Jehoram ravaged "the land of Moab with fire and sword," but his cruelties caused the King of Judah to desert his alliance and return to his own kingdom. Before the end of his reign the worship of Baal was restored in Israel. Jehoram renewed the war with the Syrians of Damascus by seizing Ramoth-Gilead. Being wounded in the battle with the Syrians, he went to Jezreel to be healed, and was there visited by his ally, Ahaziah, King of Judah. During his stay at Jezreel, JEHU was proclaimed king by the army. Jehu went to Jezreel, and slew both Jehoram and Ahaziah, after which he caused Jezebel, Ahab's wicked widow, to be thrown from the walls of Jezreel, thus exterminating all of Ahab's family, in accordance with the prophecy of Elijah.

Jehu began to reign B. C. 884. He violently suppressed the worship of Baal, but retained the idolatry of Jeroboam. Hazael of Damascus deprived Jehu of his provinces east of the Jordan, and at one time he paid tribute to Shalmaneser II. of Assyria, the Black Obelisk King. JEHOAHAZ, Jehu's son, became king B. C. 856, and under him the kingdom of Israel was still further weakened by Syrian conquests, the King of Damascus even forcing Jehoahaz to limit the strength of his standing army. JEHOASH, the son of Jehoahaz, became king B. C. 839, and was a vigorous and warlike monarch. He defeated Ben-hadad III. of Damascus in three successive engagements, and re-conquered a part of the territory wrested from Israel. He likewise defeated Amaziah, King of Judah, and entered Jerusalem in triumph. He was succeeded by his son, JEROBOAM II. B. C. 825. This king raised Israel to the highest pinnacle of power and glory. He conquered Moab and Ammon, thus recovering all the territory lost by Israel east of the Jordan, and attacked Damascus, which had been weakened by the sudden rise of Assyria, adding a large portion of the Syrian territory to the Kingdom of Israel.

ZACHARIAH, the son of Jeroboam II., who succeeded his father about B. C. 772, was assassinated six months later by SHALLUM, who thus put an end to the house of Jehu and usurped the throne of Israel, but was himself murdered after a reign of little over a month by MENAHEM, who became his successor. Menahem invaded the Assyrian territory east of the Euphrates and took Thapsacus, but the Assyrian king defeated him and reduced him to tribute. In B. C. 762 Menahem was succeeded by his son PEKAHIAH, who was murdered by PEKAH, one of his generals, who then usurped the throne, B. C. 760.

Pekah's reign of thirty-three years was marked by a series of calamities. He formed an alliance with Rezin, King of Damascus, to protect his kingdom against Assyria and to conquer Judah. The allied armies of Pekah and Rezin then invaded Judah and reduced that kingdom to great extremities; but Ahaz, King of Judah, called in the aid of Tiglath-Pileser II., King of Assyria, who came to the rescue of Judah and forced Pekah to make peace. The Assyrian monarch again invaded Israel, ravaged its provinces east of the Jordan, and carried the inhabitants captive to Assyria.

Pekah was assassinated by HOSHEA, who then usurped the throne, B. C. 730. Hosbea was the last King of Israel. That monarchy was now rapidly nearing its end. Hoshea vainly endeavored to suppress idolatry. He began to reign as a tributary of Assyria, but soon renounced his allegiance to the Assyrian monarch and entered into an alliance with Egypt to recover his country's independence. Thereupon Shalmaneser IV., King of Assyria, invaded Israel, overran the country and besieged Samaria, its capital, which held out heroically for two years, but was taken by Sargon, Shalmanezer's successor; and with its capture ended the Kingdom of Israel, after having lasted two hundred and fifty-five years (B. C. 975-721). In accordance with the policy of the Assyrian monarchs, the inhabitants of the conquered kingdom were carried captive to remote portions of the Assyrian Empire; and with the "Assyrian Captivity" the history of the "ten tribes" is ended forever, B. C. 721.

The Israelite territory remained depopulated until Esar-haddou, King of Assyria, Sargon's grandson and second successor, in the seventh century before Christ, colonized this fertile region with Babylonians, Susianians and others. These strangers brought their idolatrous worship with them. The depopulation of the country rendered it so desolate that for a time wild beasts multiplied in the cities. The new settlers considered themselves free to serve their own national gods, and their religion was a strange mixture of the worship of Jehovah with their own polytheism, which the Hebrew Scriptures describe thus: "They feared Jehovah and served their own gods." The descendants of these colonists were known in the later Jewish history as Samaritans, and were the most inveterate enemies of the Hebrew race. We are told that "the Jews had no dealings with the Samaritans."

SECTION VI.—THE KINGDOM OF JUDAH.

HE Kingdom of Judah occupied the southern and least fertile part of the Holy Land. It began its separate national existence at the same time with Israel, but survived that kingdom one hundred and thirty-five years. It embraced the two tribes of Judah and Benjamin, with great numbers of refugees from the ten revolted tribes, who willingly sacrificed home and lands for the religion of Jehovah. The people were thus closely united in bonds of common interest in the wonderful traditions of the past and the hopes for the future.

Though territorially smaller and numerically weaker than the Kingdom of Israel, Judah was really the stronger and more important kingdom of the two. Its inhabitants were thoroughly convinced that they were the true people of God and the legitimate heirs of Jehovah's promises, and they exhibited remarkable vigor and wonderful recuperative powers. It was less given to apostasy from Jehovah than the Kingdom of Israel, and suffered fewer calamities. The indomitable spirit of its people enabled them to defy successively the power of Assyria and of Egypt, and required the exertion of the whole force of the Babylonian Empire to crush it. Although exposed to peril from the attacks of many enemies, because of its situation between the two great rival empires of Egypt and Assyria, this little kindom maintained its existence for almost four centuries, and was governed during all that period by monarchs of but one dynasty, the House of David.

The reign of REHOBOAM, the first King of Israel, lasted eighteen years, and was one of disaster. In B. C. 970, Shishak, King of Egypt (called Sheshonk in Egyptian history), invaded Judah in support of the ten revolted tribes, captured Jerusalem and plundered the Temple and the palace of their treasures, and, after reducing Judah to tribute, retired from the country. Rehoboam was constantly at war with the Kingdom of Israel, and during his reign a considerable portion of the people lapsed into idolatry.

ABIJAH, the son of Rehoboam, became King of Judah upon his father's death, B. C. 958. He prosecuted the war with Israel with great vigor, defeated Jeroboam at Zemaraim, in Mount Ephraim, and captured Bethel, Jeshanah and Ephraim, which closed the struggle for ten years. ASA, who succeeded to the throne upon his father Abijah's death, in B. C. 955, was a devout follower of Jehovah. He sternly put down idolatry, and replaced the treasures of the Temple carried away by Shishak with rich offerings of gold and silver. He strengthened the fortifications of his cities and increased his army. About B. C. 941 Judah was invaded by a strong army led by "Terah the Egyptian," believed to be Osorkon II. of Egypt; but Asa routed this army at Mareshah, pursued it to Gerar, and returned to Jerusalem with the spoils of victory and of the cities around Gerar. Urged by the prophet Azariah, Asa summoned a convocation at Jerusalem in B. C. 940, when the nation entered into a solemn covenant to be faithful to the worship of Jehovah. Many devout Israelites from the Northern kingdom attended this assemblage; and this migration of the worshipers of Jehovah in Israel to Judah so alarmed Baasha, King of Israel, that he fortified Ramah, on the road between Judah and Israel, to check this emigration, and made war upon Asa, who, in alarm, purchased the alliance of Ben-hadad I., King of Damascus, with the treasures of the Temple. Ben-hadad at once invaded Israel, and the Israelitish army was withdrawn from Judah to meet this invasion. Asa was engaged in constant war during the remainder of his reign, and died in B. C. 916.

Asa's son and successor, JEHOSHAPHAT, passed much of his reign in crushing out idolatry, and in fortifying the cities of his kingdom, and likewise those captured by his father in Mount Ephraim. Jehoshaphat reigned twenty-five years. He reduced the Moabites and the Philistines to the condition of tributaries. He contracted an alliance with Ahab, King of Israel, by the marriage of his eldest son Jehoram with Athaliah, the daughter of Ahab and Jezebel, a union productive of very much trouble for Judah. He aided Ahab in his wars with the Syrians of Damascus, and was with that king at Ramoth-Gilead, where Ahab was defeated and killed in battle. This defeat of the forces of Judah and Israel encouraged the Moabites, the Ammonites and the Edomites to invade Judah in great force. It is said that the invaders were miraculously defeated by Jehovah, in response to the prayer of Jehoshaphat. This victory of Judah terrified all the neighboring nations and secured peace for the remainder of Jehoshaphat's reign. Jehoshaphat, in alliance with Ahaziah, King of Israel, Ahab's successor, en-

THE KINGDOM OF JUDAH.

deavored to renew the maritime enterprises of Solomon by way of the Red Sea, but his fleet was wrecked at Ezion-géber, it is said, in punishment for his alliance with Ahaziah, whereupon Jehoshaphat relinquished the enterprise.

Jehoshaphat died B. C. 889, and his son JEHORAM, whom he had associated with him in the government for three years, became his successor. Jehoram's reign was short and disastrous. He was utterly corrupted by his marriage with Athaliah, the daughter of Ahab, and he introduced the worship of Ashtoreth, with all its immoral rites, into Judah. To avoid a disputed succession he murdered all his brothers, but we are told that Jehovah punished his wickedness, inflicting dire calamities upon his kingdom. Edom successfully revolted and recovered its independence under its own kings, and, though afterwards defeated in battle by Judah, it never again became tributary to it. The Philistines and the Arabs, who had been tributary to Jeshoshaphat, invaded Judah and captured and pillaged Jerusalem, and carried away all the king's wives except Athaliah, and all his children except Ahaziah, the youngest son.

AHAZIAH came to the throne upon his father's death in B. C. 885. He entered into an alliance with his uncle, Jehoram, King of Israel, the brother of his mother, Athaliah. He was with his uncle in the battle of Ramoth-Gilead, where Jehoram was wounded, and was slain shortly afterward by Jehu in the revolt which made that warrior King of Israel, B. C. 884. His mother, ATHALIAH, became his successor and slew all the royal family of Judah, except Joash, a newly-born infant, the youngest son of Ahaziah, and made herself queen. Joash was hidden in the Temple by his aunt, the wife of the High Priest, Jehoiada. Athaliah reigned six years, during which Joash remained concealed in the Temple.

At length Jehoiada headed a rebellion, and was supported by the army and the people. JOASH was proclaimed king and Athaliah was put to death, B. C. 878. Jehoiada became regent. For the first twenty-three years of his reign, during which period Jehoiada was his chief counselor, Joash administered the government with success, and the kingdom was prosperous. Idolatry was stamped out and mercilessly punished. Joash repaired the Temple, and put an end to the peculations of the Levites who had squandered the sacred funds. After the death of Jehoiada, Joash plunged into idolatry. Hazael, King of Damascus, attacked Judah and compelled Joash to purchase peace by surrendering all the treasures of the Temple and the palace, including the sacred vessels.

In B. C. 839 Joash was murdered by two of his servants and was succeeded by his son AMAZIAH, who at once executed his father's assassins. Amaziah attempted to reconquer Edom, which had revolted from Jehoram. He defeated the Edomites and took their capital Pétra, where he massacred ten thousand Edomites, but he failed to subdue Edom. He made war on Jehoash, King of Israel, but was defeated and taken prisoner at Beth-shemesh. The King of Israel led his captive in triumph to Jerusalem, where he plundered the Temple and the palace, and broke down the north wall of the city. After taking hostages for the future peaceable conduct of Judah, Jehoash returned to Samaria. Amaziah grew so tyrannical and corrupt in his last years that his subjects hated him, and he was finally assassinated at Lachish, B. C. 809.

Amaziah's successor was his son UZZIAH, who was a great and warlike monarch. At the beginning of his reign he recovered and rebuilt the ancient port of Elath, at the head of the eastern arm of the Red Sea. He reigned sixty-two years, during which his kingdom enjoyed great prosperity. He subdued the greater part of Philistia, and received tribute from Ammon. His arrogance in assuming sacerdotal functions, we are told, was punished, as he was attacked with leprosy while offering incense in the Temple. This obliged him to remain secluded, and for the remaining six or seven years of his reign his son and successor, Jotham, conducted the government.

JOTHAM became sole sovereign upon his father's death in B. C. 757. He was a pious and prosperous monarch, but during his reign the people of Judah grew more and more corrupt. Jotham fortified Jerusalem, and compelled the Ammonites to pay tribute. In the latter part of his reign Pekah, King of Israel, and Rezin, King of Damascus, began the war with Judah which was eventually so disastrous to them.

At his death, in B. C. 742, Jotham was succeeded by his son, AHAZ, who reëstablished the worship of Baal and corrupted the people. The war began against Judah by the Kings of Israel and Damascus during the reign of Jotham was prosecuted with vigor; and Ahaz prevailed upon Tiglath-Pileser II. to come to his aid, purchasing his powerful help by becoming his tributary. The Assyrians invaded Syria, took Damascus, and put an end to the Syrian kingdom. Israel was also severely chastised and forced to make peace.

Ahaz died in B. C. 726, and his son HEZEKIAH became his successor. Hezekiah was one of the best kings of Judah, and began his reign by restoring the pure worship of Jehovah and destroying all the idols. He was a wise and virtuous ruler, and "did that which was right in the sight of Jehovah." He defeated the Philistines, and boldly attempted to cast off the Assyrian yoke. Thereupon Sennacherib, King of Assyria, attacked him and forced him to remain a tributary of Assyria; but he soon again revolted against Sennacherib and entered into an alliance with Egypt, then at war with Assyria.

In B. C. 699 Sennacherib again invaded Judah, with the design of crushing the little kingdom before invading Egypt, which he resolved to chastise severely for assisting his rebellious vassal. He marched along the coast to the southern extremity of the Philistine plain, the cities of the low country falling into his possession, and, having captured Lachish, he besieged Libnah. In the meantime he sent a message to Hezekiah demanding his unconditional submission, blasphemously asserting that Jehovah was unable to protect him against the vengeance of Assyria. Hezekiah went to the Temple, where he turned in prayer to Jehovah and "spread Sennacherib's letter before the Lord." It is said that the destruction of "one hundred fourscore and five thousand" of Sennacherib's army at Pelusium, while camping opposite the Egyptian army, was the miraculous answer which Jehovah gave to Hezekiah's prayer. Sennacherib hastily returned to Assyria, dismayed and disheartened. The prophet Isaiah is represented as announcing the purposes of Jehovah in advance and as foretelling the fate of Sennacherib's army.

Hezekiah, at his death in B. C. 697, was succeeded by his son MANASSEH, who reigned fifty-five years, and was one of the most wicked of all the Kings of Judah. He restored every system of idolatry that had ever been practiced in Judah or Israel, and these abominable rites became so firmly rooted in the nation that the Temple was closed and the laws of Moses were almost forgotten by the people, while the worshipers of Jehovah were actually persecuted in the Holy City itself. The prophets denounced this apostasy in the severest terms, and were cruelly persecuted by the idolatrous monarch. Isaiah is believed to have been among the first victims put to death by Manasseh.

About B. C. 677 Esar-haddon, King of Assyria, suspecting Manasseh of a design to rebel against him, deposed him and carried him captive to Babylon. We are told that Manasseh was brought to repentance by the hardships of his captivity, and that Jehovah was pleased to hear his prayers. Esar-haddon generously pardoned him and restored him to his throne as a vassal monarch. Thereafter Manasseh had a long and prosperous reign, and exerted himself to his utmost to suppress idolatry and to restore the religion of Jehovah. He likewise strengthened the defenses of Jerusalem. About this time the colonization of the territory of the Kingdom of Israel by direction of the Assyrian monarch took place.

AMON, the son of Manasseh, succeeded

to the throne of Judah upon his father's death in B. C. 642. Amon sought to restore idolatry, but was assassinated after a short reign of two years, and was succeeded by his son, JOSIAH, a boy of eight years, B. C. 640. Josiah at once set about uprooting idolatry and restoring the worship of Jehovah. He reigned thirty-one years, and was one of the best of the Kings of Judah. In his reign the Assyrian Empire fell. In B. C. 608 Neko, King of Egypt, declared war against Babylon, invaded Palestine, conquered the Philistine cities, and advanced along the Mediterranean coast of Palestine to Carmel, thence crossing the great plain of Esdraelon and marching toward the Euphrates. Josiah assembled his army, and, in accordance with his duty to his suzerain, the King of Babylon, prepared to resist the advance of the Egyptian monarch. Neko warned him to desist, as his expedition was simply directed against Babylon; but the Jewish king persisted in his opposition, and was defeated and slain in the battle of Megiddo, nearly on the very spot where Deborah and Barak had won their great victory over the Canaanites about six centuries before.

JEHOAHAZ, the second son of Josiah, succeeded to the throne of Judah, B. C. 608. Jehoahaz had been made king by the people, but reigned only three months, when he was dethroned by Neko, who bestowed the crown on JEHOIAKIM, the eldest son of Josiah, B. C. 608. Jehoiakim reigned four years as a tributary of the King of Egypt, when Judah was forced to submit to the supremacy of Babylon, in consequence of the great victory of the Babylonian crown-prince Nebuchadnezzar over the Egyptian king at Carchemish, B. C. 604. Many Hebrew youths, the prophet Daniel being among them, were carried captive to Babylon by the conquering Nebuchadnezzar, and were there educated "in all the learning of the Chaldæans." Daniel arrived at high honors under Nebuchadnezzar, and was made chief of the order of "wise men;" and it was at Babylon that he delivered his prophetic visions, and that he foretold the coming of the Messiah. In B. C. 602 Jehoiakim revolted against the Babylonian supremacy and endeavored to recover his absolute independence. The prophet Jeremiah uttered his first predictions during the reign of Josiah, and continued his prophecies during the reigns of his sons, Jehoahaz and Jehoiakim.

Jehoiakim opened his rebellion against Babylon under favorable auspices. He was promised the aid of Egypt; and Phœnicia, under the leadership of Tyre, had also risen in revolt against the power of Babylon. In B. C. 598 Nebuchadnezzar, who had been King of Babylon for six years, took the field against both Phœnicia and Judah, determined to reduce these rebellious provinces to submission. First entering Phœnicia, he laid siege to Tyre, but finding it too strong to be reduced speedily, he left a part of his army to continue the siege, while he himself led the remainder against Judah and moved upon Jerusalem, which submitted upon his approach. Jehoiakim was put to death, and his body was treated with indignity, contrary to general Oriental usage, thus fulfilling Jeremiah's prophecy concerning this monarch.

JEHOIACHIN, the son of Jehoiakim, a mere youth, was placed upon the throne of Judah by Nebuchadnezzar, who allowed him to reign only three months, when, distrusting him, he carried him to Babylon, and placed his uncle, ZEDEKIAH, the brother of Jehoiakim and the son of Josiah, upon the throne. Zedekiah remained loyal to the Babylonian monarch for eight years, and then entered into an alliance with Uaphris, King of Egypt, who agreed to aid him with a powerful army in his effort to throw off the Babylonian yoke; and Zedekiah at once raised the standard of rebellion, B. C. 589.

The siege of Tyre was still in progress, and Nebuchadnezzar led a large army against Jerusalem, defeating the Egyptian king in his effort to relieve his ally, the King of Judah, and took Jerusalem by storm. Zedekiah and the remnant of his army fled, and were overtaken in the plain of Jericho. Zedekiah was made a prisoner and his troops were cut to pieces. Nebuchadnezzar stained his triumph by the most shocking atrocities, causing Zedekiah's sons to be slain before the eyes of their father, and the eyes of the unfortunate monarch himself to be put out, after which he was carried captive to Babylon; while the city of Jerusalem and the House of David. This work of destruction was bewailed by the prophet Jeremiah in his *Lamentations*.

Judæa was placed under a Babylonian governor, who was murdered soon afterward. His assassins found refuge in Egypt, taking with them the prophet Jeremiah, who had

JEWS LED CAPTIVE TO BABYLON.

the Temple were then pillaged and burned, and the population, except a small remnant, were carried into the seventy years' "Babylonian Captivity," being transported as colonists to Chaldæa, B. C. 586. Thus ended the Kingdom of Judah and the dynasty of sought to dissuade them from their dangerous course. The Jews afterwards became involved in the fate of Egypt, and the remnant left in Judæa were carried into captivity in Babylon about the same time, thus almost entirely depopulating the country.

HEBREW KINGS.

BEGAN TO REIGN.	KINGS OF THE UNITED MONARCHY.	
B. C. 1095	SAUL—Reigned 40 years.	
" 1055	DAVID—Reigned 40 years.	
" 1015	SOLOMON—Reigned 40 years.	
	KINGS OF JUDAH.	KINGS OF ISRAEL.
" 975	REHOBOAM	JEROBOAM.
" 958	ABIJAH.	
" 956	ASA.	
" 954		NADAB.
" 953		BAASHA.
" 930		ELAH.
" 929		ZIMRI.
" "		OMRI.
" 918		AHAB.
" 916	JEHOSHAPHAT.	
" 897		AHAZIAH.
" 896		JEHORAM.
" 892	JEHORAM.	
" 885	AHAZIAH.	
" 884	ATHALIAH	JEHU.
" 878	JOASH.	
" 856		JEHOAHAZ.
" 839		JOASH.
" 838	AMAZIAH.	
" 823		JERODOAM II.
" 809	AZARIAH, or UZZIAH.	
" 772		ZACHARIAH.
" "		SHALLUM.
" "		MENAHEM.
" 762		PEKAHIAH.
" 760		PEKAH.
" 757	JOTHAM.	
" 742	AHAZ.	
" 730		HOSHEA.
" 726	HEZEKIAH.	
" 721		Assyrian Captivity.
" 697	MANASSEH.	
" 642	AMON.	
" 640	JOSIAH.	
" 609	JEHOAHAZ.	
" "	JEHOIAKIM.	
" 598	JEHOIACHIN.	
" 597	ZEDEKIAH.	
" 586	Babylonian Captivity.	

SECTION VII.—BABYLONIAN CAPTIVITY AND RETURN.

NEBUCHADNEZZAR colonized in Chaldæa the Jews whom he removed from their own homes. They were comforted in their captivity by the promises said to have been made by Jehovah, "through the mouths of his holy prophets," that he did not intend to exterminate His "chosen people" as a nation, but simply to chasten them for their disobedience and transgressions, and that he would restore them to their own land after they had suffered the chastisement He was then inflicting upon them.

During the Babylonian captivity of the Jews the Babylonian Empire was overthrown by Cyrus the Great, and the Babylonian dominions were absorbed in the great

1—24.-U. H.

Medo-Persian Empire. When Cyrus captured Babylon in B. C. 538 he there found the Jews "an oppressed race, in whose religion he found a considerable resemblance to his own." He became ardently interested in these people, and learning that many of them strongly desired to return to their own land, he issued an edict permitting them to do so. In pursuance of this edict, a Jewish colony of 42,360 persons, besides their servants, returned to Jerusalem from Babylonia in B. C. 535. They proceeded directly to Jerusalem under the leadership of Zerubbabel, a descendant of the legitimate royal race; and most of them at first settled on the site and in the immediate vicinity of the Holy City. The far greater portion of the Jewish nation yet remained in Chaldæa.

The restored Jews under Zerubbabel at once devoted their efforts to rebuilding the Holy City and the Temple and restoring the worship of Jehovah and the Mosaic laws. They began the work in the year of their return, but were stopped by the interference of the Samaritans, who were a mixed race occupying the old territory of Ephraim and Manasseh and descended from foreign colonists settled in that country by Esar-haddon, King of Assyria. The Samaritans, when the Jews had returned, offered to unite with them in rebuilding the Temple, desiring to make it a common sanctuary for both races. They claimed to be descendants of the ancient tribes of Israel, but the Jews repudiated their claim and "would have no dealings with the Samaritans." In consequence of this refusal to allow them a share in the work of rebuilding the Temple, the Samaritans became the bitter enemies of the Jews, and endeavored by every possible means to thwart their work. They succeeded in delaying the rebuilding of the Temple and the city for a time in B. C. 522, but it was resumed by order of the great Persian king, Darius Hystaspes, in B. C. 519, and the Temple was finished and dedicated in B. C. 515.

Through the favor shown them by Darius Hystaspes, the Jews were enabled to firmly establish themselves in their old homes, in spite of the jealousy and hostility of the Samaritans and other neighboring nations. Xerxes the Great, the successor of Darius Hystaspes on the throne of Persia, notwithstanding that he was favorably disposed towards the Jews, almost caused their extermination by weakly giving his consent to a plot with that design formed by his prime-minister, Haman. This plot was detected by Mordecai, a Jew and the uncle of Esther, the favorite wife of Xerxes. Through the efforts of Mordecai and Esther, King Xerxes was prevailed upon to put the Jews on their guard and to permit them to defend themselves against their enemies. Consequently the plot resulted in the death of Haman, who was hanged from the same scaffold which he had designed for others, and the Jews successfully defended themselves in every portion of the empire. Taking advantage of the king's permission, they caused their most prominent antagonists to be put to death. This event, which occurred about B. C. 473, is still commemorated in the Feast of Purim.

Ezra, a Jewish priest, who enjoyed the favor of the King of Persia, led a second colony of his countrymen from Babylon to Jerusalem in B. C. 458. As soon as he arrived he stopped the custom of intermarriages between his countrymen and the neighboring nations, which had already assumed proportions so formidable as to threaten the extinction of the pure Jewish race. Ezra made other essential reforms in church and state, and had the books of the Old Testament definitely and authoritatively arranged.

Nehemiah, a Jewish favorite of the Persian king Artaxerxes Longimanus, the successor of Xerxes, who had been the king's cupbearer, arrived at Jerusalem, having been given permission to restore the walls and fortifications of the Holy City. In spite of the king's orders, the surrounding nations tried to stop the work, but the vigilance of Nehemiah caused his countrymen to perform their labors under arms, and thus thwarted the plans of their enemies. The Jewish people were divided between the

Holy City and the royal districts, after the walls and fortifications of Jerusalem were restored. The laws of Moses were now re-established in Judæa. Nehemiah, as High Priest of his people, was appointed governor of Judæa, which had followed the fortunes of the other Babylonian dominions in becoming a province of the vast Medo-Persian Empire; and thenceforth Judæa was usually governed by the High Priest. Judæa was afterwards joined to the Persian satrapy of Syria. The Persian monarchs allowed the Jews to manage their domestic affairs in their own way, so long as they paid their tribute regularly.

The Babylonian Captivity thoroughly cured the Jews as a nation of their fondness for idolatry, and they were therefore careful thenceforth to shun idolatry and to avoid all intercourse with idolatrous nations. They ever afterward remained steadfast in the worship of Jehovah and faithfully observed the laws of Moses.

From the time of the return of the Jews from the Babylonian Captivity, the ancient territory of Judah was called *Judæa*, and its inhabitants were named *Jews*. The Jews in Babylonia returned by degrees to Palestine, but many remained in Babylonia and kept up a constant intercourse with their brethren in Judæa to the latest period.

Here the Old Testament history of the Jews ends, and we will give the remaining portions of Jewish history as it is connected with the history of other nations.

The Hebrew race contributed little to ancient civilization in the way of science, art or politics. Such was not the mission of the Israelites. The world has received no impulse from their national achievements or history in this respect. But their religious institutions, spiritual ideas and moral teachings have exerted a mighty influence on modern civilization. The sacred writings of the Jews, and the sublime works of the Hebrew bards and sages, reverenced by us as the body of Old Testament literature, have become the permanent possession of all mankind, and their influence pervades the most civilized nations of the globe.

Moses was the earliest sacred historian, as well as the lawgiver and founder of the Hebrew state. David's *Psalms* are among the most soul-stirring productions of lyric poetry, and Solomon's *Proverbs* are among the wisest maxims of antiquity. The most noted of the Hebrew prophets were Elijah, Elisha, Jonah, Isaiah, Jeremiah, Daniel and Ezekiel. Isaiah, in his sublime strains of lyric poetry, foretold the coming of the Messiah. Jeremiah denounced divine judgments on his people for their apostasy from Jehovah, and in his *Lamentations* vented his sorrow for their downfall. Daniel and Ezekiel, during their captivity in Babylon, delivered their prophetic visions, and Daniel arrived at high honors under the Babylonian kings. He predicted the time of the advent of the Messiah with such precision that a general expectation of his appearance prevailed among the Jews at the time of Christ's coming.

Among the sacred places or structures before the Captivity were the *Tabernacle*, with its altar and brazen laver, its golden candlestick, table of show-bread, and Ark of the Covenant; and Jerusalem, the Holy City, with its Mount Moriah and *Temple*, and the sanctuary of that Temple. The Tabernacle was the place where public worship was conducted from the time of Moses to the time of Solomon; and consisted of three parts—the area, or court, a space of about one hundred feet long and seventy-five feet wide; the Tabernacle proper located in the middle of the western side of the court, being an oblong square of about forty-five feet long and fifteen feet broad, covered on every part, and also walled up with boards; and the entrance, which was closed by means of a curtain made of cotton.

Among the sacred seasons of the Hebrews were the *Sabbath*, the *sabbatical year*, the *year* of *Jubilee*, and the great festivals of the *Passover*, *Pentecost* and the *Tabernacles*. The Passover was the Feast of Unleavened Bread. The Pentecost, the fiftieth from the second day of the Passover, is also called the Feast of the Weeks, because it followed a succession of weeks. It was a festival of thanks for the harvest. The Feast of the Tabernacles, celebrated from the fifteenth to the twenty-third of the seventh month, was to commemorate the Wanderings in the Wilderness, and was also in honor of the vintage and the gathering of the fruits. It was a season of joy and gladness.

The Israelites considered themselves as sacred and holy—as the special guardians of the only true religion; but the tribe of Levi, and particularly the priests of that tribe, called Levites, were more especially viewed in that light. Aaron and his posterity, who were from this tribe, were consecrated to the priesthood, who were given a close access to the throne of Jehovah, in the Holy Place. The other Levites performed the inferior religious duties, but were allowed servants for the more menial offices. The High Priest sustained the most exalted office of the tribe.

Among sacred things we may name *sacrifices*, of which there were many kinds and for different purposes—*purification*, the *first-born*, the *first fruits, tithes, oaths* and *vows*. Concerning these there were many particular regulations. One peculiar rite was the sending forth of the scape-goat into the wilderness, in atonement for national sins. After the lustration of the Holy Place, the Tabernacle and the altar, the High Priest was directed to procure a live goat, lay both hands upon his head, confess over him all the iniquities, transgressions and sins of the nation, putting the blame for them on the goat, and then letting him go free in the desert.

The Hebrews were taught that Jehovah is the Only God—the Creator and Ruler of the entire universe, to whom all men owe gratitude and obedience. They were only admonished to abstain from such kinds of food as were regarded unclean, to keep themselves free from moral pollution, and to be pure as God is pure. They were taught to be kind to the poor, to the widow and the orphan. They were forbidden to utter falsehoods and to spread scandal. They were not allowed to curse such magistrates as they disliked. Thus the Laws of Moses generally had a good moral tendency. The laws respecting circumcision, cleanliness, tithes, usury, slavery, property, marriage, theft, war, and the like, were adapted to the peculiar circumstances of the Hebrew nation. These laws were rigidly enforced.

Polygamy was prevalent among the Hebrews from the Mosaic times. Moses endeavored to check this institution by narrating the original institution of marriage, and showing the evils resulting from a plurality of wives—evils which are very great in all Asiatic countries. There were likewise some special regulations restraining polygamy, and the evil considerably diminished in the progress of time.

Agriculture, and likewise the keeping of flocks and herds, prevailed in the primitive ages, and the Mosaic laws specially favored the tillage of the soil. This art was held in high esteem among the Hebrews. The naturally-fertile soil of Palestine was made more fertile by the care taken to improve it. Such grains as wheat, millet, spelt, barley, beans, lentils, meadow-cumin, etc., were cultivated; while flax, cotton, melons, cucumbers and rice were likewise raised. The beasts of burden used in agriculture were bulls, cows and asses. The vine was extensively cultivated.

Agriculture was the chief pursuit of the Hebrews. Every seventh year the lands were left untilled, and whatever grew of itself was to be given to the destitute. The houses were mostly poor and low, and were built of sun-dried mud or unhewn stones until the time of the kings, when more attention was devoted to architecture. The street-doors were adorned with inscriptions from the Laws of Moses. The windows had no glass, but were latticed. The roofs were flat, and the people often resorted to them for cool air, and even slept there in summer time. Domestic implements were rare and of simple construction. Grain was ground in hand-mills by the women. Olive-oil was used in lamps to give light. The towns presented a mean appearance, because of the want of public buildings. The Hebrew books, like those of other ancient nations were in the form of rolls.

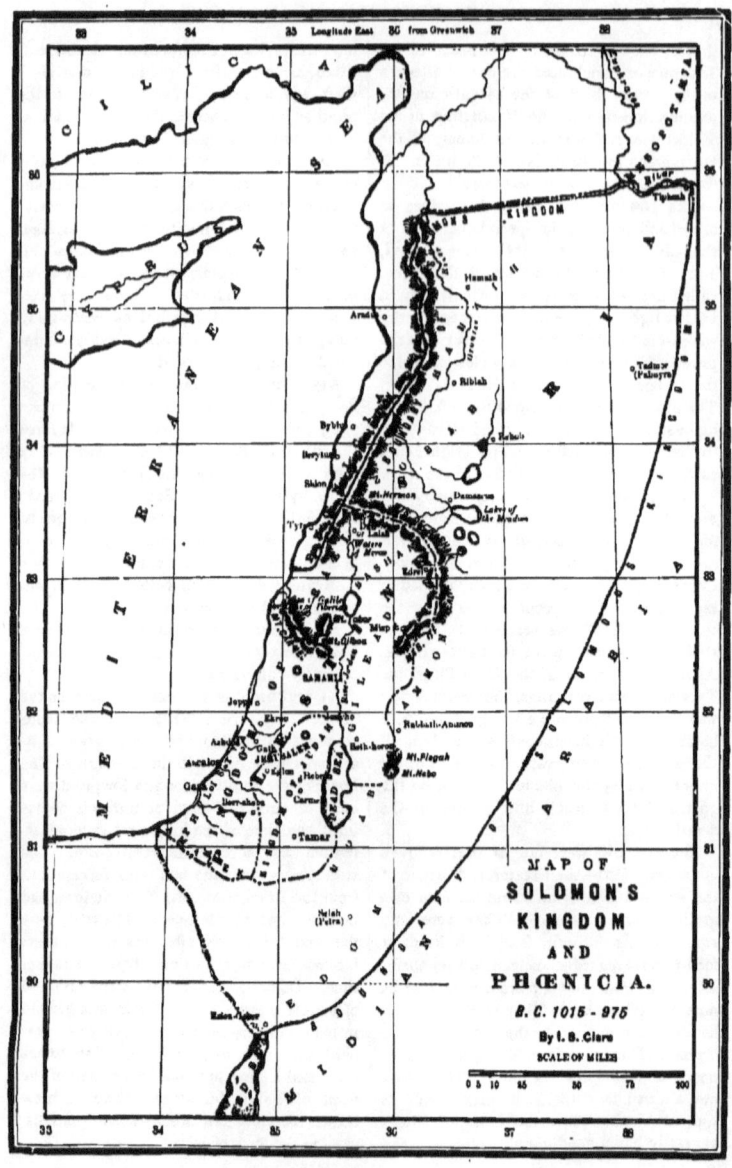

www.ingramcontent.com/pod-product-compliance
Lightning Source LLC
Chambersburg PA
CBHW030553300426
44111CB00009B/961